THE ART OF PUBLIC SPEAKING

THE ART OF PUBLIC SPEAKING

SEVENTH EDITION

STEPHEN E. LUCAS

University of Wisconsin–Madison

Boston   Burr Ridge, IL   Dubuque, IA   Madison, WI   New York   San Francisco   St. Louis
Bangkok   Bogotá   Caracas   Lisbon   London   Madrid
Mexico City   Milan   New Delhi   Seoul   Singapore   Sydney   Taipei   Toronto

McGraw-Hill Higher Education

*A Division of The **McGraw·Hill** Companies*

THE ART OF PUBLIC SPEAKING
Published by McGraw-Hill, an imprint of The McGraw-Hill Companies, Inc. 1221 Avenue of the Americas, New York, NY, 10020. Copyright © 2001, 1998, 1995, 1992, 1989, 1986, 1983, by Stephen E. Lucas. All rights reserved. No part of this publication may be reproduced or distributed in any form or by any means, or stored in a database or retrieval system, without the prior written consent of The McGraw-Hill Companies, Inc., including, but not limited to, in any network or other electronic storage or transmission, or broadcast for distance learning. Some ancillaries, including electronic and print components, may not be available to customers outside the United States.

This book is printed on acid-free paper.

domestic   6 7 8 9 0 VNH/VNH 0 9 8 7 6 5 4 3 2
international 1 2 3 4 5 6 7 8 9 0 VNH/VNH 0 9 8 7 6 5 4 3 2 1 0

ISBN 0-07-231569-5 (student edition)
ISBN 0-07-238391-7 (annotated instructor's edition)

Editorial director: *Phillip A. Butcher*
Sponsoring editor: *Nanette Kauffman*
Senior developmental editor: *Rhona Robbin*
Marketing manager: *Kelly M. May*
Senior project manager: *Susan Trentacosti*
Production supervisor: *Michael R. McCormick*
Cover design: *Keith J. McPherson*
Interior design: *Elise Lansdon*
Cover illustration: *Riccardo Vecchio*
Senior photo research coordinator: *Keri Johnson*
Photo research: *Barbara Salz*
Supplement coordinator: *Betty Hadala*
Freelance supplement editor: *Kassi Radomski*
Compositor: *York Graphic Services, Inc.*
Typeface: *10/12 Melior*
Printer: *Von Hoffmann Press, Inc.*

Library of Congress Cataloging-in-Publication Data

Lucas, Stephen.
    The art of public speaking/Stephen E. Lucas.—7th International ed.
      p. cm.
    Includes index.
    ISBN 0-07-231569-5 (student ed.: alk. paper)—ISBN 0-07-238391-7 (instructor's ed.: alk. paper)—ISBN 0-07-118003-6 (International ed.: alk. paper)
      1. Public speaking.   I. Title

PN4121 .L72 2001
 808.5'1—dc21   00-034858

INTERNATIONAL EDITION ISBN 0-07-118003-6
Copyright © 2001. Exclusive rights by The McGraw-Hill Companies, Inc. for manufacture and export.
This book cannot be re-exported from the country to which it is sold by McGraw-Hill.
The International Edition is not available in North America.

www.mhhe.com

ABOUT THE AUTHOR

Stephen E. Lucas is Professor of Communication Arts at the University of Wisconsin–Madison, where he has taught since 1972. Born in New York and raised in California, he received his bachelor's degree from the University of California, Santa Barbara, and his master's and doctorate degrees from Penn State University.

Professor Lucas has been recognized for his work as both a scholar and a teacher. His first book, *Portents of Rebellion: Rhetoric and Revolution in Philadelphia, 1765–1776,* received the Golden Anniversary Award of the Speech Communication Association in 1977 and was nominated for a Pulitzer Prize. His major articles include "The Schism in Rhetorical Scholarship" (1981), "The Renaissance of American Public Address: Text and Context in Rhetorical Criticism" (1988), "The Stylistic Artistry of the Declaration of Independence" (1990), and "The Rhetorical Ancestry of the Declaration of Independence" (1998), for which he received the Golden Anniversary Monograph Award of the National Communication Association. His most recent book is *The Quotable George Washington* (1999).

Professor Lucas has received a number of teaching awards, including the Chancellor's Award for Excellence in Teaching at the University of Wisconsin. His lecture course on "The Rhetoric of Campaigns and Revolutions" is among the most popular on campus and has twice been selected for statewide broadcast in its entirety by Wisconsin Public Radio. Professor Lucas is featured in the Educational Video Group's program on the history of American public address, and he can be seen each July fourth in the History Channel's documentary on the Declaration of Independence.

Professor Lucas has directed the introductory public speaking course at the University of Wisconsin–Madison since 1973. Over the years he has been responsible for numerous teaching innovations and has supervised the training of hundreds of graduate assistants. He has also participated in public speaking workshops and colloquia at schools throughout the United States.

Stephen Lucas and his wife, Patty, live in Madison, Wisconsin, and have two sons, Jeff and Ryan. His interests include travel, sports, art, and photography.

Contents in Brief

CONTENTS

3 LISTENING 55

PART II   SPEECH PREPARATION: GETTING STARTED

4 SELECTING A TOPIC AND PURPOSE 73

5 ANALYZING THE AUDIENCE 97

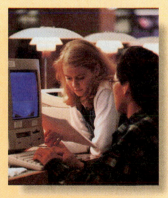

6 GATHERING MATERIALS 123

7 SUPPORTING YOUR IDEAS   163

PART III   SPEECH PREPARATION: ORGANIZING AND OUTLINING

8 ORGANIZING THE BODY OF THE SPEECH   191

9 BEGINNING AND ENDING THE SPEECH   213

10 OUTLINING THE SPEECH   237

PART IV PRESENTING THE SPEECH

11 USING LANGUAGE   255

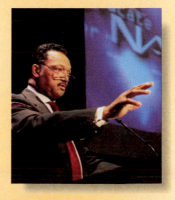

12   DELIVERY   283

13   USING VISUAL AIDS   313

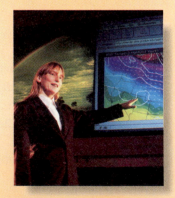

PART V   VARIETIES OF PUBLIC SPEAKING

14   SPEAKING TO INFORM   339

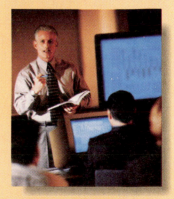

17 **SPEAKING ON SPECIAL OCCASIONS** 435

18 **SPEAKING IN SMALL GROUPS** 453

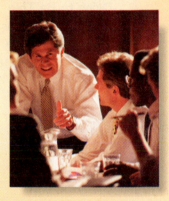

APPENDIX A GIVING YOUR FIRST SPEECH A1

APPENDIX B	SPEECHES FOR ANALYSIS AND DISCUSSION B1

PREFACE

I f it is true, as Walter Pater said, that "a book, like a person, has its fortunes," then fortune has indeed smiled upon *The Art of Public Speaking.* I am deeply appreciative to the students and teachers who have made it the leading textbook on its subject at colleges and universities across the United States.

In preparing this, the seventh edition, I have retained what readers have identified as the main strengths of previous editions. The book continues to be informed by classical and contemporary theories of rhetoric but does not present theory for its own sake. Keeping a steady eye on the practical skills of public speaking, it offers full coverage of all major aspects of speech preparation and presentation.

Throughout *The Art of Public Speaking* I have followed David Hume's advice that one "who would teach eloquence must do it chiefly by examples." Whenever possible, I have tried to *show* the principles of public speaking in action in addition to telling about them. Thus you will find in the book a large number of narratives and extracts from speeches—set off from the text in a contrasting typeface. There are also many speech outlines and sample speeches. All these are provided so students can *see* how to formulate specific purpose statements, how to analyze and adapt to audiences, how to organize ideas and construct outlines, how to assess evidence and reasoning, how to use language effectively, and so forth.

Because the immediate task facing students is to present speeches in the classroom, I have relied heavily on examples that relate directly to students' classroom needs and experiences. The speech classroom, however, is a training ground where students develop skills that will serve them throughout life. Therefore, I have also included a large number of illustrations drawn from the kinds of speaking experiences students will face after they graduate—in their careers and in their communities.

As society has changed since the first edition of *The Art of Public Speaking* was published in 1983, so has the book. In each edition, I have sought to relate the principles of effective speechmaking to students of diverse backgrounds, values, and aspirations. This new edition continues my efforts to make sure *The Art of Public Speaking* is respectful of and applicable to all of its readers. Not only does Chapter 1 place public speaking in the context of today's global multiculturalism, but attention to cultural diversity is evident throughout the book and in the instructional supplements that accompany it. Like its predecessors, this edition reflects the diversity of life in our modern world and encourages an inclusive approach to the art of public speaking.

Also as in previous editions, I have been guided by the belief that a book intended for students who want to speak more effectively should never lose sight of the fact that the most important part of speaking is thinking. The ability to think critically is vital to a world in which personality and image too often substitute for thought and substance. While helping students become capable, responsible speakers, *The Art of Public Speaking* also aims at helping them become capable, responsible thinkers.

Features of the Seventh Edition

Given the favorable response of teachers and students to the changes made in the sixth edition, I have kept the basic philosophy and approach of the book intact. At the same time, I have made a number of improvements in response to changes in technology and to the evolving needs of students and instructors. The most important of these improvements include an interactive student CD-ROM that is fully integrated with the book, a new appendix on presenting the first classroom speech, a section in Chapter 12 on question-and-answer sessions, and expanded coverage of search aids and other aspects of Internet research.

Student CD-ROM

Bridging the gap between the printed page and the spoken word has always been the greatest challenge for a public speaking textbook. Previous editions of *The Art of Public Speaking* have used videotape supplements to help bridge that gap. Taking advantage of advances in instructional technology, this edition brings the art of public speaking to life with a pathbreaking CD-ROM that is fully integrated with the book and is packaged with it. This CD consists of seven components, all of which have been carefully designed to help students master the skills, concepts, and principles discussed in the book. Let me say a word about each.

Video Clips

Forty-five minutes of video clips present speech excerpts that demonstrate the principles of public speaking in action. As students read the book, specially marked icons in the margins guide them to the appropriate video clips. Fully integrated with the text, each clip has been chosen to illustrate a specific aspect of speechmaking. So, for example, in the section on preview statements, students can click on the CD-ROM and see how the preview statements they are reading in the book were delivered by the original speakers. The same is true of subjects from ethics to visual aids, supporting materials to extemporaneous delivery, introductions and conclusions to language use and audience adaptation.

Running in length from 20 seconds to a minute and a half, the video clips are distributed throughout the book. To help students prepare their classroom speeches, two-thirds are from student presentations. The remainder are from public figures and include such models of rhetorical excellence as Winston Churchill, Martin Luther King, Ronald Reagan, Mary Fisher, Jesse Jackson, and Elizabeth Dole. In addition to helping students develop their skills, these clips give them an opportunity to experience some of the finest and most important speeches of recent time.

Interactive Study Questions

To reinforce key principles and ideas, the CD-ROM contains a comprehensive set of study questions for each chapter. These questions are fully interactive, use a variety of formats (multiple choice, true-false, fill-in, essay, and sentence-select), and systematically cover all the major concepts discussed in the book. Entirely different from items in the *Test Bank,* the questions have been written both to quiz students and to help them learn. After students enter their answer for each question, they will receive not just an indication of whether the answer is right or wrong, but feedback that *explains* the correct answer.

Speech Outliner

In addition to video clips and study questions, the CD includes a speech outliner that guides students systematically through the process of organizing and outlining their speeches. Fully revised and updated from *The Speaker's Helper* software that accompanied the fifth and sixth editions, the new speech outliner is much more powerful than its predecessors and provides a unique tool for speech preparation.

As students use the outliner, they will move step by step through each element of the speech from title through bibliography. Help screens explain the organizational methods involved in composing each part of the speech, and the outliner automatically formats the body of the speech in accordance with proper outlining principles. The program also allows students to save, revise, and print their work, as well as to export it to their own word processors.

Speech Preparation Checklists

A dozen checklists help students keep on track as they prepare their speeches. Included are checklists for ethical public speaking, for framing the specific purpose and central idea, for phrasing and organizing main points, for creating the preparation outline, for composing introductions and conclusions, for using supporting materials, and for preparing and presenting visual aids. In constructing these checklists, my aim has been to give students yet another resource that will help them apply the principles of public speaking discussed in the book.

Bibliography Formats

The CD-ROM includes a comprehensive set of sample citations for both the Modern Language Association (MLA) and American Psychological Association (APA) formats. Covering two dozen types of source material—from books, essays, and newspaper articles to government publications, personal interviews, television programs, and Internet documents—these sample citations go well beyond what I am able to cover in the book and should prove invaluable to students as they work on their speech bibliographies.

Glossary of Key Terms

Throughout the book, key terms are defined in the margin as they appear in the text. Those key terms are reproduced on the CD-ROM, where they can be accessed either by chapter or via a master glossary arranged in alphabetical order. Whether students are reviewing for exams or working with the study questions on the CD-ROM, they can instantly check the meaning of any key term at the click of a mouse.

PowerPoint Tutorial

Because more and more schools are incorporating PowerPoint into their public speaking instruction, the CD-ROM includes a brief tutorial that introduces students to the basic guidelines for effective PowerPoint presentations. This tutorial consists of 21 slides, constructed in accordance with PowerPoint principles, that cover such design elements as choosing fonts, using space and color, creating animations, and adding clip art. The tutorial also includes a hands-on guide students can follow when creating their own slides.

The First Classroom Speech

No assignment is fraught with more anxiety for students than their first classroom presentation. Usually a brief, simple talk, it is often called an ice breaker speech because it is designed to "break the ice" by getting students in front of the class as soon as possible. Unsure what to expect or how to proceed so early in the term, students are looking for clear counsel about this assignment. A new appendix titled "Giving Your First Speech" is designed to provide such counsel.

Rather than attempting to condense the entire book into a few pages, this appendix focuses specifically on the information students need to develop, organize, rehearse, and deliver their first speech. In combination with the discussion of speech apprehension in Chapter 1, it encourages students to approach this assignment in a positive frame of mind and to see it as a foundation upon which they can build throughout the rest of the class. Two complete student speeches and four CD-ROM video clips provide concrete examples of the principles discussed in the appendix.

Question-and-Answer Sessions

Answering audience questions is a common part of public speaking, whether the occasion is a press conference, business presentation, public hearing, or classroom assignment. To help students succeed in this vital skill, I have added a new section in Chapter 12 on question-and-answer sessions. After explaining how to prepare for the question period by formulating answers to possible questions and practicing the delivery of answers to those questions, I explore ways of managing the question-and-answer session so it runs smoothly and enhances the impact of the speech. This information will be of value to students not only in responding to questions about their classroom presentations but also in countless situations after they leave school.

Internet Research

One of the most popular features of the sixth edition of *The Art of Public Speaking* was its discussion of how to use the Internet efficiently and responsibly for speech research. In this edition, I have expanded upon that discussion in two ways, both of which are intended to help students locate reliable, high-quality sources of information.

First, to keep pace with changes in the Internet, I have added material on metasearch engines and virtual libraries. This material can be found in a section titled "Search Aids" (Chapter 6), which also covers standard search engines such as Yahoo, AltaVista, InfoSeek, and Northern Light. In this section, I explain the different kinds of search aids, assess the strengths and weaknesses of each, and provide URLs for a number of the best.

Second, in response to requests from readers of the sixth edition, I have augmented the section on evaluating Web documents to help students understand more fully the special issues involved in gauging the reliability of the information they find on the Internet. As in the sixth edition, I also discuss strategies for conducting focused, efficient Internet searches, and I once again identify 20 specific websites that can be used as starting points for speech research. My aim is to provide the most thorough and helpful coverage of the Internet available with any public speaking textbook.

Other Improvements

In addition to the changes described above, I have made a number of other improvements in this edition, including:

- Applying the Power of Public Speaking exercises at the end of most chapters. These real-world scenarios show how public speaking is used in everyday life and challenge students to apply their critical-thinking skills to a wide range of practical situations.

- Internet Connection boxes that point students toward websites that expand upon or complement the subjects discussed in each chapter.

- Updated discussion of library research to reflect advances in information technology and the development of new electronic databases.

- A brief discussion in Chapter 1 that highlights the centuries-old tradition of public speaking instruction in cultures around the globe.

- New student speeches with commentary in Chapters 14 and 16, two new speeches with commentary in Appendix A, and two new speeches in Appendix B for analysis and discussion.

- Thorough reworking of examples throughout the book to keep the material clear, interesting, and relevant to today's readers.

Besides these revisions, I have tried in every chapter to make sure the footnote references reflect current theory and research. My aim has been to maintain the readability of the text while using the footnotes to help students understand that the principles of effective speechmaking have been confirmed by substantial contemporary scholarship as well as by centuries of practical experience.

Instructional Resources

The Art of Public Speaking has an exceptional set of resources for students and teachers alike. Some of these resources are found in the book itself; others are supplemental to it. Taken together, they provide a fully integrated teaching and learning system.

Sample Speeches

Chapters 7, 14, 15, and 16 contain full sample speeches with commentary, as does Appendix A, "Giving Your First Speech." Chapter 10 has complete preparation and speaking outlines, both with commentary. Appendix B consists of seven additional speeches for discussion and analysis, all of which are available as part of the videotape supplement to the book.

Critical Thinking Exercises

A set of Exercises for Critical Thinking accompanies each chapter. These exercises are written assignments that students can complete on their own, in conjunction with reading assignments. They can also be used as the basis for classroom activities and discussion. In keeping with the experiential nature of speechmaking, these exercises require that students *work with* (rather than simply memorize) the principles presented in the book. The large number of exercises—in the text and in the *Instructor's Manual*—should give instructors maximum flexibility in choosing those best suited for their students.

Student Workbook

Developed in conjunction with the sixth edition, the *Student Workbook* has been fully updated. Containing exercises, checklists, worksheets, evaluation forms, and other materials, it gives students additional assistance with all the major elements of effective speechmaking. Instructors teaching distance-learning classes have found it highly valuable, but it has become a staple in many traditional classes as well.

Annotated Instructor's Edition

The *Annotated Instructor's Edition* provides a wealth of teaching aids for each chapter in the book. These aids include instructional strategies, class activities, discussion questions, speech assignments, and related readings. The *Annotated Instructor's Edition* is also cross-referenced with the *Instructor's Manual* and all the other supplements that accompany *The Art of Public Speaking* to provide a comprehensive, fully integrated teaching resource.

Instructor's Manual

A comprehensive guide to teaching from *The Art of Public Speaking,* the *Instructor's Manual* is intended primarily for the benefit of new and less experienced instructors. Providing more than 400 pages of classroom ideas, it contains outlines for each chapter of the book; discusses the end-of-chapter exercises; furnishes supplementary exercises, speeches, and classroom activities; offers suggested course outlines and speaking assignments; provides synopses of the Appendix speeches; and gives a bibliography of additional teaching and learning resources.

Test Bank

The *Test Bank* furnishes more than 1,700 examination questions based on *The Art of Public Speaking.* As a special feature, it also offers preconstructed quizzes for each chapter in the book, as well as three complete final examinations. The *Test Bank* is also available on disk and on CD-ROM for computerized test construction.

Selections from the Speech Communication Teacher

This edition marks the fourth volume of selections from *The Speech Communication Teacher* that I have compiled to accompany *The Art of Public Speaking.* Like its predecessors, the new collection covers a host of topics related to the teaching of public speaking, including audience analysis, critical thinking, diversity and multiculturalism, ethics, organization and outlining, speech anxiety, persuasion, testing and evaluation, and general instructional methods. All four volumes are available with this edition of the book. Taken together, they reprint more than 300 brief articles (1–2 pages each) that offer a wealth of practical ideas for classroom use.

Videotapes

There are several videotapes of student presentations that accompany *The Art of Public Speaking,* including a new tape developed in conjunction with this edition of the book. Instructors who adopt *The Art of Public Speaking* can also select from more than a half-dozen "Great Speeches" videotapes that accompany the book. Among the selections on these tapes are three works of exceptional merit that are also reprinted in Appendix B of the book—Martin Luther King's "I Have a Dream," Barbara Bush's 1990 commencement speech at Wellesley College, and Mary Fisher's address at the 1992 Republican National Convention.

Two other videotapes—*Be Prepared to Speak* and *Speaking Effectively to One or One Thousand*—introduce students to the public speaking process and provide helpful advice on dealing with stage fright. Both tapes are entertaining as well as informative, and either can be shown early in the course to help prepare students for their first speeches.

Overhead Transparencies

The seventh edition of *The Art of Public Speaking* comes with a binder of more than 100 full-color overhead transparencies. Created to be of maximum value for lecture presentations and classroom discussions, they include a wide range of graphics, illustrations, and exercises from the textbook, as well as additional exercises and classroom activities from the *Instructor's Manual.*

PowerPoint Slides

There is also a collection of more than 130 slides for instructors who use PowerPoint in their lectures and discussions. These slides include electronic versions of a number of the overhead transparencies, but they also incorporate additional material that is not on the transparencies. Instructors can use these slides just as they are, or they can modify them to fit the special needs of individual classes.

Instructor's CD-ROM

For the convenience of instructors, the *Instructor's Manual, Test Bank, Selections from the Speech Communication Teacher,* and PowerPoint slides are all available on a single CD-ROM.

Handbook for Teachers of Non-Native Speakers of English

Written for instructors who have ESL students in their public speaking classes, this 60-page handbook focuses on the central issues that should be considered when working with students from different linguistic and cultural backgrounds. After exploring the ways ESL students communicate, participate in, and learn from their classroom experiences, it provides more than three dozen exercises that are appropriate for ESL students enrolled in a public speaking course.

Online Resources

Instructors and students alike can take advantage of several outstanding online resources, including both *The Art of Public Speaking* website (www.mhhe.com/lucas) and the McGraw-Hill Public Speaking website (www.mhhe.com/speaking). In addition, instructors using *The Art of Public Speaking* have full access to McGraw-Hill's PageOut (www.pageout.net). This program allows teachers to create their personal course websites by plugging their class information into a professionally designed template. The process takes almost no time at all and eliminates the need for long hours of coding or knowledge of HTML. Special features of PageOut include an interactive course syllabus, an online gradebook, bookmarks, capability for posting lecture notes, and a discussion board where instructors and students can exchange ideas about topics relating to the course.

Acknowledgments

"'Tis the good reader," said Ralph Waldo Emerson, "that makes the good book." I have been fortunate to have very good readers indeed, and I would like to thank the reviewers whose names appear on page xxviii for their many helpful comments and suggestions. I am also grateful to the people listed on pages xxix–xxxi who generously offered their responses to a questionnaire about the sixth edition.

In addition, I would like to express my gratitude to the students at the University of Wisconsin whose speeches provided the material for so many of the examples in the text; to Mary Lynn Miller, Michael Newman, and Mary Rossa, who assisted with the research for this edition; to Anne Mackinnon, who lent her talents to several parts of the book; to Sue Vander Hook, who, as in previous editions, did an exceptional job formatting the *Instructor's Manual, Test Bank,* and *Student Workbook;* to Linda Loomis Steck, who prepared the PowerPoint slides for instructors and helped with the PowerPoint tutorial on the student CD-ROM; and to Jim Ferris, who once again provided a valuable sounding board on numerous issues.

I wish to extend a special thanks to Carl Burgchardt, who graciously provided permission for me to incorporate parts of his pamphlet *How to Give Your First Speech,* originally written to accompany the fifth edition of

The Art of Public Speaking, into Appendix A, "Giving Your First Speech." I am also grateful to Randy Fitzgerald, Director of Public Relations at the University of Richmond, and Paul Porterfield, Director of the Media Resource Center at the same school, for their time and effort in helping me secure the videotape of Sajjid Zahir Chinoy's "Questions of Culture."

Above all, I am indebted to my colleague Susan Zaeske, whose assistance and counsel were indispensable. In addition to spearheading the development of study questions for the student CD-ROM, she helped me select video clips for the CD, prepared the initial text of the PowerPoint tutorial, composed the first draft of the material on question-and-answer sessions, contributed to Appendix A, and provided invaluable insight on many other aspects of the book and supplements.

Members of the Communication Arts 100 and 105 teaching staffs at the University of Wisconsin have helped me by collecting sample speeches, by identifying rough spots in the sixth edition, and by piloting new assignments and exercises in the classroom. I would especially like to thank Scott Higgins, Finessa Ferrell-Smith, Matt Levine, Carmen Clark, Dorinda Hartmann, Chris Becker, Kelly Cole, Angelika Czekay, Kim Bjarkman, Bill Kirkpatrick, Lisa Dombrowski, and Jonathan Walley.

There are many people at McGraw-Hill who contributed to this edition of *The Art of Public Speaking.* Marge Byers provided a clear sense of vision and editorial direction through the early stages of the project, while Rhona Robbin did a superlative job coordinating the manuscript revisions and guiding the project into production. In addition to helping with the revision plan, Kelly May developed an exceptional marketing campaign and has worked tirelessly in behalf of the book.

Kimberly Stark oversaw the development of the student CD-ROM, as well as other technology-related aspects of the book and supplements. Elise Lansdon and Keith McPherson created a vibrant design that brings the book alive visually while simultaneously reinforcing its pedagogy. Barbara Salz did a superb job of photo research; Susan Trentacosti steered the book through production; Kassi Radomski managed the supplements program; and Betty Hadala superintended production of the supplements. Sue Driscoll helped on a number of fronts and never faltered in responding to my requests for information and materials. Phil Butcher lent his support throughout the project.

I would be remiss if I did not also thank Andrew Gardner, Marc Silver, Mary McLean, and the other talented people at Dolphin Interactive Software who were responsible for transforming the raw materials for the student CD-ROM into a final product that provides a model of instructional technology. I am also grateful to Roger Cook of the Educational Video Group for his contributions to the CD-ROM, as well as for being such a splendid person to work with over the years.

My greatest debt, as always, is to Patty, Jeff, and Ryan. They have lived with this book for the past two decades, and they have contributed to it in countless ways. More important, they have immeasurably enriched the life of its author. It is true for me, as it was for Thomas Jefferson, that "the happiest moments of my life" have been those spent "in the bosom of my family."

Stephen E. Lucas
Madison, Wisconsin

Reviewers

Julie Benson-Rosston
Red Rocks Community College

Sandra J. Berkowitz
Wayne State University

Elizabeth Berry
California State University, Northridge

Vincent L. Bloom
California State University, Fresno

John S. Bourhis
Southwest Missouri State University

Kenneth T. Broda-Bahm
Towson University

Jennifer Cochrane
Indiana University–Purdue University, Indianapolis

Thomas E. Diamond
Montana State University, Bozeman

Risa E. Dickson
California State University, San Bernardino

Joe Downing
Western Kentucky University

Amy Ebesu Hubbard
University of Hawaii, Manoa

Kerry Egdorf
Marquette University

Daniel Eness
Iowa State University

Kim E. Freeman
University of Florida

Dayle Hardy-Short
Northern Arizona University

Christopher Harlos
North Carolina State University

Robin A. Jones
Southwestern Oklahoma State University

Kimberly J. Kronvall-Jordan
South Suburban College

Sandra G. Lakey
Pennsylvania College of Technology

Victoria Leonard
College of the Canyons

Rebecca A. Litke
California State University, Northridge

Bruce Loebs
Idaho State University

Susan Messman
Pennsylvania State University

Cynthia N. Moore
Macomb County Community College

Donna R. Munde
Mercer County Community College

Donna Marie Nudd
Florida State University

Sally Perkins
California State University, Sacramento

Rick Rowland
Pepperdine University

Belinda Russell
Northeast Mississippi Community College

Joan Corey Semonella
Riverside Community College

Cheri Simonds
Illinois State University

Amy R. Slagell
Iowa State University

Jessica Stowell
Tulsa Community College

Julia McDermott Swanson
Franklin College

Jill Tyler
University of South Dakota

Marianne Adkins Ulmer
Mississippi State University

David E. Walker
Middle Tennessee State University

Nancy J. Wendt
Oregon State University

Theodore Windt
University of Pittsburgh

James L. Wolford
Joliet Junior College

QUESTIONNAIRE RESPONDENTS

Jerry Agent
Antonette M. Aragon
Bill Baines
Linda Baughman
Kristina Bendikas
Laura Garren Berry
Betty Bigby-Young
C. Jerome Binus
Tina Bishop
Mary Sue Boggs
Leila Brammer
Daniel S. Brown
J. A. Brown
Kristine Bruss
Joni M. Butcher
Rebecca Calvert
Theresa Castor
Carl M. Cates
Gil Clardy
Robert Cocettib
Sue Coffey
Frank Colbourn
Joy Cowdery
Dina Dahbany-Miraglia
Janet Davis
Linda Davis
Dan DeLozier
Joseph DiPalermo
Susan Dobie
Joan Donati
Brian Dose
Diane Dowling
Bernard Duffy
Stacey Duke
Betty Dvorson
David Easter
Rich Edwards
Michael Elkins
Scott Ellis
Kevin Erke
Ernest Ettlich

Catherine Farmer
Sharon Ferrett
F. Russell Filburn
Julie Fink
George W. Fleck
James Floss
Katherine Foerster
J. Mark Fox
Glenda Frank
Robert Friedenberg
Chrys Gabrich
David Gaer
Douglas Gaerte
Fred Garbowitz
Pam Glasnapp
Robert Glenn
Harvey Godorov
Rob Goebetz
Jerry M. Goldberg
Ava Good
Jerome A. Goodman
Catherine Gragg
Sy Grant
John Griffiths
Nicki Gutgold
Charleen Handford
Illona Hansen
Lelia J. Harkans
Philip Harwood
Wayne Hensley
Phil Hoeflich
Barbara Horn
Victoria Howitt
Barbara Hund
Carl T. Hyden
John Jamiel
M. G. Jarzabek
Stephen Jeffcoat
Sharon R. Johnston
Robin Jones
D. E. Jukes

Thom Karlsen
Richard Katula
Katherine Kinnick
Gerald R. Kish
D. K. Klein
Sharon Kleinman
Richard Knight
John Kochian
Robert Kogan
Rod Landis
Shelley D. Lane
Angela Latham
Frank Latimer Jr.
David Lawless
Edith LeFebvre
Charles E. Lester
Nathan Lilienthal
Marcia Litrenta
Bruce Loebs
Katherine Loh
J. D. Luna
Richard Lustig
Shelly Lutzweiler
Terrie MacCellan
Leslie Maggard
Mary Y. Mandeville
Vicki Marie
Ginger Martin
Marilyn Martin
Gene Matthews
Margaret G. McCain
Patrick McDonnell
Judith McPeak
Rod McVetta
Beth Merry
Cathy S. Mester
Ken Mihalik
Trudy Milburn
Jonathan Millen
Sarah Mohundro
Charlotte Morrison
Stanley Moore
Terence Morrow
David Moser
Alfred G. Mueller II
Donna Munde
George M. Muschamp Jr.
Scott A. Myers
Laura L. Nelson
Mabry M. O'Donnell

Robert Oldham
Dee Oseroff-Varnell
Pamela S. Ouellette
Valerie Peterson
Lori Polacheck
Jeff Przybyloege
Jon Radman
Norma P. Ragland
Closepet Ramesh
Diane Rao
Gerald Ratcliff
Steven L. Reagles
James Reed
Todd Rendleman
Heather Ricker-Gilbert
Craig Rickett
Rebecca Roberts
John Robertson
Paula Rodriguez
Mark C. Rogers
Eva K. Rose
Judith Rowlands
Elena Russo
Helen M. Sacco
Jeanine Samuelson
Jeanellyn Schwarzenbach
Marlene Sebeck
Joan Semonella
Gail Sharpe
Kathy Shipley
Kathleen Siskar
Kim Sisson
Cameron Smith
James Smith
Sharon E. Smith
Lin Snider
Mark Staller
Joan Steck
Joseph J. Stehno
James H. Strickler
Jeff Stromer
Gary Sullivan
David Sutton
Michael Swanson
Janet Thiede
Jerry Thomas
Roana Thornock
Rachel Tighe
Ann Tindal
Scott Titsworth

Rod Truester
Judi Truitt
Anita J. Turpin
Dudley Turner
Patrick Vaughn
Minnie Venable
Shauna Vey
Ron Vining
Ruth Wagoner
Suzanne Wallace
Tom Walton
William Wardrope
Frank Watimer, Jr.

Jean A. Weber
Bruce E. Wells
Kanda Whaley
Larry J. Whatule
Sally Wheeler
Gordon Whiting
Martistene D. Williams
Lori Wisdom-Whitley
Marianne Worthington
C. Keith Young
Patricia A. Young
Alan Zaremba
Julie G. Zink

LIST OF STUDENT CD-ROM VIDEO CLIPS

THE ART OF PUBLIC SPEAKING

CHAPTER ONE

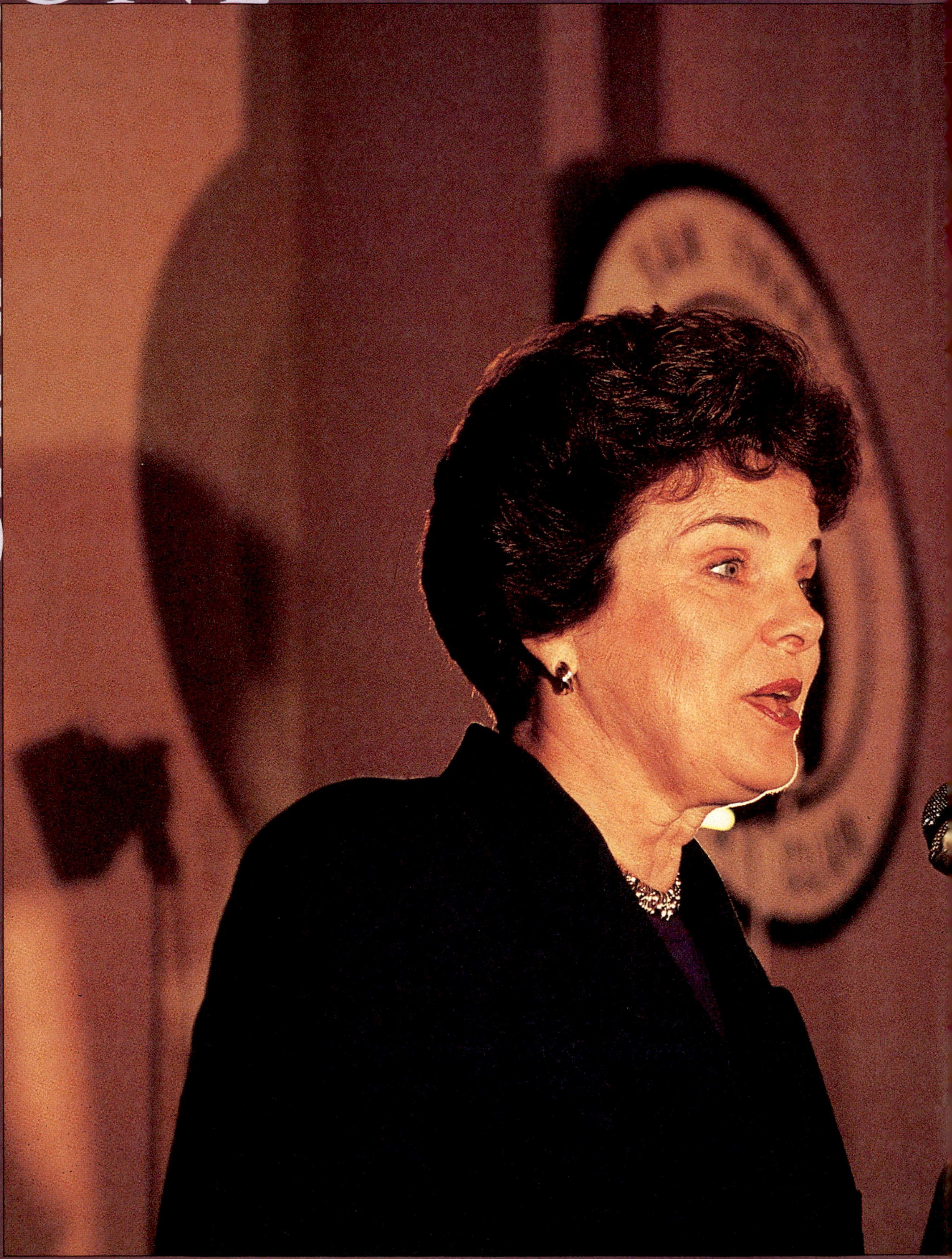

SPEAKING IN PUBLIC

An old English proverb says "talk is cheap." Whoever coined that phrase obviously did not anticipate the 1990s. Nowadays, talk—good talk—can be very expensive indeed. The burden of this expense falls heavily both on those who wish to hear accomplished speakers and on those who wish to become accomplished speakers.

Throughout the history of the United States there have been people who earned a living by working the lecture circuit—traveling from city to city, town to town, delivering speeches as a form of entertainment or information to paying audiences. Today, however, the pay for such speechmaking has reached new heights. A polished speaker with expertise in some area of interest can command thousands of dollars for a single speech. Top-ranked stars of the lecture circuit—such as Colin Powell, Oprah Winfrey, Barbara Walters, and Larry King—are paid $50,000 or more per speech.

How do such people learn the art of public speaking? A few are "naturals" who seem to be born with the talent. Some have had the benefit of public speaking courses in college, like the one you are taking now. Others do it the expensive way. They seek private instruction in speechmaking, which can cost more than $5,000 for six hours of individual work. No, talk is not cheap.

The Power of Public Speaking

We should not be surprised that people put such a high value on public speaking. Throughout history this art has been a vital means of communication. The oldest known handbook on effective speech was written on papyrus in Egypt some 4,500 years ago. Eloquence was highly prized in ancient India, Africa, and China, as well as among the Aztecs and other pre-European cultures of North and South America. In classical Greece and Rome, public speaking played a central role in education and civic life. Aristotle's *Rhetoric,* composed in the third century B.C.E., is still considered the most important work ever written on its subject.[1] Despite the many changes in the world since Aristotle's day, it is as true now as it was then that a person "who forms a judgment on any point but cannot explain" it clearly "might as well never have thought at all on the subject."[2]

View Franklin Roosevelt, Martin Luther King, Barbara Jordan, and other notable speakers in action.

CD: VIDEO CLIP 1.1

During modern times many women and men around the globe have spread their ideas and influence through public speaking. In the United States, the list would include Franklin Roosevelt, Billy Graham, Cesar Chavez, Barbara Jordan, Ronald Reagan, Martin Luther King, Jesse Jackson, and Elizabeth Dole. In other countries, we see the power of public speaking employed by people such as former British Prime Minister Margaret Thatcher, South African President Nelson Mandela, Guatemalan human rights activist Rigoberta Menchu, and Burmese democracy leader Aung San Suu Kyi.

As you read those names, you may think to yourself, "That's fine. Good for them. But what does that have to do with me? I don't plan to be a president or a preacher or a crusader for any cause." Nevertheless, the need for effective public speaking will almost certainly touch you sometime in your life—maybe tomorrow, maybe not for five years. Can you imagine yourself in any of these situations?

You are a management trainee in a large corporation. Altogether, there are seven trainees in the program. One of you will get the lower-management job that has just opened. There is to be a large staff meeting at which each of the trainees will discuss the project he or she has been developing. One by one your colleagues make their presentations. They have no experience in public speaking and are intimidated by the higher-ranking managers present. Their speeches are stumbling and awkward. You, however, call upon all the skills you learned in your public speaking course. You deliver an informative talk that is clear, well reasoned, and articulate. You get the job.

You are married and have three children. One of your children has a learning disability. You hear that your local school board has decided, for budget reasons, to eliminate the special teacher who has been helping your child. At an open meeting of the school board, you stand up and deliver a thoughtful, compelling speech on the necessity for keeping the special teacher. The school board changes its mind.

You are the assistant manager in a branch office of a national company. Your immediate superior, the branch manager, is about to retire, and there will be a retirement dinner. All the executives from the home office will attend. As his close working associate, you are asked to give a farewell toast at the party. You prepare and deliver a speech that is both witty and touching—a perfect tribute to your boss. After the speech, everyone applauds enthusiastically, and a few people have tears in their eyes. The following week you are named branch manager.

Fantasies? Not really. Any of these situations could occur. In a recent survey of 480 companies and public organizations, communication skills—including public speaking—were ranked first among the personal qualities of college graduates sought by employers.[3] The importance of such skills is true across the board—for accountants and architects, teachers and technicians, scientists and stockbrokers. Even in highly specialized fields such as civil and mechanical engineering, employers consistently rank the ability to communicate above technical knowledge when deciding whom to hire and whom to promote.

As Lee Iacocca, former president of Chrysler, explains, "You can have brilliant ideas, but if you can't get them across, your brains won't get you anywhere." To get to the top, says business leader Midge Costanza, you must have "the ability to stand on your feet, either on a one-to-one basis or before a group, and make a presentation that is convincing and believable."[4]

The same is true in community life. Look back for a moment at the second of our three hypothetical situations, the one in which you persuade the school board to keep the special teacher who has been helping your child. Why did the school board change its mind? Not simply because the facts were on your side (though they may have been) or because you know more about education than the school board (which you probably do not). The school board changed its mind because of your *speech*—in which you presented a compelling case for keeping the special teacher.

The point is that public speaking is a form of empowerment. It can—and often does—make a difference in things people care about very much. The key phrase here is "make a difference." This is what most of us want to do in life—to make a difference, to change the world in some small way. Public speaking offers you at least three possibilities for making a difference—by *persuading* people to do something you feel is right; by *inform-*

ing people about things they don't know; by *entertaining* people and making them feel happy and good about themselves. These are the three major goals of public speaking—to persuade, to inform, and to entertain. They are also the three major goals of everyday conversation.

Similarities between Public Speaking and Conversation

How much time do you spend each day talking to other people? The average adult spends about 30 percent of her or his waking hours in conversation. As you will see, there are many similarities between daily conversation and public speaking.

Children learn the art of conversation by trial and error. A toddler says, "Cookie!" to persuade her father to give her a snack. A five-year-old tells a little story to entertain Grandma and gain admiration. If neither of these things works—the cookie isn't forthcoming, Grandma is not amused—well, back to the drawing board. Next time the child will try it a slightly different way.

By the time you read this book, you will have spent much of your life perfecting the art of conversation. You may not realize it, but you already employ a wide range of skills when talking to people. These skills include the following:

1. *Organizing your thoughts logically.* Suppose you were giving someone directions to get to your house. You wouldn't do it this way:

> When you turn off the highway, you'll see a big diner on the left. But before that, stay on the highway to Exit 67. Usually a couple of the neighbors' dogs are in the street, so go slow after you turn at the blinking light. Coming from your house you get on the highway through Maple Street. If you pass the taco stand, you've gone too far. The house is blue.

Instead, you would take your listener systematically, step by step, from his or her house to your house. You would organize your message.

2. *Tailoring your message to your audience.* You are a geology major. Two people ask you how pearls are formed. One is your roommate; the other is your nine-year-old niece. You answer as follows:

> *To your roommate:* "When any irritant, say a grain of sand, gets inside the oyster's shell, the oyster automatically secretes a substance called nacre, which is principally calcium carbonate and is the same material that lines the oyster's shell. The nacre accumulates in layers around the irritant core to form the pearl."

> *To your niece:* "Imagine you're an oyster on the ocean floor. A grain of sand gets inside your shell and makes you uncomfortable. So you decide to cover it up. You cover it with a material called mother-of-pearl. The covering builds up around the grain of sand to make a pearl."

3. *Telling a story for maximum impact.* Suppose you are telling a friend about a funny incident at last week's football game. You don't begin with

Many skills used in conversation also apply in public speaking. As you learn to speak more effectively, you may also learn to communicate more effectively in other situations.

the punch line ("Keisha fell out of the stands right onto the field. Here's how it started. . . . "). Instead, you carefully build up your story, adjusting your words and tone of voice to get the best effect.

   4. *Adapting to listener feedback.* Whenever you talk with someone, you are aware of that person's verbal, facial, and physical reactions. For example:

> You are explaining an interesting point that came up in biology class. Your listener begins to look confused, puts up a hand as though to stop you, and says "Huh?" You go back and explain more clearly.

> A friend has asked you to listen while she practices a speech. At the end you say, "There's just one part I really don't like—that quotation from the attorney general." Your friend looks very hurt and says, "That was my favorite part!" So you say, "But if you just worked the quotation in a little differently, it would be wonderful."

   Each day, in casual conversation, you do all these things many times without thinking about them. You already possess these communication skills. And these are among the most important skills you will need for public speaking.

To illustrate, let's return briefly to one of the hypothetical situations at the beginning of this chapter. When addressing the school board about the need for a special teacher:

■ You *organize* your ideas to present them in the most persuasive manner. You steadily build up a compelling case about how the teacher benefits the school.

■ You *tailor your message* to your audience. This is no time to launch an impassioned defense of special education in the United States. You must show how the issue is important to the people in that very room—to their children and to the school.

■ You tell your story for *maximum impact*. Perhaps you relate an anecdote to demonstrate how much your child has improved. You also have statistics to show how many other children have been helped.

■ You *adapt to listener feedback*. When you mention the cost of the special teacher, you notice sour looks on the faces of the school board members. So you patiently explain how small that cost is in relation to the overall school budget.

In many ways, then, public speaking requires the same skills used in ordinary conversation. Most people who communicate well in daily talk can learn to communicate just as well in public speaking. By the same token, training in public speaking can make you a more adept communicator in a variety of situations, such as conversations, classroom discussions, business meetings, and interviews.

Differences between Public Speaking and Conversation

Despite their many similarities, public speaking and everyday conversation are not identical. Let's consider an example in which casual conversation expanded gradually into a true—and vital—public speaking situation. Here the speaker originally had no intention of becoming a *public* speaker and had not trained formally for that role. She was forced to learn by trial and error—in circumstances where the outcome has affected one of the vital issues of our day:

At one time, Carolyn McCarthy's world focused on the town of Mineola, New York, where she lived with her husband and son. A housewife and licensed practical nurse, McCarthy was, in her own words, an "average person" and "one of the quietest people you'd ever meet."

The incident that changed her life forever took place on December 7, 1993. On that day, a gunman opened fire with a semiautomatic weapon in a car of the Long Island Rail Road packed with commuters on their way home from work in New York City. By the time the shooting stopped, six people were fatally wounded—one of them McCarthy's husband, Dennis. Her son Kevin, also on the train, was partially paralyzed for life.

As McCarthy wrestled with her grief and anger, she swore she would do something to help stop America's plague of gun-related violence. She began talking to friends, family, neighbors—anyone who would listen. But conversations involving a few people would not solve the problem. So McCarthy started working with gun control organizations. In the process, she found herself addressing citizens' groups all across Long Island. As people started listening, she had to adapt her conversational abilities to larger audiences and more formal speaking situations. The spontaneous give-and-take of conversation evolved into structured public speeches.

When the U.S. Congressman in McCarthy's district voted in March 1996 to repeal the federal ban on assault weapons passed two years earlier, McCarthy took her speechmaking to a new level. "Determined," as she said, "to make a difference," she announced her candidacy for Congress. Again she had to adapt—this time to a cluster of newspapers and television cameras, as well as to a speaking schedule that increased from two or three presentations a week to as many as four or five a day.

Her greatest challenge came five months later, when she addressed a national television audience at the Democratic National Convention in Chicago. "This is really scary," she said before the speech. "I've got butterflies in my stomach!" Then she added, "But I believe in what I'm doing." Fired by that belief, McCarthy spoke movingly about her journey into politics and about the toll that gun violence takes in American society.

Returning home after the convention, McCarthy had to adapt yet again—this time to the speaking demands of a tough political campaign, including televised debates with her opponent. Running as a Democrat in a traditionally Republican district, she had to reach people by talking about the issues rather than by appealing to party loyalty. Often addressing several audiences a day, she communicated her ideas so effectively that she was elected to the U.S. Congress by a comfortable margin.

What a long road Carolyn McCarthy has traveled in the past few years. If someone had asked her before December 7, 1993, "Do you see yourself as a major public speaker?" she would have laughed at the idea. Yet, today she gives more than 100 speeches a year, not including radio, television, and newspaper interviews. Along the way, she has had to adapt to three major differences between conversation and public speaking.

1. *Public speaking is more highly structured.* It usually imposes strict time limitations on the speaker. In most cases, the situation does not allow listeners to interrupt with questions or commentary. The speaker must accomplish her or his purpose in the speech itself. When preparing the speech, the speaker must anticipate questions that might arise in the minds of listeners and answer them. Consequently, public speaking demands much more detailed planning and preparation than ordinary conversation.

2. *Public speaking requires more formal language.* Slang, jargon, and bad grammar have little place in public speeches. When Carolyn McCarthy addressed the Democratic National Convention, she didn't say, "We've damn well got to stop the creeps who use guns to shoot down innocent people." Despite the growing informality of all aspects of American life, listeners usually react negatively to speakers who do not elevate and polish their language when addressing an audience. A speech should be "special."

3. *Public speaking requires a different method of delivery.* When conversing informally, most people talk quietly, interject stock phrases such as "you know" and "I mean," adopt a casual posture, and use what are called vocalized pauses ("uh," "er," "um"). Effective public speakers, however, adjust their voices to be heard clearly throughout the audience. They assume a more erect posture. They avoid distracting mannerisms and verbal habits.

With study and practice, you will be able to master these differences and expand your conversational skills into speechmaking. Your speech class will provide the opportunity for this study and practice.

Developing Confidence: Your Speech Class

One of the major concerns of students in any speech class is stage fright. We may as well face the issue squarely. Many people who converse easily in all kinds of everyday situations become frightened at the idea of standing up before a group to make a speech.

stage fright
Anxiety over the prospect of giving a speech in front of an audience.

If you are worried about stage fright, you may feel better knowing that you are not alone. A survey conducted in 1973 asked more than 2,500 Americans to list their greatest fears. To the surprise of the researchers, the largest number of people—41 percent—listed speaking before a group among their greatest fears.[5] Amazing as it may seem, many Americans appear to consider public speaking a fate worse than death.

In a more recent study, researchers concentrated on social situations and, again, asked their subjects to list their greatest fears. Here is how they responded:[6]

Greatest Fear	Percent Naming
A party with strangers	74
Giving a speech	70
Asked personal questions in public	65
Meeting a date's parents	59
First day on a new job	59
Victim of a practical joke	56
Talking with someone in authority	53
Job interview	46
Formal dinner party	44
Blind date	42

Again, speechmaking ranks near the top in provoking anxiety.

Nervousness Is Normal

Actually, most people tend to be anxious before doing something important in public. Actors are nervous before a play, politicians are nervous before a campaign speech, athletes are nervous before a big game. The ones who succeed have learned to use their nervousness to their advantage. Listen to tennis star Pete Sampras, speaking after his 1999 Wimbledon title match against Andre Agassi. "I was nervous today," he admitted. "You don't want to get to this point and come up short." Putting his butterflies to good use, Sampras made sure he didn't come up short, beating Agassi in straight sets to claim his sixth Wimbledon championship.

Much the same thing happens in speechmaking. Surveys show that 76 percent of experienced speakers have stage fright before taking the floor.[7] But their nervousness is a healthy sign that they are getting "psyched up" for a good effort. Novelist and lecturer I. A. R. Wylie explains, "Now after many years of practice I am, I suppose, really a 'practiced speaker.' But I rarely rise to my feet without a throat constricted with terror and a furiously thumping heart. When, for some reason, I *am* cool and self-assured, the speech is always a failure."[8]

In other words, it is perfectly normal—even desirable—to be nervous at the start of a speech. Your body is responding as it would to any stressful situation—by producing extra *adrenaline.* This sudden shot of adrenaline is what makes your heart race, your hands shake, your knees knock, and your skin perspire. Every public speaker experiences all these reactions to some extent. The question is: How can you control your nervousness and make it work for you rather than against you?

> **adrenaline**
> A hormone released into the bloodstream in response to physical or mental stress.

Dealing with Nervousness

Rather than trying to eliminate every trace of stage fright, you should aim at transforming it from a negative force into what one expert calls *positive nervousness*—"a zesty, enthusiastic, lively feeling with a slight edge to it. . . . It's still nervousness, but it feels different. You're no longer victimized by it; instead, you're vitalized by it. You're in control of it."[9] Here are six time-tested ways you can turn your nervousness from a negative force into a positive one.

> **positive nervousness**
> Controlled nervousness that helps energize a speaker for her or his presentation.

Acquire Speaking Experience

You have already taken the first step. You are enrolled in a public speaking course, where you will learn about speechmaking and gain speaking experience. Think back to your first day at kindergarten, your first date, your first day at a new job. You were probably nervous in each situation because you were facing something new and unknown. Once you became accustomed to the situation, it was no longer threatening. So it is with public speaking. For most students, the biggest part of stage fright is fear of the unknown. The more you learn about public speaking and the more speeches you give, the less threatening speechmaking will become.

Your speech class will provide knowledge and experience to help you speak with confidence. Of course, the road to confidence will sometimes be bumpy. Learning to give a speech is not much different from learning any other skill—it proceeds by trial and error. The purpose of your speech class is to shorten the process, to minimize the errors, to give you a nonthreatening arena—a sort of laboratory—in which to undertake the "trial."

Your teacher recognizes that you are a novice and is trained to give the kind of guidance you need to get started. In your fellow students you have a highly sympathetic audience who will provide valuable feedback to help you improve your speaking skills. As the class goes on, your fears about public speaking will gradually recede until they are replaced by only a healthy nervousness before you rise to speak.[10]

Prepare, Prepare, Prepare

Another key to gaining confidence is to pick speech topics you truly care about—and then to prepare your speeches so thoroughly that you cannot help but be successful. Here's how one student combined enthusiasm for her topic with thorough preparation to score a triumph in speech class:

> Tia Betances was concerned about taking a speech class. Not having any experience as a public speaker, she got butterflies in her stomach just thinking about talking in front of an audience. But when the time came for Tia's first speech, she was determined to make it a success.
>
> Tia chose the Special Olympics as the topic for her speech. Her younger brother suffered from Down's syndrome, and for the past five years Tia had worked as a volunteer at the local Special Olympics competition. The purpose of her speech was to explain the origins, events, and philosophy of the Special Olympics.
>
> As Tia spoke, it became clear that she cared deeply about her subject and genuinely wanted her audience to care about it too. Because she was intent on communicating with her audience, she forgot to be nervous. She established eye contact with her listeners and spoke clearly, fluently, and dynamically. Soon the entire class was engrossed in her speech.
>
> Afterward, Tia conceded that she had surprised even herself. "I could hardly believe it," she said. "Once I got through the introduction, I didn't think about being nervous—I just concentrated on what I wanted to say. It was even sort of fun."

How much time should you devote to preparing your speeches? A standard rule of thumb is that each minute of speaking time requires one to two hours of preparation time—perhaps more, depending on the amount of research needed for the speech. This may seem like a lot of time, but the rewards are well worth it. Like an actor who rehearses a role until it is just right, you will find that your confidence as a speaker increases when you work on a speech until it is just right.[11] One professional speech consultant estimates that proper preparation can reduce stage fright by up to 75 percent.[12]

If you follow the techniques suggested by your teacher and in the rest of this book, you will stand up for every speech fully prepared. Imagine that the day for your first speech has arrived. You have studied your audience and selected a topic you know will interest them. You have researched the speech thoroughly and practiced it several times until it feels absolutely comfortable. You have even tried it out before two or three trusted friends. How can you help but be confident of success?

Think Positively

Confidence is mostly the well-known power of positive thinking. If you think you can do it, you usually can. On the other hand, if you predict disaster and doom, that is almost always what you will get. This is especially true when it comes to public speaking. Speakers who think negatively about themselves and the speech experience are much more likely to be overcome by stage fright than are speakers who think positively. Here are some ways you can transform negative thoughts into positive ones as you work on your speeches:

Negative Thought	Positive Thought
I wish I didn't have to give this speech.	This speech is a chance for me to share my ideas and gain experience as a speaker.
I'm not a great public speaker.	No one's perfect, but I'm getting better with each speech I give.
I'm always nervous when I give a speech.	Everyone's nervous. If other people can handle it, I can too.
No one will be interested in what I have to say.	I have a good topic and I'm fully prepared. Of course they'll be interested.

Many psychologists believe that the ratio of positive to negative thoughts in regard to stressful activities such as speechmaking should be at least five to one. That is, for each negative thought, you should counter with a minimum of five positive ones. Doing so will not make your nerves go away completely, but it will help keep them under control so you can concentrate on communicating your ideas rather than on brooding about your fears and anxieties.

Use the Power of Visualization

Visualization is closely related to positive thinking. It is a technique used by many people—athletes, musicians, actors, speakers, and others—to enhance their performance in stressful situations. How does it work? Listen to Olympic long-distance runner Vicki Huber:

> Right before a big race, I'll picture myself running, and I will try and put all of the other competitors in the race into my mind. Then I will try and imagine every possible situation I might find myself in . . . behind someone, being boxed in, pushed, shoved or cajoled, different positions on the track, laps to go, and, of course, the final stretch. And I always picture myself winning the race, no matter what happens during the event.[13]

Of course, Huber does not win every race she runs, but research has shown that the kind of mental imaging she describes can significantly increase athletic performance. Research has also shown that the same technique is of great benefit in helping speakers control their stage fright.[14]

The key to visualization is creating a vivid mental blueprint in which you see yourself succeeding in your speech. Picture yourself in your classroom rising to speak. See yourself at the lectern, poised and self-assured, making eye contact with your audience and delivering your introduction in

visualization
Mental imaging in which a speaker vividly pictures himself or herself giving a successful presentation.

Thinking positively, preparing fully, and concentrating on communicating with your audience will all help you speak with poise and confidence

a firm, clear voice. Feel your confidence growing as your listeners get more and more caught up in what you are saying. Imagine your sense of achievement as you conclude the speech knowing you have done your very best.

As you create these images in your mind's eye, be realistic but keep focused on the positive aspects of your speech. Don't allow negative images to eclipse the positive ones. Acknowledge your nervousness, but picture yourself overcoming it to give a vibrant, articulate presentation. If there is one part of the speech that always seems to give you trouble, visualize yourself getting through it without any hitches. And be specific. The more lucid your mental pictures, the more successful you are likely to be.[15]

As with your physical rehearsal of the speech, this kind of mental rehearsal of the speech should be repeated several times in the days before you speak. It doesn't guarantee that every speech will turn out exactly the way you envision it—and it certainly is no substitute for thorough preparation. But used in conjunction with the other methods of combating stage fright, it is a proven way to help control your nerves and to craft a successful presentation.

Know That Most Nervousness Is Not Visible

In addition to being anxious about giving a speech, many novice speakers are worried about appearing nervous to the audience. It's hard to speak with poise and assurance if you think you look tense and insecure. One of the most valuable lessons you will learn as your speech class proceeds is that only a fraction of the turmoil you are feeling inside is visible on the outside. "Your nervous system may be giving you a thousand shocks," says one experienced speaker, "but the viewer can see only a few of them."[16]

Even though your palms are sweating and your heart is pounding, your listeners probably won't realize how tense you are—especially if you do your best to act cool and confident on the outside. Most of the time when students confess after a speech, "I was so nervous I thought I was going to die," their classmates are surprised. To them the speaker looked calm and assured.[17]

Knowing this should make it easier for you to face your listeners with confidence. As one student stated after watching a videotape of her first classroom speech, "I was amazed at how calm I looked. I assumed everyone would be able to see how scared I was, but now that I know they can't, I won't be nearly so nervous in the future. It really helps to know that you look in control even though you may not feel that way."

Don't Expect Perfection

It may also help you to know that there is no such thing as a perfect speech. At some point in every presentation, every speaker says or does something—no matter how minor—that does not come across exactly as he or she had planned. Fortunately, as with one's nerves, such moments are usually not evident to the audience. Why? Because the audience does not know what the speaker *plans* to say. It hears only what the speaker *does* say. If you momentarily lose your place, reverse the order of a couple statements, or forget to pause at a certain spot, no one need be the wiser. When such moments occur, don't worry about them. Just proceed as if nothing happened.

Even if you do make an obvious mistake during a speech, that is no catastrophe. If you have ever listened to Martin Luther King's famous "I Have a Dream" speech, you may recall that he stumbles over his words twice during the speech. Most likely, however, you don't remember. Why? Because you were focusing on King's message rather than on the fine points of his delivery.

One of the biggest reasons people are concerned about making a mistake in a speech is that they view speechmaking as a kind of performance rather than as an act of communication. They feel the audience is judging them against a scale of absolute perfection in which every misstated word or awkward gesture will count against them. But speech audiences are not like judges in a violin recital or an ice-skating contest. They are not looking for a virtuoso performance, but for a well-thought-out address that communicates the speaker's ideas clearly and directly.[18] Sometimes an error or two can actually enhance a speaker's appeal by making her or him seem more human.

As you work on your speeches, make sure you prepare thoroughly and do all you can to get your message across to your listeners. But don't panic about being perfect or about what will happen if you make a mistake. Once you free your mind of these burdens, you will find it much easier to approach your speeches with confidence and even with enthusiasm.[19]

Besides stressing the six points just discussed, your teacher will probably give you several tips for dealing with nervousness in your first speeches. They may include:

- Be at your best physically and mentally. It's not a good idea to stay up until 4:00 A.M. partying with friends or cramming for an exam the night before your speech. A good night's sleep will serve you better.

■ As you are waiting to speak, quietly tighten and relax your leg muscles, or squeeze your hands together and then release them. Such actions help reduce tension by providing an outlet for your extra adrenaline.

■ Take a couple slow, deep breaths before you start to speak. Most people, when they are tense, take short, shallow breaths, which only reinforces their anxiety. Deep breathing breaks this cycle of tension and helps calm your nerves.

■ Work especially hard on your introduction. Research has shown that a speaker's anxiety level begins to drop significantly after the first 30 seconds of a presentation.[20] Once you get through the introduction, you should find smoother sailing the rest of the way.

■ Make eye contact with members of your audience. Remember that they are individual people, not a blur of faces. And they are your friends.

■ Concentrate on communicating with your audience rather than on worrying about your stage fright. If you get caught up in your speech, your audience will too.

■ Use visual aids. They create interest, draw attention away from you, and make you feel less self-conscious.[21]

If you are like most students, you will find your speech class to be a very positive experience. As one student wrote on her course evaluation form at the end of the class:

> I was really dreading this class. The idea of giving all those speeches scared me half to death. But I'm glad now that I stuck with it. It's a small class, and I got to know a lot of the students. Besides that, this is one class in which I got to express *my* ideas, instead of spending the whole time listening to the teacher talk. I even came to enjoy giving the speeches. I could tell at times that the audience was really with me, and that's a great feeling.

Over the years thousands of students have developed confidence in their speechmaking abilities. As your confidence grows, you will be better able to stand before other people and tell them what you think and feel and know—and to make them think and feel and know those same things. The best part about confidence is that it nurtures itself. After you score your first triumph, you will be that much more confident the next time. And as you become a more confident public speaker, you will likely become more confident in other areas of your life as well.[22]

Public Speaking and Critical Thinking

That guy at the party last night really demolished me when we got into a discussion. I know my information is right, and I'm sure there was something wrong with his argument, but I can't put my finger on it.

I need a computer, and every advertisement says its brand is state-of-the-art. But which is really the best buy for me?

I've worked hard on my term paper, but I'm not satisfied. It just doesn't seem to hang together, and I can't figure out what's wrong.

Political speeches are so one-sided. The candidates talk and talk, and they make everything sound rosy, but I still don't know whom to vote for.

Do any of these situations sound familiar? Have you ever found your-self in similar situations? If so, you may find help in your speech class. Be-sides building confidence, a course in public speaking can develop your skills as a critical thinker. Those skills can make the difference beween the articulate debater and the pushover, the careful consumer and the easy mark, the A student and the C student, the thoughtful voter and the coin tosser.

What is critical thinking? To some extent, it's a matter of logic—of be-ing able to spot weaknesses in other people's arguments and to avoid them in your own. It also involves related skills such as distinguishing fact from opinion, judging the credibility of statements, and assessing the soundness of evidence.

In the broadest sense, critical thinking is focused, organized thinking—the ability to see clearly the relationships among ideas. It has often been said that there are few new ideas in the world, only reorganized ideas. The greatest thinkers, scientists, and inventors have often taken information that was readily available and put it together differently to produce new insights. That, too, is critical thinking.[23]

If you are wondering what this has to do with your public speaking class, the answer is quite a lot. As the class proceeds, for example, you will prob-ably spend a good deal of time organizing your speeches. While this may seem like a purely mechanical exercise, it is closely interwoven with criti-cal thinking. If the structure of your speech is disjointed and confused, odds are that your thinking is also disjointed and confused. If, on the other hand, the structure is clear and cohesive, there is a good chance your thinking is too. Organizing a speech is not just a matter of arranging the ideas you al-ready have. Rather, it is an important part of shaping the ideas themselves.

What is true of organization is true of many aspects of public speaking. The skills you learn in your speech class can help you become a more ef-fective thinker in a number of ways. As you work on expressing your ideas in clear, accurate language, you will enhance your ability to think clearly and accurately. As you study the role of evidence and reasoning in speech-making, you will see how they can be used in other forms of communica-tion as well. As you learn to listen critically to speeches in class, you will be better able to assess the ideas of speakers (and writers) in a variety of situations.[24]

To return to the four examples at the beginning of this section:

That guy at the party last night—would sharpened critical thinking have helped you pounce on the flaws in his argument?

Buying a computer—are advertisements a reliable source of information, or should you try to find out more about prices and the features you need?

critical thinking
Focused, organized thinking about such things as the logical relationships among ideas, the soundness of evidence, and the differences between fact and opinion.

The term paper—would better organization and a clear outline help pull it together?

The politicians—once you filter out the fluff, are they drawing valid conclusions from sound evidence?

If you take full advantage of your speech class, you will be able to enhance your skills as a critical thinker in many circumstances. This is one reason public speaking has been regarded as a vital part of education since the days of ancient Greece.

The Speech Communication Process

As you begin your first speeches, you may find it helpful to understand what goes on when one person talks to another. Regardless of the kind of speech communication involved, there are seven elements—speaker, message, channel, listener, feedback, interference, and situation. Here we shall focus on how these elements interact when a public speaker addresses an audience.

Speaker

Speech communication begins with a speaker. If you pick up the telephone and call a friend, you are acting as a speaker. (Of course, you will also act as a listener when your friend is talking.) In public speaking, you will usually present your entire speech without interruption.

speaker
The person who is presenting an oral message to a listener.

Your success as a speaker depends on *you*—on your personal credibility, your knowledge of the subject, your preparation of the speech, your manner of speaking, your sensitivity to the audience and the occasion. But successful speaking is more than a matter of technical skill. It also requires enthusiasm. You can't expect people to be interested in what you say unless you are interested yourself. If you are truly excited about your subject, your audience is almost sure to get excited along with you. You can learn all the techniques of effective speechmaking, but before they can be of much use, you must first have something to say—something that sparks your own enthusiasm.

Message

message
Whatever a speaker communicates to someone else.

The message is whatever a speaker communicates to someone else. If you are calling a friend, you might say, "I'll be a little late picking you up tonight." That is the message. But it may not be the only message. Perhaps there is a certain tone in your voice that suggests reluctance, hesitation. The underlying message might be "I really don't want to go to that party. You talked me into it, but I'm going to put it off as long as I can."

Your goal in public speaking is to have your *intended* message be the message that is *actually* communicated. Achieving this depends both on what you say (the verbal message) and on how you say it (the nonverbal message).

Getting the verbal message just right requires work. You must narrow your topic down to something you can discuss adequately in the time allowed for the speech. You must do research and choose supporting details to make your ideas clear and convincing. You must organize your ideas so listeners can follow them without getting lost. And you must express your message in words that are accurate, clear, vivid, and appropriate.

Besides the message you send with words, you send a message with your tone of voice, appearance, gestures, facial expression, and eye contact. Imagine that one of your classmates gets up to speak about student loans. Throughout her speech she slumps behind the lectern, takes long pauses to remember what she wants to say, stares at the ceiling, and fumbles with her visual aids. Her intended message is "We must make more money available for student loans." But the message she actually communicates is "I haven't prepared very well for this speech." One of your jobs as a speaker is to make sure your nonverbal message does not distract from your verbal message.

Channel

The channel is the means by which a message is communicated. When you pick up the phone to call a friend, the telephone is the channel. Public speakers may use one or more of several channels, each of which will affect the message received by the audience.

Consider a speech to Congress by the President of the United States. The speech is carried to the nation by the channels of radio and television. For the radio audience the message is conveyed entirely by the President's voice. They can hear him, but they can't see him. For the television audience the message is conveyed by both the President's voice and the televised image of the President and his surroundings. The people in Congress have a more direct channel. They not only hear the President's voice as amplified through a microphone, but they see him and the setting firsthand.

In a public speaking class your channel is the most direct of all. Your classmates will see you and hear you without any electronic intervention.

channel
The means by which a message is communicated.

Listener

The listener is the person who receives the communicated message. Without a listener, there is no communication. When you talk to a friend on the phone, you have one listener. In public speaking you will have many listeners.

Everything a speaker says is filtered through a listener's *frame of reference*—the total of his or her knowledge, experience, goals, values, and attitudes. Because a speaker and a listener are different people, they can never have exactly the same frame of reference. And because a listener's frame of reference can never be exactly the same as a speaker's, the meaning of a message will never be exactly the same to a listener as to a speaker.

You can easily test the impact of different frames of reference. Ask each of your classmates to describe a chair. If you have 20 classmates, you'll probably get 20 different descriptions. One student might picture a large, overstuffed easy chair, another an elegant straight-backed chair, yet another an office chair, a fourth a rocking chair, and so on. Even if two or more envision the same general type—say, a rocking chair—their mental images of the chair could still be different. One might be thinking of an early American

listener
The person who receives the speaker's message.

frame of reference
The sum of a person's knowledge, experience, goals, values, and attitudes, No two people can have exactly the same frame of reference.

rocker, another of a modern Scandinavian rocker—the possibilities are unlimited. And "chair" is a fairly simple concept. What about "patriotism" or "freedom"?

Because people have different frames of reference, a public speaker must take great care to adapt the message to the particular audience being addressed. To be an effective speaker, you must be *audience-centered*. You must do everything in your speech with your audience in mind. You cannot assume that listeners will be interested in what you have to say. You must understand their point of view as you prepare the speech, and you must work to get them involved. You will quickly lose your listeners' attention if your presentation is either too basic or too sophisticated. You will also lose your audience if you do not relate to *their* experience, interests, knowledge, and values. When you make a speech that causes listeners to say, "That is important to *me,*" you will almost always be successful.

Feedback

When the President addresses the nation on television, he is engaged in one-way communication. You can talk back to the television set, but the President won't hear you. Most situations, however, involve *two-way* communication. Your listeners don't simply absorb your message like human sponges. They send back messages of their own. These messages are called feedback.

For example, when you phone your friend to say you will be late, you may hear, "Oh, no you don't! I don't care *what* your problem is; you get here on time!" That is feedback.

feedback
The messages, usually nonverbal, sent from a listener to a speaker.

The powers of critical thinking you develop in researching and organizing your speeches can also be applied in many other forms of communication.

This kind of verbal give-and-take is unusual in public speaking. Still, there is always plenty of feedback to let you know how your message is being received. Do your listeners lean forward in their seats, as if paying close attention? Do they applaud in approval? Do they laugh at your jokes? Do they have quizzical looks on their faces? Do they shuffle their feet and gaze at the clock? The message sent by these reactions could be "I am fascinated," "I am bored," "I agree with you," "I don't agree with you," or any number of others. As a speaker, you need to be alert to these reactions and adjust your message accordingly.

Like any kind of communication, feedback is affected by one's frame of reference. How would you feel if, immediately after your speech, all your classmates started to rap their knuckles on the desks? Would you run out of the room in despair? Not if you were in a European university. In many parts of Europe, students rap their knuckles on their desks to show great admiration for a classroom lecture. You must understand the feedback to be able to deal with it.

There are still two more elements we must consider to understand fully what happens in speech communication.

Interference

Interference is anything that impedes the communication of a message. When you talk on the telephone, sometimes there is static, or wires get crossed so that two different conversations are going on at once. That is a kind of interference. In public speaking, there are two kinds of interference. One, like the static or crossed wires in a phone conversation, is *external* to the audience. Many classrooms are subject to this kind of interference—from traffic outside the building, the clatter of a radiator, students conversing in the hall, a room that is stifling hot or freezing cold. Any of these can distract your listeners from what you are saying.

A second kind of interference is *internal* and comes from within your audience rather than from the outside. Perhaps one of your listeners has a bad mosquito bite or a patch of poison ivy. She may be so distracted by the itch that she doesn't pay attention to your speech. Another listener could be worrying about a test coming up in the next class period. Yet another could be brooding about an argument he had with his girlfriend.

As a speaker, you must try to hold your listeners' attention despite these various kinds of interference. In the chapters that follow you will find many ways to do this.

Situation

The situation is the time and place in which speech communication occurs. Conversation always takes place in a certain situation. Sometimes the situation helps—as when you propose marriage over an intimate candlelight dinner. Other times it may hurt—as when you try to speak words of love in competition with a blaring stereo. When you have to talk with someone about a touchy issue, you usually wait until the situation is just right.

Public speakers must also be alert to the situation. Certain occasions—funerals, church services, graduation ceremonies—require certain kinds of speeches. Physical setting is also important. It makes a great deal of difference

interference
Anything that impedes the communication of a message. Interference can be external or internal to listeners.

situation
The time and place in which speech communication occurs.

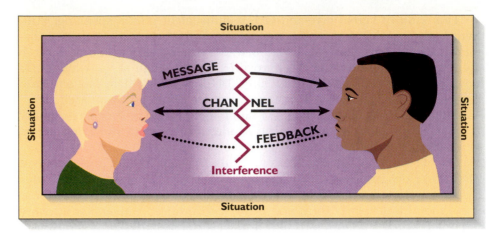

Figure 1.1

whether a speech is presented indoors or out, in a small classroom or in a gymnasium, to a densely packed crowd or to a handful of scattered souls. When you adjust to the situation of a public speech, you are only doing on a larger scale what you do every day in conversation.

Now let us look at a complete model of the speech communication process, as shown in Figure 1.1.[25]

The Speech Communication Process: Example with Commentary

The following example shows how the various components of the speech communication process interact:

Situation	It was 9:30 on a rainy Tuesday night. A series of routine reports had taken much longer than expected, and the meeting of the neighborhood association was running late.
Speaker	Angela Chiu was worried. As the founder of Pathways, a nonprofit organization devoted to operating group homes for developmentally disabled adults, she was the last speaker on the agenda. As Angela rose to address the association, she knew she faced a difficult task. She wanted to explain the purpose of Pathways and to get support for locating a group home for developmentally disabled adults in the neighborhood.
Channel Interference	Angela stepped to the microphone and began speaking. She could see members of the audience looking at their watches. They were worried about getting home on such a rainy night; some had even started putting on their coats and getting out their umbrellas.
Adapting to Interference	"Good evening," Angela began, "and thank you for staying a little longer. I promise I'll take no more than five minutes. Would anyone care to time me?" She was relieved to see several people chuckle as they checked their watches and settled back into their seats.
Message	Now that she had the attention of her audience, Angela quickly sketched the origins of Pathways and the needs of developmentally disabled adults. She ended by stating that she hoped to be able to

Feedback

address the association in more detail at a later meeting. She was delighted to see heads nodding at that suggestion, and was even more encouraged when one woman asked for Pathways' phone number. Several people jotted it down.

True to her word, Angela finished in five minutes. "Time's up," she laughed. "Thanks for listening, and don't forget your umbrellas!" Afterward, the association's president complimented Angela on dealing so well with a tough situation. "Next time, we'll make sure you're first on the agenda," the president said. "I know people are looking forward to hearing what you have to say."

Public Speaking in a Multicultural World

Cultural Diversity in the Modern World

The United States has always been a diverse society. In 1673, more than three centuries ago, a visitor to what is now New York City was astonished to find that 18 languages were spoken among the city's 8,000 inhabitants.[26] By the middle of the nineteenth century, so many people from so many lands had come to the United States that novelist Herman Melville exclaimed, "You cannot spill a drop of American blood without spilling the blood of the whole world."[27]

One can only imagine what Melville would say today! The United States has become the most diverse society on the face of the earth. For more than a century, most immigrants to the U.S. were Europeans—Irish, Germans, English, Scandinavians, Greeks, Poles, Italians, and others. Together with African-Americans, they made America the "melting pot" of the world. Today another great wave of immigration—mostly from Asia and Latin America—is transforming the United States into what one writer has called "the first universal nation," a multicultural society of unmatched diversity.[28]

The diversity of life in the United States can be seen in cities and towns, schools and businesses, community groups and houses of worship all across the land. Consider the following:

- There are 215 nations in the world, and every one of them has someone living in the United States.

- New York City has over 170 distinct ethnic communities.

- More than 32 million people in the U.S. speak a language other than English at home.

- Nonwhites and Hispanics make up a majority of high-school graduates in Hawaii, New Mexico, California, Mississippi, and Washington, D.C.

- More than 60 percent of the people in Miami were born outside the United States.

- If current trends continue, people of European descent will become a minority of U.S. citizens by the year 2050.

These kinds of changes are not limited to the United States. We are living in an age of international multiculturalism. The Internet allows for instant communication almost everywhere around the world. CNN is broadcast in more than 140 countries. International air travel has made national boundaries almost meaningless. The new global economy is redefining the nature of business and commerce. All nations, all people, all cultures are becoming part of a vast global village. For example:

- There are 60,000 transnational corporations around the world, and they account for more than a quarter of the world's economic output.

- In Brussels, the center of the European community, one in every four new babies is Arabic.

- At the University of British Columbia, in Vancouver, half of the first-year students are Asian.

- Swiss-based Nestlé sells 85 percent of its products in other countries; Gillette, located in Boston, makes 70 percent of its sales through exports.

- Restaurants in coastal towns of Queensland, Australia, print their menus in both Japanese and English.

- Four of every five new jobs in the U.S. are generated as a direct result of international trade.[29]

Cultural Diversity and Public Speaking

"That's all very interesting," you may be saying to yourself, "but what does it have to do with my speeches?" The answer is that diversity and multiculturalism are such basic facts of life that they can play a role in almost any speech you give. Consider the following situations: A business manager briefing employees of a multinational corporation. A lawyer presenting her closing argument to an ethnically mixed jury. A minister sermonizing to a culturally diverse congregation. An international student explaining the customs of his land to students at a U.S. university. A teacher addressing parents at a multiethnic urban school. These are only a few of the countless speaking situations affected by the cultural diversity of modern life.

As experts in intercultural communication have long known, speech-making becomes more complex as cultural diversity increases. Part of the complexity stems from the differences in language from culture to culture. As we will see in Chapter 11, language and thought are closely linked. So, too, are language and culture. Nothing separates one culture from another more than language. Not only do words change from language to language, but so do ways of thinking and of seeing the world. Language and culture are so closely bound that "we communicate the way we do because we are raised in a particular culture and learn its language, rules, and norms."[30]

The meanings attached to gestures, facial expressions, and other non-verbal signals also vary from culture to culture. Even the gestures for such basic messages as "yes" and "no," "hello" and "goodbye" are culturally

Public speaking is a vital mode of communication in most cultures around the world. Here Chinese President Jiang Zemin addresses an international development conference.

based. In the United States people nod their heads up and down to signal "yes" and shake them back and forth to signal "no." In Thailand the same actions have exactly the opposite meaning! To take another example, the North American "goodbye" wave is interpreted in many parts of Europe and South America as the motion for "no," while the Italian and Greek gesture for "goodbye" is the same as the U.S. signal for "come here."[31]

Many stories have been told about the fate of public speakers who fail to take into account cultural differences between themselves and their audiences. Consider the following scenario:[32]

The sales manager of a U.S. electronics firm is in Brazil to negotiate a large purchase of computers by a South American corporation. After three days of negotiations, the sales manager holds a gala reception for all the major executives to build goodwill between the companies.

As is the custom on such occasions, time is set aside during the reception for an exchange of toasts. When it is the sales manager's turn to speak, he praises the Brazilian firm for its many achievements and talks eloquently of his respect for its president and other executives. The words are perfect, and the sales manager can see his audience smiling in approval.

And then—disaster. As the sales manager closes his speech, he raises his hand and flashes the classic U.S. "OK" sign to signal his pleasure at the progress of the negotiations. Instantly the festive mood is replaced with stony silence; smiles turn to icy stares. The sales manager has given his Brazilian audience a gesture with roughly the same meaning as an extended middle finger in the United States.

The next day the Brazilian firm announces it will buy its computers from another company.

As this scenario illustrates, public speakers can ill afford to overlook their listeners' cultural values and customs. This is true whether you are speaking at home or abroad, in Atlanta or Rio de Janeiro, in a college classroom or at a meeting of community volunteers. Because of the increasing diversity of modern life, many—perhaps most—of the audiences you address will include people of different cultural backgrounds.

As you read the rest of this book, you will learn the methods of effective public speaking. Almost all of those methods will be helpful to you in speaking to culturally diverse audiences. Here we need to stress the importance of avoiding the ethnocentrism that often blocks communication between speakers and listeners of different cultural, racial, and ethnic backgrounds.

Avoiding Ethnocentrism

ethnocentrism
The belief that one's own group or culture is superior to all other groups or cultures.

Ethnocentrism is the belief that our own group or culture—whatever it may be—is superior to all other groups or cultures. Because of ethnocentrism, we identify with our group or culture and see its values, beliefs, and customs as "right" or "natural"—in comparison to the values, beliefs, and customs of other groups or cultures, which we tend to think of as "wrong" or "unnatural."[33]

Ethnocentrism is part of every culture. If you were born and raised in the United States, you may find it strange that most people in India regard the cow as a sacred animal and forgo using it as a source of food. On the other hand, if you were born and raised in India, you might well be shocked at the use of cows in the United States for food, clothing, and other consumer goods. If you are Christian, you most likely think of Sunday as the "normal" day of worship. But if you are Jewish, you probably regard Saturday as the "correct" Sabbath. And if you are Muslim, you doubtless see both Saturday and Sunday as unusual times for worship. For you, Friday is the "right" day.

Ethnocentrism can play a positive role in creating group pride and loyalty. But it can also be a destructive force—especially when it leads to prejudice and hostility toward different racial, ethnic, or cultural groups. To be an effective public speaker in a multicultural world, you need to keep in mind that all people have their special beliefs and customs.

Avoiding ethnocentrism does not mean you must agree with the values and practices of all groups and cultures. At times you might try to convince people of different cultures to change their traditional ways of doing things—as speakers from the United Nations seek to persuade farmers in Africa to adopt more productive methods of agriculture, as Muslim parents in the United States urge public school officials to accommodate Muslim customs for children who adhere to Islam, or as delegates from the U.S. and Japan attempt to influence the other country's trade policies.

If such speakers are to be successful, however, they must show respect for the cultures of the people they address. They cannot assume that their cultural assumptions and practices will be shared—or even understood—by all members of their audience. They need to adapt their message to the cultural values and expectations of their listeners.

What were the best public speeches of the twentieth century? A recent survey of communication scholars answered this question. Their list of the top 100 speeches is available at http://www.news. wisc.edu/misc/speeches/.

Thousands of people in the United States earn their living as professional public speakers. You can learn about their activities at the National Speakers Association website (http://www. nsaspeaker.org/).

The World Wide Web is rich in multicultural resources. A good starting point for accessing those resources is Yahoo: Society and Culture (http: //dir.yahoo.com/Regional/Countries/), which provides links to scores of websites dealing with countries and cultures around the world.

When you work on your speeches, keep in mind the growing diversity of life in the modern world and be alert to how cultural factors might affect the way listeners respond to your speeches. As we shall see in Chapter 5, for classroom speeches you can use audience-analysis questionnaires to learn about the backgrounds and opinions of your classmates in regard to specific speech topics. For speeches outside the classroom, the person who invites you to speak can usually provide information about the audience.

Once you know about any cultural factors that might affect the audience's response to your speech, you can work on adapting the speech to make it as effective and appropriate as possible. As you prepare the speech, try to put yourself in the place of your listeners and to hear your message through their ears. If there is a language difference between you and your audience, avoid any words or phrases that might cause misunderstanding. When researching the speech, keep an eye out for examples, comparisons, and other supporting materials that will relate to a wide range of listeners. Also, consider using visual aids in your speech. As we shall see in Chapter 13, they can be especially helpful in bridging a gap in language or cultural background.

When delivering your speech, be alert to feedback that might indicate the audience is having trouble grasping your ideas. If you see puzzled expressions on the faces of your listeners, restate your point to make sure it is understood. With some audiences, you can encourage feedback by asking, "Am I making myself clear?" or, "Did I explain this point fully enough?"

If you pose such questions, however, be aware that listeners from different cultures may respond quite differently. Most Arabs, North Americans, and Europeans will give you fairly direct feedback if you ask for it. Listeners from Asian and Caribbean countries, on the other hand, may not respond, out of concern that doing so will show disrespect for the speaker. (See Chapter 5 for a full discussion of audience analysis and adaptation.)[34]

Finally, we should note the importance of avoiding ethnocentrism when listening to speeches. As we shall see in Chapters 2 and 3, speech audiences have a responsibility to listen courteously and attentively. When you listen to a speaker from a different cultural background, be on guard against the temptation to judge that speaker on the basis of his or her appearance or manner of delivery. Too often we form opinions about people by the way they look or speak rather than by listening closely to what they *say*. No matter what the cultural background of the speaker, you should listen to her or him as attentively as you would want your audience to listen to you.

Summary

The need for effective public speaking will almost certainly touch you sometime in your life. When it does, you want to be ready. But even if you never give another speech in your life, you still have much to gain from studying public speaking. Your speech class will give you training in researching topics, organizing your ideas, and presenting yourself skillfully. This training is invaluable for every type of communication.

There are many similarities between public speaking and daily conversation. The three major goals of public speaking—to inform, to persuade, to entertain—are also the three major goals of everyday conversation. In conversation, almost without thinking about it, you employ a wide range of skills. You organize your ideas logically. You tailor your message to your audience. You tell a story for maximum impact. You adapt to feedback from your listener. These are among the most important skills you will need for public speaking.

Public speaking is also different from conversation. First, public speaking is more highly structured than conversation. It usually imposes strict time limitations on the speaker, and it requires more detailed preparation than does ordinary conversation. Second, public speaking requires more formal language. Listeners react negatively to speeches loaded with slang, jargon, and bad grammar. Third, public speaking demands a different method of delivery. Effective speakers adjust their voices to the larger audience and work at avoiding distracting physical mannerisms and verbal habits.

One of the major concerns of students in any speech class is stage fright. Actually, most successful speakers are nervous before making a speech. Your speech class will give you an opportunity to gain confidence and make your nervousness work for you rather than against you. You will take a big step toward overcoming stage fright if you think positively, prepare thoroughly, visualize yourself giving a successful speech, keep in mind that most nervousness is not visible to the audience, and think of your speech as communication rather than as a performance in which you must do everything perfectly. Like other students over the years, you too can develop confidence in your speechmaking abilities.

Besides building your confidence, a course in public speaking can help develop your skills as a critical thinker. Critical thinking is the ability to perceive relationships among ideas. It can help you spot weaknesses in other people's reasoning and avoid them in your own. Critical thinking can make a difference in many areas of your life, from your schoolwork to your activities as a consumer to your responsibilities as a citizen.

The speech communication process as a whole includes seven elements—speaker, message, channel, listener, feedback, interference, and situation. The speaker is the person who initiates a speech transaction. Whatever the speaker communicates is the message, which is sent by means of a particular channel. The listener receives the communicated message and provides feedback to the speaker. Interference is anything that impedes the communication of a message, and the situation is the time and place in which speech communication occurs. The interaction of these seven elements is what determines the outcome in any instance of speech communication.

Because of the growing diversity of modern life, many—perhaps most—of the audiences you address will include people of different cultural, racial, and ethnic backgrounds. When you work on your speeches, be alert to how such factors might affect the responses of your listeners and take steps to adapt your message accordingly. Above all, avoid the ethnocentric belief that your own culture or group—whatever it may be—is superior to every other culture or group. Also keep in mind the importance of avoiding ethnocentrism when listening to speeches. Accord every speaker the same courtesy and attentiveness you would want from your listeners.

Key Terms

stage fright (8)

adrenaline (9)

positive nervousness (9)

visualization (11)

critical thinking (15)

speaker (16)

message (16)

channel (17)

listener (17)

frame of reference (17)

feedback (18)

interference (19)

situation (19)

ethnocentrism (24)

Review Questions

After reading this chapter, you should be able to answer the following questions:

1. In what ways is public speaking likely to make a difference in your life?

2. How is public speaking similar to everyday conversation?

3. How is public speaking different from everyday conversation?

4. Why is it normal—even desirable—to be nervous at the start of a speech?

For further review, go to the Study Questions for this chapter.

CD: STUDY QUESTIONS

5. How can you control your nervousness and make it work for you in your speeches?

6. What are the seven elements of the speech communication process? How do they interact to determine the success or failure of a speech?

7. What is ethnocentrism? Why do public speakers need to avoid ethnocentrism when addressing audiences with diverse cultural, racial, or ethnic backgrounds?

Exercises for Critical Thinking

1. Think back on an important conversation you had recently in which you wanted to achieve a particular result. (*Examples:* Trying to convince your parents you should live in off-campus housing rather than in a dormitory; asking your employer to change your work schedule; explaining to a friend how to change the oil and filter in a car; trying to persuade a professor to accept your term paper a week late; attempting to talk your spouse into buying the computer you like rather than the one he or she prefers.) Work up a brief analysis of the conversation.

    In your analysis, explain the following: (1) your purpose in the conversation and the message strategy you chose to achieve your purpose; (2) the communication channels used during the conversation and how they affected the outcome; (3) the interference—internal or external—you encountered during the conversation; (4) the steps you took to adjust to feedback; (5) the strategic changes you would make in preparing for and carrying out the conversation if you had it to do over again.

2. Divide a sheet of paper into two columns. Label one column "Characteristics of an Effective Public Speaker." Label the other column "Characteristics of an Ineffective Public Speaker." In the columns, list and briefly explain what you believe to be the five most important characteristics of effective and ineffective speakers. Be prepared to discuss your ideas in class.

3. On the basis of the lists you developed for Exercise 2, candidly evaluate your own strengths and weaknesses as a speaker. Identify the three primary aspects of speechmaking you most want to improve.

Applying the POWER of Public Speaking

It has been three years since you finished college. After gaining experience as an administrative assistant at a major publishing company, you have just been promoted to marketing manager for a children's book series. Though you have occasionally given brief reports to other members of your work team, you are now facing your first speech to a large audience. At your company's annual sales meeting, you will address the sales force about the company's new books and how to sell them to wholesalers and retail bookstores.

You're pleased to have this opportunity and you know it shows the company's faith in your abilities. Yet the closer you get to the day of the speech, the harder it is to control the butterflies in your stomach. There will be 150 people in your audience, including all the senior editors and regional managers, in addition to the sales force. All eyes will be on you. It's important that you come across as confident and well-informed, but you're afraid your stage fright will send the opposite message. What strategies will you use to control your nerves and make them work for you?

Notes

[1] George A. Kennedy, *Comparative Rhetoric: An Historical and Cross-Cultural Introduction* (New York: Oxford University Press, 1998).

[2] Pericles, quoted in Richard Whately, *Elements of Rhetoric,* 7th ed. (London: John W. Parker, 1846), p. 10.

[3] *Wall Street Journal,* December 29, 1998, p. A1.

[4] Lee Iacocca, *An Autobiography* (New York: Bantam, 1984), p. 16; Midge Costanza quoted in Sharon Nelson, "Address for Success," *Nation's Business* (February 1991), pp. 43–44.

[5] What Are Americans Afraid Of?" *The Bruskin Report,* 53 (July 1973).

[6] Daniel Goleman, "Social Anxiety: New Focus Leads to Insights and Therapy," *New York Times* (December 18, 1984). "How Americans Communicate," a 1999 study commissioned by the National Communication Association, found that only 24 percent of Americans are "very comfortable" giving a speech or other formal presentation. The study can be accessed at http://www.natcom.org/research/Roper/how_americans_communicate.htm.

[7] Jeffrey C. Hahner, Martin A. Sokoloff, and Sandra L. Salisch, *Speaking Clearly: Improving Voice and Diction,* 5th ed. (New York: McGraw-Hill, 1997), p. 362.

[8] Quoted in Bert E. Bradley, *Fundamentals of Speech Communication: The Credibility of Ideas,* 6th ed. (Dubuque, Iowa: W.C. Brown, 1991), p. 36.

[9] Elayne Synder, *Speak for Yourself—With Confidence* (New York: New American Library, 1983), p. 113.

[10] A number of studies have shown that taking a public speaking course is effective in reducing stage fright. Among the most recent are Peggy Yuhas Byers and Carolyn Secord Weber, "The Timing of Speech Anxiety Reduction Treatments in the Public Speaking Classroom," *Southern Communication Journal,* 60 (1995), pp. 246–256; Rebecca B. Rubin, Alan M. Rubin, and Felicia F. Jordan, "Effects of Instruction on Communication Apprehension and Communication Competence," *Communication Education,* 46 (1997), pp. 104–114.

[11] See Kent E. Menzel and Lori J. Carrell, "The Relationship between Preparation and Performance in Public Speaking," *Communication Education,* 43 (1994), pp. 17–26.

[12] Lilly Walters, *Secrets of Successful Speakers* (New York: McGraw-Hill, 1993), pp. 32–36.

[13] Quoted in Steven Ungerleider, *Mental Training for Peak Performance* (Emmaus, Pa.: Rodale Press, 1996), p. 9.

[14] Joe Ayres, Tim Hopf, and Debbie M. Ayres "Visualization and Performance Visualization: Applications, Evidence, and Speculation," in John A. Daly, James C. McCroskey, Joe Ayres, Tim Hopf, and Debbie M. Ayres (eds.), *Avoiding Communication: Shyness, Reticence, and Communication Apprehension,* 2nd ed. (Cresskill, N.J.: Hampton Press, 1997), pp. 401–422.

[15] See Marie Dalloway, *Visualization: The Master Skill in Mental Training* (Phoenix, Ariz.: Optimal Performance Institute, 1992).

[16]Dick Cavett, quoted in Steve Allen, *How to Make a Speech* (New York: McGraw-Hill, 1986), p. 10.

[17]For research on this point, see Marianne Martini, Ralph R. Behnke, and Paul E. King, "The Communication of Public Speaking Anxiety: Perceptions of Asian and American Speakers," *Communication Quarterly,* 40 (1992), pp. 279–288.

[18]For more detail on the ideas in this paragraph, see Michael T. Motley, *Overcoming Your Fear of Public Speaking: A Proven Method* (New York: McGraw-Hill, 1995).

[19]For additional research on the benefits of viewing public speaking as an act of communication rather than a rule-governed performance, see Amy M. Bippus and John A. Daly, "What Do People Think Causes Stage Fright? Naive Attributions about the Reasons for Public Speaking Anxiety," *Communication Education,* 48 (1999), pp. 62–72.

[20]Michael T. Motley, "Taking the Terror Out of Talk," *Psychology Today* (January 1988), p. 47.

[21]For fuller discussion of these and other approaches to controlling stage fright, see Virginia P. Richmond and James C. McCroskey, *Communication: Apprehension, Avoidance, and Effectiveness,* 5th ed. (Boston: Allyn and Bacon, 1998); Peter Desberg, *No More Butterflies: Overcoming Stagefright, Shyness, Interview Anxiety, and Fear of Public Speaking* (Oakland, Calif.: New Harbinger, 1996).

[22]Several studies have documented the extent to which the confidence gained in a public speaking class benefits students in other forms of communication. See Wendy S. Zabava Ford and Andrew D. Wolvin, "The Differential Impact of a Basic Communication Course on Perceived Competencies in Class, Work, and Social Contexts," *Communication Education,* 42 (1993), pp. 215–223; Rubin, Rubin, and Jordan, "Effects of Instruction on Communication Apprehension and Communication Competence."

[23]For more detail on the dimensions of critical thinking, see Marilyn Meltzer and Susan Marcus Palau, *Acquiring Critical Thinking Skills* (Philadelphia: W.B. Saunders, 1996); M. Neil Browne and Stuart M. Keeley, *Asking the Right Questions: A Guide to Critical Thinking,* 5th ed. (Englewood Cliffs, N.J.: Prentice Hall, 1997).

[24]For a summary of research on this point, see Mike Allen, Sandra Berkowitz, Steve Hunt, and Allen Louden, "A Meta-Analysis of the Impact of Forensics and Communication Education on Critical Thinking," *Communication Education,* 48 (1999), pp. 18–30. Also see Virginia O'Keefe, *Speaking to Think; Thinking to Speak: The Importance of Talk in the Learning Process* (Portsmouth, N.H.: Boynton/Cook, 1995).

[25]For other models of the speech communication process, see Stephen W. Littlejohn, *Theories of Human Communication,* 6th ed. (Belmont, Calif.: Wadsworth, 1999); Em Griffin, *A First Look at Communication Theory,* 4th ed. (New York: McGraw-Hill, 2000).

[26]John Elson, "The Great Migration," *Time* (Fall 1993), p. 30. For a detailed look at the cultural diversity of colonial America, see Bernard Bailyn and Philip D. Morgan (eds.), *Strangers within the Realm: Cultural Margins of the First British Empire* (Chapel Hill, N.C.: University of North Carolina Press, 1991).

[27]Quoted in Ronald Takai, *A Different Mirror: A History of Multicultural America* (Boston: Little, Brown, 1993), p. 427.

[28]Ben J. Wattenberg, *The First Universal Nation: Leading Indicators and Ideas about the Surge of America in the 1990s* (New York: Free Press, 1991).

[29]Sources for this and the previous paragraphs include Harold Hodgkinson, "Demographics of Diversity for the Twenty-First Century," *Education Digest,* 64 (1998), pp. 4–7; Pico Iyer, "The Global Village Finally Arrives," *Time* (Fall 1993), pp. 86–87; Myron W. Lustig and Jolene Koester, *Intercultural Competence: Interpersonal Communication across Cultures,* 3rd ed. (New York: Longman, 1999), p. 6; David Hale, "A Second Chance," *Fortune* (November 22, 1999), pp. 189–190; Courtland L. Boveé and John V. Thill, *Business Communication Today,* 4th ed. (New York: McGraw-Hill, 1995), p. 56; *Wisconsin State Journal,* August 29, 1999, p. 9A.

[30]William B. Gudykunst and Young Yun Kim, *Communicating with Strangers: An Approach to Intercultural Communication,* 3rd ed. (New York: McGraw-Hill, 1997), p. 4. For more detail, see Larry A. Samovar and Richard E. Porter, *Communication between Cultures,* 2nd ed. (Belmont, Calif.: Wadsworth, 1995), pp. 149–179.

[31]Carly H. Dodd, *Dynamics of Intercultural Communication,* 5th ed. (New York: McGraw-Hill, 1998), pp. 133–153; Dale Marco, "Doing Business Overseas: It's a Whole New Ballgame," *USA Today* (September 1998), pp. 20–22.

[32]Adapted from Roger E. Axtell (ed.), *Do's and Taboos Around the World,* 3rd ed. (New York: John Wiley and Sons, 1993), p. 41.

[33]Lustig and Koester, *Intercultural Competence,* p. 146.

[34]For more on the ins and outs of intercultural communication, see Kenneth Cushner and Richard W. Brislin, *Intercultural Interactions: A Practical Guide* (Thousand Oaks, Calif.: Sage, 1996).

CHAPTER TWO

ETHICS AND PUBLIC SPEAKING

The Importance of Ethics

Guidelines for Ethical Speaking

Make Sure Your Goals Are Ethically Sound
Be Fully Prepared for Each Speech
Be Honest in What You Say
Avoid Name-Calling and Other Forms of Abusive
    Language
Put Ethical Principles into Practice

Plagiarism

Global Plagiarism
Patchwork Plagiarism
Incremental Plagiarism

Guidelines for Ethical Listening

Be Courteous and Attentive
Avoid Prejudging the Speaker
Maintain the Free and Open Expression of Ideas

Kathryn Luedtke, a manager in the state Department of Development and Natural Resources, was in charge of planning a multipurpose center for business and educational retreats on a little-used stretch of riverfront in the northwest tip of the state. There was just one catch. The year before, a local environmental group had raised funds to create a small wildlife park on one corner of the site. Although final plans for the center had not been drawn, Kathryn knew the park would have to be closed to make way for an access road.

Shortly before the plans were finished, Kathryn was asked to speak at a meeting of the local group. Recognizing the positive economic impact the center would have on their community, the group's members were willing to support it as long as it did not disrupt the wildlife park. Reasoning to herself that the group was small and located far from the state's media centers, Kathryn assured them the park would be protected. The group voted to endorse the proposal.

Two days after final plans for the center were presented to the legislature, a reporter who had been contacted by the local group called Kathryn to ask how she could sacrifice the park after promising to do the opposite. Kathryn tried to talk her way out of it, but she had no defense. The legislature withdrew funding for the center, a national environmental group put Kathryn on their annual "Liars List," and she was fired from her position with the Department of Development and Natural Resources.

This is not a happy story, but it shows why speechmaking needs to be guided by a strong sense of integrity. Kathryn Luedtke was persuasive when speaking to the local environmental group, but she was unethical in not telling the truth about the impact of her project on the wildlife park. As a result, the project was abandoned, Kathryn lost her job, and her reputation was left in tatters.

You might be saying to yourself, "Yes, that's very unfortunate. But lots of people lie and cheat, and many of them don't get caught." And you would be correct—many people don't get caught. But that doesn't make their behavior right. In public speaking, as in other areas of life, there are standards for ethical conduct.

The goal of public speaking is to gain a desired response from listeners—but not at any cost. Speechmaking is a form of power and therefore carries with it heavy ethical responsibilities. As the Roman rhetorician Quintilian stated 2,000 years ago, the ideal of commendable speechmaking is the good person speaking well. In this chapter, we explore that ideal by looking at the importance of ethics in public speaking, the ethical obligations of speakers and listeners, and the practical problem of plagiarism and how to avoid it.

The Importance of Ethics

ethics
The branch of philosophy that deals with issues of right and wrong in human affairs.

Ethics is the branch of philosophy that deals with issues of right and wrong in human affairs. Questions of ethics arise whenever we ask whether a course of action is moral or immoral, fair or unfair, just or unjust, honest or dishonest.[1]

We face such questions daily in almost every part of our lives. The parent must decide how to deal with a child who has been sent home from school for unruly behavior. The researcher must decide whether to shade her data "just a bit" in order to gain credit for an important scientific breakthrough. The shopper must decide what to do with the $5 extra change mistakenly given by the clerk at the grocery store. The student must decide whether to say anything about a friend he has seen cheating on a final exam.

Questions of ethics also come into play whenever a public speaker faces an audience. In an ideal world, as the Greek philosopher Plato noted, all public speakers would be truthful and devoted to the good of society. Yet history tells us that the power of speech is often abused—sometimes with disastrous results. Adolf Hitler was unquestionably a persuasive speaker. His oratory galvanized the German people into following one ideal and one leader. But his aims were horrifying and his tactics despicable. He remains to this day the ultimate example of why the power of the spoken word needs to be guided by a strong sense of ethical integrity.

As a public speaker, you will face ethical issues at every stage of the speechmaking process—from the initial decision to speak through the final presentation of the message. This is true whether you are speaking in the classroom or the courtroom, whether you are participating in a business meeting or a religious service, whether you are addressing an audience of two people or 2,000 people. And the answers will not always be easy. Consider the following example:

> Felicia Robinson is running for school board in a large eastern city. Her opponent is conducting what Felicia regards as a highly unethical campaign. In addition to twisting the facts about school taxes, the opponent is pandering to racial prejudice by raising resentment against African-Americans and newly arrived immigrants.
>
> Five days before the election, Felicia, who is slightly behind in the polls, learns that the district attorney is preparing to indict her opponent for shady business practices. But the indictment will not be formally issued until after the election. Nor can it be taken as evidence that her opponent is guilty—like all citizens, he has the right to be presumed innocent until proven otherwise.
>
> Still, news of the indictment could be enough to throw the election Felicia's way, and her advisers urge her to make it an issue in her remaining campaign speeches. Should Felicia follow their advice?

There are creditable arguments to be made on both sides of the ethical dilemma faced by Felicia Robinson. She has tried to run an honest campaign, and she is troubled by the possibility of unfairly attacking her opponent—despite the fact that he has shown no such scruples himself. Yet she knows that the impending indictment may be her last chance to win the election, and she is convinced that a victory for her opponent will spell disaster for the city's school system. Torn between her commitment to fair play, her desire to be elected, and her concern for the good of the community, she faces the age-old ethical dilemma of whether the ends justify the means.

"So," you may be saying to yourself, "what is the answer to Felicia Robinson's dilemma?" But in complex cases such as hers there are no cut-and-dried answers. As Richard Johannesen, a leader in the study of communication ethics, states, "We should formulate meaningful ethical guidelines, not inflexible rules."[2] Your ethical decisions will be guided by your values, your conscience, your sense of right and wrong.

But this does not mean such decisions are simply a matter of personal whim or fancy. Sound ethical decisions involve weighing a potential course of action against a set of ethical standards or guidelines. Just as there are

ethical decisions
Sound ethical decisions involve weighing a potential course of action against a set of ethical standards or guidelines.

guidelines for ethical behavior in other areas of life, so are there guidelines for ethical conduct in public speaking. These guidelines will not automatically solve every ethical quandary you face as a speaker, but knowing them will provide a reliable compass to help you find your way.

Guidelines for Ethical Speaking

Make Sure Your Goals Are Ethically Sound

Not long ago, I spoke with a former student—we'll call her Melissa—who had turned down a job in the public relations department of the American Tobacco Institute. Why? Not because of the salary (which was generous) or the work schedule (which was ideal). Melissa declined the job because it would have required her to lobby on behalf of the cigarette industry. Knowing that cigarettes are the number one health hazard in the United States, Melissa did not believe she could ethically promote a product that she saw as responsible for thousands of deaths and illnesses each year.

Given Melissa's view of the dangers of cigarette smoking, there can be no doubt that she made an ethically informed decision to turn down the job with the American Tobacco Institute. On the other side of the coin, someone with a different view of cigarette smoking could make an ethically informed decision to *take* the job. The point of this example is not to judge the rightness or wrongness of Melissa's decision (or of cigarette smoking), but to illustrate how ethical considerations can affect a speaker's choice of goals.

Your first responsibility as a speaker is to ask whether your goals are ethically sound. During World War II, Hitler stirred the German people to condone war, invasion, and genocide. More recently, we have seen politicians who betray the public trust for personal gain, business leaders who defraud investors of millions of dollars, preachers who lead lavish lifestyles at the expense of their religious duties. There can be no doubt that these are not worthy goals.

But think back for a moment to the examples of speechmaking given in Chapter 1. What do the speakers hope to accomplish? Report on a business project. Improve the quality of education. Pay tribute to a fellow worker. Stop the plague of gun violence in the U.S. Support the Special Olympics. Few people would question that these goals are ethically sound.

As with other ethical issues, there can be gray areas when it comes to assessing a speaker's goals—areas in which reasonable people with well-defined standards of right and wrong can legitimately disagree. But this is not a reason to avoid asking ethical questions. If you are to be a responsible public speaker, you cannot escape assessing the ethical soundness of your goals.

Be Fully Prepared for Each Speech

"A speech," as Jenkin Lloyd Jones noted, "is a solemn responsibility." You have an obligation—to yourself and to your listeners—to prepare fully every time you stand in front of an audience. The obligation to yourself is obvious: The better you prepare, the better your speech will be. But the obliga-

Among current public speakers, Burmese democracy leader Aung San Suu Kyi, winner of the Nobel Peace Prize, is highly regarded for her ethically sound goals and powerful persuasive appeal.

tion to your listeners is no less important. Think of it this way: The person who makes a bad 30-minute speech to an audience of 200 people wastes only a half hour of her or his own time. But that same speaker wastes 100 hours of the audience's time—more than four full days. This, Jones exclaimed, "should be a hanging offense!"

At this stage of your speaking career, of course, you will probably not be facing many audiences of 200 people. And you will probably not be giving many speeches in which the audience has come for the sole purpose of listening to you. But neither the size nor the composition of your audience changes your ethical responsibility to be fully prepared. Your speech classmates are as worthy of your best effort as if you were addressing a jury or a business meeting, a union conference or a church congregation, the local Rotary club or even the United States Senate.

Being prepared for a speech involves everything from analyzing your audience to creating visual aids, organizing your ideas to rehearsing your delivery. Most crucial from an ethical standpoint, though, is being fully informed about your subject. Why is this so important? Consider the following story:

Several years ago Manuel Higuera, a student at a large California university, gave a classroom speech demonstrating how to use the Heimlich maneuver to dislodge a piece of food trapped in a person's windpipe. Manuel had learned the maneuver from his mother, a Red Cross worker, but he did not rely on that knowledge alone in preparing his speech. He read several magazine articles about the Heimlich maneuver, and he picked up a pamphlet from the local fire department explaining how to perform the maneuver.

In addition to his research, Manuel gave a lot of thought to organizing and delivering his speech. He even got a friend to serve as a volunteer on whom he could demonstrate the steps of the Heimlich maneuver for his classmates. By the day of his speech, Manuel was thoroughly prepared—and he gave an excellent presentation.

No more than a week later, one of Manuel's classmates, Alison Bartlett, was eating dinner in her apartment when her roommate began choking on a piece of food. Remembering Manuel's speech, Alison went into action with the Heimlich maneuver. First she got her roommate to stand up. Then she put her arms around her roommate's waist, made a fist with one hand, pressed it into her roommate's abdomen, and exerted several quick upward thrusts until the food popped out. Alison saved her roommate's life, thanks to Manuel's speech.

This is an especially dramatic case, but it demonstrates how your speeches can have a genuine impact on your listeners' lives. As a speaker, you have an ethical responsibility to consider that impact and to make sure you prepare fully so as not to communicate erroneous information or misleading advice. Imagine what might have happened if Manuel had not done such a thorough job researching his speech. He might have given his classmates faulty instructions about the Heimlich maneuver—instructions that might have had tragic results.

No matter what the topic, no matter what the audience, you need to explore your speech topic as thoroughly as possible. Investigate the whole story, learn about all sides of an issue, seek out competing viewpoints, get the facts right. Not only will you give a better speech, you will also fulfill one of your major ethical obligations.

Be Honest in What You Say

Nothing is more important to ethical speechmaking than honesty. Public speaking rests on the unspoken assumption that "words can be trusted and people will be truthful."[3] Without this assumption, there is no basis for communication, no reason for one person to believe anything that another person says. Once the bond of trust between a speaker and listener is broken, it can never be fully restored.

Does this mean *every* speaker must *always* tell "the truth, the whole truth, and nothing but the truth"? We can all think of situations in which this is impossible (because we do not know the whole truth) or inadvisable (because it would be tactless or imprudent). Consider a presidential press secretary who denies the existence of secret diplomatic negotiations because she does not know they are taking place. Or a parent who tells his two-year-old daughter that her screeching violin solo is "beautiful." Or a speaker who tells a falsehood in circumstances when disclosing the truth might touch off mob violence. Few people would find these actions unethical.[4]

In contrast, think back to the case of Kathryn Luedtke at the start of this chapter. Kathryn knew the center she was developing would require closing the local wildlife park. Yet she told the environmental group that the center could be built without harming the park. The group accepted her word and voted to support the center. There is no way to excuse Kathryn's conduct. She told a flat-out lie without regard to its consequences on the audience.

Such blatant contempt for the truth is one kind of dishonesty in public speaking. But there are more subtle forms of dishonesty that are just as unethical. They include juggling statistics, quoting out of context, misrepresenting the sources of facts and figures, painting tentative findings as firm conclusions, portraying a few details as the whole story, citing unusual cases as typical examples, and substituting innuendo and half-truths for evidence and proof. All of these violate the speaker's duty to be accurate and fair in presenting information.

While on the subject of honesty in speechmaking, we should also note that ethically responsible speakers do not present other people's words as their own. They do not plagiarize their speeches. This subject is so important that we devote a separate section to it later in this chapter.

Avoid Name-Calling and Other Forms of Abusive Language

"Sticks and stones can break my bones, but words can never hurt me." This popular children's chant could not be more wrong. Words may not literally break people's bones, but they are powerful weapons that can leave psychological scars as surely as sticks and stones can leave physical scars. As one writer explains, "Our identities, who and what we are, how others see us, are greatly affected by the names we are called and the words with which we are labeled."[5] This is why almost all communication ethicists warn public speakers to avoid name-calling and other forms of abusive language.

Name-Calling and Personal Dignity

Name-calling is the use of language to defame, demean, or degrade individuals or groups. When applied to various groups in America, it includes such epithets as "fag," "kike," "nigger," "wop," "jap," "chink," and "spic." Such terms have been used to debase people because of their ethnic background, religious beliefs, or sexual orientation. These words dehumanize the groups they are directed against. They imply that the groups are inferior and do not deserve to be treated with the same dignity and respect as other members of society.

The same is true of sexist language. We have come to understand in recent years how the English language is riddled with sexism. Most blatant is the generic "he," which excludes women from whatever group is being discussed—as in, "When a college student studies for an exam, he should be sure to review all his lecture notes." Not only does this statement imply that women do not attend college, but it overlooks the fact that women now outnumber men on most campuses. There are also countless words and phrases that convey negative, stereotyped, or misleading views of women. Some disparage, patronize, or ridicule ("little woman," "chick," "dumb blonde"); others imply second-class status ("the other sex," "the weaker sex"); still others classify women in ways that are seldom applied to men ("coed," "woman pioneer," "unchaste").[6]

name-calling
The use of language to defame, demean, or degrade individuals or groups.

In Chapter 11 we will look at ways you can avoid sexist language in your speeches. For now the point to remember is that, contrary to what some people claim, avoiding racist, sexist, and other kinds of abusive language is not simply a matter of "political correctness." Such language is ethically suspect because it devalues the people in question and stereotypes them in ways that assume the innate superiority of one group over another. This principle applies whether the group is being maligned for its gender, religion, ethnic background, sexual orientation, or physical or mental disability. The issue is not one of politics, but of respecting the dignity of the diverse groups in contemporary society.

Name-Calling and Free Speech

Name-calling and abusive language also pose ethical problems in public speaking when they are used to silence opposing voices. A democratic society depends upon the free and open expression of ideas. In the United States, all citizens have the right to join in the never-ending dialogue of democracy. As a public speaker, you have an ethical obligation to help preserve that right by avoiding tactics such as name-calling that automatically impugn the accuracy or respectability of public statements made by groups or individuals who voice opinions different from yours.[7]

This obligation is the same regardless of whether you are black or white, Asian or Latino, male or female, Republican or Democrat, liberal or conservative. A pro-environmentalist office seeker who castigated everyone opposed to her ideas as an "enemy of wildlife" would be on as thin ice ethically as a politician who labeled all his adversaries "tax-and-spend liberals" when he knew full well that the charge was untrue. No matter what your stand on particular issues, you have an ethical responsibility to avoid name-calling and other tactics that harm the free and open expression of ideas.

Bill of Rights
The first 10 amendments to the United States Constitution.

Like other ethical questions in public speaking, name-calling raises some thorny issues. Although name-calling can be hazardous to free speech, it is still protected under the free-speech clause of the Bill of Rights. This is why the American Civil Liberties Union, a major defender of constitutional rights, has opposed broadly worded codes against abusive speech on college campuses. Such codes usually prohibit threatening or insulting speech against racial or religious minorities, women, gays and lesbians, and people with physical disabilities. To date, these codes have not survived legal challenges, and a number of schools are now developing more narrowly focused regulations that they hope will stand up in court.[8]

But whatever the legal outcome may be, it will not alter the ethical responsibility of public speakers—on or off campus—to avoid name-calling and other kinds of abusive language. Legality and ethics, though related, are not identical. There is nothing illegal about falsifying statistics in a speech, but there is no doubt that it is unethical. The same is true of name-calling. It may not be illegal to cast racial, sexual, or religious slurs at people in a speech, but it is still unethical. Not only does it demean the dignity of the groups or individuals being attacked, but it undermines the right of all groups in the U.S. to be fairly heard.

THE INTERNET *Connection*

Questions of right and wrong arise whenever people communicate—whether it be through public speaking, group discussion, everyday conversation, or the mass media. To help foster responsible communication, the National Communication Association has developed a Credo for Ethical Communication, which you can access at http://www.natcom.org/lc/nov99/rescredo.htm.

The question of speech codes on campus is very controversial. To learn why the American Civil Liberties Union opposes such codes, read its briefing paper "Hate Speech on Campus" (http://www.aclu.org/library/pbp16.html). For links to other sites dealing with free speech issues, visit the ACLU's Free Speech website at http://www.aclu.org/issues/freespeech/hmfs.html.

Put Ethical Principles into Practice

We are all familiar with people who say one thing and do another. It is easy to pay lip service to the importance of ethics. It is much harder to act ethically. Yet that is just what the responsible public speaker must do. As one popular book on ethics states, "Being ethical means behaving ethically *all the time*—not only when it's convenient."[9]

As you work on your speeches, you will ask yourself such questions as, "Is my choice of topic suitable for the audience?" "Are my supporting materials clear and convincing?" "How can I phrase my ideas to give them more punch?" These are *strategic* questions. As you answer them, you will try to make your speech as informative, as persuasive, or as entertaining as possible.

But you will also face moments of *ethical* decision—similar, perhaps, to those faced by Kathryn Luedtke, Felicia Robinson, and the other speakers in this chapter. When those moments arrive, don't simply brush them aside and go on your way. Take your ethical responsibilities as seriously as your strategic objectives. Keep in mind the guidelines for ethical speechmaking we have discussed and do your best to follow them through thick and thin. Make sure you can answer yes to all the questions on the Checklist for Ethical Public Speaking on page 42 (Figure 2.1).

Plagiarism

"Plagiarism" comes from *plagiarius,* the Latin word for kidnapper. To plagiarize means to present another person's language or ideas as your own—to give the impression you have written or thought something yourself when you have actually taken it from someone else.[10] We often think of plagiarism as an ethical issue in the classroom, but it can have repercussions in other situations:

plagiarism
Presenting another person's language or ideas as one's own.

Figure 2.1

CHECKLIST FOR ETHICAL PUBLIC SPEAKING

1.   Have I examined my goals to make sure they are ethically sound?

   a.   Can I defend my goals on ethical grounds if they are questioned
        or challenged?
   b.   Would I want other people to know my true motives in presenting this speech?

2.   Have I fulfilled my ethical obligation to prepare fully for the speech?

   a.   Have I done a thorough job of studying and researching the topic?
   b.   Have I prepared diligently so as not to communicate erroneous or misleading
        information to my listeners?

3.   Is the speech free of plagiarism?

   a.   Can I vouch that the speech represents my own work, my own thinking, my own
        language?
   b.   Do I cite the sources of all quotations and paraphrases?

4.   Am I honest in what I say in the speech?

   a.   Is the speech free of any false or deliberately deceptive statements?
   b.   Does the speech present statistics, testimony, and other kinds of
        evidence fairly and accurately?
   c.   Does the speech contain valid reasoning?
   d.   If the speech includes visual aids, do they present facts honestly and reliably?

5.   Do I use the power of language ethically?

   a.   Do I avoid name-calling and other forms of abusive language?
   b.   Does my language show respect for the right of free speech and expression?

6.   All in all, have I made a conscious effort to put ethical principles into practice in preparing
     my speech?

In 1987, Senator Joe Biden of Delaware was emerging as a strong candidate for the Democratic Party's presidential nomination. Handsome, articulate, and a dynamic speaker, Biden seemed ready to make a serious run for the nomination, when it was reported that his eloquent conclusion to a speech at the Iowa State Fair was lifted, almost word for word, from an address by British political leader Neil Kinnock.

Biden claimed the similarity between his speech and Kinnock's was purely accidental, but it was soon discovered that in an earlier speech he had pirated, almost verbatim, the words of Robert Kennedy. Even more damage was done a few days later when Biden admitted he had been found guilty of plagiarism while a law student at Syracuse University.

Although Biden tried to pass the whole matter off as "much ado about nothing," his standing in the polls plummeted and his presidential campaign never recovered. In the view of many experts, Biden's credibility was so damaged as to permanently injure any hopes he might have had of becoming President.

As this story shows, plagiarism is a serious matter. If you are caught plagiarizing a speech in class, the punishment can range from a failing grade to expulsion from school. If you are caught plagiarizing outside the classroom, you stand to forfeit your good name, to damage your career, or, if you are sued, to lose a large amount of money. It is worth your while, then, to make sure you know what plagiarism is and how to avoid it.[11]

Global Plagiarism

Global plagiarism is stealing your speech entirely from another source and passing it off as your own. The most blatant—and unforgivable—kind of plagiarism, it is grossly unethical.

> **global plagiarism**
> Stealing a speech entirely from a single source and passing it off as one's own.

When global plagiarism takes place in a college classroom, it is sometimes the result of deliberate dishonesty. More often it happens because a student puts off the assignment until the last minute. Then, in an act of desperation, the student gets an old speech from a friend or roommate, a fraternity or sorority file, and hands it in as his or her own. Or the student dashes to the library, finds a suitable magazine article or encyclopedia entry, copies it more or less verbatim, and turns that in as the assigned speech.

The best way to avoid this, of course, is not to leave your speech until the last minute. Most teachers explain speech assignments far enough in advance that you should have no trouble getting an early start. By starting early, you will give yourself plenty of time to prepare a first-rate speech—a speech of your own.

If, for some reason, you fail to get your speech ready on time, do not succumb to the lure of plagiarism. Whatever penalty you suffer from being late will pale in comparison with the consequences if you are caught plagiarizing. Here, as in other aspects of life, honesty is the best policy.

Patchwork Plagiarism

Unlike global plagiarism, in which a speaker pirates an entire speech from a single source, patchwork plagiarism occurs when a speaker pilfers from two or three sources. Here's an example:

patchwork plagiarism
Stealing ideas or
language from two or
three sources and
passing them off as one's
own.

Kevin Moss chose "The Paintings of Georgia O'Keeffe" as the topic for his first informative speech. In his research, Kevin found three especially helpful sources. The first was a pamphlet about O'Keeffe published by the local art center, which was showing an exhibit of her work. The second was an entry in the *Encyclopaedia Britannica*. The third was an article in *Art Digest*. Working from these sources, Kevin put together a speech dealing with O'Keeffe's early life, the major features of her paintings, and her contributions to modern art.

Unfortunately, instead of using his research materials creatively to generate a speech in his own words, Kevin lifted long passages from the pamphlet, the encyclopedia entry, and the magazine article and patched them together with a few transitions. When he was finished, he had a speech that sounded wonderful—but it was not truly *his* speech since it was composed almost entirely of other people's words.

As it turned out, Kevin's teacher had been to the same art show and thought parts of his speech sounded very familiar. After checking her copy of the art center's pamphlet at home that evening, her suspicions were confirmed. Fearful that Kevin might have filched from more than the pamphlet, she stopped at the library the next morning. In a short while, she found both the encyclopedia entry and the magazine article. Kevin was caught red-handed.

This story illustrates an important point about plagiarism. Kevin did not take his speech from a single source. He even did a little research. But copying word for word from a few sources is no less plagiarism than is copying from a single source. When you give a speech, it is just like putting your name on a paper in your English class. You declare that the speech is your work—that it is the product of your thinking, your beliefs, your language. Kevin's speech did not contain any of these. Instead it was cut and pasted wholly from other people's ideas, other people's words.

"But," you may be thinking, "not many students are experts on their speech topics. Why should they be expected to come up with new ideas that even the experts haven't thought of?" The answer is they aren't. The

Speakers who consult a wide range of research materials are less likely to fall into the trap of plagiarism than are speakers who rely on a limited number of sources.

key is not whether you have something absolutely original to say, but whether you do enough research and thinking to come up with your own slant on the topic.

How can you do this? There is no formula, but perhaps an example will help. In the Appendix, you will find a speech on anorexia titled "Dying to Be Thin." The speaker, Jennifer Breuer, a biochemistry major, is hardly an expert on eating disorders. The inspiration for her speech came from a high-school friend who had died of anorexia nervosa. Because of that experience, Jennifer cared deeply about the topic and wanted to inform her audience about it.

As Jennifer did her research, she learned a number of important facts about anorexia—many more than she could ever include in a six-minute speech. Noticing that much of what she found dealt with the causes, effects, and treatment of anorexia, she decided to focus her speech on those three areas. From all the materials she gathered in her research, she selected for her speech those that best illustrated her ideas. Because those ideas were truly hers, she had no trouble expressing them in her words. By the time she was done, she had blended the raw materials amassed during her research into a speech that was distinctively her own.

As with global plagiarism, one key to averting patchwork plagiarism is to start working on your speech as soon as you possibly can. The longer you work on it, the more apt you are to come up with your own approach. It is also vital to consult a large number of sources in your research. If you have only two or three sources to turn to for inspiration, you are far more likely to fall into the trap of patchwork plagiarism than if you consult a wide range of research materials.

Incremental Plagiarism

In global plagiarism and patchwork plagiarism the entire speech is cribbed more or less verbatim from a single source or a few sources. But plagiarism can exist even when the speech as a whole is not pirated. This is called incremental plagiarism. It occurs when the speaker fails to give credit for particular parts—increments—of the speech that are borrowed from other people. The most important of these increments are quotations and paraphrases.

incremental plagiarism
Failing to give credit for particular parts of a speech that are borrowed from other people.

Quotations

Whenever you quote someone directly, you must attribute the words to that person. Suppose you are giving a speech on Malcolm X, the famous African-American leader of the 1960s. While doing your research, you run across the following passage from Bruce Perry's acclaimed biography, *Malcolm: The Life of a Man Who Changed Black America:*

> Malcolm X fathered no legislation. He engineered no stunning Supreme Court victories or political campaigns. He scored no major electoral triumphs. Yet because of the way he articulated his followers' grievances and anger, the impact he had upon the body politic was enormous.[12]

This is a fine quotation that summarizes the nature and importance of Malcolm's impact on American politics. It would make a strong addition to your speech—as long as you acknowledge Perry as the author. The way to avoid plagiarism in this instance is to introduce Perry's statement by saying something like:

> In his 1991 biography, *Malcolm: The Life of a Man Who Changed Black America,* historian Bruce Perry says the following about Malcolm's impact on American politics. . . .

Or,

> According to historian Bruce Perry in his 1991 book, *Malcolm: The Life of a Man Who Changed Black America,* . . .

Now you have clearly identified Perry and given him credit for his words rather than presenting them as your own.

Paraphrases

When you paraphrase an author, you restate or summarize her or his ideas in your own words. Suppose, once again, that your topic is Malcolm X. But this time you decide to paraphrase the statement from Bruce Perry's biography rather than quoting it. You might say:

> Malcolm X was not a politician. He did not pass any laws, or win any Supreme Court victories, or get elected to any office. But he stated the grievances and anger of his followers so powerfully that the whole nation took notice.

paraphrase
To restate or summarize an author's ideas in one's own words.

Even though you do not quote Perry directly, you still appropriate the structure of his ideas and a fair amount of his language. Thus you still need to give him credit—just as if you were repeating his words verbatim.

It is especially important in this case to acknowledge Perry because you are borrowing his opinion—his judgment—about Malcolm X. If you simply recount basic facts about Malcolm's life—he was born in Omaha, Nebraska, converted to the Nation of Islam while in prison, traveled to Mecca toward the end of his life, was assassinated in February 1965—you do not have to report the source of your information. These facts are well known and can be found in any standard reference work on Malcolm X.

On the other hand, there is still considerable debate about Malcolm's views of other African-American leaders, the circumstances surrounding his death, and what he might have done had he lived. If you were to cite Perry's views on any of these matters—regardless of whether you quoted or paraphrased—you would need to acknowledge him as your source. If you did not, you could very well be charged with plagiarism.

As more than one speaker (and writer) has discovered, it is possible to commit incremental plagiarism quite by accident. This is less offensive than deliberate plagiarism, but it is plagiarism nonetheless. There are two ways to guard against incremental plagiarism. The first is to be careful when taking research notes to distinguish among direct quotations, paraphrased material, and your own comments. (See Chapter 6 for a full discussion of research methods.) The second way to avoid incremental plagiarism is to err on the side of caution. In other words, when in doubt, cite your source. This way, you cannot go wrong.

Guidelines for Ethical Listening

So far in this chapter we have focused on the ethical duties of public speakers. But speechmaking is not a one-way street. Listeners also have ethical obligations. They are (1) to listen courteously and attentively; (2) to avoid prejudging the speaker; and (3) to maintain the free and open expression of ideas. Let us look at each.

Be Courteous and Attentive

Imagine that you are giving your first classroom speech. You have put a great deal of time into writing the speech, and you have practiced your delivery until it is just right. You have not had much experience giving speeches, but you are confident you can do well—especially once you get over the initial rush of stage fright.

You have worked hard on your introduction, and your speech gets off to a fine start. You are pleased to see that most of your classmates are paying close attention. But you also notice that some are not. One appears to be doing homework for another class. Another keeps sneaking glances at the school newspaper. Two or three are gazing out the window, and one is leaning back in his chair with his eyes shut!

You try to block them out of your mind—especially since the rest of the class seems interested in what you are saying—but the longer you speak, the more concerned you become. "What am I doing wrong?" you wonder to yourself. "How can I get these people to pay attention?" The more you think about your inconsiderate and inattentive listeners, the more your confidence and concentration waver.

When you momentarily lose your place halfway through the speech, you start to panic. Your nerves, which you have held in check so far, take the upper hand. Your major thought now becomes, "How can I get this over as fast as possible?" Flustered and distracted, you rush through the rest of your speech and sit down.

It is vital for a democratic society to maintain the free and open expression of ideas. This is an important ethical responsibility for speakers and listeners alike.

How would you feel if this happened to you? Angry? Frustrated? Discouraged? Certainly you would not regard your speech as a positive experience. Nor would you be brimming with confidence as you worked on your next speech. Perhaps you would be soured on speechmaking altogether.

Just as public speakers have an ethical obligation to prepare fully for each speech, so listeners have a responsibility to be courteous and attentive during the speech. This responsibility—which is a matter of civility in any circumstance—is especially important in speech class. You and your classmates are in a learning situation in which you need to support one another. Professional speakers are trained to deal with inconsiderate or unresponsive audiences, but novices need encouraging, sympathetic listeners to help maintain their morale and confidence.[13]

When you listen to speeches in class, give your fellow students the same courtesy and attention you want from them. Come to class prepared to listen to—and to learn from—your classmates' speeches. As you listen, be conscious of the feedback you are sending the speaker. Sit up in your chair rather than slouching; maintain eye contact with the speaker; show support and encouragement in your facial expressions. Keep in mind the power you have as a listener over the speaker's confidence and composure, and exercise that power with a strong sense of ethical responsibility.

Avoid Prejudging the Speaker

We have all heard that you can't judge a book by its cover. The same is true of speeches. You can't judge a speech by the name, race, lifestyle, appearance, or reputation of the speaker.

As we shall see in Chapter 3, jumping to conclusions about a speaker's ideas before hearing the speech is one of the major barriers to effective listening. But it also has ethical implications. If a speaker has fulfilled her or his responsibility to prepare fully and conscientiously, the audience has an obligation to listen to that speaker before deciding whether to accept or reject what she or he is saying. As the National Communication Association states in its Credo for Ethical Communication, listeners should "strive to understand and respect" speakers "before evaluating and responding to their messages."[14]

This does not mean you must agree with every speaker you hear. You do not want to be a "rubber-stamp" listener any more than you want to be a closed-minded one. Your aim is to listen carefully to the speaker's ideas, to assess the evidence and reasoning offered in support of those ideas, and to reach an intelligent judgment about the speech. In Chapter 3, we will discuss specific steps you can take to improve your listening skills. For now it is enough to know that if you prejudge a speaker—either positively or negatively—you will fail in one of your ethical responsibilities as a listener.

Maintain the Free and Open Expression of Ideas

As we saw earlier in this chapter, a democratic society depends on the free and open expression of ideas. The right of free expression is so important that it is protected by the First Amendment to the U.S. Constitution, which declares, in part, that "Congress shall make no law . . . abridging the freedom of speech." Without the right of individual citizens to speak their minds on public issues, free government cannot survive. Just as public speakers need to avoid name-calling and other tactics that can undermine free speech, so listeners have an obligation to maintain the right of speakers to be heard.

As with other ethical issues, the extent of this obligation is open to debate. Disputes over the meaning and scope of the First Amendment arise almost daily in connection with issues such as abortion, pornography, and hate speech on college campuses. The question underlying such disputes is whether *all* speakers have a right to be heard.

There are some kinds of speech that are not protected under the First Amendment—including defamatory falsehoods that destroy a person's reputation, threats against the life of the President, and inciting an audience to illegal action in circumstances where the audience is likely to carry out the action. Otherwise, the Supreme Court has held—and most experts in communication ethics have agreed—that public speakers have an almost unlimited right of free expression.[15]

In contrast to this view, it has been argued that some ideas are so dangerous, so misguided, or so offensive that society has a duty to suppress them. But who is to determine which ideas are too dangerous, misguided, or offensive to be uttered? Who is to decide which speakers are to be heard and which are to be silenced? As Edward Kennedy explains in his acclaimed speech "Truth and Tolerance in America," once we succumb to the temptation of censoring ideas with which we disagree, "we step onto a slippery slope where everyone's freedom is at risk."[16]

View Edward Kennedy's warning against censorship in his "Truth and Tolerance in America."

CD: VIDEO CLIP 2.1

No matter how well intentioned they may be, efforts to "protect" society by restricting free speech usually end up repressing minority viewpoints and unpopular opinions. In U.S. history such efforts were used to keep women off the public platform until the 1840s, to stop abolitionist orators from exposing the evils of slavery before the Civil War, to muzzle labor organizers during the 1890s, and to impede civil rights leaders in the 1960s. Imagine what American society might be like if these speakers had been silenced!

It is important to keep in mind that ensuring a person's freedom to express her or his ideas does not imply agreement with those ideas. You can disagree entirely with the message but still support the speaker's right to express it. As Colin Powell stated in a highly publicized presentation at Howard University in 1994, "freedom of speech means permitting the widest range of views to be presented, however controversial those views may be. The First Amendment right of free speech is intended to protect the controversial and even the outrageous word and not just comforting platitudes too mundane to need protection."[17] In the long run, there is no better way to maintain liberty and protect human dignity than to protect the free and open expression of ideas.

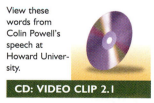

View these words from Colin Powell's speech at Howard University.

CD: VIDEO CLIP 2.1

Summary

Because public speaking is a form of power, it carries with it heavy ethical responsibilities. Today, as for the past 2,000 years, the good person speaking well remains the ideal of commendable speechmaking.

There are five basic guidelines for ethical public speaking. The first is to make sure your goals are ethically sound—that they are consistent with the welfare of society and your audience. The second is to be fully prepared for each speech. Every audience you address—in class and out—deserves your best effort. You do not want to waste their time or mislead them through shoddy research or muddled thinking. The third guideline is to be honest in what you say. Responsible speakers do not distort the truth for personal gain. They are accurate and fair in their message and in their methods.

The fourth guideline for ethical speaking is to avoid name-calling and other forms of abusive language. Name-calling is the use of language to defame or degrade other individuals or groups. It is ethically suspect because it demeans the dignity of the people being attacked and because it can undermine the right of all groups in American society to be fairly heard. The final guideline is to put ethical principles into practice—to follow them through thick and thin, not just when it is convenient.

Of all the ethical lapses a public speaker can commit, few are more serious than plagiarism. Global plagiarism is lifting a speech entirely from a single source and passing it off as your own. Patchwork plagiarism involves stitching a speech together by copying more or less verbatim from a few sources. Whenever you give a speech, you must be sure it represents your work, your thinking, your language. You must also take care to avoid incremental plagiarism, which occurs when a speaker fails to give credit for specific quotations and paraphrases that are borrowed from other people.

In addition to your ethical responsibilities as a speaker, you have ethical obligations as a listener. The first is to listen courteously and attentively. The second is to avoid prejudging the speaker. The third is to support the free and open expression of ideas. In all these ways, your speech class will offer a good testing ground for questions of ethical responsibility.

Key Terms

ethics (34)

ethical decisions (35)

name-calling (39)

Bill of Rights (40)

plagiarism (41)

global plagiarism (43)

patchwork plagiarism (44)

incremental plagiarism (45)

paraphrase (46)

Review Questions

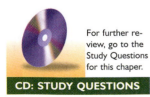

For further review, go to the Study Questions for this chaper.

CD: STUDY QUESTIONS

After reading this chapter, you should be able to answer the following questions:

1. What is ethics? Why is a strong sense of ethical responsibility vital for public speakers?

2. What are the five guidelines for ethical speechmaking discussed in this chapter?

3. What is the difference between global plagiarism and patchwork plagiarism? What are the best ways to avoid these two kinds of plagiarism?

4. What is incremental plagiarism? How can you steer clear of it when dealing with quotations and paraphrases?

5. What are the three basic guidelines for ethical listening discussed in this chapter?

Exercises for Critical Thinking

1. Look back at the story of Felicia Robinson on page 35. Evaluate her dilemma in light of the guidelines for ethical speechmaking presented in this chapter. Explain what you believe would be the most ethical course of action in her case.

2. The issue of insulting and abusive speech—especially slurs directed against people on the basis of race, religion, gender, or sexual orientation—is extremely controversial. Do you believe society should punish such speech with criminal penalties? To what degree are colleges and universities justified in trying to discipline students who engage in such speech? Do you feel it is proper to place any boundaries on free expression in order to prohibit insulting and abusive speech? Why or why not? Be prepared to explain your ideas in class.

3. All of the following situations could arise in your speech class. Identify the ethical issues in each and explain what, as a responsible speaker or listener, your course of action would be.

   a. You are speaking on the topic of prison reform. In your research, you run across two public opinion polls. One of them, an independent survey by the Gallup poll, shows that a majority of people in your state oppose your position. The other poll, suspect in its methods and conducted by a partisan organization, says a majority of people in your state support your position. Which poll do you cite in your speech? If you cite the second poll, do you point out its shortcomings?

   b. When listening to an informative speech by one of your classmates, you realize that much of it is plagiarized from a magazine article you read a couple weeks earlier. What do you do? Do you say something when your instructor asks for comments about the speech? Do you mention your concern to the instructor after class? Do you talk with the speaker? Do you remain silent?

   c. While researching your persuasive speech, you find a quotation from an article by a highly respected expert that will nail down one of your most important points. But as you read the rest of the article, you realize the author does not in fact support the policy you are advocating. Should you still include the quotation in your speech?

Applying the POWER of **Public Speaking**

Having graduated with a degree in public administration and hoping to pursue a career in politics, you have been fortunate to receive a staff position with one of the leading senators in your state legislature. Since your arrival two months ago, you have answered phones, ordered lunch, made copies, stapled mailings, and stuffed envelopes. Finally you have been asked to look over a speech the senator will deliver at your alma mater. Surely, you think, this will be the first of many important assignments once your value is recognized.

After reading the speech, however, your enthusiasm is dampened. You agree wholeheartedly with its support of a bill to fund scholarships for low-income students, but you're dismayed by its attack on opponents of the bill as "elitist bigots who would deny a college education to those who need it most." You haven't been asked to comment on the ethics of the speech and you certainly don't want to jeopardize your position on the senator's staff. At the same time, you think his use of name-calling may actually arouse sympathy for the opposition. The senator would like your comments in two hours. What will you tell him?

Notes

[1]James A. Jaska and Michael S. Pritchard, *Communication Ethics: Methods of Analysis,* 2nd ed. (Belmont, Calif.: Wadsworth, 1994), pp. 3–6.

[2]Richard L. Johannesen, *Ethics in Human Communication,* 4th ed. (Prospect Heights, Ill.: Waveland Press, 1996), p. 16.

[3]Johannesen, *Ethics in Human Communication,* p. 14.

[4]See, for example, David Nyberg, *The Varnished Truth: Truth Telling and Deceiving in Ordinary Life* (Chicago: University of Chicago Press, 1993).

[5]Haig A. Bosmajian, *The Language of Oppression* (Washington, D.C.: Public Affairs Press, 1974), p. 5.

[6]The discussion in this paragraph is modeled on William Zinsser, *On Writing Well,* 6th ed. (New York: HarperCollins, 1998), pp. 81–83.

[7]Donald K. Smith, *Man Speaking: A Rhetoric of Public Speech* (New York: Dodd, Mead, 1969), p. 244.

[8]Thomas L. Tedford, *Freedom of Speech in the United States,* 3rd ed. (State College, Pa.: Strata Publishing, 1997), pp. 173–179. Also see Cass R. Sunstein, *Democracy and the Problem of Free Speech* (New York: Free Press, 1993), pp. 197–204.

[9]Kenneth Blanchard and Norman Vincent Peale, *The Power of Ethical Management* (New York: Ballantine Books, 1988), p. 64.

[10]Joseph Gibaldi, *MLA Handbook for Writers of Research Papers,* 5th ed. (New York: Modern Language Association of America, 1999), p. 30.

[11]For a fascinating look at the history of plagiarism in a variety of contexts, see Thomas Mallon, *Stolen Words: Forays into the Origins and Ravages of Plagiarism* (New York: Penguin Books, 1991).

[12]Bruce Perry, *Malcolm: The Life of a Man Who Changed Black America* (Tarrytown, N.Y.: Station Hill, 1991), p. 380.

[13]For research on the impact of audience members on a speaker's self-confidence, see Peter D. MacIntyre, Kimly A. Thivierge, and J. Renee MacDonald, "The Effect of Audience Interest, Responsiveness, and Evaluation on Public Speaking Anxiety and Related Variables," *Communication Research Reports,* 14 (1997), pp. 157–168.

[14]The entire credo, which was ratified in November 1999, is printed in *Spectra* (January 2000), p. 10. It is also available online at the National Communication Association website (http://www.natcom.org).

[15]See, for example, Rodney A. Smolla, *Free Speech in an Open Society* (New York: Knopf, 1992); Franklyn S. Haiman, *"Speech Acts" and the First Amendment* (Carbondale, Ill.: Southern Illinois University Press, 1994).

[16]Edward M. Kennedy, "Truth and Tolerance in America," October 3, 1983, in Lloyd Rohler and Roger Cook (eds.), *Great Speeches for Criticism and Analysis,* 3rd ed. (Greenwood, Ind.: Alistair Press, 1998), pp. 313–314.

[17]Colin Powell, Commencement Address at Howard University, May 14, 1994, in Rohler and Cook, *Great Speeches,* p. 319.

LISTENING

t had been a long day at the office, and the going-home traffic was bumper to bumper. By the time Jason Whitehawk pulled his late-model car into the driveway at home, he was exhausted. As he trudged into the house, he routinely asked his wife, "How did things go with you at work today?"

"Oh, pretty well," she replied, "except for the terrorist attack in the morning and the outbreak of bubonic plague in the afternoon."

Jason nodded his head as he made his way toward the sofa. "That's nice," he said. "At least someone had a good day. Mine was awful."

hearing
The vibration of sound waves on the eardrums and the firing of electrochemical impulses in the brain.

listening
Paying close attention to, and making sense of, what we hear.

This story illustrates what one research study after another has revealed—most people are shockingly poor listeners. We fake paying attention. We can look right at someone, appear interested in what that person says, even nod our head or smile at the appropriate moments—all without really listening.

Not listening doesn't mean we don't hear. *Hearing* is a physiological process, involving the vibration of sound waves on our eardrums and the firing of electrochemical impulses from the inner ear to the central auditory system of the brain.[1] But *listening* involves paying close attention to, and making sense of, what we hear. Even when we think we are listening carefully, we usually grasp only 50 percent of what we hear. After two days we can remember only half of that—or 25 percent of the original message. It's little wonder that listening has been called a lost art.[2]

Listening Is Important

Although most people listen poorly, there are exceptions. Top-flight business executives, successful politicians, brilliant teachers—nearly all are excellent listeners. So much of what they do depends on absorbing information that is given verbally—and absorbing it quickly and accurately. If you had an interview with the president of a major corporation, you might be shocked (and flattered) to see how closely that person listened to your words. One business executive admitted, "Frankly, I had never thought of listening as an important subject by itself. But now that I am aware of it, I think that perhaps 80 percent of my work depends upon my listening to someone, or upon someone listening to me."[3]

In our communication-oriented age, listening is more important than ever. This is why, in most companies, effective listeners hold higher positions and are promoted more often than people who are ineffective listeners.[4] When business managers are asked to rank-order the communication skills most crucial to their jobs, they usually rank listening number one.[5] Listening is so important that in one survey of America's Fortune 500 companies, almost 60 percent of the respondents said they provide some kind of listening training for their employees.[6]

Even if you don't plan to be a corporate executive, the art of listening can be helpful in almost every part of your life. This is not surprising when you realize that people spend more time listening than doing any other communicative activity—more than reading, more than writing, more even than speaking.

Think for a moment about your own life as a college student. Close to 90 percent of class time in U.S. colleges and universities is spent listening to discussions and lectures. A number of studies have shown a strong correlation between listening and academic success. Students with the highest grades are usually those with the strongest listening skills. The reverse is also true—students with the lowest grades are usually those with the weakest listening skills.[7]

There is plenty of reason, then, to take listening seriously. Employers and employees, parents and children, wives and husbands, doctors and patients, students and teachers—all depend on the apparently simple skill of listening. Regardless of your profession or walk of life, you never escape the need for a well-trained ear.

Listening is also important to you as a speaker. It is probably the way you get most of your ideas and information—from television, radio, conversation, and lectures. If you do not listen well, you will not understand what you hear and may pass along your misunderstanding to others.

Besides, in class—as in life—you will listen to many more speeches than you give. It is only fair to pay close attention to your classmates' speeches; after all, you want them to listen carefully to *your* speeches. An excellent way to improve your own speeches is to listen attentively to the speeches of other people. One student, reflecting on her speech class, said, "As I listened to the speeches, I discovered things that seemed to work—things I could try. I also learned what didn't work—what to avoid. That helped a lot in my own speeches." Over and over, teachers find that the best speakers are usually the best listeners.

A side benefit of your speech class is that it offers an ideal opportunity to work on the art of listening. During the 95 percent of the time when you are not speaking, you have nothing else to do but listen and learn. You can sit there like a stone—or you can use the time profitably to master a skill that will serve you in a thousand ways.

Listening and Critical Thinking

One of the ways listening can serve you is by enhancing your skills as a critical thinker. We can identify four kinds of listening:[8]

- *Appreciative listening*—listening for pleasure or enjoyment, as when we listen to music, to a comedy routine, or to an entertaining speech.

- *Empathic listening*—listening to provide emotional support for the speaker, as when a psychiatrist listens to a patient or when we lend a sympathetic ear to a friend in distress.

- *Comprehensive listening*—listening to understand the message of a speaker, as when we attend a classroom lecture or listen to directions for finding a friend's house.

- *Critical listening*—listening to evaluate a message for purposes of accepting or rejecting it, as when we listen to the sales pitch of a used-car dealer, the campaign speech of a political candidate, or the closing arguments of an attorney in a jury trial.

appreciative listening
Listening for pleasure or enjoyment.

empathic listening
Listening to provide emotional support for a speaker.

comprehensive listening
Listening to understand the message of a speaker.

Although all four kinds of listening are important, this chapter deals primarily with the last two—comprehensive listening and critical listening. They are the kinds of listening you will use most often when listening to speeches in class, when taking lecture notes in other courses, when communicating at work, and when responding to the barrage of commercials and other persuasive appeals you face every day in our fast-paced society. They are also the kinds of listening that are most closely tied to critical thinking.

As we saw in Chapter 1, critical thinking involves a number of skills. Some of those skills—summarizing information, recalling facts, distinguishing main points from minor points—are central to comprehensive listening. Other skills of critical thinking—separating fact from opinion, spotting weaknesses in reasoning, judging the soundness of evidence—are especially important in critical listening. When you engage in comprehensive listening or critical listening, you must use your mind as well as your ears. When your mind is not actively involved, you may be hearing, but you are not *listening*.[9] In fact, listening and critical thinking are so closely allied that training in listening is also training in how to think.

At the end of this chapter, we'll discuss steps you can take to improve your skills in comprehensive and critical listening. If you follow these steps, you may also become a better critical thinker at the same time.

Four Causes of Poor Listening

Not Concentrating

The brain is incredibly efficient. Although we talk at a rate of 120 to 150 words a minute, the brain can process 400 to 800 words a minute.[10] This would seem to make listening very easy, but actually it has the opposite effect. Because we can take in a speaker's words and still have plenty of spare "brain time," we are tempted to interrupt our listening by thinking about other things. And thinking about other things is just what we do. Here's what happens:

Rico Salazar is the youngest member of the public relations team for a giant oil company. He is pleased to be included in the biweekly staff meetings. After two dozen or so meetings, however, he is beginning to find them tedious.

This time the vice president is droning on about executive speechwriting—an area in which Rico is not directly concerned. The vice president says, "When the draft of a speech hits the president's desk . . . "

"Desk," thinks Rico. "That's my big problem. It's humiliating to have a metal desk when everyone else has wood. There must be some way to convince my boss that I need a new wooden desk." In his imagination, Rico sees himself behind a handsome walnut desk. He is conducting an interview, and his visitor is so impressed . . .

Sternly, Rico pulls his attention back to the meeting. The vice president has moved on to a public relations problem in Latin America. Rico listens carefully for a while, until he hears the words "especially in the Caribbean."

"Oh, if only I could get away for a winter vacation this year," he thinks. He is lost in a reverie featuring white beaches, tropical drinks, exotic dances, scuba diving, sailboats, himself tanned and windblown . . .

People spend more time listening than in any other communicative activity. One benefit of your speech class is that it gives you a chance to improve your listening skills.

" . . . will definitely affect salary increases this year" brings him back to the meeting with a jolt. What did the vice president say about salary increases? Oh, well, he can ask someone else after the meeting. But now the vice president is talking about budgets. All those dreary figures and percentages . . . And Rico is off again.

His date last night, Celine, really seemed to like him and yet . . . Was it something he did that made her say goodnight at the door and go inside alone? Could she have been *that* tired? The last time she invited him in for coffee. Of course, she really did have a rough day. Anybody can understand that. But still . . .

" . . . an area Rico has taken a special interest in. Maybe we should hear from him." Uh, oh! *What* area does the vice president mean? Everyone is looking at Rico, as he tries frantically to recall the last words said at the meeting.

It's not that Rico *meant* to lose track of the discussion. But there comes a point at which it's so easy to give in to physical and mental distractions—to let your thoughts wander rather than to concentrate on what is being said. After all, concentrating is hard work. Louis Nizer, the famous trial lawyer, says, "So complete is this concentration that at the end of a court day in which I have only listened, I find myself wringing wet despite a calm and casual manner."[11]

Later in this chapter, we will look at some things you can do to concentrate better on what you hear.

Listening Too Hard

Until now we have been talking about not paying close attention to what we hear. But sometimes we listen *too* hard. We turn into human sponges, soaking up a speaker's every word as if every word were equally important. We try to remember all the names, all the dates, all the places. In the process we often miss the speaker's point by submerging it in a morass of details. What is worse, we may end up confusing the facts as well.

Hilary Schneider was about to see her last patient when she got a phone call from her husband, Joel. "Guess what!" he exclaimed. "I left work early so I could come home and fix us a nice dinner. By the way, do you remember how your sister makes that incredible chocolate cake?"

"Sure," Hilary said. "The secret is to beat the egg whites separately. But the oven isn't working. I tried it yesterday, and the temperature control is all messed up."

"I just need to know where to find the recipe," Joel answered. "I'm sure it's in one of our cookbooks."

"If you really want to know," Hilary told him, "I think it's in the *American Regional Cookbook,* the one with the picture of an old farmhouse on the cover. It's on the second shelf of the cabinet with all the other cookbooks—just above the shelf with the cooking wine and spices."

"I'm sure I can find it," Joel declared. "There are a ton of great recipes in that book. But I've got to hustle if I'm going to get everything done by the time you get home. Bye."

"Joel, wait a minute," Hilary said. "How in heaven's name are you going to bake the cake?"

"How am I going to bake the cake?" Joel asked in surprise. "In the oven, of course." And he hung up.

This is a typical example of losing the main message by concentrating on details. Joel had set his mind to find the cookbook with the great chocolate cake recipe—period. In so doing, he blocked out everything else—including the information that the oven was not working.

The same thing can happen when you listen to a speech: you pick up the details but miss the point. It just isn't possible to remember everything a speaker says. Efficient listeners usually concentrate on main ideas and evidence. We'll discuss these things more thoroughly later in the chapter.

Jumping to Conclusions

Renee Anello, a recent college graduate, took a job as an editorial assistant in the research department of a regional magazine. Shortly after Renee arrived, the editor in charge of the research department left the magazine for another job. For the next two months, Renee struggled to handle the work of the research department by herself. She often felt in over her head, but she knew this was a good opportunity to learn, and she hated to give up her new responsibilities.

One day Seiji Tomasu, the editor in chief of the magazine, comes into Renee's office to talk. The following conversation takes place:

Seiji: You've done a great job these last two months, Renee. But you know we really need a new editor. So we've decided to make some changes.

Renee: I'm not surprised. I know I've made my share of mistakes.

Seiji: Everyone makes mistakes when they're starting out. And you've been carrying a lot of responsibility. Too much. That's why . . .

Renee: That's okay. I'm grateful to have had a chance to try my hand at this. I know I'm inexperienced, and this is an important department.

Seiji: Yes, it is. And it's not an easy job. We really need an editor and an assistant to handle all the work. That's why I wanted to tell you . . .

Renee: You're right, of course. I hope you've found somebody good to be the new editor.

Seiji: I think so. But, Renee, I don't think you understand . . .

Renee: No, I understand. I knew all along that I was just filling in.

Seiji: Renee, you're not listening.

Renee: Yes, I am. You're trying to be nice, but you're here to tell me that you've hired a new editor and I'll be going back to my old job.

Seiji: No, that's not it at all. I think you've done a fine job under difficult circumstances. You've proved yourself, and I intend to make *you* the editor. But I think you'll need an assistant to help you.

Why is there so much confusion here? Clearly, Renee is unsure about her future at the magazine. Although she has worked hard, she knows she has made some mistakes that a more experienced person might have avoided. So when Seiji starts to talk about making some changes, Renee jumps to a conclusion and assumes the worst. The misunderstanding could have been avoided if, when Seiji had said, "We've decided to make some changes," Renee had asked, "What changes?"—and then *listened.*

This is one form of jumping to conclusions—putting words into a speaker's mouth. It is one reason why we sometimes communicate so poorly with people we are closest to. Because we are so sure we know what they mean, we don't listen to what they actually say. Sometimes we don't even hear them out.

Another way of jumping to conclusions is prematurely rejecting a speaker's ideas as boring or misguided. We may decide early on that a speaker has nothing valuable to say. Suppose you are passionately committed to animal rights and a speaker's announced topic is "The Importance of Animals to Scientific Research." You may decide in advance not to listen to anything the speaker has to say. This would be a mistake. You might pick up useful information that could either strengthen or modify your thinking. In another situation, you might jump to the conclusion that a speech will be boring. Let's say the announced topic is "Looking Toward Jupiter: Science and the Cosmos." It sounds dull. So you tune out—and miss a fascinating discussion of possible extraterrestrial life-forms.

Nearly every speech has something to offer you—whether it be information, point of view, or technique. You are cheating yourself if you prejudge and choose not to listen.

Focusing on Delivery and Personal Appearance

Even though Tim and Suzanne had been born in Nebraska, they had lived in Brooklyn for 15 years and had come to love it. But when Suzanne's company offered her a promotion and a new position in the Ohama office, they decided to move.

Soon after they arrived in Omaha, Suzanne saw a notice in the local paper about an Audubon Society lecture on the annual Sandhill Crane migration. She asked Tim if he'd like to attend, and they decided to go the following weekend. "This may come as a surprise," Tim said when they arrived at the lecture, "but I'm really looking forward to this. I remember watching the crane migration with my grandfather when I was a kid. It's an amazing spectacle."

The speaker, a professor at a nearby college, began by discussing the geography of the migration and pointing out the stretch of wetlands on the Platte River where half a million cranes stop every year. He explained how cranes have followed the same route from Mexico to Alaska for more than nine million years, and he showed dramatic color slides of the birds that had most of the audience spellbound.

"That was great," exclaimed Suzanne when they got back to the car. "I definitely want to see the migration next spring." But Tim was scowling. "What's wrong?" Suzanne asked.

"I know you're going to think this is stupid," Tim began, "but once I realized the speaker had a Brooklyn accent, I didn't hear a word he said."

"But you love Brooklyn," Suzanne protested. "That professor is a great speaker, and he gave a terrific presentation."

"I know, I know," Tim admitted. "I guess I just wanted him to sound like my grandfather."

This story illustrates a very common problem. We tend to judge people by the way they look or speak and therefore don't listen to what they *say*. Some people become so distracted by a speaker's accent, personal appearance, or vocal mannerisms that they lose sight of the message. As in Tim's case, this can happen even when a listener is interested in the topic and looking forward to the presentation. Focusing on a speaker's delivery or personal appearance is one of the major sources of interference in the speech communication process, and it is something we always need to guard against.

How to Become a Better Listener

Take Listening Seriously

The first step to improvement is always self-awareness. Analyze your shortcomings as a listener and commit yourself to overcoming them. Good listeners are not born that way. They have *worked* at learning how to listen effectively. Good listening does not go hand in hand with intelligence, education, or social standing. Like any other skill, it comes from practice and self-discipline.

You should begin to think of listening as an active process. So many aspects of modern life encourage us to listen passively. We "listen" to the radio while studying or "listen" to the television while moving about from room to room. This type of passive listening is a habit—but so is active listening. We can learn to identify those situations in which active listening is important. If you work seriously at becoming a more efficient listener, you will reap the rewards in your schoolwork, in your personal and family relations, and in your career.

Resist Distractions

In an ideal world, we could eliminate all physical and mental distractions. In the real world, however, this is not possible. Because we think so much faster than a speaker can talk, it's easy to let our attention wander while we listen. Sometimes it's very easy—when the room is too hot, when construction machinery is operating right outside the window, when the speaker is

Effective listeners take their task seriously. By approaching listening as an active process, you will sharpen your powers of concentration and comprehension.

tedious. But our attention can stray even in the best of circumstances—if for no other reason than a failure to stay alert and make ourselves concentrate.

Whenever you find this happening, make a conscious effort to pull your mind back to what the speaker is saying. Then force it to stay there. One way to do this is to think a little ahead of the speaker—try to anticipate what will come next. This is not the same as jumping to conclusions. When you jump to conclusions, you put words into the speaker's mouth and don't actually listen to what is said. In this case you *will* listen—and measure what the speaker says against what you had anticipated.

Another way to keep your mind on a speech is to review mentally what the speaker has already said and make sure you understand it. Yet another is to listen between the lines and assess what a speaker implies verbally or says nonverbally with body language. Suppose a politician is running for reelection. During a campaign speech to her constituents she makes this statement: "Just last week I had lunch with the President, and he assured me that he has a special concern for the people of our state." The careful listener would hear this implied message: "If you vote for me, there's a good chance more tax money will flow into the state."

To take another example, suppose a speaker is introducing someone to an audience. The speaker says, "It gives me great pleasure to present to you my very dear friend, Nadine Zussman." But the speaker doesn't shake hands with Nadine. He doesn't even look at her—just turns his back and leaves the podium. Is Nadine really his "very dear friend"? Certainly not.

Attentive listeners can pick up all kinds of clues to a speaker's real message. At first you may find it difficult to listen so intently. If you work at it, however, your concentration is bound to improve.

Don't Be Diverted by Appearance or Delivery

If you had attended Abraham Lincoln's momentous Cooper Union speech of 1860, this is what you would have seen:

The long, ungainly figure upon which hung clothes that, while new for this trip, were evidently the work of an unskilled tailor; the large feet and clumsy hands, of which, at the outset, at least, the orator seemed to be unduly conscious; the long, gaunt head, capped by a shock of hair that seemed not to have been thoroughly brushed out, made a picture which did not fit in with New York's conception of a finished statesman.[12]

But although he seemed awkward and uncultivated, Lincoln had a powerful message about the moral evils of slavery. Fortunately, the audience at Cooper Union did not let his appearance stand in the way of his words.

Similarly, you must be willing to set aside preconceived judgments based on a person's looks or manner of speech. Gandhi was a very unimpressive looking man who often spoke dressed in a simple white cotton cloth. Helen Keller, deaf and blind from earliest childhood, always had trouble articulating words distinctly. Renowned physicist Stephen Hawking is severely disabled and can speak only with the aid of a voice synthesizer. Yet imagine if no one had listened to them. Even though it may tax your tolerance, patience, and concentration, don't let negative feelings about a speaker's appearance or delivery keep you from listening to the message.

On the other hand, try not to be misled if the speaker has an unusually attractive appearance. It's all too easy to assume that because someone is good-looking and has a polished delivery, he or she is speaking eloquently. Some of the most unscrupulous speakers in history have been handsome people with hypnotic delivery skills. Again, be sure you respond to the message, not to the package it comes in.

Suspend Judgment

Unless we listen only to people who think exactly as we do, we are going to hear things with which we disagree. When this happens, our natural inclination is to argue mentally with the speaker or to dismiss everything she or he says. But neither response is fair—to the speaker or to ourselves. In both cases we blot out any chance of learning or being persuaded.

Does this mean you must agree with everything you hear? Not at all. It means you should hear people out *before* reaching a final judgment. Try to understand their point of view. Listen to their ideas, examine their evidence, assess their reasoning. *Then* make up your mind. If you're sure of your beliefs, you need not fear listening to opposing views. If you're not sure, you have every reason to listen carefully. It has been said more than once that a closed mind is an empty mind.

Focus Your Listening

As we have seen, skilled listeners do not try to absorb a speaker's every word. Rather, they focus on specific things in a speech. Here are three suggestions to help you focus your listening.

Listen for Main Points

Most speeches contain from two to four main points. Here, for example, are the main points of a speech delivered by Bill Clinton on the challenges facing the United Nations in the twenty-first century.[13]

1. The first challenge facing the U.N. is to use the benefits of global prosperity to combat poverty and disease in developing nations.

2. The second challenge facing the U.N. is to prevent ethnic cleansing and other incidents of mass killing and displacement.

3. The third challenge facing the U.N. is to ensure that nuclear, chemical, and biological weapons will never be used again.

These three main points are the heart of Clinton's message. As with any speech, they are the most important things to listen for.

Unless a speaker is terribly scatterbrained, you should be able to detect his or her main points with little difficulty. Often a speaker will give some idea at the outset of the main points to be discussed in the speech. For example, at the end of his introduction, Clinton said he was going to offer "three resolutions for the new millennium." Noticing this, a sharp listener would have been prepared for a speech with three main points, each dealing with a different resolution. As the speech progressed, Clinton enumerated each main point to help his listeners keep track of them. He also summarized them in his conclusion. After this, only the most inattentive of listeners could have been in the dark about Clinton's main points.

Listen for Evidence

Identifying a speaker's main points, however, is not enough. You must also listen for supporting evidence. By themselves, Clinton's main points are only assertions. You may be inclined to believe them just because they were stated by the President of the United States. Yet a careful listener will be concerned about evidence no matter who is speaking. Had you been listening to Clinton's speech, you would have heard him support his claim about the need to combat proverty and disease with a mass of verifiable evidence. Here is an excerpt:

We are still squandering the potential of far too many: 1.3 billion people still live on less than a dollar a day. More than half the population of many countries have no access to safe water. A person in South Asia is 700 times less likely to use the Internet than someone in the United States. And 40 million people a year still die of hunger—almost as many as the total number killed in World War II. . . . Over the next 10 years in Africa, AIDS is expected to kill more people and orphan more children than all the wars of the twentieth century combined.

There are four basic questions to ask about a speaker's evidence:

Is it *accurate?*

Is it taken from *objective* sources?

Is it *relevant* to the speaker's claims?

Is it *sufficient* to support the speaker's point?

In Clinton's case, the answer to each question is yes. His figures about economic conditions, water quality, Internet use, hunger, and the AIDS epidemic in Africa are well established in the public record and can be verified by independent sources. The figures are clearly relevant to Clinton's claim about the problems of poverty and disease in developing nations, and they are sufficient to support that claim. If Clinton's evidence were inaccurate, biased, irrelevant, or insufficient, you should be wary of accepting his claim.

Listen for Technique

We said earlier that you should not let a speaker's delivery distract you from the message, and this is true. However, if you want to become an effective speaker, you should study the methods other people use to speak effectively. When you listen to speeches—in class and out—focus above all on the content of a speaker's message; but also pay attention to the techniques the speaker uses to get the message across.

Analyze the introduction: What methods does the speaker use to gain attention, to relate to the audience, to establish credibility and goodwill? Assess the organization of the speech: Is it clear and easy to follow? Can you pick out the speaker's main points? Can you follow when the speaker moves from one point to another?

Study the speaker's language: Is it accurate, clear, vivid, appropriate? Does the speaker adapt well to the audience and occasion? Finally, diagnose the speaker's delivery: Is it fluent, dynamic, convincing? Does it strengthen or weaken the impact of the speaker's ideas? How well does the speaker use eye contact, gestures, and visual aids?

As you listen, focus on the speaker's strengths and weaknesses. If the speaker is not effective, try to determine why. If he or she is effective, try to pick out techniques you can use in your own speeches. If you listen in this way, you will be surprised how much you can learn about successful speaking.

This is why many teachers require students to complete evaluation forms on their classmates' speeches. Figure 3.1 on page 68 is an example of such a form. To fill in the form conscientiously, you must listen carefully. But the effort is well worth the rewards. Not only will you provide valuable feedback to your classmates about their speeches, you will also find yourself becoming a much more efficient listener.

Develop Note-Taking Skills

Speech students are often amazed at how easily their teacher can pick out a speaker's main points, evidence, and techniques. Of course, the teacher knows what to listen for and has had plenty of practice. But the next time you get an opportunity, watch your teacher during a speech. Chances are she or he will be listening with pen and paper. When note taking is done properly, it is a surefire way to improve your concentration and keep track of a speaker's ideas.

The key words here are *when done properly*. Unfortunately, many people don't take notes effectively. Some try to write down everything a speaker says. They view note taking as a race, pitting their handwriting agility against the speaker's rate of speech. As the speaker starts to talk, the note taker starts to write. But soon the speaker is winning the race. In a desperate effort to keep up, the note taker slips into a scribbled writing style with incomplete sentences and abbreviated words. Even this is not enough. The speaker pulls so far ahead that the note taker can never catch up. Finally, the note taker concedes defeat and spends the rest of the speech grumbling in frustration.[14]

Some people go to the opposite extreme. They arrive armed with pen, notebook, and the best of intentions. They know they can't write down everything, so they settle comfortably in their seats and wait for the speaker to say something that grabs their attention. Every once in a while the speaker rewards them with a joke, a dramatic story, or a startling fact. Then the note taker seizes pen, jots down a few words, and leans back dreamily to await the next fascinating tidbit. By the end of the lecture the note taker has a set of tidbits—and little or no record of the speaker's important ideas.

As these examples illustrate, most inefficient note takers suffer from one or both of two problems: they don't know *what* to listen for, and they don't know *how* to record what they do listen for. The solution to the first problem is to focus on a speaker's main points and evidence. But once you know what to listen for, you still need a sound method of note taking.

Although there are a number of systems, most students find the *key-word outline* best for listening to classroom lectures and formal speeches. As its name suggests, this method briefly notes a speaker's main points and supporting evidence in rough outline form. Suppose a speaker says:

key-word outline
An outline that briefly notes a speaker's main points and supporting evidence in rough outline form.

Figure 3.1

Speaker _____   **Topic** _____

Rate the speaker on each point by using this scale:

E	G	A	F	P
excellent	good	average	fair	poor

Introduction:

_____ Gained attention and interest

_____ Introduced topic clearly

_____ Related topic to audience

_____ Established speaker's credibility

_____ Previewed body of speech

Body:

_____ Made main points clear

_____ Fully supported main points

_____ Organized the material well

_____ Used accurate language

_____ Used clear language

_____ Used appropriate language

_____ Used effective connectives

Conclusion:

_____ Prepared audience for ending

_____ Reinforced central idea of speech

_____ Presented vivid ending

Delivery:

_____ Began speech without rushing

_____ Maintained strong eye contact

_____ Avoided distracting mannerisms

_____ Articulated words clearly

_____ Used pauses effectively

_____ Used vocal variety to add impact

_____ Presented visual aids well

_____ Departed from lectern without rushing

Overall Evaluation:

_____ Chose a challenging topic

_____ Chose the specific purpose well

_____ Adapted message to audience

_____ Completed speech within time limit

_____ Held interest of audience

What did the speaker do most effectively? _____

_____

What should the speaker pay special attention to next time? _____

_____

General comments: _____

_____

Listening carefully and taking clear notes are vital skills for success in college. They will also benefit you in countless situations throughout life.

Elephants have long been hunted for their ivory tusks. In the 1920s thousands of elephants were killed to meet demand in the United States for 60,000 ivory billiard balls every year and hundreds of thousands of piano keys. Today the ivory trade is centered in the Far East—especially Japan and China—where ivory ornaments are highly prized. According to *Time* magazine, more than 3,900 tons of ivory were imported into Hong Kong alone during the 1980s. That represents the death of more than 400,000 elephants.

Despite international agreements designed to reduce the ivory trade, poaching continues to take its toll. As recently as 1980, 1.3 million elephants roamed Africa. According to the World Wildlife Federation, today that number has been reduced by at least 50 percent, and in some locations by more than 75 percent. *U.S. News and World Report* states that if the carnage continues, elephants will be threatened with extinction.

A key-word note taker would record something like this:

Elephants long hunted
    1920s—U.S.
    Today—Far East
        Hong Kong: 3,900 tons
        Death of 400,000 elephants

How serious a problem?
    1.3 million elephants in 1980
    Reduced by 50–75 percent today
    U.S. News: could threaten extinction

Notice how brief the notes are. They contain only 35 words (compared to the speaker's 155), yet they accurately summarize the speaker's ideas. Also notice how clear the notes are. By separating main points from subpoints and evidence, the outline format shows the relationships among the speaker's ideas.

Perfecting this—or any other—system of note taking requires practice. But with a little effort you should see results soon. As you become a better note taker, you will become a better listener. There is also a good chance you will become a better student. Common sense and experience suggest that students who take effective notes usually receive higher grades than those who do not.

Summary

Most people are poor listeners. Even when we think we are listening carefully, we usually grasp only half of what we hear, and we retain even less. Improving your listening skills can be helpful in every part of your life, including speechmaking. The best speakers are often the best listeners. Your speech class gives you a perfect chance to work on your listening skills as well as your speaking skills.

The most important cause of poor listening is giving in to physical and mental distractions. Many times we let our thoughts wander rather than concentrating on what is being said. Sometimes, however, we listen *too* hard. We try to remember every word a speaker says, and we lose the main message by concentrating on details. In other situations, we may jump to conclusions and prejudge a speaker without hearing out the message. Finally, we often judge people by their appearance or speaking manner instead of listening to what they say.

You can overcome these poor listening habits by taking several steps. First, take listening seriously. Think of listening as an active process and commit yourself to becoming a better listener. Second, resist distractions. Make a conscious effort to keep your mind on what the speaker is saying. Third, try not to be diverted by appearance or delivery. Set aside preconceived judgments based on a person's looks or manner of speech. Fourth, suspend judgment until you have heard the speaker's entire message— even if you think you are going to disagree. Fifth, focus your listening by paying attention to main points, to evidence, and to the speaker's techniques. Finally, develop your note-taking skills. When done properly, note taking is an excellent way to improve your concentration and to keep track of a speaker's ideas. It almost forces you to become a more attentive and creative listener.

Key Terms

hearing (56)

listening (56)

appreciative listening (57)

empathic listening (57)

comprehensive listening (57)

critical listening (58)

spare "brain time" (58)

key-word outline (67)

Review Questions

After reading this chapter, you should be able to answer the following questions:

1. What is the difference between hearing and listening?

2. Why is listening important to you as a public speaker?

3. What are the four main causes of poor listening?

4. What are six ways to become a better listener?

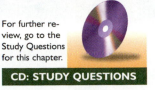

For further re-
view, go to the
Study Questions
for this chapter.

CD: STUDY QUESTIONS

Exercises for Critical Thinking

1. Which of the four causes of poor listening do you consider the most important? Choose a specific case of poor listening in which you were involved. Explain what went wrong.

2. Write a candid evaluation of your major strengths and weaknesses as a listener. Explain what steps you need to take to become a better listener. Be specific.

3. Watch the lead story on *60 Minutes* this week. Using the key-word method of note taking, record the main ideas of the story.

4. Choose a lecture in one of your other classes. Analyze what the lecturer does most effectively. Identify three things the lecturer could do better to help students keep track of the lecture.

Notes

[1]Hayes A. Newby and Gerald R. Popelka, *Audiology,* 6th ed. (Englewood Cliffs, N.J.: Prentice Hall, 1992), pp. 5–59.

[2]Michael P. Nichols, *The Lost Art of Listening* (New York: Guilford, 1995).

[3]Quoted in Ralph G. Nichols and Leonard A. Stevens, *Are You Listening?* (New York: McGraw-Hill, 1957), p. 141.

[4]Beverly Davenport Sypher, Robert N. Bostrom, and Joy Hart Seibert, "Listening, Communication Abilities, and Success at Work," *Journal of Business Communication,* 26 (1989), pp. 293–303.

[5]See the studies cited by Andrew D. Wolvin and Carolyn Gwynn Coakley, "A Survey of the Status of Listening Training in Some Fortune 500 Corporations," *Communication Education,* 40 (1991), p. 153.

[6]Wolvin and Coakley, "A Survey of the Status of Listening Training," pp. 152–162.

[7]Carolyn Coakley and Andrew Wolvin, "Listening in the Educational Environment," in Deborah Borisoff and Michael Purdy (eds.), *Listening in Everyday Life: A Personal and Professional Approach* (Lanham, Md.: University Press of America, 1991), pp. 163–164.

[8]Andrew W. Wolvin and Carolyn Gwynn Coakley, *Listening,* 5th ed. (Dubuque, Iowa: Brown and Benchmark, 1995), pp. 223–396.

[9]Mortimer J. Adler, *How to Speak, How to Listen* (New York: Macmillan, 1983), pp. 85–86.

[10]Florence I. Wolff and Nadine C. Marsnik, *Perceptive Listening,* 2nd ed. (Fort Worth, Tex.: Harcourt Brace Jovanovich, 1992), p. 66.

[11]Louis Nizer, *My Life in Court* (New York: Doubleday, 1961), pp. 297–298.

[12]George H. Putnam, *Abraham Lincoln* (New York: Putnam, 1909), pp. 44–45.

[13]Bill Clinton, "Peace in the New Millennium," *Vital Speeches,* 66 (1999), pp. 2–5.

[14]Nichols and Stevens, *Are You Listening?,* pp. 113–114.

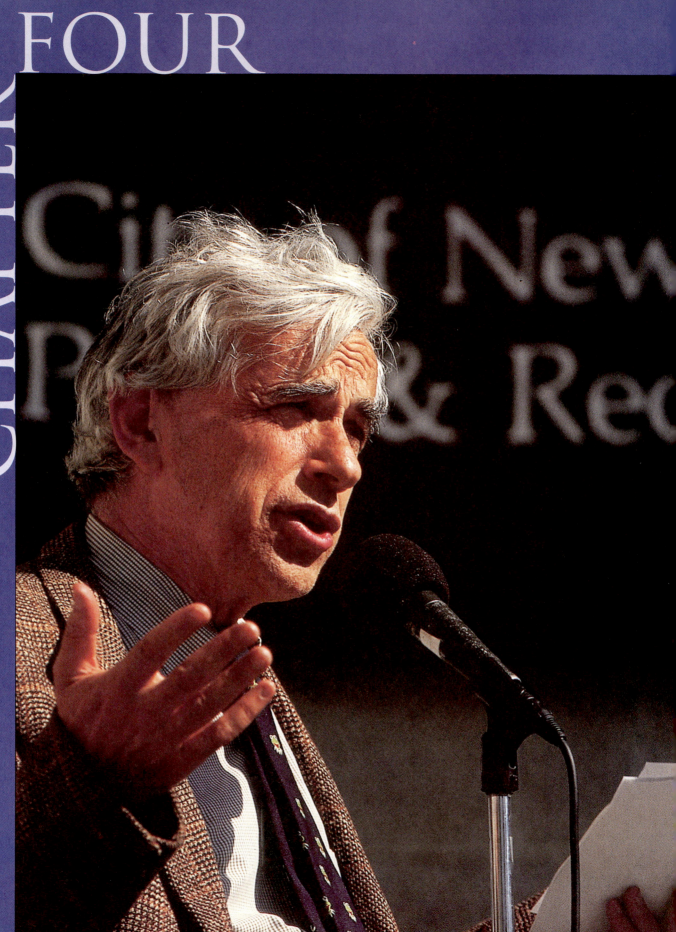

CHAPTER FOUR

SELECTING
A TOPIC
AND PURPOSE

Choosing a Topic

Topics You Know a Lot About
Topics You Want to Know More About
Brainstorming for Topics

Determining the General Purpose

Determining the Specific Purpose

Tips for Formulating the Specific Purpose Statement
Questions to Ask About Your Specific Purpose

Phrasing the Central Idea

What Is the Central Idea?
Guidelines for the Central Idea

A s you read through this book, you will find examples of hundreds of speeches that were delivered in classrooms, in the political arena, in community and business situations. Here is a very small sample of the topics they cover:

African storytelling	Navajo sandpainting
breast cancer	opera
Cesar Chavez	prison reform
doctor-assisted suicide	Quinceanera
E. coli bacteria	Rosh Hashanah
Frederick Douglass	Special Olympics
genetic engineering	tae kwon do
Habitat for Humanity	Underground Railroad
Internet	value-added tax
Japanese internment camps	women's gymnastics
Kashmir	x-rays
life on Mars	Yucatán peninsula
Mount Everest	zoos

Undoubtedly you noticed that the list runs from A to Z. This array of topics wasn't planned. It happened naturally in the course of presenting many different kinds of speeches. The list is given here simply to show you that there are literally endless possibilities for speech topics—from A to Z.

Choosing a Topic

topic
The subject of a speech.

The first step in speechmaking is choosing a topic. For speeches outside the classroom this is seldom a problem. Usually the speech topic is determined by the occasion, the audience, and the speaker's qualifications. When Toni Morrison lectures on a college campus, she is invited to speak about literature and the African-American experience. Elizabeth Dole will discuss politics and current events. Roger Ebert might share his views about the latest in filmmaking. The same is true of ordinary citizens. The doctor is asked to speak with high-school athletes and their parents about sports injuries. The stockbroker discourses on investment procedures, the florist on how to grow thriving houseplants.

In a public speaking class the situation is different. Most of your speech assignments will not come with a designated topic. Students generally have great leeway in selecting subjects for their speeches. This would appear to be an advantage, since it allows you to talk about matters of personal interest. Yet there may be no facet of speech preparation that causes more gnashing of teeth than selecting a topic.

It is a constant source of amazement to teachers that students who regularly chat with their friends about almost any subject under the sun become mentally paralyzed when faced with the task of deciding what to talk about in their speech class. Fortunately, once you get over this initial paralysis, you should have little trouble choosing a good topic.

There are two broad categories of potential topics for your classroom speeches: (1) subjects you know a lot about and (2) subjects you want to know more about. Let's start with the first.

Topics You Know a Lot About

Most people speak best about subjects with which they are most familiar. You can't go too far wrong by drawing on your own knowledge and experience. You may think to yourself, "That's impossible. I've never done anything fascinating. My life is too ordinary to interest other people." Everyone knows things or has done things that can be used in a speech.

Think for a moment about unusual experiences you may have had. Think also about special knowledge or expertise you may have acquired. You are bound to come up with something. One student, who grew up in Pakistan, presented a fascinating speech about daily life in that country. Another used her knowledge as a jewelry store salesperson to prepare a speech on how to judge the value of cut diamonds. A third student, who had lived through a tornado, gave a gripping speech about that terrifying experience.

Too dramatic? Nothing in your life is as interesting? Yet another student, who described herself as "just a housewife who is returning to school to finish the education she started 20 years ago," delivered a witty and highly entertaining speech on the adjustments she had to make in coming back to college. This speaker talked about the strange feelings of sitting in class with students young enough to be her children, the difficulty of balancing her academic work against her family commitments, and the satisfaction of completing the education she had begun years earlier.

Here are a few more examples of speech topics based largely on the students' personal knowledge and experience:

Hong Kong: City of Paradox

Working in a Television Newsroom

Iguanas: The Ideal Pets

A Tour of Old Jerusalem

Jai Alai: The World's Fastest Sport

Scuba Diving: A New World Under Water

Performing with the Native American Dance Troupe

Diabetes: You Can Live with It

How to Have a Successful Job Interview

When you look for a speech topic, keep in mind sports, hobbies, travel, and other personal experiences that would make for an interesting presentation.

Topics You Want to Know More About

On the other hand, you may decide to make your speech a learning experience for yourself as well as for your audience. You may choose a subject about which you already have some knowledge or expertise but not enough to prepare a speech without doing additional research. You may even select a topic that hasn't touched you at all before but that you want to explore. Say, for example, you've always been interested in extrasensory perception but never knew much about it. This would be a perfect opportunity to research a fascinating subject and turn it into a fascinating speech.

Or suppose you run across a subject in one of your other classes that catches your fancy. Why not investigate it further for your speech class? One student used this approach to develop a speech on the use of edible insects as a human food source. After hearing about the topic in a biology lecture, the student checked with his professor for additional readings, which he was able to find in the library. As it turned out, the professor was an internationally known expert on the role of insects as a food source, so the student also arranged an interview with the professor. (See Chapter 6 for information on conducting a research interview.) Using what he learned in his research, the student put together a captivating speech that kept everyone's attention from beginning to end.

Still another possibility—especially for persuasive speeches—is to think of subjects about which you hold strong opinions and beliefs. Imagine you are at dinner with a friend and find yourself arguing that television broadcasters should not report the projected results of presidential elections until polls have closed throughout the country. Why not give a speech in class on the same topic? Or suppose you believe your school should set up a program to help reduce burglaries on campus. Why not try to convince your classmates and get them to petition for such a program?

View an excerpt from Chinaka Steady, "Edible Insects."

CD: VIDEO CLIP 4.1

Like everyone else, you surely have issues about which you care deeply. They may include national or international concerns such as gun control, protection of the environment, or the threat of cyberterrorism. Or perhaps you are closely involved in a local issue, such as a teachers' strike, the campaign for mayor, or a proposal to increase tuition. Not all such topics must be "political." They can deal with anything from graduation requirements to helping people with physical disabilities, from vegetarianism to preserving a nature sanctuary, from dormitory regulations to building a church recreation center.

Brainstorming for Topics

After all this, you may still be thinking, "I *don't* care about edible insects. I've *never* been to Pakistan. I'm *not* active in politics. WHAT am I going to talk about?" If you are having trouble selecting a topic, there are a number of brainstorming procedures you can follow to get started.

brainstorming
A method of generating ideas for speech topics by free association of words and ideas.

Personal Inventory

First make a quick inventory of your experiences, interests, hobbies, skills, beliefs, and so forth. Jot down anything that comes to mind, no matter how silly or irrelevant it may seem. From this list may come a general subject area out of which you can fashion a specific topic. This method has worked for many students.

Clustering

If the first method doesn't work, try the second. It's a technique called clustering. Take a sheet of paper and divide it into nine columns as follows: People, Places, Things, Events, Processes, Concepts, Natural Phenomena, Problems, and Plans and Policies. Then list in each column the first five or six items that come to mind. The result might look like this:

People	Places	Things
Nelson Mandela	Miami	cartoons
Hillary Clinton	New York	high-definition TV
my family	Ellis Island	dream catchers
Oprah Winfrey	Grand Canyon	churches
Dave Matthews	my hometown	mosques
Oscar de la Hoya	Los Angeles	Koran

Events	Processes
Passover	writing a job resumé
World Cup	creating a personal website
marriage	investing in the stock market
Chinese New Year	how acupuncture works
graduation	what happens when people dream
Cinco de Mayo	adapting to a different culture

Concepts	Natural Phenomena
free trade	hurricanes
Afrocentrism	earthquakes
music theory	lightning
conservatism	global warming
multiculturalism	planets
Confucianism	asteroids

Problems	Plans and Policies
sweatshops	online voting
school violence	building a new library
identity theft	campaign finance reform
sickle-cell anemia	same-sex marriages
sleep deprivation	school vouchers
campus crime	protecting Indian tribal rights

Very likely, several items on your lists will strike you as potential topics. If not, take the items you find most intriguing and compose sublists for each. Try to free-associate. Write down a word or idea. What does that trigger in your mind? Whatever it is, write that down next, and keep going until you have six or seven ideas on your list. For example, working from the lists printed above, one student composed sublists for cartoons, campus crime, and lightning:

Cartoons	Campus Crime	Lightning
television	vandalism	thunder
movies	police	noise
Academy Awards	fingerprints	traffic
prizes	hands	air pollution
lotteries	gloves	gasoline
gambling	cold weather	motorcycles

Can you follow her trail of association? In the first column cartoons made her think of television. Television reminded her of movies. Movies suggest the Academy Awards. The Academy Awards are prizes. Prizes reminded her of lotteries. Lotteries are a form of gambling. Suddenly, this student remembered a magazine article she had read on the growing problem of gambling addiction in America. The idea clicked in her mind. After considerable research she developed an excellent speech entitled "Gambling Addiction: Why You Can't Beat the Odds."

That's a far cry from cartoons! If you started out free-associating from cartoons, you would doubtless end up somewhere completely different. This is what clustering is all about.

Reference Search

By clustering, most people are able to come up with a topic rather quickly. But if you are still stymied, don't despair. There is a third technique you can use. Go to the reference room of the library and browse through an encyclopedia, the *Reader's Guide to Periodical Literature,* the *New York Times Index,* or some other reference work until you stumble across what might be a good speech topic. As an experiment, one student decided to scan the CD-ROM version of *The American Heritage Dictionary,* limiting herself to the letter *b.* Within 10 minutes she had come up with these potential topics:

Bible	bonsai	Baja California	bar mitzvah
backpacking	blackjack	braille	backgammon
Bill of Rights	bioethics	bicycle	Beatles
ballet	Beethoven	Beijing	beer
beta-carotene	birthstones	botulism	Buddhism

With proper research and development, any one of these could make an excellent speech.

Internet Search

Yet another possibility, if you have access to the World Wide Web via the Internet, is to connect to a subject-based search engine such as Yahoo or the Librarians' Index to the Internet. You will see a screen much like the one in Figure 4.1, which lists the major categories of subjects indexed by Yahoo. If you select one of those categories—say, Health—the next screen will show all subcategories indexed under that heading. The result will look something like Figure 4.2 (page 80), which lists 26 subcategories for Health, any one of which might strike your fancy as a potential speech topic.

One of the advantages of using Yahoo as a brainstorming aid is that you can continue to make your search more and more specific until you find just the right topic. Suppose, for example, that as you look at the subheadings

Figure 4.1

Figure 4.2

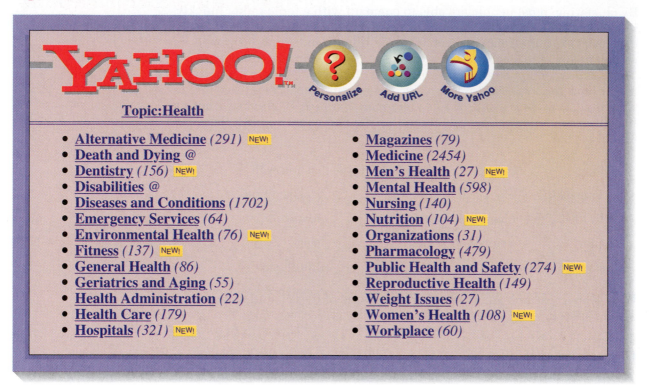

for Health, your attention is grabbed by the first item—Alternative Medicine. If you click on this item, you will get another screen with a detailed list of subheadings for Alternative Medicine. Working from that list, you can link up to other sites that will help you narrow and focus your topic even further. This process is much faster than leafing through reference works in the library, and it can be a great spur to thinking creatively about a topic.

Whatever the means you use for selecting a topic, *start early*. The major reason students have difficulty choosing speech topics is that, like most people, they tend to procrastinate—to put off starting projects for as long as possible. Since choosing a topic is your first step in the process of speech preparation, it is only natural to postpone facing up to it. But if you postpone it for too long, you may dig yourself into a hole from which you cannot escape.

Start thinking about your topic as soon as each assignment is announced. Pay attention to interesting subjects in class and conversation, on the radio and television, in newspapers and magazines. Jot down in your notebook ideas for topics as they occur to you. Having an inventory of possible topics to choose from is much better than having to rack your brain for one at the last minute. If you get an early start on choosing a topic, you will have plenty of time to pick just the right one and prepare a first-rate speech.

Determining the General Purpose

Along with choosing a topic, you need to determine the *general purpose* of your speech. Usually it will fall into one of two overlapping categories—to inform or to persuade. (As noted in Chapter 1, there is a third possible category—the speech to entertain. But classroom speeches are rarely of this type.)

> **general purpose**
> The broad goal of a speech. The three major kinds of general purposes are to inform, to persuade, and to entertain.

When your general purpose is to *inform,* you act as a teacher or lecturer. Your goal is to convey information—and to do so clearly, accurately, and interestingly. If you give an account of your trip to Spain, describe how to lift weights, narrate the major events of the latest Middle East crisis, report on your sorority's financial position, or explain how genetic testing for hereditary diseases works, you are speaking to inform. Your aim is to enhance the knowledge and understanding of your listeners—to give them information they did not have before.

When your general purpose is to *persuade,* you act as an advocate or a partisan. You go beyond giving information to espousing a cause. You want to *change* or *structure* the attitudes or actions of your audience. The difference between informing and persuading is the difference between explaining and exhorting.[1] If you try to convince your listeners that they should start a regular program of weight lifting, that the United States should modify its policy in the Middle East, that more students should take advantage of the study-abroad program, that your sorority should start a fund-raising drive to balance its budget, or that the federal government should prohibit businesses from using genetic testing when hiring employees—then you are speaking to persuade. In doing so, you cannot help but give information; but your primary goal is to win over your listeners to your point of view—to get them to believe something or do something as a result of your speech.

In speech classes, the general purpose is usually specified as part of the speech assignment. For speeches outside the classroom, however, you have to make sure of your general purpose yourself. Usually this is easy to do. Are you going to explain, report, or demonstrate something? Then your general purpose is to inform. Are you going to sell, advocate, or defend something? Then your general purpose is to persuade. But no matter what the situation, you must be certain of exactly what you hope to achieve by speaking. Knowing your general purpose is the first step. The next step is determining your specific purpose.

Determining the Specific Purpose

Once you have chosen a topic and a general purpose, you must narrow your choices to determine the *specific purpose* of your speech. The specific purpose should focus on one aspect of a topic. You should be able to state your specific purpose in a single infinitive phrase (to inform my audience about . . . ; to persuade my audience to . . .) that indicates *precisely* what you hope to accomplish with your speech. Perhaps an example will help to clarify the process of choosing a specific purpose.

specific purpose
A single infinitive phrase that states precisely what a speaker hopes to accomplish in his or her speech.

Meg Fugate, a student at the University of Wisconsin, decided to give her first classroom speech on a topic from her personal experience. In her job as a lifeguard during the previous four summers, Meg had dealt with emergencies ranging from drownings to second-degree burns to heart attacks. Knowing that most people will face an emergency at some point in their lives, Meg wanted to share what she had learned with her classmates. This gave her a topic and a general purpose, which she stated this way:

Topic: Emergencies

General Purpose: To inform.

So far, so good. But what aspect of her topic would Meg discuss? The different kinds of emergencies? The emergency situations she had faced? Specific techniques such as water rescue, applying first aid, or preventing a person from going into shock? She had to choose something interesting that she could cover in a six-minute speech. Finally, she settled on explaining the major steps involved in responding to an emergency. She stated her specific purpose this way:

Specific Purpose: To inform my audience of the major steps in responding to an emergency.

This turned out to be an excellent choice, and Meg's speech was among the best in the class.

Notice how clear the specific purpose statement is. Notice also how it relates the topic directly to the audience. That is, it states not what the *speaker* wants to *say,* but what the speaker wants the *audience* to *know* as a result of the speech. This is very important, for it helps keep the audience at the center of your attention as you prepare the speech.

Look what happens when the specific purpose statement does not include the audience.

Specific Purpose: To explain the major steps in responding to an emergency.

Explain to whom? To a group of medical students? To an introductory Red Cross class? Those would be two different speeches. The medical students already know the basic facts about responding to an emergency. For them the speaker might provide a more advanced discussion. But the people in the basic Red Cross class will not have anywhere near the knowledge of the medical students. To communicate effectively with them, the speaker will need to prepare a more general speech.

When the audience slips out of the specific purpose, it may slip out of the speaker's consciousness. You may begin to think your task is the general one of preparing "an informative speech," when in fact your task is the specific one of informing a particular group of people. This may seem like a small point right now, but as we shall see in the next chapter, it is almost impossible to prepare a good speech without keeping constantly in mind the *people* for whom it is intended.

THE INTERNET Connection

Having trouble choosing a speech topic? Try browsing through the subject categories at the Librarians' Index to the Internet (http://lii.org/). You will find a wealth of high-quality materials that can help get your creative juices flowing.

Another valuable website for anyone thinking about speech topics is http://www.britannica.com/, which provides an electronic version of the complete *Encyclopaedia Britannica,* as well as hundreds of links to other resources.

Tips for Formulating the Specific Purpose Statement

Formulating a specific purpose is the most important early step in developing a successful speech. When writing your purpose statement, try to follow the general principles outlined below.

Write the Purpose Statement as a Full Infinitive Phrase, Not as a Fragment

Ineffective: Calendars.

More Effective: To inform my audience about the four major kinds of calendars used in the world today.

Ineffective: Halloween.

More Effective: To inform my audience about the history of Halloween observances.

The ineffective statements above are adequate as announcements of the speech topic, but they are not thought out fully enough to indicate the specific purpose.

Express Your Purpose as a Statement, Not as a Question

Ineffective: What is Quinceanera?

More Effective: To inform my audience about the origins, ceremonies, and importance for young women of the traditional Quinceanera celebration in Mexico.

Ineffective: Is the U.S. space program necessary?

More Effective: To persuade my audience that the U.S. space program provides many important benefits to people here on earth.

The questions might make adequate titles, but they are not effective as purpose statements. They give no indication about what direction the speech will take or what the speaker hopes to accomplish.

Avoid Figurative Language in Your Purpose Statement

Ineffective: To inform my audience that yoga is totally sweet.

More Effective: To inform my audience of the ways yoga can reduce their stress, improve their health, and even help them get better grades.

Ineffective: To persuade my audience that banning all fraternities because there have been hazing abuses at some schools would be like throwing out the baby with the bath water.

More Effective: To persuade my audience that banning all fraternities because there have been hazing abuses at some schools would punish the vast majority for the actions of a few.

Although the ineffective statements indicate something of the speaker's viewpoint, they do not state concisely what he or she hopes to achieve. Metaphors, analogies, and the like are effective devices for reinforcing ideas within a speech, but they are too ambiguous for specific purpose statements.

Limit Your Purpose Statement to One Distinct Idea

Ineffective: To persuade my audience to become literacy tutors and to donate time to Habitat for Humanity.

This purpose statement expresses two unrelated ideas, either of which could be the subject of a speech. The easiest remedy is to select one or the other as a focus for your presentation.

More Effective: To persuade my audience to become literacy tutors.

Or:

More Effective: To persuade my audience to donate time to Habitat for Humanity.

Make Sure Your Specific Purpose Is Not Too Vague or General

Ineffective: To inform my audience about the Civil War.

More Effective: To inform my audience about the role of African-American soldiers in the Civil War.

The ineffective purpose statement above falls into one of the most common traps—it is too broad and ill-defined. It gives no clues about what aspect of the Civil War the speaker will cover. The more effective purpose statement is sharp and concise. It reveals clearly what the speaker plans to discuss.
    Here is another example, this time from a persuasive speech:

Ineffective: To persuade my audience that something should be done about medical care.

More Effective: To persuade my audience that the federal government should adopt a system of national health insurance for all people in the United States.

Library resources can provide ideas for speech topics, as well as material for developing the speech itself.

Again, the ineffective purpose statement is vague and indistinct. It gives no indication of the speaker's stance toward the topic. The "something" that "should be done" could include anything from clamping down on abuses by HMOs to reforming Medicare and Medicaid. The more effective purpose is crisp and clear. It does not leave us guessing what the speaker hopes to accomplish.

The more precise your specific purpose, the easier it will be to prepare your speech. Consider this topic and specific purpose:

Topic: Hot-air balloons

Specific Purpose: To inform my audience about hot-air balloons.

With such a hazy purpose, you have no systematic way of limiting your research or of deciding what to include in the speech and what to exclude. The origins of hot-air balloons, how they work, their current popularity— all could be equally relevant to a speech designed "to inform my audience about hot-air balloons."

In contrast, look at this topic and specific purpose:

Topic: Hot-air balloons

Specific Purpose: To inform my audience about the scientific uses of hot-air balloons.

Now it is easy to decide what is germane and what is not. The origins of hot-air balloons, how they work, their current popularity—all are interesting, but none is essential to the specific purpose of explaining "the scientific uses of hot-air balloons." Thus you need not worry about researching these matters or about explaining them in your speech. You can spend your preparation time efficiently.

Questions to Ask About Your Specific Purpose

Sometimes you will arrive at your specific purpose almost immediately after choosing your topic. At other times you may do quite a bit of research before deciding on a specific purpose. Much will depend on how familiar you are with the topic, as well as on any special demands imposed by the assignment, the audience, or the occasion. But whenever you settle on your specific purpose, ask yourself the following questions about it.

Does My Purpose Meet the Assignment?

Students occasionally stumble over this question. Be sure you understand your assignment, and shape your specific purpose to meet it. If you have questions, check with your instructor.

Can I Accomplish My Purpose in the Time Allotted?

Most classroom speeches are quite short, ranging from four to five minutes to ten minutes. That may seem like a lot of time if you have never given a speech before. But you will quickly find what generations of students have discovered, much to their surprise—time flies when you are giving a speech! Most people speak at an average rate of 120 to 150 words a minute. This means that a six-minute speech will consist of roughly 720 to 900 words. That is not long enough to develop a highly complex topic. Here are some specific purpose statements that would defy being handled well in the time normally allocated for classroom speeches:

> To inform my audience about the role of technology in human history.
>
> To inform my audience about the rise and fall of the Roman Empire.
>
> To persuade my audience to convert to Buddhism.

You are much better off with a limited purpose that you have some reasonable hope of achieving in the short span of four to ten minutes.

The Specific Purpose Checklist can help you prepare your speeches.

CD: SPEECH CHECKLIST

Is the Purpose Relevant to My Audience?

The price of retirement homes in Sun City might be an engrossing topic for older citizens who are in the market for such dwellings. And the quality of hot lunches in the elementary schools is of great concern to the students who eat them and the parents who pay for them. But neither subject has much relevance for an audience of college students. No matter how well you construct your speeches, they are likely to fall flat unless you speak about matters of interest to your listeners.

This is not to say you must select only topics that pertain *directly* to the college student's daily experience—the grading system, dormitory conditions, parking spaces on campus, and the like. Most students have wide-ranging backgrounds, interests, ideas, and values. And most of them are intellectually curious. They can get involved in an astonishing variety of subjects. Follow your common sense, and make sure *you* are truly interested in the topic. Also, when speaking on a subject that is not obviously relevant to your listeners, take time in your speech to tie the subject in with their goals, values, interests, and well-being. We'll discuss how to do this in the next chapter.

Is the Purpose Too Trivial for My Audience?

Just as you need to avoid speech topics that are too broad or complicated, so you need to steer clear of topics that are too superficial. How to build a fire without matches might absorb a group of Cub Scouts, but your classmates would probably consider it frivolous. Unfortunately, there is no absolute rule for determining what is trivial to an audience and what is not. Here are some examples of specific purposes that most people would find too trivial for classroom speeches:

> To inform my audience about the parts of a backpack.

> To inform my audience how to tie a bow tie.

> To persuade my audience that Tommy Hilfiger makes the best jeans.

Is the Purpose Too Technical for My Audience?

Nothing puts an audience to sleep faster than a dry and technical speech. Beware of topics that are inherently technical, as well as of treating ordinary subjects in a technical fashion. Although you may be perfectly familiar with the principles and vocabulary of quantum physics, physical anthropology, molecular biology, clinical psychology, or constitutional law, most of your classmates probably are not. There are aspects of these and similar subjects that can be treated clearly, with a minimum of jargon. But if you find that you can't fulfill your specific purpose without relying on technical words and concepts, you should reconsider your purpose. Here are some examples of specific purposes that are overly technical for most classroom speeches:

> To inform my audience about the solution to Fermat's Last Theorem.

> To inform my audience about the complexities of Aristotelian metaphysics.

> To inform my audience about the methods of econometrics.

We shall discuss the details of audience analysis and adaptation in Chapter 5. For the moment, remember to make sure that your specific purpose is appropriate for your listeners. If you have doubts, ask your instructor, or circulate a questionnaire among your classmates (see pages 113–116).

Phrasing the Central Idea

What Is the Central Idea?

The specific purpose of a speech is what you hope to accomplish. The *central idea* is a concise statement of what you *expect to say.* Sometimes it is called the thesis statement, the subject sentence, or the major thought. Whatever the term, the central idea is usually expressed as a simple, declarative sentence that refines and sharpens the specific purpose statement.

central idea
A one-sentence statement that sums up or encapsulates the major ideas of a speech.

Imagine you run into a friend on your way to speech class. She says, "I have to dash to my history lecture, but I hear you're giving a speech today. Can you tell me the gist of it in one sentence?" "Sure," you reply. "America's prison system suffers from three major problems—overcrowding of inmates, lack of effective rehabilitation programs, and high expense to taxpayers."

Your answer is the central idea of your speech. It is more precise than your topic (America's prison system) or your specific purpose statement ("To inform my audience of the three major problems facing America's prison system"). By stating exactly what the three major problems are, the central idea "sums up" your speech in a single sentence.

residual message
What a speaker wants the audience to remember after it has forgotten everything else in a speech.

Another way to think of the central idea is as your *residual message*—what you want your audience to remember after they have forgotten everything else in the speech. Most of the time the central idea will encapsulate the main points to be developed in the body of the speech. To show how this works, let's take a few of the examples we saw earlier in this chapter and develop them from the topic, general purpose, and specific purpose to the central idea.

We can start with the speech about responding to an emergency situation.

Topic: Emergencies

General Purpose: To inform.

Specific Purpose: To inform my audience of the major steps in responding to an emergency.

Central Idea: The three major steps in responding to an emergency are surveying the scene, contacting an emergency medical service, and starting CPR if needed.

View the introduction from Meg Fugate, "CPR."

CD: VIDEO CLIP 4.2

Look carefully at this example. It shows how the speaker might start with a broad subject (emergencies) that becomes narrower and narrower as the speaker moves from the general purpose to the specific purpose to the central idea. Notice also how much more the central idea suggests about the content of the speech. From it we can expect the speaker to develop three main points in the speech—each corresponding to one of the three major steps in responding to an emergency.

This sharpening of focus as one proceeds to the central idea is crucial. Here is another example:

Topic:	Calendars
General Purpose:	To inform.
Specific Purpose:	To inform my audience of the four major calendars used in the world today.
Central Idea:	The four major calendars used in the world today are the Gregorian calendar, the Hebrew calendar, the Chinese calendar, and the Islamic calendar.

This central idea is especially well worded. We can assume from it that the body of the speech will contain four main points—on the Gregorian calendar, the Hebrew calendar, the Chinese calendar, and the Islamic calendar.

Much the same is true of the following example:

Topic:	Campus parking
General Purpose:	To persuade.
Specific Purpose:	To persuade my audience to petition against our school's plan to reduce the number of campus parking spaces assigned to students.
Central Idea:	Our school's plan to reduce student parking spaces is an infringement of student rights and will result in widespread illegal parking.

From this central idea we can deduce that the speaker will develop two main points in the speech: (1) students have a right to park on campus; and (2) if this right is limited, the students' only recourse is to park illegally.

There is something else important about these examples. Notice in each case how much more the central idea reveals about the content of the speech than does the specific purpose. This is not accidental. Often you can settle on a specific purpose statement early in preparing your speech. The central idea, however, usually emerges later—after you have done your research and have decided on the main points of the speech. The process may work like this:

As an environmental science major, Marcia Esposito had learned that many experts fear the world may face a severe water shortage by the year 2020. She decided this would make a good topic for her informative speech. Tentatively, she adopted the following specific purpose statement: "To inform my audience about the seriousness of the growing international water crisis." Then Marcia started her research.

An article in *Newsweek,* which she located through the *InfoTrac Magazine Index,* explained how the population in countries such as China, Egypt, and Mexico is outstripping the available supply of fresh water. According to the article, one-third of the wells in Beijing, China's largest city, have gone dry, and the water table in Mexico City is dropping at the rate of 11 feet per year.

Next Marcia found a report on the Worldwatch Institute website about the impact of pollution on the water supply. The report stated that, in many parts of the world, urban and industrial contamination is creating "a water supply too polluted for their people to drink."

Then Marcia hit upon the idea of interviewing one of her environmental science professors. In addition to confirming Marcia's research about the impact of population growth and pollution, the professor mentioned the problems caused by mismanagement of water supplies. Around the world 65 to 70 percent of the water people use is lost to waste, evaporation, and other inefficiencies; the rate in the United States is about 50 percent.

Marcia digested all this information. Now she was ready to formulate her central idea: "Population growth, pollution, and mismanagement are creating a serious shortage of fresh water in many parts of the world."

Guidelines for the Central Idea

What makes a well-worded central idea? Essentially the same things that make a well-worded specific purpose statement. The central idea should be expressed in a full sentence, should not be in the form of a question, should avoid figurative language, and should not be vague or overly general.

Here, for example, are four poorly written central ideas. See if you can identify the problem with each and figure out how each might be phrased more effectively:

Ineffective: Paying college athletes a salary is a good idea.

Ineffective: Problems of fad diets.

Ineffective: How does indoor soccer differ from outdoor soccer?

Ineffective: Mexico's Yucatán Peninsula is an awesome place for a vacation.

The first, of course, is too general. To say that paying college athletes a monthly salary is a "good idea" does not convey the speaker's viewpoint sharply and clearly. What does the speaker mean by a "good idea"? That paying athletes a monthly salary is justified given the millions of dollars generated for universities by sports such as football and basketball? That the salary should be paid to all athletes, or just to those in major revenue-producing sports? That the salary should be $200 a month? If so, the central idea should say as much. A revised central idea for this speech might be:

More Effective: Because college athletes in revenue-producing sports such as football and basketball generate millions of dollars in revenue for their schools, the NCAA should allow such athletes to receive a $200 monthly salary as part of their scholarships.

The second ineffective central idea is also too general, but it suffers further from not being written as a complete sentence. "Problems of fad diets" might work as a topic statement, but it does not reveal enough about the content of the speech to serve as the central idea. It should be rewritten as a full sentence that identifies the problems of fad diets to be discussed in the speech:

Unlike the specific purpose, which you can often settle on early, the central idea usually takes shape as a result of your research and analysis of the topic.

More Effective: Although fad diets produce quick weight loss, they can lead to serious health problems by creating deficiencies in vitamins and minerals and by breaking down muscle tissue as well as fat.

The third poorly written central idea is phrased as a question rather than as a full declarative sentence. Asking "How does indoor soccer differ from outdoor soccer?" might be a good way to catch the interest of your listeners, but it does not encapsulate the main points to be developed in the speech. A more effective central idea would be:

More Effective: Played on a smaller, enclosed field that resembles a hockey rink with artificial turf, indoor soccer involves faster action, more scoring, and different strategies than outdoor soccer.

The final ineffective central idea is flawed by its use of figurative language. To say that the Yucatán Peninsula is an "awesome" place for a vacation does not state the speaker's central idea clearly and concisely. It does not indicate what characteristics of the Yucatán Peninsula the speaker intends to discuss. Moreover, "awesome" could mean quite different things to different people. A better central idea might be:

The Central Idea Checklist can help you prepare your speeches.

CD: SPEECH CHECKLIST

More Effective: Mexico's Yucatán Peninsula has many attractions for vacationers, including a warm climate, excellent food, and extensive Mayan ruins.

Notice that in all these examples the more effective central idea encapsulates or sums up the main points of the speech in a single sentence. If you are having trouble phrasing your central idea, the reason may be that you do not yet have a firm grasp on the main points of your speech. Do not worry too much about your central idea until after you have developed the body of your speech (see Chapter 8). If, at that point, you still cannot come up with a clear, concise central idea, it may be that your speech itself is not very clear or concise. Keep working on the speech until you can compose a central idea that fits the criteria just discussed. The result will be a sharper central idea and a tighter, more coherent speech.

Summary

The first step in speechmaking is choosing a topic. For classroom speeches it is often best to choose a subject you know well or in which you have personal experience, but you can also succeed with a topic you research especially for the speech. If you have trouble picking a topic, you can follow at least four brainstorming procedures. First, make a quick inventory of your hobbies, interests, skills, experiences, beliefs, and so forth. Second, use the technique of clustering and write down on a sheet of paper the first topics that come to mind in several categories. Third, look through a reference work for ideas. Fourth, use a World Wide Web subject directory such as Yahoo to help you scan possible topics.

After you choose a topic, you need to settle on the general purpose of your speech. Usually the general purpose will be to inform or to persuade. When your general purpose is to inform, you act as a teacher. Your goal is to communicate information clearly, accurately, and interestingly. When your general purpose is to persuade, you act as an advocate. You go beyond giving information to espousing a cause. Your goal is to win listeners over to your point of view.

Once you know your topic and general purpose, you must narrow in on a specific purpose that you can express as a single infinitive phrase. The phrase should indicate precisely what your speech seeks to achieve; for example, "To inform my audience of the major kinds of canoe races." The specific purpose statement should (1) be a full infinitive phrase, not a fragment; (2) be phrased as a statement, not a question; (3) avoid figurative language; (4) concentrate on one distinct idea; (5) not be too vague or too general.

In addition, keep several questions in mind as you formulate your specific purpose statement: Does my purpose meet the assignment? Can I accomplish my purpose in the time allotted? Is the purpose relevant to my audience? Is the purpose too trivial or too technical for my audience?

The central idea refines and sharpens your specific purpose. It is a concise statement of what you will say in your speech, and it usually crystallizes in your thinking after you have done your research and have decided on the main points of your speech. An example of a central idea is, "The three major kinds of canoe races are marathon races, white-water races, and flat-water races." As you can see, the central idea usually encapsulates the main points to be developed in the body of your speech.

Key Terms

topic (74)

brainstorming (77)

general purpose (81)

specific purpose (82)

central idea (88)

residual message (88)

Review Questions

After reading this chapter, you should be able to answer the following questions:

1. What four brainstorming methods can you follow if you are having trouble choosing a topic for your speech?

2. What are the two general purposes of most classroom speeches? How do they differ?

3. Why is determining the specific purpose such an important early step in speech preparation? Why is it important to include the audience in the specific purpose statement?

4. What are five tips for formulating your specific purpose?

5. What are five questions to ask about your specific purpose?

6. What is the difference between the specific purpose and the central idea of a speech? What are four guidelines for an effective central idea?

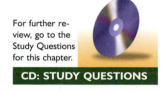

For further review, go to the Study Questions for this chapter.

CD: STUDY QUESTIONS

Exercises for Critical Thinking

1. Using one of the four brainstorming methods described in this chapter, come up with three topics you might like to deal with in your next classroom speech. For each topic, devise two possible specific purpose statements suitable for the speech assignment. Make sure the specific purpose statements fit the guidelines discussed in the chapter.

2. At the top of page 94 is a list of nine topics. Choose three, and for each of the three compose two specific purpose statements—one suitable for an informative speech and one suitable for a persuasive speech.

   Example

   Topic: School buses

   Informative: To inform my audience of the dangerous conditions of many school buses in the United States.

   Persuasive: To persuade my audience that the federal government should impose stronger safety standards for school buses in the United States.

education   technology   crime
sports   politics   prejudice
science   music   health

3. Here are several specific purpose statements for classroom speeches. Identify the problem with each, and rewrite the statement to correct the problem.

    To inform my audience how to make perfect popcorn every time.

    To inform my audience about the growth of credit card fraud and the methods of sound financial planning.

    What is obsessive compulsive disorder?

    To inform my audience why square grooves are superior to U-shaped grooves on golf clubs.

    To inform my audience about Thailand.

    Donate blood.

    To persuade my audience that something has to be done about the problem of antibiotic-resistant bacteria.

4. Below are two sets of main points for speeches. For each set supply the general purpose, specific purpose, and central idea.

    General Purpose:

    Specific Purpose:

    Central Idea:

    Main Points: I.   The first major race in alpine skiing is the downhill.
                        II. The second major race in alpine skiing is the slalom.
                        III. The third major race in alpine skiing is the giant slalom.

    General Purpose:

    Specific Purpose:

    Central Idea:

    Main Points: I.   You should support the school bond referendum because it will improve classroom facilities.

                        II. You should support the school bond referendum because it will increase the number of teachers.

                        III. You should support the school bond referendum because it will upgrade instructional resources.

Applying the POWER of Public Speaking

Your chemistry degree and excellent communication skills have helped you land a job in the office of Public Information in your state's Department of Health. With a particularly dangerous strain of type-A influenza moving through your state, a news briefing has been scheduled to inform residents about the disease. You are selected to present the briefing.

After gathering information from your agency's medical personnel, you plan what you will say in the briefing. You decide that you will (1) report the symptoms of the disease, (2) identify the people—young children, the elderly, and others—who are most at risk to catch the disease, (3) explain preventive measures to avoid getting the disease, and (4) relate how to treat the disease if one does come down with it.

Following the format used in this chapter, state the general purpose, specific purpose, main points, and central idea of your speech.

Notes

[1]James C. Humes, *Roles Speakers Play* (New York: Harper & Row, 1976), p. 5.

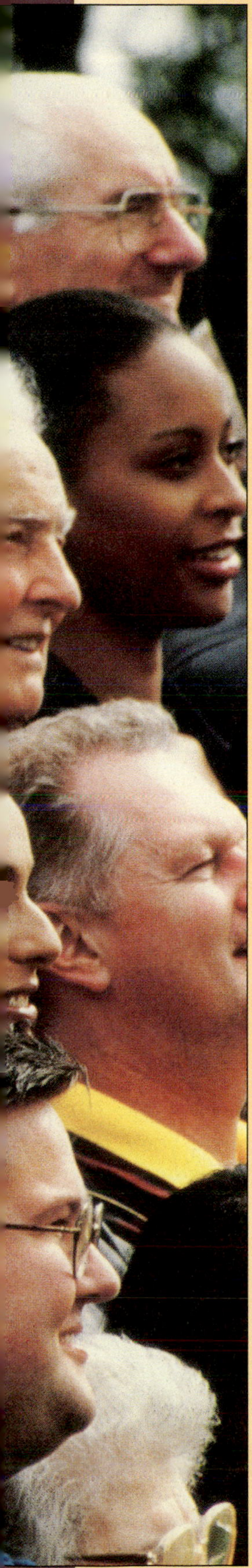

CHAPTER FIVE

ANALYZING
THE AUDIENCE

Audience-Centeredness

Your Classmates as an Audience

The Psychology of Audiences

Demographic Audience Analysis

Age
Gender
Racial, Ethnic, or Cultural Background
Religion
Group Membership

Situational Audience Analysis

Size
Physical Setting
Disposition toward the Topic
Disposition toward the Speaker
Disposition toward the Occasion

Getting Information about the Audience

Interviewing
Questionnaires

Adapting to the Audience

Audience Adaptation before the Speech
Audience Adaptation during the Speech

Few speakers in recent memory have faced a tougher situation than Barbara Bush when she delivered the commencement address at Wellesley College on June 1, 1990. Bush was invited to speak after the students' first choice, author Alice Walker, had declined. In protest of Bush's selection, more than one-fourth of the graduating class signed a petition charging that she was not a good role model for career-oriented women and had been chosen simply because she was the wife of the President of the United States.

The petition ignited a month-long national controversy. As educators, politicians, and editorialists debated the students' actions, Bush remained silent. By the day of the speech, interest had grown to the point that her remarks were broadcast live by all the television networks. The public wanted to hear what she would say and to see how the students would react.

Speaking with a blend of grace and humor, Bush acknowledged that the students had preferred Walker, "known for *The Color Purple,*" and had instead got her, "known for the color of my hair!" Rather than being defensive or scolding the students, Bush spoke with them personally about her views on the difficult choices facing women in balancing their careers with commitments to friends and family. She capped off the speech by suggesting that someone in the audience might follow in her footsteps and one day preside over the White House as the President's spouse. "I wish *him* well," she added, to thunderous cheering and applause.

Deemed "a triumph" by the *New York Times,* the speech garnered universal praise. Even students who had been critical of Bush beforehand were impressed. "She was wonderful and funny," one of them stated. "She could have addressed more women's issues. But she was sincere and she touched our hearts." NBC News anchor Tom Brokaw called it "one of the best commencement speeches I've ever heard."

View excerpts from Barbara Bush's commencement speech at Wellesley College.

CD: VIDEO CLIP 5.1

Audience-Centeredness

audience-centeredness
Keeping the audience foremost in mind at every step of speech preparation and presentation.

Bush's speech points up an important fact: Good public speakers are *audience-centered.* They know the primary purpose of speechmaking is not to lord it over the audience or to blow off steam. Rather, it is to gain a *desired response* from listeners. No matter what Barbara Bush felt about the petition against her selection as speaker, she had nothing to gain by complaining about it. Nor, under the circumstances, could she ignore it. By respecting the students and their concerns, she was able to establish common ground with her audience and gain a hearing for her ideas.

Being audience-centered does not involve taking any means to an end. You need not prostitute your beliefs to get a favorable response from your audience. Nor should you use devious, unethical tactics to achieve your goals. As with Barbara Bush, you can remain true to yourself while adapting your message to the needs of a particular audience. When working on your speeches you should keep several questions in mind:

To whom am I speaking?

What do I want them to know, believe, or do as a result of my speech?

What is the most effective way of composing and presenting my speech to accomplish that aim?

The answers to these questions will influence every decision you make along the way—selecting a topic, determining a specific purpose, settling on your main points and supporting materials, organizing the message, and, finally, delivering the speech.

It can be instructive to watch how political candidates deal with audience-centeredness. Suppose a person is running for Congress. To an audience of senior citizens she or he might talk about Social Security benefits; to a group of farmers the speech might emphasize agricultural price supports; to urban apartment dwellers the candidate might stress methods to counteract street crime. This strategy is perfectly legitimate, provided all the policies are part of the candidate's overall program. If the candidate were to concentrate on agricultural price supports before a group of white-collar workers, they simply wouldn't care. The speaker's aim is to adjust to the concerns of the audience, not to show how much she or he knows about a wide variety of issues.

This is not very different from what you do in your daily social contacts. Few people would walk into a party and announce, "What a jerk the governor is!" Or, "You know, those people protesting at the administration building are way over the edge!" If you made either of these statements, you would risk having among your listeners (1) an ardent suporter of the governor, (2) someone who participated in the protest at the administration building, (3) both of the above. The resulting situation could be rather embarrassing.

People usually prefer to open controversial topics with a fairly noncommittal position, to see how their listeners respond. You might say, "Did you hear what the governor did today?" Or, "What's going on at the administration building?" Then when you have heard and processed your companion's response, you can tailor your statements accordingly. (You don't have to *agree* with a viewpoint different from your own, but neither do you have to hit your listeners over the head with your own opinion.)

When you make a speech, either in class or in some other forum, you can't just wait to see how your audience responds and then change the rest of the speech. But you can find out in advance as much as possible about your listeners' positions on various subjects. Unless you know what your listeners believe *now,* you cannot hope to change their beliefs.

At this point you may be nodding your head and saying, "Of course, everyone knows that. It's only common sense." But knowing a precept and putting it into practice are two different matters. The aim of this chapter is to introduce the basic principles necessary in order to understand audiences. Chapters 14–16 will deal with those features of audience analysis and adaptation unique to informative and persuasive speaking.

Your Classmates as an Audience

There is a tendency—among students and teachers alike—to view the classroom as an artificial speaking situation. In a way, it is. Your speech class is a testing ground where you can develop your communication skills before applying them outside the classroom. No elections, no verdicts, no business decisions, no promotions ride on your performance. The most serious measure of success or failure is your grade, and that is determined ultimately by your teacher.

Because of this, it is easy to lose sight of your fellow students as an authentic audience. But each of your classmates is a real person with real ideas, attitudes, and feelings. Your speech class offers an enormous opportunity to inform and persuade other people. As one student wrote on her evaluation form at the end of her speech class, "I thought the speeches would all be phony, but they weren't. Some of them really hit me hard. I've not only learned a lot about speaking—I've learned a lot about other things from listening to the speeches in class."

The best classroom speeches are those that take the classroom audience as seriously as a lawyer, a politician, a minister, or an advertiser takes an audience. Public speaking is not acting. The essence of speechmaking is not to learn a role that can be played over and over without variation, but to adapt one's ideas to particular audiences on particular occasions. If you regard your audience as artificial, you will probably give a speech that sounds artificial.

One key to successful speaking is to consider every audience—inside the classroom and out—as worthy of your best efforts to communicate your knowledge or convictions. At the least you show respect for your listeners. At the most you could make a real difference in their lives. The following story demonstrates the latter:

Crystal Watkins gave an informative speech on the subject of small claims court, where ordinary people can press lawsuits involving up to $2,000 without lawyers. Part of her speech went like this: "It's two weeks after you have moved into a new apartment. A letter arrives from your old landlord. Expecting to get back your $400 security deposit, you joyfully tear open the envelope. Inside is a form letter explaining why your security deposit is not being refunded. What can you do about it? Nothing, right? Wrong! You can file a claim in small claims court."

Lee Callaway, one of Crystal's classmates, paid close attention. At the end of the previous term, he had run into a situation just like the one Crystal described. Not having money to hire a lawyer, he assumed he would have to forfeit his security deposit. But now, as he listened to Crystal's speech, Lee decided he would try to get his money back in small claims court. He filed suit the next week, and within a month he had his money back—thanks in part to his classmate's speech!

Most of your classroom speeches won't have this much immediate impact. Nevertheless, any topic that you handle conscientiously can influence your listeners—can enrich their experience, broaden their knowledge, perhaps change their views about something important.

The Psychology of Audiences

What do you do when you listen to a speech? Sometimes you pay close attention; at other times you let your thoughts wander. People may be compelled to attend a speech, but no one can make them listen unless they want to. It's up to the speaker to make the audience *choose* to pay attention.

The best classroom speeches, like those in other settings, are audience-centered. Each of your speeches provides an opportunity to inform, persuade, or inspire your classmates.

Even when people do pay attention, they don't process a speaker's message exactly as the speaker intends. Auditory perception is always selective. Every speech contains two messages—the one sent by the speaker and the one received by the listener. As we saw in Chapter 1, what a speaker says is filtered through a listener's frame of reference—the sum of her or his needs, interests, expectations, knowledge, and experience. As a result, we constantly listen and respond to speeches not as they are, but as we are. Or, to borrow from Paul Simon's classic song "The Boxer," people hear what they want to hear and disregard the rest.

What do people want to hear? Very simply, they usually want to hear about things that are meaningful to them. People are *egocentric.* They pay closest attention to messages that affect their own values, their own beliefs, their own well-being. Listeners typically approach speeches with one question uppermost in mind: "Why is this important to *me?*" As Harry Emerson Fosdick, the great preacher, once said: "There is nothing that people are so interested in as themselves, their own problems, and the way to solve them. That fact is basic. . . . It is the primary starting point of all successful public speaking."[1]

What do these psychological principles mean to you as a speaker? First, they mean your listeners will hear and judge what you say on the basis of what they already know and believe. Second, they mean you must relate your message to your listeners—show how it pertains to them, explain why they should care about it as much as you do. Here's an example:

> Cheryl Amato had graduated with a degree in public health and was thrilled to be hired to develop a new program on domestic violence at a local hospital. A survey of patients had shown that almost none of the battered women who came into the

egocentrism
The tendency of people to be concerned above all with their own values, beliefs, and well-being.

emergency room had ever told their doctors they were being abused—and that their doctors hadn't asked. It would be Cheryl's job to train physicians in the hospital's managed care network to recognize the warning signs of abuse in their patients and to intervene quickly.

Drawing on the latest research, Cheryl put together a cutting-edge presentation complete with video clips and PowerPoint slides. After practicing it several times, she asked a couple doctors in the network for their feedback. "You obviously know a lot about the subject," one of them said. "But let's be realistic. Because of managed care, even doctors who are well informed about domestic violence have almost no time to spend with their patients. When are we supposed to talk with them about such a complex issue?"

Cheryl was taken aback, but she answered quickly: "You're right. So what are some simple, practical things a concerned physician can do?" In the discussion that followed, the doctors came up with a number of suggestions.

The next day, Cheryl reworked her presentation and gave it a new title: "Preventing Domestic Violence: Tips for the Busy Physician." When the first group of doctors came for training the following week, she began: "A survey of patients here in our own hospital showed that most abused women who come to the emergency room have never talked about domestic violence with their doctors. One reason is that doctors today are too busy to spend much time with their patients. Today I'd like to share some tips from doctors like yourselves about how to spot the warning signs of domestic violence, even in a busy practice." In a few moments, Cheryl had everyone's attention and her speech was off to a great start.

As Cheryl's experience shows, you need some grasp of what your listeners know, believe, and care about. As Saul Alinksy, the noted community organizer, advises, "People only understand things in terms of their experience," which means that to communicate with them, "you must get inside their experience."[2]

Of course, you can't actually get inside another person's experience. But you can learn enough about your audience to know what you should do to make your ideas clear and meaningful. How you can do this is our next topic.

Demographic Audience Analysis

demographic audience analysis
Audience analysis that focuses on demographic factors such as age, gender, religious orientation, group membership, and racial, ethnic, or cultural background.

One of the ways speakers analyze audiences is by looking for observable traits such as age, gender, religious orientation, racial, ethnic, or cultural background, group membership, and the like. This is called *demographic audience analysis.* It consists of two steps: (1) identifying the general demographic features of your audience; (2) gauging the importance of those features to a particular speaking situation. Here are a few of the major factors you will need to consider.

Age

Are you a member of Generation X? Generation Next? Twenty-something or thirty-something? A baby boomer or a senior citizen? To some extent these are merely labels. All Gen X'ers do not think alike; all baby boomers do not buy the same products; all senior citizens do not vote for the same political candidates.

Yet, as Aristotle noted over 2,000 years ago and as researchers have confirmed many times since, few things affect a person's outlook more than his or her age. Each generation has more or less common values and experiences that set it apart from other generations. No matter how hard they try, for example, many people who grew up during the 1940s will never be fully comfortable with hip-hop, body piercing, and couples living together outside of marriage. On the other hand, to people in their late teens or early 20s, Pearl Harbor, Marilyn Monroe, Vietnam, John Kennedy, Watergate—all are just people and events out of the past. Whatever your age, you are a product of your world.

You can see what this means for your speeches. Suppose you address an audience of older people. If you refer offhandedly to your "roommate"— making it clear that your roommate is someone of the opposite sex—your audience may be disturbed and tune out the rest of your speech. Similarly, if you speak to an audience of young adults and casually mention Joseph McCarthy (an anti-Communist Senator of the 1950s) or the Tet offensive (an important campaign of the Vietnam War), they may not know what you are talking about. Even if younger listeners do recognize the names, they will not have the emotional associations of older people who lived through the 1950s or the war in Vietnam.

Depending on the composition of your speech class, you may face an audience that is mostly in their late teens and early 20s. If so, you can assume a common level of age experience. On the other hand, 45 percent of college students today are age 25 or older, and many classrooms include students in their 30s, 40s, 50s, and beyond. You may then have to tackle two or three generations. This will give you good practice for speeches outside the classroom, where age is usually a major factor in audience analysis.

Gender

As the new sales director for a national computer firm, Alex Kvalo was looking forward to his first meeting with the company's district managers. Everyone arrived on time, and Alex's presentation went extremely well. He decided to end the meeting with a conversation about the importance of the district managers to the company's plans.

"I believe we are going to continue to increase our share of the market," he began, "because of the quality of the people in this room. The district manager is the key to the success of the sales representatives in his district. He sets the tone for everyone else. If he has ambitious goals and is willing to put in long hours, everyone in his unit will follow his example."

When Alex was finished, he received polite applause, but hardly the enthusiastic response he had hoped for. Later, he spoke with one of the senior managers. "Things were going so well until the end," Alex lamented. "Obviously, I said the wrong thing."

"Yes," the district manager replied. "Half of our managers are women. Most have worked their way up from sales representatives, and they're very proud of the role they've played in the company's growth. They don't care a hoot about political correctness, but they were definitely surprised, and distressed, to be referred to as *he*."

Alex should not have been surprised at the lukewarm response to his speech. Although he did not mean to cause offense, by calling all the district managers "he," Alex disregarded half of his audience and their contributions to the company. The same would have been true if he had referred to all the managers as "she." A speaker who ignores the gender of his or her listeners is almost certain to offend some members of the audience.

In speechmaking you must be wary of making assumptions with respect to gender until you have tested those assumptions and found them to be correct. Social distinctions between the sexes have been eroding for some years. Men now cook, keep house, work as receptionists, and volunteer in their children's schools. Women work in construction trades, run corporations, enlist in the armed forces, and serve as college athletic directors. Men and women today share a much broader range of experiences, interests, and aspirations than they once did.

In addition, the "typical" composition of audiences has also changed. At one time local civic groups such as Kiwanis and Rotary clubs were all-male. Today most have sizable contingents of women. Parent associations, which were once composed almost solely of women, now include plenty of interested fathers. Here, as in other areas, the old stereotypes no longer apply.

This is not to say that women and men are alike in all their values and beliefs. When it comes to politics, for instance, American women tend to be more concerned about issues such as education, health care, and social justice, whereas men tend to stress economics and military defense. But keep in mind that these are generalizations. There are lots of women who believe military defense comes first, just as there are plenty of men who give priority to social issues. An astute speaker will be equally attuned to both the differences *and* the similarities between the sexes.

An astute speaker will also take care to avoid using sexist language. Almost any audience you address will contain people—men and women alike—who will take offense at words and phrases that convey stereotyped or demeaning views of women. In Chapter 11, we will look more closely at sexist language and how to avoid it in your speeches. For now, it is enough to know that refraining from sexist language is an important part of being an audience-centered public speaker.[3]

Racial, Ethnic, or Cultural Background

As we saw in Chapter 1, the United States is becoming more and more a multiracial, multicultural society. Twenty-five percent of all Americans identify themselves as Hispanic or nonwhite, a figure that will continue to increase in the years ahead. Despite their similarities as Americans, people of European descent, blacks, Latinos, Asians, and others may have different customs and beliefs that bear upon your speech topic. So, too, may international students. Here's what happened to one student who forgot to allow for such differences:

After spending an exciting summer as an intern in a law firm, Lindsey Feldman decided to give her informative speech on how successful women handle themselves in professional situations. Part of her speech dealt with the importance of making a positive first impression.

"One of the things I learned from my internship," she said, "is how much depends on that initial handshake. A strong handshake is essential to any woman who wants to be taken seriously in law or business. It conveys confidence, honesty, and friendliness, all at once. You have to reach forward energetically, grasp firmly, and look the person straight in the eye. Most men know how to do this. And so does every successful woman."

Lindsey expected her audience to nod their heads on this line, but the reaction seemed lukewarm at best. At the end of class, Lindsey spoke with her classmate Daniela, a Chilean student spending a year in the U.S. "I really liked your speech," Daniela said, "except for the part about shaking hands. In Chile, we greet people with a kiss. To us, a handshake is cold and impersonal."

"But in business," objected Lindsey, "you really need to shake hands, especially if you're a woman."

"Maybe here," replied Daniela, "but not at home. My mother is a very successful lawyer in Santiago. For her, a kiss on the cheek works better every time."

What happened to Lindsey, of course, could happen to anyone who is not familiar with South American culture. Even business leaders and heads of state sometimes misstep when speaking to people of different racial, ethnic, or cultural background. During his first trip to a foreign land after being elected President of the U.S., Bill Clinton rose to make a speech during a state dinner in South Korea. He asked the translator to stand between him and South Korean President Kim Young-sam, creating an awkward moment in a country where it is an insult for anyone to stand between two heads of state. At the same dinner, Clinton also referred several times to Kim's wife as "Mrs. Kim." But Korean women keep their birth names. Clinton should have addressed President Kim's wife as "Mrs. Sohn Myong-suk," or as "Mrs. Sohn."[4]

How can you avoid these kinds of gaffes in your speeches? The first step is to recognize that some of your listeners may indeed have special racial, ethnic, or cultural orientations that bear upon your speech topic. The second step is to try to determine what those orientations are and how they are likely to affect the audience's response to your message. The third step is to adjust your message so it will be as clear, suitable, and convincing as possible given the racial, ethnic, or cultural background of your listeners—as in the following example:

Gwen Smith, a middle-school teacher, chaired the planning committee for Black History Month celebrations in her community. Gwen was known as a good speaker, and each year she prepared a talk on African-American history for interested clubs, churches, schools, and civic groups. This year her subject was the vast migration of black Americans during the 1920s and 30s from farms in the southern states to northern cities like Chicago, Detroit, Cleveland, and New York. This migration was a pivotal chapter in the lives of many African-American families, including Gwen's own.

One evening in early February, Gwen was invited to speak to a new neighborhood group in an area she hadn't visited in several years. Knowing that the neighborhood was home to many recent arrivals from the Caribbean, Gwen decided she would need to modify her usual presentation for this audience.

When she arrived at the meeting, she was greeted by about 50 local residents, nearly all of whom had immigrated from Jamaica, Barbados, Haiti, and other islands in the past 10 years. She began by saying: "My talk is titled 'The Great Migration,' but meeting you tonight makes me wonder if I should change it to 'The *First* Great Migration.' As we talk about the forces that caused so many black Americans to move north during the early years of the twentieth century, I also hope we'll be able to explore how their journey compares with your own."

Throughout the rest of her speech, Gwen could see that she had the full attention of her audience. Afterward, the chair of the speaker's committee who had invited Gwen told her, "What a wonderful speech. The historical information was fascinating, and I particularly appreciate your sensitivity to the fact that the culture of Caribbean blacks is often quite different from that of blacks in the United States. It made everyone want to listen closely to what you were saying."

As in Gwen's case, good speakers are alert to the cultural background of their listeners. No matter who the speaker, no matter what the occasion, adapting one's message to people of diverse cultures is a vital aspect of the art of public speaking.

Religion

Russell Middleton, the director of the town's public library, was delighted to be invited to address his local civic association. He needed volunteers to help paint the reading rooms, and he felt sure he could recruit some from the association.

On the evening of his speech, Russell explained the painting project, making special mention of the fact that anyone who volunteered would help the library save money for more books and better programs. "Most of our work will be on Saturdays," he said. "We might also work in the evening, or maybe on a Sunday afternoon. But don't worry. We won't work on Sunday morning because that's when everyone will be at church." He finished by asking volunteers to sign up on a clipboard near the door.

At the end of the evening, Russell was pleased to see plenty of names on his clipboard, but he also found the following note. "Mr. Middleton," it began, "your project seems excellent, and I will be pleased to help. But I think you should remember that there are people in this community who do not go to church or worship on Sunday morning. I am Muslim, and some of the people sitting near me are Jewish. Fortunately,

I had a chance to hear about your project before the comment about attending church on Sunday. If I hadn't, I might have concluded that you were not interested in my help. Please give me a call when you are ready to start the painting. Hamid Shakir."

This story illustrates a factor you must take into account in all your speeches. You cannot assume that your views on religion—whatever they may be—are shared by your listeners. And religious views are among the most emotionally charged and passionately defended of all human concerns. Even your small speech class might include a wide range of faiths, as well as atheists and agnostics.

As the United States becomes more diverse culturally, it is also becoming more diverse religiously. The traditional mix of Protestantism, Catholicism, and Judaism is being enriched by growing numbers of Muslims, Buddhists, Hindus, Sikhs, and others. You can see this diversity in cities large and small across the land. There are 15 Buddhist temples in the greater Seattle area, two Taoist temples in Denver, a Sikh gurdwara in Phoenix, six Muslim mosques in Dallas, and a Jain center in Blairstown, New Jersey. Islam, with over 5.5 million adherents, is the fastest-growing religion in the United States. Nationwide there are more than 1,100 houses of worship for Muslims, 1,500 for Buddhists, and 400 for Hindus.[5]

There is also great diversity within different faiths. You cannot assume that all Catholics support the official view of their church on such matters as birth control or women in the priesthood, any more than you can stereotype all Baptists as being born-again. In matters of religion, the United States is truly a nation of many faiths, many voices, many views.

Whenever you speak on a topic with religious dimensions, then, be sure to consider the religious orientations of your listeners. At the least, failure to do so can weaken your speech. At the most, you may be seriously embarrassed.

Group Membership

"Tell me thy company," says Don Quixote, "and I'll tell thee what thou art." For all of our talk about rugged individualism, Americans are very group-oriented. Workers belong to unions, businesspeople to chambers of commerce. Hunters join the National Rifle Association, environmentalists the Sierra Club, feminists the National Organization for Women. Doctors enroll in the American Medical Association, lawyers in the American Bar Association. There are thousands of such voluntary organizations in the United States.

Similar groups abound on campus. Some of your classmates may belong to fraternities or sororities, some to Campus Crusade for Christ, some to the Young Republicans, some to the film society, some to the ski club, and so forth. For speeches in the classroom, as well as for those outside the classroom, the group affiliations of your audience may provide excellent clues about your listeners' interests and attitudes.

Age; gender; religion; racial, ethnic, or cultural background; group membership—these are just a few of the variables to consider in demographic audience analysis. Others include occupation, economic position, social standing, education, intelligence, and place of residence. Indeed, *anything* characteristic of a given audience is potentially important to a speaker addressing that audience. For your classroom speeches, you may want to learn about your classmates' academic majors, years in school, extracurricular activities, living arrangements, and job aspirations.

Perhaps the most important thing to keep in mind about demographic audience analysis is that it is not an end in itself. Your aim is not just to list the major traits of your listeners but to find in those traits clues about how your listeners will respond to your speech. Once you have done that, you are ready to move on to the second stage of audience analysis.

Situational Audience Analysis

situational audience analysis
Audience analysis that focuses on situational factors such as the size of the audience, the physical setting for the speech, and the disposition of the audience toward the topic, the speaker, and the occasion.

Situational audience analysis usually builds on the demographic analysis. It identifies traits of the audience unique to the speaking situation at hand. These traits include the size of the audience, attitudes influenced by the physical setting, and the disposition of the audience toward the subject, the speaker, and the occasion.

Size

Outside the classroom, the size of an audience can, with the aid of television and radio, range in the millions. Most speech classes, however, consist of between 15 and 30 people—a small- to medium-sized audience. This is a good size for beginning speakers, most of whom are horrified at the prospect of addressing a huge crowd. As you gain more experience, though, you may welcome the challenge of speaking to larger groups. Some speakers actually prefer a large audience to a small one.

No matter what size group you are addressing, bear in mind one basic principle: The larger the audience, the more formal your presentation must be. Audience size will have the greatest impact on your delivery, but it may also affect your language, choice of appeals, and use of visual aids.

Physical Setting

The receptivity of listeners to your speech frequently will be influenced by factors beyond their control—and sometimes beyond your control. Which of the following would you rather address?

An audience assembled immediately after lunch, crammed into an overheated room with inadequate seating

An audience assembled at 10:00 in the morning, comfortably seated in an airy, well-lighted room

Undoubtedly you chose the second option. Any of the adverse conditions listed in the first could seriously impair your audience's willingness to accept your ideas or even listen to you at all.

Situational audience analysis is a vital element in public speaking. Effective speakers work at adjusting their remarks to the size of the audience and the physical setting of the speech.

When you face any speaking situation, it is important to know in advance if there will be any difficulties with the physical setting. For classroom speeches, of course, you already do know. But speeches outside the classroom can confront you with many unpleasant surprises unless you do your homework beforehand.

When you are invited to speak, don't be shy about asking questions of the person who arranged the speech. If possible, look over the room yourself a few days in advance, or else arrive early on the day of your speech to give the room a quick inspection. If it is too warm or too cold, see about adjusting the thermostat. Check the seating arrangements and the location of the lectern to be sure your audience can see you properly. In short, do everything you can to control the influence of physical setting on your audience.

But, you may wonder, what about circumstances you can't control? Your speech *is* scheduled directly after lunch or dinner. The room *is* too small for the audience expected. The heat *cannot* be regulated. Then you are simply going to have to work harder to adapt to these aspects of your listeners' discomfort. When faced with an audience that is potentially hot, sleepy, and cross, do your best to make the speech as interesting and lively as you can. Above all, don't let *yourself* be influenced by the poor physical setting. If your audience sees that you are energetic, alert, and involved with your topic, chances are they will forget their discomfort and come right along with you.

Disposition toward the Topic

As we saw in Chapter 4, you should keep your audience in mind when choosing a topic. Ideally, you will pick a topic that suits them as well as it suits you. Once you have your topic, however, you must consider in more detail how your listeners will react to it. In particular, you need to assess their interest in the topic, their knowledge about it, and their attitudes toward it.

Interest

Outside the classroom, people do not often expend the time and effort to attend a speech unless they are interested in the topic. But the members of your speech class are a captive audience. Sometimes they will be deeply interested in your topic, particularly if it relates directly to them. Most of the time they will range from fairly interested to mildly curious to downright indifferent.

One of your tasks will be to assess their interest in advance and to adjust your speech accordingly. Most important, if your topic is not likely to generate great interest, you must take special steps to get your classmates involved. Here are two brief examples of how to do this:

Jennifer wanted to persuade her classmates to donate blood on a regular basis. At the beginning of her speech, she said: "Are you at least 17 years old? Do you weigh more than 110 pounds? Do you consider yourself fairly healthy? If you answered yes to all of these questions, you should be donating blood every two months."

View the beginning of Jennifer Conard. "The Ultimate Gift," and Rob Kowolski, "Smile."

CD: VIDEO CLIP 5.2

Rob's speech was about the need for better dental hygiene among college students. He started by saying: "Slide your tongue along your teeth. Does your tongue burn? Can you feel the millions and billions of bacteria called *Streptococcus Mutans* gnawing away at the inside of your mouth? Can you feel the highly concentrated acids they produced from the sugars left behind from this morning's breakfast?"

In the chapters that follow, we'll look closely at all the ways you can develop interest in your topic—by an arresting introduction, provocative supporting materials, vivid language, dynamic delivery, visual aids, and so forth.

Knowledge

There is often a strong correlation between interest in a topic and knowledge about it. People tend to be interested in what they know about. Likewise, they are inclined to learn about subjects that interest them. But there are exceptions. Few students know much about handwriting analysis, yet most would find it an absorbing topic. On the other hand, almost all know a lot about checking books out of the library, but few would find it a fascinating subject for a speech.

Why is it important to gauge your listeners' knowledge about your topic? Quite simply, because it will to a large extent determine what you can say in your speech. If your listeners know little about your topic—whether or not they find it interesting—you will have to talk at a more elementary level. If they are reasonably well informed, you can take a more technical and detailed approach.

Attitude

The attitude of your listeners toward your topic can be extremely important in determining how you handle the material. If you know in advance the prevailing attitude among members of your audience, you can adjust what you say to what your audience needs to hear. Consider the experiences of the following two students—one who did not account for listener attitude and one who did:

> Brad Kaminski spoke about the effects on human health of pesticides and other chemicals found in the environment. On the basis of his research, he believed that the dangers of exposure to pesticide residues in our food have been exaggerated by the popular press. His position was interesting but highly controversial. Unfortunately, rather than citing his sources and acknowledging that his point of view was unusual, Brad presented his material as though it were general knowledge.
>
> The speech was not well received. In fact, the class found Brad's approach so inconsistent with everything they had read about pesticides and food that they couldn't accept it. As one student said after the speech, "You may be right in what you said, but I have trouble believing it. We've all heard so much about the dangers of pesticides—can it all be wrong? I think you would have been more persuasive if you had looked at both sides of the issue rather than just your own."

Had Brad taken the skepticism of his audience into account, he could have established the scientific credibility of his material, and thereby made his audience more receptive to his point of view.

Compare the approach of Lee Hawkins, who also espoused a controversial viewpoint:

> A firm opponent of capital punishment, Lee decided to give his persuasive speech in opposition to the death penalty. After distributing a questionnaire among his classmates, Lee found that three-fourths of them favored capital punishment. They gave two reasons. First, they believed the death penalty was a just punishment for someone who commits a crime such as murder. Second, they believed capital punishment works as a deterrent to crime.
>
> Although Lee disagreed with those beliefs, he realized he could neither ignore them nor insult his classmates for holding them. He knew he would have to discuss these points logically and with hard evidence if he were to have any chance of persuading his audience.

As it turned out, Lee did convince some members of the class to reconsider their beliefs. He could not have done so without first investigating what those beliefs were and then adapting his message to them.[6]

Disposition toward the Speaker

Let's return for a moment to Brad's speech about pesticide residues in food. Brad was a sophomore business major with no special scientific or nutritional background. It's not surprising that his classmates took his statements with a large grain of salt. But suppose Brad had been a recognized expert on pesticides and the food chain. Then his listeners would have found him much more believable. Why? Because an audience's response to a message is invariably colored by their perception of the speaker.

attitude
A frame of mind in favor of or opposed to a person, policy, belief, institution, etc.

View an excerpt from Lee Hawkins, "Capital Punishment."

CD: VIDEO CLIP 5.3

The more competent listeners believe a speaker to be, the more likely they are to accept what the speaker says. Likewise, the more listeners believe that a speaker has their best interests at heart, the more likely they are to respond positively to the speaker's message.

We will come back to this subject in detail when we deal with strategies for persuasive speaking in Chapter 16. For now, keep in mind that your listeners will always have *some* set of attitudes toward you as a speaker. Estimating what those attitudes are and how they will affect your speech is a crucial part of situational audience analysis.

Disposition toward the Occasion

It was Martin Luther King Day, and the city was holding a public program celebrating King's life and legacy. More than 1,000 people, including hundreds of schoolchildren, were in attendance. All the prominent figures of the city—politicians, clergy, business-people, community leaders—were on the platform. Between songs and other performances, they came to the microphone to talk briefly about the great civil rights leader and what his memory meant to them.

One of the last to speak was James Irvin, the developer of a proposed business complex that he hoped to locate in one of the city's more impoverished neighborhoods. Irvin began his speech by invoking the memory of Dr. King. He then continued: "Some people say I'm out to exploit the poor people of this city and get tax breaks for myself. All I want to do is bring money into the community and make a fair profit on my investment. But to do that I need the support of every one of the people sitting up here with me today, and I want all of you to hold them accountable."

The people on the platform merely looked uncomfortable, but the audience reacted with boos and hisses.

On other occasions Irvin's comments would not have touched off such an angry response. But the Martin Luther King Day gathering was understood by the organizers—and the audience—to be an occasion for commemoration and reverence. The last thing they expected to hear was a pitch for a business project. What angered the audience was not what Irvin said, but that he exploited the occasion for his own purposes.

No matter what the situation, listeners have fairly definite ideas about the speeches they consider appropriate. They expect to hear political speeches in Congress, sermons in church, after-dinner speeches after dinner, and so forth. Speakers who seriously violate these expectations can almost always count on infuriating the audience.

Perhaps most important, the occasion will dictate how long a speech should be. When you are invited to speak, the chairperson will usually say how much time you have for your talk. If not, be sure to ask. And once you know, pare down your speech so it fits easily within the allotted time. Do not exceed that time under any circumstances, for you are likely to see your audience dwindle as you drone on. (This is one reason why most teachers insist that classroom speeches be kept within the designated time limit. It provides crucial training for speeches you will give outside the classroom.)

There are other audience expectations that apply to your classroom situation. One is that speeches will conform to the assignment. Another is that speakers will observe appropriate standards of taste and decorum. Failure to adhere to these expectations may disturb your classmates and will almost certainly damage your grade.

Poll-taking helps political candidates keep track of public opinion. For classroom speeches, you can use an audience questionnaire to gauge the knowledge and opinions of your listeners.

Getting Information About the Audience

Now that you know *what* to learn about an audience, the next question is *how* do you learn it? A person running for high political office can rely on hired professional pollsters. If, as is more likely, you are invited sometime to address a particular group—say a meeting of the local Rotary club—the person who invites you can usually provide a good sketch of the audience. Ask your contact with the group where you can find out more about its history and purpose. Best of all, if you know someone who has spoken to the same group, be sure to sound out that person.

What about your classmates as an audience? You can learn a lot about them just by observation and conversation. Still, you probably will need to know more about their backgrounds and opinions in relation to specific speech topics. Some teachers require students to do a formal audience analysis—either through interviews or through written questionnaires—for at least one of their speeches.

Interviewing

The face-to-face interview (see Chapter 6) is highly flexible and allows for in-depth questioning. When properly planned, structured, and conducted, it can be a superb way of learning about individual members of an audience. The great drawback is the cost in time and energy. Interviewing each member of a class before every speech may be the most thorough method of audience analysis, but it is seldom practical. Therefore, most teachers encourage their students to rely on questionnaires.

Questionnaires

Like interviewing, constructing a good questionnaire is an art you cannot be expected to master in a speech class. By following a few basic guidelines, however, you can learn to develop a questionnaire that will be more than adequate for analyzing your classroom audience.

There are three major types of questions to choose from: fixed-alternative questions, scale questions, and open-ended questions.

Fixed-alternative questions, as their name implies, offer a fixed choice between two or more responses. For example:

Do you know what the insanity plea is in the U.S. legal system?

Yes _____

No _____

Not sure _____

Do you know of any legal cases in which the insanity plea was used?

Yes _____

No _____

Not sure _____

By limiting the possible responses, such questions produce clear, unambiguous answers. They also tend to yield superficial answers. Other techniques are needed to get beneath the surface.

Scale questions resemble fixed-alternative questions, but they allow more leeway in responding. For example:

How often do you believe the insanity plea is used in U.S. court cases?

Very
seldom ———————————|————————|————————|————————|——————— Very
often

Do you agree or disagree with the following? Expert psychologists can determine with a high degree of accuracy whether or not a defendant is criminally insane.

| Strongly agree | Mildly agree | Undecided | Mildly disagree | Strongly disagree |

———————|————————|————————|————————|————————

Questions like these are especially useful for getting at the strength of a respondent's attitudes.

Open-ended questions give maximum leeway in responding. For example:

What is your opinion about the insanity plea in U.S. court cases?

Under what circumstances do you think the insanity plea is legitimate in a criminal trial? Please explain.

Although open-ended questions invite more detailed responses than the other two types of questions, they also increase the likelihood of getting answers that do not give the kind of information you need.

Because each type of question has its advantages and disadvantages, many questionnaires contain all three types. Figure 5.1 shows a question-

fixed-alternative questions
Questions that offer a fixed choice between two or more alternatives.

scale questions
Questions that require responses at fixed intervals along a scale of answers.

open-ended questions
Questions that allow respondents to answer however they want.

Figure 5.1 Sample Questionnaire.

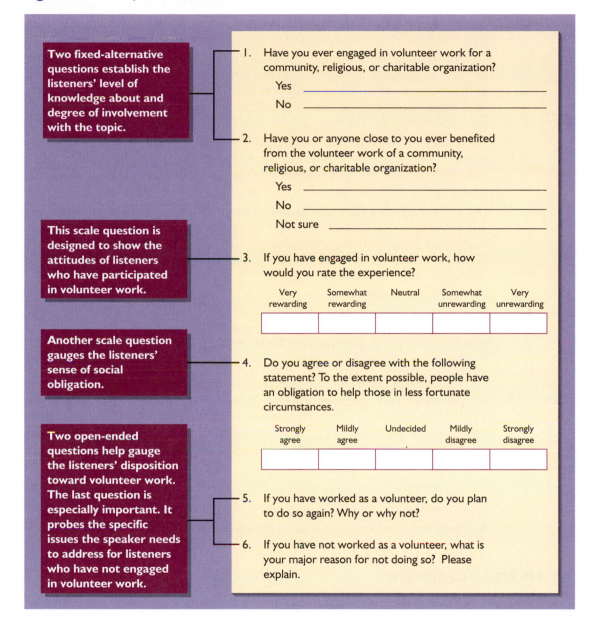

Two fixed-alternative questions establish the listeners' level of knowledge about and degree of involvement with the topic.

1. Have you ever engaged in volunteer work for a community, religious, or charitable organization?

   Yes _____

   No _____

2. Have you or anyone close to you ever benefited from the volunteer work of a community, religious, or charitable organization?

   Yes _____

   No _____

   Not sure _____

This scale question is designed to show the attitudes of listeners who have participated in volunteer work.

3. If you have engaged in volunteer work, how would you rate the experience?

Very rewarding	Somewhat rewarding	Neutral	Somewhat unrewarding	Very unrewarding

Another scale question gauges the listeners' sense of social obligation.

4. Do you agree or disagree with the following statement? To the extent possible, people have an obligation to help those in less fortunate circumstances.

Strongly agree	Mildly agree	Undecided	Mildly disagree	Strongly disagree

Two open-ended questions help gauge the listeners' disposition toward volunteer work. The last question is especially important. It probes the specific issues the speaker needs to address for listeners who have not engaged in volunteer work.

5. If you have worked as a volunteer, do you plan to do so again? Why or why not?

6. If you have not worked as a volunteer, what is your major reason for not doing so? Please explain.

naire that was distributed before a classroom speech on volunteering for a community, religious, or charitable organization. By using all three types of questions, the speaker did two things—elicited specific information about the audience and probed more deeply into their attitudes toward the speech topic. The results of the questionnaire survey broke down as follows:

1. Less than half of the class had participated as a volunteer. Therefore, the speaker knew she would have to explain clearly what was involved in this kind of work.

2. Five students knew someone close to them who had benefited from volunteer work by a community, religious, or charitable organization; most said they were not sure. Thus the speaker could not depend on a high degree of personal involvement among the audience.

3. All but one of the students who had engaged in volunteer work rated it as "very rewarding" or "somewhat rewarding." Not only would this portion of the audience be inclined to support the speaker's position, but the speaker could point to their attitude as proof that work as a volunteer is a rewarding experience.

4. Nearly 75 percent of the respondents either "strongly agreed" or "mildly agreed" that people have an obligation to help those in less fortunate circumstances. No one strongly disagreed. The speaker could therefore depend on an audience favorably inclined to the basic premise underlying volunteer work.

5. Answers to the fifth question—"If you have worked as a volunteer, do you plan to do so again? Why or why not?"—were interesting. All the respondents indicated that they planned to engage in volunteer work again, but most said they were not likely to do so while in college because they were too busy with other activities.

6. Nearly 90 percent of the students who had not engaged in volunteer work stated that their major reason for not doing so was a lack of time. In combination with the answers to question 5, these responses showed that the speaker would have to deal persuasively with the time issue if she were to be successful in convincing people to volunteer while they were enrolled in school.

This questionnaire worked extremely well. It revealed a great deal about the listeners' knowledge, attitudes, and concerns. You should be able to put together an equally useful questionnaire. In doing so, keep the following principles in mind:

1. Plan the questionnaire carefully to elicit precisely the information you need.

2. Use all three types of questions—fixed-alternative, scale, and open-ended.

3. Make sure the questions are clear and unambiguous.

4. Keep the questionnaire relatively brief.

View how the speakers in Video Clips 5.2 and 5.3 used audience surveys in their speeches.

CD: VIDEO CLIP 5.4

Adapting to the Audience

Once you have completed the audience analysis, you should have a pretty clear picture of your listeners. You should know their relevant demographic characteristics, their interest in and knowledge about the topic, their attitudes toward the topic and the speaker, and their expectations about the occasion. Knowing all this, however, does not guarantee a successful speech. The key is how well you *use* what you know in preparing and presenting the speech.

This point deserves special attention because it poses one of the hardest tasks facing novice speakers. Most people can identify the major characteristics of their audience, but many have trouble *adapting* their ideas to the audience. There are two major stages in the process of audience adaptation—the first occurs before the speech, as part of your preparation and rehearsal; the second occurs during the presentation of the speech itself.

Audience Adaptation before the Speech

As we have seen, you must keep your audience in mind at every stage of speech preparation. "Keeping your audience in mind," however, involves more than simply remembering who your listeners will be. Above all, it means two things: (1) assessing how your audience is likely to respond to what you will say in your speech and (2) adjusting what you say to make it as clear, appropriate, and convincing as possible.

This is not always easy to do. We are all so wrapped up in our own ideas and concerns that we have trouble seeing things from other people's perspective—especially if their perspective is quite different from ours. If, for example, you speak on a subject in which you are expert, you may find it hard to put yourself in the place of someone who knows nothing about it. To step outside your own frame of reference and see things from another person's point of view is a real achievement.

Yet this is what a successful speaker eventually learns to do. You must submerge your own views so completely that you can adopt, temporarily, those of your listeners. When you do this, you will begin to hear your speech through the ears of your audience and to adjust it accordingly.

You must keep your listeners constantly in mind as you prepare your speech. Try to imagine what they will like, what they will dislike, where they will have doubts or questions, whether they will need more details here or fewer there, what will interest them and what will not.

At every point you must *anticipate* how your audience will respond. How will they react to your introduction and conclusion? Will they find your examples clear and convincing? Will your visual aids help them grasp your ideas? How will they respond to your language and manner of delivery? As you answer these questions, consciously identify with your listeners. Put yourself in their place and respond to your speech as they would.

Here is how one student worked out his problems of audience adaptation:

Juan Ruiz, a junior geology major, decided to give an informative speech about how earthquakes occur. From his audience analysis he learned that only two or three of his classmates knew much of anything about geology. To most of them, a tectonic plate would be found on a dinner table rather than below the surface of the earth. Juan realized, then, that he must present his speech at an elementary level and with a minimum of scientific language.

As he prepared the speech, Juan kept asking himself, "How can I make this clear and meaningful to someone who knows nothing about earthquakes or geological principles?" Since he was speaking in the Midwest, he decided to begin by noting that the most severe earthquake in American history took place not in California or Alaska, but at New Madrid, Missouri, in 1811. If such an earthquake happened today, it would be felt from the Rocky Mountains to the Atlantic Ocean and would flatten most of the cities in the Mississippi Valley. That, he figured, should get his classmates' attention.

Throughout the body of the speech, Juan dealt only with the basic mechanics of earthquakes and carefully avoided technical terms such as "asthenosphere," "lithosphere," and "subduction zones." He also prepared visual aids diagramming fault lines so his classmates wouldn't get confused.

To be absolutely safe, Juan asked his roommate—who was not a geology major—to listen to the speech. "Stop me," he said, "anytime I say something you don't understand." Juan's roommate stopped him four times, and at each spot Juan worked out a way to make his point more clearly. Finally, he had a speech that was interesting and perfectly understandable to his audience.

As you work on your speeches, try to keep your listeners constantly in mind. Anticipate how they will respond to your ideas. Be creative in thinking about ways to adapt your message to them. Like Juan, you will give a much better speech.

Audience Adaptation during the Speech

No matter how hard you work ahead of time, things may not go exactly as planned on the day of your speech. For speeches in the classroom you may find that the easel for your visual aids is not available or that another student has the same topic as you. For speeches outside the classroom you might learn that the room for your speech has been changed, that the audience will be much larger (or smaller) than you had anticipated, or even that the amount of time available for your speech has been cut in half because a previous speaker has droned on for too long.

If something like this happens to you, don't panic. Find another way to present your visual aids. Modify your introduction to mention the other student's speech on your topic. Adjust your delivery to the changed audience size. And if you find you have less time for your speech than you had planned, don't simply talk twice as fast to get everything in—that would be worse than not talking at all. Instead, condense your speech to its most essential points and present them in the time available. Your listeners will sympathize with your predicament and will appreciate your regard for their time. This will more than compensate for your lost speaking time.

Finally, be sure to keep an eye out during your speech for audience feedback. If your listeners are sitting forward in their chairs, looking at you with interest, and nodding their heads in approval, you can assume things are going well. But suppose you find them frowning or responding with quizzical looks. Then you may need to back up and go over your point again, as in this example:

Michelle Voss, a business major, had worked diligently to make sure her informative speech on investing in the stock market was not too technical for her classmates, most of whom were engineering and humanities students. She explained everything from the ground up, prepared two excellent visual aids, and practiced giving the speech to her best friend, an art major and self-confessed "economics imbecile."

On the day of Michelle's speech, everything went well until she got to her second main point, when she noticed that several of her classmates seemed puzzled by the relationship between common stock and preferred stock. Knowing they would be lost for the rest of the speech if they didn't understand that relationship, Michelle paused and said, "I can see some of you are confused by my explanation. Let me try it again from another angle."

As Michelle went through the material a second time, she could see her classmates nodding their heads in understanding. She could now go on with her speech, confident that her audience was ready to go with her.

Adapting to your audience—both before the speech and during it—is one of the most important keys to successful public speaking. Like other aspects of speechmaking, it is sometimes easier said than done. But once you master it, you'll see that it pays dividends in more personal facets of your life—when you adapt to an audience of one.

Summary

Good speakers are audience-centered. They know that the aim of speech-making is to gain a desired response from listeners. When working on your speeches, keep three questions in mind: To whom am I speaking? What do I want them to know, believe, or do as a result of my speech? What is the most effective way of composing and presenting my speech to accomplish that aim? Your classroom speeches will give you excellent practice in dealing with these questions, provided you always think of your classmates as a *real* audience.

To be an effective speaker, you should know something about the psychology of audiences. Auditory perception is selective. Even when people pay close attention, they don't process a speaker's message exactly as the speaker intended. People hear what they want to hear. People also are egocentric. They typically approach speeches with one question uppermost in mind: "Why is this important to *me?*" Therefore, you need to study your audience and adapt your speech directly to their beliefs and interests.

The first stage in learning about your audience is to undertake a demographic audience analysis. This involves identifying important demographic traits of your audience such as age, gender, religion, group membership, and racial, ethnic, or cultural background. The second stage in learning about your audience is to conduct a situational audience analysis. This involves identifying traits of the audience unique to the particular speaking situation at hand. These traits include the size of the audience, attitudes influenced by the physical setting, and your listeners' disposition toward the topic, toward you as a speaker, and toward the occasion.

For speeches outside the classroom, you can best get information about the audience by asking the person who invites you to speak. If possible, you should also sound out someone else who has spoken to the same group. For your classroom speeches, you can learn much about your audience by observation and conversation. You also can do a more formal audience analysis by interviewing members of the audience or by circulating a questionnaire.

Once you complete the audience analysis, you must adapt your speech so it will be clear and convincing to your listeners. Keep them in mind constantly as you prepare the speech. Put yourself in their place. Try to hear the speech as they will. Anticipate questions and objections, and try to answer them in advance.

When you deliver your speech, keep an eye out for audience feedback. If you see frowns or puzzled looks on your listeners' faces, you may need to adjust your remarks in response. Like other aspects of audience adaptation, this may be difficult at first, but if you work at it, you should soon see results.

Key Terms

audience-centeredness (98)

egocentrism (101)

demographic audience analysis (102)

situational audience analysis (108)

attitude (111)

fixed-alternative questions (114)

scale questions (114)

open-ended questions (114)

Review Questions

For further re-
view, go to the
Study Questions
for this chapter.

CD: STUDY QUESTIONS

After reading this chapter, you should be able to answer the following questions:

1. Why must a public speaker be audience-centered?

2. What does it mean to say that people are egocentric? What implications does the egocentrism of audiences hold for you as a public speaker?

3. What are the five demographic traits of audiences discussed in this chapter? Why is each important to audience analysis?

4. What is situational audience analysis? What factors do you need to consider in situational audience analysis?

5. How can you get information about an audience?

6. What are the three kinds of questions used in questionnaires? Why is it a good idea to use all three in audience analysis?

7. What methods can you use to adapt your speech to your audience before the speech? During the speech?

Exercises for Critical Thinking

1. Advertisers are usually very conscious of their audience. Choose an issue of a popular magazine such as *Time, Newsweek, Sports Illustrated, Cosmopolitan,* or the like. From that issue select five advertisements to analyze. Try to determine the audience being appealed to in each advertisement, and analyze the appeals (verbal and visual) used to persuade buyers. How might the appeals differ if the ads were designed to persuade a different audience?

2. Below are three general speech topics and, for each, two hypothetical audiences to which a speech might be delivered. For each topic, write a brief paragraph explaining how you might adjust your specific purpose and message according to the demographic characteristics of the audience.

   a. *Topic:*   "Superconductivity"
      Audience #1: 50% physics majors, 30% engineering majors, 20% music majors
      Audience #2: 40% English majors, 40% business majors, 20% physics majors

   b. *Topic:*   "Sexual Assault: The Biggest Campus Crime"
      Audience #1: 80% female, 20% male
      Audience #2: 80% male, 20% female

   c. *Topic:*   "The *Challenger* Explosion"
      Audience #1: Day class: 70% age 18 to 22, 30% age 23 and over
      Audience #2: Evening class: 50% age 35 and over, 30% age 23 to 34, 20% age 18 to 22

3. For your next speech, design and circulate among your classmates an audience analysis questionnaire like that discussed on pages 113–116. Use all three kinds of questions explained in the text—fixed-alternative questions, scale questions, and open-ended questions. After you have tabulated the results of the questionnaire, write an analysis explaining what the questionnaire reveals about your audience and what steps you must take to adapt your speech to the audience.

4. Read the speech in Appendix B by Barbara Bush ("Choices and Change"). Focus on how Bush adapts her message to her audience in light of the controversy that preceded her speech. Be prepared to discuss your ideas in class.

Applying the POWER of Public Speaking

As a university professor, your research, writing, and teaching in the area of gender communication has attracted media attention. It seems that nearly everyone is interested in the differences between the communication styles of men and women. You have been asked to address the managers of a large local manufacturing company on the topic of gender communication in the workplace.

To prepare for your speech, you have scheduled a meeting with the company's human resource director who contacted you. Having taken a public speaking class in college, you know how important it is to analyze the audience you will be addressing. List (1) the three most important questions you want to ask the resource director about the demographics of your audience, and (2) the three most important questions you want to ask about the situational traits of your audience. Be specific in your questions, and be prepared, if necessary, to explain your choice of questions.

Notes

[1]Quoted in Halford R. Ryan, "Harry Emerson Fosdick," in Bernard K. Duffy and Halford R. Ryan (eds.), *American Orators of the Twentieth Century* (New York: Greenwood Press, 1987), p. 148.
[2]Saul Alinsky, *Rules for Radicals* (New York: Random House, 1971), p. 81.
[3]For a broader discussion of gender issues in communication, see Julia T. Wood, *Gendered Lives: Communication, Gender, and Culture* 3rd ed. (Belmont, Calif.: Wadsworth, 1999); and Diana K. Ivy and Phil Backlund, *Exploring GenderSpeak: Personal Effectiveness in Gender Communication,* 2nd ed. (New York: McGraw-Hill, 2000).
[4]David Foster, "Cultural Concierges on Alert," *Wisconsin State Journal* (November 19, 1993).
[5]Richard N. Ostling, "One Nation Under Gods," *Time* (Fall 1993), p. 62; *2000 World Almanac and Book of Facts* (Mahwah, N.J.: World Almanac Books, 1999), pp. 692–693.
[6]There is a substantial body of research to show that speakers are usually more persuasive when they attempt to refute opposing arguments rather than ignoring them. See Richard M. Perloff, *The Dynamics of Persuasion* (Hillsdale, N.J.: Lawrence Erlbaum, 1993), pp. 166–168.

GATHERING MATERIALS

uppose you want to build an entertainment center for your home. You need to provide space for all the components (television, receiver, CD player, VHS, DVD, and so on) as well as storage for tapes and discs. How do you go about it? You can talk to people who have built their own centers and ask them for details. You can write away to a magazine for plans. You can get books from the library or download instructions from the Internet. On the other hand, if you've worked on an entertainment center before, you can fall back on your experience and adapt it to your current needs. Since you want your center to be perfect, you gather as much information as you can before starting to build.

Gathering material for a speech is like gathering information for any project. Many resources are available to you if you take advantage of them. How do you get material for your speeches? There are several ways. You can interview people with specialized knowledge on a given topic. You can write or call organizations that collect information on your subject and are set up to provide it to the public. You can do research in the library or on the Internet. Sometimes you can use yourself as a resource—whenever you have personal experience or more-than-average knowledge about a subject. Let's turn first to the resource of your own experience.

Using Your Own Knowledge and Experience

Everybody is an expert on something, whether it is auto mechanics or baking brownies or simply "Why I Failed Calculus." As we saw in Chapter 4, we usually speak best about subjects with which we are familiar. This is why teachers encourage students to capitalize on their own knowledge and experience in developing speech topics.

When you choose a topic from your own experience, you may be tempted to depersonalize it by relying solely on facts and figures from books. Such outside information is almost always necessary. But supplementing it with the personal touch can really bring your speeches to life.

One student, afflicted with diabetes, chose to explain how a person can live with the disease on a daily basis. He cited statistics on the incidence of diabetes in the United States, identified symptoms of the disease, and related how it is treated. Along the way he illustrated his points by talking about his personal experiences. Here is part of what he said:

> Being a diabetic presents a challenge one cannot afford to lose. On a personal note, I have tried not to let my diabetes affect my lifestyle. Last year I spent nine months traveling in Central and South America. The trip was very memorable, but I had one particularly frightening experience that quickly makes you realize just how vulnerable a diabetic is. On the fifth day of a two-week excursion down the Amazon River in Brazil, our canoe tipped, dumping everything into the river.
>
> Although I recovered my pack, part of its contents—including my insulin—were swallowed up by the river. Without insulin I could not eat any food, for if I did, my blood sugar level would become too high and I could eventually go into convulsions, slip into a coma, and die. We returned back up the Amazon and traveled three days until we reached the first village and I could radio for more medicine. I was hot and hungry, but alive.

This speech has color and emotion. By drawing on his own experience, the speaker conveyed his point much more meaningfully than he could have in any other way.

Even if your life stories are not that dramatic, you can still put them to work for you. After all, you are the one who was there. You did, saw, felt, heard whatever it is you are speaking about. By thinking over your past experiences—gathering material from yourself—you can find many supporting details for your speeches.

Doing Library Research

Some students regard the library as a sinner regards a church—as a place to be entered only in the most desperate circumstances. Then they take a speech class and discover that the library is not so forbidding after all. You will get many of the materials for your speeches from the library. Thus you need to know the basic techniques of doing library research. Of course, you may know them already, in which case you need only review this section of the book.

There are quick, easy, systematic ways to find whatever you need in the library. The first step is to learn your way around. Take the orientation tour offered by your library. While on the tour, you will probably receive a brief handbook or series of leaflets explaining what is in the library and how to find it. Keep this material with your class notes. It takes only a few minutes to read and will be helpful later.

Ultimately, the only way to become adept at library research is to do it—and to do it properly. You have five important resources for finding what you need in the library: librarians, the library catalogue, periodical indexes, newspaper indexes, and reference works. We'll look at each in turn.[1]

Librarians

Thanks to movies, comic strips, and television commercials, librarians have a bad image. They are typically portrayed as cold, stuffy, bespectacled people whose main goal in life is to keep people from speaking above a whisper. In fact, most librarians are friendly men and women who can be of enormous help.

Too often students waste their time wandering aimlessly in search of a source because they are afraid to ask for assistance. They don't want to appear stupid or to "bother" anyone. But would you be as sensitive about asking a doctor for help with a medical problem? Librarians are experts in their own field, trained in library use and research methods. If you have a question, don't hesitate to ask a librarian. She or he can help you find your way, locate sources, even track down a specific piece of information.

Catalogues

There are two kinds of library catalogues—the card catalogue and the computer catalogue. Although most libraries now have fully computerized catalogue systems, some use both kinds of catalogues and a few continue to rely solely on the card catalogue. Regardless of the setup at your school, one fact remains constant: the catalogue is the key to finding materials in the library. If you learn how to use the catalogue effectively, you can save yourself a great deal of time.

The Card Catalogue

In the card catalogue you will find listed alphabetically on 3×5 cards all the books and periodicals owned by the library. For each book, there will be at least three cards—one listing it by the *author's last name,* one listing it by *title,* and one (or more) listing it by *subject.* If you know who wrote a book or you know the book's title, your first step is to locate the catalogue card under the author or title. When you do not know the author or title, or simply want to see what books are available on a given subject, check the catalogue under the appropriate subject.

The Online Catalogue

Like the card catalogue, the online catalogue lists books by author, title, and subject. Unlike the card catalogue, it allows you to conduct *keyword searches,* which means you can locate a book by typing in a significant word or phrase, even if that word or phrase is not part of the book's title. Another advantage of the online catalogue is that it tells you whether the book you want is available on the shelves or is already checked out.

Figure 6.1 shows a sample book entry from an online catalogue. As you can see, it gives quite a bit of information about the book. The key to finding the book on the shelves is the *call number.* Once you have the call num-

card catalogue
A catalogue that lists on 3×5 cards all the books and periodicals owned by a library.

online catalogue
An electronic listing of the books and periodicals owned by a library.

Figure 6.1   Online Catalogue Entry for a Book.

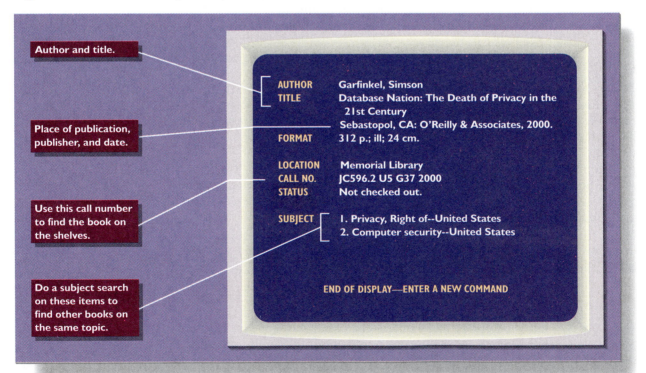

Author and title.

Place of publication, publisher, and date.

Use this call number to find the book on the shelves.

Do a subject search on these items to find other books on the same topic.

AUTHOR	Garfinkel, Simson
TITLE	Database Nation: The Death of Privacy in the 21st Century
	Sebastopol, CA: O'Reilly & Associates, 2000.
FORMAT	312 p.; ill; 24 cm.
LOCATION	Memorial Library
CALL NO.	JC596.2 U5 G37 2000
STATUS	Not checked out.
SUBJECT	1. Privacy, Right of--United States
	2. Computer security--United States

END OF DISPLAY—ENTER A NEW COMMAND

ber, all you have to do is find the right section of the shelves (or stacks, as they are called in some libraries) and retrieve your book.

Periodicals are listed by title in both the card catalogue and the online catalogue. Figure 6.2 shows an online catalogue entry for a periodical. Libraries usually have a special room in which they keep the latest issues of magazines and newspapers. Bound volumes of issues from past years are kept on the book shelves.

Because there are many different online catalogue systems, you should spend some time learning how to use the one at your library. The best time to do this is early in your speech class, before you have library assignments to complete. Learning how to use the catalogue *and* doing research for a speech at the same time can be a frustrating experience.

call number
A number used in libraries to classify books and periodicals and to indicate where they can be found on the shelves.

Periodical Indexes

The catalogue tells you what books and periodicals are in the library. But suppose you are trying to locate recent magazine articles on a topic such as "bilingual education in the Southwest" or "military tactics in the battle of Gettysburg." You could rummage through a dozen magazines in hopes of stumbling across what you need. But the easy, efficient way to get the information is to consult one of the library's periodical indexes.

Periodical indexes do for articles in magazines and journals what the library catalogue does for books. Just as the catalogue helps you locate specific books from among all the books in the library, a periodical index helps

periodical index
A research aid that catalogues articles from a large number of journals or magazines.

Figure 6.2   Online Catalogue Entry for a Periodical.

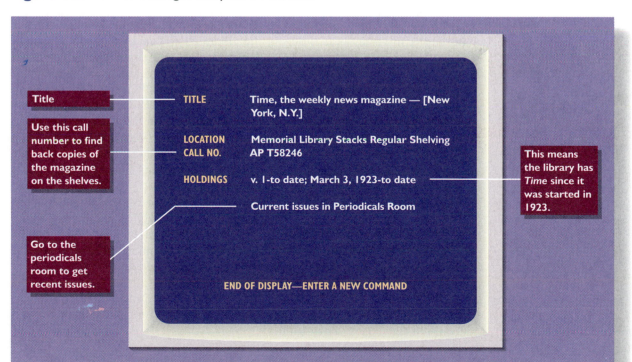

you locate specific magazine or journal articles. Until recently, periodical indexes were thick, multivolume books. Today most are computerized, which greatly simplifies the task of finding what you need.

Accessing a computerized periodical index—or database, as it is also called—is as easy as using the library's online catalogue. You simply enter the subject on which you want information, and citations of articles on your subject appear on the screen. You can choose the citations that interest you, and a printer hooked up to the computer will print them out for you. You can then use the citations to locate the articles you need on the shelves or in the periodicals section of the library. Depending on the index or database you are using, you may be able to produce the full text of the articles on screen for immediate viewing or printing.

abstract
A summary of a magazine or journal article, written by someone other than the original author.

Even if the full text is not available online, you may be able to print *abstracts* that summarize the articles on your list of citations. Keep in mind, however, that an abstract is only a summary of an article, written by someone other than the original author. The purpose of the abstract is to help you decide whether or not the article will be of use for your speech. You should never cite an article in your speech on the basis of the abstract alone. You should always consult the full article.

Altogether there are hundreds of periodical indexes, covering topics from agriculture to zoology. The specific indexes you can use will depend on what is available in your library. Here are a few of the major ones you are most likely to use in preparing your speeches. They are divided into two groups—general indexes and special indexes. Knowing how to use them will be of value to you long after you have finished your speech class.

General Indexes

The best-known general index is the *Reader's Guide to Periodical Literature,* which provides an up-to-date listing of more than 240 of the most widely read magazines in the United States. Included are *Time, Newsweek, Scientific American, Sports Illustrated, Aviation Week and Space Technology, Consumer Reports, Ebony, Ms., Vital Speeches, Rolling Stone,* and *Psychology Today.* In addition to the print version of the *Reader's Guide,* there is an electronic version titled *Reader's Guide Abstracts and Full-Text,* which also includes entries from the *New York Times.* In addition to furnishing abstracts of all the items it indexes, the online *Reader's Guide* provides full-text articles for more than 120 periodicals.

As with most periodical indexes, articles in the print *Reader's Guide* are catalogued alphabetically by author and subject. Each entry gives all the necessary information for finding articles in the magazines—title of article, author, name of magazine, volume number, page numbers, and date. If you were giving a speech on recent developments in electronic commerce, you would look in the *Reader's Guide* under "Electronic Commerce." Figure 6.3 shows what you would find.

In addition to the *Reader's Guide,* there are a number of other general periodical databases. They include:

General Reference Center. An easy-to-use guide to more than 410 popular magazines on topics such as current affairs, education, leisure

Figure 6.3 Sample *Reader's Guide* Entry. *(Reader's Guide to Periodical Literature.* Copyright 2000 by the H. W. Wilson Company. Material reproduced by permission of the publisher.)

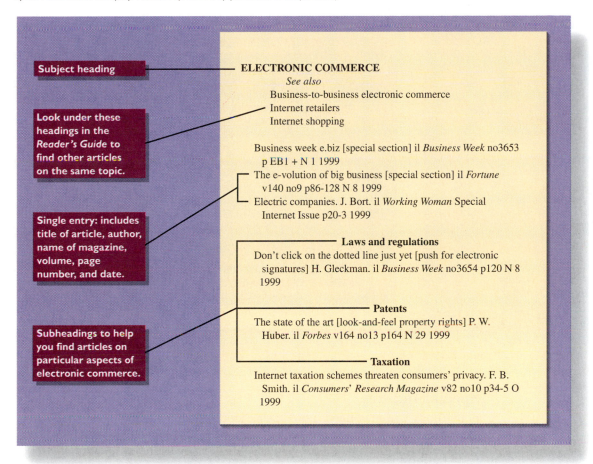

and travel, science, and the arts. In addition to indexing all titles, it provides the full text of articles from 315 of the publications it indexes.

ProQuest Research Library. An excellent database that indexes more than 2,000 general-interest, business, and scholarly journals published since 1988 and provides the full text of articles from nearly 1,000 of them. Figure 6.4 (page 130) shows a sample screen from *ProQuest Research Library* with a typical magazine citation and abstract.

Academic Search. An extremely valuable resource that provides the full text of articles from more than 1,200 English-language journals, popular and scholarly alike. It also indexes and abstracts articles from an additional 1,800 publications, including the *New York Times.*

Public Affairs Information Service International. A wide-ranging database that, in addition to indexing journal articles, includes citations for government documents and other works relating to public policy from all over the world.

Figure 6.4   Sample Entry from ProQuest Research Library.

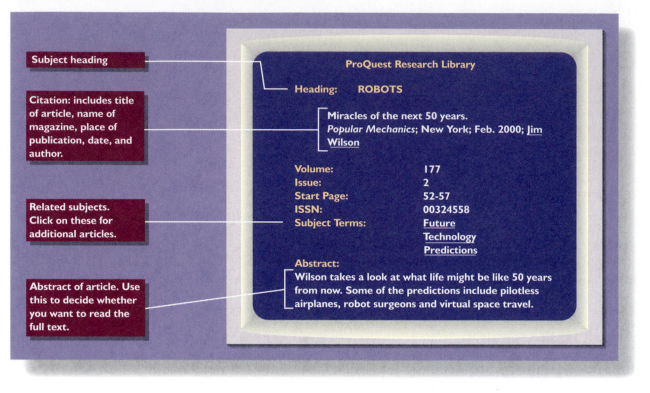

Special Indexes

Sometimes you may need more specialized information than you can find in the kinds of publications covered in the general periodical indexes. If so, check with your librarian, who will direct you to a special index. Examples are:

Applied Science and Technology Index

Social Sciences Index

Art Index

Hispanic American Periodicals Index

Business Abstracts

ERIC (Education Resources Information Center)

Education Index

Women's Resources International

Ethnic NewsWatch

Index to Black Periodicals

Newspaper Indexes

Newspapers are invaluable for research on many topics, historical as well as current. Fortunately, back issues of several major U.S. newspapers are now indexed, including the *New York Times, The Wall Street Journal, Christian Science Monitor, Los Angeles Times, Washington Post, Atlanta Constitution,* and *USA Today.* Of these papers, your library is most likely to carry back issues of the *New York Times* on microfilm or computer. To find what you are looking for in the *New York Times,* look under your subject in the *New York Times Index.*

> **newspaper index**
> A research aid that catalogues articles from one or more newspapers.

If you are hunting for information from a newspaper, you may also be able to find it in *NewsBank's NewsSource.* This helpful resource reprints the full text of more than 3,000 newspaper articles each month from more than 100 U.S. newspapers and international wire services. If your library does not have *NewsBank's NewsSource,* it may have a similar database, such as the *National Newspaper Index,* UMI's *Newspaper Abstracts,* or *ProQuest Newspapers.* (See Figure 6.5 for a sample screen from the *National Newspaper Index.*)

Another resource available in a growing number of campus libraries is *Lexis/Nexis Academic Universe,* an online service composed of approximately 5,000 legal, news, reference, and business sources, including a large number of U.S. and international newspapers. It also provides daily updates from news wire services such as Reuters, United Press International, and the Associated Press. If you have access to *Lexis/Nexis,* you will find it an invaluable research tool—especially for topics that require up-to-the-minute information.

Finally, you should know about more specialized newspaper reference sources such as *Editorials on File* and *Black Newspapers Index. Editorials*

Figure 6.5 Sample Entry from *National Newspaper Index.*

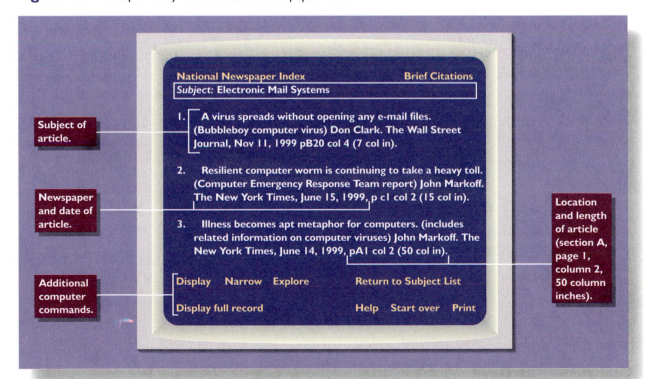

on File reprints editorials on important public issues from hundreds of newspapers across the United States and is an excellent source of informed opinion on current events. *Black Newspapers Index* provides a helpful guide to articles printed in African-American newspapers, including the *Amsterdam News, Chicago Defender,* and *Los Angeles Sentinel.*

Reference Works

reference work
A work that synthesizes a large amount of related information for easy access by researchers.

How far is it from Los Angeles to Tokyo? What are the origins of the phrase "raining cats and dogs"? How many people in the United States die in fires each year? Who won the Academy Award for Best Actor in 1993? Which city has the highest murder rate in the U.S.?

These are all questions that could arise in the process of researching a speech. You could try to answer them by rummaging through a dozen books or thumbing through a batch of magazines or newspapers in hopes of finding what you need. The easy, efficient approach, however, would be to consult the library's collection of reference works.

Reference works are usually kept in a separate part of the library called the reference section. The right reference work can save you hours of time by putting at your fingertips a wealth of information that might be difficult to locate through an index or the library catalogue. The major kinds of reference works are encyclopedias, yearbooks, dictionaries, biographical aids, atlases, and gazetteers. Here are the ones you should find most valuable in preparing your speeches.

Encyclopedias

general encyclopedia
A comprehensive reference work that provides information about all branches of human knowledge.

We are all familiar with general encyclopedias such as the *Encyclopaedia Britannica* and the *Encyclopedia Americana.* They seek to provide accurate, objective information about all branches of human knowledge and are an excellent place to begin your research. Both *Britannica* and *Americana* are arranged alphabetically and issue annual supplements to update what is contained in the basic volumes. Many general encyclopedias—including *Britannica* and *Americana*—can also be accessed online.

special encyclopedia
A comprehensive reference work devoted to a specific subject such as religion, art, law, science, music, etc.

In addition to general encyclopedias, there are special encyclopedias devoted to particular subjects such as religion, art, law, science, literature, music, education, and the like. They cover their fields in much more depth and detail than do general encyclopedias. Some of the most frequently used special encyclopedias are:

Encyclopedia of Philosophy

International Encyclopedia of the Social Sciences

Encyclopedia of World Art

Encyclopedia of Religion

Grove's Dictionary of Music and Musicians

Grzimek's Animal Life Encyclopedia

Encyclopedia of World Crime

McGraw-Hill Encyclopedia of Science and Technology

Food and Nutrition Encyclopedia

Encyclopedia of Computer Science

African American Encyclopedia

Latino Encyclopedia

Asian American Encyclopedia

Yearbooks

As the name implies, yearbooks are published annually. They contain an amazing amount of current information that would otherwise be all but impossible to track down. Here are three of the most valuable yearbooks.

Statistical Abstract of the United States. Published since 1878 by the U.S. Bureau of the Census and now available online as well, the *Statistical Abstract* is the standard reference work for numerical information on the social, political, and economic aspects of American life. Among the incredible array of facts it contains are the U.S. fertility rate, labor union membership, death rates from various diseases, median family income by state, and so on.

World Almanac and Book of Facts. Unlike the *Statistical Abstract,* the *World Almanac* is not limited to the United States or to numerical data. Among the things you can discover in it are all the Nobel Prize winners since 1901, the most-watched television shows of the previous year, records for professional and collegiate sports, the literacy rate in Afghanistan, and the natural resources of Peru.

Facts on File. Available in both print and electronic versions, *Facts on File* is a weekly digest of national and foreign news events. It covers politics, sports, medicine, education, religion, crime, economics, and the arts. At the end of the year, all the weekly issues are published together as *Facts on File Yearbook.* This is an excellent place to check up quickly on something that happened in a given year.

> **yearbook**
> A reference work published annually that contains information about the previous year.

Dictionaries

There are several excellent dictionaries of the English language, including *Webster's* and the *American Heritage Dictionary,* both of which are available on disc as well as in book form. If you are interested more in the history of a word than its present meaning, you should turn first to the *Oxford English Dictionary.* There are also a number of specialized dictionaries that cover a wide range of topics. Some examples are the *Computer Dictionary, Black's Law Dictionary,* the *Dictionary of Feminist Theory,* and the *Morris Dictionary of Word and Phrase Origins.*

Quotation Books

The best-known collection of quotations is *Bartlett's Familiar Quotations.* With more than 25,000 quotations from historical and contemporary figures, it has long been regarded as an indispensable source for speakers and writers alike. Other excellent quotation books include:

Oxford Dictionary of Quotations

Harper Book of American Quotations

The New Quotable Woman

My Soul Looks Back, 'Less I Forget: A Collection of Quotations by People of Color

Ancient Echoes: Native American Words of Wisdom

Fire in Our Souls: Quotations of Wisdom and Inspiration by Latino Americans

A Treasury of Jewish Quotations

All of these works are indexed to help you locate quotations by subject as well as by author.

Biographical Aids

biographical aid
A reference work that provides information about people.

When you need information about people in the news, you should go first to the reference section, where you will find books that contain brief life and career facts about contemporary men and women. Here are some of the ones you are likely to find most useful:

International Who's Who

Who's Who in America

The reference section of the library provides encyclopedias, yearbooks, biographical aides, atlases, and many other resources you can use when researching your speeches.

Who's Who of American Women

Contemporary Black Biography

Dictionary of Hispanic Biography

Native American Women

Who's Who Among Asian Americans

If you need more detailed information than these guides provide, your best bet is *Current Biography,* an exceedingly helpful magazine that is published every month except December. During each year it offers some 400 independent and highly readable articles about newsworthy people all over the world. Each article is three to four pages long, and the fields covered include politics, science, the arts, labor, sports, and industry. At the end of the year, the articles are revised and collected alphabetically in a single volume entitled *Current Biography Yearbook.* An excellent cumulative index makes it easy to find the article you want from any year.

If you are having trouble finding what you need about a person, you should turn to *Biography Index.* It won't give you biographical information, but it will tell you where to find it. Available in print and electronic form, *Biography Index* provides citations for biographical material appearing in more than 3,000 periodicals and some 2,500 current books.

Atlases and Gazetteers

Atlases, of course, contain maps. But most modern atlases also include a variety of charts, plates, and tables that furnish information about the geography of states, regions, and countries. The leading all-purpose atlas is the *Rand McNally Cosmopolitan World Atlas,* which includes maps of the world by region, as well as maps of each state of the United States. It also gives a wealth of facts and figures about the population, politics, and geography of the U.S. and other parts of the world.

atlas
A book of maps.

Gazetteers, or geographical dictionaries, follow the same alphabetical format as regular dictionaries, but all entries deal with geographical topics. The best-known gazetteer is *Merriam-Webster's Geographical Dictionary.* This fascinating volume lists more than 48,000 places around the world—countries, regions, cities, islands, mountains, rivers—and gives concise facts about each. You should look here to find such things as the height of Mount Everest, the state flower of Florida, and all the places in the world named Athens.

gazetteer
A geographical dictionary.

Searching the Internet

The Internet has been called the world's biggest library. A global collection of interlinked computer networks, it includes everything from e-mail to the World Wide Web. Through it you can read electronic versions of the *New York Times,* the *Tokyo Shimbun,* and the *Jerusalem Post.* You can visit the great museums of Europe, browse through the Library of Congress, and get up-to-the-minute bulletins from CNN and Reuters News Service. You can access government agencies and most major corporations. You can read texts

Internet
A global collection of interlinked computer networks.

of Supreme Court decisions and of the latest bills proposed in Congress. You can check stock market prices, conduct word searches of the Bible, and find statistics on virtually every topic under the sun.

Unlike a library, however, the Internet has no central information desk, no librarians, no catalogue, and no reference section. Nor does it have a person or department in charge of choosing new materials to make sure they are of high quality. You can unearth a great deal of information on the Internet, but you cannot always find the same range and depth of research materials as in a good library. This is why experts advise that you use the Internet to supplement, not to replace, library research.

The most widely used part of the Internet for research purposes is the World Wide Web. Created in 1991 by scientists at the European Particle Physics Laboratory, the Web is one of the great success stories of the computer age. As recently as 1994 it was relatively unknown to the general public. Today it is used by millions of people the world over to navigate their way through the vast galaxy of cyberspace.

In this section, we will look at ways you can go beyond surfing the Web and turn it into a powerful research tool for your speeches. We'll begin by looking at browsers, search aids, and other resources for conducting efficient, focused inquiries. Then we'll look at some specialized research resources that are especially valuable for classroom speeches. Finally, we'll explain how to evaluate the reliability and objectivity of the research materials you find on the Web.

Browsers

The explosive growth of the Web is due largely to the development of graphical *browsers* that allow you to move easily among the millions of websites. The two most popular browsers are Netscape and Microsoft's Internet Explorer. Commercial services such as America Online also offer their own browsers.

Each document on the Web contains *links* that connect to another spot in the same document or to an entirely different document someplace else on the Web. These links are usually represented by underlined or distinctively colored words or phrases. When you use your computer's mouse to click on one of these links, the document connected to that link appears on your screen. If you want to return to your original document, you click the "Back" or "Previous" button at the top of your screen. If you want to continue exploring, you do so by clicking on other interesting links as they appear.

The ease with which Netscape and other browsers allow you to skip from link to link puts a huge fund of information literally at your fingertips. But unless you have a systematic method of finding the precise materials that you need for a speech, you can spend hours browsing with little in the way of practical results. Clicking from one website to another without a research strategy is like driving through a strange city without a road map. After a while, you realize you've been going around in circles without getting any closer to your desired destination. There is a better way.

World Wide Web
A global hypertext information system that allows users to access text, graphics, audio, and moving images from the Internet.

browser
A computer program for navigating the World Wide Web.

link
A connection between two documents or sections of a document on the World Wide Web.

Search Aids

Instead of haphazardly browsing the Web, the smart approach is to use a search aid to find exactly what you need. Because there are so many documents on the Web, no search aid can provide a comprehensive catalogue of all of them. Each aid has its strengths and weaknesses, and each has its own procedures for in-depth searches. New search aids keep cropping up, and existing ones continue to be refined. The three major kinds of aids are search engines, metasearch engines, and virtual libraries.

search aid
A program used in combination with a browser to find information on the World Wide Web.

Search Engines

Search engines index Web pages and search them to find what you want. Because each works a little differently and indexes different pages, the results of any search will vary depending on the engine you use. Taken together, the major search engines cover less than half the total number of Web pages, and no single search engine covers much more than a third.[2] Depending on the topic of your speech and the information you're looking for, you may find exactly what you need right away. If not, don't despair— it may well show up on another search engine.

search engine
A search aid that indexes Web pages and checks them for sites that match a researcher's request.

Here are some of the major search engines currently in operation:

Yahoo! (http://www.yahoo.com)

AltaVista (http://www.altavista.com)

Google (http://www.google.com)

InfoSeek (http://www.infoseek.go.com)

HotBot (http://www.hotbot.com)

Northern Light (http://northernlight.com)

FastSearch (http://www.alltheweb.com)

Excite (http://www.excite.com)

About.com (http://www.about.com)

Metasearch Engines

Metasearch engines are the search engines of search engines.[3] They send your request to several search engines at the same time, allowing you to cast a much broader net than is possible with a single engine. This can be a great advantage—especially when you are looking for something very obscure. Trying to find it by going through a number of search engines one by one would be extremely time-consuming. By using a metasearch engine, you can scan a dozen or more search engines simultaneously. One expert recommends that you use a metasearch engine only when you don't want to generate more than 10 sites and when your search involves a single word or phrase.[4]

metasearch engine
A search aid that sends a researcher's request to several search engines at the same time.

It's also important to know that metasearch engines vary in the specific search engines they cover, the number of search engines they can access at one time, the length of time they devote to searching each engine, and the number of records they can retrieve from it. If you decide to use a metasearch engine, be sure to check which engines it includes so you will know if there are others you want to access in addition.

There are currently more than 130 metasearch engines. Here are 8 of the better ones:

Dogpile (http://www.dogpile.com)

Inference Find (http://www.infind.com)

InvisibleWeb (http://www.invisibleweb.com)

Ixquick Metasearch (http://www.ixquick.com)

MetaCrawler (www.metacrawler.com)

SavvySearch (www.savvysearch.com)

ProFusion (http://www.profusion.com)

Cyber 411 (http://cyber411.com)

Virtual Libraries

virtual library
A search aid that combines Internet technology with traditional library methods of cataloguing and assessing data.

Search engines and metasearch engines help you find what's on the Web, but few evaluate the quality of the sources they retrieve. Faced with the fact that anyone can post anything on the Internet, librarians and other information specialists are working to make it easier to locate reliable, high-quality Web resources. One result of their efforts is the creation of *virtual libraries*—search aids that combine Internet technology with traditional library methods of cataloguing and assessing data to create first-class research collections.

Mostly nonprofit ventures associated with colleges or universities, virtual libraries are much smaller than commercial search engines. What they lack in size, however, they more than make up in quality. You will not retrieve nearly as many sources with a virtual library as with a commercial search engine, but you can be confident that the ones you do get have been screened for accuracy and reliability.

As time goes on, we can expect more virtual libraries to be developed. For now, here are seven that you may find helpful as you work on your speeches. All have clear, user-friendly category systems that make searching for information easy and efficient.[5]

Librarian's Index to the Internet (http://lii.org)

Argus Clearinghouse (http://www.clearinghouse.net)

Internet Public Library (http://www.ipl.org)

Infomine (http://infomine.ucr.edu)

WWW Virtual Library (http://vlib.org)

Social Science Information Gateway (http://www.sosig.ac.uk)

Britannica.com (http://www.britannica.com)

Once you have selected a search aid, you will proceed by conducting either a keyword search or a subject search. Both methods are similar to conducting keyword or subject searches in the library, and both are equally effective depending on the topic of your speech and the kind of information you are seeking.

Keyword Searches

When you undertake a keyword search with a search aid that you have not used before, you should start by clicking on the "Help" or "Tips" button on the search aid's homepage. The resulting screen will tell you how to use that particular search aid most efficiently. This is especially important if you are using multiple words in your search.

Suppose, for example, that you are using the AltaVista search engine to look for information on attention deficit disorder. If you simply enter the words *attention deficit disorder* in the search box, you will get a list of every document catalogued by AltaVista that contains the word "attention," "deficit" or "disorder" in its index field—more than 100,000 documents in all. Many of these will pertain to attention deficit disorder, but others will not. Some will deal with the federal budget deficit, others with a variety of clinical disorders. You will also get links for an advertising studio known as Attention Design and an Internet consulting firm named Attention, Inc. Scanning through everything to find what you need would be a daunting task.

search box
The space provided by a search engine for entering the terms to be used in a keyword search.

How do you limit your search to get more manageable results? Sticking with AltaVista, you start by typing "attention deficit disorder" in quotation marks in the search box. Doing so will yield only citations in which the words *attention deficit disorder* appear next to each other—in this case, about 5,000 documents. This is better than 100,000, but it's still too many to go through one by one.

So you narrow your search even further. Let's assume you are interested primarily in attention deficit disorder among adults. This time you type the following entry into AltaVista's search box:

+adult+"attention deficit disorder"

The + signs before *adult* and before *"attention deficit disorder"* restrict the search to items that contain both sets of keywords. Bingo! This time you get a list of 200 documents, all of which deal with attention deficit disorder among adults.

If you were using a different search aid than AltaVista, you would enter different commands. But the basic principles for doing precise, pinpointed keyword searches are similar from search aid to search aid. If you understand those principles, you will greatly increase your odds of finding exactly what you need for your speeches.

Subject Searches

In addition to searching the Web by keyword, you can explore it by subject. The most popular subject-based search aid is Yahoo. If you access the Yahoo homepage, you will find links to a number of general topic areas, including Business and Economy, Education, Government, Health, News and Media, Science, and Society and Culture. If you click on one of these topic areas, you will get a screen with a list of subtopics. If you click on one of the subtopics, you will get a screen that divides the subtopic into smaller categories. You continue moving from screen to screen until you find the websites you want to visit.

Exploring the Web by subject has many advantages. Suppose you need information about a bill currently being debated in the U.S. Congress. You could try to find it with a keyword search, but looking by subject would be much faster. The first step is to access the Yahoo homepage and click on "Government." The next screen will give you several options, including "U.S. Government."

If you select "U.S. Government" from this screen and "Legislative Branch" from the next, you will come to a screen that includes "Bills" among its options. By choosing "Bills," you will get a screen similar to that in Figure 6.6. Click on "Search Full Text of Bills" and pick the particular bill you want from the subsequent screen. What could be easier?

Bookmarks

Whether you are searching the Web by subject or by keyword, you need to keep track of all the useful-looking resources you uncover. Otherwise, you may never find them again.

Figure 6.6

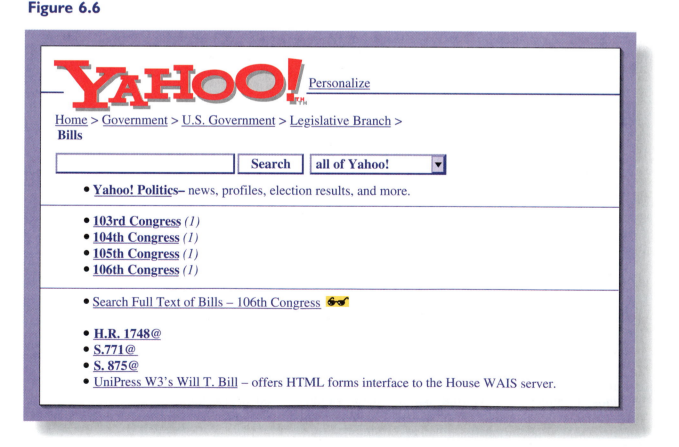

As a library book or periodical is identified by its call number, an Internet site is identified by its URL (Uniform Resource Locator). Sometimes referred to as a site's "address," the URL consists of a string of letters or numbers that identifies the site's precise location on the Internet. If you look back at the search aids listed earlier in this section, you will see the URL for each in parentheses.

Once you find a document that looks as if it may be relevant to your speech, you should record it in your preliminary bibliography (see page 155 for a sample bibliography entry for an Internet document). If you are doing your research at an on-campus computer center, you can write the site's URL by hand. A better method, however, is to use the computer's copy-and-paste function to transfer the URL to a floppy disk. This way you avoid the possibility of handwriting errors and ensure that the URL is recorded with absolute accuracy.[6]

If you have your own computer, you can record the URL by using your browser's "Bookmark" or "Favorites" feature. In Microsoft Explorer, for example, you will see the word "Favorites" at the top of the screen. If you click on that word, one of your choices in the resulting menu will be "Add to Favorites." By clicking on "Add to Favorites," you will automatically store the URL of the website currently on your screen. Not only does this give you a record of the URL for your bibliography, but you can revisit the same site whenever you want simply by calling it up from your list of favorites.

> **URL (Uniform Resource Locator)**
> A string of letters or numbers that identify the location of a given website on the Internet.

> **bookmark**
> A feature in a Web browser that stores links to sites so they can be easily revisited.

Specialized Research Resources

Search aids are extremely helpful, but they are not the only vehicles for finding information on the Web. Because the Web is so vast, you may find it helpful to have a brief list of stable, high-quality websites that you can turn to with confidence in case a search aid doesn't turn up what you're looking for. In compiling the following list, I have concentrated on the kinds of sites that are most likely to be helpful as you work on your speeches.

Given the dynamic nature of the Internet, some sites may change their addresses by the time you read this book. If they do, you will probably find a new address at the old URL. If there is no new address, use a search engine to look for the site by name. (It's possible, of course, that a site will cease to exist, but most of those listed below should be around for some time.)

Government Resources

One of the great strengths of the Internet as a research tool is the access it provides to government documents and publications. Whether you are looking for information from a federal bureau in Washington, D.C., or from a state or local agency, chances are you can find it by starting your search at one of these websites:

Federal Web Locator (http://www.infoctr.edu/fwl). One-stop shopping site for federal government information on the Web. Contains links to all major U.S. government websites, including Congress, the White House, the FBI, the Department of Education, the Food and Drug

Administration, the Centers for Disease Control, the Environmental Protection Agency, and so on.

Fed World Information Network (http://www.fedworld.gov). Despite a somewhat confusing homepage, this is a fine site for accessing government information. Click on "Explore U.S. Government Web Sites" for links to a subject directory that cuts across federal agencies and commissions.

State and Local Government on the Net (http://www.piperinfo.com/ state/states.html). Provides links to all 50 state governments, to Guam, Puerto Rico, and other U.S. territories, and to cities and towns throughout the nation. Whether you're looking for the police department in Soldotna, Alaska, or the mayor's office in New York City, this is the website for you.

Reference Resources

The Internet cannot take the place of your library's reference section, with its encyclopedias, yearbooks, biographical aids, and the like. But it does contain a growing number of sites that can come in handy when you need a reference source. These sites include:

Virtual Reference Collection (http://www.lib.uci.edu/rraz.genref.html). A superior reference guide with links to electronic dictionaries, encyclopedias, phone directories, geographic works, U.S. historical documents, and much more.

Virtual Reference Desk (http://thorplus.lib.purdue.edu/reference/ index.html). Offers links to a wide range of reference sources, including the Television News Archive at Vanderbilt University and a large number of foreign language dictionaries. A great spot as well for finding e-mail addresses and phone numbers of people all over the world.

Galaxy Quotations (http://galaxy.einet.net/galaxy/Reference/ Quotations.html). A comprehensive roster of links to collected quotations on the Web. Includes everything from Shakespeare to an electronic version of *Bartlett's.*

World Factbook (http://www.odci.gov/cia/publications/factbook/ index.html). Published annually by the U.S. Central Intelligence Agency, the *World Factbook* is a rich compendium of information on every country of the world. Topics include people, government, economy, communication, transportation, and transnational issues.

Statistical Abstract (http://www.census.gov/pub/statab/www). Provides frequently requested tables and other selected data from the annual *Statistical Abstract of the United States.* Despite being less comprehensive than the printed *Statistical Abstract,* this is a superior site for quantitative information on life in the U.S.

Periodical Resources

Not only are *Time, Newsweek, U.S. News and World Report,* and many other leading magazines available online, but there is a growing roster of periodicals that exist only in electronic form. You can access any given publication by looking for it by name with a search engine, or you can go through one of the sites listed below. The Web is also home to an extraordinary on-line bibliographic service that indexes thousands of periodicals—including academic journals—from all over the world.

NewsDirectory.com (http://www.ecola.com). One of the largest and most diverse media resources on the Web. Provides links to hundreds of English-language magazines around the globe, as well as to newspapers and television stations. Has excellent search capabilities and allows browsing of magazines by subject or country.

CMPA Reading Room (http://www.cmpa.ca/maghome.html). Sponsored by the Canadian Magazine Publishers Association, this site provides links to more than 260 online Canadian magazines, including *Maclean's.*

UnCoverWeb (http://uncweb.carl.org). Indexes 17,000 scholarly journals and popular magazines. For a fee, you can get articles faxed to you within a day, but you can search the entire database for free. The ultimate periodical index!

News Resources

Most U.S. newspapers have their own websites—as do the major television news organizations. If you are looking for a particular newspaper or

Researching on the Internet has many advantages, especially if you learn how to conduct efficient, focused searches that lead you to high-quality sources of information.

network, try typing its name, in quotation marks, in the AltaVista search box. To cast a wider net, log on to one of the following:

Media Links: Online Media Directory (http://emedia1.mediainfo.com/ emedia). One-stop shopping for U.S. online newspapers. Contains links to everything from the *New York Times* and *Washington Post* to the Pueblo, Colorado, *Chieftain* and the Amarillo, Texas, *Globe-News.* With a click of the mouse, you can also access newspapers around the globe.

Newsroom (http://www.auburn.edu/~vestmon/gif/news.html). Provides links to most leading newspapers and broadcast news organizations, including Reuters, CNN, ABC, and CBS. An excellent site as well for business and financial news.

NewsLink (http://www.newslink.org). Claims to be the Web's most comprehensive news site, with links to thousands of newspapers, magazines, and broadcasters. Also provides access to campus papers from colleges and universities across the U.S.

The Ultimate Collection of News Links (http://pppp.net/links/news/). Provides links to 10,000 electronic newspapers and magazines around the world. An especially valuable resource for international news and perspectives.

Multicultural Resources

As its name implies, the World Wide Web is a global phenomenon, and it mirrors the internationalism and diversity of our modern age. If you are speaking on a topic with multicultural dimensions, you may find help at one of the following sites:

Yahoo!: Regional (http://www.yahoo.com/Regional). A great starting point that offers links to scores of countries and regions around the world, as well as to each of the 50 United States.

WWW Virtual Library: American Indians (http://www.hanksville.org/ NAresources). Comprehensive, well-organized resource with hundreds of links to sites dealing with Native American history, language, culture, education, health, art, and the like.

Asian American Resources (http://www.mit.edu/activities/aar/aar. html). Provides links to scores of websites that feature topics, writings, and organizations of special interest to Asian-Americans.

Latino/Hispanic Resources (http://www-rcf.usc.edu/~cmmr/Latino. html). Maintained by the University of Southern California's Center for Multilingual, Multicultural Research, this outstanding site provides links to a treasure trove of resources devoted to Latino- and Latina-related issues.

African American Web Connection (http://www.aawc.com). Award-winning website that deals with all aspects of African-American life, including history, business, politics, and religion. Also provides links to organizations such as the National Urban League, Congressional Black Caucus, and NAACP.

Of course, there are thousands of other useful websites. But the ones discussed above, in conjunction with one of the Web's search aids, should help get your research started on the right foot.

Evaluating Internet Documents

When you do research in a library, everything you find has been evaluated in one way or another before it gets to you. Books, magazines, and journals have editorial procedures to determine whether a given work should or should not be published. Once a work is published, it has to be approved by the acquisitions staff for inclusion in the library.

The Internet, of course, is a very different story. The most trusted resources on the World Wide Web are those derived from printed works—government records, newspaper articles, research reports, and the like. But most Web documents exist only in electronic form. Of these, few have gone through the kind of editorial review that is designed to assure a basic level of reliability in printed works. The Web is "the largest self-publishing experiment in history."[7] Anyone with a computer and access to the Internet can share his or her opinions with a discussion group, publish an electronic newsletter, or create a personal Web page. Charlatans, extremists, and malcontents circulate their ideas on equal footing with CNN, the Library of Congress, and Nobel prize winners. Never has the old adage been more true than when applied to the Internet: Don't believe everything you read.[8]

In Chapter 7, we will discuss how to judge the soundness of supporting materials in general. Here we look at three criteria you can use to help distinguish between the jewels and the junk on the Internet.[9]

Authorship

Is the author of the Web document you are assessing clearly identified? If so, what are her or his qualifications? Is the author an expert on the topic? Can her or his data and opinions be accepted as objective and unbiased? Just as you should not cite a book or magazine article without identifying the author and his or her credentials, so you should not cite an electronic work in the absence of this information.

In a book or magazine article, information about the author is usually fairly easy to find. Too often, however, it is not made available on the Internet. If you can't find information about the author in a document itself, look for a link to the author's homepage or to another site that may explain the author's credentials. Some Internet documents include the author's e-mail address, which you can use to request further information.

Another option is to access the Virtual Reference Desk (http://thorplus.lib.purdue.edu/reference/index.html) and click on "Phone Books and Email Directories," where you will find links to a score of electronic directories. If that doesn't work, try checking one of the printed biographical aids discussed earlier in this chapter (pages 134–135).

Sponsorship

Many Web documents are published by businesses, government agencies, public-interest groups, and the like rather than by individual authors. In such cases, you must judge whether the sponsoring organization is impartial enough to cite in your speech. Is the organization objective in its research and fair-minded in its statements? Is it economically unbiased with regard to the issue under discussion? Does it have a history of accuracy and nonpartisanship?

Over the years, some organizations have developed strong reputations for their expertise and objectivity. Many of these are public-interest groups such as Consumer's Union, Common Cause, and the American Cancer Society. Others include the National Archives, Centers for Disease Control, and similar government agencies. Private think tanks such as the Rand Corporation and the Cato Institute often have definite political leanings, but are usually well respected for the quality and substance of their research.

On the other hand, you need to be wary of groups that sound respectable but in fact are not. Don't let a fancy-sounding name trick you into accepting a sponsoring organization's credibility at face value. For example, the World Internet News Distributory Source sounds like a nonpartisan news service. In fact, it is categorized by Yahoo as a white pride and racialism group, and it refuses to identify the names or credentials of the authors who write under its sponsorship.

One way to gauge the credibility of a website is by clicking on the "About" or "Welcome" link on its homepage. Often the resulting screen will identify the site's founders, purpose, or philosophy. In the case of the World Internet News Distributory Source, it is clear from the "Welcome" page that the site does not meet the necessary standards of objectivity and expertise.

What do you do if you cannot verify the credentials of an author or identify a credible sponsoring organization for an Internet document? The answer is easy: Don't use the document in your speech! In this regard, the same standards apply whether you are dealing with a printed work or an electronic one.

sponsoring organization
An organization that, in the absence of a clearly identified author, is responsible for the content of a document on the World Wide Web.

Recency

One of the advantages of using the Internet for research is that it often has more recent information than you can find in print sources. But just because a document is on the Internet does not mean its facts and figures are up-to-the-minute. There are several ways to gauge the recency of an Internet document.

The easiest way is to look for a copyright date, publication date, or date of last revision at the top or bottom of the document. If none of these are present, and you are using Netscape Navigator 4.5, select "Page Info" from the "View" menu at the top of your screen and see if there is a date in the "Last Modified" entry. If you are using Microsoft Explorer, click on the "File" menu at the top of your screen, select "Properties," and look under "Modified." There is no guarantee that either Netscape or Microsoft Explorer will have the information you need, but it is worth checking.

Once you know the date of the document, you can determine whether it is current enough to use in your speech. This is especially important with regard to statistics, which you should never cite from an undated source, whether in print or on the Internet. If you can't fix the date on which a Web document was created or last modified, you should search for another work whose recency you can verify.

Interviewing

Most people think of interviewing in terms of job interviews or conversations with celebrities. But there is another kind of interview—the research (or investigative) interview. Among journalists it is a time-honored way to collect information. It is also an excellent way to gather materials for speeches.

> **research interview**
> An interview conducted to gather information for a speech.

Suppose you are explaining the latest advances in personal computers. Why not contact a local computer dealer as one source of information? Or suppose you are dealing with the problem of binge drinking among college students. Why not get in touch with the dean of students to find out the situation at your school? Once you begin to think about the possibilities, you will discover many people on your campus and in your community who can contribute to your speeches.

When done well, interviewing (like many things) looks deceptively easy. In practice, it is a complex and demanding art. So before you dash off to conduct your interviews à la Larry King or Barbara Walters, you should understand a few basic principles of effective interviewing. They fall into three groups—what to do before the interview, what to do during the interview, and what to do after the interview.

To illustrate, we'll follow the entire interview process for a hypothetical speech about gender equity in college athletics.

Before the Interview

Just as the outcome of most speeches is decided by how well the speaker prepares, so the outcome of most interviews is decided by how well the interviewer prepares. Here are five steps you should take ahead of time to help ensure a successful interview.

Define the Purpose of the Interview

You have done library research about the issue of gender equity in college athletics and have begun to grasp the major points of view fairly well. At this stage you think it would be helpful to know the status of men's and women's athletics at your school. You get some information from the newspaper, and some more from a handbook put out by the athletic department. But you still have many questions. You decide the only way to get answers is to interview someone associated with the athletic program. In that decision you have begun to formulate a purpose for the interview.

Decide Whom to Interview

There are several possibilities—players, coaches, administrators. You elect to start at the top—with the athletic director. Isn't that a bit presumptuous? Why not begin with someone a little further down the line—an assistant director or a coach, for instance? You could. But in dealing with administrative organizations it is usually best to go to the leaders first. They are likely to have a broad understanding of the issues. And if you need more specific information than they have, they can get it for you or put you in touch with the right person.

Arrange the Interview

In this case, let's assume the athletic director is a man. The subject of gender equity may be a delicate issue. Furthermore, he is a very busy person. So you work out a plan for convincing him to agree to talk with you. Knowing that it is easier to brush someone off over the telephone than in person, you go to the athletic office to request the interview. You introduce yourself, identify your exact purpose, and explain why the interview is important. The athletic director agrees, and you set up the interview for three days later.

(You are astonished to get the interview, but you shouldn't be. Nearly everyone likes to be interviewed. If your purpose is a serious one and you conduct yourself well, the person you ask to interview is likely to cooperate.)

Decide Whether or Not to Use a Tape Recorder

If your subject does not want the interview tape-recorded, then the decision is made. Otherwise, you must choose. There are two major advantages of using a tape recorder: (1) Since you don't have to spend all your time taking notes, you can concentrate on the interviewee's message and on formulating your questions. (2) Your record of the interview will be exact—there will be no possibility of misquoting or of forgetting important facts.

There are also two disadvantages to using a tape recorder during an interview: (1) Many interviewees are so uncomfortable with a recorder in the room that this may spoil the interview. (2) You will have to spend a lot of time after the interview playing the tape over and over to distill the recorded material. When you take notes, on the other hand, that distillation process takes place during the interview because you write down only the important points.

If you decide to use a tape recorder, never smuggle it in without the knowledge or consent of the person being interviewed. Not only is it unethical, but the interviewee is bound to find out and you will cause yourself more trouble than you had hoped to avoid.

Prepare Your Questions

You now face the most important part of your preinterview tasks—working out the questions you will ask during the interview. Keep in mind the old adage, "Ask a stupid question, you'll get a stupid answer." You should devise questions that are sensible, intelligent, and meaningful. Here are some types of questions to *avoid:*

- Questions you can answer without the interview. (How long has the school had a women's athletic program? What sports does it include?) Queries like these just waste the subject's time and make you look foolish. Research this information yourself before the interview.

- Leading questions. (You *do* think women should have as many athletic scholarships as men, *don't you*?)

- Hostile, loaded questions. (I think it's disgraceful that most of the women's athletic teams at this school are still coached by men. Don't you think women can coach as well as men? What do you say to *that,* hmmm?)

You need not shy away from tough questions. Just phrase them as neutrally as possible and save them until near the end of the interview. That way, if your interviewee becomes irritated or uncooperative, you'll still get most of the information you want.

When you are finished preparing, you should have a set of direct, specific, reasonable questions, such as the following:

- Gender equity seems to be the major issue facing college athletic programs today. How does our school plan to deal with decisions about gender equity made by the federal courts and the NCAA?

- I understand you are considering adding three additional sports for women. What sports will those be and when will they get under way?

- How does the athletic department intend to pay for the cost of reaching equity between men's and women's sports? Will any men's sports be cut in order to achieve gender equity?

- Last month the women's gymnastics team complained that while the athletic department spends a lot of money on women's basketball and volleyball, it still does not provide adequate facilities or practice time for other women's sports. Is the complaint justified? If so, are steps being taken to deal with it?

- Given the controversy over gender equity, how do you see the future of intercollegiate athletics in the United States? What do you think athletic programs will look like 10 years from now?

Although some experienced journalists conduct interviews with only a few key-word notes on the areas to be covered, you want to be sure not to forget anything during the interview. So you arrange your questions in the order you want to ask them and take the list with you to the interview.

During the Interview

Every interview is unique. Just as a speaker adapts to the audience during a speech, so must an interviewer adapt to the person being interviewed. Because the session will seldom go exactly as you plan, you need to be alert and flexible. Here are several steps you can take to help make the interview proceed smoothly.

Dress Appropriately and Be on Time

The athletic director has a busy schedule and is doing you a favor by agreeing to an interview, so you make every effort to show up on time. Since the interview is a special occasion, you dress appropriately. This is one way of telling the athletic director that you regard the interview as serious business. In return, he is likely to take you more seriously.

Repeat the Purpose of the Interview

The athletic director invites you into his office; you exchange a few introductory remarks. Now, before you plunge into your questions, you take a minute or two to restate the purpose of the interview. This refreshes the athletic director's memory and gives the interview a sharper focus. You are more likely to get clear, helpful answers if your subject knows why you are following a certain line of questioning.

Set Up the Tape Recorder, If You Are Using One

If your subject has agreed to being recorded, keep one principle in mind: the tape recording should be as casual and inconspicuous as possible. Don't thrust the microphone into your subject's face. Don't fiddle endlessly with the tape or the machine. You should have practiced in advance to make sure you understand how the recorder works. Set up the recorder, start the tape, and then try to ignore it for the rest of the interview. With luck, your subject will ignore it too.

For this exercise, we'll assume the athletic director does not want the interview tape-recorded.

Keep the Interview on Track

You ask the athletic director the first question on your list. He answers it. You ask him the second question. He answers it, but in doing so he also answers question 4. What do you do now? Do you go on to question 5 or return to question 3?

Sometimes a personal interview can provide information from people with special expertise on your speech topic. When conducting an interview, be sure to prepare your questions carefully and to listen attentively.

Either approach is fine. As it turns out, you go back to question 3 (while also checking off question 4 from your list). Now, in answering question 3, the athletic director raises an important issue that is not covered anywhere in your list of questions. Do you pursue that issue or forge doggedly ahead with question 5?

You make the wise decision to veer slightly from your prearranged order of questioning to pursue the new issue. You pose a couple questions about it, get helpful answers, then keep the interview on track by returning to your list of prepared questions.

This is more or less how things go for the rest of the interview. You pursue new leads when they appear, improvise probing follow-up questions when called for, then lead on again in an orderly fashion. The interview is freewheeling at times, but you never let it get out of control. When it is over, you have answers to all your prepared questions—and a lot more.

Listen Carefully

During the interview, you listen attentively while taking key-word notes (see Chapter 3). When you don't understand something, you ask for clarification. If you hear a statement you want to quote directly, you have the athletic director repeat it to make sure you get it exactly right. Chances are a prominent person like him will have been misquoted more than once in the press, so he'll be happy to oblige.

Don't Overstay Your Welcome

Try to keep within the stipulated time period for the interview, unless your subject clearly wants to prolong the session. When the interview is over, you thank the athletic director for having given of his time and insights.

After the Interview

Although the interview is over, the interviewing process is not. You must now review and transcribe your notes.

Review Your Notes As Soon As Possible

When you leave the athletic director's office, the interview is fresh in your mind. You know what the cryptic comments and scrawls in your notes mean. But as time passes, the details will become hazy. Don't let something like this true story happen to you:

Years ago, a prominent woman—writer and diplomat—was being interviewed by a young reporter. Among other things, the reporter asked about hobbies and leisure activities. The woman replied that she enjoyed skeet shooting and raised Siamese cats. The reporter scribbled in her notes "shoots" and "cats"—but didn't bother to put a comma or a dash between the words. The interview was published. And ever since, that prominent woman has been trying to live down the reputation that she "shoots cats."

In reviewing your notes, try to concentrate on two things—discovering the main points that emerged during the interview and pulling out specific information that might be useful in your speech.

The best way to locate the main points is to decide what you would answer if someone asked you to summarize the interview in one minute or less. As you look through your notes, you see three ideas that surface over and over in the athletic director's comments: (1) Gender equity is mandated by Title IX legislation passed by Congress in 1972 and has been consistently upheld by the courts. (2) In the absence of significant new sources of revenue, your school cannot create additional sports for women without trimming men's sports. (3) To prevent harming the men's athletic program, the school should contribute money from its general funds to help pay for the achievement of gender equity.

As you review the interview, you also seize on several specific items—figures, anecdotes, quotations—that look promising as supporting details for your speech. If any of them are unclear, call the athletic director to make sure you have the facts right.

Transcribe Your Notes

After reviewing the notes, you transcribe important ideas and information onto index cards. Since this requires filling in from memory various details of the interview, you do it as soon as possible. It's important to use index cards because that is how you will record materials gathered in your library research (see pages 155–156). Thus you will have all your research materials in the same format, so they can be arranged and rearranged easily when you begin to organize your speech.[10]

Writing and Calling for Information

If the subject of your speech is at all controversial, you can be pretty sure that somewhere there is an organization for it or against it—and probably there are both. Take the issue of reforming the U.S. Social Security system. The Concord Coalition is for it; the American Association of Retired People is against it. Cigarette smoking? Companies such as R.J. Reynolds vigorously promote it; numerous organizations, including the American Cancer Society, are actively opposed to it.

There are thousands of special-interest groups in this country, and most of them offer free pamphlets and other literature related to their concerns. The *Encyclopedia of Associations,* available in the reference section of most libraries, will give you a list of these groups along with their telephone numbers, mailing addresses, and websites. You can also get information at Associations on the Net, an online directory of groups available through the Internet Public Library (http://www.ipl.org/ref.AON).

However, a bit of caution is needed when using material obtained from such groups. Since these organizations exist specifically to promote or oppose a particular cause, their information may be biased, slanted, even downright wrong. Whenever possible, check facts and statistics against a more independent source.

Government agencies are another excellent source of information on a wide range of topics. Suppose you plan to speak on a subject related to farming. The Department of Agriculture publishes hundreds of bulletins, all available at little or no cost. If you are in doubt about which government agency is responsible for a particular subject, try calling or writing your congressional representative. His or her staff can point you in the right direction.

If you call or write for information, be sure to do it as soon as possible once you have chosen your speech topic. Unless you are contacting a local organization, it will usually take at least a week for the information to reach you.

Tips for Doing Research

Few people regard doing research as one of life's great joys. There are, however, ways to make it less tedious and more productive. Here are four ways that are guaranteed to help.

Start Early

The biggest mistake students make when faced with a research project is waiting too long to begin. The longer you wait, the more problems you will encounter. You may find that a vital book has been checked out of the library or that you no longer have time to arrange a crucial interview. Starting early also eases the tension of completing an assignment. Instead of sweating under intense time pressure, you can work at your convenience. No matter what kind of research you do, you can be sure of one thing. It will *always* take longer than you expect. So get started early and avoid the pitfalls that come from procrastinating.

Starting early also gives you plenty of time to think about what you find. In researching, you will collect much more material than you will actually use in the speech. Preparing a speech is a little like constructing a jigsaw puzzle. Once you gather the pieces, you have to decide how they fit together. The more time you give yourself, the more likely you are to get the pieces to fit just right.

Make a Preliminary Bibliography

In your research, you will run across the titles of books, magazine articles, Internet documents, and so on that look as if they might contain helpful information about your speech topic. Enter each item you find in your preliminary bibliography. If you are taking research notes by hand, fill out a separate index card for each item. (It's important to use index cards because they can be put in alphabetical order quickly.) If you are using a computer, create a separate file for your preliminary bibliography and enter citations in alphabetical order.

For books, record the author, title, place of publication, publisher, date of publication, and call number. You may also want to include a brief comment indicating why the book may be valuable for your speech. Figure 6.7 (page 154) shows a sample bibliography card for a book.

For magazine articles, record the author, title of the article, name of the magazine, date of publication, and page numbers. You should also indicate where you can find the full text of the article—computerized database or

preliminary bibliography
A list compiled early in the research process of works that look as if they might contain helpful information about a speech topic.

Figure 6.7 Sample Bibliography Card for a Book.

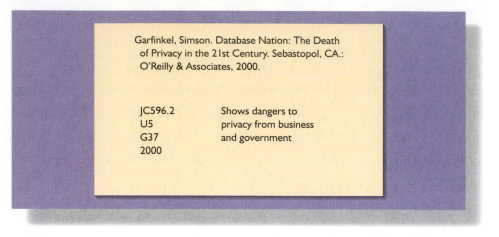

> Garfinkel, Simson. Database Nation: The Death
> of Privacy in the 21st Century. Sebastopol, CA.:
> O'Reilly & Associates, 2000.
>
> JC596.2   Shows dangers to
> U5   privacy from business
> G37   and government
> 2000

call number in the library shelves. As with book entries, you may also want to include a note to yourself about the article. Figure 6.8 shows a sample bibliography card for a magazine article.

Figure 6.8 Sample Bibliography Card for a Magazine Article.

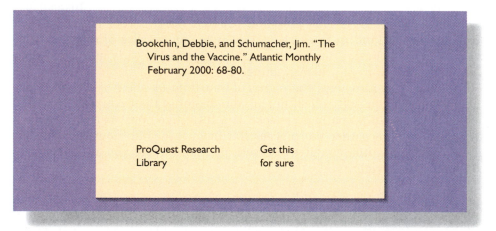

> Bookchin, Debbie, and Schumacher, Jim. "The
> Virus and the Vaccine." Atlantic Monthly
> February 2000: 68-80.
>
> ProQuest Research   Get this
> Library   for sure

For Internet documents, cite the author or sponsoring organization, title of the document, date of Internet publication or of latest update, URL, and the date on which you accessed the document. Figure 6.9 shows a sample bibliography card for an Internet document.[11]

One important point needs to be stressed. You should include in your preliminary bibliography *each* book, article, Internet document, and the like that looks as if it *could be* helpful in preparing your speech. As a result, you may well have 15 or 20 items in your preliminary bibliography. But remember that you have not yet examined the works listed on the cards. Of the 15 or 20 preliminary sources, only 7 or 8 are likely to be of much use in drafting the speech. It is an inevitable fact of research that you must sift through many sources to find what you need. If you prepare a skimpy preliminary bibliography, you may well end up with a skimpy speech.

Go to the Bibliography Formats for details on citing Internet sources and other works in a speech bibliography.

CD: BIBLIOGRAPHY FORMATS

Figure 6.9   Sample Bibliography Card for an Internet Document.

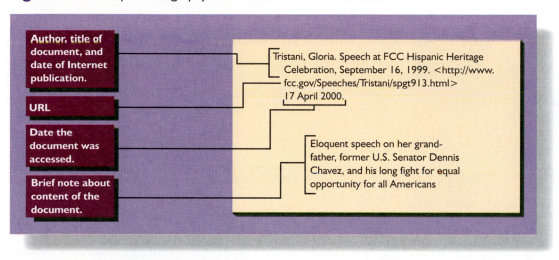

Take Notes Efficiently

Asia Marshall started her speech preparation with the best of intentions. She was excited about her topic, "Great Women of Jazz," and she logged on to the Internet to begin researching the same day the assignment was announced. She found several interesting sources and took some notes about them on index cards. That evening she went to the library, checked out a book about Billie Holiday, and brought it back to her room. The book was so interesting that she read it straight through. She didn't bother taking notes because she was sure she'd remember it all. The next day, she stopped by the reference section of the library to look through the *Encyclopedia of Jazz*. When she got there, she realized she had forgotten her index cards, so she jotted a few notes on the back of her speech syllabus.

Then Asia remembered she had a test in another class. Somewhat panicked, she put aside her speech research to study for the test. When she got back to working on the speech, the deadline was only four days away. She dug out the notes she had made, but what did they mean? Most of them were far too brief to be of much help. One said, "Medford—*important!!!*" But who or what was Medford? An author? A musician? Or could it be a place? Asia had thought she'd remember all about the Billie Holiday book, but without notes it was mostly a blur by now. With a sense of doom, she faced up to the fact that she would have to start over—and finish in four days.

Sound familiar? This has happened to almost everyone at least once. But once is enough. There is a better way to take research notes. Here is a method that has worked well for many students:

1. Record notes on index cards. Many people prefer the 4×6 or 5×8 size. Both are large enough to hold quite a bit of information, yet they can be sorted easily when you start to organize the speech. The importance of using index cards cannot be overemphasized. It is the first step to more efficient note taking. Once you begin to use them, you'll be surprised at how much time and frustration they save.

2. On each card write the note, the source of the note, and a heading indicating the subject of the note (see Figure 6.10, page 156). The subject

Figure 6.10   Sample Research Note.

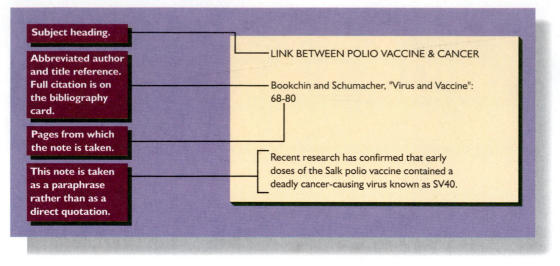

heading is crucial, for it allows you to tell at a glance what the note is about. This simplifies the task of arranging your notes when you start to organize the speech. Use the same format for notes taken from an interview.

3. Use a separate card for each note. Many students try to write down all the information from one source on a single card. This defeats the purpose of using index cards because it makes your notes almost impossible to review and organize. You can avoid this problem by making a separate card for each quotation or piece of information you record. Although you may end up with several cards from the same document, you will find that this method allows you to keep better track of your research.

4. Distinguish among direct quotations, paraphrases, and your own ideas. As we saw in Chapter 2, it is easy to plagiarize accidentally by not taking careful research notes. As you do research for your speeches, be sure to use quotation marks on your note cards whenever you copy the exact words of a source. If you paraphrase, rather than quote verbatim, make sure to cite the source on your note card. By keeping track of quotations and paraphrases, you will be able to separate your own words and ideas from those of other people. This will help you avoid the trap of inadvertent plagiarism when you put your speech together.

5. Take plenty of notes. Few things are more aggravating than trying to recall some bit of information you ran across in your research but neglected to record on a note card. You might have said to yourself, "That's sort of interesting, but I don't know whether it's important. I'll remember it if I need it." Now, of course, you don't remember it exactly. Worse yet, you don't remember where you read it. So you head back to the library or log onto the Internet hoping you can relocate the information. But even if you do find it, you have wasted a lot of time. The moral is clear: If there is even an outside chance you may need a piece of information, jot it down. This procedure will take a little extra time in the short run, but in the long run it can save you much grief.

Think about Your Materials as You Research

Students often approach research as a mechanical routine that simply involves gathering the materials to be used in a speech or paper. But when done properly, research can be extremely creative.

If you *think about* what you are finding in your research, you will see your topic just a little bit differently with each note you take. You will find new relationships, develop new questions, explore new angles. You will, in short, begin to write the speech in your head even as you do the research. As you learn more about the topic, you will formulate a central idea, begin to sketch out main points and supporting points, experiment with ways of organizing your thoughts. You may even change your point of view, as did this student:

> Francesca Lopez began her speech preparation with this central idea in mind: "Wild animals make more interesting pets than dogs and cats." She went about her research conscientiously, spending many hours in the library. On her third day she came upon some disturbing information about the capture of wild animals. She read that young chimpanzees and other apes were literally snatched out of their mothers' arms, and that the mothers were afterward heard to cry almost like humans. Back in her room that night, Francesca couldn't get her mind off the baby chimpanzees.
>
> The next day at the library Francesca found some more disturbing material. One source told about the extraordinarily high death rate of wild animals during shipment to the United States. Again, that night, Francesca brooded about the young animals dying of fear and cold in the cargo holds of airplanes.
>
> By the time she finished her research, Francesca's central idea was completely different. When she spoke, her central idea was "The importation of wild animals for use as pets is inhumane."

This is an example of creative research—and of critical thinking. Francesca kept her mind open, read everything she could find about her topic, and thought seriously about what she found. Because of this thoughtful approach, she changed her mind.

Your own speech preparation may not cause you to reverse your position, but it should give you new insights into your topic. If you approach research in this way, you may well find that the time you spend researching is the most productive of all the time you devote to preparing your speech.[12]

Summary

Gathering materials for a speech is like gathering information for any project. Many resources are available if you take advantage of them. When you have personal experience or more-than-average knowledge about a topic, you can use yourself as a resource. Most of the time, however, you will need outside information, which you can get in several ways. You can do research in the library or on the Internet. You can interview people with specialized knowledge about your topic. You can write away or call for information.

Finding what you need in the library is largely a matter of knowing how to search for information. The library catalogue lists all the books and periodicals owned by the library. Periodical indexes and newspaper indexes provide an efficient way to locate articles from newspapers and magazines.

The reference section contains a wealth of resources—including encyclopedias, yearbooks, dictionaries, biographical aids, atlases, and gazetteers. If you have trouble finding something, don't hesitate to ask a librarian.

The most widely used part of the Internet for research purposes is the World Wide Web. The best approach to exploring systematically on the Web is to use a search aid to find exactly what you need. Both keyword and subject searches can be equally effective depending on the topic of your speech and the kind of information you are seeking. Given the lack of editorial review for most documents on the Web, it is especially important to evaluate the authorship, sponsoring organization, and recency of the research materials you find there.

You can also get information by conducting a personal interview with someone on campus or in the community. Before the interview, you should define its purpose, decide whom you are going to interview, and make an appointment with that person. You should also prepare the questions you are going to ask during the interview. Once the interview begins, be sure to keep it on track, to listen attentively, and to take accurate notes. Afterward, review and transcribe your notes as soon as possible, while they are still fresh in your mind.

Writing away or calling for information is a good way to gather material if you have enough time before your speech. Government agencies, corporations, and special-interest groups all offer free or very inexpensive publications.

No matter what sources you draw upon in gathering your information, your research will be more effective if you start early and make a preliminary bibliography to keep track of all the books, articles, and Internet documents that look as if they might be helpful. By learning to take research notes effectively, you will save yourself time and energy every step of the way. And if you think about your materials as you research, you may find that gathering materials is the most creative part of your speech preparation.

Key Terms

card catalogue (126)

online catalogue (126)

call number (127)

periodical index (127)

abstract (128)

newspaper index (131)

reference work (132)

general encyclopedia (132)

special encyclopedia (132)

yearbook (133)

biographical aid (134)

atlas (135)

gazetteer (135)

Internet (135)

World Wide Web (136)

browser (136)

link (136)

search aid (137)

search engine (137)

metasearch engine (137)

virtual library (138)

search box (139)

URL (Uniform Resource Locator) (141)

bookmark (141)

sponsoring organization (146)

research interview (147)

preliminary bibliography (153)

Review Questions

After reading this chapter, you should be able to answer the following questions:

1. Why is it important to draw on your own knowledge and experience in gathering materials for your speeches?

2. What are five important resources for finding what you need in the library?

3. What are three kinds of search aids you can use to find information systematically on the World Wide Web?

4. What are the major criteria for evaluating the soundness of research materials that you find on the Web?

5. What are the three stages of interviewing? What should you do as an interviewer in each stage to help ensure a successful interview?

6. Why is it important to start your speech research early?

7. What is a preliminary bibliography? Why is it helpful to you in researching a speech?

8. What five things should you do to take research notes efficiently?

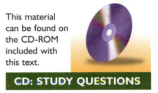

This material can be found on the CD-ROM included with this text.

CD: STUDY QUESTIONS

Exercises for Critical Thinking

1. Using the *Reader's Guide to Periodical Literature* or one of the other general periodical indexes discussed on pages 127–129, find three articles on the subject of your next speech. Prepare a preliminary bibliography card for each article. Locate the full text of the article and assess its value for your speech.

2. Use one of the newspaper indexes discussed on pages 130–132 to find three articles on the subject of your next speech. Prepare a preliminary bibliography card for each article. Read the full text of each article and assess its value for your speech.

3. Find two Internet documents on the topic of your next speech and prepare a preliminary bibliography card for each. Assess both documents in light of the criteria discussed on pages 145–147 for evaluating Internet documents. Be specific.

4. Plan to conduct an interview for one of your classroom speeches. Be sure to follow the guidelines presented in this chapter for effective interviewing. Afterward, evaluate the interview. Did you prepare for it adequately? Did you get the information you needed? What would you do differently if you could conduct the interview again?

5. This exercise is designed to give you firsthand experience with some of the major reference works discussed on pages 132–135. Your task is to answer each of the following questions. Some of the questions indicate where you will find the answer, and some do not. If

necessary, look back through the chapter to see in which reference works you are most likely to find the answers. For each question, record both your answer and where you found it.

Example

Question: Who said, "Who knows what women can be when they are finally free to become themselves"?

Answer: Betty Friedan said, "Who knows what women can be when they are finally free to become themselves." *Bartlett's Familiar Quotations,* 15th edition, page 898.

a. According to the *Encyclopedia Judaica,* when was the first kibbutz founded?

b. What were listed in *Facts on File* as the three top-rated prime-time television programs for the period January 31–February 27, 2000?

c. As explained in the *Latino Encyclopedia,* what does the historical holiday Cinco de Mayo commemorate?

d. Which issue of the *New York Times* in 1999 reported that college students living on campus are three times more likely to develop meningitis than are students living off campus?

e. What is Jesse Jackson's mailing address?

f. When, according to the *Encyclopedia of Computer Science,* was the first computer virus program created?

g. According to the 1998 *Statistical Abstract of the United States,* what was the average monthly bill for cellular telephone users in 1990? In 1997?

h. As noted in *Who's Who among Asian Americans,* what award did film director Ismail Merchant receive in 1993?

i. What two bodies of water does the Torres Strait connect?

Applying the POWER of Public Speaking

Your four-year-old daughter has recently been diagnosed with asthma, making her one of the growing number of urban children with this chronic disease. After speaking with other people in your neighborhood, you discover there are a number of other families facing the same medical situation. For the last year an informal group has been meeting to exchange ideas on balancing treatment plans, medication, and preventive strategies while maintaining regular family life. Now you have volunteered to research information on creating a formal support group allied with one of the national asthma and allergy organizations. You will report on your findings at the next neighborhood meeting.

Find the information you need by conducting a subject search through the Librarians' Index to the Internet.

Notes

[1] I would like to thank the reference staff of Memorial Library, University of Wisconsin–Madison, for their assistance in providing materials for this section of the chapter.

[2]Randolph Hock, *The Extreme Searcher's Guide to Web Search Engines: A Handbook for the Serious Searcher* (Medford, N.J.: CyberAge Books, 1999), p. 13.

[3]Timothy K. Maloy, *The Internet Research Guide,* 2nd ed. (New York: Allworth Press, 1999), p. 41.

[4]Hock, *Extreme Searcher's Guide,* pp. 166–167.

[5]For more information on these and other virtual libraries, see Amy Tracy Wells, Susan Calcari, and Travis Koplow, *The Amazing Internet Challenge: How Leading Projects Use Library Skills to Organize the Web* (Chicago: American Library Association, 1999), on which my discussion is based.

[6]Andrew Harnack and Eugene Kleppinger, *Online! A Reference Guide to Using Internet Sources* (New York: St. Martin's, 1997), pp. 55–56.

[7]Evan Morris, *The Book Lover's Guide to the Internet* (New York: Fawcett Columbine, 1996), p. 106.

[8]"Call It Cybernoia," *Philadelphia Daily News,* March 1, 1997, p. 11.

[9]These criteria are adapted from Elizabeth Kirk, "Evaluating Information Found on the Internet," January 4, 2000. URL: http://milton.mse.jhu.edu:8001/research/education/net.html (February 21, 2000).

[10]For more detail on all aspects of interviewing, see Charles J. Stewart and William B. Cash, Jr., *Interviewing: Principles and Practices,* 9th ed. (New York: McGraw-Hill, 2000).

[11]Criteria for citing Internet documents continue to evolve. The most extensive discussion is Xia Li and Nancy B. Crane, *Electronic Styles: A Handbook for Citing Electronic Information,* 2nd ed. (Medford, N.J.: Information Today, 1996). Salient parts of this work can be accessed online at "Bibliographic Formats for Citing Electronic Information" (http://www.uvm.edu/~ncrane/estyles).

[12]For a fascinating discussion of the creative dimensions of research, see Howard S. Becker, *Tricks of the Trade: How to Think about Your Research while You're Doing It* (Chicago: University of Chicago Press, 1998).

CHAPTER SEVEN

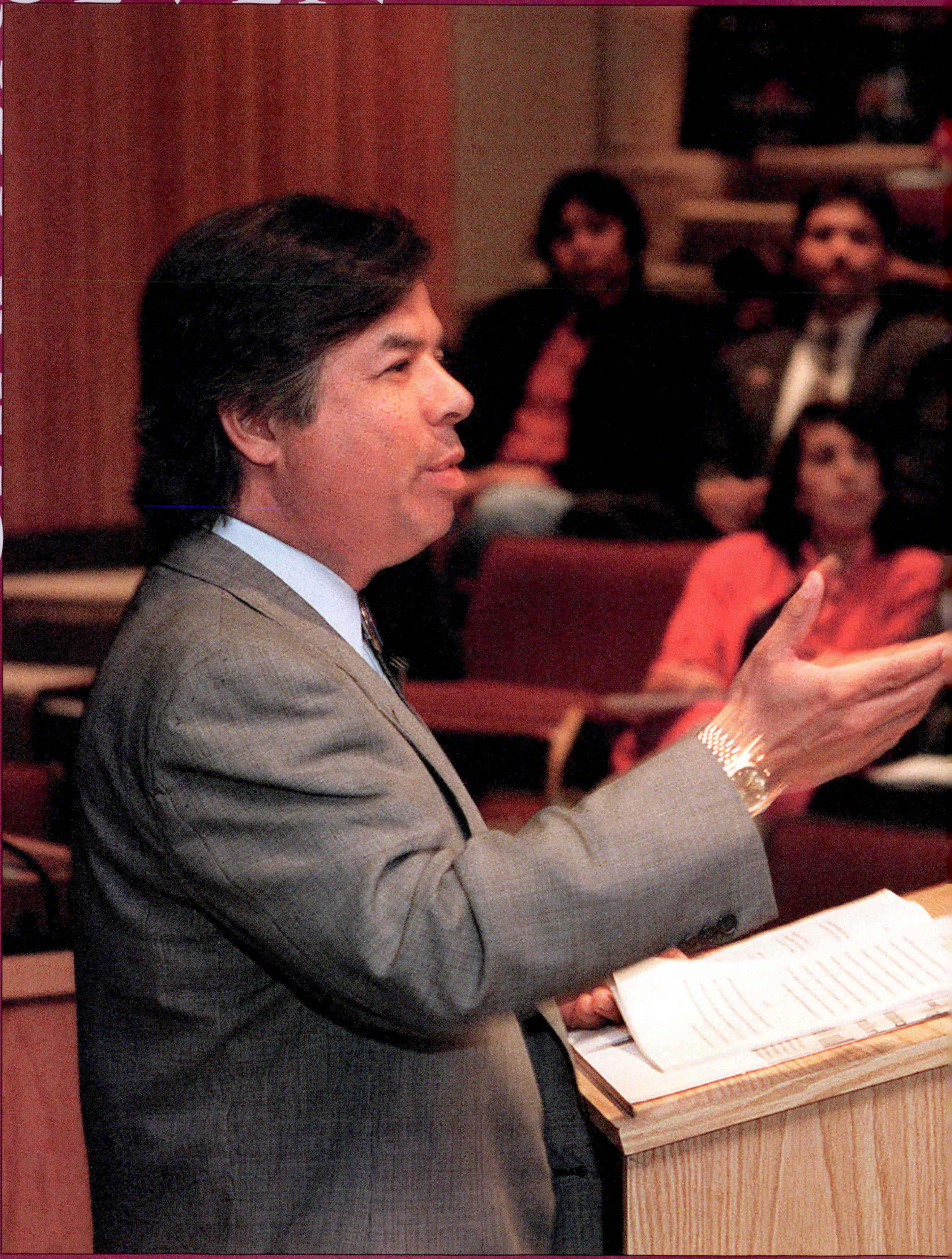

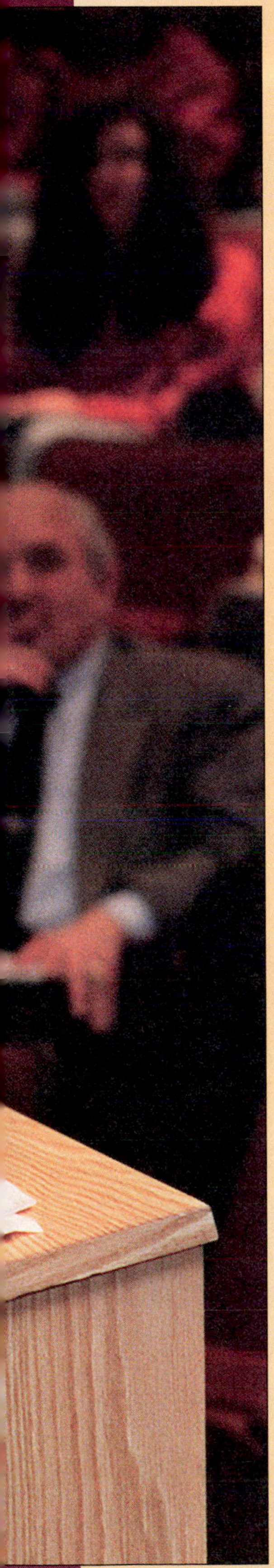

SUPPORTING YOUR IDEAS

Supporting Materials and Critical Thinking

Examples

Brief Examples
Extended Examples
Hypothetical Examples
Tips for Using Examples

Statistics

Understanding Statistics
Tips for Using Statistics
Where to Find Statistics

Testimony

Expert Testimony
Peer Testimony
Quoting versus Paraphrasing
Tips for Using Testimony

Sample Speech with Commentary

Heather Kolpin decided to give her first classroom speech on the benefits of good nutrition. A dedicated fitness enthusiast, she had recently switched to a high-protein diet. Part of her speech ran like this:

"For years we've been told that meat, eggs, and cheese are bad for us and that we should eat more carbohydrates like cereal, grains, pasta, and rice. But too many carbohydrates can unbalance the body and make you tired and overweight. Do you want more energy? Do you want to concentrate better and get higher grades? Do you want to enjoy real meals and still lose those unsightly pounds? If so, you should eat more protein. I've been on a high-protein diet for six months, and I've never felt better or done better in my classes!"

After the speech, Heather's classmates were interested but skeptical. As one remarked, "I know high-protein diets are popular right now, but Heather's no expert on nutrition. Besides, there are lots of diets around, and they all claim to work wonders. Personally, I'd be more convinced if Heather gave some scientific evidence to back up her opinion."

Good speeches are not composed of hot air and generalizations. They need strong supporting materials to bolster the speaker's point of view. In Heather's case, although there is plenty of evidence on the need to balance protein and carbohydrate consumption, many nutritionists have warned about the dangers of overloading on protein. So Heather's listeners were right to be skeptical. Heather made the mistake of generalizing from her own experience with nothing concrete to support her ideas.

The problem with generalizations is that they do not answer the three questions listeners always mentally ask of a speaker: "What do you mean?" "Why should I believe you?" "So what?" Consider, for example, the following sets of statements:

General	Less General	Specific
AIDS is a serious problem in Africa.	The AIDS plague is taking a fearsome toll throughout sub-Saharan Africa.	By the year 2000, more than 12 million people in sub-Saharan Africa had died of AIDS—2.2 million in 1999 alone. Every minute, 11 people worldwide are infected with AIDS, 10 of them in sub-Saharan Africa. Annually, the world's wars take only one-tenth as many lives as AIDS claims in Africa.[1]
Museums are very popular.	Attendance at museums outstrips many other forms of culture and entertainment.	More people in the United States visit museums each year than attend all major-league sports events combined. New York's largest tourist attraction

is not the Statue of Liberty or the Empire State Building, but the Metropolitan Museum of Art, which draws more than 5 million visitors annually.

Racial and ethnic blending is a growing phenomenon.	The blending of racial and ethnic lines is dramatically changing the face of America.	Today there are more than 1.5 million interracial marriages in the U.S.—10 times as many as in 1960. The Census Bureau reports that by 2020 more and more Americans will be of mixed ancestry: black, white, and Hispanic, like singer Mariah Carey. Or black, Asian, American Indian, and white, like golfer Tiger Woods.

Which group of statements do you find most interesting? Most convincing? Chances are you will prefer those in the right-hand column. They are sharp and specific, clear and credible—just the sort of thing a speech needs to come alive.

Supporting Materials and Critical Thinking

The skillful use of supporting materials often makes the difference between a poor speech and a good one. It is also closely related to critical thinking. Using supporting materials is not a matter of haphazardly tossing facts and figures into your speech. You must decide which ideas need to be supported given your audience, topic, and specific purpose. You must do research to find materials that will bring your ideas across clearly and creatively. And you must evaluate your supporting materials to make sure they really do back up your ideas.

As you put your speeches together, you will need to make sure your supporting materials are accurate, relevant, and reliable. You will find yourself asking questions such as "Are my examples representative?" "Am I using statistical measures correctly?" "Am I quoting reputable, qualified sources?" Assessing the supporting materials in your speeches—as well as in the speeches of your classmates—is yet another way in which critical thinking is part of public speaking.

In Chapters 14 and 16, we will look at special uses of supporting materials in informative and persuasive speeches. In this chapter, we focus on the basic kinds of supporting materials—examples, statistics, and testimony—and on general principles for using them effectively and responsibly.

supporting materials The materials used to support a speaker's ideas. The three major kinds of supporting materials are examples, statistics, and testimony.

Examples

Across from a small, grassy park dedicated to Greek and Irish immigrants, Joe Cogliano, whose grandparents were Italian, sells mangoes to Hispanic customers from the back of his truck. Children play tag while chattering in Spanish on O'Brien Terrace, part of a housing project built in 1939 for Irish laborers. The pungent odor of Vietnamese fish sauce fills a Southeast Asian restaurant where Giavis' Greek Grocery once thrived for more than 70 years.[2]

These were the opening lines of an article in *Time* magazine about the interaction of cultures in Lowell, Massachusetts. It illustrates a device well known to magazine writers—and speechmakers: get the audience involved.

example
A specific case used to illustrate or to represent a group of people, ideas, conditions, experiences, or the like.

See how skillfully this example accomplishes the goal. It begins by focusing attention on a particular person (Joe Cogliano). It then provides details of time and place that set the scene vividly before our eyes. We almost feel ourselves there in Lowell buying mangoes from the back of Cogliano's truck, listening to the sound of children, smelling the Vietnamese fish sauce. We would not be nearly as involved if the article had merely said, "Many cultural groups interact in Lowell on a daily basis." The *example* touches something in us that no generalization can.

Research has shown that vivid, concrete examples have strong impact on listeners' beliefs and actions.[3] Without examples, ideas often seem vague, impersonal, and lifeless. With examples, ideas become specific, personal, and lively. This is nowhere better illustrated than in the Bible, which uses all manner of stories, parables, and anecdotes to make abstract principles clear and compelling. There are several kinds of examples you may want to try in your speeches.

Brief Examples

Brief examples—also called specific instances—may be referred to in passing to illustrate a point. The following excerpt uses a brief example to illustrate the miraculous nature of recent advances in creating artificial limbs for accident victims:

brief example
A specific case referred to in passing to illustrate a point.

Changes in technology have made it possible for doctors to work wonders that once seemed impossible. *Roger Charter, for example, lost both his feet when they were crushed in a truck accident. Now he has new feet—made of a springy plastic alloy that duplicates a normal arch. Not only can Roger walk normally, but he can run and play sports again!*

A brief example may also be used to introduce a topic:

When archaeologists broke the seal on Tutankhamen's tomb in the autumn of 1922, they uncovered an amazing treasure—a storehouse of ancient Egyptian art of priceless beauty that had lain, untouched and unseen, for more than 3,000 years. Archaeology is a profession of endless drudgery, painstaking research, and the occasional—very rare—marvelous find.

Another way to use brief examples is to pile them one upon the other until you create the desired impression. Here is how the technique might be used to reinforce the point that Chinese Americans have made many valuable contributions to U.S. life and culture:

> We all know the achievements of current Chinese Americans such as tennis player Michael Chang, novelist Amy Tan, and newscaster Connie Chung. But throughout the twentieth century many other Chinese Americans have played a vital role in U.S. life. The Bing cherry was developed in Oregon by horticulturist Ah Bing. In Florida, frost-resistant oranges were first bred by Lue Gim Gong. Architect I. M. Pei has designed some of America's most important buildings, including the John F. Kennedy Library and the National Gallery of Art. Another architect, Maya Ying Lin, created the design for the Vietnam Veterans Memorial in Washington, D.C.

Extended Examples

Extended examples are often called illustrations, narratives, or anecdotes. They are longer and more detailed than brief examples. By telling a story vividly and dramatically, they pull listeners into the speech. Here is such an example, from a student speech about the astonishing similarities that sometimes exist between identical twins:

> After 40 years of separation from his identical twin, James Lewis began his search for his long-lost brother. They had been separated a few weeks after birth and were adopted by different families. Their reunion took place at the home of the other twin—James Springer. Upon meeting, they found that they had more in common than their first names.
>
> Both had married a woman named Betty, been divorced, and remarried a woman named Sally. Both had similar jobs as deputy sheriffs, McDonald's employees, and gas station attendants. Both liked to build wood furniture in their basement workshops. Both put on 10 pounds as teenagers and lost it later. Both had the same favorite subjects in school, were bad spellers, and suffered from migraine headaches and sleeping problems. All in all, they shared 27 matching characteristics.

This long example captures vividly the many likenesses that often exist between identical twins. The speaker could merely have said, "identical twins are a lot alike," but the story makes the point far more vividly.

Hypothetical Examples

Whether brief or extended, examples can be either factual or hypothetical. All the examples presented up to now have been factual; the incidents they refer to really happened. Sometimes, however, speakers will use a hypothetical example—one that describes an imaginary situation. Usually such examples are brief stories that relate a general principle.

Here is how one student used a hypothetical example to illustrate the need for college students to protect themselves against crime:

> You're tired; you're hungry. You've just spent a long day at College Library and you can't wait to get back to your room. Glancing outside, you remember how quickly it becomes dark. You don't think much of it, though, as you bundle up and head out into the gusty wind. Not until you spy the shadows on the sidewalk or hear the leaves rustling beside you do you wish you weren't alone. You walk quickly, trying to stop

extended example
A story, narrative, or anecdote developed at some length to illustrate a point.

hypothetical example
An example that describes an imaginary or fictitious situation.

Personal examples are an excellent way to clarify ideas and build audience interest. To be most effective, they should be delivered sincerely and with strong eye contact.

View this portion of Rebecca Hanson, "Self-Defense on Campus."

CD: VIDEO CLIP 7.1

your imagination from thinking of murderers and rapists. Only when you are safely inside your room do you relax and try to stop your heart from pounding out of your chest.

Can you remember a time when you felt this way? I would be surprised if you never have. The FBI reported last year that there were three murders, approximately 430 aggravated assaults, 1,400 burglaries, and 80 rapes here in Madison alone. And while these statistics are quite alarming, they don't compare to the numbers of larger metropolitan areas.

This hypothetical example is particularly effective. The speaker creates a realistic scenario, relates it directly to her listeners, and gets them involved in the speech. In addition, she uses figures from the FBI to show that the scenario could really happen to any of her classmates. Whenever you use a hypothetical example, it is a good idea to follow it with statistics or testimony to show that the example is not far-fetched.

Tips for Using Examples

Use Examples to Clarify Your Ideas

You probably use clarifying examples all the time in everyday conversation. If you were explaining to a friend about different body types, you might say, "Look at Professor Shankar. He's a typical ectomorph—tall, thin, and bony."

Examples are an excellent way to clarify unfamiliar or complex ideas. This is why so many teachers use examples in the classroom. Examples put abstract ideas into concrete terms that listeners can easily understand.

This principle works exceptionally well in speeches. Suppose you are talking about suspension bridges. You could give a technical description:

> The suspension bridge has a roadway suspended by vertical cables attached to two or more main cables. The main cables are hung on two towers and have their ends anchored in concrete or bedrock.

If your audience were made up of people familiar with structural systems, they might be able to visualize what a suspension bridge looks like. But for listeners lacking this background, you might want to add a simple example:

> Two well-known suspension bridges are the Golden Gate Bridge in San Francisco and the Brooklyn Bridge in New York.

Because almost everyone has at least seen a picture of the Golden Gate Bridge or the Brooklyn Bridge, using them as examples clarifies your meaning quickly and effectively.

Use Examples to Reinforce Your Ideas

In a speech entitled "Boxing: The Most Dangerous Sport," Rob Goeckel, a student at the University of Wisconsin, argued that professional boxing should be banned in the United States. In addition to noting the dozens of deaths caused by boxing, he deplored the irreparable brain damage sustained by many fighters. He explained that a punch thrown by a heavyweight boxer lands with a force of more than 1,000 pounds, and he provided testimony from neurologists about the consequences of receiving repeated blows to the head. To reinforce his point, Rob cited the example of Muhammad Ali, who suffers from a severe case of Parkinson's diease brought on by his years in the ring. His symptoms include impaired hand-eye coordination, slurred speech, reduced muscle strength, and chronic fatigue. Once the heavyweight champion of the world, Ali "has been reduced to a mere shell of a man, a shaking, silent reminder of the brutality of boxing."

View this portion of Rob Goeckel, "Boxing: The Most Dangerous Sport."

CD: VIDEO CLIP 7.2

This example was especially effective. It put the medical facts about boxing and brain damage in vivid, human terms that everyone could understand. When you use such an example, make sure it is representative—that it does not deal with unusual or exceptional cases. Your listeners are sure to feel betrayed if they suspect you have chosen an atypical example to prove a general point.

Use Examples to Personalize Your Ideas

People are interested in people. As social psychologist Eliot Aronson explains, "Most people are more deeply influenced by one clear, vivid, personal example than by an abundance of statistical data."[4] Whenever you talk to a general audience (such as your speech class), you can include examples that will add human interest to your speech. So far in this section we have seen a number of such examples—the people of Lowell,

Massachusetts, accident victim Roger Charter, and so on. The abstract becomes more meaningful when applied to a person. Which of the following would you be more likely to respond to?

There are many hungry families in our community who could benefit from food donations.

Or:

Let me tell you about Arturo. Arturo is four years old. He has big brown eyes and a mop of black hair and an empty belly. In all his four years on this earth, Arturo has never once enjoyed three square meals in a single day.

Try using examples with human interest in your speeches. You will soon discover why accomplished speakers consider them "the very life of the speech."[5]

Make Your Examples Vivid and Richly Textured

The richly textured example supplies everyday details that bring the example to life. Recall the example on page 167 of identical twins James Lewis and James Springer. The speaker provided us with many details about the twins. They were separated a week after birth and reunited 40 years later. Despite being apart for so long, both had married a woman named Betty. Both had worked as deputy sheriffs and gas station attendants. Both had the same favorite subjects in school. Both were bad spellers and suffered from migraine headaches.

How much less compelling the example would have been if the speaker had merely said:

One set of identical twins actually shared more than two dozen personal traits.

Instead, the details let us see the astounding similarities between James Lewis and James Springer. Those details are much more likely to stay in our minds than a vague statement about "twins who are a lot alike." Remember, the more vivid your examples—brief or extended—the more impact they are likely to have on your audience.

Practice Delivery to Enhance Your Extended Examples

An extended example is just like a story, and the impact of your story will depend as much on delivery as on content. Many students have discovered this the hard way. After spending much time and energy developing a splendid example, they have seen the example fall flat on the day of the speech because they did not take the extra step to make it vivid and gripping for listeners.

When you use an extended example, think of yourself as a storyteller. Don't race through the example as though you were reading a newspaper, but instead use your voice to get listeners involved. Speak faster here to create a sense of action, slower there to build suspense. Raise your voice in some places, lower it in others. Pause occasionally for dramatic effect.

Most important, maintain eye contact with your audience. The easiest way to ruin a fine example is to read it dully from your notes. As you practice the speech, "talk through" your extended examples without relying on your notes. By the day of your speech, you should be able to deliver your extended examples as naturally as if you were telling a story to a group of friends.

Statistics

We live in an age of statistics. Day in and day out we are bombarded with a staggering array of numbers: Elton John has sold over 70 million albums; 12 percent of U.S. children under the age of 18 suffer from some form of psychological illness; France produces almost 2 billion gallons of wine every year; the literacy rate of Iraq is 71 percent; Americans consume more than 700 million pounds of peanut butter annually.

What do all these numbers mean? Most of us would be hard-pressed to say. Yet we feel more secure in our knowledge when we can express it numerically. According to Lord Kelvin, the nineteenth-century physicist, "When you can measure what you are speaking about, and express it in numbers, you know something about it. But when you cannot measure it, when you cannot express it in numbers, your knowledge is . . . meager and unsatisfactory." It is this widely shared belief that makes statistics, when used properly, such an effective way to clarify and support ideas.[6]

statistics
Numerical data.

Like brief examples, statistics are often cited in passing to clarify or strengthen a speaker's points. The following examples show how three students used statistics in their speeches:

To document the perilous state of the earth's animal population: "Worldwatch Institute reports that extinction threatens 11 percent of the world's bird species, 25 percent of mammal species, and 34 percent of fish species."

To emphasize the need for breast cancer research: "According to the Surgeon General's office, a new case of breast cancer is diagnosed every three minutes, and someone dies from breast cancer every twelve minutes."

To illustrate the U.S. teacher shortage: "As stated by the Department of Education, 200,000 new teachers will need to be hired each year for the next 10 years to keep pace with the growing number of students."

Statistics can also be used in combination—stacked up to show the magnitude or seriousness of an issue. We find a good instance of this technique in a student presentation on the dangers of chewing tobacco. To help demonstrate her point that the use of chewing tobacco is a widespread problem, the speaker cited the following figures:

View this portion of Catherine Twohig, "The Dangers of Chewing Tobacco."
CD: VIDEO CLIP 7.3

According to the American Cancer Society, one in every twelve Americans is a regular user of chewing tobacco. The average age of first use is just 10 years old, which means that many children are chewing tobacco when they are in fourth grade. The American Cancer Society also reports that 40 percent of high-school boys have tried chewing tobacco—and, what's worse, 21 percent of kindergartners have tried it. Children are using chewing tobacco before they can even read the warning labels.

This is a well-supported argument. But what if the speaker had merely said:

> Lots of people, including many children, use chewing tobacco.

The second statement is neither as clear nor as convincing as the one containing statistics. The statistics make the speaker's claim credible and specific. Of course, the audience didn't remember all the numbers, but that's all right. The purpose of presenting a series of figures is to create an *overall* impact on listeners. What the audience did recall is that an impressive array of statistics supported the speaker's position.

Understanding Statistics

In his classic book *How to Lie with Statistics,* Darrell Huff exploded the notion that numbers don't lie. Strictly speaking, they don't. But they can be easily manipulated and distorted. For example, which of the following statements is true?

a. Enriched white bread is more nutritious than whole-wheat bread because it contains as much or more protein, calcium, niacin, thiamine, and riboflavin.

b. Whole-wheat bread is more nutritious than white bread because it contains seven times the amount of fiber, plus more iron, phosphorus, and potassium.

As you might expect, *both* statements are true. And you might hear either one of them—depending on who is trying to sell you the bread.

One can play with statistics in all kinds of areas. Which of these statements is true?

a. The cheetah, clocked at 70 miles per hour, is the fastest animal in the world.

b. The pronghorn antelope, clocked at 61 miles per hour, is the fastest animal in the world.

The cheetah, right? Not necessarily. It's true the cheetah can go faster, but only for short sprints. The antelope can maintain its high speed over a much greater distance. So which is faster? It depends on what you're measuring. Put in terms of human races, the cheetah would win the hundred-yard dash, but the antelope would win the marathon.

When you are dealing with money, statistics become even trickier. For instance, consider the following facts:

a. In 1947 President Harry Truman earned a salary of $75,000.

b. In 1967 President Lyndon B. Johnson earned a salary of $100,000.

c. In 1997 President Bill Clinton earned a salary of $200,000.

Which President was paid the most money? It depends. In purely mathematical terms, Clinton is the highest earner. But as we all know, a dollar today does not buy nearly as much as it did when Harry Truman was President. One measure of the inflation rate is the Consumer Price Index, which gauges the value of the dollar in any given year against its purchasing power in 1967. If we apply the Consumer Price Index to the three Presidents' salaries, we can see how much each earned in 1967 dollars:

a. In 1947 President Harry Truman earned a salary of $104,000.

b. In 1967 President Lyndon B. Johnson earned a salary of $100,000.

c. In 1997 President Bill Clinton earned a salary of $59,000.

In other words, although Clinton had the highest salary, the value of his $200,000 was considerably less than the value of Truman's $75,000.

The point is that there is usually more to statistics than meets the eye.[7] When you track down statistics for your speeches, be sure to evaluate them in light of the following questions.

Are the Statistics Representative?

Say that on your way to class you choose ten students at random and ask them whether they favor or oppose government tax credits for students attending private schools. Say also that six approve of such funding and four do not. Would you then be accurate in claiming that 60 percent of the students on your campus favor spending government money for private schools?

Of course not. Ten students is not a big enough sample. But even if it were, other problems would arise. Do the ten students interviewed accurately reflect your school's proportion of freshmen, sophomores, juniors, and seniors? Do they mirror the proportion of male and female students? Are the various majors accurately represented? What about part-time and full-time students? Students of different cultural and religious backgrounds?

In short, make sure your statistics are representative of what they claim to measure.

Are Statistical Measures Used Correctly?

Here are two groups of numbers:

Group A	Group B
7,500	5,400
6,300	5,400
5,000	5,000
4,400	2,300
4,400	1,700

Let us apply to each group three basic statistical measures—the mean, the median and the mode.

The *mean*—popularly called the average—is determined by summing all of the items in a group and dividing by the number of items. The mean for group A is 5,520. For group B it is 3,960.

mean
The average value of a group of numbers.

median
The middle number in a group of numbers arranged from highest to lowest.

The *median* is the middle figure in a group once the figures are put in order from highest to lowest. The median for both group A and group B is exactly the same—5,000.

The *mode* is the number that occurs most frequently in a group of numbers. The mode for group A is 4,400. For group B it is 5,400.

Notice the results:

	Group A	Group B
Mean	5,520	3,960
Median	5,000	5,000
Mode	4,400	5,400

mode
The number that occurs most frequently in a group of numbers.

All of these measures have the same goal—to indicate what is typical or characteristic of a certain group of numbers. Yet see how different the results are, depending on which measure you use.

The differences among the various measures can be striking. For instance, the *mean* salary of local TV news anchorpersons outside of major media centers such as New York, Los Angeles, and Chicago is $60,800 a year. But most local anchors don't earn anywhere near that amount. The mean is inflated by the huge salaries (up to $600,000 a year) paid to star anchors at a few local stations. In contrast, the *median* salary of local news anchors is $43,000—not a sum to scoff at, but still $17,800 less than the average salary.[8]

How might a speaker use these different measures? The owner of a television station would probably cite the *mean* ($60,800) to show that local news anchors are handsomely compensated for their work. An organization of news anchors might emphasize the *median* ($43,000) to demonstrate that salaries are not nearly as high as the station owner makes them out to be. Both speakers would be telling the truth, but neither would be completely honest unless they made clear the meaning of the statistics.

Are the Statistics from a Reliable Source?

Which is the more reliable estimate of the environmental dangers of toxic waste in a landfill—one from the U.S. Environmental Protection Agency or one compiled by the company that owns the landfill? Easy—the estimate by the EPA, which does not have a vested interest in what the figures look like. What about nutritional ratings for fast foods offered by Consumer's Union (a highly respected nonprofit organization) or by Burger King? That's easy too—Consumer's Union, whose claims are not manipulated by advertising executives.

But now things get tougher. What about the competing statistics offered by groups for and against Medicare reform? Or the conflicting numbers tossed out by a school board and the teachers striking against it? In these cases the answer is not so clear, since both sides would present the facts according to their own partisan motives.

As a speaker, you must be aware of possible bias in the use of numbers. Since statistics can be interpreted so many ways and put to so many uses, you should seek figures gathered by objective, nonpartisan sources.

Tips for Using Statistics

Use Statistics to Quantify Your Ideas

The main value of statistics is to give your ideas numerical precision. This can be especially important when you are trying to document the existence of a problem. Examples can bring the problem alive and dramatize it in personal terms. But your listeners may still wonder how many people the problem actually affects. In such a situation, you should turn to statistics. Research has shown that the impact of examples is greatly enhanced when they are followed by statistics that show the examples to be typical.[9]

Suppose you are talking about the need for tougher driver's license requirements for elderly drivers. Part of your speech deals with the growing number of auto accidents caused by drivers age 70 and older. You give an example, you personalize it, you provide many details, as follows:

Marie Wyman's 87th birthday celebration at the Lobster Trap and Steakhouse in Winslow, Maine, ended with a bang. As Wyman backed out of her parking spot, she lost control of her Buick and plowed right through the restaurant's crowded dining room. Tables and chairs scattered as terrified diners scrambled for cover. Twenty-seven people were injured, and police say it was a miracle that no one was killed.

Confronted with this example, a listener might think, "Yes, that's very unfortunate, but is the accident rate of older drivers really that serious a problem?" Anticipating just such a response, a sharp speaker would include figures to quantify the problem:

As explained in *Time* magazine, fatal crashes involving drivers 70 and older have risen 42 percent in the last decade, to more than 5,000 a year. In 20 years, there will be more than 30 million drivers over age 70 in the United States, and highway safety experts warn that the number of people killed in crashes involving elderly motorists is likely to exceed the drunk-driving death toll.

Now the audience is much more likely to agree that there may indeed be a need for tougher licensing requirements.

Use Statistics Sparingly

As helpful as statistics can be, nothing puts an audience to sleep faster than a speech cluttered with numbers from beginning to end. Insert statistics only when they are needed, and then make sure they are easy to grasp. Even the most attentive listener would have trouble sorting out this barrage of figures:

According to the Department of Health and Human Services, life expectancy at birth in the United States ranks eighteenth among 39 industrialized countries for females, twenty-second for males. For comparison, life expectancy for an American male is 71.5 years; for a Japanese male it is 75.8 years. The United States ranks twenty-second among 39 industrialized countries on infant mortality, with a rate almost twice as great as Japan's. Canada ranks seventh. The per capita health expenditure for the U.S. is currently 40 percent higher than Canada and 127 percent higher than Japan.

Instead of drowning your audience in a sea of statistics, use only those that are most important. For example:

Strong supporting materials often make the difference between a poor speech and a good one. This is as true for speeches in business, politics, and the community as for speeches in the classroom.

According to the Department of Health and Human Services, people in the United States have one of the lower life expectancies among industrialized nations. We also have one of the highest rates of infant mortality. Yet we spend much more for health care than other countries—40 percent more per person than Canada and 127 percent more than Japan.

This second statement makes the same point as the first statement, but now the ideas emerge more clearly because they are not lost in a torrent of numbers.

Identify the Sources of Your Statistics

As we have seen, figures are easy to manipulate. This is why careful listeners keep an ear out for the sources of a speaker's statistics. One student learned this by experience. In a speech entitled "Improving American Education: Fact versus Fiction," he claimed that the United States spends more money on education than Japan, Germany, or Sweden—all of which are often pointed to as having superior education systems. The U.S., he said, spends 7 percent of its gross domestic product on education. In comparison, Japan spends 4.8 percent, Germany 4.9 percent, and Sweden 6.8 percent. These are startling statistics—especially given recent concerns about inadequate funding for education in the U.S. But because the student did not say where he got the figures, his classmates were not willing to accept them. They were sure he must be wrong.

As it turned out, the figures were quite reliable. They had come from a lengthy report on education published in *Newsweek* magazine. If the speaker had mentioned the source in his speech, he would have been more successful.[10]

Explain Your Statistics

Statistics don't speak for themselves. They need to be interpreted and related to your listeners. Notice how effectively one speaker did this:

> Children throughout America dream about growing up to be a professional athlete, but the odds of that dream coming true are extremely slim. To take but one sport, of the 20,000 students who play college basketball in any given year, usually no more than 40 will make it to the National Basketball Association. John Slaughter, President of Occidental College, put these figures in perspective when he stated, "The odds of becoming a brain surgeon are greater than the odds of winning a starting spot on the Boston Celtics."

Explaining what statistics mean is particularly important when you deal with large numbers, since they are hard to visualize. How, for example, can we comprehend $5.7 trillion of the U.S. national debt? We could explain that a trillion is a thousand billion and a billion is a thousand million. But that doesn't do much good, since millions and billions are almost as hard to visualize as trillions. Suppose, instead, we translate the huge numbers into terms a listener can relate to. Here is one speaker's solution:

> How much money is a trillion dollars? Think of it this way. If you had $1 million and spent it at the rate of $1,000 a day, you would run out of money in less than three years. If you had $1 billion and spent it at the rate of $1,000 a day, you would not run out of money for almost 3,000 years. And if you had $1 trillion and spent it at the rate of $1,000 a day, you wouldn't run out of money for nearly 3 million years!

Whenever you use statistics in your speeches, think of how you can make them meaningful to your audience. Rather than simply reciting figures about, say, the short-term and long-term consequences of excessive drinking on college campuses, find a way to bring those figures home to your audience. You might say, as did one speaker:

> According to the Office for Substance Abuse Prevention, alcohol is the leading cause of death among young adults. Furthermore, of college students currently enrolled in the United States, more than 240,000 will eventually lose their lives to alcohol. Two hundred and forty thousand—that's the current student population of this university six times over.

Or suppose you're discussing the crime rate in the United States. You could say, "The Foundation for Crime Prevention Education reports that the rate of assault is six times higher than in 1960, and the FBI indicates that every 16 seconds a murder, rape, robbery, or assault takes place." These are alarming statistics, but they are likely to go in one ear and out the other unless you bring them home to your audience. Here's what one student said in her speech:

View Joveta Dixon, "Responsible Drinking," and Rebecca Hanson, "Self-Defense on Campus."

CD: VIDEO CLIP 7.4

According to the Foundation for Crime Prevention Education, violence and crime have dramatically increased. An American is six times more likely to be assaulted with a weapon today than in 1960. The FBI reports that someone is either murdered, raped, assaulted, or robbed every 16 seconds. This means that today, at the end of our 50-minute class period, approximately 187 people will have been victims of a violent crime.

Be creative in thinking of ways to relate your statistics to your audience. This is probably the single most important step you can take to make statistics work in your speeches.

Round Off Complicated Statistics

Mount Kilimanjaro is 19,341 feet high; the official world land speed record is 622.287 miles per hour; the world's highest waterfall has a total drop of 3,212 feet; the greatest attendance at any boxing match was 135,132 people; the moon is 238,855 miles from earth.

These are intriguing figures, but they are too complicated to be readily understood by listeners. Unless there is an important reason to give exact numbers, you should round off most statistics. You might say that Mount Kilimanjaro is 19,300 feet high; the world land speed record is more than 622 miles per hour; the world's highest waterfall has a drop of some 3,200 feet; the greatest attendance at any boxing match was 135,000; and the moon is 239,000 miles from earth.

Use Visual Aids to Clarify Statistical Trends

Visual aids can save you a lot of time, as well as make your statistics easier to comprehend. Suppose you are discussing the number of major strikes by labor unions in the United States since World War II. You could start by explaining that after the war, during the early 1950s, there were a record number of strikes involving 1,000 or more workers—including the 1950 walkout of 370,000 United Mine Workers that crippled the nation's industries. Then, after the start of Dwight Eisenhower's presidency in 1953, the number of strikes declined fairly steadily until 1964, when they started climbing to a peak of more than 400 in 1968. After a sharp decline in the early 1970s, they jumped again in 1975 to the highest level in two decades. Finally, the number of strikes took a dramatic turn downward during the Reagan years of the 1980s and reached a record low in 1999 under President Clinton.

These are interesting statistics, and you could build a good speech around them. But strung together in a few sentences they are hard to digest. Figure 7.1 shows how much more clearly the points can be made with a simple graph. We shall discuss visual aids in detail in Chapter 13. For the moment, keep in mind that they can be helpful in presenting statistical information.

Where to Find Statistics

Statistics can be found in any kind of reputable publication—books, magazines, newspapers, scholarly journals, government documents, business reports, and so forth. A world almanac (there are several established versions) can be a treasure house of interesting numbers.

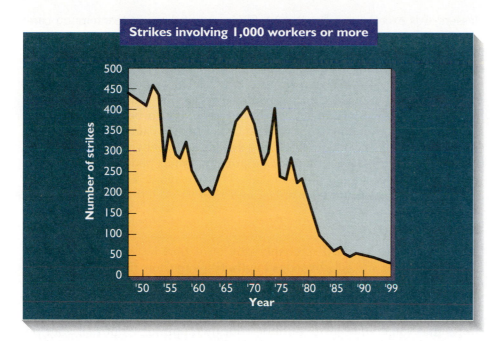

Strikes involving 1,000 workers or more

Figure 7.1

There are also some sources devoted solely to statistics. They include the *Statistical Yearbook* (put out by the United Nations) and the *Statistical Abstract of the United States* (published annually since 1878 and also available on CD-ROM). These sources contain statistics on everything from the U.S. economy to world population trends. The *Guinness Book of World Records* offers more esoteric information, such as the weight of the world's largest polished diamond, the internal temperature of the sun, and how many hours of television the average child watches by the age of 18.

You will find these and other handy sources of statistics in the reference room of your library (see Chapter 6). Besides being easy to use, they can be fascinating to look through. This is why the *Guinness Book of World Records* remains a best-seller year after year.

You can also garner a wealth of statistics from the Internet. Many sites on the World Wide Web provide numerical data—much of it more current than that found in printed works. As with any kind of information acquired off the Internet, you need to make sure your statistics come from reliable sources such as universities, government agencies, nonpartisan organizations, and the like. One excellent source is the *Statistical Abstract of the United States* website (http://www.census.gov/statab/www). Another is FedStats, which provides links to more than 70 federal agencies that produce statistics of public interest (http://www.fedstats.gov).

Testimony

Imagine you are talking with a friend about the classes you plan to take next term. You are not sure whether to sign up for Psychology 230 or Accounting 181. Both are requirements; both meet at the same time of day. Your friend says, "I took those classes last year. They're both good, but Professor

Hassam was excellent in Psych 230. She's one of the best teachers on campus. If she's teaching the course next term, I'd take it for sure." You check the timetable and find that Professor Hassam is indeed slated for Psychology 230. You sign up for her course.

As this story illustrates, we are often influenced by the *testimony* of other people when making decisions in everyday life. Much the same thing happens in public speaking. Just as you are likely to be swayed by your friend's recommendation about which class to take, so audiences tend to respect the opinions of people who have special knowledge or experience on the topic at hand. By quoting or paraphrasing such people, you can give your ideas greater strength and impact. The two major kinds of testimony are expert testimony and peer testimony.

testimony
Quotations or paraphrases used to support a point.

Expert Testimony

expert testimony
Testimony from people who are recognized experts in their fields.

In most speeches you will probably rely on expert testimony—testimony from people who are acknowledged authorities in their fields. Expert testimony is especially helpful for student speakers because students are seldom recognized as experts on their speech topics. Citing the views of people who are experts is a good way to lend credibility to your speeches. It shows that you are not just mouthing your own opinions, but that your position is supported by people who are knowledgeable about the topic.[11]

Expert testimony is even more important when a topic is controversial or when the audience is skeptical about a speaker's point of view. The following story explains how one speaker enlisted expert testimony for a speech on reforming the U.S. Social Security system:

As Julia Wang did her research on how to make Social Security more equitable for younger taxpayers, she became convinced that individual citizens should be allowed to invest their Social Security funds directly in the stock market. Yet Julia was not an expert on the matter. Nor did she have any firsthand experience with the Social Security system. How could she convince her audience to accept her ideas?

Statistics helped, and so did examples. But on such a controversial topic, that was not enough. So to reinforce her credibility, Julia quoted a wide range of experts who agreed with her—Illinois Congressman John Porter; Jeffrey Sachs, a Harvard economics professor; former U.S. Social Security Commissioner Dorcas Hardy; Jose Piñera, president of the International Center for Pension Reform; former U.S. Secretary of Commerce Peter G. Peterson; and Timothy Penny of the Democratic Leadership Council. By citing the views of these experts—some of whom might be expected to disagree with her point of view—Julia made her speech much more persuasive.

Peer Testimony

peer testimony
Testimony from ordinary people with firsthand experience or insight on a topic.

Another type of testimony often used in speeches is peer testimony—opinions of people like ourselves; not prominent figures, but ordinary citizens who have firsthand experience on the topic. This kind of testimony is especially valuable because it gives a more personal viewpoint on issues than can be gained from expert testimony. It conveys the feelings, the knowledge, the insight of people who speak with the voice of genuine experience.

For example, if you were speaking about the barriers faced by people with physical disabilities, you would surely include testimony from doctors and other medical authorities. But in this case, the expert testimony would be limited because it cannot communicate what it really means to have a physical disability. To communicate that, you need statements from people who have physical disabilities—such as the following:

Itzhak Perlman, the world-renowned violinist whose legs are paralyzed, once said: "When you are in a wheelchair, people don't talk to you. Perhaps they think it is contagious, or perhaps they think crippled legs mean a crippled mind. But whatever the reason, they treat you like a thing."

Paul Longmore, who lost the use of his legs as a child, notes that most people are uncomfortable in the presence of someone who is handicapped. "It's only when they really go out of their way to get to know us," he says, "that they realize we are just as bright, witty, and companionable as they are."

There is no way expert testimony can express these ideas with the same authenticity and emotional impact.

Quoting versus Paraphrasing

The statements from Itzhak Perlman and Paul Longmore are presented as direct quotations. Testimony can also be presented by paraphrasing. Rather than quoting someone verbatim, you present the gist of that person's ideas in your own words—as did one student in her speech about America's potential water crisis:

Writing in *Audubon* magazine, Dr. Peter Bourne, president of Global Water, a nonpartisan educational group in Washington, D.C., said most Americans do not yet realize the extent and urgency of the water problem. At the present rate, he says, we are headed for a crisis that will change the way we live in every part of the nation.

direct quotation
Testimony that is presented word for word.

When should you use a direct quotation as opposed to paraphrasing? The standard rule of thumb is that quotations are most effective when they are brief, when they convey your meaning better than you can, and when they are particularly eloquent, witty, or compelling. If you find a quotation that fits these criteria, then recite the quotation word for word.

Paraphrasing is better than direct quotation in two situations: (1) when the wording of a quotation is obscure or cumbersome, as is often the case with government documents; (2) when a quotation is longer than two or three sentences. Audiences often tune out partway through lengthy quotations, which tend to interrupt the flow of a speaker's ideas. Since the rest of the speech is in your own words, you should put longer quotations in your own words as well.

paraphrase
To restate or summarize a source's ideas in one's own words.

Tips for Using Testimony

Quote or Paraphrase Accurately

Accurate quotation involves three things: making sure you do not misquote someone; making sure you do not violate the meaning of statements you paraphrase; making sure you do not quote out of context. Of these, the last is the most subtle—and the most dangerous. By quoting out of context, you can twist someone's remarks so as to prove almost anything. Take movie advertisements. A critic pans a movie with these words:

quoting out of context
Quoting a statement in such a way as to distort its meaning by removing the statement from the words and phrases surrounding it.

> This movie is a colossal bore. From beginning to end it is a disaster. What is meant to be brilliant dialogue is about as fascinating as the stuff you clean out of your kitchen drain.

But when the movie is advertised in the newspapers, what appears in huge letters over the critic's name? "COLOSSAL! FROM BEGINNING TO END— BRILLIANT! FASCINATING!"

This is so flagrant as to be humorous. But quoting out of context can have serious consequences. In 1992 Janet Gastil was challenging incumbent U.S. Representative Duncan Hunter for election in California's 52nd congressional district. In a public forum featuring the candidates, Gastil was asked her opinion about a 10-cent-per-gallon gasoline tax, which had been proposed by presidential candidate Ross Perot. Gastil replied as follows:

> The 10-cent tax on gasoline—most Americans would vote against that; most Americans would vote their Congressman out of office if their Congressman proposed it. *However, it would go a long way toward improving America's infrastructure.* The price of gasoline in this country is artificially low—look what it is in Europe, and you'll see what I mean. But I'm not proposing any tax increases of any kind.

Gastil's line about America's deteriorating infrastructure was a throwaway. The main point of her full statement was that she did not favor any new taxes. When Hunter responded to the same question, he acknowledged Gastil's opposition and stated that he, too, disapproved of a gas tax. But several weeks later, Hunter ran television ads quoting Gastil's words about infrastructure improvements and claiming that she favored a gas tax—except that the words were quoted out of context, without the rest of Gastil's original statement opposing the gas tax.

Despite Gastil's protests, Hunter refused to withdraw the ads. They ran throughout the crucial final week of the campaign and helped turn the election in Hunter's favor. When the votes were counted, Gastil had lost and Hunter had won. According to KGTV, Channel 10, in San Diego, Hunter's "twisting and distorting the truth" had cost Gastil the election.

Clearly, quoting or paraphrasing accurately is an important ethical responsibility for all communicators.

Use Testimony from Qualified Sources

We have all become accustomed to the celebrity testimonial in television and magazine advertising. The professional golfer endorses a particular brand of clubs. The movie star praises a certain hair spray or shampoo. The basketball player plugs a type of athletic shoe. So far, so good. These are the tools of the trade for the people who endorse them.

But what happens when a comedian endorses a long-distance company? A tennis player represents a line of cameras? A retired golfer extols the virtues of a brand of motor oil? Do they know more about these products than you or I? Probably not. They have been paid large sums of money to be photographed with the product in hopes that their popularity will rub off on it.

Being a celebrity or an authority in one area does not make someone competent in other areas. Listeners will find your speeches much more credible if you use testimony from sources qualified *on the subject at hand.* As we have seen, this may include either recognized experts or ordinary citizens with special experience on the speech topic.

Use Testimony from Unbiased Sources

In a speech about the controversial sleeping pill Halcion, which has been blamed for causing side effects such as amnesia, anxiety, delusions, and hostility, a student said:

> Pharmacologist Robert Shaw, director of project management at the Upjohn Company, the Michigan-based manufacturer of Halcion, maintains that it has no more serious side effects than any other sleeping pill when it is used properly. "The vast majority of studies," Shaw says, "back us up on that point."

As you might expect, the student's classmates were not persuaded. After all, what would you expect someone at Upjohn to say—that its product is unsafe and causes psychiatric disorders? One listener reacted in this way: "For all I know, the statement by Shaw may be true, but he is hardly an unbiased source. I wish you had cited an impartial expert instead."

Careful listeners are suspicious of opinion from biased or self-interested sources. Be sure to use testimony from credible, competent, objective authorities.

Identify the People You Quote or Paraphrase

The usual way to identify your source is to name the person and sketch her or his qualifications before presenting the testimony. The following excerpt is from a student speech titled "Dandelions: The Uncommon Weed":

> In addition to being tasty, dandelions are extremely nutritious. According to Peter Gail, a professor of economic botany at Cleveland State University, "The dandelion's nutrient qualities read almost like a One-a-Day vitamin. Dandelion greens have 50 percent more vitamin C than tomatoes, twice as much protein as eggplant, and double the fiber of asparagus."

Had the speaker not identified Peter Gail, listeners would not have had the foggiest notion who he is or why his opinion should be heeded.

For another example, look at this statement from a speech in favor of beginning foreign language instruction in the elementary schools:

The Supporting Materials Checklist can help you prepare your speeches.

CD: SPEECH CHECKLIST

View Susan Hirsch, "Dandelions," and Renee Varghese, "Multicultural, Multilingual."

CD: VIDEO CLIP 7.5

John Silber, Chancellor of Boston University and Chairman of the Massachusetts Board of Education, remarks: "It is quite clear that remarkable competence in a language can be achieved in three years—if these years are the ages three, four, and five. There is no question that for the average child to become bilingual, the earlier the better."

After this statement, there is no doubt about Silber's qualifications or why the audience should respect his judgment on the subject of education.

Nor are students the only speakers who need to identify their sources. Whether you are speaking in a classroom or a courtroom, at a business meeting or a technical conference, to a community organization or a religious gathering, you will be much more effective if you make clear to your audience why they should accept the testimony of the people you quote or paraphrase. As we saw in Chapter 2, identifying the source of testimony is also an important ethical responsibility. If you use another person's words or ideas without giving credit to that person, you will be guilty of plagiarism. This is true whether you paraphrase the original source or quote it verbatim.

Examples, statistics, and testimony are all helpful devices for the speaker. Depending on your topic, you may want to use some of them, all of them, or none of them. Remember, they are tools, and they all serve the same purpose—getting your message across to your listeners.

Sample Speech with Commentary

The following speech illustrates how to work supporting materials into a presentation. As you read, study how the speaker uses a variety of examples, statistics, and quotations to make the ideas clear, credible, and convincing.

Suffer the Children

Commentary	Speech
The speaker begins with an extended example to gain attention and interest. The example is specific and detailed. We are told Matthew Garvey's name and age, where he lived, the kind of work he did, and how he was injured. These are the kinds of details that bring examples to life and help get listeners involved in a speech.	Matthew Garvey was just 13 years old when he was hired by Quality Car Wash in Laurel, Maryland, to towel-dry cars as they came off the line. Not long after he began working, Matthew lost his right leg when it got caught in an industrial machine used to suck the moisture out of the towels. After investigating, the U.S. Department of Labor fined the car wash for illegally hiring a minor and for operating a machine with a broken safety lid.
The speaker moves smoothly into testimony suggesting that the opening story is representative of a major problem in the U.S. When you use an extended example, it is usually a good idea to precede or follow	This is just one of the more tragic examples of what Jeffrey Newman of the National Child Labor Committee calls the "crisis" of child labor law abuses in the United States. In researching this speech, I discovered that employers from New York to California are breaking the law by hiring children from

the example with statistics or testimony showing that the example is not unusual or exceptional.

In her first main point the speaker explores the problem of child labor law violations in the United States. She begins by summarizing the provisions of the law. Notice how she identifies the source of her information and integrates that information deftly into the speech.

Statistics in this and the next paragraph back up the speaker's point that violations of child labor laws are widespread in the U.S. Rather than giving the exact number of violations, she rounds them off, making them easier to grasp and recall.

The speaker uses a combination of statistics and testimony to support her point about child labor law abuses in the garment industry. The statement from Thomas Gubiak is an example of expert testimony; the closing quotation from Faviola Flores is an instance of peer testimony.

A series of brief examples supports the speaker's claim about the pervasiveness of child labor law violations. Because the examples deal with large companies such as Sears and Toys 'R Us, they provide strong evidence to reinforce the speaker's point that violations of the law are widespread.

ages 7 to 17 who often put in long, hard hours in dangerous conditions. Today I would like to show you the extent of the problem and how it jeopardizes the education and safety of millions of young people.

To understand the problem of child labor law violations, we need to begin by looking at the provisions of the law. As explained in a 1997 study by Douglas Kruse of the School of Management and Labor Relations at Rutgers University, the U.S. Fair Labor Standards Act sets a minimum working age of 14. It limits 14-year-olds and 15-year-olds to three hours of work on school days, prohibits them from working after 7 at night, and allows them a total of 18 work hours per week during the school year. The law also restricts employment of children under 18 in dangerous jobs such as construction, meat-cutting, and mining.

Passed in 1938 and amended several times since, the Fair Labor Standards Act was designed to prevent the exploitation of child labor that took place during the nineteenth century. Yet today violations of the law are shockingly widespread. According to the Associated Press, 148,000 minors in the U.S. are employed illegally in nonagricultural jobs during an average week, working too many hours or in hazardous conditions. In addition, the National Child Labor Committee reported in 1996 that more than 110,000 children work illegally on U.S. farms.

Some of the most serious violations occur in garment industry factories known as sweatshops that hire immigrant children at rates well below minimum wage. The Associated Press estimates that as many as 2,600 minors are employed illegally in New York City sweatshops. Thomas Gubiak, head of the city's garment district task force, says "most of the children in these factories are below 18, some as young as 8." Like Faviola Flores, a 15-year-old Mexican girl in a Manhattan sweatshop, they toil long days in unsafe conditions for as little as $3.00 an hour. "I don't like working here," Flores says, "but I have no choice."

Although the exploitation of child labor has been a problem in the garment trade since the 1800s, it can be found in almost every industry that employs minors. In May 1999, Sears, Roebuck and Company was fined $325,000 for using minors to operate hazardous equipment. In January 2000, the national retailer Toys 'R Us was fined $200,000 for scheduling 14- and 15-year-olds for too many hours. Also in January 2000, Wagner's Meats of New Orleans was fined nearly $150,000 for illegally employing 27 minors in dangerous jobs and for exceeding federal hour limits.

The speaker begins her second main point—that violations of child labor laws have serious consequences for the education and physical safety of young workers.

The quotation from Hugh McDaid, like others in the speech, is short and forceful. There is no reason to use a direct quotation unless it makes the point more clearly and forcefully than you can in your own words.

Here the speaker paraphrases rather than quoting verbatim. Notice that she gives the name of the book she is paraphrasing from and identifies its authors. As we saw in Chapter 2, speakers have an ethical obligation to indicate the sources of paraphrases, as well as of quotations.

The examples in this paragraph show specific cases in which teenagers were injured or killed by the violation of child labor laws. The extended example about Michael Hurcone is especially effective. Filled with specific details that make it interesting and credible, it puts the speaker's point in human terms with which the audience can identify.

In this paragraph the speaker presents testimony and statistics to prove that the examples in the previous paragraph are not atypical.

The speaker begins her conclusion by summarizing the two main points she had made in the body of the speech. She then ends with a dramatic quotation. As we shall see in Chapter 9, this is an effective way to pull a speech together and to reinforce its central idea.

Like other businesses caught breaking child labor laws, Sears and Wagner's have tried to downplay the seriousness of their offenses. But the growing epidemic of child labor law violations threatens both the education and the physical safety of young workers.

The educational consequences are most damaging to illegal underage employees who work instead of attending school. As Hugh McDaid of New York City's garment task force says, illegal underage workers "sacrifice their education and literally commit themselves to a life of working in a sweatshop. They have no future." But even for children who do attend school, too many hours at work can harm their education. In their book *When Teenagers Work,* psychology professors Ellen Greenberger and Laurence Steinberg note that intensive levels of work among youth tend to produce higher truancy and lower grades. According to Greenberger and Steinberg, one study after another has found that working more than a very few hours a week has a negative impact on teenagers' academic performance.

Not only do child workers harm their education, but they often endanger their physical safety as well. Recall the story I told in my introduction about Matthew Garvey, the 13-year-old who lost his leg while working at a car wash. Even more tragic is the case of Michael Hurcone, a 17-year-old Pennsylvania high-school student. While employed at a supermarket, he was working with a bailer—a machine that crushes and binds cardboard boxes and is supposed to be off-limits to minors. Noticing that some material was stuck in the bailer, Michael tried to free up the jam when he got caught in the machine. It crushed his body for 30 minutes before he suffocated.

Nor are these isolated examples. As U.S. Labor Secretary Alexis Herman stated in June 1999, "too many young people are being killed or hurt" on the job. According to Herman, nearly 70 minors are killed at work each year and another 200,000 are injured—most in accidents involving infractions of child labor laws.

In the light of all this evidence, there can be no doubt that the violation of child labor laws is a widespread problem with serious consequences. The issue is well summarized by former U.S. Senator Howard Metzenbaum of Ohio, who stated after congressional hearings on the subject, "I shudder to think that children the same age as my own grandchildren are being robbed of an education, their limbs, and indeed, their lives through illegal child labor."

Summary

Good speeches are not composed of hot air and unfounded assertions. They need strong supporting materials to bolster the speaker's point of view. In fact, the skillful use of supporting materials often makes the difference between a good speech and a poor one. The three basic types of supporting materials are examples, statistics, and testimony.

In the course of a speech you may use brief examples—specific instances referred to in passing—and sometimes you may want to give several brief examples in a row to create a stronger impression. Extended examples—often called illustrations, narratives, or anecdotes—are longer and more detailed. Hypothetical examples describe imaginary situations and can be quite effective for relating ideas to the audience. All three kinds of examples help to clarify ideas, to reinforce ideas, or to personalize ideas. To be most effective, though, they should be vivid and richly textured.

Statistics can be extremely helpful in conveying your message as long as you use them sparingly and explain them so that they are meaningful to your audience. Above all, you should understand your statistics and use them fairly. Numbers can easily be manipulated and distorted. Make sure your figures are representative of what they claim to measure, that you use statistical measures correctly, and that you take statistics only from reliable sources.

Testimony is especially helpful for student speakers because students are seldom recognized as experts on their speech topics. Citing the views of people who are experts is a good way to make your ideas more credible. When you include testimony in a speech, you can either quote someone verbatim or paraphrase his or her words. As with statistics, there are guidelines for using testimony. Be sure to quote or paraphrase accurately and to cite qualified, unbiased sources. If the source is not generally known to your audience, be certain to establish his or her credentials.

Key Terms

supporting materials (165)
example (166)
brief example (166)
extended example (167)
hypothetical example (167)
statistics (171)
mean (173)
median (174)

mode (174)
testimony (180)
expert testimony (180)
peer testimony (180)
direct quotation (181)
paraphrase (181)
quoting out of context (181)

Review Questions

After reading this chapter, you should be able to answer the following questions:

1. Why do you need supporting materials in your speeches?

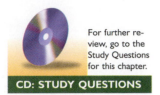

For further review, go to the Study Questions for this chapter.

CD: STUDY QUESTIONS

2. What are the three kinds of examples discussed in this chapter? How might you use each kind to support your ideas?

3. What are five tips for using examples in your speeches?

4. Why is it so easy to lie with statistics? What three questions should you ask to judge the reliability of statistics?

5. What are six tips for using statistics in your speeches?

6. What is testimony? Explain the difference between expert testimony and peer testimony.

7. What are four tips for using testimony in your speeches?

Exercises for Critical Thinking

1. Each of the following statements violates at least one of the criteria for effective supporting materials discussed in the chapter. Identify the flaw (or flaws) in each statement.

   a. In the words of one expert, "Internet growth will continue to be a major economic fact of life for at least the next 10 years. If I were looking for a place to invest, I'd look first to Internet stocks, whose value will keep going up and up."

   b. According to the *New York Times Almanac,* San Francisco has the highest per capita annual income of any U.S. city—$41,128. The lowest per capita annual income belongs to McAllen-Edinburg-Mission, Texas, at $12,005. The average per capita annual income for all U.S. metropolitan areas is $26,840.

   c. In a random survey taken last month of 320 members of the American Association of Retired Persons, 96 percent of those interviewed opposed any major changes in the Social Security system. Clearly, then, the American people oppose such changes.

   d. As Brad Pitt noted in a recent interview, global warming is one of the world's most serious problems. If the industrialized nations do not take greater action to bring it under control, Pitt said, the ecosystem of the entire planet will be permanently damaged.

   e. According to statistics compiled by the Board of Regents, the median salary for professors at our state university is $56,938. This shows that professors average almost $57,000 a year in salary.

   f. It's just not true that media violence has a strong influence on crimes by young people. All my friends watch television, go to the movies, and play video games, and none of us has ever committed a violent crime.

   g. According to a poll conducted for ATT, most people prefer ATT's long-distance service to that of MCI or Sprint.

2. Analyze the speech in Appendix B by Renee Varghese ("Multicultural, Multilingual"). Identify the main points of the speech and the supporting materials used for each. Evaluate the speaker's use of supporting materials in light of the criteria discussed in this chapter.

Applying the POWER of Public Speaking

While driving home from Thanksgiving dinner with your family, you are blind-sided by a drunk driver. Miraculously, everyone involved is uninjured, but you know the outcome could easily have been different. Shaken by the experience, you have become committed to working for tougher legal and judicial action against drunk driving.

Your state ranks among the lowest in the fight against drunk drivers, but you know a bill will be introduced in the next session of the state senate to change that. To build support for the bill, you will be speaking to several local service organizations. You will tell them about your personal experience and provide testimony in support of the new legislation, but you will also need to support your speech with national and state drunk-driving statistics. Because your accident occurred on Thanksgiving, you also want to know if anyone has compiled figures that correlate drunk-driving accidents with specific holidays throughout the year.

As part of your research, you decide to check the website of Mothers Against Drunk Driving (http://www.madd.org/). What do you find that will help you in your speech? Be specific.

Notes

[1]George Will, "AIDS Crushes a Continent," *Newsweek* (January 10, 2000), p. 64.

[2]Ann Blackman, "Lowell's Little Acre," *Time* (Fall 1993), p. 34.

[3]Dean C. Kazoleas, "A Comparison of the Persuasive Effectiveness of Qualitative versus Quantitative Evidence: A Test of Explanatory Hypotheses," *Communication Quarterly,* 41 (1993), pp. 40–50.

[4]Eliot Aronson, *The Social Animal,* 7th ed. (New York: W. H. Freeman, 1995), p. 93.

[5]James A. Winans, *Speech-Making* (New York: Appleton-Century-Crofts, 1922), p. 141. W. Lance Haynes, "Public Speaking Pedagogy in the Media Age," *Communication Education,* 39 (1990), p. 100, suggests that examples may be especially valuable in speeches because they fit with the fluid, personal nature of oral experience.

[6]Over the years, there has been much debate over whether statistics or examples have more impact on listeners. For a recent study that gives the nod to statistics, see Mike Allen and Raymond W. Preiss, "Comparing the Persuasiveness of Narrative and Statistical Evidence Using Meta-Analysis," *Communication Research Reports,* 14 (1997), pp. 125–131.

[7]For two fascinating works on the use and misuse of statistics, see John Allen Paulos, *A Mathematician Reads the Newspaper* (New York: Basic Books, 1995), and Cynthia Crossen, *Tainted Truth: The Manipulation of Fact in America* (New York: Simon & Schuster, 1994).

[8]Bob Papper, Andrew Sharma, and Michael Gerhard, "Salaries Moving Up," *Communicator* (February 1996), pp. 16–23.

[9]John C. Reinard, "The Empirical Study of the Persuasive Effects of Evidence: The Status After Fifty Years of Research," *Human Communication Research,* 15 (1988), p. 25.

[10]For research confirming the preference of listeners for unbiased, objective evidence, see Reinard, "Persuasive Effects of Evidence," p. 34.

[11]See Daniel J. O'Keefe, *Persuasion: Theory and Research* (Newbury Park, Calif.: Sage, 1990), pp. 135–136.

CHAPTER EIGHT

ORGANIZING THE BODY OF THE SPEECH

Organization Is Important

Main Points

Number of Main Points
Strategic Order of Main Points
Tips for Preparing Main Points

Supporting Materials

Connectives

Transitions
Internal Previews
Internal Summaries
Signposts

I f you thumb through any mail-order catalogue today, you will discover that many of the items for sale are *organizers*—closet organizers, kitchen organizers, office organizers, audio and video equipment organizers. Read enough catalogues, and you must conclude that if something exists, it can be organized.

Why all this quest for organization? Obviously, when the objects you possess are well organized, they serve you better. There's little point in having multiple possessions if you can't find them when you need them. Organization allows you to see what you have and to put your hands immediately on the garment, the tool, the tape, the piece of paper, the CD you want without a frenzied search.

Much the same is true of your speeches. If they are well organized, they will serve you better. Organization allows you—and your listeners—to see what ideas you have and to put mental "hands" on the most important ones.

Organization Is Important

Several years ago a college professor took a well-organized speech and scrambled it by randomly changing the order of its sentences. He then had a speaker deliver the original version to one group of listeners and the scrambled version to another group. After the speeches, he gave a test to see how well each group understood what they had heard. Not surprisingly, the group that heard the original, unscrambled speech scored much higher than the other group.[1]

A few years later, two professors repeated the same experiment at another school. But instead of testing how well the listeners comprehended each speech, they tested to see what effects the speeches had on the listeners' attitudes toward the speakers. They found that people who heard the well-organized speech believed the speaker to be much more competent and trustworthy than did those who heard the scrambled speech.[2]

These are just two of many studies that show the importance of organization in effective speechmaking. They confirm what most of us know from experience. How many times have you listened to someone who rambled aimlessly from one idea to another? You realize how difficult it is to pay attention to the speaker, much less to understand the message. In fact, when students explain what they hope to learn from their speech class, they almost always put "the ability to organize my ideas more effectively" near the top of the list.

This ability is especially vital for speechmaking. Listeners demand coherence. They have little patience with speakers who bounce wildly from idea to idea. Keep in mind that listeners—unlike readers—cannot flip back to a previous page if they have trouble grasping a speaker's ideas. In this respect a speech is much like a movie. Just as a director must be sure viewers can follow the plot of a film from beginning to end, so must a speaker be sure listeners can follow the progression of ideas in a speech from beginning to end. This requires that speeches be organized *strategically*. They should be put together in particular ways to achieve particular results with particular audiences.

Speech organization is important for other reasons as well. As we saw in Chapter 1, it is closely connected to critical thinking. When you work to organize your speeches, you gain practice in the general skill of establishing clear relationships among your ideas. This skill will serve you well throughout your college days and in almost any career you may choose. In addition, there is evidence that using a clear, specific method of speech organization can boost your confidence as a speaker and improve your ability to deliver a message fluently.[3]

The first step in developing a strong sense of speech organization is to gain command of the three basic parts of a speech—introduction, body, and conclusion—and the strategic role of each. In this chapter we deal with the body of the speech. The next chapter will take up the introduction and conclusion.

There are good reasons for talking first about the body of the speech. The body is the longest and most important part. Also, you will usually prepare the body first. It is much easier to create an effective introduction after you know exactly what you will say in the body.

The process of organizing the body of a speech begins when you determine the main points.

strategic organization
Putting a speech together in a particular way to achieve a particular result with a particular audience.

Main Points

The main points are the central features of your speech. You should select them carefully, phrase them precisely, and arrange them strategically. Here are the main points of a student speech about the medical uses of hypnosis:

Specific Purpose: To inform my audience about the major uses of hypnosis.

Central Idea: The major uses of hypnosis today are to control pain in medical surgery, to help people stop smoking, and to help students improve their academic performance.

Main Points:

I. Hypnosis is used in surgery as an adjunct to chemical anesthesia.
II. Hypnosis is used to help people stop smoking.
III. Hypnosis is used to help students improve their academic performance.

main points
The major points developed in the body of a speech. Most speeches contain from two to five main points.

These three main points form the skeleton of the body of the speech. If there are three major *uses* of hypnosis for medical purposes, then logically there can be three *main points* in the speech.

How do you choose your main points? Sometimes they will be evident from your specific purpose statement. Suppose your specific purpose is "To inform my audience about the origins, events, and philosophy of the Special Olympics." Obviously, your speech will have three main points. The first will deal with the origins of the Special Olympics, the second with the events of the Special Olympics, the third with the philosophy of the Special Olympics. Written in outline form, the main points might be:

Specific Purpose: To inform my audience about the origins, events, and philosophy of the Special Olympics.

Central Idea: The Special Olympics gives people who are mentally or physically challenged a chance to experience athletic competition.

Main Points:
   I. The Special Olympics was founded in 1968 to promote fitness for the mentally and physically challenged.
  II. Held locally every year and internationally every four years, the Special Olympics has sports events similar to those in the Olympic Games.
 III. Although medals are awarded, the Special Olympics stresses effort and participation rather than winning.

Even if your main points are not stated expressly in your specific purpose, they may be easy to project from it. Let's say your specific purpose is "To inform my audience of the basic steps in making stained-glass windows." You know each of your main points will correspond to a step in the window-making process. They might look like this in outline form:

Specific Purpose: To inform my audience of the basic steps in making stained-glass windows.

Central Idea: There are four steps in making stained-glass windows.

Main Points:
   I. The first step is designing the window.
  II. The second step is cutting the glass to fit the design.
 III. The third step is painting the glass.
 IV. The fourth step is assembling the window.

You will not always settle on your main points so easily. Often they will emerge as you research the speech and evaluate your findings. Suppose your specific purpose is "To persuade my audience that our state should not approve proposals for online voting." You know that each main point in the speech will present a *reason* why online voting should not be instituted in your state. But you aren't sure how many main points there will be or what they will be. As you research and study the topic, you decide there are two major reasons to support your view. Each of these reasons will become a main point in your speech. Written in outline form, they might be:

Specific Purpose: To persuade my audience that our state should not approve proposals for online voting.

Central Idea: Our state should not approve online voting because it will increase voter fraud and disfranchise people without Internet access.

Main Points:
   I. Our state should not approve online voting because it will increase voter fraud.
  II. Our state should not approve online voting because it will disfranchise people without access to the Internet.

Now you have two broad areas around which to organize your ideas.

Number of Main Points

You will not have time in your classroom speeches to develop more than four or five main points, and most speeches will contain only two or three. Regardless of how long a speech might run, if you have too many main points, the audience will have trouble sorting them out. When everything is equally important, nothing is important.

Imagine, for example, that you have a particularly lenient professor who gives everyone in the class an A. Your A won't have much value for you. But if only three students in the class get an A and you are one of them, then you stand out from the crowd. That is what you must aim to do in your speeches—to make a few main points stand out and be remembered.

If, when you list your main points, you find you have too many, you may be able to condense them into categories. Here is a set of main points for a speech about lasers:

Specific Purpose: To inform my audience about the uses of lasers.

Central Idea: Lasers harness the power of light for a wide range of uses.

Main Points:
    I. Laser gravity wave detectors allow astronomers to "see" deep into space.
    II. Automobile manufacturers use lasers for many purposes in making cars.
    III. Neurosurgeons use lasers to vaporize brain tumors.
    IV. Lasers help create billions of industrial goods every year.
    V. With lasers, scientists can chart the fastest of chemical reactions.
    VI. The telephone industry sends phone calls underseas to Europe with lasers.
    VII. Eye specialists routinely use lasers to "weld" loose retinas back in place.
    VIII. Lasers allow doctors to make early diagnoses of certain kinds of cancer.

You have eight main points—which is too many. But if you look at the list, you see that the eight points fall into three broad categories: lasers in science, lasers in industry, lasers in medicine. You might, therefore, restate your main points this way:

  I. Lasers have many important uses in science.
  II. Lasers have become indispensable to industry.
  III. Lasers are revolutionizing the practice of medicine.

Strategic Order of Main Points

Once you establish your main points, you need to decide in what order you will present them in your speech. This is extremely important, for it will affect both the clarity and the persuasiveness of your ideas.

The most effective order depends on three things—your topic, your purpose, and your audience. Chapters 14 and 15 will deal with special aspects of organizing informative speeches and persuasive speeches. Here let us look briefly at the five basic patterns of organization used most often by public speakers.

Chronological Order

chronological order
A method of speech organization in which the main points follow a time pattern.

Speeches arranged chronologically follow a time pattern. They may narrate a series of events in the sequence in which they happened. For example:

Specific Purpose: To inform my audience how the Great Wall of China was built.

Central Idea: The Great Wall of China was built in three major stages.

Main Points: I. Building of the Great Wall began during the Chou dynasty in the fourth century B.C.
II. New sections of the Great Wall were added during the Ch'in, Han, and Sui dynasties from 221 B.C. to 618 A.D.
III. The Great Wall was completed during the Ming dynasty of 1368–1644.

Chronological order is also used in speeches explaining a process or demonstrating how to do something. For example:

Specific Purpose: To inform my audience of the steps in getting a professional tattoo.

Central Idea: There are four main steps in getting a professional tattoo.

The main points of a speech should be organized to communicate the speaker's message. For a speech explaining how the Great Wall of China was built, chronological order might be highly effective.

Main Points: I. First, the skin is shaved and sterilized in the area to be tattooed.

                II. Second, the main lines of the tattoo are traced on the skin with a machine called an outliner.

              III. Third, colored pigments are applied inside the outline with a machine called a shader.

              IV. Fourth, the tattoo is sterilized and bandaged.

As this outline shows, chronological order is especially useful for informative speeches.

Spatial Order

Speeches arranged in spatial order follow a directional pattern. That is, the main points proceed from top to bottom, left to right, front to back, inside to outside, east to west, or some other route. For example:

spatial order
A method of speech organization in which the main points follow a directional pattern.

Specific Purpose: To inform my audience about the design of the Eiffel Tower.

Central Idea: The Eiffel Tower is divided into three sections.

Main Points: I. The lowest section of the tower contains the entrance, a gift shop, and a restaurant.

              II. The middle section of the tower consists of stairs and elevators that lead to the top.

              III. The top section of the tower includes an observation deck with a spectacular view of Paris.

Or:

Specific Purpose: To inform my audience of five major civilizations that existed in different parts of North America centuries before the arrival of Columbus.

Central Idea: Centuries before the arrival of Columbus there were major civilizations in what is today New York, Florida, New Mexico, the Pacific Northwest, and the Mississippi Valley.

Main Points: I. In New York, the Onondaga were skilled agriculturalists and fierce warriors.

              II. In Florida, the Calusa developed one of the most advanced cultures to flourish without agriculture.

              III. In New Mexico, the people of Chaco Canyon were sophisticated architectural planners and builders.

              IV. In the Pacific Northwest, the Makah were expert mariners and foresters.

              V. In the Mississippi Valley, the Cahokia created a complex, prosperous society whose burial mounds are still evident today.

Spatial order, like chronological order, is used most often in informative speeches.

Causal Order

Speeches arranged in causal order organize main points so as to show a cause-effect relationship. When you put your speech in causal order, you have two main points—one dealing with the causes of an event, the other dealing with its effects. Depending on your topic, you can either devote your first main point to the causes and the second to the effects, or you can deal first with the effects and then with the causes.

Suppose your specific purpose is "To persuade my audience that the use of aging airplanes by U.S. airline companies is a serious problem." You would begin with the causes of the airline companies' use of aging planes and work toward its effects:

Specific Purpose: To persuade my audience that the use of aging airplanes by U.S. airline companies is a serious problem.

Central Idea: The use of aging planes by U.S. airline companies threatens the safety of air travel.

Main Points: I. To meet the demand for air travel, airline companies are keeping more and more old planes in service.
II. If this trend continues, it will create serious problems for airline safety.

When the effects you are discussing have already occurred, you may want to reverse the order and talk first about the effects and then about their causes—as in this speech about the Mayan civilization of Central America:

Specific Purpose: To inform my audience about the possible causes for the collapse of Mayan civilization.

Central Idea: The causes for the collapse of Mayan civilization have not yet been fully explained.

Main Points: I. Mayan civilization flourished for over a thousand years until 900 A.D., when it mysteriously began to disintegrate.
II. Scholars have advanced three major explanations for the causes of this disintegration.

Because of its versatility, causal order can be used both for persuasive speeches and informative speeches.

Problem-Solution Order

Speeches arranged in problem-solution order are divided into two main parts. The first shows the existence and seriousness of a problem. The second presents a workable solution to the problem. For example:

Specific Purpose: To persuade my audience that legislation is needed to control the abuses of fraudulent charity fund-raisers.

Central Idea: Fraudulent fund-raising for charities is a serious problem that requires action by government and individuals alike.

| *Main Points:* | I. | Fraudulent charity fund-raising has become a widespread national problem. |
| | II. | The problem can be solved by a combination of government initiative and individual awareness. |

Or:

| *Specific Purpose:* | To persuade my audience that the United States should act now to protect its citizens against electronic invasions of their personal privacy. |

| *Central Idea:* | The loss of personal privacy in our electronic society is a serious problem that requires decisive action. |

| *Main Points:* | I. | The use of electronic data gathering by business and government poses a serious threat to personal privacy. |
| | II. | The problem could be greatly reduced by federal privacy laws that impose strict controls on the collection of personal information by businesses and government agencies. |

As these examples indicate, problem-solution order is most appropriate for persuasive speeches.

Topical Order

Speeches that are not in chronological, spatial, causal, or problem-solution order usually fall into topical order. Topical order results when you divide the speech topic into *subtopics,* each of which becomes a main point in the speech. The main points are not part of a chronological, spatial, causal, or problem-solution sequence, but are simply parts of the whole. If this sounds confusing, a few examples should help to make it clearer.

Suppose your specific purpose is "To inform my audience of the major kinds of fireworks." This topic does not lend itself to chronological, spatial, causal, or problem-solution order. Rather, you separate the subject—kinds of fireworks—into its constituent parts, so that each main point deals with a single kind of fireworks. Your central idea and main points might look like this:

topical order
A method of speech organization in which the main points divide the topic into logical and consistent subtopics.

| *Specific Purpose:* | To inform my audience of the major kinds of fireworks. |

| *Central Idea:* | The major kinds of fireworks are skyrockets, Roman candles, pinwheels, and lances. |

Main Points:	I.	Skyrockets explode high in the air, producing the most dramatic effects of all fireworks.
	II.	Roman candles shoot out separate groups of sparks and colored flames with a series of booming noises.
	III.	Pinwheels throw off sparks and flames as they whirl on the end of a stick.
	IV.	Lances are thin, colorful fireworks used in ground displays.

Regardless of the speaker and occasion, organizing ideas strategically to communicate with the audience is vital to effective public speaking.

To take another example, let's say your specific purpose is "To inform my audience about the athletic achievements of Babe Didrikson." Didrikson, who is considered the greatest American female athlete of all time, competed during the 1930s, 1940s, and 1950s. So you could organize your speech chronologically—by discussing Didrikson's exploits during each decade of her career. On the other hand, you could arrange the speech topically—by dividing Didrikson's accomplishments into categories. Then your central idea and main points might be:

Specific Purpose: To inform my audience about the athletic achievements of Babe Didrikson.

Central Idea: Babe Didrikson was a world-class athlete in track and field, basketball, and golf.

Main Points:
    I. As a track-and-field athlete, Didrikson set two world records in the Olympic Games.
    II. As a basketball player, Didrikson was twice named to the women's All-America team.
    III. As a professional golfer, Didrikson set a record that still stands by winning seventeen tournaments in a row.

Notice that in both of the preceding examples, the main points subdivide the speech topic logically and consistently. In the first example, each main point deals with a single category of fireworks. In the second example, each main point isolates one aspect of Didrikson's achievements as an athlete. But suppose your main points look like this:

I. As a track-and-field athlete, Didrikson set two world records in the Olympic Games.

II. As a basketball player, Didrikson was twice named to the women's All-America team.
III. In the 1940s Didrikson dominated American women's sports.

This would *not* be a good topical order because main point III is inconsistent with the rest of the main points. It deals with a *period* in Didrikson's career, whereas main points I and II deal with *kinds* of athletic events.

All the examples so far refer to informative speeches. But topical order also works for persuasive speeches. Usually the topical subdivisions are the *reasons* why a speaker believes in a certain point of view. Here, for example, are the main points of a speech by NASA official Daniel Goldin on why the United States should expand its program of space exploration:[4]

Specific Purpose: To persuade my audience that the United States should expand its program of space exploration.

Central Idea: The United States should expand its program of space exploration because it will open access to vital natural resources, expand scientific knowledge, and further the search for extraterrestrial life.

Main Points:
I. Space exploration will open access to vital natural resources that are in limited supply on earth.
II. Space exploration will produce scientific knowledge that will benefit life on earth.
III. Space exploration will further the search for extraterrestrial life.

Because it is applicable to almost any subject and to any kind of speech, topical order is used more often than any other method of speech organization.[5]

Tips for Preparing Main Points

Keep Main Points Separate

Each main point in a speech should be clearly independent of the other main points. Take care not to lump together what should be separate main points. Compare these two sets of main points for a speech about the process of producing a Broadway play:

Ineffective

I. The first step is choosing the play.
II. The second step is selecting the cast.
III. The third step is conducting rehearsals and then performing the play.

More Effective

I. The first step is choosing the play.
II. The second step is selecting the cast.
III. The third step is conducting the rehearsals.
IV. The fourth step is performing the play.

The problem with the left-hand list is that point III contains two main points. It should be divided, as shown in the right-hand list.

Try to Use the Same Pattern of Wording for Main Points

Consider the following main points for an informative speech about the benefits of exercise.

Ineffective

   I. Regular exercise increases your endurance.
  II. Your sleeping pattern is is improved by regular exercise.
 III. It is possible to help control your weight by regular exercise.

More Effective

   I. Regular exercise increases your endurance.
  II. Regular exercise improves your sleeping pattern.
 III. Regular exercise helps control your weight.

The set of main points on the right follows a consistent pattern of wording throughout. Therefore, it is easier to understand and easier to remember than the set on the left.

You will find that it is not always possible to use this kind of parallel wording for your main points. Some speeches just don't lend themselves to such a tidy arrangement. But try to keep the wording parallel when you can, for it is a good way to make your main points stand out from the details surrounding them.

Balance the Amount of Time Devoted to Main Points

Because your main points are so important, you want to be sure they all receive enough emphasis to be clear and convincing. This means allowing sufficient time to develop each main point. Suppose you discover that the proportion of time devoted to your main points is something like this:

   I. 85 percent
  II. 10 percent
 III. 5 percent

A breakdown of this sort indicates one of two things. Either points II and III aren't really *main* points and you have only one main point, or points II and III haven't been given the attention they need. If the latter, you should revise the body of the speech to bring the main points into better balance.

This is not to say that all main points must receive exactly equal emphasis, but only that they should be roughly balanced. For example, either of the following would be fine:

   I. 30 percent   I. 20 percent
  II. 40 percent   II. 30 percent
 III. 30 percent   III. 50 percent

The amount of time spent on each main point depends on the amount and complexity of supporting materials for each point. Supporting materials are, in effect, the "flesh" that fills out the skeleton of your speech.

Supporting Materials

By themselves, main points are only assertions. As we saw in Chapter 7, listeners need supporting materials to accept what a speaker says. When the supporting materials are added, the body of a speech looks like the following in outline form:

I. Hypnosis is used in surgery as an adjunct to chemical anesthesia.
   A. Hypnosis reduces both the physical and psychological aspects of pain.
      1. Hypnosis can double a person's pain threshold.
      2. It also reduces the fear that intensifies physical pain.
   B. Hypnosis is most useful in cases when the patient is known to have problems with general anesthesia.
      1. Quotation from Dr. Harold Wain of Walter Reed Army Hospital.
      2. Story of Linda Kuay.
      3. Statistics from *Psychology Today.*
II. Hypnosis is used to help people stop smoking.
   A. Many therapists utilize hypnosis to help people break their addiction to cigarettes.
      1. The U.S. Department of Health and Human Services considers hypnosis a safe and effective means of stopping smoking.
      2. Success rates are as high as 70 percent.
         a. Story of Alex Hamilton.
         b. Quotation from New York psychiatrist Dr. Herbert Spiegel.
   B. Hypnosis does not work for all smokers.
      1. A person must want to stop smoking for hypnosis to work.
      2. A person must also be responsive to hypnotic suggestion.
III. Hypnosis is used to help students improve their academic performance.
   A. Hypnosis enables people to use their minds more effectively.
      1. The conscious mind uses about 10 percent of a person's mental ability.
      2. Hypnosis allows people to tap more of their mental power.
   B. Studies show that hypnosis can help people overcome many obstacles to academic success.
      1. Improves ability to concentrate.
      2. Increases reading speed.
      3. Reduces test anxiety.

In Chapter 7 we discussed the major kinds of supporting materials and how to use them. Here, we need stress only the importance of *organizing* your supporting materials so they are directly relevant to the main points they are supposed to support. Misplaced supporting materials are confusing. Here's an example:

supporting materials The materials used to support a speaker's ideas. The three major kinds of supporting materials are examples, statistics, and testimony.

I. There are several reasons why people immigrate to the United States.
   A. Over the years, millions of people have immigrated to the United States.
   B. Many people immigrate in search of economic opportunity.
   C. Others immigrate to attain political freedom.
   D. Still others immigrate to escape religious persecution.

The main point deals with the reasons immigrants come to the United States, as do supporting points B, C, and D. Supporting point A ("Over the years, millions of people have immigrated to the United States") does not. It is out of place and should not be included with this main point.

If you find such a situation in your own speeches, try to reorganize your supporting points under appropriate main points, like this:

I. Over the years, millions of people have immigrated to the United States.
   A. Since the American Revolution, an estimated 60 million people have immigrated to the U.S.
   B. Today there are over 20 million Americans who were born in other countries.
II. There are several reasons why people immigrate to the United States.
   A. Many people immigrate in search of economic opportunity.
   B. Others immigrate to attain political freedom.
   C. Still others immigrate to escape religious persecution.

Now you have two supporting points to back up your "millions of people" point and three supporting points to back up your "reasons" point.

Once you have organized your main points and supporting points, you must give attention to the third element in the body of a speech—connectives.

Connectives

Carla Maggio was speaking to her class about the need for students to vote in state and local elections. She had rehearsed the speech several times, had a well-defined central idea, three sharp main points, and strong evidence to support her position. But when Carla delivered the speech, she said "All right" every time she moved from one thought to the next. All told, she said "All right" 10 times in six minutes. After a while, her classmates started counting. By the end of the speech, most had stopped listening. They were too busy waiting for the next "All right." Afterward, Carla said, "I never even thought about saying 'All right.' I guess it just popped out when I didn't know what else to say."

This experience is not unusual. We all have stock phrases that we habitually use to fill the space between thoughts. In casual conversation they are seldom troublesome. But in speechmaking they create a problem—particularly when they call attention to themselves.

What Carla's speech lacked were strong *connectives*—words or phrases that join one thought to another and indicate the relationship between them. Connectives in the body of a speech are like ligaments and tendons in a human body. Without connectives, a speech is disjointed and uncoordinated—much as a person would be without ligaments and tendons to join the bones and hold the organs in place. Four types of speech connectives are transitions, internal previews, internal summaries, and signposts.

Transitions

Transitions are words or phrases that indicate when a speaker has just completed one thought and is moving on to another. Technically, the transitions

connective
A word or phrase that connects the ideas of a speech and indicates the relationship between them.

transition
A word or phrase that indicates when a speaker has finished one thought and is moving on to another.

state both the idea the speaker is leaving and the idea she or he is coming up to. In the following examples the transitional phrases are underlined:

In addition to being discriminary, capital punishment is also immoral.

Now that we have a clear understanding of the problem, let me share the solution with you.

Not only is boxing dangerous to its participants, but it can hurt our society as well.

So the evidence is strongly in favor of wearing seatbelts. That brings me to the next question—why don't people wear seatbelts?

Now that we've seen how drinking too much is a serious problem for students and their communities, let's look at some causes.

Notice how these phrases remind the listener of the thought just completed, as well as reveal the thought about to be developed.

View these transitions from student speeches.

CD: VIDEO CLIP 8.1

Internal Previews

Internal previews let the audience know what the speaker will take up next, but they are more detailed than transitions. In effect, an internal preview works just like the preview statement in a speech introduction, except that it comes in the body of the speech—usually as the speaker is starting to discuss a main point. For example:

In discussing how Asian Americans have been stereotyped in the mass media, we'll look first at the origins of the problem and second at its continuing impact today.

internal preview
A statement in the body of the speech that lets the audience know what the speaker is going to discuss next.

When you organize your speeches, make sure to include transitions, internal summaries, and other connectives to help listeners keep track of your ideas.

After hearing this, the audience knows exactly what to listen for as the speaker develops the "problem" main point.

Internal previews are often combined with transitions. For example:

> [*Transition*]: Now that we have seen how serious the problem of faulty credit reports is, let's look at some solutions. [*Internal Preview*]: I will focus on three solutions—instituting tighter government regulation of credit bureaus, holding credit bureaus financially responsible for their errors, and giving individuals easier access to their credit reports.

You will seldom need an internal preview for each main point in your speech, but be sure to use one whenever you think it will help listeners keep track of your ideas.

Internal Summaries

internal summary
A statement in the body of the speech that summarizes the speaker's preceding point or points.

Internal summaries are the reverse of internal previews. Rather than letting listeners know what is coming up next, internal summaries remind listeners of what they have just heard. Such summaries are generally used when a speaker finishes a complicated or particularly important main point or set of main points. Rather than moving immediately to the next point, the speaker takes a moment to summarize the preceding point or points. For example:

> In short, palm reading is an ancient art. Developed in China more than five thousand years ago, it was practiced in classical Greece and Rome, flourished during the Middle Ages, survived the Industrial Revolution, and remains popular today in many parts of the world.

> I hope I've made clear the benefits of walking as a form of exercise. Unlike running, which often causes as many injuries as it prevents, walking is a gentle but no less effective way to keep in shape. Regular walking at a brisk pace strengthens the heart, increases lung capacity, improves blood circulation, and burns calories—all without the strain on the knees and ankles caused by running.

Such internal summaries are an excellent way to clarify and reinforce ideas. By combining them with transitions, you can also lead your audience smoothly into your next main point:

> [*Internal Summary*]: So far we have seen that the normal individual's need for a three-minute burst of stimuli has produced a growing demand for thrill rides and has helped launch a coaster war between amusement parks. Then we looked at the roller coaster's past and present. [*Transition*]: Now I'd like to show you what's in store for us in the future.

> [*Internal Summary*]: To summarize what we've seen so far, mercury vapor light produces light pollution, which harms both astronomy and the environment, while the light fixtures themselves are costing the U.S. millions of dollars. [*Transition*]: Luckily for all of us, a solution exists which can put a stop to all of these problems.

View these excerpts from "The Thrilling World of Roller Coasters" and "The Battle of the Bulbs."

CD: VIDEO CLIP 8.2

Signposts

Signposts are very brief statements that indicate exactly where you are in the speech. They can be as simple as numbers, but they are crucial to effective speechmaking no matter who the speaker or what the occasion. Here is how President George Bush used numerical signposts to help his audience keep track of the principles underlying U.S. action in the Persian Gulf War:

> Four simple principles guide our policy. <u>First</u>, we seek the immediate, unconditional, and complete withdrawal of all Iraqi forces from Kuwait.
>
> <u>Second</u>, Kuwait's legitimate government must be restored to replace the puppet regime.
>
> <u>Third</u>, my administration, as has been the case with every President from President Roosevelt to President Reagan, is committed to the security and stability of the Persian Gulf.
>
> And <u>fourth</u>, I am determined to protect the lives of American citizens abroad.

View this portion of George Bush's "Defense of Saudi Arabia."

CD: VIDEO CLIP 8.3

The signposts are underscored. Notice how they enumerate each of Bush's points and make them easier to remember.

Another way to accomplish the same thing is to introduce your main points with a question, as did one student in his speech about mail-order fraud. His first main point dealt with the continuing growth of mail-order fraud. He introduced it this way:

> What makes mail-order fraud such a persistent problem? Why do people keep falling for gimmicks that are obviously too good to be true?

His second main point dealt with ways to curb mail-order fraud. He introduced it like this:

> How can we solve this problem? Is there a way to protect the rights of legitimate mail-order companies while attacking the fraudulent ones?

Questions are particularly effective as signposts because they invite subliminal answers and thereby get the audience more involved with the speech.

Besides using signposts to indicate where you are in the speech, you can use them to focus attention on key ideas. You can do this with a simple phrase, as in the following example:

> <u>The most important thing to remember</u> about abstract art is that it is always based on forms in the natural world.

The underlined words alert the audience to the fact that an especially significant point is coming up. So do phrases such as these:

> Be sure to keep this in mind . . .
>
> This is crucial to understanding the rest of the speech . . .
>
> Above all, you need to know . . .
>
> Let me repeat that last statement . . .

Depending on the needs of your speech, you may want to use two, three, or even all four kinds of connectives in combination. You needn't worry too

signpost
A very brief statement that indicates where a speaker is in the speech or that focuses attention on key ideas.

much about what they are called—whether this one is a signpost and that a transition. In fact, many people lump them all together as "transitions." The important thing is to be aware of their functions. Properly applied, connectives can make your speeches much more unified and coherent.

Summary

Clear organization is vital to speechmaking. Listeners demand coherence. They get only one chance to grasp a speaker's ideas, and they have little patience for speakers who ramble aimlessly from one idea to another. A well-organized speech will enhance your credibility and make it easier for the audience to understand your message.

Speeches should be organized strategically. They should be put together in particular ways to achieve particular results with particular audiences. The first step in organizing speeches is to gain command of the three basic parts of a speech—introduction, body, conclusion—and the strategic role of each. In this chapter we have dealt with the body of the speech.

The process of planning the body of a speech begins when you determine the main points. These are the central features of your speech. You should choose them carefully, phrase them precisely, and organize them strategically. Because listeners cannot keep track of a multitude of main points, most speeches should contain no more than two to five main points. Each main point should focus on a single idea, should be worded clearly, and should receive enough emphasis to be clear and convincing.

You can organize main points in various ways. The strategic order will be determined by your topic, your purpose, and your audience. Chronological order means that your speech follows a time pattern. Speeches arranged in spatial order follow a directional pattern. To put your speech in causal order, you organize main points according to their cause-effect relationship. Topical order results when you divide your main topic into subtopics, each of which covers one aspect of the main topic. For problem-solution order you break the body of your speech into two main parts—the first showing a problem, the second giving a solution.

Supporting materials are the backup ideas for your main points. When organizing supporting materials, make sure they are directly relevant to the main points they are supposed to support.

Once you have organized your main points and supporting materials, you are ready to work out the third element in the body of your speech: connectives. Connectives help tie a speech together. They are words or phrases that join one thought to another and indicate the relationship between them. The four major types of speech connectives are transitions, internal previews, internal summaries, and signposts. Using them effectively will make your speeches more unified and coherent.

Key Terms

strategic organization (193)
main points (193)
chronological order (196)
spatial order (197)
causal order (198)
problem-solution order (198)
topical order (199)

supporting materials (203)
connective (204)
transition (204)
internal preview (205)
internal summary (206)
signpost (207)

Review Questions

After reading this chapter, you should be able to answer the following questions:

1. Why is it important that speeches be organized clearly and coherently?

2. How many main points will your speeches usually contain? Why is it important to limit the number of main points in your speeches?

3. What are the five basic patterns of organizing main points in a speech? Which are appropriate for informative speeches? Which is used only in persuasive speeches? Which is used most often?

4. What are three tips for preparing your main points?

5. What is the most important thing to remember when organizing supporting materials in the body of your speech?

6. What are the four kinds of speech connectives? What role does each play in a speech?

For further review, go to the Study Questions for this chapter.
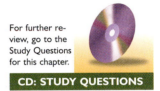
CD: STUDY QUESTIONS

Exercises for Critical Thinking

1. Identify the organizational method used in each of the following sets of main points.

    I. Cesar Chavez is best known for his efforts to protect the rights of Hispanic farmworkers in California.
    II. Cesar Chavez was also a tireless advocate for Hispanic racial and cultural pride in general.

    I. Rodeos began in the Old West as contests of skill among cowboys during cattle roundups.
    II. By 1920 rodeos had become a popular spectator sport for the general public.
    III. Today rodeos combine traditional western events with a circuslike atmosphere and the marketing techniques of big business.

    I. Many citizens are victimized every year by incompetent lawyers.
    II. A bill requiring lawyers to stand for recertification every 10 years will do much to help solve the problem.

    I. The outermost section of the ancient Egyptian burial tomb was the entrance passage.

    II. The next section of the Egyptian burial tomb was the antechamber.

    III. The third section of the Egyptian burial tomb was the treasury.

    IV. The innermost section of the Egyptian burial tomb was the burial chamber.

    I. Sickle-cell anemia is a hereditary blood disease caused by abnormal blood cells.

    II. The effects of sickle-cell anemia include liver damage, blindness, paralysis, and early death.

2. What organizational method (or methods) might you use to arrange main points for speeches with the following specific purpose statements?

   To inform my audience about the major events in the development of the civil rights movement from 1955 to 1970.

   To inform my audience of the causes and effects of the erosion of America's seacoasts.

   To inform my audience about the educational philosophy of Maria Montessori.

   To inform my audience about the geographical regions of the Philippines.

   To persuade my audience that our state legislature should enact tougher laws to deal with the problem of child abuse.

   To inform my audience about the major kinds of symbols used in traditional Native American art.

3. Turn to the outline of main points and supporting materials for the speech about hypnosis on page 203. Create appropriate transitions, internal previews, internal summaries, and signposts for the speech.

Applying the POWER of Public Speaking

After working for two other firms, you have spent the last several years at a Fortune 500 company that, as part of its operations, is a major manufacturer of lawn care equipment. The company has recently acquired three specialized European businesses that produce similar products. With your engineering degree and experience as part of the fast-growing Product Quality Group, you were the logical candidate to visit the newly acquired companies and evaluate their products for safety, quality, and emissions controls.

You have just returned from a week-long trip to the three sites in Scotland, France, and Germany. You will deliver your findings and recommendations to the management group for new acquisitions, but you're unsure how best to organize your speech. Your major choices are chronological order, spatial order, and topical order. What might be the main points of your speech in each of these methods of organization? Explain which method you think would be most effective for your presentation.

Notes

[1]Ernest C. Thompson, "An Experimental Investigation of the Relative Effectiveness of Organizational Structure in Oral Communication," *Southern Speech Journal,* 20 (1960), pp. 59–69.

[2]Harry Sharp, Jr., and Thomas McClung, "Effect of Organization on the Speaker's Ethos," *Speech Monographs,* 33 (1966), pp. 182–183.

[3]John O. Greene, "Speech Preparation Processes and Verbal Fluency," *Human Communication Research,* 11 (1984), pp. 61–84.

[4]Daniel S. Goldin, "The Light of a New Age: Space Exploration," *Vital Speeches,* 58 (1992), pp. 741–744.

[5]For an interesting study of the role of structure in speeches and other public discourses, see Regina M. Hoffman, "Temporal Organization as a Rhetorical Resource," *Southern Communication Journal,* 57 (1992), pp. 194–204.

CHAPTER NINE

BEGINNING AND ENDING THE SPEECH

The Introduction

The Conclusion

O n the night of October 9, 1986, a conductor stepped up to the podium at Her Majesty's Theater in London, tapped his baton, raised his arms, and signaled the orchestra to play. Moments later the public first heard the dramatic opening chords of the song "The Phantom of the Opera."

Like most musical stage plays, *Phantom of the Opera* begins with an overture—an orchestral introduction that captures the audience's attention and gives them a preview of the music they are going to hear. Without such an introduction—if the characters simply walked onstage and began singing or speaking—the beginning of the play would seem too abrupt, and the audience would not be suitably "primed" for the entertainment.

Similarly, nearly all musicals end with a finale, when the whole cast is onstage, elements of the dramatic plot are resolved, portions of the principal songs are recalled, and the music is brought to a dramatic climax. If there were no such conclusion, if the actors merely stopped and walked off-stage, the audience would be left unsatisfied.

Just as musical plays need appropriate beginnings and endings, so do speeches. The beginning, or introduction, prepares listeners for what is to come. The conclusion ties up the speech and alerts listeners that the speech is going to end. Ideally, it is a satisfying conclusion.

In this chapter we explore the roles played by an introduction and a conclusion in speechmaking. We also discuss techniques aimed at fulfilling those roles. If you apply these techniques imaginatively, you will take a big step toward elevating your speeches from the ordinary to the splendid.

The Introduction

First impressions are important. A poor beginning may so distract or alienate listeners that the speaker can never fully recover. Moreover, getting off on the right foot is vital to a speaker's self-confidence. What could be more encouraging than watching your listeners' faces begin to register interest, attention, and pleasure? The hardest part of any presentation is the beginning. If you get through the opening stages of your speech without blundering, the rest will go much more smoothly. A good introduction, you will find, is an excellent confidence booster.

In most speech situations, there are four objectives you need to accomplish at the outset:

■ Get the attention and interest of your audience.

■ Reveal the topic of your speech.

■ Establish your credibility and goodwill.

■ Preview the body of the speech.

We'll look at each of these objectives in turn.

Get Attention and Interest

"Unless a speaker can interest his audience at once, his effort will be a failure." So said the great lawyer Clarence Darrow. If your topic is not one of extraordinary interest, your listeners are likely to say to themselves, "So what? Who cares?" No matter how famous the speaker or how vital the topic, the speaker can quickly lose an audience if she or he doesn't use the introduction to get their attention and quicken their interest.

Getting the initial attention of your audience is usually easy to do—even before you utter a single word. After you are introduced and step to the lectern, your audience will normally give you their attention. If they don't, merely wait patiently. Look directly at the audience without saying a word. In a few moments all talking and physical commotion will stop. Your listeners will be attentive. You will be ready to start speaking.

Keeping the attention of your audience once you start talking is more difficult. Here are the methods used most often. Employed individually or in combination, they will help get the audience caught up in your speech.

Relate the Topic to the Audience

People pay attention to things that affect them directly. If you can relate the topic to your listeners, they are much more likely to be interested in it.

Suppose, for example, one of your classmates begins her speech like this:

> Today I am going to talk about collecting postcards—a hobby that is both fascinating and financially rewarding. I would like to explain the basic kinds of collectible postcards, why they are so valuable, and how collectors buy and sell their cards.

This is certainly a clear introduction, but it is not one to get you hooked on the speech. Now what if your classmate were to begin her speech this way—as one student actually did.

> It's Saturday morning, and you are helping clean out your grandmother's attic. After working a while, you stumble upon a trunk, open it, and discover inside hundreds of old postcards. Thinking about getting to the football game on time, you start tossing the cards into the trash can. Congratulations! You have just thrown away a year's tuition.

This time the speaker has used just the right bait. Chances are you will be hooked.

Even when you use other interest-arousing lures, you should *always* relate your topic to the audience. At times this will test your ingenuity, but it pays dividends. Here are two excellent examples. The first is from a speech entitled "Making Campus Accessible for Disabled Students." Notice how the speaker gets her classmates to put themselves in the place of people who are unable to get to class on time because they can't get their wheelchairs through the snow.

> I'd like to ask you to use your imaginations and think how it would feel if you'd spent an evening studying for an exam, you get up in the morning all set to go to class, you go down, you get to your door, and it won't open. You think, "Oh, I can just use my back door." But you go to your back door, and that won't open either.
>
> It would be pretty frustrating, wouldn't it? That's the kind of frustration handicapped students feel when they can't get to class because of the snow.

View the beginning of Diane Bright, "Making Campus Accessible for Disabled Students."

CD: VIDEO CLIP 9.1

The second example is from a speech about Mother Teresa. This is how the speaker began her remarks.

> Imagine you are a small child lying on the dirt roads of Calcutta, India. You are severely dehydrated because no one you ask will offer you some of their water. You are weak and malnourished because you have not eaten for days. You are hysterically and painfully coughing from your tuberculosis. You have no family, no friends, and, it seems, no future.
>
> As you begin to shut your eyes, gentle but strong arms reach out and pick you up off the dirt road. You regain enough strength to focus your eyes on the face before you. Her face is wrinkled with age and love and is like a ray of light in your dark world.
>
> This is a familiar story for the many poor and needy of India who were touched by Mother Teresa.

View the beginning of Mei Chu, "Mother of Love."

CD: VIDEO CLIP 9.2

By using vivid language, the speaker helps her classmates identify with the poor and downtrodden who Mother Teresa helped during her years as a Catholic nun in India.

State the Importance of Your Topic

Presumably, you think your speech topic is important. Tell your audience why they should think so, too. Here is how Postmaster General Anthony M. Frank began his speech to the Economic Club of Indianapolis on the future of the U.S. Postal Service.

> Thank you for giving me the opportunity to tell you about the United States Postal Service . . .
>
> We are a huge enterprise—40,000 locations staffed by about 800,000 full- and part-time employees, with income and expenses exceeding $40 billion this year. . . . We faithfully complete an enormous task by delivering 535 million pieces of mail every day, six days a week. We deliver 41 percent of the world's mail volume and we do it faster and at postage rates that are up to 50 percent less expensive than, say, the postal services of Great Britain and Germany.[1]

These are striking statistics. By citing them in the introduction, Frank emphasized the importance of his topic and captured the attention of his audience.

Clearly, this technique is easy to use when discussing social and political issues such as the postal service, poor schools, drug abuse, toxic waste, or drunk driving, but it is appropriate for other kinds of topics as well. Here is how one student handled it in a speech about starting a home aquarium:

> It is very hard to cuddle a fish. Fish won't roll over or fetch the morning paper. You won't find them curling up on your lap, chasing a ball of string, or rescuing a child from a burning building.
>
> Yet despite these shortcomings, 250 million tropical fish have found their way into 10 million American homes. Tropical fish make up 50 percent of all live animal sales in the United States, and they have earned a spot next to the all-American dog and the cuddly kitten in the hearts of millions of people. Today I would like to explain how you can start a home aquarium and discover the pleasures of owning tropical fish.

The first paragraph—with its clever opening line—grabs the listener's attention. But it is the second paragraph that keeps the attention. Indeed, whenever you discuss a topic whose importance may not be clear to the audience, you should think about ways to demonstrate its significance in the introduction.

Startle the Audience

One surefire way to arouse interest quickly is to startle your listeners with an arresting or intriguing statement. Everyone in the audience paid close attention after this speaker's introduction:

> Take a moment and think of the three women closest to you. Who comes to mind? Your mother? Your sister? Your girlfriend? Your wife? Your best friend? Now guess which one will be sexually assaulted during her lifetime. It's not a pleasant thought, but according to the U.S. Department of Justice, one of every three American women will be sexually assaulted sometime during her life.

Notice the gradual buildup to the speaker's arresting statement, "Now guess which one will be sexually assaulted during her lifetime." This statement startles the audience—especially the men—and drives home at a personal level the problem of sexual assault against women. The effect would have been much less if the speaker had said, "Sexual assault against women is a serious problem."

Sometimes you may want to startle your audience in the very first sentence of your speech. Here is how one student began a speech about the environmental problems created by the 3 billion disposable batteries tossed away in the United States each year:

> One day the Energizer bunny will die.[2]

A good introduction will get your speech off to a strong start. To be most effective, it should be delivered smoothly, from a minimum of notes, and with strong eye contact.

And here is a slightly longer example of the same technique.

> Yesterday, millions of dollars in United States currency was burned while a group of people stood and watched. They did nothing to stop the burning—in fact, they encouraged it. They are employees of the United States Mint in Washington, D.C., and they were witnessing the destruction of counterfeit money.

This technique is highly effective and easy to use. Just be sure the startling introduction relates directly to the subject of your speech. The example cited above made a good beginning for an informative speech about counterfeiting. It would not work for a speech about the U.S. banking system. If you choose a strong opening simply for its shock value and then go on to talk about something else, your audience will be confused and possibly annoyed.

Arouse the Curiosity of the Audience

People are curious. One way to draw them into your speech is with a series of statements that progressively whet their curiosity about the subject of the speech. For example:

> It is the most common chronic disease in the United States. Controllable but incurable, it is a symptomless disease. You can have it for years and never know until it kills you. Some 40 million Americans have this disease, and 300,000 will die from it before the year is out. Odds are that five of us in this class have it.
>
> What am I talking about? Not cancer. Not AIDS. Not heart disease. I am talking about hypertension—high blood pressure.

As another example, consider this clever opening from a student informative speech titled "The Licnep":

> The licnep is one of the most common objects on a college campus. First marketed in England in 1564, its core is usually made of graphite and its exterior of cedar. It comes in different strengths and sizes. It can be hard or soft, colored or plain, and its length tends to change throughout its lifetime.
>
> With a little help from us, the licnep has the power to ace a math exam, evaluate our professor, give a message to a loved one, or put our name on the dotted line. Most of us have a licnep in our purse or backpack at this very moment.
>
> What is a licnep? As many of you have no doubt figured out, a "licnep" is pencil spelled backward.

Not only does this student relate the topic directly to his classmates, he gets them further involved by building suspense about what a "licnep" is. Imagine how much less effective his introduction would have been if he had simply said, "Today I am going to talk about pencils." When used appropriately, arousing curiosity is a surefire way to capture and hold your listeners' interest.

Question the Audience

rhetorical question
A question that the audience answers mentally rather than out loud.

Asking a *rhetorical question* is another way to get your listeners thinking about your speech. Sometimes a single question will do:

Do you know how it feels to be an international student?

What would you think if you went to a doctor because you were ill and she told you to watch *The Simpsons* as part of your treatment?

If you had exciting news that you wanted to share with someone, whom would you tell first?

In other circumstances you may want to pose a series of questions, each of which draws the audience deeper into the speech. Here is how one student developed this method.

Do you surf the Web for hours on end? Do you spend more time scanning bulletin boards in cyberspace than reading books for your classes? Are you more connected emotionally with people in your chat groups than with friends or family members? Do you feel a sense of depression or aimlessness when you can't get on the Internet? Is logging on the high point of your day? If so, you may be part of that growing portion of the population whom psychologists identify as Internet addicts.

Like beginning with a startling statement, opening with a question works best when the question is meaningful to the audience and firmly related to the content of the speech. It also works most effectively when you pause for just a moment after each question. This adds dramatic impact and gives the question time to sink in. The audience, of course, will answer mentally—not out loud.

Begin with a Quotation

Another way to arouse the interest of your audience is to start with an attention-getting quotation. You might choose your quotation from the words of a famous speaker or writer, from Shakespeare or Confucius, from the Bible or Talmud, from a poem or song, even from a television show. One student used the last of these to introduce a speech about the role of women in the United States space program:

"Space—the final frontier. These are the voyages of the Starship *Enterprise.* Its five-year mission: To explore new worlds. To seek out new life and new civilizations. To boldly go where no man has gone before."

These well-known words, which opened every episode of the original *Star Trek* television series, captured the spirit of adventure that marked American attitudes toward space exploration during the 1960s and 1970s. They also captured the notion that space exploration was essentially a male activity: "To boldly go where no *man* has gone before."

Today, of course, times have changed. Not only are women central characters in both of the later *Star Trek* series, but they are playing more and more important roles in the U.S. space program itself. Today I would like to discuss the current status and future prospects of women in the space program.

You need not use a well-known or famous quotation. The following made an effective introduction for a speech about bird-watching:

"Even to this day I cannot describe what happened without feeling the excitement of the moment. I glimpsed a flash of color in the thicket. I raised my binoculars to my eyes, and then I saw it—a Bachman's Warbler, one of the rarest birds in all of America.

THE **INTERNET** *Connection*

Looking for a quotation to use in the introduction or conclusion of your speech? Visit Yahoo: Reference: Quotations (http://www.yahoo.com/reference/quotations/) for a comprehensive roster of links to collected quotations on the Web.

Are you interested in reading introductions and conclusions from important speeches in U.S. history? You can find them at Douglass: Archives of American Public Address (http://douglass.speech.nwu.edu/).

For me, this was the equivalent of a coin collector discovering a rare silver dollar, or of a football player scoring a touchdown in the Super Bowl."

This statement was made by my father. He is just one of the millions of people who have discovered the joys and thrills of bird-watching.

A humorous quotation can afford double impact, as in this speech about the need to impose term limitations on members of the U.S. Congress:

Mark Twain once said, "It could probably be shown by facts and figures that there is no distinctly American criminal class except Congress."

By opening with Twain's words, the speaker not only got the audience's attention, she also foreshadowed a central theme of her speech. Notice, too, that all the quotations used here as examples are relatively short. Opening your speech with a lengthy quotation is a sure way to set your audience yawning.

Tell a Story

We all enjoy stories—especially if they are provocative, amusing, dramatic, or suspenseful. To work well as introductions, they should also be clearly relevant to the main point of the speech. Used in this way, stories are perhaps the most effective way to begin a speech.

Consider, for example, the story one student, an education major, told to open his speech about the ways American teachers are adapting to the cultural diversity of today's school-age population:

On a cloudy winter afternoon, Florann Greenberg, a teacher at P.S. 14 in New York City, noticed that her first-grade class was growing fidgety. One girl, dropping all pretense of work, stared at the snow falling outside the schoolroom windows. Annoyed, Greenberg asked her, "Haven't you seen snow before?" The girl whispered, "No." Her classmates began nodding their heads in agreement.

Then it dawned on Greenberg. Of course these children had never seen snow—almost all were immigrants from Colombia and the Dominican Republic. Immediately Greenberg changed her lesson plans. New topics: What is snow? How is it formed? How do you dress in the snow? What games do you play?

This story, reported in *Time* magazine, illustrates the cultural diversity now found in thousands of school classrooms across the United States and how creative teachers are adjusting to that diversity.

Like many good introductions, this one does a double job—it arouses the interest of the audience and gets listeners emotionally involved in the subject of the speech.

You can also use stories based on your personal experience. Here is how one student used such a story in his commencement speech at the University of Richmond. The student had come from Bombay, India, to attend college in the United States. He began by explaining the questions and uncertainties that were running through his mind as he prepared to leave his native land:

I can visualize the scene again and again: 11:30 P.M., Saturday night, the 15th of August, 1992, Bombay International Airport, India. I was leaving home for the University of Richmond. And as I said that final goodbye to my parents, my family, and my friends; and as I saw hope, expectation, even a tinge of sadness, in their eyes; and as I stepped aboard the Boeing 747 in front, I knew my life had changed forever.

View the beginning of Sajjid Zahir Chinoy, "Questions of Culture."

CD: VIDEO CLIP 9.3

The effectiveness of any story—especially a personal one—hinges as much on the speaker's delivery as on the content of the story. As you can see from the clip of this speech on the CD-ROM, the speaker used pauses, eye contact, and changes in his tone of voice to heighten the impact of his words and draw his audience into the speech. See if you can do the same in your speech introductions.

The seven methods discussed above are the ones used most often by student speakers to gain attention and interest. Other methods include referring to the occasion, inviting audience participation, using audio equipment or visual aids, relating to a previous speaker, and beginning with humor. For any given speech, try to choose the method that is most suitable for the topic, audience, and occasion.

Reveal the Topic

In the process of gaining attention, be sure to state clearly the topic of your speech. If you do not, your listeners will be confused. And once they are confused, your chances of getting them absorbed in the speech are almost nil. This is a basic point—so basic that it may hardly seem worth mentioning. Yet you would be surprised how many students need to be reminded of it. You may hear speeches in your own class in which the topic is not clear by the end of the introduction. So that you will know what to avoid, here is such an introduction, presented in a public speaking class.

When Roseanne Taos went to the hospital for knee surgery, her biggest concern was how soon she would be able to go skiing again. Tragically, the answer was never. No, Roseanne didn't die, but an overdose of general anesthesia during surgery left her permanently disabled. She will live the rest of her life under custodial supervision. As this example demonstrates, the use of anesthesia can be the most dangerous part of surgery. Today, I would like to discuss this issue with you.

What is the topic of this speech? The potential dangers of anesthesia? No. The need for periodic recertification of anesthesiologists? No. The limits of modern medicine in general? No. This student was speaking about the ancient Chinese practice of acupuncture as an alternative to anesthesia. But he did not make that clear to his audience. Listening to the introduction, they expected him to talk about the hazards of anesthesia.

This student found a dramatic introduction but ignored the fact that it didn't relate properly to his speech. Certainly the story of Roseanne Taos is an excellent attention getter. But in this case it was wasted. Suppose, instead, the student had begun his speech with a different story:

> The young woman on the operating table at the Institute of Tuberculosis in Beijing, China, is having a diseased lung removed. She has not received any painkilling drugs. Even though she is fully conscious, she experiences no pain and even talks periodically with her surgeons. Her only anesthetic is the array of stainless-steel acupuncture needles in her hands and feet.

This opening would have provided drama and a way to get the listeners' attention, but it also would have related directly to the speech topic.

If you beat around the bush in your introduction, you may lose your listeners. Even if they already know your topic, you should restate it clearly and concisely at some point in the introduction.

Establish Credibility and Goodwill

Besides getting attention and revealing the topic, there is a third objective you may need to accomplish in your introduction—establishing your credibility and goodwill.

Credibility is mostly a matter of being qualified to speak on a given topic—and of being *perceived* as qualified by your listeners. If, for instance, Tom Cruise got up before an audience to speak about nuclear physics, he would have to take drastic steps to establish his credibility on the subject.

Here is how one student established her credibility on the subject of weight lifting without sounding like a braggart:

> What is the fastest-growing sport today among American women? If you answered weight lifting, you are absolutely correct. Once seen as an exclusively male activity, weight lifting has crossed the gender barrier—and with good reason. Regardless of whether you are male or female, weight lifting can give you a sense of strength and power, enhance your self-esteem, and make you look and feel better.
>
> I started lifting weights when I was in high school, and I have kept at it for the past eight years. I have also taught weight lifting in several health clubs, and I am a certified instructor through the Aerobics and Fitness Association of America.
>
> Using some of my experience, I would like to explain the basic kinds of weights and how to use them properly.

Whether or not you lift weights, you will probably be more interested in the speech when you realize the speaker knows what she is talking about.

Your credibility need not be based on firsthand knowledge and experience. It can come from reading, from classes, from interviews, from friends—as in these cases:

credibility
The audience's perception of whether a speaker is qualified to speak on a given topic.

Using the introduction to establish goodwill toward the audience is often a major concern for speakers who deal with controversial public issues—as in the case of this advocate for Tibetan independence.

I have been interested in the history of the civil rights movement for several years, and I have read a number of books and articles about it.

The information I am going to share with you today comes mostly from my biology class and an interview with Reyna Vasquez of the local Audubon Society.

I've learned a great deal about the problems of early childhood education from my mother, who is a teacher in the San Francisco school system.

Whatever the source of your expertise, be sure to let the audience know.

Establishing your *goodwill* is a slightly different problem. It is often crucial outside the classroom, where speakers have well-established reputations and may be identified with causes that arouse hostility among listeners. In such a situation, the speaker must try to defuse that hostility right at the start of the speech.[3]

Occasionally you may have to do the same thing in your classroom speeches. Suppose you advocate a highly unpopular position. You will need to make a special effort at the outset to ensure that your classmates will at least consider your point of view. This is how one student tried to minimize his classmates' opposition at the start of a speech in favor of building more nuclear power plants to meet America's energy needs during the 21st century.

> The development of new nuclear power plants in the United States came to a standstill during the 1980s. As *Discover* magazine stated just last month, however, the time has come to look again at the benefits of nuclear power. Unlike fossil fuels, it does not contribute to the greenhouse effect; it does not leave America at the mercy of foreign oil; and, with advances in technology, it is much safer than before.
>
> That is why I am speaking in favor of building more nuclear power plants to meet our future energy needs. I know that most of you oppose nuclear power—I did, too,

goodwill
The audience's perception of whether the speaker has the best interests of the audience in mind.

until I started researching this speech. Today I would like to share with you some of the facts I have found. I know I can't change all your minds. But I do ask you to listen with an open mind and to consider the merit of my arguments.

What reasonable listener could ignore such a sincere, forthright plea?

Preview the Body of the Speech

As we saw in Chapter 3, most people are poor listeners. Even good listeners need all the help they can get in sorting out a speaker's ideas. One way to help your listeners is to tell them in the introduction what they should listen for in the rest of the speech. Here is an excellent example, from a student speech about the potential effects of birth order on personality development:

> Where do you fit in your family structure? Are you at the top of the totem pole, partway down, or at the bottom? And how might your place in the family structure influence who you are? This morning I would like to explore how personality development can be affected by each of the four major patterns of birth order—the only child, the first child followed by younger brothers or sisters, the second or middle child, and the youngest child.

preview statement
A statement in the introduction of a speech that identifies the main points to be discussed in the body of the speech.

After this introduction, there is no doubt about the speaker's topic, central idea, or main points.

In some types of persuasive speeches, you may not want to reveal your central idea until later in the speech. But even in such a situation you must be sure your audience is not left guessing about the main points they should listen for as the speech unfolds. Nearly always, you should include some *preview statement* similar to the following:

> In order for you to understand why the mariachis are significant to Hispanic culture, I will be giving you a brief overview of the history of the mariachi, what the word "mariachi" means, their style of dress, and the ways they are used in entertainment today.

> Today I'd like to share some of this information with you by first exposing the presence of insects in our everyday foods. Then we'll consider a history of edible insects, next their nutritional value, and finally we'll see what the possibilities are for making insects a more prevalent part of our diet.

> As you can see, I use a scooter to get around campus, and I have found that this campus is inaccessible due to the uncleared snow. I'd like to share that problem with you and then share my solution.

View these preview statements from student speeches.

CD: VIDEO CLIP 9.4

Preview statements such as these serve another purpose as well. Because they usually come at the very end of the introduction, they provide a smooth lead-in to the body of the speech. They signal that the body of the speech is about to begin.

There is one other aspect you may want to cover in previewing your speech. You can use your introduction to give specialized information—definitions or background—that your listeners will need if they are to understand the rest of the speech. Often you can do this very quickly, as in the following examples:

"Cryonics" is the science of freezing human organs or body parts in liquid nitrogen to preserve them for later use.

A "triathlon" is a race made up of three different events completed in succession. The events are usually swimming, biking, and running, though canoeing is sometimes substituted for one of these.

In other circumstances, you may have to explain an important term in more detail. Here is how one student handled the problem in a speech about the Underground Railroad used by slaves to escape from the South before the Civil War. Although most people have heard the phrase "Underground Railroad," many are not sure exactly what it means. Knowing this, the speaker took time in her introduction to give a precise definition:

The term "Underground Railroad" was first used about 1830. But in fact, the Underground Railroad was neither underground nor a railroad. It was an informal network that provided runaway slaves food, clothing, directions, and places to hide on their escape routes to the North and to Canada.

Why was it called the Underground Railroad? Because of its secrecy and because many of the people involved used railroad terms as code words. Hiding places, for example, were called "stations," and people who helped the slaves were called "conductors." Over the years, the Underground Railroad helped thousands of slaves make their way from bondage to freedom.

Sample Introduction with Commentary

So far we have seen many excerpts showing how to fulfill the various objectives of an introduction. Now here is a complete introduction from a student speech. The side comments indicate the principles used in developing the introduction.

Canine Companions

Commentary	Introduction
The speaker uses a story to gain attention. This story works particularly well because it is richly detailed and arouses our curiosity about Frances's peculiar behavior.	The doorbell rings. Instantly, Frances jumps up from where she has been sitting, spins around three times, and runs back and forth from the door to the sofa. Next she hops onto the sofa and begins bouncing up and down. Is Frances deranged? No, Frances is a "canine companion," and she has just alerted her deaf owner to the fact that a visitor is at the door.
Now the speaker reveals her topic. She defines what canine companions are and uses statistics to show how many are currently at work. This helps to strengthen the audience's interest.	Canine companions are dogs that have been trained to assist people who are hearing-impaired or who have physical disabilities. In addition to answering the door, canine companions perform a wide range of tasks that include locking and unlocking wheelchairs, turning light switches on and off, retrieving books from shelves, even fetching a beer from the refrigera-

tor. According to *Smithsonian* magazine, there are some 3,500 canine companions at work throughout the United States, in addition to the 7,000 "seeing eye" dogs that help guide blind people.

The speaker does an excellent job of establishing her credibility and explaining her personal interest in the topic.

> I became interested in canine companions two years ago when my older sister, who was paralyzed in a car accident, received a canine companion named Lucky. Since then I have learned about the subject by watching Lucky, by talking with my sister, and by reading a number of articles and pamphlets.

Here the speaker relates the topic directly to her audience and suggests why they should care about it.

> As a result of my sister's accident, I have also gained a greater appreciation of the fact that being physically disabled is the one minority we can all join at any time. Due to an accident or serious illness, any of us could one day be in a situation where we—or someone we love—might require the services of a canine companion. So this afternoon I would like to tell you about canine companions—how they are trained and the many benefits they provide for the people they assist.

By previewing the main points of her speech, the speaker lets her audience know what to listen for. She also provides a good lead-in to the body of the speech.

Tips for Preparing the Introduction

1. Keep the introduction relatively brief. Under normal circumstances it should not constitute more than about 10 to 20 percent of your speech.

2. Be on the lookout for possible introductory materials as you do your research. File them with your notes, so they will be handy when you are ready for them.

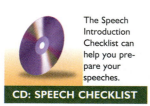

The Speech Introduction Checklist can help you prepare your speeches.

CD: SPEECH CHECKLIST

3. Be creative in devising your introduction. Experiment with two or three different openings and choose the one that seems most likely to get the audience interested in your speech. (Don't hesitate to discard a "great" introduction that doesn't quite fit your speech. You'll think of another great one.)

4. Don't worry about the exact wording of your introduction until you have finished preparing the body of the speech. After you have determined your main points, it will be much easier to make final decisions about how to begin the speech.

5. Work out your introduction in detail. Some teachers recommend that you write it out word for word; others prefer that you outline it. Whichever method you use, practice the introduction over and over until you can deliver it smoothly from a minimum of notes and with strong eye contact. This will get your speech off to a good start and give you a big boost of confidence.

The Conclusion

"Great is the art of beginning," said Longfellow, "but greater the art is of ending." Longfellow was thinking of poetry, but his insight is equally applicable to public speaking. Many a speaker has marred an otherwise fine speech by a long-winded, silly, or antagonistic conclusion. Your closing remarks are your last chance to drive home your ideas. Moreover, your final impression will probably linger in your listeners' minds. Thus you need to craft your conclusion with as much care as your introduction.

No matter what kind of speech you are giving, the conclusion has two major functions:

- To let the audience know you are ending the speech.
- To reinforce the audience's understanding of, or commitment to, the central idea.

Let us look at each.

Signal the End of the Speech

It may seem obvious that you should let your audience know you are going to stop soon. However, you will almost certainly hear speeches in your class in which the speaker concludes so abruptly that you are taken by surprise. Even in casual conversation you expect some signal that the talk is coming to an end. You are taken aback when the person you are talking with suddenly walks off without warning. The same is true of speechmaking. Too sudden an ending leaves the audience puzzled and unfulfilled.

How do you let an audience know your speech is ending? One way is through what you say. "In conclusion," "One last thought," "In closing," "My purpose has been," "Let me end by saying"—these are all brief cues that you are getting ready to stop.

You can also let your audience know the end is in sight by your manner of delivery. The conclusion is the climax of a speech. A speaker who has carefully built to a peak of interest and involvement will not need to say anything like "in conclusion." By use of the voice—its tone, pacing, intonation, and rhythm—a speaker can build the momentum of a speech so there is no doubt when it is over.

One method of doing this has been likened to a musical crescendo. As in a symphony in which one instrument after another joins in until the entire orchestra is playing, the speech builds in force until it reaches a zenith of power and intensity.[4] (This does *not* mean simply getting louder and louder. It is a combination of many things, including vocal pitch, choice of words, dramatic content, gestures, pauses—and possibly loudness.)

> **crescendo ending**
> A conclusion in which the speech builds to a zenith of power and intensity.

A superb example of this method is the memorable conclusion to Martin Luther King's "I've Been to the Mountaintop," the speech he delivered the night before he was assassinated in April 1968. Speaking to an audience of 2,000 people in Memphis, Tennessee, he ended his speech with a stirring declaration that the civil rights movement would succeed despite the many threats on his life:

> Like anybody, I would like to live a long life. Longevity has its place, but I'm not concerned about that now. I just want to do God's will, and he's allowed me to go up to the mountain, and I've looked over and I've seen the Promised Land. I may not get there with you, but I want you to know tonight that we as a people will get to the Promised Land. So I'm happy tonight. I'm not worried about anything; I'm not fearing any man. Mine eyes have seen the glory of the coming of the Lord.[5]

View the ending of Martin Luther King's "I've Been to the Mountaintop."

CD: VIDEO CLIP 9.5

Another effective method might be compared to the dissolve ending of a concert song that evokes deep emotions: "The song seems to fade away while the light on the singer shrinks gradually to a smaller and smaller circle until it lights only the face, then the eyes. Finally, it is a pinpoint, and disappears with the last note of the song."[6] Here is a speech ending that does much the same thing. It is from General Douglas MacArthur's moving farewell to the cadets at the U.S. Military Academy:

> In my dreams I hear again the crash of guns, the rattle of musketry, the strange, mournful mutter of the battlefield. But in the evening of my memory always I come back to West Point. Always there echoes and re-echoes: duty, honor, country.
>
> Today marks my final roll call with you. But I want you to know that when I cross the river, my last conscious thoughts will be of the Corps, and the Corps, and the Corps.
>
> I bid you farewell.[7]

The final words fade like the spotlight, bringing the speech to an emotional close.

You may think that you couldn't possibly end a speech with that much pathos—and you'd be right. MacArthur was an eloquent speaker discussing a grave issue with extraordinary poignance. This combination rarely occurs. But that doesn't mean you can't use the dissolve ending effectively. One student used it with great effect in a speech about visiting her grandparents' family farm as a young girl. During the body of the speech, the student spoke about the sights and sounds of the farm, the love and laughter she shared there as a child. Then, in conclusion, she evoked the images and sentiments of the farm one last time to create a moving dissolve ending:

> Now, as with so much of our childhood, the farm is no longer the same. Grandpa is gone. The barn has been rebuilt. The softball sits idly on the shelf. Grandma no longer cooks her huge family dinners. Going to the farm is different without these pleasures. But still the memories remain. I can still see the fields. I can still smell the hay. I can still hear the laughter. I can still feel the love.

Both the crescendo and the dissolve endings must be worked out with great care. Practice until you get the words and the timing just right. The benefits will be well worth your time.

Reinforce the Central Idea

The second major function of a conclusion is to reinforce the audience's understanding of, or commitment to, the central idea. There are many ways to do this. Here are the ones you are most likely to use.

Summarize Your Speech

Restating the main points is the easiest way to end a speech. One student used this technique effectively in her informative speech about color psychology:

dissolve ending
A conclusion that generates emotional appeal by fading step by step to a dramatic final statement.

The conclusion is a speaker's last chance to drive home her or his ideas. Successful speakers, such as Hillary Rodham Clinton, craft their conclusions with great care to leave a strong final impression.

As we have seen, color psychology is a fascinating subject that is not yet totally understood by researchers. What I have tried to do, through information from books and articles, is to explain why different colors affect people in certain ways and how this knowledge is being used in advertising, interior decorating, and health care. I hope this will help you understand how seemingly minor things such as the color of our clothes, of our homes, and even of the food we eat can have such an important impact on our daily lives.

The value of a summary is that it explicitly restates the central idea and main points one last time. But as we shall see, there are more imaginative and compelling ways to end a speech. They can be used in combination with a summary or, at times, in place of it.

End with a Quotation

A quotation is one of the most common and effective devices to conclude a speech. Here is a fine example, from a speech on the misuse of television advertisements in political campaigns:

We cannot ignore the evils of television commercials in which candidates for the highest offices are sold to the voters in 30-second spots. These ads cheapen the elective process and degrade our political institutions. In the words of historian Arthur Schlesinger, Jr., "You cannot merchandise candidates like soap and hope to preserve a rational democracy."

The closing quotation is particularly good because its urgency is exactly suited to the speech. When you run across a *brief* quotation that so perfectly captures your central idea, keep it in mind as a possible conclusion.

Make a Dramatic Statement

Rather than using a quotation to give your conclusion force and vitality, you may want to devise your own dramatic statement. Some speeches have become famous because of their powerful closing lines. One is Patrick Henry's legendary "Liberty or Death" oration. It takes its name from the final sentences Henry uttered on March 23, 1775, as he exhorted his audience to resist British tyranny:

> Is life so dear, or peace so sweet, as to be purchased at the price of chains and slavery? Forbid it, Almighty God! I know not what course others may take; but as for me, give me liberty, or give me death.[8]

Although your classroom speeches are not likely to become famous, you can still rivet your listeners—as Henry did—with a dramatic concluding statement. What follows is a particularly striking example, from a speech on suicide prevention. Throughout the speech, the student referred to a friend who had tried to commit suicide the previous year. Then, in the conclusion, she said:

> My friend is back in school, participating in activities she never did before—and enjoying it. I'm happy and proud to say that she's still fighting for her life and even happier that she failed to kill herself. Otherwise, I wouldn't be here today trying to help you. You see, I am my "friend," and I'm more than glad to say, I've made it.

As you can imagine, the audience was stunned. The closing lines brought the speech to a dramatic conclusion.

Here is another example of the same technique—this time from a less unusual situation:

> It is so easy to label the homeless as "bums" and "bag ladies." It is also easy to see them as people who are just looking for a handout—and often we give it to them and walk away. But as we have seen, most homeless people are not simply looking for a handout—they are reaching for a hand. Don't you think we should extend it to them?

This conclusion works because it takes the listener slightly by surprise and creates a lingering impression in the audience. Here the speaker made it even more effective by pausing for just a moment before the last sentence and by using his voice to give the closing words extra emotional force.

Refer to the Introduction

An excellent way to give your speech psychological unity is to conclude by referring to ideas in the introduction. This is an easy technique to use, and it may give your speech an extra touch of class. Here is how one student used the method in her speech about cryonics, the process of freezing people after death in the hope that medical science will be able to revive them in the future:

Introduction: The time is now. Imagine your mother or father has suffered a heart attack. Deprived of its vital blood supply, a part of their heart is dying. Or imagine your grandmother or grandfather lying nearly motionless in their nursing home bed. Advanced age, complicated by pneumonia, is about to end their lives. Or imagine a close friend has just entered the hospital with a massive systemwide infection. AIDS has left their body ravaged by multiple disease.

For most people, these circumstances would herald the end of life. Today's medicine can no longer help them. But all of you may be able to meet again in the far future. Does this sound like science fiction? Perhaps. But it may one day be possible. How? Through the process of cryonics.

In the body of her speech the student explained the origins of cryonics, the scientific methods used to freeze people, and the problems that must be overcome if they are to be thawed and returned to life in the future. Then, in her conclusion, she returned to the scenarios mentioned in her introduction to tie the whole speech together:

Conclusion: So think again of your father or mother suffering a heart attack, your grandmother or grandfather dying of pneumonia, or your close friend stricken with AIDS. If they chose to be buried or cremated in traditional fashion, their physical minds and bodies would be destroyed. That is absolutely certain. By contrast, being cryonically frozen offers some small chance that they may be revived in the future. Even if that chance is small, it's more than no chance at all.

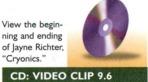

View the beginning and ending of Jayne Richter, "Cryonics."

CD: VIDEO CLIP 9.6

Summarizing the speech, ending with a quotation, making a dramatic statement, referring to the introduction—all these techniques can be used separately. But you have probably noticed that speakers often combine two or more in their conclusions. Actually, all four techniques can be fused into one—for example, a dramatic quotation that summarizes the central idea while referring to the introduction.

One other concluding technique is making a direct appeal to your audience for action. This technique applies only to a particular type of persuasive speech, however, and will be discussed in Chapter 15. The four methods covered in this chapter are appropriate for all kinds of speeches and occasions.

Sample Conclusion with Commentary

How do you fit these methods together to make a conclusion? Here is an example, from the same speech about canine companions whose introduction we looked at earlier (pages 225–226).

Commentary	Conclusion
The speaker gives an excellent summary of her speech. This is particularly important when you are speaking to inform because it	We have seen, then, that training a canine companion takes a great deal of time and money—up to $10,000 per dog. We have also seen that people who receive the dogs must go through their own training to make sure they and their dog will

gives you one last chance to make sure the audience remembers your main points.

By referring back to her sister, whom she had mentioned in the introduction, the speaker unifies the entire speech. Her closing quotation reinforces the central idea and ends the speech on a strong note.

work as a team. Finally, we have seen the amazing tasks canine companions can perform to help people with physical disabilities enjoy more independent lives.

It has now been two years since my sister received her canine companion. During that time, Lucky has become her hands, her feet, and her best friend. She says of Lucky, "I don't know what I would do without him. He has given my life new meaning."

Tips for Preparing the Conclusion

1. As with the introduction, keep an eye out for possible concluding materials as you research and develop the speech.

2. Conclude with a bang, not a whimper. Be creative in devising a conclusion that hits the hearts and minds of your audience. Work on several possible endings, and select the one that seems likely to have the greatest impact.

The Speech Conclusion Checklist can help you prepare your speeches.

CD: SPEECH CHECKLIST

3. Don't be long-winded. The conclusion will normally make up no more than about 5 to 10 percent of your speech. Nothing aggravates audiences more than a speaker who says "In conclusion" and then drones on interminably.

4. Don't leave anything in your conclusion to chance. Work it out in detail, and give yourself plenty of time to practice delivering it. Many students like to write out the conclusion word for word to guarantee it is just right. If you do this, make sure you can present it smoothly, confidently, and with feeling—without relying on your notes or sounding wooden. Make your last impression as forceful and as favorable as you can.

Summary

First impressions are important. So are final impressions. This is why speeches need strong introductions and conclusions.

In most speech situations you need to accomplish four objectives with your introduction—get the attention and interest of the audience, reveal the topic of your speech, establish your credibility and goodwill, and preview the body of the speech. Gaining attention and interest can be done in several ways. You can show the importance of your topic, especially as it relates to your audience. You can startle or question your audience or arouse their curiosity. You can begin with a quotation or a story.

Be sure to state the topic of your speech clearly in your introduction; otherwise, your audience may be confused and wonder where the speech is going. Establishing credibility means that you tell the audience why you are qualified to speak on the topic at hand; establishing goodwill, although less important for classroom speeches than for speeches outside the classroom, may be necessary if your point of view is unpopular. Previewing the body of the speech helps the audience listen effectively and provides a smooth lead-in to the body of the speech.

The conclusion of a speech is particularly important, because the final impression is often what will stick in your listeners' minds. The conclusion has two major objectives—to let the audience know you are ending the speech, and to reinforce their understanding of, or commitment to, your central idea. Too sudden an ending may leave your audience puzzled; it is always a good idea to alert them that you are finishing. You can do this either by your words or by your manner of delivery.

You can use a number of techniques to reinforce your central idea in the conclusion. They include summarizing the speech, ending with a pertinent quotation, making a dramatic statement, and referring to the introduction. Sometimes you may want to combine two or more of these techniques. Be creative in devising a vivid, forceful conclusion.

Key Terms

rhetorical question (218)

credibility (222)

goodwill (223)

preview statement (224)

crescendo ending (227)

dissolve ending (228)

Review Questions

After reading this chapter, you should be able to answer the following questions:

1. What are four objectives of a speech introduction?

2. What are seven methods you can use in the introduction to get the attention and interest of your audience?

3. Why is it important to establish your credibility at the beginning of your speech?

4. What is a preview statement? Why should you nearly always include a preview statement in the introduction of your speech?

5. What are five tips for preparing your introduction?

6. What are the major functions of a speech conclusion?

7. What are two ways you can signal the end of your speech?

8. What are four ways to reinforce the central idea when concluding your speech?

9. What are four tips for preparing your conclusion?

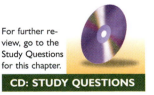

For further review, go to the Study Questions for this chapter.

CD: STUDY QUESTIONS

Exercises for Critical Thinking

1. Here are six speech topics. Explain how you might relate each to your classmates in the introduction of a speech.

Social Security	laughter
illiteracy	steroids
soap operas	blood donation

2. Think of a speech topic (preferably one for your next speech in class). Create an introduction for a speech dealing with any aspect of the topic you wish. In your introduction be sure to gain the attention of the audience, to reveal the topic and relate it to the audience, to establish your credibility, and to preview the body of the speech.

3. Using the same topic as in Exercise 2, create a speech conclusion. Be sure to let your audience know the speech is ending, to reinforce the central idea, and to make the conclusion vivid and memorable.

Applying the POWER of Public Speaking

Since leaving college with a degree in education, you have been a classroom teacher, high-school principal, and now assistant superintendent in a large urban school district—the same district in which you, yourself, attended high school. Because of your excellent public speaking skills, you have been chosen to represent the district at a meeting of parents, alumni, and neighborhood residents called to protest the closing of the city's oldest high school. With 1,200 current students and thousands of graduates still in the city, the school has produced many top scholars, as well as championship athletic teams.

At the meeting, you will need to explain the decision to close the school and to demolish the 1907 building. Architects, engineers, and city planners agree that renovation of the old structure is impractical and that the city's changing population requires construction of a new school in a new location.

As a graduate of the high school, you understand the feelings of people who want it to remain open. As a member of the school district administration, you understand why it must be closed. You also know that if your speech is to be persuasive, you must use the introduction to establish your credibility and goodwill so the audience will be willing to listen receptively to what you say in the body.

Write a draft of your introduction. In it, be sure to address all four functions of a speech introduction discussed in this chapter.

Notes

1. Anthony M. Frank, "The U.S. Postal Service: Making Progress," *Vital Speeches,* 56 (1990), p. 336.
2. Jeffrey E. Jamison, "Alkali Batteries: Powering Electronics and Polluting the Environment," in *Winning Orations, 1991* (Mankato, Minn.: Interstate Oratorical Association, 1991), p. 43.

[3]For research on the importance of goodwill to speakers in a variety of situations, see James C. McCroskey and Jason J. Teven, "Goodwill: A Reexamination of the Construct and Its Measurement," *Communication Monographs,* 66 (1999), pp. 90–103.

[4]Dorothy Sarnoff, *Speech Can Change Your Life* (Garden City, N.Y.: Doubleday, 1970), p. 189.

[5]Martin Luther King, Jr., "I've Been to the Mountaintop," in Lloyd E. Rohler and Roger Cook (eds.), *Great Speeches for Criticism and Analysis,* 3rd ed. (Greenwood, Ind.: Alistair Press, 1998), p. 358.

[6]Sarnoff, *Speech Can Change Your Life,* p. 190.

[7]Douglas MacArthur, "Farewell to the Cadets," May 12, 1962, in Richard L. Johannesen, R. R. Allen, Wil A. Linkugel, and Ferald J. Bryan (eds.), *Contemporary American Speeches,* 8th ed. (Dubuque, Iowa: Kendall/Hunt, 1997), pp. 403–404.

[8]Patrick Henry, "Give Me Liberty or Give Me Death," in Ronald F. Reid (ed.), *American Rhetorical Discourse,* 2nd ed. (Prospect Heights, Ill.: Waveland Press, 1995), p. 116.

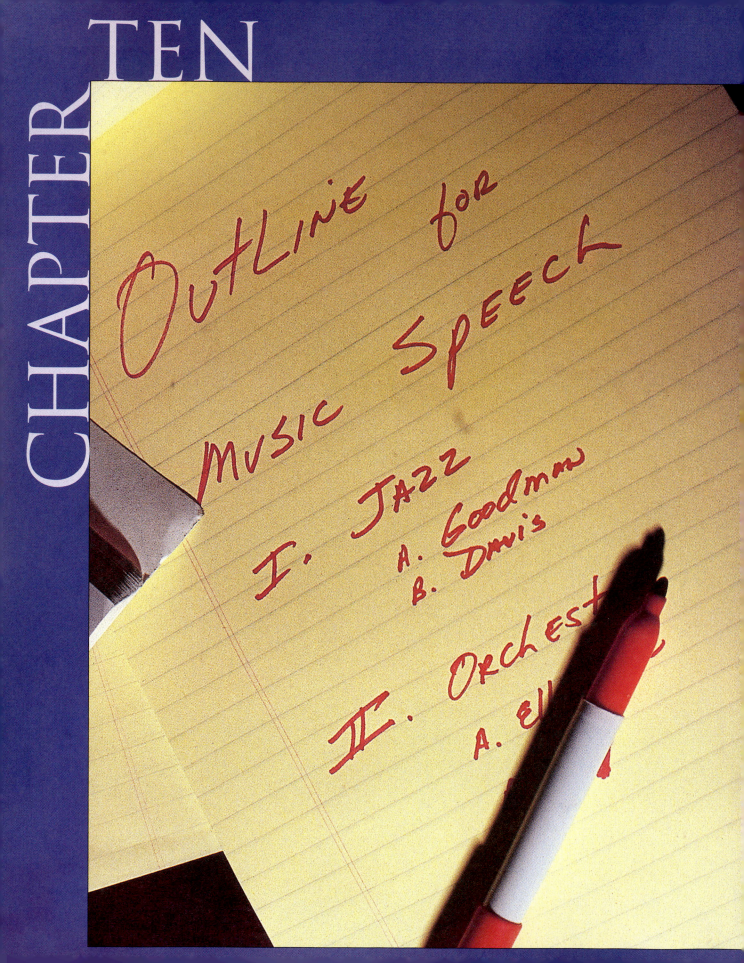

OUTLINING THE SPEECH

The Preparation Outline

Guidelines for the Preparation Outline
Sample Preparation Outline with Commentary

The Speaking Outline

Guidelines for the Speaking Outline
Sample Speaking Outline with Commentary

T
hink what might happen if you tried to build a house without a floor plan or an architect's blueprint. You build the kitchen next to the driveway to make it convenient for carrying in groceries. But the dining room turns up at the other end of the house. When you cook and serve a meal, you have to run with the plates to keep the food from getting cold. You put the bathroom at the head of the stairs to make it accessible to visitors. But the door opens in such a way that the unwary guest is catapulted down the steps. You think it's a wonderful idea to have almost no interior walls. After all, the modern living space is supposed to be free and open. But when the first snowfall comes, your (unsupported) roof collapses.

Plans and blueprints are essential to architecture. So, too, are outlines essential to effective speeches. An outline is like a blueprint for your speech. By outlining, you make sure that related items are together, that ideas flow from one to another, that the structure of your speech will "stand up"—and not collapse.

Probably you will use two kinds of outlines for your speeches—one very detailed, for the planning stage, and one very brief, for the delivery of the speech.

The Preparation Outline

The preparation outline is just what its name implies—an outline that helps you prepare the speech. Writing a preparation outline means actually putting your speech together. It is the stage at which you decide what you will say in the introduction, how you will organize the main points and supporting materials in the body of the speech, and what you will say in the conclusion.

Guidelines for the Preparation Outline

preparation outline
A detailed outline developed during the process of speech preparation that includes the title, specific purpose, central idea, introduction, main points, subpoints, connectives, conclusion, and bibliography of a speech.

Over the years, a relatively uniform system for preparation outlines has developed. It is explained below and is exemplified in the sample outline on pages 243–245. You should check with your teacher to see exactly what format you are to follow.

State the Specific Purpose of Your Speech

The specific purpose statement should be a separate unit that comes before the text of the outline itself. Including the specific purpose with the outline makes it easier to assess how well you have constructed the speech to accomplish your purpose.

Identify the Central Idea

Some teachers prefer that the central idea be given immediately after the purpose statement. Others prefer that it be given and identified in the text of the outline itself. Check to see which your teacher wants.

Label the Introduction, Body, and Conclusion

If you label the parts of your speech, you will be sure that you indeed *have* an introduction and conclusion and have accomplished the essential objectives of each. Usually the names of the speech parts are placed in the middle of the page or in the far left margin. They are technical labels only and are not included in the system of symbolization used to identify main points and supporting materials.

Use a Consistent Pattern of Symbolization and Indentation

In the most common system of outlining, main points are identified by Roman numerals and are indented equally so as to be aligned down the page. Subpoints (components of the main points) are identified by capital letters and are also indented equally so as to be aligned with each other. Beyond this, there may be sub-subpoints and even sub-sub-subpoints. For example:

  I. Main point
    A. Subpoint
    B. Subpoint
       1. Sub-subpoint
       2. Sub-subpoint
          a. Sub-sub-subpoint
          b. Sub-sub-subpoint
 II. Main point
    A. Subpoint
       1. Sub-subpoint
       2. Sub-subpoint
    B. Subpoint

The clear *visual framework* of this outline immediately shows the relationships among the ideas of the speech. The most important ideas (main points) are farthest to the left. Less important ideas (subpoints, sub-subpoints, and so on) are progressively farther to the right. This pattern reveals the structure of your entire speech.

> **visual framework**
> The pattern of symbolization and indentation in a speech outline that shows the relationships among the speaker's ideas.

Once you have organized the body of your speech (see Chapter 8), you should have identified the main points. You need only flesh out your outline with subpoints and sub-subpoints, as necessary, to support the main points. But suppose, as sometimes happens, you find yourself with a list of statements and are not sure which are main points, which are subpoints, and so forth. Such a list might look like this:

There were 13 people at the Last Supper—Jesus and his 12 disciples.

One of the most common sources of superstition is numbers.

In the United States, 13 is often omitted in the floor numbering of hotels and skyscrapers.

The number 13 has meant bad luck as long as anyone can remember.

Which statement is the main point? The second statement ("One of the most common sources of superstition is numbers"), which is broader in scope than any of the other statements. This would be one of the main ideas of your speech. The fourth statement is the subpoint; it immediately supports the main point. The other two statements are sub-subpoints; they illustrate the subpoint. Rearranged properly, they look like this:

I. One of the most common sources of superstition is numbers.
  A. The number 13 has meant bad luck as long as anyone can remember.
    1. There were 13 people at the Last Supper—Jesus and his 12 disciples.
    2. In the United States, 13 is often omitted in the floor numbering of hotels and skyscrapers.

Above all, remember that all points at the same level should immediately support the point that is just above and one notch to the left in your outline. If this sounds confusing, think of it as a business organization chart:

I. President
  A. Vice president—Operations
    1. Manager—Domestic Operations
      a. Assistant manager—East
      b. Assistant manager—West
    2. Manager—Foreign Operations
      a. Assistant manager—Europe and Asia
      b. Assistant manager—Africa
      c. Assistant manager—Americas
  B. Vice president—Administration
    1. Manager—Finance
    2. Manager—Personnel

As you can see, every person on this chart reports to the person who is above and one notch to the left—except, of course, the President, who is the "main point."

State Main Points and Subpoints in Full Sentences

Below are two sets of main points and subpoints for the same speech on the life of Martin Luther King.

Ineffective	More Effective
I. Montgomery	I. King began his civil rights career in the Montgomery bus boycott of 1955–1956.
II. 1960s	II. King's greatest triumphs came during the early 1960s.
A. Birmingham	A. In 1963 he campaigned against segregation in Birmingham, Alabama.
B. March	B. Later that year he participated in the famous march on Washington, D.C.
1. 200,000	1. More than 200,000 people took part.
2. "Dream"	2. King gave his "I Have a Dream" speech.

As blueprints are essential to architecture, so outlines are essential to speechmaking. Writing an outline helps ensure that your ideas are fully developed and that the structure of your speech is coherent.

C. Prize	C. In 1964 he received the Nobel Peace Prize.
III. Final years	III. King faced great turmoil during his final years.
A. Criticized	A. He was criticized by more militant blacks for being nonviolent.
B. Vietnam	B. He protested against the war in Vietnam.
C. Assassination	C. He was assassinated in Memphis, Tennessee, on April 4, 1968.

The sample at left might serve adequately as a speaking outline, but it is virtually useless as a preparation outline. It gives only vague labels rather than distinct ideas. It does not indicate clearly the content of the main points and subpoints. Nor does it reveal whether the speaker has thought out his or her ideas. But there is no concern about any of these matters with the outline on the right.

In sum, a skimpy preparation outline is of little value. Stating your main points and subpoints in full sentences will ensure that you develop your ideas fully.

Label Transitions, Internal Summaries, and Internal Previews

One way to make sure you have strong transitions, internal summaries, and internal previews is to include them in the preparation outline. Usually they are not incorporated into the system of symbolization and indentation, but are labeled separately and inserted in the outline where they will appear in the speech.

Attach a Bibliography

bibliography
A list of all the sources used in preparing a speech.

You should include with the outline a list of the sources you consulted in preparing the speech. The bibliography will show all the books, magazines, newspapers, and Internet sources you consulted, as well as any interviews or field research you conducted. You may use any one of a number of bibliographical formats, or your teacher may have a preference. No matter which format you adopt, make sure your statement of sources is clear, accurate, and consistent.

Give Your Speech a Title, If One Is Desired

Go to the Bibliography Formats for details on how to cite sources in a speech bibliography.

CD: BIBLIOGRAPHY FORMATS

In the classroom you probably do not need a title for your speech unless your teacher requires one. In some other situations, however, a speech title is necessary—as when the speech is publicized in advance, when the group inviting you to speak requests a title, or when the speech is going to be published. Whatever the reason, if you do decide to use a title, it should (1) be brief, (2) attract the attention of your audience, and (3) encapsulate the main thrust of your speech.

A good title need not have what Madison Avenue would call "sex appeal"—lots of glitter and pizzazz. By the same token, there is certainly nothing wrong with a catchy title—as long as it is germane to the speech. Here are two groups of titles. Those on the left are straightforward and descriptive. Those on the right are figurative alternatives to the ones on the left.

Group I	Group II
Unsafe Drinking Water	Toxins on Tap
Living with Deafness	The Sounds of Silence
The Rage to Diet	The Art of Wishful Shrinking
The United States Mint	The Buck Starts Here
Gambling Addiction	Against All Odds

Which group do you prefer? Neither is perfect. There are advantages and disadvantages to both. Those in the first group clearly reveal the topic of the speech, but they are not as provocative as those in the second group. Those in the second group are sure to arouse interest, but they do not give as clear an idea of what the speeches are about.

There is one other kind of title you should consider—the question. Phrasing your title as a question can be both descriptive and provocative. Using this method, we can construct a third set of titles combining the virtues of groups I and II:

Group III

Is Your Water Safe to Drink?

Can You See What I'm Saying?

Diets: How Effective Are They?

Where Is Making Money a Way of Life?

Do You Really Think You Can Beat the Odds?

The Speech Outliner will guide you through the steps in creating a preparation outline.

CD: SPEECH OUTLINER

Sometimes you will choose a title for your speech very early. At other times you may not find one you like until the last minute. Either way, try to be resourceful about creating titles for your speeches. Experiment with several and choose the one that seems most appropriate.

Sample Preparation Outline with Commentary

The following outline for a six-minute informative speech illustrates the guidelines just discussed.[1] The commentary explains the procedures used in organizing the speech and writing the outline. (Check with your teacher to see if she or he wants you to include a title with your outline.)

India: Land of Diversity	
Commentary	**Outline**
	Neera Nijhawan
Stating your specific purpose and central idea as separate units before the text of the outline makes it easier to judge how well you have constructed the outline to achieve your purpose and to communicate your central idea.	*Specific Purpose:* To inform my audience about the diversity of India's geography and languages. *Central Idea:* India is a country of great geographical and linguistic diversity.
Labeling the introduction marks it as a distinct section that plays a special role in the speech.	*Introduction*
Opening with a non-English word helps to get attention.	I. "Namaste." A. Do you know what I just said? B. I greeted you the way I would in India. II. The same word—"Namaste"—is also used when saying good-bye. A. The identical word can have two entirely different meanings. B. This is just one example of the diversity of life in India.
Here the speaker moves from her attention getter to reveal the topic of her speech.	

Now the speaker establishes her credibility and previews the main points to be discussed in the body of the speech.

Including transitions ensures that the speaker has worked out how to connect one idea to the next. Notice that the transition is not included in the system of symbolization and indentation used for the rest of the speech.

Labeling the body marks it as a distinct part of the speech.

Main point I is phrased as a full sentence. As the outline progresses, notice that the main points are arranged in topical order.

The three subpoints are shown by the capital letters A, B, and C, and are written in complete sentences to ensure that the speaker has thought them out fully.

Points below the level of subpoint are indicated by Arabic numerals and lowercase letters. Often they are not written in full sentences. Check to see what your teacher prefers.

When this speech was presented in class, the speaker used a large map as a visual aid throughout main point I so she could point out the regions of India as she discussed them.

The transition shows how the speaker will move from main point I to main point II.

Main point II, like main point I, is phrased as a full sentence.

III.   As a first-generation Indian-American, I have had firsthand experience with Indian life and culture.
IV.   Today I would like to give you a glimpse of India's diversity by looking at its geography and languages.

(*Transition:* Let's start with geography.)

Body

I.   India is a land of great geographical diversity.
   A. The northernmost part of India consists of the Himalaya Mountains.
     1. The highest mountain system in the world, the Himalaya separate India from China.
     2. The Indian Himalaya have many mountains more than 20,000 feet high.
   B. The central part of India consists of the Northern Plains.
     1. About 200 miles wide, the Northern Plains stretch across India from the Arabian Sea on the west to the Bay of Bengal on the east.
     2. Within the Northern Plains, there is considerable diversity.
       a. There is fertile farmland.
       b. There are major cities such as Delhi and Calcutta.
       c. There is the great Indian Desert.
   C. The southern part of India consists of the Deccan plateau.
     1. Extending from the edge of the Northern Plains to the southern tip of India, the Deccan plateau is more than 1,200 miles long.
     2. The Deccan plateau includes many geographical features.
       a. It contains farming and grazing land.
       b. It contains tropical forests.
       c. It contains most of India's seacoast.

(*Transition:* Now that you know something about the geographical diversity of India, let's look at its linguistic diversity.)

II.   India is a land of great linguistic diversity.
   A. The official language is Hindi.
     1. Hindi is spoken by 40 percent of the people.
     2. The opening word of my speech—"Namaste"—is Hindi.

Notice the pattern of subordination in this section. Subpoint B announces that there are 17 languages besides Hindi recognized in the Indian constitution. Sub-subpoint 1 deals with the distinctiveness of those languages. Because items a and b expand upon the distinctiveness point, they are subordinated to it.

The progressive indentation shows visually the relationships among main points, subpoints, sub-subpoints, etc.

Throughout main point II, the speaker uses well-chosen supporting materials to illustrate India's linguistic diversity in a clear and interesting fashion.

Labeling the conclusion marks it as a distinct part of the speech.

Summarizing the main points is usually standard procedure in an informative speech.

The closing line provides unity by relating back to the introduction.

This is the final bibliography. It lists the sources actually used in writing the speech and is shorter than the preliminary bibliography compiled in the early stages of research. (See Chapter 6 for a discussion of the preliminary bibliography.)

This bibliography follows the format recommended by the *MLA Handbook for Writers of Research Papers*. Check with your instructor to see what format you should use for your bibliography.

B. In addition to Hindi, there are 17 regional languages recognized in the Indian constitution.
  1. These languages are as distinct from each other as English is from French.
    a. Each has its own grammar and pronunciation.
    b. Some have their own alphabet.
  2. Many of these languages have literary traditions that are 2,000 years old.

C. India also has more than 1,000 minor languages and dialects.
  1. These can change entirely from village to village.
  2. This often makes communication very difficult.

D. Most educated Indians also speak English.
  1. The use of English comes from 300 years of British rule.
  2. English is spoken by 2 percent of the population.
  3. It is widely used in colleges and universities.

E. As linguist Kamala Singh has stated, the diversity of India's language is "unrivaled by any other nation."

Conclusion

I. I hope you can see from India's geography and languages why it is such a diverse—and fascinating—country.

II. Thank you and "Namaste."

Bibliography

Books

Arnett, Robert. *India Unveiled.* 2nd ed. Columbus, GA: Atman Press, 1999.

Kulke, Hermann, and Rothermund, Dietmar. *A History of India.* 3rd ed. London: Routledge, 1998.

Articles

Kinzer, Stephen. "Nehru Spoke It, but It's Still 'Foreign.'" *New York Times* 28 Jan. 1998: A4.

Tharoor, Shashi. "Who Is an Indian?" *New Perspectives Quarterly* Summer 1999: 27–28.

Internet Sources

Gupta, Sourendu. "Major Indian Languages." 14 Aug. 1999 [last update]. <http://theory.theory.tifr.res.in/bombay/history/people/language/> 12 April 2000.

United States Central Intelligence Agency. "India." *World Factbook,* 4 Feb. 2000 [last update]. <http://www.odci.gov/cia/publications/factbook/in.html > 12 April 2000.

The Speaking Outline

"I was never so excited by public speaking before in my life," wrote one listener in 1820 after listening to Daniel Webster. "Three or four times I thought my temples would burst with the gush of blood. . . I was beside myself, and am so still."[2]

Such reactions were not unusual among Webster's audiences. He thrilled two generations of Americans with his masterful orations. Incredible as it seems today, he did so while speaking for three, four, even five hours at a time. Equally incredible, he often spoke without using any notes! A reporter once asked how he managed this. "It is my memory," Webster said. "I can prepare a speech, revise and correct it in my memory, then deliver the corrected speech exactly as finished."[3]

Few people have Webster's remarkable powers of memory. Fortunately, it is no longer customary to speak from memory. Today most people speak extemporaneously—which means the speech is thoroughly prepared and carefully practiced in advance, but much of the exact wording is selected while the speech is being delivered (see Chapter 12). Your speeches will probably be of this type. You should know, then, about the *speaking outline*—the most widely recommended form of notes for extemporaneous speeches.

The aim of a speaking outline is to help you remember what you want to say. In some ways it is a condensed version of your preparation outline. It should contain key words or phrases to jog your memory, as well as essential statistics and quotations that you do not want to risk forgetting. But it should also include material *not* in your preparation outline—especially cues to direct and sharpen your delivery.

Most speakers develop their own variations on the speaking outline. As you acquire more experience, you, too, should feel free to experiment. But for now, you cannot go wrong by following the basic guidelines below and by imitating the sample speaking outline on pages 249–250.

speaking outline
A brief outline used to jog a speaker's memory during the presentation of a speech.

Guidelines for the Speaking Outline

Follow the Visual Framework Used in the Preparation Outline

Your speaking outline should use the same visual framework—the same symbols and the same pattern of indentation—as your preparation outline. This will make it much easier to prepare the speaking outline. More important, it will allow you to see instantly where you are in the speech at any given moment while you are speaking. You will find this a great advantage. As you speak, you will look down at your outline periodically to make sure you are covering the right ideas in the right order. It will be of little help if you have to hunt around to find where you are every time you look down.

Compare the following two versions of a partial speaking outline. They are from an informative speech about the history of feminism in the United States.

The Preparation Outline Checklist can help you prepare your outline.

CD: SPEECH CHECKLIST

Novice speakers tend to rely on too many notes when delivering their speeches. Accomplished speakers often use a minimum of notes, or no notes at all, which helps them communicate directly with the audience.

Ineffective

I. 1840–1860
A. World Anti-Slavery Convention
B. Seneca Falls convention
1. Lucretia Mott
2. Elizabeth Cady Stanton
3. Declaration of Sentiments
II. 1900–1920
A. National American Woman Suffrage Association
1. Founding
2. Objectives
B. Nineteenth Amendment
1. Campaign
2. Ratification

More Effective

I. 1840–1860
   A. World Anti-Slavery Convention
   B. Seneca Falls convention
       1. Lucretia Mott
       2. Elizabeth Cady Stanton
       3. Declaration of Sentiments
II. 1900–1920
   A. National American Woman Suffrage Association
       1. Founding
       2. Objectives
   B. Nineteenth Amendment
       1. Campaign
       2. Ratification

The wording of both outlines is exactly the same. But the visual framework of the one on the right makes it easier to take in at a glance and reduces the odds of the speaker losing his or her place.

Make Sure the Outline Is Plainly Legible

You would be surprised how many students try to speak from messy, scribbled notes that would be hard to decipher at leisure, much less under the pressures of a speech situation. Your speaking outline is all but worthless unless it is instantly readable at a distance. When you make your outline, use dark ink and large lettering, leave extra space between lines, provide ample margins, and write or type on one side of the paper only.

Some speakers put their notes on index cards. Most find the 3×5 size too cramped and prefer the 4×6 or 5×8 sizes instead. Other people write their speaking outlines on regular paper. Either practice is fine, as long as your notes are immediately legible to you while you are speaking.

Keep the Outline as Brief as Possible

If your notes are too detailed, you will have difficulty maintaining eye contact with your audience. A detailed outline will tempt you to look at it far too often, as one student discovered:

Mike Spagnola was speaking about the joys of roller blading. He had prepared the speech thoroughly and practiced it until it was nearly perfect. But when he delivered the speech in class, he referred constantly to his detailed notes. As a result, his delivery was choppy and strained. After the speech, Mike's classmates remarked on how often he had looked at his notes, and he was amazed. "I didn't even know I was doing it," he said. "Most of the time I wasn't even paying attention to the outline. I knew the speech cold."

Many students have had the same experience. Having lots of notes is a psychological security blanket against the possibility that something will go terribly wrong. The feeling seems to be, "As long as I have plenty of notes, disaster will not strike." In fact, most beginning speakers use far too many notes. Like Mike, they find they don't need all of them to remember the speech. They also discover that too many notes can actually interfere with good communication.

To guard against having too many notes, keep your speaking outline as brief as possible. It should contain key words or phrases to help you remember major points, subpoints, and connectives. If you are citing statistics, you will probably want to include them in your notes. Unless you are good at memorizing quotations, write them out fully as well. Finally, there may be two, three, or four key ideas whose wording is so important that you want to state them in simple complete sentences. The best rule of thumb is that your notes should be the *minimum* you need to jog your memory and keep you on track. At first you may find it risky to speak from a brief outline, but you will soon become more comfortable with it.

Give Yourself Cues for Delivering the Speech

A good speaking outline reminds you not only of *what* you want to say but also of *how* you want to say it. As you practice the speech, you will decide that certain ideas and phrases need special emphasis—that they should be spoken more loudly, softly, slowly, or rapidly than other parts of the speech. You will also determine how you want to pace the speech—how you will control its timing, rhythm, and momentum. But no matter how you work these things out ahead of time, no matter how often you practice, it is easy to forget them once you get up in front of an audience.

delivery cues
Directions in a speaking outline to help a speaker remember how she or he wants to deliver key parts of the speech.

The solution is to include in your speaking outline *delivery cues*—directions for delivering the speech. One way to do this is by underlining or otherwise highlighting key ideas that you want to be sure to emphasize. Then, when you reach them in the outline, you will be reminded to stress them. Another way is to jot down on the outline explicit cues such as "pause," "repeat," "slow down," "louder," and so forth. Both techniques are good aids for beginning speakers, but they are also used by most experienced speakers.

Sample Speaking Outline with Commentary

Below is a sample speaking outline for a six-minute informative talk about the geographical and linguistic diversity of India. By comparing it with the preparation outline for the same speech on pages 243–245, you can see how a detailed preparation outline is transformed into a concise speaking outline.

Commentary	Outline
	Eye Contact!! *Slow Down*

These comments remind the speaker to establish eye contact and not to race through the speech.	I. "Namaste."
	   A. Know what I said?
	   B. Greeted as if in India.

	— *Pause* —

The word "pause" reminds the speaker to pause after her opening lines.	II. "Namaste" also used when saying good-bye.
	   A. Two different meanings.
	   B. Example of India's diversity.
	III. First-generation Indian-American.
	IV. Today—India's diversity in geography and languages.
	(Let's start with geography.)

Including the main ideas of the introduction helps keep the speaker on track at the start of the speech.	
It's usually a good idea to pause briefly before launching into the first main point. This is another way of signaling that you are moving from the introduction to the body.	— *Pause* —

Most speakers find it helpful to demarcate the body of the speech in the speaking outline as well as in the preparation outline.	*Body*
	I. Great geographical diversity.
	   A. Himalaya Mountains.
	     1. Separate India from China.
	     2. 20,000 feet high.
	   B. Northern Plains.
	     1. 200 miles wide.

Notice how the body of the speech follows the same visual format as the preparation outline. This makes the outline easy to read at a glance.	2. Diversity of Northern Plains.
	       a. Farmland.
	       b. Cities: Delhi and Calcutta.
	       c. Great Indian Desert.

Throughout the outline key words are used to jog the speaker's memory. Because the final wording of an extemporaneous speech is chosen at the moment of delivery, it will not be exactly the same as that in the preparation outline.

Inserting transitions makes sure the speaker doesn't forget them.

Underlining reminds the speaker to stress key words or ideas.

Quotations are usually written out in full in the speaking outline.

It's usually a good idea to pause before entering the conclusion.

Most speakers label the conclusion in the speaking outline as well as in the preparation outline.

Including the last sentence jogs the speaker's memory and ensures that the speech will end as planned.

C. Deccan plateau.
   1. 1,200 miles long.
   2. Geographical features.
      a. Farming and grazing land.
      b. Tropical forests.
      c. Seacoasts.

(Now you know geographical . . . look at linguistic.)

II. Great linguistic diversity.
   A. Official language is Hindi.
     1. Spoken by 40 percent.
     2. "Namaste" is Hindi.
   B. 17 other <u>major</u> languages in constitution.
     1. Distinct as English and French.
       a. Grammar and pronunciation.
       b. Alphabet.
     2. Literary traditions—<u>2,000</u> years.
   C. <u>1,000</u> minor languages and dialects.
     1. Change from village to village.
     2. Communication <u>very</u> difficult.
   D. Educated also speak English.
     1. 2 percent
     2. Colleges and universities.
   E. Kamala Singh: linguistic diversity "unrivaled by any other nation."

— Pause —

Conclusion

I. Hope you see diversity from geography and languages.
II. Thank you and "Namaste."

Summary

Outlines are essential to effective speeches. By outlining, you make sure that related ideas are together, that your thoughts flow from one to another, and that the structure of your speech is coherent. You will probably use two kinds of outlines for your speeches—the detailed preparation outline and the brief speaking outline.

The preparation outline helps you prepare your speech. In this outline you state your specific purpose and central idea, label the introduction, body, and conclusion, and designate transitions, internal summaries, and internal previews. You should identify main points, subpoints, and sub-subpoints by a consistent pattern of symbolization and indentation. It is usually advisable to state at least main points and subpoints in full sentences. Your teacher may require a bibliography with your preparation outline.

The speaking outline consists of brief notes to help you while you deliver the speech. It should contain key words or phrases to jog your memory, as well as essential statistics and quotations. In making up your speaking outline, follow the same visual framework used in your preparation outline. Keep the speaking outline as brief as possible, and be sure it is plainly legible. You can also give yourself cues for delivering the speech—when to speak more softly or more slowly, when to pause, and so forth.

Key Terms

preparation outline (238)

speaking outline (246)

visual framework (239)

delivery cues (248)

bibliography (242)

Review Questions

After reading this chapter, you should be able to answer the following questions:

1. Why is it important to outline your speeches?

2. What is a preparation outline? What are the eight guidelines discussed in the chapter for writing a preparation outline?

3. What is a speaking outline? What are four guidelines for your speaking outline?

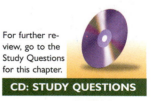

For further review, go to the Study Questions for this chapter.

CD: STUDY QUESTIONS

Exercises for Critical Thinking

1. In the left-hand column at the top of page 252 is a partially blank outline from a speech about sleep deprivation. In the right-hand column, arranged in random order, are the subpoints to fill in the outline. Choose the appropriate subpoint for each blank in the outline.

Outline	**Subpoints**
I. Most Americans do not get the sleep they need on a regular basis.	Sleep deprivation has been linked to a number of health problems.
	The *Times* also blames falling asleep at the wheel for 6,500 U.S. traffic deaths each year.
A.	
	The typical adult needs about eight hours of sleep each night to function effectively during the day.
B.	
1.	Second, it increases the risk of heart disease.
2.	The same study showed that 20 percent of the population gets less than six hours sleep a night.
II. Sleep deprivation is a major cause of traffic accidents and deaths.	
	The statistics linking sleep deprivation to traffic accidents and deaths are alarming.
A.	
	Yet most Americans consistently get less than eight hours sleep a night.
1.	
2.	First, it weakens the immune system.
B.	Sleep deprivation is second only to alcohol as the leading cause of traffic accidents and deaths.
III. Sleep deprivation also contributes to poor personal health.	*Newsweek* reports that "sleep deprivation has become one of the most pervasive health problems facing the U.S."
A.	
B.	A Stanford study showed that over half the population gets less than seven hours sleep a night.
1.	
2.	Third, it contributes to gastrointestinal illness.
3.	The *Los Angeles Times* reports that drowsiness causes 200,000 auto accidents each year.

2. Following the format used in the sample preparation outline on pages 243–245, outline "Cryonics," the sample speech at the end of Chapter 14. Be sure to include a specific purpose statement, to identify the central idea, to label the introduction, body, and conclusion, to use a consistent pattern of symbolization and indentation, to state the main points and subpoints in full sentences, and to label transitions and internal summaries.

3. From the preparation outline you constructed in Exercise 2, create a speaking outline that you might use in delivering the speech. Follow the guidelines for a speaking outline discussed in this chapter.

*A*pplying the POWER of Public Speaking

As the defense attorney in a car theft case, you need to prepare your closing argument to the jury before it begins its deliberations. After reviewing evidence from the trial, you decide to stress the following points to demonstrate the innocence of your client:

a. The stolen car was found abandoned three hours after the theft with the engine still warm; at the time the car was found, your client was at the airport to meet the flight of a friend who was flying into town.
b. Lab analysis of muddy shoe prints on the floor mat of the car indicates that the prints came from a size 13 shoe; your client wears a size 10.
c. Lab anlaysis shows the presence of cigarette smoke in the car, but your client does not smoke.
d. The only eyewitness to the crime, who was 50 feet from the car, said the thief "looked like" your client; yet the eyewitness admitted that at the time of the theft she was not wearing her corrective lenses, which had been prescribed for improving distance vision.
e. The car was stolen at about 1 P.M.; your client testified that he was in a small town 175 miles away at 11 A.M.
f. In a statement to police, the eyewitness described the thief as blond; your client has red hair.

   As you work on the outline of your speech, you see that these points can be organized into three main points, each with two supporting points. Compose an outline that organizes the points in this manner.

Notes

[1]Reprinted with permission of Neera Nijhawan.
[2]Robert T. Oliver, *History of Public Speaking in America* (Boston: Allyn and Bacon, 1965), p. 143.
[3]Oliver, *History of Public Speaking*, p. 145.

CHAPTER ELEVEN

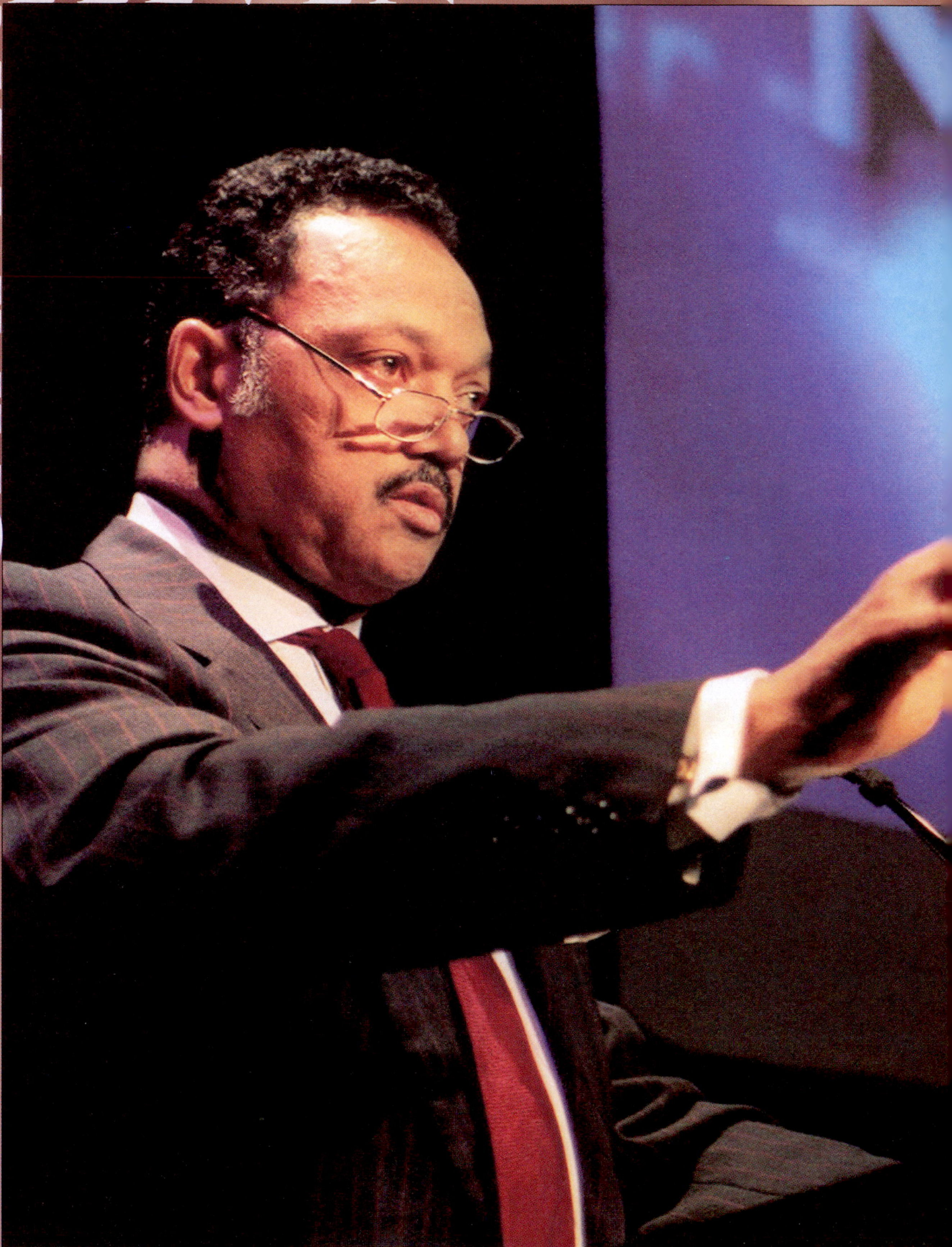

USING LANGUAGE

Have you ever played *Pictionary?* The point of the game is to draw words so people watching you can guess them. Some words are easy—"house," "bird," and "television," for instance. Even people without artistic talent can draw these in such a way that observers catch on immediately. But other kinds of words are more challenging. Try drawing "numb," "embarrass," or "dehydrated." The more abstract the word the more difficult it is to represent visually. How would you draw "improvement" or "appropriate"?

This is why language has evolved. Human beings need to communicate at a level far above what can be shown by pictures. But for language to work there must be a common understanding of what words mean. In effect, we've all made a pact that a certain collection of letters and sounds will mean the same thing to everybody. If you say "book," everybody who speaks English will picture something like what you're holding right now. On the other hand, when you don't use words properly, you "break the pact" and communication breaks down. Suppose you say to a friend, "Abby, you're so pedestrian." You may mean she walks a lot; but Abby is likely to become angry, because you actually called her boring and ordinary.

Language Is Important

Good speakers respect language and how it works. How well do you use language? Do you say Shaquille O'Neal plays basketball *good,* when you mean he plays *well*? Do you say *in the eventuality of* when *if* will do? Do you describe a hurricane as a *terrible disaster,* as if there were such a thing as a *good disaster*? Do you litter your speech with such meaningless words as *you know, like, man,* and *really*?

If you do these things, you are bound to be less effective as a speaker. And, unfortunately, you are not alone. Much American speech is turning into the linguistic equivalent of junk food. For example:

Newspaper headline: "Lost sisters reunited after 18 years at grocery checkout counter." (Amazing. What about the other people in line for all those years?)

Classified ad: "For sale: Unique home in downtown Craigsville. Large lot. Many trees. One you will enjoy living in." (What do tree houses cost these days, anyway?)

Pittsburgh Steelers football coach Bill Cowher, discussing his quarterback: "Certainly that position is the one that's going to burden the blunt of the responsibilities." (Excuse me?)

Announcement in a campus bulletin: "Dean of Students promises to stop drinking on campus." (It's about time!)

The problem with these statements is not that they violate elitist standards of "good English." People in the United States have always talked casually. Our language has grown with as much vigor and variety as our population. We have borrowed words from other languages. We have coined new words and dropped old ones.[1] The first edition of *Webster's Collegiate Dictionary,* published in 1898, contained about 70,000 words.[2] The tenth edition, reprinted in 1998, has 170,000 words—and these are just the words deemed necessary for a college education. One expert has estimated that the

English language has more than 2 million words, with a thousand new ones being added each year.[3]

There is a big difference, however, between the natural growth of a living language and the misuse of that language. To misuse our language is much more than a matter of mere words. Contrary to popular belief, language does not mirror reality. It does not simply describe the world as it is. Instead, language helps create our sense of reality by giving meaning to events. Language is not neutral. The words we use to label an event determine to a great extent how we respond to it.[4]

Consider the continuing public debate over euthanasia. If you see euthanasia as "immoral," as a form of "murder," as "a violation of the doctor's duty to save lives," you will likely oppose efforts to allow it in any form. But if you see euthanasia as "moral," as a way to provide "death with dignity," as "an acceptable alternative to needless pain and suffering" for the terminally ill, you will likely support efforts to permit it in some circumstances.

What separates these two viewpoints? Not the capabilities of modern medicine; not the conditions of terminally ill patients; not even the act of euthanasia itself. All those are the same for both sides. The difference is in the *meaning* given to them by the words that label them. This is why, as one writer has said, a choice of words is also a choice of worlds.[5]

Words are vital to thinking itself. Thought and language are closely linked. We do not get an idea and then come up with words to express it. Rather, we usually think in words. How often have you said, "I know what I want to say, but I just don't know how to say it." In fact, if you truly knew what you wanted to say, you probably would be able to say it. On most occasions when we are looking for "just the right word," what we are really looking for is just the right *idea.*[6]

As a speaker, once you get the right idea, you must decide how best to *communicate* it to listeners. To do this, you need to be especially conscious of what language can do. Unless you use language accurately and clearly, no one will understand your ideas.

Words are the tools of a speaker's craft. They have special uses, just like the tools of any other profession. Have you ever watched a carpenter at work? The job that would take you or me a couple of hours is done by the carpenter in 10 minutes—with the right tools. You can't drive a nail with a screwdriver or turn a screw with a hammer. It is the same with public speaking. You must choose the right words for the job you want to do.

Good speakers are aware of the meanings of words—both their obvious and their subtle meanings. They also know how to use language accurately, clearly, vividly, and appropriately. The balance of this chapter will explore each of these aspects of language use. We will also give special attention to nonsexist language in public speaking.

Meanings of Words

Words have two kinds of meanings—denotative and connotative. *Denotative* meaning is precise, literal, and objective. It simply describes the object, person, place, idea, or event to which the word refers. One way to think of

denotative meaning
The literal or dictionary meaning of a word or phrase.

connotative meaning
The meaning suggested by the associations or emotions triggered by a word or phrase.

a word's denotative meaning is as its dictionary definition. For example, denotatively, the noun "school" means "a place, institution, or building where instruction is given."

Connotative meaning is more variable, figurative, and subjective. Put simply, the connotative meaning of a word is what the word suggests or implies. For instance, the connotative meaning of the word "school" includes all the feelings, associations, and emotions that the word touches off in different people. For some people, "school" might connote personal growth, childhood friends, and a special teacher. For others, it might connote frustration, discipline, and boring homework assignments.

Connotative meaning gives words their intensity and emotional power. It arouses in listeners feelings of anger, pity, love, fear, friendship, nostalgia, greed, guilt, and the like. Speakers, like poets, often use connotation to enrich their meaning. For example:

> Terrorists neither listen to reason nor engage in reasoning with others. Their aim is to generate fear—to frighten people into submission. They measure success by the magnitude of the fear they generate through brutal, savage acts of violence. Terrorists are prepared to kill to further whatever cause they claim to be pursuing. And the heinousness of these murders is accentuated by the fact that terrorists murder without passion. They murder with cool deliberation and deliberate planning. They are utterly amoral.

The underlined words in this passage have powerful connotations that are almost certain to produce a strong emotional revulsion to terrorism.

Here, in contrast, is another version of the same statement—this time using words with a different set of connotations:

> Terrorists do not seek to negotiate with their opponents. They seek victory by using political and psychological pressure, including acts of violence that may endanger the lives of some people. To the terrorist, ultimate objectives are more important than the means used to achieve them.

With the exception of "terrorist," the words in this statement are less likely to evoke an intensely negative response than those in the first statement.

Which statement is preferable? That depends on the audience, the occasion, and the speaker's purpose. Do you want to stir up your listeners' emotions, rally them to some cause? Then select words with more intense connotative meanings. Or are you addressing a controversial issue and trying to seem completely impartial? Then stick with words that touch off less intense reactions. Choosing words skillfully for their denotative and connotative meanings is a crucial part of the speaker's craft.

Using Language Accurately

Using language accurately is as vital to a speaker as using numbers accurately is to an accountant. One student found this out the hard way. In a speech about America's criminal justice system, he referred several times to "crimi-

Good speakers use words accurately and correctly. If you are unsure about the meaning of a word, be sure to look it up in a dictionary, thesaurus, phrase book, or similar work.

nal *persecution.*" What he meant, of course, was "criminal *prosecution.*" This one error virtually ruined his speech. As one of his classmates said, "How can I believe what you say about our courts when you don't even know the difference between prosecution and persecution?"

Sometimes inaccuracy results from a misguided attempt to be elegant. This happened to the business manager of a magazine.

Mary Jo Hundt had a special fondness for adding "istic" to the end of a word. Addressing the magazine's editorial staff one day, she said, "We are going to streamline our paperwork to make it more *simplistic.* That's the *modernistic* way to do things. With less paperwork, we'll have more time to devote to the magazine, and that will be *impressionistic* to management."

Mary Jo clearly did not realize that "simplistic" doesn't mean simple or easy but instead refers to *over*simplification on shaky grounds. And "modernistic" refers to a particular style of design, not the general condition of being modern. "Impressionistic," of course, has nothing to do with making an impression on someone; it describes a certain type of art or music. But the editorial staff knew all these things, and they were embarrassed for Mary Jo.

The moral of this story is obvious. Don't use a word unless you are sure of its meaning. If you are not sure, look up the word in a dictionary.

Fortunately, such outright blunders are relatively rare among college students. However, we all commit more subtle errors—especially using one word when another will capture our ideas more precisely. Every word has shades of meaning that distinguish it from every other word. As Mark Twain said, "The difference between the right word and the almost right word is the difference between lightning and the lightning bug."

thesaurus
A book of synonyms.

If you look in a thesaurus, you'll find the following words given as synonyms:

drop   collapse

decline   dive

All mean roughly the same thing—to fall from a higher place to a lower one. But all these words have different shades of meaning. See if you can fill in the best word to complete each of the sentences below:

1. One should never _____ into the shallow end of a pool.

2. After losing in the last minute to its archrival, the football team seemed to suffer a total _____.

3. Be careful unloading the dishwasher. You don't want to _____ the fine china.

4. In a day of heavy trading, the stock market witnessed a sharp _____ in commodity prices.

The best answers for the four statements are:

1. dive   3. drop

2. collapse   4. decline

Each of the words is a little different from the others, and each says something special to listeners.

As you prepare your speeches, ask yourself constantly, "What do I *really* want to say? What do I *really* mean?" Choose words that are precise, exact, accurate. When in doubt, consult the dictionary or thesaurus to make sure you have the best words to express your ideas.

If you have serious aspirations as a speaker, you should work out a systematic plan to improve your vocabulary. Years ago Malcolm X, the famous African-American leader, did this by copying the dictionary, word by word! This method is extreme, and few people would take the time for it. A less arduous plan might be to try using one new word every day—and using the word correctly. The purpose of this is not to learn a lot of big words, but to "learn when certain words should be used, . . . to use the proper word at the proper time."[7]

Using Language Clearly

Suppose you are standing on a street corner and you see a careless pedestrian about to step into the path of an oncoming car. Do you say, "It would appear from available empirical evidence as if an unsuspecting person is in danger of being struck and injured by an approaching automotive vehicle"? Of course not. You yell, "Look out!"

As many people have discovered, much to their dismay, it is possible to use language accurately without using it clearly. Here is a well-known story that shows how much trouble can be caused by not communicating clearly. A plumber wrote to a government agency to ask whether there was any harm in using hydrochloric acid to clean out drain pipes. The agency replied:

> The efficacy of hydrochloric acid is indisputable, but the corrosive effect is incompatible with metallic permanence.

The plumber thanked the agency for approving the use of hydrochloric acid. The agency wrote back, saying:

> We cannot assume responsibility for the production of toxic and noxious residue with hydrochloric acid and suggest you use an alternative procedure.

Once more the plumber thanked the agency for its approval. Finally, the agency, alarmed at the prospect of hundreds of ruined drain pipes, called in another scientist. He wrote:

> Don't use hydrochloric acid. It eats holes in the pipes!

Remember, people are different. What makes perfect sense to some may be gobbledygook to others. You cannot assume that what is clear to you is clear to your audience. This is particularly true in speechmaking. Listeners, unlike readers, cannot turn to a dictionary or reread an author's words to discover their meaning. A speaker's meaning must be *immediately* comprehensible; it must be so clear that there is virtually no chance of misunderstanding. You can ensure this by using familiar words, by choosing concrete words over abstract words, and by eliminating verbal clutter.

Use Familiar Words

It may seem obvious that familiar words are better than unfamiliar ones. But you would be amazed at how many speakers persist in bombarding listeners with complicated words—usually out of the mistaken belief that such words sound impressive. In truth, filling a speech with long, multisyllabic words only marks the speaker as stuffy and pretentious. Worse, it usually destroys understanding. One of the greatest barriers to clear speech is using big, bloated words where short, sharp ones will do the job better.[8]

Here, for example, are two passages expressing much the same idea. Which is easier to understand?

> Is this a genuine affirmation that the utterances you anticipate communicating during the time period immediately succeeding the present shall be entirely veracious and devoid of deception, complete in all pertinent minutiae and particularities, and absent of all misleading obfuscation or superfluous and undocumentable specificities, on the authority of your allegiance and fidelity to the supreme deity?

Or,

> Do you swear that the testimony you are about to give shall be the truth, the whole truth, and nothing but the truth, so help you God?

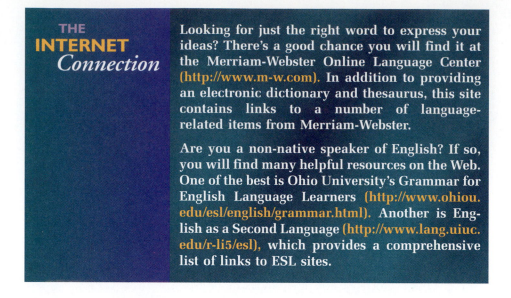

THE **INTERNET** *Connection*

Looking for just the right word to express your ideas? There's a good chance you will find it at the Merriam-Webster Online Language Center (http://www.m-w.com). In addition to providing an electronic dictionary and thesaurus, this site contains links to a number of language-related items from Merriam-Webster.

Are you a non-native speaker of English? If so, you will find many helpful resources on the Web. One of the best is Ohio University's Grammar for English Language Learners (http://www.ohiou.edu/esl/english/grammar.html). Another is English as a Second Language (http://www.lang.uiuc.edu/r-li5/esl), which provides a comprehensive list of links to ESL sites.

The second passage is the standard oath taken by a witness before testifying in a court of law. It consists of short, simple, familiar words that are easy to comprehend. Its meaning comes across without forcing you to perform complex mental gymnastics. The first passage says essentially the same thing as the second, but is full of stuffy, ostentatious words that make its meaning almost impossible to decipher.

When speaking about technical subjects, you may not be able to avoid unfamiliar words. If this happens, keep the technical terms to a minimum and define clearly those that your audience may not understand. If you work at it, you will almost always be able to translate even the most specialized topic into clear, familiar language.

Here, for instance, are three passages explaining the devastating effects of a pregnant woman's drinking on her unborn child. The first passage is in medical jargon, and it defies comprehension by ordinary listeners:

> Alcohol consumption by the pregnant woman seriously influences the intrauterine milieu and therefore contributes to the morbidity and mortality of children born to these mothers. In regard to the pathophysiology of this syndrome, genetic polymorphism of enzymes for ethanol metabolism may alter fetal susceptibility. There may also be poor microsomal or mitochondrial function or decreased ATP activity.

Even an educated person without a medical background would have trouble with "pathophysiology" and "polymorphism" and "mitochondrial," much less be able to put them all together.

The second passage represents an attempt to adapt to a nonmedical audience. It is in more familiar language but retains enough obscure words to be difficult:

> The deleterious effects of alcohol on the unborn child are very serious. When a pregnant mother consumes alcohol, the ethanol in the bloodstream easily crosses the placenta from mother to child and invades the amniotic fluid. This can produce a num-

ber of abnormal birth syndromes, including central-nervous-system dysfunctions, growth deficiencies, a cluster of facial aberrations, and variable major and minor malformations.

Well-informed listeners could probably figure out "deleterious effects," "central-nervous-system dysfunctions," and "facial aberrations." But these terms don't create a sharp mental image of what the speaker is trying to say. We still need to go one step further away from medical jargon toward ordinary language.

So we come to the third passage, which is utterly clear. It is from a speech by Annmarie Mungo, a student at Eastern Michigan University, and shows what can be done with work, imagination, and a healthy respect for everyday words:

When the expectant mother drinks, alcohol is absorbed into her bloodstream and distributed throughout her entire body. After a few beers or a couple of martinis, she begins to feel tipsy and decides to sober up. She grabs a cup of coffee, two aspirin, and takes a little nap. After a while she'll be fine.

But while she sleeps, the fetus is surrounded by the same alcoholic content as its mother had. After being drowned in alcohol, the fetus begins to feel the effect. But it can't sober up. It can't grab a cup of coffee. It can't grab a couple of aspirin. For the fetus's liver, the key organ in removing alcohol from the blood, is just not developed. The fetus is literally pickled in alcohol.[9]

This kind of plain talk is what listeners want. You cannot go wrong by following the advice of Winston Churchill to speak in "short, homely words of common usage." If you think big words (or a lot of words) are needed to impress listeners, bear in mind that the Gettysburg Address—considered the finest speech in the English language—contains 271 words, of which 251 have only one or two syllables.

Choose Concrete Words

Concrete words refer to tangible objects—people, places, and things. They differ from abstract words, which refer to general concepts, qualities, or attributes. "Carrot," "pencil," "nose," and "door" are concrete words. "Humility," "science," "progress," and "philosophy" are abstract words.

Of course, few words are completely abstract or concrete. Abstractness and concreteness are relative. "Apple pie" is concrete, but the phrase also has abstract values of patriotism and conventional morals. Usually, the more specific a word, the more concrete it is. Let us say you are talking about golf. Here are several words and phrases you might use:

physical activity   abstract/general

sports

golf

professional golf

Tiger Woods   concrete/specific

concrete words
Words that refer to tangible objects.

abstract words
Words that refer to ideas or concepts.

As you move down the list, the words become less abstract and more concrete. You begin with a general concept (physical activity), descend to one type of activity (sports), to a particular sport (golf), to a division of that sport (professional golf), to one specific professional golfer (Tiger Woods).

The more abstract a word, the more ambiguous it will be. Although abstract words are necessary to express certain kinds of ideas, they are much easier to misinterpret than are concrete words. Also, concrete words are much more likely to claim your listeners' attention. Suppose you make a speech about fire ants, which have long plagued the South and are now attacking western states. Here are two ways you could approach the subject— one featuring abstract words, the other concrete words:

Abstract Words:

Fire ants have been a problem ever since they came to the United States from South America. They have spread across the South and now threaten various parts of the West as well. This is a serious problem because fire ants are highly aggressive. There have even been human casualties from fire ant stings.

Concrete Words:

Since fire ants arrived here from South America sometime before World War II, they have spread like a biblical plague across eleven states from Florida to Texas. Now they are invading New Mexico, Arizona, and California. Fire ants attack in swarms and they will climb any foot that is left in the wrong spot for a few seconds. They have even turned up indoors, in clothes hampers, beds, and closets. Fortunately, fewer than 1 percent of people who are stung have to see a doctor, but toddlers who have fallen on fire ant mounds have sometimes died from stings, as have highly allergic adults.[10]

Notice how much more persuasive the second version is. A speech dominated by concrete words will almost always be clearer, more interesting, and easier to recall than one dominated by abstract words.

Eliminate Clutter

Cluttered speech has become a national epidemic. Whatever happened to such simple words as "before," "if," and "now"? When last seen they were being routed by their cluttered counterparts—"prior to," "in the eventuality of," and "at this point in time." By the same token, why can't weather forecasters say, "It's raining," instead of saying, "It appears as if we are currently experiencing precipitation activity"? And why can't politicians say, "We have a crisis," instead of saying, "We are facing a difficult crisis situation that will be troublesome to successfully resolve"?

clutter
Discourse that takes many more words than are necessary to express an idea.

This type of clutter is deadly to clear, compelling speech. It forces listeners to hack through a tangle of words to discover the meaning. When you make a speech, keep your language lean and lively. Beware of using several words where one or two will do. Avoid flabby phrases. Let your ideas emerge sharply and firmly. Above all, watch out for redundant adjectives and adverbs. Inexperienced speakers (and writers) tend to string together two or three synonymous adjectives, such as "a learned and educated person," or "a hot, steamy, torrid day."

Here is part of a student speech that has been revised to eliminate clutter:

Sitting Bull was one of the most important ~~and significant of all~~ Native American leaders.
He was born in ~~the year of~~ 1831 near Grand River, in ~~an area that is now part of the~~ *present-day*
~~state of~~ South Dakota. A fearless ~~and courageous~~ warrior, he ~~ended up being~~ *was* elected
chief of the Hunkpapa Sioux in 1867. In the following years, he also attracted a large
~~and numerous~~ following among the ~~tribes of the~~ Cheyenne and Arapaho. He is best
known ~~to people in this day and age~~ *today* for his ~~instrumental~~ role in ~~helping to lead the~~ *defeating*
~~defeat of~~ General Custer at the Battle of Little Bighorn in 1876. Although eventually
~~required against his will~~ *forced* to live ~~his life~~ on the Standing Rock Reservation in South Dakota,
he never surrendered ~~to anyone~~ his dignity or his ~~personal~~ devotion to the Sioux way
of life.

Notice how much cleaner and easier to follow the revised version is. No longer are the speaker's ideas hidden in a thicket of wasted words.

This kind of pruning is easy once you get the knack of it. The hardest part—and it is often very hard—is recognizing clutter for what it is and then forcing yourself to throw away the unnecessary words. Watch for clutter when you write your speech outlines. Be prepared to revise the outline until your ideas emerge as clearly and crisply as possible. As with revising an essay or a term paper, this will take extra time. But if you keep at it, you will become a much more effective speaker—and writer.

You can also help eliminate clutter by practicing your speeches with one or more reliable friends. Ask your friends to keep an ear out not just for flabby phrases but for verbal fillers such as "you know," "like," and "really." (If you are a habitual "like"-er, you will find this exasperating at first, but try to stay with it. You will discover that people listen to you much more seriously when you conquer this verbal tic.)

After your friends have helped you trim the clutter, practice delivering the speech again. At first you may feel awkward and unnatural because you are forcing yourself to break old habits. But if you practice regularly and concentrate on trimming your speeches of wasted words, you will gradually develop a new habit of speaking naturally without all that clutter. This will not only make you a better public speaker, but it will help you present ideas more effectively in meetings, conversations, and group discussions.

Using Language Vividly

Just as you can be accurate without being clear, so you can be both accurate and clear without being interesting. Here, for example, is how Martin Luther King *might have* phrased part of his great "I Have a Dream" speech:

> Turning back is something we cannot do. We must continue to work against police brutality, segregated housing, disfranchisement, and alienation. Only when these problems are solved will we be satisfied.

Here is what King *actually* said:

> We cannot turn back. There are those who ask the devotees of civil rights, "When will you be satisfied?" We can never be satisfied as long as the Negro is the victim of the unspeakable horrors of police brutality. We can never be satisfied as long as our bodies, heavy with the fatigue of travel, cannot gain lodging in the motels of the highways and the hotels of the cities. . . . We cannot be satisfied as long as a Negro in Mississippi cannot vote and a Negro in New York believes he has nothing for which to vote. No, no, we are not satisfied, and we will not be satisfied until justice rolls down like waters and righteousness like a mighty stream.[11]

Much more stirring, isn't it? If you want to move people with your speeches, use moving language. Dull, dreary words make for dull, dreary speeches. Bring your speeches to life by using vivid, animated language. Although there are several ways to do this, here are two of the most important—imagery and rhythm.

Imagery

One sign of a good novelist is the ability to create word pictures that get you totally involved with a story. These word pictures let you "see" the haunted house, or "feel" the bite of the snow against your face, or "hear" the birds chirping on a warm spring morning, or "smell" the bacon cooking over an open campfire, or "taste" the hot enchiladas at a Mexican restaurant.

imagery
The use of vivid language to create mental images of objects, actions, or ideas.

Speakers can use imagery in much the same way to make their ideas come alive. Three ways to generate imagery are by using concrete words, simile, and metaphor.

Concrete Words

As we saw earlier in this chapter, choosing concrete words over abstract words is one way to enhance the clarity of your speeches. Concrete words are also the key to effective imagery. Consider the following excerpt from Ronald Reagan's famous address commemorating the fortieth anniversary of D-Day. Speaking at the scene of the battle, Reagan dramatically recounted the heroism of the U.S. Rangers who scaled the cliffs at Pointe du Hoc to help free Europe from Hitler's stranglehold:

> We stand on a lonely, windswept point on the northern shore of France. The air is soft, but 40 years ago at this moment, the air was dense with smoke and the cries of men, and the air was filled with the crack of rifle fire and the roar of cannon.

Words are the tools of a speaker's craft. Ann Richards, former governor of Texas, is well known for her use of vivid, concrete language to bring her ideas to life.

At dawn, on the morning of the 6th of June, 1944, 225 Rangers jumped off the British landing craft and ran to the bottom of these cliffs. . . . The Rangers looked up and saw the enemy soldiers—at the edge of the cliffs shooting down at them with machine guns and throwing grenades. And the American Rangers began to climb. They shot rope ladders over the face of these cliffs and began to pull themselves up.

When one Ranger fell, another would take his place. When one rope was cut, a Ranger would grab another and begin his climb again. They climbed, shot back, and held their footing. Soon, one by one, the Rangers pulled themselves over the top, and in seizing the firm land at the top of these cliffs, they began to seize back the continent of Europe.[12]

View this excerpt from Ronald Reagan's speech at Pointe du Hoc.

CD: VIDEO CLIP 11.1

Concrete words call up mental impressions of sights, sounds, touch, smell, and taste. In the speech just quoted, we do not merely learn that the U.S. Rangers helped win the battle of D-Day. We visualize the Rangers landing at the foot of the cliffs. We see them fighting their way up the cliffs in the face of enemy grenades and machine guns. We hear the crack of rifle fire and the cries of the soldiers. The concrete words create images of sights and sounds, feelings and emotions that pull us irresistibly into the speech.

Simile

Another way to create imagery is through the use of simile. Simile is an explicit comparison between things that are essentially different yet have something in common. It always contains the words "like" or "as." Here are some examples from student speeches:

Walking into my grandparents' home when I was a child was like being wrapped in a giant security blanket.

Air pollution is eating away at the monuments in Washington, D.C., like a giant Alka-Seltzer tablet.

simile
An explicit comparison, introduced with the word "like" or "as," between things that are essentially different yet have something in common.

These are bright, fresh similes that clarify and vitalize ideas. Some similes, however, have become stale through overuse. Here are a few:

fresh as a daisy	hungry as a bear
fit as a fiddle	busy as a bee
strong as an ox	big as a mountain
stubborn as a mule	happy as a lark
blind as a bat	light as a feather

cliché
A trite or overused expression.

Such *clichés* are fine in everyday conversation, but you should avoid them in speechmaking. Otherwise, you are likely to be "dull as dishwater" and to find your audience "sleeping like a log"!

Metaphor

You can also use metaphor to create imagery in your speeches. Metaphor is an implicit comparison between things that are essentially different yet have something in common. Unlike simile, metaphor does not contain the words "like" or "as." For example:

metaphor
An implicit comparison, not introduced with the word "like" or "as," between two things that are essentially different yet have something in common.

In recent years, issues related to fairness have been relegated to the back of the bus, while issues of economic efficiency are in the driver's seat. (John E. Jacob)

America's cities are the windows through which the world looks at American society. (Henry Cisneros)

These are both brief metaphors. Sometimes, however, a speaker will develop a longer metaphor. Here is an excellent example from Elizabeth Cady Stanton's classic speech "The Solitude of Self":

No matter how much women prefer to lean, to be protected and supported, nor how much men desire to have them do so, they must make the voyage of life alone, and for safety in an emergency they must know something of the laws of navigation. To guide our own craft, we must be captain, pilot, engineer; with compass and chart to stand at the wheel; to watch the wind and waves and know when to take in the sail, and to read the signs in the firmament over all.[13]

mixed metaphor
A metaphor that combines two or more incompatible or illogical comparisons.

As you can see, metaphor is an excellent way to turn a phrase. Sometimes, however, metaphors get out of control. The result is a *mixed metaphor,* in which two or more incongruous comparisons are run together—often with comic results. Here, for example, is what one speaker (a U.S. Senator, no less!) said about a proposal to change the current method of funding Social Security:

This thing could sprout wings and become an irresistible political juggernaut that will thunder through the halls of Congress like a locomotive.

The speaker began by saying that the plan could "sprout wings." Having done so, he then needed to make the plan behave like a bird (not an airplane, because airplanes do not "sprout" wings). Instead, he turned it into a juggernaut, which the *Random House Dictionary* defines as a "large, over-powering, destructive force or object." It's hard to imagine a juggernaut with wings. Still, the speaker could have recovered a bit by having the juggernaut act like a winged creature. So what did he do? He had it "thunder through the halls of Congress like a locomotive"!

Needless to say, such a metaphor does more harm than good. When used effectively, however, metaphor—like simile—is an excellent way to bring color to a speech, to make abstract ideas concrete, to clarify the unknown, and to express feelings and emotions.

Rhythm

Language has a rhythm created by the choice and arrangement of words. Sometimes the appeal of a statement depends almost entirely on its rhythm—as in this children's verse:

> Pease porridge hot,
>   Pease porridge cold,
> Pease porridge in the pot,
>   Nine days old.

There is little meaning here. The appeal comes from the combination of sounds, which gives the passage an almost musical cadence.[14]

Speakers, like poets, sometimes seek to exploit the rhythm of language. By catching up their listeners in an arresting string of sounds, speakers can enhance the impact of their words—and therefore of their ideas.[15] Winston Churchill was a master at this. Here is a passage from one of his famous speeches during World War II. To emphasize its cadence, the passage has been printed as if it were poetry rather than prose:

> We cannot tell what the course
>   of this fell war will be
> as it spreads remorseless
>   through ever-wider regions.
> We know it will be hard;
>   we expect it will be long.
> We cannot predict or measure
>   its episodes or its tribulations. . . .
> We cannot yet see
>   how deliverance will come,
> or when it will come.
>   But nothing is more certain
> than that every trace of Hitler's footsteps,
>   every stain of his infected and corroding fingers,
> will be sponged and purged
>   and, if need be,
> blasted from the surface of the earth.[16]

The impact of the passage was heightened by Churchill's superb delivery; but even by themselves the words take on an emphatic rhythm that reinforces the message. You can see why John Kennedy said later that Churchill "mobilized the English language and sent it into battle."

rhythm
The pattern of sound in a speech created by the choice and arrangement of words.

View this excerpt from Winston Churchill's speech of June 12, 1941.

CD: VIDEO CLIP 11.2

A speech, however, is not a poem. You should never emphasize sound and rhythm at the expense of meaning. And you may never have paid much conscious attention to the rhythm and flow of language. But you can develop an ear for vocal rhythms by study and practice. What's more, you can easily begin now to use four basic stylistic devices employed by Churchill and other fine speakers to enhance the rhythm of their prose.

Parallelism

parallelism
The similar arrangement of a pair or series of related words, phrases, or sentences.

The first device is parallelism—the similar arrangement of a pair or series of related words, phrases, or sentences. For example:

Rich and poor, intelligent and ignorant, wise and foolish, virtuous and vicious, man and woman—it is ever the same, each soul must depend wholly on itself. (Elizabeth Cady Stanton)

The denial of human rights *anywhere is a threat to* human rights *everywhere.* Injustice *anywhere is a threat to* justice *everywhere.* (Jesse Jackson)

The effects of parallelism are perhaps best illustrated by seeing what happens when it is absent. For instance, compare this statement:

I speak as a Republican. I speak as a woman. I speak as a United States Senator. I speak as an American. (Margaret Chase Smith)

with this one:

I speak as a Republican. I speak as a woman. I speak as a United States Senator. And I am also addressing you as an American.

The first statement is clear, consistent, and compelling. The second is not. By violating the principle of parallel structure, its final sentence ("And I am also addressing you as an American") destroys the progression begun by the preceding three sentences ("I speak as a Republican. I speak as a woman. I speak as a United States Senator"). It thereby turns a strong, lucid, harmonious statement into one that is fuzzy and jarring.

Repetition

repetition
Reiteration of the same word or set of words at the beginning or end of successive clauses or sentences.

The second device you can use to lend rhythm to your speeches is repetition. This means repeating the same word or set of words at the beginning or end of successive clauses or sentences. For example:

We left America safe, *we left America* secure, *we left America* free—*still a* beacon of hope to mankind, *still a* light unto the nations. (Ronald Reagan)

We are a people in a quandary about the present. *We are a people* in search of our future. *We are a people* in search of a national community. (Barbara Jordan)

As you can see, repetition inevitably results in parallelism. In addition to building a strong cadence, it also unifies a sequence of ideas, emphasizes an idea by stating it more than once, and helps to create a strong emotional effect.

Alliteration

The third device you can use to enhance the rhythm of your speeches is alliteration. The most common method of alliteration is repeating the initial consonant sound of close or adjoining words. For example:

alliteration
Repetition of the initial consonant sound of close or adjoining words.

> We should not *d*emean our *d*emocracy with the politics of *d*istraction, *d*enial, and *d*espair. (Al Gore)

> In a nation founded on the promise of human dignity, our colleges, our communities, our country should challenge hatred wherever we find it. (Hillary Rodham Clinton)

By highlighting the sounds of words, alliteration catches the attention of listeners and can make ideas easier to remember. Used sparingly, it is a marvelous way to spruce up your speeches. Used to excess, however, it can be laughable and draw too much attention, so that listeners get more involved in listening for the next alliteration than in absorbing the content of the speech.

Antithesis

Finally, you might try using antithesis—the juxtaposition of contrasting ideas, usually in parallel structure. For example:

antithesis
The juxtaposition of contrasting ideas, usually in parallel structure.

> Ask not what your country can do for you; ask what you can do for your country. (John F. Kennedy)

> Your success as a family, our success as a society, depends not on what happens at the White House, but on what happens inside your house. (Barbara Bush)

Antithesis has long been a favorite device of accomplished speakers. Because it nearly always produces a neatly turned phrase, it is a fine way to give your speeches a special touch of class.

You may be thinking that imagery and rhythm are fine for famous people but are too fancy for ordinary speeches like yours. This is not true. Imagery and rhythm are easy to use and can enliven even the most routine of speeches. As an example, take a look at the following excerpt from one student's speech about her grandparents and other survivors of the Holocaust:

> When my grandparents are gone, I will continue to tell their story. I will tell my children about the men and women who were murdered for no cause. . . . And I hope that you, too, will tell stories. For as the Holocaust survivor and writer Elie Wiesel once said, "Not to transmit an experience is to betray it."
> To the millions who died in the Holocaust, lie peacefully in your graves, for you have not been forgotten.

View the ending of Andrea Besikof, "The Survivors."

CD: VIDEO CLIP 11.3

To the survivors of the Holocaust, rest assured that we have listened to your stories, have learned by your examples, and we, too, are willing to fight for freedom and peace.

May no person around the globe again fall to his or her death murmuring, "How could this happen."

This is vivid, moving language. The imagery is sharp and poignant, the rhythm strong and insistent. Think of how you can do similar things in your own speeches.

Using Language Appropriately

Here is part of a famous oration given by John Hancock in 1774, during the American Revolution. Speaking of the British soldiers who killed five Americans in the Boston Massacre, Hancock exclaimed:

Ye dark designing knaves, ye murderers, parricides! How dare you tread upon the earth, which has drank in the blood of slaughtered innocents shed by your wicked hands? How dare you breathe that air which wafted to the ear of heaven the groans of those who fell a sacrifice to your accursed ambition? . . . Tell me, ye bloody butchers, ye villains high and low, ye wretches . . . do you not feel the goads and stings of conscious guilt pierce through your savage bosoms?[17]

This is certainly vivid language—and Hancock's audience loved it. But can you imagine speaking the same way today? In addition to being accurate, clear, and vivid, language should be appropriate—to the occasion, to the audience, to the topic, and to the speaker.

Appropriateness to the Occasion

Language that is appropriate for some occasions may not be appropriate for others. "There is a time for dialect, a place for slang, an occasion for literary form. What is correct on the sports page is out of place on the op-ed page; what is with-it on the street may well be without it in the classroom."[18] As a simple example, a coach might address the football team as "you guys" (or worse!), whereas the speaker in a more formal situation would begin with "distinguished guests." Try reversing these two situations, and see how ridiculous it becomes. It's only common sense to adjust your language to different occasions.

Appropriateness to the Audience

Appropriateness also depends on the audience. If you keep this in mind, it will help you greatly when dealing with technical or scientific topics. When addressing an audience of physicians, you might use the word "parotitis" to refer to a viral disease marked by the swelling of the parotid glands. Your

Language needs to be appropriate to a speaker's topic, as well as to the audience and occasion. A speech on downhill skiing, for example, would probably use more action-oriented words than a speech about theories of psychology.

audience would know just what you meant. But when talking to a non-medical audience, such as your classmates, a word like "parotitis" would not be appropriate. The appropriate word in this case would be "mumps."

You should be especially careful to avoid language that might offend your audience. If you were a stand-up comedian, off-color humor or profanity might be appropriate in a nightclub routine, but most listeners would find it offensive in a formal public speech. Remember, speakers are expected to elevate and polish their language when addressing an audience.

They are also expected to avoid name-calling and other forms of abusive language. As we saw in Chapter 2, such language is ethically suspect because it demeans the basic human worth of the people against whom it is directed. In addition, most listeners take offense at statements that denounce people on the basis of their religious beliefs or ethnic heritage. If you include such statements in your speeches, you will not only violate an important ethical responsibility, you will almost surely alienate a good portion of your audience. (You will also have problems with appropriateness if you pepper your speeches with sexist language. This has become such an important issue for speakers that we discuss it in detail later in this chapter.)

Of course, you cannot always be sure of how listeners will respond to what you say. As a general rule, bend over backward to avoid language that may confuse or offend your listeners. When it comes to appropriateness, you will seldom go wrong by erring on the side of caution. (Put simply, "erring on the side of caution" means "when in doubt—don't.")

Appropriateness to the Topic

Language should also be appropriate to the topic. You would not use metaphor, antithesis, and alliteration when explaining how to change a bicycle tire or how to perform routine maintenance on a car. But you might use all three in a speech celebrating the genius of Leonardo da Vinci or honoring the American soldiers who served in the Persian Gulf War. The first two topics call for straightforward description and explanation. The latter two call for special language skills to evoke emotion, admiration, and appreciation.

Appropriateness to the Speaker

No matter what the occasion, audience, or topic, language should also be appropriate to the speaker. Imagine the effect if Al Gore tried to adopt the religious imagery and rhythmical cadence of Jesse Jackson. The results would be comical. Every public speaker develops her or his own language style. Ann Richards and Mario Cuomo seek to create striking phrases through imagery, antithesis, and metaphor. Elizabeth Dole and Colin Powell seldom use such devices. Yet all four are among the most successful speakers in America.

"Terrific," you may be thinking. "I have my own style too. I feel more comfortable using abstract words, slang, and technical jargon. That's just me. It's *my* way of speaking." But to say language should be appropriate to the speaker does not justify ignoring the other needs for appropriateness. There is a difference between one's everyday personal style and one's *developed* style as a public speaker. Dole, Powell, and other accomplished speakers have developed their speaking styles over many years of trial, error, and practice. They have *worked* at using language effectively.

You can do the same if you become language-conscious. Analyze your strengths and weaknesses. Read and listen to the speeches of people like Richards, Powell, Churchill, and King. Study their techniques for achieving accuracy, clarity, and vividness, and try to adapt those techniques to your own speeches. But do not try to "become" someone else when you speak. Learn from other speakers, blend what you learn into your own language style, and seek to become the best possible you.

A Note on Nonsexist Language

"Above all it is language that separates man from the other creatures."

"When a soldier goes to war, he should have the best possible equipment."

"The major responsibility of an elementary-school teacher is to make sure her students learn reading, writing, and arithmetic."

Thirty years ago, most people in the United States who heard these statements in a speech would not have given them a second thought. Today the same statements would raise more than a few eyebrows—and perhaps tempers—in almost any audience. Here's why:

It's not just "man" but all people who are separated from the other creatures by the use of language. To use "man" as a generic word for all people leaves out half of humanity. You can test this by rewording the original statement as follows: "Above all it is language that separates woman from the other creatures."

Soldiers in the U.S. military include women as well as men. To say, "When a soldier goes to war, he should have the best possible equipment," ignores the existence of female soldiers. It also can be interpreted as meaning that only male soldiers should go to war with the finest equipment—hardly a comforting thought to female soldiers or their loved ones!

It may be the major job of an elementary-school teacher to teach reading, writing, and arithmetic, but the third statement ignores the fact that not all elementary-school teachers are female. The statement stereotypes this occupational group as being suitable only for women, in the same way that the second statement stereotypes all soldiers as men.

For centuries, English has been a male-dominated language with countless words and phrases that favor men and convey stereotyped, misleading, or demeaning views of women. Today that is changing—not as fast, perhaps, as some people might like, and doubtless too fast for other people—but changing nonetheless. If current trends continue, 30 years from now the statements at the beginning of this section will seem as outdated as bloomers and corsets.

Whatever your feelings about these trends, avoiding sexist language is important as a matter of accuracy in speechmaking. To speak as if all soldiers (or doctors, or lawyers, or firefighters) are men is incorrect—just as it is erroneous to speak as if all elementary-school teachers (or secretaries, or nurses, or flight attendants) are women. Being accurate in such matters is no less important than being accurate in other aspects of your language.[19]

As we saw in Chapter 5, avoiding sexist language is also a vital part of audience adaptation. Even if you do not care about sexist language yourself, you can be sure that almost any audience you address will contain people—men and women alike—who do care and who will be upset if you use it in your speech. In this respect, as in others, an effective speaker must adjust to the values and expectations of the audience.

When editors, linguists, and others first proposed nonsexist alternatives to traditional words and phrases, some people reacted with shock and indignation. You cannot change the language, they said, without destroying its beauty and purity. But the English language has been changing for centuries—just as it will continue to change in the future. Today a number of nonsexist usages have become so widely accepted that no aspiring speaker (or writer) can afford to ignore them. Let's look at four of these usages.

sexist language
Language that promotes the stereotyping of people on the basis of gender.

nonsexist language
Language that does not stereotype people on the basis of gender.

Avoid the Generic "He"

generic "he"
The use of "he" to refer to both women and men.

Ineffective: Each time a surgeon walks into the operating room, *he* risks being sued for malpractice.

More Effective: Each time a surgeon walks into the operating room, *she or he* risks being sued for malpractice.

Often, a more graceful way to solve this problem is to pluralize. For example:

More Effective: Whenever surgeons walk into the operating room, *they* risk being sued for malpractice.

Avoid the Use of "Man" When Referring to Both Men and Women

Ineffective: If a large comet struck the earth, it could destroy all of mankind.

More Effective: If a large comet struck the earth, it could destroy all human life.

Ineffective: No matter how popular cats have become, the dog is still man's best friend.

More Effective: No matter how popular cats have become, the dog is still a person's best friend.

Avoid Stereotyping Jobs and Social Roles by Gender

Ineffective: Being a small businessman in the current economic climate is not easy.

More Effective: Being a small businessperson in the current economic climate is not easy.

stereotype
A widely held, over-simplified opinion or image.

Sometimes you can solve this problem with a simple twist in sentence construction. For example:

More Effective: Owning a small business is not easy in the current economic climate.

Avoid Unnecessary or Patronizing Gender Labels

Ineffective: Sandra Day O'Connor is an outstanding lady judge.

More Effective: Sandra Day O'Connor is an outstanding judge.

Ineffective: When I phoned the registrar's office this morning, a male receptionist told me to call back during the afternoon.

More Effective: When I phoned the registrar's office this morning, the receptionist told me to call back during the afternoon.

Like many other aspects of modern life, questions of sexist and non-sexist language can sometimes be confusing. Although "steward" and "stewardess" gave way long ago to "flight attendant," most people—including those who bestow the Academy Awards—continue to distinguish between "actor" and "actress."[20] Is this logical? Hardly—and it could change any time. If you do a lot of public speaking (or writing), you should consider purchasing a guidebook to nonsexist language such as Rosalie Maggio's *Talking about People: A Guide to Fair and Accurate Language*.

Summary

Of all human creations, language may be the most remarkable. Through language we share experiences, formulate values, exchange ideas, transmit knowledge, and sustain culture. Indeed, language is vital to thinking itself. Contrary to popular belief, language does not simply mirror reality, but helps create our sense of reality by giving meaning to events.

Good speakers have respect for language and how it works. Words are the tools of a speaker's craft. They have special uses, just like the tools of any other profession. As a speaker, you should be aware of the meanings of words and know how to use language accurately, clearly, vividly, and appropriately.

Words have two kinds of meanings—denotative and connotative. Denotative meaning is precise, literal, and objective. One way to think of a word's denotative meaning is as its dictionary definition. Connotative meaning is more variable, figurative, and subjective. It is whatever the word suggests or implies. Connotative meaning includes all the feelings, associations, and emotions that a word touches off in different people.

Using language accurately is as vital to a speaker as using numbers accurately is to an accountant. Never use a word unless you are sure of its meaning. If you are not sure, look up the word in a dictionary. As you prepare your speeches, ask yourself constantly, "What do I *really* want to say? What do I *really* mean?" Choose words that are precise and accurate.

Using language clearly allows listeners to grasp your meaning immediately. You can assure this by using familiar words that are known to the average person and require no specialized background; by choosing concrete words in preference to more abstract ones; and by eliminating verbal clutter.

Using language vividly helps bring your speech to life. One way to make your language more vivid is through imagery, or the creation of word pictures. You can develop imagery by using concrete language, simile, and metaphor. Simile is an explicit comparison between things that are essentially different yet have something in common; it always contains the words "like" or "as." Metaphor is an implicit comparison between things that are different yet have something in common; it does not contain the words "like" or "as."

Another way to make your speeches vivid is by exploiting the rhythm of language. Four devices for creating rhythm are parallelism, repetition, alliteration, and antithesis. Parallelism is the similar arrangement of a pair or series of related words, phrases, or sentences. Repetition is the use of the same word or set of words at the beginning or end of successive clauses or sentences. Alliteration is the repetition of the initial consonant sounds of close or adjoining words. Antithesis is the juxtaposition of contrasting ideas, usually in parallel structure.

Using language appropriately means adapting to the particular occasion, audience, and topic at hand. It also means developing your own language style instead of trying to copy someone else's. If your language is appropriate in all respects, your speech is much more likely to succeed.

You will also be more likely to succeed if you do not pepper your speech with sexist language. Although the topic of sexist language is complex and controversial, a number of nonsexist usages are so widely accepted that no aspiring speaker can afford to ignore them. They include avoiding the generic "he," dropping the use of "man" when referring to both men and women, refraining from stereotyping jobs and social roles by gender, and discarding unnecessary or patronizing gender labels.

Key Terms

denotative meaning (258)

connotative meaning (258)

thesaurus (260)

concrete words (263)

abstract words (263)

clutter (264)

imagery (266)

simile (267)

cliché (268)

metaphor (268)

mixed metaphor (268)

rhythm (269)

parallelism (270)

repetition (270)

alliteration (271)

antithesis (271)

sexist language (275)

nonsexist language (275)

generic "he" (276)

stereotype (276)

Review Questions

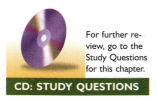

For further review, go to the Study Questions for this chapter.

CD: STUDY QUESTIONS

After reading this chapter, you should be able to answer the following questions:

1. How does language help shape our sense of reality?

2. What is the difference between denotative and connotative meaning? How might you use each to convey your message most effectively?

3. What are the four criteria for using language effectively in your speeches?

4. What are three things you should do to use language clearly in your speeches?

5. What are two ways to bring your speeches to life with vivid, animated language?

6. What does it mean to say you should use language appropriately in your speeches?

7. Why is sexist language a problem for public speakers? What are four nonsexist language usages which have become so widely accepted that no speaker can afford to ignore them?

Exercises for Critical Thinking

1. Arrange each of the sequences below in order, from the most abstract word to the most concrete word.

   a. housing complex, building, dining room, structure, apartment
   b. *Mona Lisa,* art, painting, creative activity, portrait
   c. Communication Department, college, educational institution, Stanford, school
   d. automobile, vehicle, Ferrari, transportation, sports car

2. Rewrite each of the following sentences using clear, familiar words.

   a. Some students were not cognizant of the fact that the professor made a modification in the assignment subsequent to the last class meeting.
   b. My employment objective is to attain a position of maximum financial reward.
   c. All professors at this school are expected to achieve high standards of excellence in their instructional duties.
   d. The burglar evaded security personnel and is no longer on the premises.
   e. In the eventuality of a fire, it is imperative that all persons evacuate the building without undue delay.

3. Each of the statements below uses one or more of the following stylistic devices: metaphor, simile, parallelism, repetition, alliteration, antithesis. Identify the device (or devices) used in each statement.

   a. "It will be up to you who are graduating today to take from Harvard not just knowledge, but wisdom; not just intelligence, but humanity; not just a drive for self-fulfillment, but a sense of service and a taste for hard work." (Colin Powell)
   b. "The vice presidency is the sand trap of American politics. It's near the prize, and designed to be limiting." (Howard Fineman)
   c. "For too long American leadership has waffled and wiggled and wavered." (Bill Bradley)
   d. "America is not like a blanket—one piece of unbroken cloth, the same color, the same texture, the same size. America is more like a quilt—many patches, many sizes, and woven and held together by a common thread." (Jesse Jackson)

4. Analyze Martin Luther King's "I Have a Dream" (Appendix B). Identify the methods King uses to make his language clear, vivid, and appropriate. Look particularly at King's use of familiar words, concrete words, imagery, and rhythm.

Applying the POWER of Public Speaking

Since graduating from college, you have developed a successful business that is located near the campus. As part of its plan to involve more alumni and community members in college affairs, the school has asked you to speak with new students during registration week for the fall term. In the opening section of your speech, you want the audience to feel what you felt the first few days you were on campus as a new student. The best strategy, you decide, is to present two or three similes that complete the sentence, "Beginning college is like . . . " Write your similes.

Notes

[1] For a highly readable study on this subject, see Bill Bryson, *Made in America: An Informal History of the English Language in the United States* (New York: Avon Books, 1996).

[2] Raymond Gozzi, Jr., *New Words and a Changing American Culture* (Columbia S.C.: University of South Carolina Press, 1990), p. 97.

[3] Richard Lederer, *The Miracle of Language* (New York: Simon and Schuster, 1991), p. 32.

[4] See, for example, John McCrone, *The Ape That Spoke: Language and the Evolution of the Human Mind* (New York: Morrow, 1991); Steven Pinker, *The Language Instinct: How the Mind Creates Language* (New York: HarperCollins, 1994).

[5] James R. Andrews, *A Choice of Worlds: The Practice and Criticism of Public Discourse* (New York: Harper and Row, 1973).

[6] This has been understood for many years by teachers of rhetoric. See the comment of Hugh Blair, in his *Lectures on Rhetoric and Belles Lettres* (London: W. Strahan, 1783), I, p. 245: "We may rest assured, that whenever we express ourselves ill, there is, besides the mismanagement of language, for the most part, some mistake in conceiving the subject. Embarrassed, obscure, and feeble sentences are generally, if not always, the result of embarrassed, obscure, and feeble thought. Thought and language react upon each other mutually. . . . He that is learning to arrange his sentences with accuracy and order is learning, at the same time, to think with accuracy and order."

[7] Quoted in Edward P. J. Corbett and Robert J. Connors, *Classical Rhetoric for the Modern Student,* 4th ed. (New York: Oxford University Press, 1999), p. 372.

[8] Dorothy Sarnoff, *Speech Can Change Your Life* (New York: Doubleday, 1970), p. 71.

[9] Annmarie Mungo, "A Child Is Born," *Winning Orations, 1980* (Mankato, Minn.: Interstate Oratorical Association, 1980), pp. 49–50.

[10] Adapted from Richard Conniff, "You Never Know What the Fire Ant Is Going to Do Next," *Smithsonian,* July 1990, p. 49.

[11] See Appendix B for the full text of King's speech.

[12] "Remarks at the U.S. Ranger Monument," Pointe du Hoc, France, June 6, 1984, in Ronald Reagan, *Speaking My Mind: Selected Speeches* (New York: Simon and Schuster, 1989), pp. 217–222.

[13] Elizabeth Cady Stanton, "The Solitude of Self," in Karlyn Kohrs Campbell (ed.), *Man Cannot Speak for Her: Key Texts of the Early Feminists* (New York: Praeger, 1989), p. 374.

[14] Thomas R. Arp, William Kornblum, and Laurence Perrine, *Sound and Sense: An Introduction to Poetry,* 9th ed. (Fort Worth, Texas: Harcourt, Brace, Jovanovich, 1996), p. 193.

[15] For an interesting discussion of rhythm in speechmaking, see Paula Wilson, "The Rhythm of Rhetoric: Jesse Jackson at the 1988 Democratic National Convention," *Southern Communication Journal,* 61 (1996), pp. 253–264.

[16]Winston Churchill, Speech at St. James Palace, London, June 12, 1941, in Lloyd Rohler and Roger Cook (eds.), *Great Speeches for Analysis and Criticism,* 3rd ed. (Greenwood, Ind.: Alistair Press, 1998), p. 102.

[17]John Hancock, Boston Massacre Oration, March 5, 1774, in Ronald F. Reid (ed.), *American Rhetorical Discourse,* 2nd ed. (Prospect Heights, Ill.: Waveland Press, 1995), pp. 99–108.

[18]William Safire, *On Language* (New York: Times Books, 1980), p. xiv.

[19]For discussion of these and other gender issues in communication, see Diana K. Ivy and Phil Backlund, *Exploring GenderSpeak: Personal Effectiveness in Gender Communication,* 2nd ed. (New York: McGraw-Hill, 2000); Julia T. Wood, *Gendered Lives: Communication, Gender, and Culture,* 3rd ed. (Belmont, Calif.: Wadsworth, 1999).

[20]Frederick Crews, Sandra Schor, and Michael Hennessy, *The Borzoi Handbook for Writers,* 3rd ed. (New York: McGraw-Hill, 1993), p. 185.

CHAPTER TWELVE

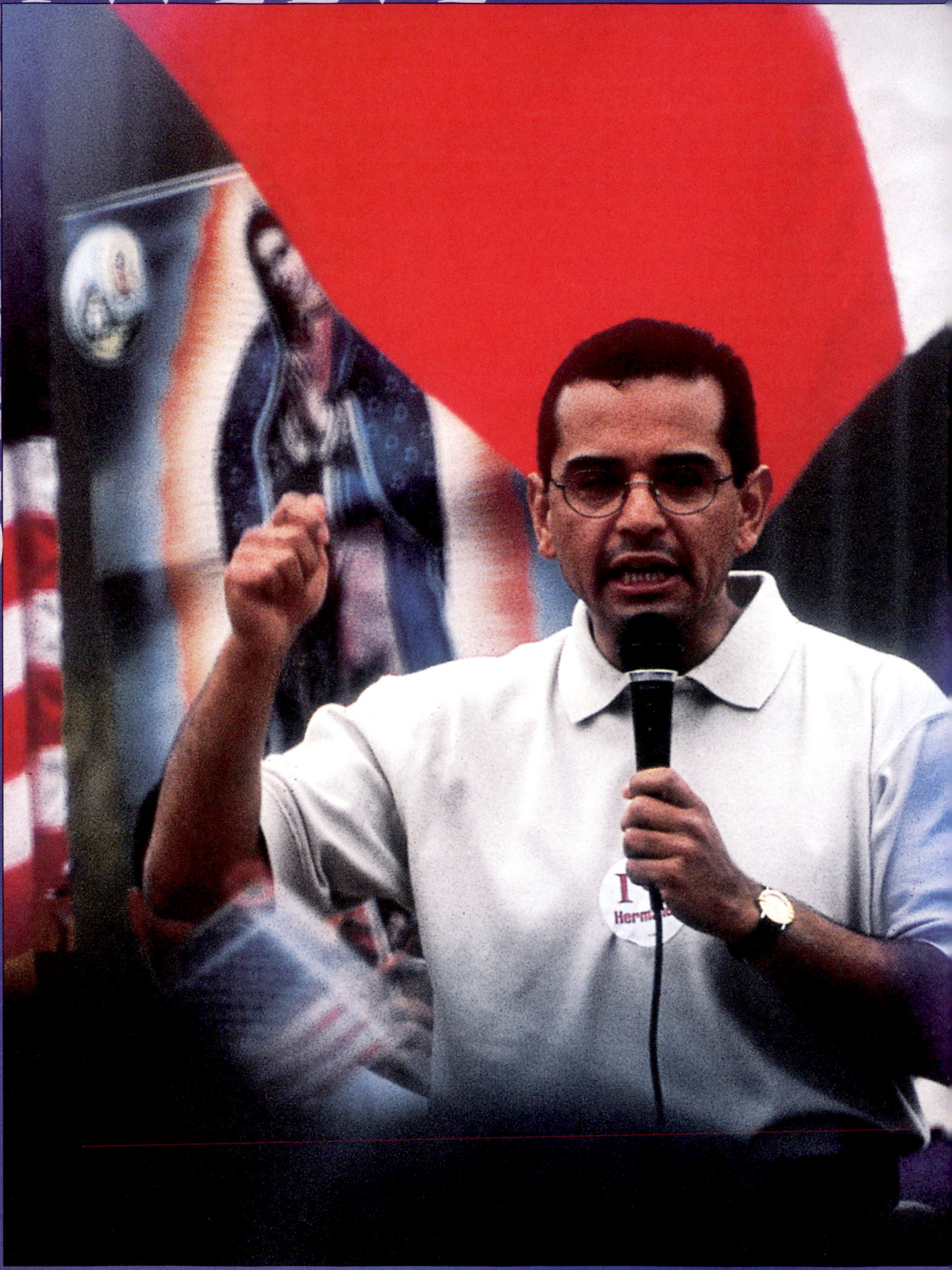

DELIVERY

What Is Good Delivery?

Methods of Delivery
Reading from a Manuscript
Reciting from Memory
Speaking Impromptu
Speaking Extemporaneously

The Speaker's Voice
Volume
Pitch
Rate
Pauses
Vocal Variety
Pronunciation
Articulation
Dialect

Nonverbal Communication
Personal Appearance
Bodily Action
Gestures
Eye Contact

Practicing Delivery

Answering Audience Questions
Preparing for the Question-and-Answer Session
Managing the Question-and-Answer Session

f you were to tape-record one of David Letterman's comedy routines, memorize it word for word, and stand up before your friends to recite it, would you get the same response Letterman does? Not very likely. And why not? Because you would not *deliver* the jokes as Letterman does. Of course, the jokes are basically funny. But David Letterman brings something extra to the jokes—his manner of presentation, his vocal inflections, his perfectly timed pauses, his facial expressions, his gestures. All these are part of an expert delivery. It would take you years of practice—as it took Letterman—to duplicate his results.

No one expects your speech class to transform you into a multimillion-dollar talk show host. Still, this example demonstrates how important delivery can be to any public speaking situation. Even a mediocre speech will be more effective if it is presented well, whereas a wonderfully written speech can be ruined by poor delivery.

This does not mean dazzling delivery will turn a mindless string of nonsense into a triumphant oration. You cannot make a good speech without having something to say. But having something to say is not enough. You must also know *how* to say it.

What Is Good Delivery?

Wendell Phillips was a leader in the movement to abolish slavery in the United States during the 1800s. Some people considered him the greatest speaker of his time. The following story suggests one reason why:

> Shortly before the Civil War an Andover student, learning that Phillips was to lecture in Boston, made a 22-mile pilgrimage on foot to hear him. At first the trip seemed hardly worthwhile, for the student discovered that Phillips was not an orator in the grand manner, but spoke in an almost conversational style. He stood on the platform, one hand lightly resting on a table, talked for what seemed to be about 20 minutes, concluded, and sat down. When the student looked at his watch, he found to his astonishment that he had been listening for an hour and a half![1]

Good delivery does not call attention to itself. It conveys the speaker's ideas clearly, interestingly, and without distracting the audience. If you mumble your words, shuffle your feet, gaze out the window, or talk in a monotone, you will not get your message across. Nor will you be effective if you show off, strike a dramatic pose, or shout in ringing tones. Most audiences prefer delivery that combines a certain degree of formality with the best attributes of good conversation—directness, spontaneity, animation, vocal and facial expressiveness, and a lively sense of communication.

When you begin speaking in public, you will probably have many questions about delivery: "Should I be strong and aggressive or low-key?" "Where should I stand?" "How should I gesture?" "How should I handle my notes?" "How fast should I speak?" "When should I pause?" "Where should I look?" "What do I do if I make a mistake?"

There are no hard-and-fast answers to these questions. Speech delivery is an art, not a science. What works for one speaker may fail for another. And what succeeds with today's audience may not with tomorrow's. You cannot become a skilled speaker just by following a set of rules in a textbook. In the long run, there is no substitute for experience. But take heart! A textbook *can* give you basic pointers to get you started in the right direction.

When you plan your first speech (or second or third), you should concentrate on such basics as speaking intelligibly, avoiding distracting mannerisms, and establishing eye contact with your listeners. Once you get these elements under control and begin to feel fairly comfortable in front of an audience, you can work on polishing your delivery to enhance the impact of your ideas. Eventually, you may find yourself able to control the timing, rhythm, and momentum of a speech as skillfully as a conductor controls an orchestra.

Methods of Delivery

There are four basic methods of delivering a speech: (1) reading verbatim from a manuscript; (2) reciting a memorized text; (3) speaking impromptu; and (4) speaking extemporaneously. Let us look at each.

Reading from a Manuscript

Certain speeches *must* be delivered word for word, according to a meticulously prepared manuscript. Examples include a Pope's religious proclamation, an engineer's report to a professional meeting, or a President's message to Congress. In such situations, absolute accuracy is essential. Every word of the speech will be analyzed by the press, by colleagues, perhaps by enemies. In the case of the President, a misstated phrase could cause an international incident.

> **manuscript speech**
> A speech that is written out word for word and read to the audience.

Timing may also be a factor in manuscript speeches. Much of today's political campaigning is done on radio and television. If the candidate buys a one-minute spot and pays a great deal of money for it, that one minute of speech must be just right.

Although it looks easy, delivering a speech from a manuscript requires great skill. Some people do it well. Their words "come alive as if coined on the spot."[2] Others seem to ruin it every time. Instead of sounding vibrant and conversational, they come across as wooden and artificial. They falter over words, pause in the wrong places, read too quickly or too slowly, speak in a monotone, and march through the speech without even glancing at their audience. In short, they come across as *reading to* their listeners, rather than *talking with* them.

Among current public figures, no one is better at avoiding these problems than former Texas governor Ann Richards. Through years of practice, she has learned to sound spontaneous and to communicate heartfelt emotion even though she is delivering the speech word for word. You can see this in the excerpt from her 1996 eulogy to Barbara Jordan on CD-ROM Video Clip 12.1. Speaking before a packed audience of 1,500 people at Houston's Good Hope Missionary Baptist Church, Richards spoke movingly of Jordan's life and achievements. She communicated as directly with the audience as if she had been speaking informally to a small group of friends.

View an excerpt from Ann Richards's eulogy to Barbara Jordan.

CD: VIDEO CLIP 12.1

If you are in a situation where you must speak from a manuscript, do your best to follow Richards's lead. Practice aloud to make sure the speech sounds natural. Work on establishing eye contact with your listeners. Be certain the final manuscript is legible at a glance. Above all, reach out to your audience with the same directness and sincerity that you would if you were speaking extemporaneously.[3]

Reciting from Memory

Among the feats of the legendary orators, none leaves us more in awe than their practice of presenting even the longest and most complex speeches entirely from memory. Nowadays it is no longer customary to memorize any but the shortest of speeches—toasts, congratulatory remarks, acceptance speeches, introductions, and the like. If you are giving a speech of this kind and want to memorize it, by all means do so. However, be sure to memorize it so thoroughly that you will be able to concentrate on communicating with the audience, not on trying to remember the words. Speakers who gaze at the ceiling or stare out the window trying to recall what they have memorized are no better off than those who read dully from a manuscript.

Speaking Impromptu

impromptu speech
A speech delivered with little or no immediate preparation.

An impromptu speech is delivered with little or no immediate preparation. Few people choose to speak impromptu, but sometimes it cannot be avoided. In fact, many of the speeches you give in life will be impromptu. You might be called on suddenly to "say a few words" or, in the course of a class discussion, business meeting, or committee report, want to respond to a previous speaker.

When such situations arise, don't panic. No one expects you to deliver a perfect speech on the spur of the moment. If you are in a meeting or discussion, pay close attention to what the other speakers say. Take notes of major points with which you agree or disagree. In the process, you will automatically begin to formulate what you will say when it is your turn to speak.

Whenever you are responding to a previous speaker, try to present your speech in four simple steps: First, state the point you are answering. Second, state the point you wish to make. Third, support your point with appropriate statistics, examples, or testimony. Fourth, summarize your point. This four-step method will help you organize your thoughts quickly and clearly.

If time allows, sketch a quick outline of your remarks on a piece of paper before you rise to speak. Use the same method of jotting down key words and phrases followed in a more formal speaking outline (see Chapter 10). This will help you remember what you want to say and will keep you from rambling.

In many cases, you will be able to speak informally without rising from your chair. But if the situation calls for you to speak from a lectern, walk to it calmly, take a deep breath or two (not a visible gasp), establish eye contact with your audience, and begin speaking. No matter how nervous you are inside, do your best to look calm and assured on the outside.

Once you begin speaking, maintain strong eye contact with the audience. If you are prone to talking rapidly when you are nervous, concentrate on speaking at a slower pace. Help the audience keep track of your ideas with signposts such as "My first point is . . . ; second, we can see that . . . ; in conclusion, I would like to say. . . . " If you have had time to prepare notes, stick to what you have written. By stating your points clearly and concisely, you will come across as organized and confident.

Whether you realize it or not, you have given thousands of impromptu "speeches" in daily conversation—as when you informed a new student how to register for classes, or explained to your boss why you were late for work, or answered questions in a job interview, or tried to persuade your roommate to lend you 10 dollars until next week. There is no reason to fall apart when you are asked to speak impromptu in a more formal situation. If you keep cool, organize your thoughts, and limit yourself to a few remarks, you should do just fine.

As with other kinds of public speaking, the best way to become a better impromptu speaker is to practice. If you are assigned an impromptu speech in class, do your best to follow the guidelines discussed here. You can also practice impromptu speaking on your own. Simply choose a topic on which you are already well informed, and give a one- or two-minute impromptu talk on some aspect of that topic. Any topic will do—no matter how serious or frivolous it may be. Nor do you need an audience—you can speak to an empty room. Better yet, you can speak to a tape recorder and play the speech back to see how you sound. The purpose is to gain experience in pulling your ideas together quickly and stating them succinctly. Over the years, many people have found this an effective way to improve their skills of impromptu speaking.

Speaking Extemporaneously

In popular usage, "extemporaneous" means the same as "impromptu." But technically the two are different. Unlike an impromptu speech, which is totally off the cuff, an extemporaneous speech is carefully prepared and practiced in advance. In presenting the speech, the extemporaneous speaker uses only a set of brief notes or a speaking outline to jog the memory (see Chapter 10). The exact wording is chosen at the moment of delivery.

This is not as hard as it sounds. Once you have your outline (or notes) and know what topics you are going to cover and in what order, you can begin to practice the speech. Every time you run through it, the wording will be slightly different. As you practice the speech over and over, the best way to present each part will emerge and stick in your mind.

The extemporaneous method has several advantages. It gives more precise control over thought and language than does impromptu speaking; it offers greater spontaneity and directness than does speaking from memory or from a full manuscript; and it is adaptable to a wide range of situations. It also encourages the conversational quality audiences look for in speech delivery. "Conversational quality" means that no matter how many times a speech has been rehearsed, it still *sounds* spontaneous to the audience. When you speak extemporaneously—and have prepared properly—you

extemporaneous speech
A carefully prepared and rehearsed speech that is presented from a brief set of notes.

conversational quality
Presenting a speech so it sounds spontaneous no matter how many times it has been rehearsed.

Extemporaneous speeches are fully prepared ahead of time, but the exact words are chosen at the moment of delivery. This allows for stronger eye contact and more direct delivery than does reading from a manuscript.

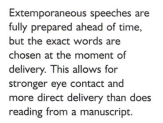

View excerpts from Elizabeth Dole's speech at the 1996 Republican National Convention.

CD: VIDEO CLIP 12.2

have full control over your ideas, yet you are not tied to a manuscript. You are free to establish strong eye contact, to gesture naturally, and to concentrate on talking *with* the audience rather than declaiming *to* them.[4]

There is no better example of the power of extemporaneous delivery than Elizabeth Dole's renowned speech to the 1996 Republican National Convention in support of her husband's bid for the White House. Speaking to the delegates assembled in San Diego and to a national television audience, Dole broke 150 years of tradition by leaving the lectern and presenting her speech while walking among her listeners on the floor of the auditorium. Speaking extemporaneously, with no notes (and no teleprompter), she was able to break through the physical and psychological barriers that would otherwise have separated her from the audience. As numerous observers commented, it was more like listening to a conversation than to a formal speech.

Dole, of course, is one of the most accomplished speakers in the United States. You can't be expected in your speech class to reach the same mastery that she has worked years to achieve. Yet, like thousands of students before you, can develop your skills of extemporaneous delivery to the point that you become quite adept by the end of the term and have a solid foundation on which to build in the future. As one student commented in looking back on his speech class, "At the start, I never thought I'd be able to give my speeches without a ton of notes, but I'm amazed at how much progress I made. It's still a bit nerve-wracking to speak extemporaneously, but I'm confident I can do it, and I know I'll connect better with the audience as a result. This is one of the most valuable things I learned in the entire class."

Most experienced speakers prefer the extemporaneous method, and most teachers emphasize it. Later in this chapter (pages 301–302), we'll look at a step-by-step program for practicing your extemporaneous delivery.

The Speaker's Voice

What kind of voice do you have? Is it rich and resonant like James Earl Jones's? Soft and alluring like Michelle Pfeiffer's? Thin and nasal like Dana Carvey's? Deep and raspy like Whoopi Goldberg's? Harsh and irritating like Fran Drescher's?

Whatever the characteristics of your voice, you can be sure it is unique. Because no two people are exactly the same physically, no two people have identical voices. This is why voiceprints are sometimes used in criminal trials as guides to personal identity. The human voice is produced by a complex series of steps that starts with the exhalation of air from the lungs. (Try talking intelligibly while inhaling and see what happens.) As air is exhaled, it passes through the larynx (or voice box), where it is vibrated to generate sound. This sound is then amplified and modified as it resonates through the throat, mouth, and nasal passages. Finally, the resonated sound is shaped into specific vowel and consonant sounds by the movement of the tongue, lips, teeth, and roof of the mouth. The resulting sounds are combined to form words and sentences.

The voice produced by this physical process will greatly affect the success of your speeches. A golden voice is certainly an asset, but you can manage without. Some of the most famous speakers in history had undistinguished voices. Abraham Lincoln had a harsh and penetrating voice; Winston Churchill suffered from a slight lisp and an awkward stammer; Will Rogers spoke with a nasal twang. Like them, you can overcome natural disadvantages and use your voice to the best effect. If you speak too softly to be heard, constantly stumble over words, spit out your ideas at machine-gun speed, or plod along as if you were reading a grocery list, your speeches will fail. Lincoln, Churchill, and Rogers learned to *control* their voices. You can do the same thing.

The aspects of voice you should work to control are volume, pitch, rate, pauses, variety, pronunciation, articulation, and dialect.

Volume

At one time a powerful voice was all but essential for an orator. Today, electronic amplification allows even the most feeble of speakers to be heard in any setting. But in the classroom you will speak without a microphone. When you do, be sure to adjust your voice to the acoustics of the room, the size of the audience, and the level of background noise. If you speak too loudly, your listeners will think you boorish. If you speak too softly, they will not understand you. Remember that your own voice always sounds louder to you than to a listener. Soon after beginning your speech, glance at the people farthest away from you. If they look puzzled, are leaning forward in their seats, or are otherwise straining to hear, you need to talk louder.

volume
The loudness or softness of the speaker's voice.

Pitch

Pitch is the highness or lowness of the speaker's voice. The faster sound waves vibrate, the higher their pitch; the slower they vibrate, the lower their pitch. Pitch distinguishes the sound produced by the keys at one end of a piano from that produced by the keys at the other end.

pitch
The highness or lowness of the speaker's voice.

In speech, pitch can affect the meaning of words or sounds. Pitch is what makes the difference between the "Aha!" triumphantly exclaimed by Sherlock Holmes upon discovering a seemingly decisive clue and the "Aha" he mutters when he learns the clue is not decisive after all. If you were to read the preceding sentence aloud, your voice would probably go up in pitch on the first "Aha" and down in pitch on the second.

inflections
Changes in the pitch or tone of a speaker's voice.

Changes in pitch are known as *inflections.* They give your voice luster, warmth, and vitality. It is the inflection of your voice that reveals whether you are asking a question or making a statement; whether you are being sincere or sarcastic. Your inflections can also make you sound happy or sad, angry or pleased, dynamic or listless, tense or relaxed, interested or bored.

monotone
A constant pitch or tone of voice.

In ordinary conversation we instinctively use inflections to convey meaning and emotion. People who do not are said to speak in a *monotone*—a trait whose only known benefit is to cure insomnia in one's listeners. Few people speak in an absolute monotone, with no variation whatever in pitch, but many fall into repetitive pitch patterns that are just as hypnotic as a monotone. You can guard against this problem by tape-recording your speeches as you practice them. If all your sentences end on the same inflection—either upward or downward—work on varying your pitch patterns to fit the meaning of your words. As with breaking any other habit, this may seem awkward at first, but it is guaranteed to make you a better speaker.

Rate

rate
The speed at which a person speaks.

Rate refers to the speed at which a person speaks. People in the U.S. usually speak at a rate between 120 and 150 words per minute, but there is no uniform rate for effective speechmaking. Daniel Webster spoke at roughly 90 words per minute, Franklin Roosevelt at 110, John Kennedy at 180. Martin Luther King opened his "I Have a Dream" speech at a pace of 92 words per minute and finished it at 145. The best rate of speech depends on several things—the vocal attributes of the speaker, the mood she or he is trying to create, the composition of the audience, and the nature of the occasion.

For example, if you wanted to convey the excitement of the Daytona 500 car race, you would probably speak rather quickly, but a slower rate would be more appropriate to describe the serenity of the Alaskan wilderness. A fast rate helps to create feelings of happiness, fear, anger, and surprise, while a slow rate is better for expressing sadness or disgust. A slower tempo is called for when you explain complex information, a faster tempo when the information is already familiar to the audience. Finally, research suggests that in most situations listeners will find a speaker with a somewhat faster rate than normal to be more competent and more persuasive than a speaker with a slower rate.[5]

Two obvious faults to avoid are speaking so slowly that your listeners become bored or so quickly that they lose track of your ideas. Novice speakers are particularly prone to racing through their speeches at a frantic rate. Fortunately, once a speaker begins to work on it, this is usually an easy habit to break, as is the less common one of crawling through one's speech at a snail's pace.

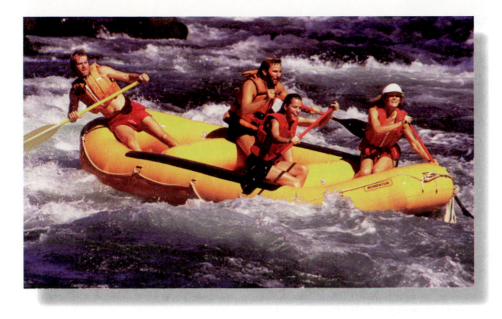

The best rate of speech depends partly on the mood the speaker is trying to create. If you wanted to communicate the excitement of white-water rafting, you would probably speak at a faster-than-normal rate.

The key in both cases is becoming aware of the problem and concentrating on solving it. Use a tape recorder to check how fast you speak. Pay special attention to rate when practicing your speech. Finally, be sure to include reminders about delivery on your speaking outline, so you won't forget to make the adjustments when you give your speech in class.

Pauses

Learning how and when to pause is a major challenge for most beginning speakers. Even a moment of silence can seem like an eternity. As you gain more poise and confidence, however, you will discover how useful the pause can be. It can signal the end of a thought unit, give an idea time to sink in, and lend dramatic impact to a statement. "The right word may be effective," said Mark Twain, "but no word was ever as effective as a rightly timed pause."

As Twain knew, the crucial factor is timing. "For one audience," he cautioned, "the pause will be short, for another a little longer, for another a shade longer still." Looking back on his own career as a speaker, he recalled: "When the pause was right the effect was sure; when the pause was wrong . . . the laughter was only mild, never a crash."

Developing a keen sense of timing is partly a matter of common sense, partly a matter of experience. You will not always get your pauses just right at first, but keep trying. Listen to accomplished speakers to see how they use pauses to modulate the rate and rhythm of their messages. Work on pauses when you practice your speeches.

When you do pause, make sure you pause at the end of thought units and not in the middle. Otherwise, you may distract listeners from your ideas. Most important, do not fill the silence with "uh," "er," or "um." These *vocalized pauses,* as they are called, are always annoying, and they can be devastating. Not only do they create negative perceptions about a speaker's intelligence, but they often make a speaker appear deceptive.[6]

pause
A momentary break in the vocal delivery of a speech.

vocalized pause
A pause that occurs when a speaker fills the silence between words with vocalizations such as "uh," "er," and "um."

Vocal Variety

Just as variety is the spice of life, so is it the spice of public speaking. A flat, listless, unchanging voice is just as deadly to speechmaking as a flat, listless, unchanging routine is to daily life.

Try reading this limerick aloud:

> I sat next to the Duchess at tea.
> It was just as I feared it would be:
>   Her rumblings abdominal
>   Were simply abominable
> And everyone thought it was me!

Now recite this passage from James Joyce's "All Day I Hear the Noise of Waters":

> The gray winds, the cold winds are blowing
>   Where I go.
> I hear the noise of many waters
>   Far below.
> All day, all night, I hear them flowing
>   To and fro.[7]

Certainly you did not utter both passages the same way. You instinctively varied the rate, pitch, volume, and pauses to distinguish the light-hearted limerick from the solemn melancholy of Joyce's poem. When giving a speech, you should modulate your voice in just this way to communicate your ideas and feelings.

For an excellent example of vocal variety, look at CD-ROM Video Clip 12.3. The speaker is Sajjid Zahir Chinoy, who was born and raised in Bombay, India, before coming to the United States to attend college at the University of Richmond. At the end of his senior year, Chinoy was selected as the student commencement speaker in a campuswide competition. He spoke of the warm reception he received at Richmond and of how cultural differences can be overcome by attempting to understand other people.

At the end of his speech, Chinoy received thunderous applause—partly because of what he said, but also because of how he said it. Addressing the audience of 3,000 people without notes, he spoke extemporaneously with strong eye contact and excellent vocal variety. The speech was so inspiring that the main commencement speaker, Harvard psychiatrist Robert Coles, began his presentation by paying tribute to Chinoy. "I've been to a number of commencements," said Coles, "but I've never heard a speech quite like that!"

How can you develop a lively, expressive voice? Above all, by approaching every speech as Chinoy approached his—as an opportunity to share with your listeners ideas that are important to you. Your sense of conviction and your desire to communicate will help give your voice the same spark it has in spontaneous conversation.

Diagnose your present speaking voice to decide which aspects need improvement. Tape-record your speeches to hear how they sound. Try them out on members of your family, a friend, or a roommate. Check with your

vocal variety
Changes in a speaker's rate, pitch, and volume that give the voice variety and expressiveness.

View an excerpt from Sajjid Zahir Chinoy, "Questions of Culture."

CD: VIDEO CLIP 12.3

teacher for suggestions. Practice the vocal variety exercise at the end of this chapter. Vocal variety is a natural feature of ordinary conversation. There is no reason it should not be as natural a feature of your speeches.

Pronunciation

We all mispronounce words now and again. Here, for example, are six words with which you are probably familiar. Say each one aloud.

genuine	err
arctic	nuclear
theater	February

Very likely you made a mistake on at least one, for they are among the most frequently mispronounced words in the English language. Let's see:

Word	Common Error	Correct Pronunciation
genuine	gen-u-wine	gen-u-win
arctic	ar-tic	arc-tic
theater	thee-até-er	theé-a-ter
err	air	ur
nuclear	nu-cu-lar	nu-cle-ar
February	Feb-u-ary	Feb-ru-ary

Every word leads a triple life: it is read, written, and spoken. Most people recognize and understand many more words in reading than they use in ordinary writing, and about three times as many as occur in spontaneous speech.[8] This is why we occasionally stumble when speaking words that are part of our reading or writing vocabularies. In other cases, we may mispronounce the most commonplace words out of habit.

The problem is that we usually don't *know* when we are mispronouncing a word; otherwise we would say it correctly. If we are lucky, we learn the right pronunciation by hearing someone else say the word properly or by having someone gently correct us in private. If we are unlucky, we mispronounce the word in front of a roomful of people, who may raise their eyebrows, groan, or laugh. Even experienced speakers sometimes fall into this trap. In reporting about a recent presidential election, a local TV news anchor referred several times to the number of votes needed to capture a majority in the e-lec-tor-*e*-al college. When he had finished, his coanchor said (on the air!), "And it also takes 270 votes to win a majority in the e-lec-tor-al college." The first announcer tried to shrug it off, but he was noticeably embarrassed.

All of this argues for practicing your speech in front of as many trusted friends and relatives as you can corner. If you have any doubts about the proper pronunciation of certain words, be sure to check a dictionary.

Articulation

Articulation and pronunciation are not identical. Sloppy articulation is the failure to form particular speech sounds crisply and distinctly. It is one of several causes of mispronunciation; but not all errors in pronunciation stem from poor articulation.[9] You can articulate a word sharply and still mispronounce it. For example, if you say the "s" in "Illinois" or the "p" in "pneumonia," you are making a mistake in pronunciation, regardless of how precisely you articulate the sounds.

Errors in articulation can be caused by a cleft palate, by an overly large tongue, by a misaligned jaw, even by a poorly fitted dental plate or braces on the teeth. Serious problems require the aid of a certified speech therapist. But most of the time poor articulation is caused by laziness—by failing to manipulate the lips, tongue, jaw, and soft palate so as to produce speech sounds clearly and precisely. Whether or not people in the U.S. have "the worst articulation in the Western world,"[10] as one scholar claims, many of us are unquestionably sloppy speakers. We habitually chop, slur, and mumble our words, rather than enunciating them plainly.

Among college students, poor articulation is more common than ignorance of correct pronunciation. We know that "let me" is not "lemme," that "going to" is not "gonna," that "did you" is not "didja," yet we persist in articulating these words improperly. Here are some other common errors in articulation you should work to avoid:

Word	Misarticulation
ought to	otta
didn't	dint
for	fur
don't know	dunno

pronunciation
The accepted standard of sound and rhythm for words in a given language.

articulation
The physical production of particular speech sounds.

have to	hafta
them	em
want to	wanna
will you	wilya

If you have sloppy articulation, work on identifying and eliminating your most common errors. Like other bad habits, careless articulation can be broken only by persistent effort—but the results are well worth it. Not only will your speeches be more intelligible, but employers will be more likely to hire you, to place you in positions of responsibility, and to promote you. As Shakespeare advised, "Mend your speech a little, lest you may mar your fortunes."

Dialect

Most languages have dialects, each with a distinctive accent, grammar, and vocabulary. Dialects are usually based on regional or ethnic speech patterns. The United States has four major regional dialects—Eastern, New England, Southern, and General American. These dialects affect the way people talk in different parts of the country. In New York people may get "idears" about "dee-ah" friends. In Alabama parents tell their children to stop "squinching" their eyes while watching television and to go clean up their rooms "rat" now. In Utah people praise the "lard" and put the "lord" in the refrigerator.[11]

There are also several well-established ethnic dialects in the United States, including Black English, Jewish English, Hispanic English, and Cajun English.[12] In recent years we have also seen the emergence of newer dialects such as Haitian English and Cuban English. As the United States becomes more diverse culturally, it is also becoming more diverse linguistically.

Over the years linguists have done a great deal of research on dialects. They have concluded that no dialect is inherently better or worse than another. There is no such thing as a right or wrong dialect. Dialects are not linguistic badges of superiority or inferiority. They are usually shaped by our regional or ethnic background, and every dialect is "right" for the community of people who use it.[13]

When is dialect appropriate in public speaking? The answer depends above all on the composition of your audience. Heavy use of any dialect—regional or ethnic—can be troublesome for a speaker when the audience does not share that dialect. In such a situation, the dialect may cause listeners to make negative judgments about the speaker's personality, intelligence, and competence.[14] This is why professional speakers have been known to invest large amounts of time (and money) to master the General American dialect used by most television news broadcasters. This dialect has become so widely accepted throughout the United States that it is suitable for almost any audience.

Does this mean you must talk like a television news broadcaster if you want to be successful in your speeches? Not at all. Regional or ethnic dialects do not pose a problem as long as the audience is familiar with them

dialect
A variety of a language distinguished by variations of accent, grammar, or vocabulary.

and finds them appropriate to the occasion. When speaking in the North, for example, a southern politician will probably avoid heavy use of regional dialect. But when addressing audiences in the South, the same politician may intentionally include regional dialect as a way of creating common ground with his or her listeners.

Although not strictly speaking a matter of dialect, the proficiency of non-native speakers of English often arises in the speech classroom. Fortunately, teachers and students alike usually go out of their way to be helpful and encouraging with international students and others for whom English is not the primary language. Over the years many non-native speakers of English have found speech class a supportive environment in which to improve their proficiency in spoken English.

Sometimes a speaker may be able to overcome a lower proficiency level by discussing it in her or his speech. Consider the experience of Myung Yi, an international student from Hong Kong. In a speech on human rights abuses in China, a subject about which she felt deeply, Myung included the following statement as part of her introduction:

I know my English is not yet perfect. I know at times it may be hard for some of you to understand me. But I ask you to listen carefully because my message is important. We may speak different languages, but we should all be concerned about the violations of democracy and human rights by the Chinese government.

By dealing head-on with the rough edges in her spoken English, Myung turned a potential barrier to communication into a positive factor that enhanced her credibility and generated sympathy for her position.[15]

Nonverbal Communication

Imagine you are at a party. During the evening you form impressions about the people around you. Tyrone seems relaxed and even-tempered, Nicole tense and irritable. Dorinda seems open and straightforward, Amy hostile and evasive. Amin seems happy to see you; Seth definitely is not.

How do you reach these conclusions? To a surprising extent, you reach them not on the basis of what people say with words, but because of what they say *nonverbally*—with their posture, gestures, eyes, and facial expressions. Suppose you are sitting next to Amin, and he says, "This is a great party. I'm really glad to be here with you." However, his body is turned slightly away from you, and he keeps looking at someone across the room. Despite what he says, you know he is *not* glad to be there with you.

Much the same thing happens in speechmaking. Here is the story of one student's first two classroom speeches and the effect created by his nonverbal actions on each occasion:

Sean O'Connor's first speech did not go very well. Even though he had chosen an interesting topic, researched the speech with care, and practiced it faithfully, he did not take into account the importance of nonverbal communication. When the time came for him to speak, a stricken look crossed his face. He got up from his chair like a condemned man and plodded to the lectern as though going to the guillotine. His

nonverbal communication
Communication that occurs as a result of appearance, posture, gesture, eye contact, facial expressions, and other nonlinguistic factors.

vocal delivery was good enough, but all the while his hands were living a life of their own. They fidgeted with his notes, played with the buttons of his shirt, and drummed on the lectern. Throughout the speech Sean kept his head down, and he looked at his watch repeatedly. Regardless of what his *words* were saying, his *body* was saying, "I don't want to be here!"

Finally it was over. Sean rushed to his seat and collapsed into it, looking enormously relieved. Needless to say, his speech was not a great success.

Fortunately, when Sean's problem with nonverbal communication was pointed out to him, he worked hard to correct it. His next speech was quite a different story. This time he got up from his chair and strode to the lectern confidently. He kept his hands under control and concentrated on making eye contact with his listeners. This was truly an achievement, because Sean was just as nervous as the first time. However, he found that the more he made himself *look* confident, the more confident he *became*. After the speech his classmates were enthusiastic. "Great speech," they said. "You really seemed to care about the subject, and you brought this caring to the audience."

In fact, the wording of Sean's second speech wasn't much better than that of the first. It was his nonverbal signals that made all the difference. From the time he left his seat until he returned, his actions said, "I am confident and in control of the situation. I have something worthwhile to say, and I want you to think so too."

Posture, facial expression, gestures, eye contact—all affect the way listeners respond to a speaker. How we use these and other body motions to communicate is the subject of a fascinating area of study called kinesics. One of its founders, Ray Birdwhistell, estimates that more than 700,000 possible physical signals can be sent through bodily movement. Studies have shown that in some situations these signals account for much of the meaning communicated by speakers. Research has also confirmed what the Greek historian Herodotus observed more than 2,400 years ago: "People trust their ears less than their eyes." When a speaker's body language is inconsistent with his or her words, listeners tend to believe the body language rather than the words.[16]

kinesics
The study of nonverbal body motions as a systematic mode of communication.

Here are the major aspects of nonverbal communication that will affect the outcome of your speeches.

Personal Appearance

If you were Madonna, you could show up to make an Academy Award presentation speech wearing a bizarre creation that left little to the imagination. If you were Albert Einstein, you could show up to address an international science conference wearing wrinkled trousers, a sweater, and tennis shoes. While the members of your audience would certainly comment on your attire, your reputation would not be harmed. In fact, it might be enhanced. You would be one of the few, the very few, who live outside the rules, who are expected to be unusual.

Now imagine what would happen if the president of a corporation showed up to address a stockholders' meeting attired like Madonna, or if the President of the United States spoke on national television wearing wrinkled clothes and tennis shoes. Both presidents would soon be looking for work. Barring the occasional eccentric, every speaker is expected by her or his audience to exhibit a personal appearance in keeping with the occasion of the speech.

The President of the United States can be photographed in golfing clothes or hiking clothes for a quick weekend interview at Camp David, but that same president will don a conservative suit and tie to address a joint session of Congress. Similarly, a business executive speaking at a winter sales conference in Acapulco would probably wear slacks and a casual shirt or blouse because a business suit, in this atmosphere, would seem too formal. But back home in San Francisco, Chicago, or New York, the same executive will be immaculately dressed in a well-tailored suit.

A number of studies have confirmed that personal appearance plays an important role in speechmaking.[17] Listeners always see you before they hear you. Just as you adapt your language to the audience and the occasion, so should you dress and groom appropriately. Although the force of your speech can sometimes overcome a poor impression created by personal appearance, the odds are against it. (In a survey of top business executives, 84 percent revealed that their companies do not hire people who appear at job interviews improperly attired.)[18] Regardless of the speaking situation, you should try to evoke a favorable first impression—an impression that is likely to make listeners more receptive to what you say.

Bodily Action

Novice speakers are often unsure about what to do with their body while giving a speech. Some pace nonstop back and forth across the podium, fearing that if they stop, they will forget everything. Others are perpetual-motion machines, constantly shifting their weight from one foot to the other, bobbing their shoulders, fidgeting with their notes, or jingling coins in their pockets. Still others turn into statues, standing rigid and expressionless from beginning to end.

Such quirks usually stem from nervousness. If you are prone to distracting mannerisms, your teacher will identify them so you can work on controlling them in later speeches. With a little concentration, these mannerisms should disappear as you become more comfortable speaking in front of an audience.

As important as how you act during the speech is what you do just *before* you begin and *after* you finish. As you rise to speak, try to appear calm, poised, and confident, despite the butterflies in your stomach. When you reach the lectern, don't lean on it, and don't rush into your speech. Give yourself time to get set. Arrange your notes just the way you want them. Stand quietly as you wait to make sure the audience is paying attention. Establish eye contact with your listeners. Then—and only then—should you start to talk.

When you reach the end of your speech, maintain eye contact for a few moments after you stop talking. This will give your closing line time to sink in. Unless you are staying at the lectern to answer questions, collect your notes and return to your seat. As you do so, maintain your cool, collected demeanor. Whatever you do, don't start to gather your notes before you have finished talking; and don't cap off your speech with a huge sigh of relief or some remark like "Whew! Am I glad that's over!"

All of this advice is common sense; yet you would be surprised how many people need it. When practicing your speeches, spend a little time re-

Good speakers use a lively voice to help bring their ideas to life. They also use gestures, eye contact, and facial expressions to create a bond with their listeners.

hearsing how you will behave at the beginning and at the end. It is probably one of the easiest—and one of the most effective—things you can do to improve your image with an audience.

Gestures

Few aspects of delivery seem to cause students more anguish than deciding what to do with their hands. "Should I clasp them behind my back? Let them hang at my sides? Put them in my pockets? Rest them on the lectern? And what about gesturing? When should I do that—and how?" Even people who normally use their hands expressively in everyday conversation seem to regard them as awkward appendages when speaking before an audience.

Over the years, more nonsense has been written about gesturing than about any other aspect of speech delivery. Adroit gestures *can* add to the impact of a speech; but there is nothing to the popular notion that public speakers must have a vast repertoire of graceful gestures. Some accomplished speakers gesture frequently; others hardly at all. The primary rule is this: Whatever gestures you make should not draw attention to themselves and distract from your message. They should *appear* natural and spontaneous, help to clarify or reinforce your ideas, and be suited to the audience and occasion.[19]

gestures
Motions of a speaker's hands or arms during a speech.

At this stage of your speaking career, you have many more important things to concentrate on than how to gesture. Gesturing tends to work itself out as you acquire experience and confidence. In the meantime, make sure your hands do not upstage your ideas. Avoid flailing them about, wringing them together, cracking your knuckles, or toying with your rings. Once you have eliminated these distractions, forget about your hands. Think about communicating with your listeners, and your gestures will probably take care of themselves—just as they do in conversation.

Eye Contact

eye contact
Direct visual contact with the eyes of another person.

The eyeball itself expresses no emotion. Yet by manipulating the eyeball and the areas of the face around it—especially the upper eyelids and the eyebrows—we are able to convey an intricate array of nonverbal messages. So revealing are these messages that we think of the eyes as "the windows of the soul." We look to them to help gauge the truthfulness, intelligence, attitudes, and feelings of a speaker.

Like many aspects of communication, eye contact is influenced by cultural background. When engaged in conversation, Arabs, Latin Americans, and Southern Europeans tend to look directly at the person with whom they are talking. People from Asian countries and parts of Africa tend to engage in less eye contact. In Kenya a discussion between a woman and her son-in-law may well be conducted with each person turning her or his back to the other![20]

When it comes to public speaking, there appears to be fairly wide agreement across cultures on the importance of some degree of eye contact.[21] In most circumstances, one of the quickest ways to establish a communicative bond with your listeners is to look at them personally and pleasantly. Avoiding their gaze is one of the surest ways to lose them. There is a great deal of research to show that speakers in the United States who refuse to establish eye contact are perceived as tentative or ill at ease and may be seen as insincere or dishonest.[22] It is no wonder, then, that teachers urge students to look at the audience 80 to 90 percent of the time they are talking.

You may find this disconcerting at first. But after one or two speeches, you should be able to meet the gaze of your audience fairly comfortably. As you look at your listeners, be alert for their reactions. Can they hear you? Do they understand you? Are they awake? Your eyes will help you answer these questions.

It isn't enough just to look at your listeners; *how* you look at them also counts. A blank stare is almost as bad as no eye contact at all. So is a fierce, hostile glower or a series of frightened, bewildered glances. Also beware of the tendency to gaze intently at one part of the audience while ignoring the rest. In speech class some students look only at the section of the room where the teacher is sitting. Others avoid looking anywhere near the teacher and focus on one or two sympathetic friends. You should try to establish eye contact with your whole audience.

Look at CD-ROM Video Clip 12.4 for an excellent example of eye contact. The speech is by Kristin Berg, a student at the University of Wisconsin. Kristin's assignment was to interview one of her classmates, Reva, and to give a brief talk introducing her to the rest of the class. In her speech,

Kristin explained how Reva's parents had worked to help their growing family adapt to a new culture after immigrating to the United States. As you can see from the CD, the impact of Kristin's speech was greatly enhanced by her strong eye contact (as well by her vocal variety and communicative gestures).

When addressing a small audience such as your class, you can usually look briefly, as Kristin did, from one person to another. For a larger group, you will probably scan the audience rather than trying to engage the eyes of each person individually. No matter what the size of your audience, you want your eyes to convey confidence, sincerity, and conviction. They should say, "I am pleased to be able to talk with you. I believe deeply in what I am saying, and I want you to believe in it too."[23]

View an excerpt from Kristin Berg, "A Family Tradition.

CD: VIDEO CLIP 12.4

Practicing Delivery

Popular wisdom promises that practice makes perfect. This is true, but only if we practice properly. No matter how long and hard you practice playing the piano, you will never make beautiful music if you don't know the difference between a sharp and a flat. By the same token, you will do little to improve your speech delivery unless you practice the right things in the right ways. Here is a five-step method that has worked well for many students:

1. Go through your preparation outline *aloud* to check how what you have written translates into spoken discourse. Is it too long? Too short? Are the main points clear when you speak them? Are the supporting materials distinct, convincing, interesting? Do the introduction and conclusion come across well? As you answer these questions, revise the speech as needed.

2. Prepare your speaking outline. In doing so, be sure to follow the guidelines discussed in Chapter 10. Use the same visual framework as in the preparation outline. Make sure the speaking outline is easy to read at a glance. Keep the outline as brief as possible. Give yourself cues on the outline for delivering the speech.

3. Practice the speech aloud several times using only the speaking outline. Be sure to "talk through" all examples and to recite in full all quotations and statistics. If your speech includes visual aids, use them as you practice. The first couple of times you will probably forget something or make a mistake, but don't worry about that. Keep going and complete the speech as well as you can. Concentrate on gaining control of the *ideas;* don't try to learn the speech word for word. After a few tries you should be able to get through the speech extemporaneously with surprising ease.

4. Now begin to polish and refine your delivery. Practice the speech in front of a mirror to check for eye contact and distracting mannerisms. Tape-record the speech to gauge volume, pitch, rate, pauses, and vocal variety. Most important, try it out on friends, roommates, family members—anyone who will listen and give you an honest appraisal. Don't be shy about asking. Most people love to give their opinion about something. Since your speech is designed for people rather than for mirrors or tape recorders, you need to find out ahead of time how it goes over with people.

5. Finally, give your speech a dress rehearsal under conditions as close as possible to those you will face in class. Some students like to try the speech a couple of times in an empty classroom the day before the speech is due. No matter where you hold your last practice session, you should leave it feeling confident and looking forward to speaking in your class.

If this or any practice method is to work, you must start early. Don't wait until the day of your speech, or even the night before, to begin working on delivery. A single practice session—no matter how long—is rarely enough. Allow yourself *at least* a couple of days, preferably more, to gain command of the speech and its presentation. No matter how brilliant your preparation outline, what counts is how the speech comes across when you deliver it. Give yourself plenty of time to make sure it comes across well.[24]

Answering Audience Questions

As director of the city municipal building, Delia Sedano was responsible for presenting a plan she and her colleagues had developed to improve security. City employees, citizens, and the media gathered in the building's auditorium to hear her describe the plan. After outlining the main points she would cover, she assured the audience that she would be happy to answer questions at the end.

Delia realized that the plan was expensive and somewhat controversial, so she was not surprised to see a number of hands go up as soon as she finished. An employee in the city clerk's office asked, "How will the security system affect the daily lives of people who work in the building?" Delia had anticipated this question and had an answer ready. After repeating the question so everyone could hear it, she replied that the only change would be a new requirement to carry a security card. "A small inconvenience for safeguarding our employees and the public," she added.

The next question was more confrontational: "How can you justify spending half a million dollars on a security system for one building when it's not safe to walk through entire neighborhoods in our city?" The journalist who asked the question seemed hostile, but Delia was careful not to adopt a defensive tone. She pointed out that voters had authorized the spending in a referendum.

A third question—about the mechanics of the alarm system—was rather technical, so Delia clarified the gist of the question. She then introduced the specialist who had worked with the planning committee and asked him to make a brief reply. Delia also offered to remain after the session to answer additional questions of a technical nature.

Near the end of the 25 minutes she had allotted, Delia said she would take two more questions. When those were finished, she concluded the session with a brief restatement of how the new system would improve security and peace of mind in the municipal building.

After Delia closed, Art Shafer, a member of the planning committee for the security system, came forward to congratulate her on a successful briefing. "Your presentation was great," he said, "but the Q&A was really important. It showed the audience that we've looked at this from all angles."

If you have ever watched a press conference or heard a speaker answer questions after a talk, you know that the question-and-answer session can make or break a presentation. A speaker who handles questions well, like

Delia Sedano, can enhance her credibility and strengthen the impact of her speech. On the other hand, a speaker who evades questions or shows annoyance will almost certainly create the opposite effect.

The question-and-answer session is a common part of public speaking, whether the occasion is a press conference, business presentation, public hearing, or classroom assignment. Depending on the situation, questioning may take place throughout the presentation, or it may be reserved until after the speaker has completed his or her remarks. In either case, an answer to a question is often the final word an audience hears and is likely to leave a lasting impression. Effective speakers recognize that the question period can be as important as the speech itself.

Preparing for the Question-and-Answer Session

The first step to doing well in a question-and-answer session is to take it as seriously as the speech itself. Even experienced speakers have been known to stumble if they fail to prepare thoroughly for the question-and-answer part of their presentation. The two major steps in preparing are working out answers to possible questions and practicing the delivery of those answers.

Formulate Answers to Possible Questions

Once you know your presentation will include questions from the audience, you should be thinking about possible questions even as you are writing your speech. If you practice your speech in front of friends, family, or coworkers, ask them to jot down any questions they may have. Keep track of all the questions and take the time to formulate answers. In Delia Sedano's case, she knew people working in the municipal building were likely to ask how the security plan would affect them. Because she had prepared an answer for this question, she was able to answer it clearly and convincingly. She also knew some people would challenge the city's expenditure on the security system, and she had resolved in advance not to allow herself to be drawn into an argument on this issue.

In the same way, you should anticipate questions and prepare answers to them. Write your answers in full to make sure you have thought them through completely. If you are giving a persuasive speech, be sure to work out answers to objections the audience may have to your proposal. No matter how careful you are to deal with those objections in your speech, you can be sure they will come up at some point in the question-and-answer session.

If you are speaking on a topic with technical aspects, be ready to answer specialized inquiries about them, as well as questions that seek clarification in nontechnical terms. You might even prepare a handout that you can distribute afterward for people who want more information than you can provide in the question-and-answer period.

Practice the Delivery of Your Answers

You would not present a speech to a room full of people without rehearsing. Neither should you go into a question-and-answer session without practicing the delivery of your answers. As many speakers have discovered, writing out answers in the privacy of your home or office and vocalizing them articulately under the pressure of an open forum are two different matters. Since you will be presenting your answers out loud, you should rehearse them out loud. Otherwise, you may find that the answers you have so carefully prepared come out garbled and incoherent.

One possibility is to have a friend or colleague listen to your presentation, ask questions, and critique your answers. This method is used extensively by political candidates and business leaders, whose staff members grill them with questions before debates or press conferences. Another possibility is to tape-record your answers to anticipated questions, play them back, and revise your answers until you get them just right.

As you rehearse, work on making your answers brief and to the point. Many simple questions can be answered in 10 seconds, and even complex ones should be answered in less than a minute. If you practice answering questions beforehand, you will find it much easier to keep to these time limits.

Of course, no matter how much you work ahead of time, there is no way to predict every question you will receive. Some people will ask questions you had not anticipated, and some of the questions you did anticipate may not get asked at all. But if you go into the question-and-answer period fully prepared, you will find it much easier to adapt to unforeseen questions and circumstances.

Managing the Question-and-Answer Session

If you have ever watched a skillful speaker field questions from the audience, you know there is an art to managing a question-and-answer session so it runs smoothly and enhances the speech. Entire books have been written on this subject, but the following suggestions will help get you started on the right foot.

Clarify the Format

If there is any doubt about when you will entertain questions, take time early in your speech to clarify the format you prefer. You can do this very simply by saying something like, "Feel free to ask questions throughout my speech," or "I am happy to answer questions at the end of my talk." Of course, if the gound rules are already clear, there is no need to say anything about them.

Approach Questions with a Positive Attitude

A positive attitude will help you answer questions graciously and respectfully. Try to view questions from the audience as signs of genuine interest and a desire to learn more about your subject. This is particularly important when an audience member asks a question about material you feel you have covered or a point that seems clear to you. Instead of replying, "I discussed that at the beginning of my talk," or "The answer to that is obvious," use moments like these to reiterate or expand upon your ideas. If you insult a questioner by dismissing his or her question, the audience is likely to make negative judgments about your character.

Similarly, a speaker who adopts a sharp or defensive tone while answering questions will probably alienate many people in the audience.

The ability to answer questions effectively is an important skill for public speakers. Here John McCain responds to inquiries from the press during the 2000 New Hampshire presidential primary.

Think of the question-and-answer session as another opportunity to communicate your ideas rather than as a challenge to your competence, intelligence, or personhood. If someone in the audience has misunderstood a portion of your speech, the Q&A is a perfect time to clarify your ideas.

Even if you are asked a hostile question, keep your cool. Avoid the temptation to answer defensively, sarcastically, or argumentatively. Most people in the audience will respect you for trying to avoid a quarrel.

Listen Carefully

It's hard to answer a question well if you don't listen carefully to it. Give the questioner your full attention. Look directly at her or him rather than glancing around the room, at the floor, or at the ceiling. If the audience member is having a difficult time stating the question, you might even nod in encouragement to help them along.

When faced with an unclear or unwieldy question, try to rephrase it by saying something like, "If I understand your question, it seems to me that you are asking . . . " Another option is simply to ask the audience member to repeat the question. Most people will restate it more succinctly and clearly. If you still don't understand, ask the questioner to give an example of what he or she means.

Direct Answers to the Entire Audience

When you are being asked a question, look at the questioner. Direct your answer, however, to the entire audience. Make occasional eye contact with the questioner as you answer, but speak primarily to the audience as a whole. This will help you keep everyone's attention. If you speak just to the questioner, you may well find the rest of your audience drifting off.

When speaking to a large audience, be sure to repeat or paraphrase each question after it is asked. This helps ensure that you understand the question properly. It also involves the entire audience and guarantees that they know the question you are addressing. In addition, repeating or paraphrasing the question gives you a moment to frame an answer before you respond.

Be Honest and Straightforward

Some speakers dread question-and-answer sessions because they are afraid of being derailed by a question they can't answer. The world won't end if you can't answer every possible question. If you don't know the answer, say so. Don't apologize, don't evade, and most important, don't try to bluff. Do, however, let the questioner know that you take the question seriously. Offer to check into the answer as soon as possible after the speech. If a more knowledgeable person is at hand, ask if he or she knows the answer.

Stay on Track

It is easy to get diverted or to lose control of time in the give and take of a lively question-and-answer session. Unless there is a moderator for the session, the speaker is responsible for keeping things on track. Sometimes that means preventing a single questioner from dominating the session. Allow one follow-up question from each person, and don't let yourself be dragged into a personal debate with any questioner. If someone attempts to ask more than two questions, respond graciously yet firmly by saying, "This is an interesting line of questioning, but we need to give other people a chance to ask questions."

Sometimes, a listener will launch into an extended monologue instead of posing a question. When this happens, you can regain control of the situation by saying something like, "Those are very interesting ideas, but do you have a specific question I can answer?" If the person continues, offer to talk individually with him or her after the session.

On some occasions, the length of the question-and-answer session is predetermined by the moderator or by the schedule of the audience. On other occasions, it's up to the speaker to decide how much time to devote to answering questions. Often this requires adapting to the kind and number of questions you are receiving. Make sure you allow enough time to get through issues of major importance, but don't let things drag on after the momentum of the session has started winding down. As the end approaches, offer to respond to another question or two. After answering them, wrap things up by thanking the audience for its time and attention.[25]

Summary

The impact of a speech is strongly affected by how the speech is delivered. You cannot make a good speech without having something to say. But having something to say is not enough. You must also know *how* to say it.

Good delivery does not call attention to itself. It conveys the speaker's ideas clearly, interestingly, and without distracting the audience. In your earliest speeches you should concentrate on speaking intelligibly, avoiding distracting mannerisms, and establishing eye contact with your listeners. Once you get these elements under control, you can work on refining your delivery so that it adds to the impact of your ideas.

There are four basic methods of delivering a speech: reading verbatim from a manuscript, reciting a memorized text, speaking impromptu, and speaking extemporaneously. The last of these—speaking extemporaneously—is the method you probably will use for classroom speeches and for most speeches outside the classroom. When speaking extemporaneously, you will have only a brief set of notes or a speaking outline. You will choose the exact wording of your speech at the moment of delivery.

A primary factor in delivery is the speaker's voice. To use your voice effectively you should work on controlling your volume, pitch, rate, pauses, vocal variety, pronunciation, articulation, and dialect. Volume is the relative loudness of your voice, and pitch is the relative highness or lowness. Rate refers to the speed at which you talk. Pauses, when carefully timed, can add great impact to your speech, but you should avoid vocalized pauses ("er," "um," and the like). Vocal variety refers to changes in volume, pitch, rate, and pauses, and is crucial to making your voice lively and animated. Most of us speak casually in everyday conversation, but for public speaking you should be sure to pronounce words correctly and to articulate them distinctly. You should also avoid heavy use of dialect in situations where the audience does not share the dialect or will find it inappropriate to the occasion.

Nonverbal communication is another vital factor in delivery. Posture, personal appearance, facial expression, bodily movement, gestures, and eye contact all affect the way listeners respond to speakers. You can do little to change your face or body, but you can dress and groom appropriately for the situation at hand. You can also learn to control gestures and bodily movements so they enhance your message, rather than distract from it. Making eye contact with listeners is the quickest way to establish a communicative bond with them.

You should practice all these aspects of delivery along with the words of your speech. Start your practice sessions early, so you will have plenty of time to gain command of the speech and its presentation.

If your speech includes a question-and-answer session, you will need to prepare for that as well, since it can have a strong impact on the audience's final impression. Anticipate the most likely questions, prepare answers to them, and practice delivering those answers. Once the question-and-answer period is underway, listen carefully to the questions, approach them positively, and respond to them briefly, graciously, and straightforwardly. Direct your answers to the full audience, rather than to the questioner alone, and make sure to end the session in a timely fashion.

Key Terms

manuscript speech (285)

impromptu speech (286)

extemporaneous speech (287)

conversational quality (287)

volume (289)

pitch (289)

inflections (290)

monotone (290)

rate (290)

pause (290)

vocalized pause (291)   nonverbal communication (296)

vocal variety (292)   kinesics (297)

pronunciation (294)   gestures (299)

articulation (294)   eye contact (300)

dialect (295)

Review Questions

For further review, go to the Study Questions for this chapter.

CD: STUDY QUESTIONS

After reading this chapter, you should be able to answer the following questions:

1. What is good speech delivery? Why is good delivery important to successful speaking?

2. What are the four methods of speech delivery?

3. Why is every person's voice unique?

4. What are the eight aspects of voice usage you should concentrate on in your speeches?

5. Why is nonverbal communication important to a public speaker?

6. What are the four aspects of nonverbal communication you should concentrate on in your speeches?

7. What are the five steps you should follow in practicing your speech delivery?

8. What steps should you take when preparing for a question-and-answer session? What are six things you should do when responding to questions during the session itself?

Exercises for Critical Thinking

1. An excellent way to improve your vocal variety is to read aloud selections from poetry that require emphasis and feeling. Choose one of your favorite poems that falls into this category, or else find one by leafing through a poetry anthology. Practice reading the selection aloud. As you read, use your voice to make the poem come alive. Vary your volume, rate, and pitch. Find the appropriate places for pauses. Underline the key words or phrases you think should be stressed. Modulate your tone of voice; use inflections for emphasis and meaning.

   For this to work, you must overcome your fear of sounding affected or "dramatic." Most beginning speakers do better if they exaggerate changes in volume, rate, pitch, and expression. This will make you more aware of the many ways you can use your voice to express a wide range of moods and meanings. Besides, what sounds overly "dramatic" to you usually does not sound that way to an audience. By adding luster, warmth, and enthusiasm to your voice, you will go a long way toward capturing and keeping the interest of your listeners.

If possible, practice reading the selection into a tape recorder. Listen to the playback. If you are not satisfied with what you hear, practice the selection some more and record it again.

2. Watch a 10-minute segment of a television drama with the sound turned off. What do the characters say with their dress, gestures, facial expressions, and the like? Do the same with a television comedy. How do the nonverbal messages in the two shows differ? Be prepared to report your observations in class.

3. Attend a speech on campus. You may choose either a presentation by a guest speaker from outside the college or a class session by a professor who has a reputation as a good lecturer. Prepare a brief report on the speaker's vocal and nonverbal communication.

In your report, first analyze the speaker's volume, pitch, rate, pauses, vocal variety, pronunciation, and articulation. Then evaluate the speaker's personal appearance, bodily action, gestures, and eye contact. Explain how the speaker's delivery added to or detracted from what the speaker said. Finally, note at least two techniques of delivery used by the speaker that you might want to try in your next speech.

Applying the POWER of Public Speaking

Utilizing your business degree and computer savvy, you have made a success of the online marketing company you started after graduating from college. Now in its third year, the company has prepared a proposal to design the e-commerce site for a major sporting goods retailer. In your 30-minute presentation to the retailer's management team, you will review the home page designs, site maps, and security protocols.

You notice on the agenda that another 30 minutes has been allotted after your presentation for questions and answers. Knowing from your previous experience with clients how important the Q&A session can be, you want to be sure you are ready for it. What steps will you take to prepare?

Notes

[1] Irving Bartlett, *Wendell Phillips: Boston Brahmin* (Boston: Beacon Press, 1961), p. 192.
[2] A. Craig Baird, *Rhetoric: A Philosophical Inquiry* (New York: Ronald Press, 1965), p. 207.
[3] There is still no better guide to the techniques of manuscript speaking than James C. Humes, *Talk Your Way to the Top* (New York: McGraw-Hill, 1980), pp. 125–135.
[4] For research on the importance of conversational quality, see Robert James Branham and W. Barnett Pearce, "The Conversational Frame in Public Address," *Communication Quarterly,* 44 (1996), pp. 423–439.

[5]See, for example, David B. Buller, Beth A. LePoire, R. Kelly Aune, and Sylvia V. Eloy, "Social Perceptions as Mediators of the Effect of Speech Rate Similarity on Compliance," *Human Communication Research,* 19 (1992), pp. 286–311.

[6]This is confirmed by a large number of research studies, including Steven W. Knowlton and Charles R. Berger, "Message Planning, Communication Failure, and Cognitive Load: Further Explorations of the Hierarchy Principle," *Human Communication Research,* 24 (1997), pp. 4–30.

[7]James Joyce, "Chamber Music," stanza XXXV, from *The Portable James Joyce,* ed. Harry Levin (New York: Viking, 1946–1947). Copyright renewed 1974, 1975. Reprinted by permission of Viking Penguin, Inc.

[8]Dorothy Sarnoff, *Speech Can Change Your Life* (Garden City, N.Y.: Doubleday, 1970), p. 73.

[9]The relationship between articulation and pronunciation is a matter of some dispute among experts and is far from clear in many books. I would like to thank Professor Raymond D. Kent of the Department of Communicative Disorders, University of Wisconsin, Madison, for helping me sort out the distinctions.

[10]William Norwood Brigance, *Speech: Its Techniques and Disciplines in a Free Society* (New York: Appleton-Century-Crofts, 1961), p. 349.

[11]The most authoritative guide to regional dialects in the United States is Frederic G. Cassidy and Joan H. Hall (eds.), *Dictionary of American Regional English* (Cambridge, Mass.: Harvard University Press). The first three volumes of this work were published in 1985, 1991, and 1996, respectively. Two more volumes are in preparation.

[12]Tom McArthur (ed.), *The Oxford Companion to the English Language* (New York: Oxford University Press, 1992).

[13]For an interesting discussion of this point, see Patrick L. Courts, *Multicultural Literacies: Dialect, Discourse, and Diversity* (New York: Peter Lang, 1997).

[14]Mary M. Gill, "Accents and Stereotypes: Their Effect on Perceptions of Teachers and Lecture Comprehension," *Journal of Applied Communication Research,* 22 (1994), pp. 348–361.

[15]For a more detailed guide on vocal communication, consult Jeffrey C. Hahner, Martin A. Sokoloff, and Sandra L. Salisch, *Speaking Clearly: Improving Voice and Diction,* 5th ed. (New York: McGraw-Hill, 1996).

[16]See, for example, April R. Trees and Valerie Manusov, "Managing Face Concerns in Critics: Integrating Nonverbal Behaviors as a Dimension of Politeness in Female Friendship Dyads," *Human Communication Research,* 24 (1998), pp. 564–583.

[17]Richard M. Perloff, *The Dynamics of Persuasion* (Hillsdale, N.J.: Erlbaum, 1993), pp. 149–152.

[18]John T. Malloy, *Dress for Success* (New York: Warner, 1975), p. 36. For a later work on the same subject, see Susan Bixler, *Professional Presence* (New York: Perigee Books, 1991), pp. 141–170.

[19]For the importance of coordinating gestures and other nonverbal cues with one's verbal message, see Mary Mino, "The Relative Effects of Vocal Delivery during a Simulated Employment Interview," *Communication Research Reports,* 13 (1996), pp. 225–238.

[20]Mark L. Knapp and Judith A. Hall, *Nonverbal Communication in Human Interaction,* 4th ed. (Fort Worth, Tex.: Harcourt Brace Jovanovich, 1997), p. 386.

[21]See James C. McCroskey, Aino Sallinen, Joan M. Fayer, Virginia P. Richmond, and Robert A. Barraclough, "Nonverbal Immediacy and Cognitive Learning: A Cross-Cultural Investigation," *Communication Education,* 45 (1996), pp. 200–211.

[22]Mark T. Palmer and Karl B. Simmons, "Communicating Intentions through Nonverbal Behaviors," *Human Communication Research,* 22 (1995), pp. 128–160.

[23]For an excellent collection of writings on the impact of nonverbal messages in a variety of communication contexts, see Laura K. Guerrero, Joseph A. DeVito, and Michael L. Hecht (eds.), *The Nonverbal Communication Reader: Classic and Contemporary Readings,* 2nd ed. (Prospect Heights, Ill.: Waveland Press, 1999).

[24]For a recent study that underscores the importance of practicing speech delivery, see John O. Greene, Marianne S. Sassi, Terri L. Malek-Madani, and Christopher N.

Edwards, "Adult Acquisition of Message-Production Skills," *Communication Monographs,* 64 (1997), pp. 181–200.

[25]For more on managing question-and-answer sessions, consult Claudyne Wilder, *The Presentations Kit: 10 Steps for Selling Your Ideas,* rev. ed. (New York: Wiley, 1994), pp. 207–225; and Thomas K. Mira, *Speak Smart* (New York: Random House, 1997), pp. 115–123.

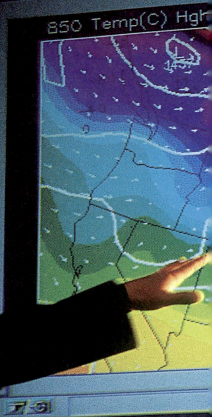

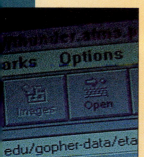

USING VISUAL AIDS

Advantages of Visual Aids

Kinds of Visual Aids

Objects
Models
Photographs
Drawings
Graphs
Charts
Slides and Videotapes
Computer-Generated Graphics
Transparencies
Multimedia Presentations
The Speaker

Guidelines for Preparing Visual Aids

Prepare Visual Aids in Advance
Keep Visual Aids Simple
Make Sure Visual Aids Are Large Enough
Use Fonts That Are Easy to Read
Use a Limited Number of Fonts
Use Color Effectively

Tips for Presenting Visual Aids

Avoid Using the Chalkboard for Visual Aids
Display Visual Aids Where Listeners Can See Them
Avoid Passing Visual Aids among the Audience
Display Visual Aids only while Discussing Them
Talk to Your Audience, Not to Your Visual Aid
Explain Visual Aids Clearly and Concisely
Practice with Your Visual Aids

"Magnificent!" *New York Times.*

"Spellbinding!" Ian Brodie, *London Daily Telegraph.*

"A classic!" David Zucchino, *Philadelphia Inquirer.*

Reviews of Julia Roberts' latest movie? John Grisham's most recent novel? Andrew Lloyd Weber's newest Broadway play?

In fact, these are the words used to describe General Norman Schwarzkopf's famous press briefing at the end of the Persian Gulf War. Delivered to the press corps in Riyadh, Saudi Arabia, on February 27, 1991, and shown live around the world by CNN, the briefing was hailed as a public speaking masterpiece. Not only was it rebroadcast on all the U.S. networks within hours of its original presentation, but it became a best-selling home video when released as part of ABC News' "Schwarzkopf: How the War Was Won."

View an excerpt from Norman Schwarzkopf's briefing of February 27, 1991.

CD: VIDEO CLIP 13.1

Speaking flawlessly and without notes, Schwarzkopf led viewers step by step through a half-dozen maps that showed Allied troop movements and military strategy from the beginning of the war to its end. Wielding a collapsible metal pointer, he moved from map to map as adroitly as a conductor leading an orchestra. Viewers sat mesmerized as he explained how each map showed a different stage in the development of the war. It was "as spellbinding as the toniest of Hamlets," raved the *Washington Post,* and it could not have been achieved without Schwarzkopf's masterful use of visual aids.

As the old saying tells us, one picture is worth a thousand words. People find a speaker's message more interesting, grasp it more easily, and retain it longer when it is presented visually as well as verbally. Can you picture the deployment of allied and Iraqi troops in the Persian Gulf War? You could if you had watched Schwarzkopf use his maps to illustrate those deployments. Their dramatic visual impact brought home Schwarzkopf's points more effectively than any recitation of facts and figures alone.

Advantages of Visual Aids

Visual aids offer several advantages. The primary advantage is *clarity.* If you are discussing an object, you can make your message clearer by showing the object or some representation of it. If you are citing statistics, showing how something works, or demonstrating a technique, a visual aid will make your information more vivid to your audience. After all, we live in a visual age. Television and movies have conditioned us to expect a visual image. By using visual aids in your speeches, you often will make it easier for listeners to understand exactly what you are trying to communicate.[1]

Another advantage of visual aids is *interest.* The interest generated by visual images is so strong that visual aids are now used routinely in many areas, not just speechmaking. A generation or so ago, most college textbooks were rather dry—page after page of words. Today they are enlivened with photographs, drawings, and other visual aids that clarify the material and make it more interesting. Encyclopedias have blossomed with photographs and maps; even dictionaries contain small drawings to highlight word definitions. You can do the same thing with your speeches.

Still another advantage of visual aids is *retention.* Visual images often stay with us longer than verbal ones. The people who saw Norman

Schwarzkopf's briefing may not remember exactly where allied troops were deployed on any given day of the Persian Gulf War. But they certainly remember the maps that showed those deployments. And they doubtless can recall more about the allies' strategy as a result of the maps. We've all heard that words can "go in one ear and out the other." Visual images tend to last.[2]

In fact, when used well, visual aids can enhance almost *every* aspect of a speech. One study showed that an average speaker who uses visual aids will come across as better prepared, more credible, and more professional than a dynamic speaker who does not use visual aids. According to the same study, visual aids can increase the persuasiveness of a speech by more than 40 percent.[3] There is also research to indicate that visual aids are an excellent way to combat stage fright. They heighten audience interest, shift attention away from the speaker, and give the speaker greater confidence in the speech as a whole.[4]

For all these reasons, you will find visual aids of great value in your speeches. In this chapter we will concentrate primarily on visual aids suitable for classroom speeches. However, the principles outlined here are true for all circumstances. For speeches outside the classroom—in business or community situations, for instance—you should have no difficulty applying the general suggestions given here.

Let us look first at the kinds of visual aids you are likely to use, then at guidelines for preparing visual aids, and finally at some tips for using visual aids effectively.

Kinds of Visual Aids

Objects

Tracy Collins is an avid downhill skier. When it came time for her informative speech, she chose as her specific purpose "To inform my audience how to choose the right ski equipment." On the day of her speech, she brought to class a pair of skis, boots, bindings, and ski clothing. It was then easy for her to explain exactly what to look for in each item.

By *showing* her classmates the equipment rather than just telling them about it, Tracy presented her ideas much more effectively than she could have by using words alone. She also made her speech more interesting to nonskiers. As one of her classmates said afterward, "I don't ski, but I found your speech fascinating. Using the skis and other equipment as visual aids really helped get me involved. Now I have a little better idea of what my friends who ski are talking about. Without the visual aids I would have been lost."

As in Tracy's speech, bringing the object of your talk to class can be an excellent way to clarify your ideas and give them dramatic impact. If you talk about guitars, why not bring one to class to show your listeners? If you plan to explain the different kinds of golf clubs, what could be better than showing a sample of each kind? Or suppose you want to inform your audience about the Japanese art of doll making. You could bring several dolls to class and explain to your classmates how they were made.

In certain situations you might use living objects as visual aids. This worked well for a high-school wrestling coach who returned to college to take a night class in public speaking. Not surprisingly, the coach gave one of his speeches about wrestling. On the night of his speech he brought along two of his high-school students, who demonstrated each of the basic holds as the coach discussed them.

Many objects, however, cannot be used effectively in classroom speeches. Some are too big to be hauled into a classroom. Others are too small to be seen clearly by the audience. Still others may not be available to you. If you were speaking about a rare suit of armor in the local museum, you could, theoretically, transport it to class, but it is most unlikely that the museum would let you borrow it. You would have to look for another kind of visual aid.

Models

model
An object, usually built to scale, that represents another object in detail.

If the item you want to discuss is too large, too small, or unavailable, you may be able to work with a model. One kind is a small-scale model of a large object. One speaker used such a model to help explain the events connected with the sinking of the ocean liner *Titanic.* Another speaker brought to class a scaled-down model of a hang glider to demonstrate the equipment and techniques of hang gliding.

A second kind of model is a large-scale representation of a small object. Science teachers use such models to help students visualize minuscule structures like molecules. A good example of this kind of model came in a speech about extended-wear contact lenses. The speaker wanted to demonstrate the differences in flexibility among hard contact lenses, soft lenses, and extended-wear lenses. Since the lenses themselves were too small for his classmates to see, he used a glass plate, a paper plate, and a sheet of clear plastic wrap to illustrate the differences among the three kinds of lenses. As you can see from CD-ROM Video Clip 13.2, it worked to perfection and allowed the speaker to communicate his ideas far more effectively than he could have by words alone.

View the use of visual aids in "Extended-Wear Contact Lenses."

CD: VIDEO CLIP 13.2

Finally, models can be life-size. To demonstrate the techniques of cardiopulmonary resuscitation, one speaker borrowed a life-size dummy of a human torso from the Red Cross. Another speaker, an anthropology major, used a full-scale model of a human skull to show how archaeologists use bone fragments to reconstruct the forms of early humans.

Photographs

In the absence of an object or a model, you may be able to use photographs. Lawyers often employ photographs in trials to show the crime scene or to dramatize evidence for the jury. Business speakers use them to illustrate new product lines; architects to show prospective clients other buildings the firm has designed; drunk-driving activists to show the tragic results of combining alcohol with driving.

Photographs will not work in a speech, however, unless you have access to oversize enlargements. Normal-size photos are not big enough to be seen clearly without being passed around—which only diverts the audience from what you are saying. The same is true of photographs in a book. Even oversize books are too small to be seen clearly by all members of an audience.

When used well, visual aids make a speaker's message clearer, more interesting, and easier to retain. Using a live object as a visual aid can have an especially dramatic impact.

How can you get large-scale photos for use in a speech? One student, who had his own darkroom, showed 2 × 3–foot enlargements to demonstrate the differences between professional and amateur photography. A second student used large art posters to illustrate her points in a speech about the painter Vincent van Gogh. Yet another speaker used enlargements produced by a color copier to show the spectacular markings of various species of saltwater tropical fish. The enlargements were 18 × 24 inches, and the speaker mounted them on white poster board to make them easier to see.

There is yet another option. Copy services can now convert photographs (or slides) into transparencies that can be used with an overhead projector. The projector enlarges the image and displays it on a screen, where it can be seen clearly even by large audiences. If you have photographs that are essential to your speech, you might want to explore this option. The cost is fairly minimal, and the results can be dramatic.

Drawings

Diagrams, sketches, and other kinds of drawings are superb alternatives to photographs. They are inexpensive to make. Moreover, since they are drawn specifically for one speech, they can be designed to illustrate your points exactly. This more than compensates for what they may lack in realism.

For example, Figure 13.1 (page 318) is a drawing used by a student in a speech about Navajo sandpainting. The student wanted to show his audience what sandpainting looks like and to explain its symbolism and religious significance. As you can imagine, it would have been almost impossible for him to do so without some kind of visual aid.

Figure 13.2 (page 318) shows a drawing used in a speech about the kinds of problems faced by people who suffer from dyslexia. This aid was particularly effective because it allowed the speaker to translate complex ideas into visual terms the audience could grasp almost immediately.

Figure 13.1

Figure 13.2

Maps are another kind of drawing that is easy to prepare. You can trace the basic outlines from an atlas and then enlarge the scale to make your visual aid. Figure 13.3 is a map used in a speech about the Central American country of Costa Rica. The map places Costa Rica in relation to its neighbors, Panama and Nicaragua, shows the major regions of the country (the Caribbean Lowlands, the Central Highlands, and the Pacific Coastal Strip), and identifies the location of its capital (San José). Each site on the map illustrated a different point in the speech.

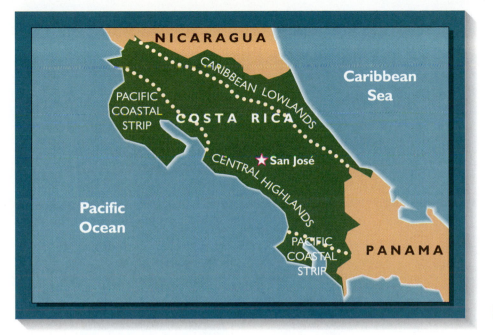

Figure 13.3

Graphs

Graphs are a good way to simplify and clarify statistics. Audiences often have trouble grasping a complex series of numbers. You can ease their difficulty by using graphs to show statistical trends and patterns.

The most common type is the *line graph.* Figure 13.4 shows such a graph, used in a speech about the American movie industry. The speaker explained the graph as follows:

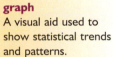

graph
A visual aid used to show statistical trends and patterns.

line graph
A graph that uses one or more lines to show changes in statistics over time or space.

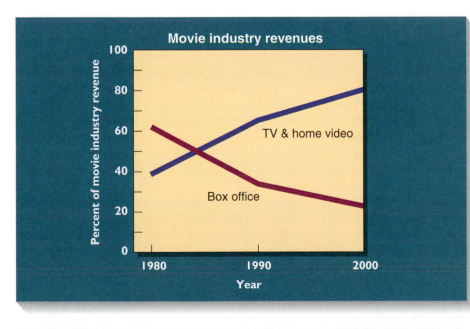

Figure 13.4

As you can see from this graph based on figures in *Newsweek* magazine, the video revolution has had a major impact on the American movie industry. From 1981 to 1999, the percent of movie industry revenues generated by box office receipts fell dramatically—from 61 percent to 22 percent. At the same time, the percent of movie industry revenues generated by videocassettes and films shown on television doubled—from 39 percent in 1981 to 78 percent in 1999.

pie graph
A graph that highlights segments of a circle to show simple distribution patterns.

The *pie graph* is best suited for illustrating simple distribution patterns. You will see such a graph in your newspaper each year to show the division of the national budget. Figure 13.5 shows how one speaker used a pie graph to help listeners visualize changes in marital status among working women in the past century. The graph on the left shows the percentages of working women who were single, married, and widowed or divorced in 1900. The graph on the right shows percentages for the same groups in 2000.

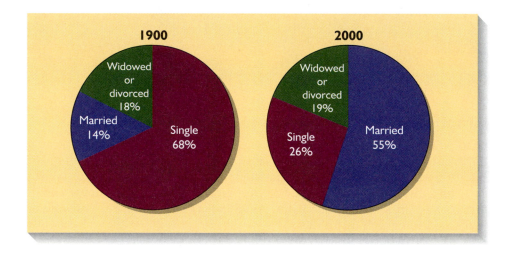

Figure 13.5

These pie graphs helped the speaker make three points: (1) The percentage of working women who are widowed or divorced has remained relatively stable since 1900; (2) the percentage of working women who are single has declined greatly during the past century; (3) the percentage of working women who are married has more than tripled, to the point that they are now far and away the largest group of working women in the United States.

Because a pie graph is used to dramatize relationships among the parts of a whole, you should keep the number of different segments in the graph as small as possible. A pie graph should ideally have from two to five segments; under no circumstances should it have more than eight.

bar graph
A graph that uses vertical or horizontal bars to show comparisons among two or more items.

The *bar graph* is a particularly good way to show comparisons between two or more items. It also has the advantage of being easy to understand, even by people who have no background in reading graphs. Figure 13.6 is an example of a bar graph from a speech entitled "The Politics of Race in America." It shows visually the relative standing of whites and blacks with respect to median household income, infant mortality, unemployment, and college education. By using a bar graph, the speaker made her points much more vividly than if she had just cited the numbers orally.

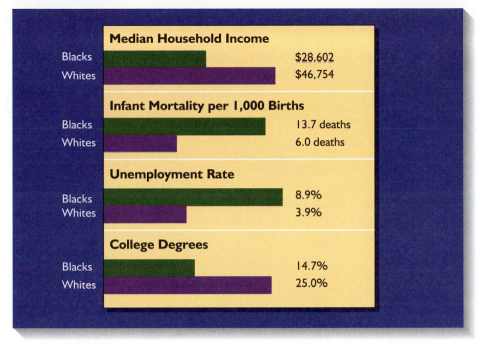

Figure 13.6

Charts

Charts are particularly useful for summarizing large blocks of information. One student, in a speech titled "The United States: A Nation of Immigrants," used a chart to show the leading countries of birth for foreign-born U.S. residents (Figure 13.7). These are too many categories to be presented effectively in a pie graph or a bar graph. By listing them on a chart, the speaker made it easier for listeners to keep the information straight.

chart
A visual aid that summarizes a large block of information, usually in list form.

Country of Birth	Number of U.S. Residents
Mexico	6.7 million
Philippines	1.2 million
China/Taiwan/Hong Kong	816,000
Cuba	797,000
Canada	695,000
El Salvador	650,000
Great Britain	617,000
Germany	598,000

Figure 13.7

Charts are also valuable for presenting the steps of a process. One speaker used several charts in a speech about survival techniques in the wilderness, including one outlining the steps in emergency treatment of snakebites. Another speaker used charts effectively to help her listeners keep track of the steps involved in making cappuccino and other specialty coffee drinks.

You can also use charts to present information that your audience may want to write down. In a speech about consumer protection organizations, for example, a speaker might use a chart to let the audience know exactly where to write or phone for consumer services.

The biggest mistake that beginning speakers make when using a chart is to include so much information that the chart is jumbled and hard to read. As we will discuss later, visual aids should be clear, simple, and uncluttered. Lists on a chart should rarely exceed seven or eight items, with generous spacing between items. If you cannot fit everything on a single chart, make a second one.

Slides and Videotapes

Slides and videotapes can be extremely effective as visual aids. If you are talking about the major sites in Paris, Jerusalem, or Buenos Aires, what could be better than showing slides of them? Or suppose you are explaining the different kinds of roller coasters found in U.S. amusement parks. Your best visual aid would be a videotape showing those coasters in action. The detail, immediacy, and vividness of slides and videotapes are hard to match. This is why they are so often used in business speeches and other kinds of professional presentations.

When used with care, slides and videotapes can also be employed in classroom speeches. Until a few years ago, the only way to present slides was with a slide projector that required a darkened room. Today slides can be converted into full-color transparencies that can be shown in a lighted room with an overhead projector. This makes it much easier to integrate slides with the rest of a speech. The conversion process is not overly expensive and can be done quickly by most copy services.

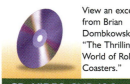

View an excerpt from Brian Dombkowski, "The Thrilling World of Roller Coasters."

CD: VIDEO CLIP 13.3

Despite its many advantages, using videotape in a speech can be complicated. It requires cumbersome equipment, distracts attention from the speaker, and may do more harm than good if used carelessly. If you decide to use videotape in one of your speeches, you need to follow the lead of Brian Dombkowski, the student who gave the speech on roller coasters mentioned earlier in this section. Brian sent away to Arrow Dynamics, Inc., the leading manufacturer of custom roller coasters for a videotape of their rides. He then went to the audiovisual center on campus and edited several snippets from that tape onto his own tape, which he then showed during his speech.

Knowing that a sloppily edited tape is of less value than no tape at all, Brian made sure his editing was clean and expert and would not distract from his ideas. He also included the videotape every time he rehearsed the speech, so it would be smoothly integrated with the rest of his presentation. He even made a special trip to campus to practice with the playback equipment in the classroom so he would be able to use it flawlessly on the day of the speech. The result was a memorable presentation that took full advantage of the benefits of videotape without falling prey to its potential drawbacks.

Computer-Generated Graphics

If you own a personal computer or have access to a computer center on campus, you may be able to create computer-generated graphics for your speeches. Depending on the kind of software you use, these graphics can include anything from simple diagrams to highly sophisticated, full-color charts and graphs. Most graphics programs also include ready-made drawings, symbols, and other clip art that you can add to your visual aids.

Computer-generated graphics allow you to have dramatic, professional-looking visual aids regardless of your artistic talent. Creating the graphic, however, is only the first step in making it suitable for use in a speech. When used in classroom speeches, computer-generated graphics are usually presented on transparencies that can be shown with an overhead projector.

If you have access to an ink-jet or laser printer, you may be able to print your graphic directly on a transparency. If you use a dot matrix printer, you will probably have to print your graphic on a regular sheet of paper. Because this graphic will be too small for your audience to see from a distance, you should take it to a copy service, which will convert it to a transparency. The cost is minimal, and the conversion process works with both color and black-and-white originals.

Another possibility is to design your visual aid on a computer and then have it enlarged and printed directly from disk by a professional copy service. For an additional fee, most copy services will also mount the final product on foamcore or poster board. This process is usually too expensive for student speeches, but it is often used by businesses, political groups, and public-interest organizations.

> **computer-generated graphic**
> A diagram, chart, graph, or the like created with the aid of a computer.

Transparencies

Several times in this chapter we have mentioned the possibility of converting photographs, slides, and computer-generated graphics to transparencies, which can be shown with an overhead projector. You can also use transparencies to present drawings, graphs, and charts. Transparencies are inexpensive, easy to create, and produce a strong visual image. For all of these reasons, they are one of the most widely used methods of presenting visual aids.

Transparencies are made of clear acetate and are the same size as a regular sheet of paper. You can use them to create visual aids in one of two ways. The first is to draw or write directly on the transparency with a special felt-tipped pen. The second is to take a photograph, drawing, graph, or chart to a copy service, where you can have it copied onto a transparency. This conversion is no more work—and little more expense—than xeroxing from one sheet of paper to another.

Despite their many advantages, transparencies can present pitfalls for the unwary. Unless you are a very experienced speaker, trying to write or draw on a transparency while you are speaking is an almost certain recipe

> **transparency**
> A visual aid drawn, written, or printed on a sheet of clear acetate and shown with an overhead projector.

for disaster. Prepare your transparencies well in advance and make sure any writing is large enough to be seen from the back of the room. A good rule of thumb is that all numbers and letters—whether typed or handwritten—should be at least one-quarter inch high (about three times as large as the print on this page).

In addition, check your overhead projector ahead of time to make sure it is working and that you know how to operate it. Better yet, arrange to practice with the projector when you rehearse the speech. Practicing with the projector will help ensure that your transparencies are well coordinated with the rest of your presentation.

Multimedia Presentations

multimedia presentation
A speech that uses special computer software to combine several kinds of visual and/or audio aids in the same presentation.

You may have heard of presentation software programs such as Microsoft PowerPoint, Lotus Freelance, Adobe Persuasion, and Corel Presentation. In addition to creating computer-generated graphics that can be used in speeches, these programs allow a speaker to produce *multimedia presentations* that combine charts and graphs, slides and photographs, even animations, video clips, and sound in the same talk. Depending on the technological resources at your school, you may be able to give multimedia presentations in your speech class. Such presentations provide training for speeches outside the classroom—especially in business settings, where multimedia resources are used every day.

Although each multimedia presentation program operates a bit differently, all allow you to import a wide range of material for use in a speech. Suppose, for example, that you are talking about Mayan architecture and you want to show your audience a photograph of the famous ruins at Chichén Itzá. If the photograph is from the Internet, you can download it directly to your computer for use with your other visual aids. If the photograph is from a book or magazine, you can transfer it to disk with a piece

Multimedia presentations allow a speaker to include charts, graphs, slides, photographs, even video clips and sound in the same talk.

of equipment called a scanner. Or suppose you are explaining the special effects in movies such as *Armageddon* or *The Matrix*. You can import video clips from the movies—including sound—for presentation in your speech.

Once the images and sounds are stored on your computer, you can call them up in any order you want for presentation in your speech. You can also program your photographs, slides, animations, video clips, and other visuals to appear automatically at preset times—leaving you free to concentrate on communicating with your audience. In addition, most multimedia software packages allow you to create a link to the Internet right on your visual aid. With the click of a mouse, your visual aid can become connected to information anywhere in the world.

Go to the PowerPoint Tutorial for a brief guide to using PowerPoint in your speeches.

CD: POWERPOINT TUTORIAL

During the speech, you use a computer to control the order, content, and timing of your multimedia presentation. The computer is connected to a television monitor, a large-screen video projector, a digital light projection (DLP) unit, or an LCD projector. Some systems have a wireless mouse or remote control that lets you move through your presentation with a minimum of fuss.

For all of their advantages, multimedia presentations do have drawbacks—not the least of which is the high cost of the equipment required to show them. It also takes considerable time to learn how to use the software, to design graphs and charts, to edit sound and video clips, and to organize and rehearse a presentation so it is smooth and professional. If you plan to make a multimedia presentation, be sure to give yourself plenty of time to make sure it comes off just right.

As with any complex technology, there is always the chance of faulty equipment. If possible, set up your computer, projection unit, and so forth early enough that you can double-check them before your audience arrives. Make sure you know the equipment well enough to handle any basic technical difficulties that may arise. Always carry a backup disk of your presentation in case you should happen to need it. Most important, be prepared to give your speech even if all the multimedia equipment were to fall apart. It may not be as dazzling as the speech you had planned, but it will be much better than no speech at all. Your audience will sympathize with your predicament and will give you credit for adapting to a difficult situation.[5]

The Speaker

Sometimes you can use your own body as a visual aid—by showing how to perform sign language for the deaf, by demonstrating the skills of modern dance, by doing magic tricks, and so forth. One student gave an informative speech on the art of mime. Throughout the speech she illustrated her points by performing mime routines. In addition to clarifying her ideas, this demonstration kept her classmates deeply engrossed in the speech. Many students have also found that doing some kind of demonstration reduces their nervousness during a speech by providing an outlet for their extra adrenaline.

Doing a demonstration well requires special practice to coordinate your actions with your words and to control the timing of your speech. You can see an excellent example in CD-ROM Video Clip 13.4. The subject of the speech is cardiopulmonary resuscitation (CPR). To demonstrate how to ad-

minister CPR, the speaker borrowed a life-size dummy of a human torso from the local Red Cross. She used the dummy in her practice sessions, and on the day of her speech, she was able to move effortlessly between explaining her ideas and performing the techniques of CPR without breaking eye contact or stumbling in her delivery. Afterward, one of her classmates commented that the speech was better than the CPR demonstration he had seen at the Red Cross!

Special care is required if you are demonstrating a process that takes longer to complete than the time allocated for your speech. If you plan to show a long process, you might borrow the techniques of television personalities such as Martha Stewart. They work through most of the steps in making a perfect enchilada or holiday decoration, for example, but they have a second, finished enchilada or decoration ready to show you at the last minute.

Guidelines for Preparing Visual Aids

Whether you are creating visual aids by hand or designing them on a computer, there are six basic guidelines you should follow to make your aids clear and visually appealing. These guidelines apply whether you are speaking in or out of the classroom, at a business meeting or a political forum, to an audience of 20 or of 200.

Prepare Visual Aids in Advance

No matter what visual aids you plan to use, prepare them well before the day your speech is due. This has two advantages. First, it means you will have the time and resources to devise creative, attractive aids that will truly enhance your speech. Audiences respond much more favorably to speakers who have obviously put a great deal of thought and effort into their visual aids.

Second, preparing your visual aids ahead of time means you can use them while practicing your speech. Visual aids are effective only when they are integrated smoothly with the rest of the speech. If you lose your place, drop your aids, or otherwise stumble around when presenting them, you will distract your audience and shatter your concentration. You can avoid such disasters by preparing your visual aids far enough in advance.

Keep Visual Aids Simple

The purpose of a visual aid is to communicate your ideas, not to display your virtuosity as an artist or wizardry with computer graphics. Visual aids should be simple, clear, and to the point. Limit each aid to a manageable amount of information, and beware of the tendency to go overboard with computer-generated graphics. It is possible, using software such as PowerPoint or Persuasion, to create a graphic that displays two charts, a photograph, and ten lines of text in five different typefaces with 250 colors on the same visual aid. But who would be able to read it? Rather than enhancing your speech, such a graphic would detract from it.

The basic rule of thumb is to include in your visual aid only what you need to make your point. If you look back at the aids presented earlier in this chapter, you will see that all of them are clear and uncluttered. They contain enough information to communicate the speaker's point, but not so much as to confuse or distract the audience. The average visual aid is on display for thirty to forty seconds during a speech. That is not long enough for listeners to decipher a highly intricate graph or drawing. The less complicated your visual aids, the better chance you have of being understood.

Make Sure Visual Aids Are Large Enough

A visual aid is useless if no one can see it. This is one of those points that seems so obvious as to need no comment. But as many speakers have discovered, it is one thing to nod your head in agreement and another to prepare a visual aid properly. Beginning speakers in particular tend to design visual aids that are too small.

When you design a visual aid, keep in mind the size of the room in which you will be speaking. Make sure the aid is big enough to be seen easily by everyone in the room. If you compose a diagram, chart, or graph by hand, guard against the tendency to write and draw too small. You will probably need a piece of poster board or foamcore 2 × 3 feet in size. Use dark ink and an extra-wide marker, so whatever you write or draw can be seen from the back of the room. Lettering for titles should be three inches tall, other lettering two inches. As you prepare the aid, check its visibility by moving to a point as far away from it as your most distant listener will be sitting. If you have trouble making out the words or drawings, your audience will too. By making sure your visual aid is large enough, you will avoid having to introduce it with the lame comment, "I know some of you can't see this, but . . . "

If you are preparing a computer-generated graphic, remember that regular-size type (such as that in this book) may be easy to read from two feet away on a computer screen, but it is much too small for a visual aid—even

The Checklist for Preparing Visual Aids can help you develop effective visual aids.

CD: SPEECH CHECKLIST

for one that is enlarged with a video unit or an overhead projector. Most experts recommend printing all words and numbers in bold and using 36-point type for titles, 24-point type for subtitles, and 18-point type for other text. Figure 13.8 shows these type sizes in comparison to standard 12-point type.

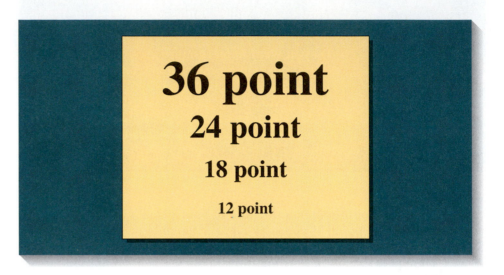

Figure 13.8

What about using all capital letters? That might seem a great way to ensure that your print is large enough to be read easily. But research has shown that a long string of words in ALL CAPS is actually harder to read than is normal text. Reserve ALL CAPS for titles or for individual words that require special emphasis.

Use Fonts That Are Easy to Read

font
A complete set of type of the same design.

Most computer programs come with a large number of fonts (or typefaces, as they are sometimes called), which you can use to vary the style of your visual aids. High-powered programs such as PowerPoint or Persuasion allow you to choose from among hundreds of fonts. Although it can be fun to experiment with the fonts, not all are suitable for visual aids. For the most part, you should avoid decorative fonts such as those on the left in Figure 13.9. They are hard to read and can easily distract the attention of listeners.

In contrast, look at the fonts on the right in Figure 13.9. They are less exciting than those on the left, but they are clear and easy to read. If you use fonts such as these, your visual aids will be audience-friendly.

Use a Limited Number of Fonts

Some variety of fonts in a visual aid is appealing, but too much can be distracting—as in the aid on the left in Figure 13.10, which uses a different font for each line. Most experts recommend using no more than two fonts

Ineffective	More Effective
Airfoil Script	AHD Symbol
Bauble	Arial
Black Tie Engraved	**Antique Olive**
Corruga	Courier
Marker Board	Times New Roman
Twinkie	Univers
TWOSIE	**Swiss 721**

Figure 13.9

in a single visual aid—one for the title or major headings, another for subtitles or other text. Standard procedure is to use a block typeface for the title and a rounder typeface for subtitles and text—as in the aid on the right in Figure 13.10.

Ineffective	More Effective
MAJOR CLASSES *Of* WINE	MAJOR CLASSES OF WINE
appetizer wines	Appetizer Wines
Table Wines	Table Wines
Dessert Wines	Dessert Wines
Sparkling Wines	Sparkling Wines

Figure 13.10

Use Color Effectively

Color adds clout to a visual aid. When used effectively, it increases recognition by 78 percent and comprehension by 73 percent.[6] The key words, of course, are "when used effectively." Some colors do not work well together. Red and green are a tough combination for anyone to read, and they look the same to people who are color-blind. Many shades of blue and green are too close to each other to be easily differentiated—as are orange and red, and blue and purple.

It is also possible to have too many colors on a visual aid. In most circumstances, charts and graphs should be limited to a few colors that are used consistently and solely for functional reasons. The usual procedure is to use dark print or lettering on a light background—especially if you are using poster board or an overhead transparency. If you are using an LCD projector or a large-screen video projector as part of a multimedia presentation, you may find that light print on a dark background works better. In either case, make sure there is enough contrast between the background and the text that listeners can see everything clearly.

You can also use color to highlight key points in a visual aid. One student, in a speech about noise pollution, used a chart to summarize the sound levels of everyday noise and to indicate their potential danger for hearing loss (Figure 13.11). Notice, when you look at the chart, how the speaker used color to emphasize the different levels. He put sounds that are definitely harmful to hearing in red, sounds that may cause hearing loss in blue, and sounds that are loud but safe in green. These colors reinforced the speaker's ideas and, at the same time, made his chart easier to read.[7]

IMPACT ON HEARING	DECIBEL LEVEL	TYPE OF NOISE
Harmful	140	Firecracker
to	130	Jackhammer
hearing	120	Jet engine
Risk	110	Rock concert
hearing	100	Chain saw
loss	90	Motorcycle
Loud	80	Alarm clock
but	70	Busy traffic
safe	60	Air conditioner

Figure 13.11

Tips for Presenting Visual Aids

In addition to selecting and preparing your visual aids with care, you need to give attention to how you will *present* the aids in your speech. No matter how well designed your visual aids may be, they will be of little value unless you display them properly, discuss them clearly, and integrate them effectively with the rest of your presentation. Here are seven tips that will help you get the maximum impact out of your visual aids.

Avoid Using the Chalkboard for Visual Aids

At first thought, using the chalkboard in your classroom to present visual aids seems like a splendid idea. Usually, however, it is not. You have too much to do during a speech to worry about drawing or writing legibly on the board. Many students have marred an otherwise fine speech by turning their backs on the audience to use the chalkboard. Even if your visual aid is put on the chalkboard ahead of time, it seldom is as vivid or as neat as one composed on posterboard, on a flip chart, or on a transparency.

In some speaking situations, however, use of the chalkboard is essential. A teacher giving a lecture or a coach explaining a new play will write on the board while speaking. If you ever need to do this, make sure your writing is clear and large enough for all to read.

Display Visual Aids Where Listeners Can See Them

Check the classroom ahead of time to decide exactly where you will display your visual aids. Keep in mind that inexpensive poster board is too flimsy to stand by itself in front of a lectern or on the edge of a chalkboard. It can even be unsteady when placed on an easel. Instead, look for a sturdy piece of poster board that can be displayed without curling up or falling over. An even better choice is foamcore, a thin sheet of styrofoam with graphics-quality paper on both sides. Sturdy, rigid, and lightweight, it is an excellent material for displaying graphs, charts, and drawings.

If you are displaying an object or a model, be sure to place it where it can be seen easily by everyone in the room. Setting it on a table next to the lectern may be fine for listeners seated in front, but the table may be too low for the aid to be visible to people seated farther back. If necessary, hold up the object or model while you are discussing it.

Once you have set the aid in the best location, don't undo all your preparation by standing where you block the audience's view of the aid. Stand to one side of the aid, and point with the arm nearest it. If possible, use a pencil, a ruler, or some other pointer. Using a pointer will allow you to stand farther away from the visual aid, thereby reducing the likelihood that you will obstruct the view of people sitting on the same side of the room as you are standing.

Avoid Passing Visual Aids among the Audience

Once visual aids get into the hands of your listeners, you are in trouble. At least three people will be paying more attention to the aid than to you—the person who has just had it, the person who has it now, and the person waiting to get it next.[8] By the time the visual aid moves on, all three may have lost track of what you are saying.

Nor do you solve this problem by preparing a handout for every member of the audience. There is no guarantee they will pay attention to it only when you want them to. In fact, they are likely to spend a good part of the speech looking over the handout at their own pace, rather than listening to you. Although handouts can be valuable, they usually just create competition for beginning speakers.

Every once in a while, of course, you will want listeners to have copies of some material to take home. When such a situation arises, keep the copies until after you've finished talking and can distribute them without creating a distraction. Keeping control of your visual aids is essential to keeping control of your speech.

Display Visual Aids only while Discussing Them

Just as circulating visual aids distracts attention, so does displaying them throughout a speech. Whenever an aid is visible, at least some people will spend their time looking at it rather than listening to you.

If you are using an object or a model, keep it out of sight until you are ready to discuss it. When you finish your discussion, place the object or model back out of sight. The same is true of charts, graphs, or drawings prepared on poster board. If you are using an easel, put a blank sheet of poster board in front of the sheet with the visual aid. When the time comes, remove the blank sheet to show the aid. When you are finished with the aid, remove it from the easel or cover it back up with a blank piece of poster board so it will not divert the attention of your listeners.

Talk to Your Audience, Not to Your Visual Aid

When explaining a visual aid, it is easy to break eye contact with your audience and speak to the aid. Of course, your listeners are looking primarily at the aid, and you will need to glance at it periodically as you talk. But if you keep your eyes fixed on the visual aid, you may lose your audience. By keeping eye contact with your listeners, you will also pick up feedback about how the visual aid and your explanation of it are coming across.

Explain Visual Aids Clearly and Concisely

Visual aids don't explain themselves. Like statistics, they need to be translated and related to the audience. For example, Figure 13.12 is an excellent visual aid, but do you know what it represents? You may if you suffer from migraine headaches, since it shows the different regions of pain experienced during a cluster migraine attack. But even then the full meaning of the drawing may not be clear until it is explained to you. And it certainly will not be clear to a person who knows little about migraines.

A visual aid can be of enormous benefit—but only if the viewer knows what to look for and why. Unfortunately, beginning speakers often rush over their visual aids without explaining them clearly and concisely. Be sure to adapt your visual aids to the audience. Don't just say, "As you can see . . . " and then pass quickly over the aid. Tell listeners what the aid means. Describe its major features. Spell out the meaning of charts and graphs. Interpret statistics and percentages. Remember, a visual aid is only as useful as the explanation that goes with it.

As you can see from CD-ROM Video Clip 13.5, the speaker who used the diagram of the migraine headache discussed above did an excellent job of explaining how each color on the drawing corresponds with an area of

View an excerpt from Kris Recker, "The Agony of Migraines."

CD: VIDEO CLIP 13.5

Figure 13.12

intense pain suffered during a cluster migraine. Having used the drawing during her practice sessions, she was able to integrate it into the speech smoothly and skillfully—and to maintain eye contact with her listeners throughout her discussion of it. You should strive to do the same when you present visual aids in your speeches.

Practice with Your Visual Aids

This chapter has mentioned several times the need to practice with visual aids, but the point bears repeating. You do not want to suffer through an experience like the one that follows.

This is the story of a young man who was a brilliant designer and a good inventor, but who failed to realize that to complete his work he had to be able to explain it and to convince his supervisors that his invention was a worthwhile investment.

He had designed a machine that used several new and patentable ideas. The stage was set for him not only to show off his invention but to show himself to the managers, who would help him shape his ideas and give him additional opportunities. This was the part of the test he flunked.

He knew who his audience would be. He had been told to compose his talk thoughtfully, to prepare slides and other visual aids, and to practice in the conference room, using its rather complex lectern and public address system. At the lectern he could control the lights, show his slides in any sequence he chose, and have his choice of microphones and other visual and speaking aids.

Unfortunately, although he had done a brilliant job on the engineering project, he neglected to plan his presentation with similar care. His worst mistake was not practicing with the equipment he was now called on to operate. When he dimmed the lights, he could not read his text. When the first slide came on, it was not his but belonged to a former speaker. When the first correct slide was reached, the type was too small for anyone but the people in the first row to see. He could not turn on the light arrow indicator to point out the line he was talking about, so he walked away from the lectern to point things out directly on the screen. But he left the microphone behind, so people in the back rows could neither see nor hear.

When a picture of his machine appeared, he was too close to see the critical parts. Since he could not read his text because of the darkness, he lost track of what he was supposed to say. Reaching for a steel-tipped pointer because he could not operate the optical one, he managed to punch a hole through the screen.

In desperation, he abandoned the slides, turned up the lights, and in utter consternation raced through the rest of his talk so fast and with such poor enunciation that he was almost completely unintelligible. Finally, in embarrassment both for himself and for the audience, he sat down.[9]

This sounds like a routine from *Saturday Night Live,* but it is a true story. What makes the story especially sad is that it didn't have to happen. With some effort, thought, and preparation, the young inventor could have made a success of his presentation instead of turning it into a fiasco.

You can avoid following in his footsteps if you practice with the visual aids you have chosen. Rehearse with your equipment to be sure you can set up the visual aid with a minimum of fuss. Run through the entire speech several times, practicing the handling of the aids, the gestures you will make, the timing of each move. If necessary, practice removing the visual aid when you are finished with it. In using visual aids, as in other aspects of speech-making, there is no substitute for the Boy Scout motto—"Be prepared."

The Checklist for Presenting Visual Aids can help you use visual aids effectively.

CD: SPEECH CHECKLIST

Summary

There are many kinds of visual aids. Most obvious is the object about which you are speaking, or a model of it. Diagrams, sketches, and other kinds of drawings are valuable because you can design them to illustrate your points exactly. Graphs are an excellent way to illustrate any subject dealing with numbers, while charts are used to summarize large blocks of information. Although videotapes can be useful as visual aids, they need to be carefully edited and integrated into the speech. Photographs, slides, and computer-generated graphics often work best when they are converted to transparencies that can be shown with an overhead projector. If you have access to the right equipment, you may be able to combine several kinds of visual aids—plus sound—in a multimedia presentation. Finally, you can act as your own visual aid by performing actions that demonstrate processes or ideas.

No matter what kind of visual aid you use, you need to prepare it carefully. You will be most successful if you prepare your visual aids in advance, keep them simple, make sure they are large enough to be seen by all your listeners, and use color effectively for emphasis and visual appeal. If you are creating visual aids on a computer, use a limited number of typefaces and make sure the ones you select will be easy for your audience to read.

In addition to being designed with care, visual aids need to be presented skillfully. Try to avoid writing or drawing visual aids on the chalkboard. Nor should you pass visual aids among the audience. Instead, display each aid only while you are talking about it, and be sure to display it where everyone can see it without straining. When presenting a visual aid, maintain eye contact with your listeners. Talk to the audience, not to the aid, and explain the aid clearly and concisely. Above all, practice with your visual aids so they fit into your speech smoothly and expertly.

Key Terms

model (316)

graph (319)

line graph (319)

pie graph (320)

bar graph (320)

chart (321)

computer-generated graphic (323)

transparency (323)

multimedia presentation (324)

font (328)

Review Questions

After reading this chapter, you should be able to answer the following questions:

1. What are the major advantages of using visual aids in your speeches?

2. What kinds of visual aids might you use in a speech?

3. What guidelines are given in the chapter for preparing visual aids?

4. What tips are given in the chapter for presenting visual aids?

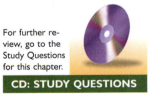

For further review, go to the Study Questions for this chapter.

CD: STUDY QUESTIONS

Exercises for Critical Thinking

1. Watch a "how-to" type of television program (a cooking or gardening show, for example) or the weather portion of a local newscast. Notice how the speaker uses visual aids to help communicate the message. What kinds of visual aids are used? How do they enhance the clarity, interest, and retainability of the speaker's message? What would the speaker have to do to communicate the message effectively without visual aids?

2. Consider how you might use visual aids to explain each of the following:

   a. How to perform the Heimlich maneuver to help a choking victim.

   b. The location of the five boroughs of New York City.

   c. The proportion of the electorate that votes in major national elections in the United States, France, Germany, England, and Japan, respectively.

   d. Where to write for information about student loans.

   e. The wing patterns of various species of butterflies.

   f. The increase in the amount of money spent by Americans on health care since 1985.

   g. How to change a bicycle tire.

   h. The basic equipment and techniques of rock climbing.

3. Plan to use visual aids in at least one of your classroom speeches. Be creative in devising your aids, and be sure to follow the guidelines discussed in the chapter for using them. After the speech, analyze how effectively you employed your visual aids, what you learned about the use of visual aids from your experience, and what changes you would make in using visual aids if you were to deliver the speech again.

Applying the POWER of Public Speaking

As a veterinarian and owner of a small animal practice, you work closely with your local humane society to help control a growing population of unwanted dogs and cats. You and your staff devote many hours annually in free and reduced-cost medical services to animals adopted from the society. Now you have been asked to speak to the city council in support of legislation proposed by the society for stronger enforcement of animal licensing and leash laws.

In your speech, you plan to include statistics that (1) compare estimates of the city's dog population with the number of licenses issued during the past five years and (2) show the small number of citations given by local law enforcement for unleashed pets during the same period of time. Knowing from your college public speaking class how valuable visual aids can be in presenting statistics, you decide to illustrate one set of statistics with a chart and the other with a graph.

For which set of statistics will a chart be more appropriate? For which set will a graph be more appropriate? Of the three kinds of graphs discussed in this chapter (bar, line, pie), which will work best for your statistics and why?

Notes

[1]Richard E. Mayer and Valerie K. Sims, "For Whom Is a Picture Worth a Thousand Words? Extensions of a Dual-Coding Theory of Multimedia Learning," *Journal of Educational Psychology,* 86 (1994), pp. 389–401.

[2]Michael E. Patterson, Donald F. Danscreau, and Dianna Newbern, "Effects of Communication Aids on Cooperative Teaching," *Journal of Educational Psychology,* 84 (1992), pp. 453–461.

[3]Douglas R. Vogel, Gary W. Dickson, and John A. Lehman, *Persuasion and the Role of Visual Presentation Support: The UM/3M Study* (Minneapolis: University of Minnesota School of Management, 1986).

[4]Joe Ayres, "Using Visual Aids to Reduce Speech Anxiety," *Communication Research Reports,* 8 (June–December 1991), pp. 73–79.

[5]For more information on computer-generated graphics and multimedia presentations, see Jo Robbins, *High-Impact Presentations: A Multimedia Approach* (New York: Wiley, 1997); Molly W. Joss and Roger C. Parker, *Looking Good in Presentations*, 3rd ed. (Scottsdale, Ariz.: Coriolis, 2000).

[6]Claudyne Wilder, *The Presentations Kit: 10 Steps for Selling Your Ideas,* rev. ed. (New York: John Wiley, 1994), p. 101.

[7]See Alan L. Brown, *Power Pitches: How to Produce Winning Presentations Using Charts, Slides, Video and Multimedia* (Burr Ridge, Ill.: Irwin, 1997), for further information on preparing effective visual aids.

[8]Bert E. Bradley, *Fundamentals of Speech Communication: The Credibility of Ideas,* 6th ed. (Dubuque, Iowa: W. C. Brown, 1991), p. 280.

[9]Adapted from Eric A. Walker, "About the 'Death' of an Engineer," *Centre Daily Times,* April 25, 1972.

CHAPTER FOURTEEN

SPEAKING TO INFORM

Mei-Lan Deng is the pharmacy director at a major metropolitan hospital. One morning, after responding to her usual flurry of new e-mail messages, Mei-Lan greeted a pharmaceutical sales rep who had dropped by to discuss a new pain medication the FDA had recently approved for use. She looked through the materials the salesperson brought along, asked numerous questions about how the drug could be used with her hospital's patient population, and took careful notes.

Later that morning, Mei-Lan decided to review the PowerPoint slides for the lunch talk she would be giving in a couple of hours. It was her turn to address a group of pharmacists from area hospitals who met monthly to share ideas. She double-checked the slides on her laptop. They looked terrific, and she knew she could use them again when she spoke to her hospital's administrative council the next week.

The lunch talk went well, and Mei-Lan was back in her office in time for a two o'clock department meeting. She wanted to get her staff members' thoughts on the new pain medication, so she passed around the materials she had received that morning and answered questions based on the notes she had taken.

Back at her desk, Mei-Lan switched on her computer and groaned—20 new messages! What a relief when she realized half were from members of her lunch group, congratulating her on her "fascinating" talk and asking her to e-mail them copies of her "very informative" slides.

Mei-Lan doesn't consider herself a "public speaker," but much of her job involves absorbing and communicating information clearly and effectively. Although Mei-Lan is just one person, her experience is not unusual. In a recent survey, graduates from five U.S. colleges were asked to rank the speech skills most important to their jobs. They rated informative speaking number one.[1] In another survey, 62 percent of the respondents said they used informative speaking "almost constantly."[2]

Public speaking to inform occurs in a wide range of everyday situations. What kinds of people make informative speeches? The business manager explaining next year's budget. The architect reviewing plans for a new building. The military officer briefing subordinates. The union leader informing members about details of a new contract. The church worker outlining plans for a fund drive. The teacher in a classroom. There are endless situations in which people need to inform others. Competence in this form of communication will prove valuable to you throughout your life.

One of your first classroom assignments probably will be to deliver an informative speech in which you will act as a lecturer or teacher. You may describe an object, show how something works, report on an event, explain a concept. Your aim will be to convey knowledge and understanding—not to advocate a cause. Your speech will be judged in light of three general criteria:

Is the information communicated *accurately?*

Is the information communicated *clearly?*

Is the information made *meaningful* and *interesting* to the audience?

informative speech
A speech designed to convey knowledge and understanding.

In this chapter, we will look at four types of informative speeches and the basic principles of informative speaking. Along the way, we will apply various general principles discussed in previous chapters.

Types of Informative Speeches: Analysis and Organization

There are many ways to classify informative speeches. Here we focus on the four kinds of informative speeches you are most likely to give in your speech class: (1) speeches about objects, (2) speeches about processes, (3) speeches about events, and (4) speeches about concepts. These are not hard-and-fast categories, but they provide an effective method of analyzing and organizing informative speeches.

Speeches about Objects

As the word is used here, "objects" include anything that is visible, tangible, and stable in form. Objects may have moving parts or be alive; they may include places, structures, animals, even people. Here are examples of subjects for speeches about objects:

object
Anything that is visible, tangible, and stable in form.

Sitting Bull	subways
Grand Canyon	stock market
the human eye	Elizabeth Cady Stanton
seaweed	digital cameras
comic strips	U.S. Army

You will not have time to tell your classmates everything about any of these subjects. Instead, you will choose a specific purpose that focuses on one aspect of your subject. Working from the topics presented above, the following are examples of good specific purpose statements for informative speeches about objects:

To inform my audience about the social functions of comic strips.

To inform my audience about the geological features of the Grand Canyon.

To inform my audience about the role of Elizabeth Cady Stanton in the U.S. women's rights movement.

To inform my audience what to look for when buying a digital camera.

To inform my audience about the commercial uses of seaweed.

Notice how precise these statements are. As we saw in Chapter 4, you should select a specific purpose that is not too broad to achieve in the allotted time. "To inform my audience about cameras" is far too general for a classroom speech. "To inform my audience what to look for when buying a digital camera" is more exact and is a purpose you could reasonably hope to achieve in a brief talk.

If your specific purpose is to explain the history or evolution of your subject, you will put your speech in *chronological* order. For example:

Specific Purpose: To inform my audience about the major achievements of Frederick Douglass.

Central Idea: Although born in slavery, Frederick Douglass became one of the greatest African Americans in history.

Main Points:
I. Douglass spent the first 20 years of his life as a slave in Maryland.
II. After escaping to the North, Douglass became a leader in the abolitionist movement to end slavery.
III. During the Civil War, Douglass helped to establish black regiments in the Union Army.
IV. After the war, Douglass was a tireless champion of equal rights for his race.

If your specific purpose is to describe the main features of your subject, you may organize your speech in *spatial* order:

Specific Purpose: To inform my audience about the major land regions in Spain.

Central Idea: There are five major land regions in Spain.

Main Points:
I. The Northern Mountains extend across northernmost Spain from the Atlantic Ocean to the Coastal Plains.
II. The Ebro Basin consists of broad plains that extend along the Ebro River in northeastern Spain.
III. The Coastal Plains stretch along Spain's entire east coast.
IV. The Guadalquivir Basin is a dry but extremely fertile region in southern Spain.
V. The Meseta is a huge plateau that covers central Spain.

As often as not, you will find that speeches about objects fall into *topical* order. Here is an example:

Specific Purpose: To inform my audience about the major alternative-fuel cars now being developed.

Central Idea: The major alternative-fuel cars now being developed are powered by electricity, natural gas, methanol, or hydrogen.

Main Points:
I. One kind of alternative-fuel car is powered by electricity.

  II. A second kind of alternative-fuel car is powered by natural gas.

  III. A third kind of alternative-fuel car is powered by methanol.

  IV. A fourth kind of alternative-fuel car is powered by hydrogen.

No matter which of these organizational methods you use—chronological, spatial, or topical—be sure to follow the guidelines discussed in Chapter 8: (1) limit your speech to between two and five main points; (2) keep main points separate; (3) try to use the same pattern of wording for all main points; (4) balance the amount of time devoted to each main point.

Speeches about Processes

A process is a systematic series of actions that leads to a specific result or product. Speeches about processes explain how something is made, how something is done, or how something works. Here are examples of good specific purpose statements for speeches about processes:

> To inform my audience how hurricanes develop.
>
> To inform my audience how to write an effective job resumé.
>
> To inform my audience how to save people from drowning.
>
> To inform my audience how oriental rugs are made.
>
> To inform my audience how to create their own Web pages.

process
A systematic series of actions that leads to a specific result or product.

As these examples suggest, there are two kinds of informative speeches about processes. One kind explains a process so that listeners will *understand* it better. Your goal in this kind of speech is to have your audience know the steps of the process and how they relate to one another. If your specific purpose is "To inform my audience how a nuclear bomb works," you will explain the basic steps in making a bomb and how they result in a nuclear explosion. You will not instruct your listeners how they can *make* a nuclear bomb.

A second kind of speech explains a process so listeners will be better able to *perform* the process themselves. Your goal in this kind of speech is to have the audience learn a particular skill. Suppose your specific purpose is "To inform my audience how to take pictures like a professional photographer." You will present the basic techniques of professional photography and show your listeners how they can utilize those techniques. You want the audience to be able to *use* the techniques as a result of your speech.

Both kinds of speeches about processes may require visual aids. At the very least, you should prepare a chart outlining the steps or techniques of your process. In some cases you will need to demonstrate the steps or techniques by performing them in front of your audience. One student did sleight-of-hand magic tricks to show the techniques behind them. Another acted out the basic methods of mime. Yet another executed elementary karate maneuvers. In each case, the demonstration not only clarified the speaker's process, but captivated the audience as well. (If you are using visual aids of any kind, be sure to review Chapter 13 before your speech.)

When informing about a process, you will usually arrange your speech in *chronological* order, explaining the process step by step from beginning to end. For example:

Specific Purpose: To inform my audience how to create their own Web pages.

Central Idea: There are four major steps in creating one's own Web page.

Main Points:
    I. The first step is deciding on the content of your Web page.
    II. The second step is designing your Web page.
    III. The third step is saving your Web page as an HTML file.
    IV. The fourth step is uploading your Web page onto the Internet.

Sometimes, rather than leading your audience through a process step by step, you will focus on the major principles or techniques involved in performing the process. Then you will organize your speech in *topical* order. Each main point will deal with a separate principle or technique. For example:

Specific Purpose: To inform my audience of the common methods used by stage magicians to perform their tricks.

Informative speeches can be organized in several ways. A speech about the history of Cinco de Mayo would probably be structured chronologically, while a speech about the major elements of Cinco de Mayo celebrations today would most likely follow topical order.

Central Idea: Stage magicians use two common methods to perform their tricks—mechanical devices and sleight of hand.

Main Points: I. Many magic tricks rely on mechanical devices that may require little skill by the magician.
        II. Other magic tricks depend on the magician's skill in fooling people by sleight-of-hand manipulation.

Concise organization is especially important in speeches about processes. You must make sure each step in the process is clear and easy to follow. If your process has more than four or five steps, group the steps into units so as to limit the number of main points. Otherwise, you will have too many main points for listeners to grasp and recall. For example, in a speech explaining how to set up a home aquarium, a student presented the following main points:

  I. First you must choose the size of your tank.
  II. Then you must determine the shape of your tank.
 III. You must also decide how much you can afford to pay for a tank.
 IV. Once you have the tank, you need a filter system.
  V. A heater is also absolutely necessary.
 VI. You must also get an air pump.
 VII. Once this is done, you need to choose gravel for the tank.
VIII. You will also need plants.
 IX. Other decorations will round out the effects of your aquarium.
  X. Now you are ready to add the fish.
 XI. Freshwater fish are the most common.
 XII. Saltwater fish are more expensive and require special care.

Not surprisingly, this was too much for the audience to follow. The speaker should have organized the points something like this:

 I. The first step in establishing a home aquarium is choosing a tank.
  A. The size of the tank is important.
  B. The shape of the tank is important.
  C. The cost of the tank is important.
 II. The second step in establishing a home aquarium is equipping the tank.
  A. You will need a filter system.
  B. You will need a heater.
  C. You will need an air pump.
  D. You will need gravel.
  E. You will need plants.
  F. You may also want other decorations.
III. The third step in establishing a home aquarium is adding the fish.
  A. Freshwater fish are the most common for home aquariums.
  B. Saltwater fish are more expensive and require special care.

As you can see, the subpoints cover the same territory as that originally covered by the twelve main points. But three main points are much easier to understand and remember than twelve.

event
Anything that happens
or is regarded as
happening.

Speeches about Events

The *Random House Dictionary* defines an event as "anything that happens
or is regarded as happening." By this definition, the following are examples
of suitable subjects for informative speeches about events:

Holocaust	mountain climbing
civil rights movement	Paralympics
figure skating	job interviews
Cinco de Mayo	therapeutic massage
attention deficit disorder	Battle of Little Big Horn

As usual, you will need to narrow your focus and pick a specific purpose you can accomplish in a short speech. Here are examples of good specific purpose statements for informative speeches about events:

To inform my audience about the equipment used in mountain climbing.

To inform my audience of the festivities at Mexico's Cinco de Mayo celebration.

To inform my audience about what happened at the Battle of Little Big Horn.

To inform my audience about the techniques of therapeutic massage.

To Inform my audience about the internment of Japanese Americans during
World War II.

As you can see, there are many ways to discuss events. If your specific
purpose is to recount the history of an event, you will organize your speech
in *chronological* order, relating the incidents one after another in the order
they occurred. For example:

Specific Purpose: To inform my audience about the history of the
disability rights movement.

Central Idea: The disability rights movement has made major strides
during the past 30 years.

Main Points:
   I. The disability rights movement began in Berkeley,
California, during the mid-1960s.
   II. The movement achieved its first major victory in
1973 with passage of the federal Rehabilitation
Act.
   III. The movement reached another milestone in 1990
when Congress approved the Americans with
Disabilities Act.
   IV. Today the movement is spreading to countries
beyond the United States.

Instead of recounting the history of an event, you might take a more an-
alytical approach and explain its causes and/or effects. In such a case, you
will organize your speech in *causal* order. Let's say your specific purpose

is "To inform my audience why so many lives were lost when the 'unsinkable' ocean liner *Titanic* sank." Working from cause to effect, your outline might look like this:

Specific Purpose: To inform my audience why so many lives were lost when the "unsinkable" ocean liner *Titanic* sank.

Central Idea: Inability to remove the passengers and crew from the doomed *Titanic* caused the death of more than two-thirds of those on board.

Main Points:
    I. There were two major causes for the great loss of life when the *Titanic* went down.
        A. The *Titanic* carried insufficient lifeboats for the number of people on board.
        B. On the ship *Californian,* which was nearby, the radio operator had shut down the radio and gone to sleep.
    II. The effects of these two situations were disastrous.
        A. When all usable lifeboats had been filled, more than 1,500 people remained on board the *Titanic.*
        B. The *Californian,* unaware of the distress signal, steamed on while the *Titanic* went to the bottom.

There are other ways to deal with an event besides telling what happened or why it happened. Indeed, you can approach an event from almost any angle or combination of angles—features, origins, implications, benefits, future developments, and so forth. In such cases, you will put your speech together in *topical* order. And you should make sure your main points subdivide the subject logically and consistently. For instance:

Specific Purpose: To inform my audience about the four traditional events in women's gymnastics.

Central Idea: The four traditional events in women's gymnastics are floor exercise, vault, balance beam, and uneven parallel bars.

Main Points:
    I. The floor exercise combines dancing, acrobatics, and tumbling.
   II. The vault features explosive strength and dramatic midair maneuvers.
 III. The balance beam requires precise routines and perfect coordination.
 IV. The uneven parallel bars demand great strength, flexibility, and agility.

Speeches about Concepts

concept
A belief, theory, idea, notion, principle, or the like.

Concepts include beliefs, theories, ideas, principles, and the like. They are more abstract than objects, processes, or events. The following are some examples of subjects for speeches about concepts:

Confucianism	film theory
philosophies of education	principles of feminism
original-intent doctrine	Afrocentrism
concepts of science	theories of psychology
religious beliefs	Keynesian economics

Taking a few of these general subjects, here are some good specific purpose statements for speeches about concepts:

To inform my audience about the basic principles of Afrocentrism.

To inform my audience about the doctrine of original intent in constitutional interpretation.

To inform my audience about the different philosophies of education in Europe and the United States.

To inform my audience about the concept of patriarchy in feminist thought.

To inform my audience about the major principles of film theory.

Speeches about concepts are usually organized in *topical* order. One common approach is to enumerate the main features or aspects of your concept. For example:

Specific Purpose: To inform my audience about the basic principles of Afrocentrism.

Central Idea: The basic principles of Afrocentrism have a theoretical and a practical dimension.

Main Points:
  I. The theoretical dimension of Afrocentrism looks at historical and social events from an African rather than a European perspective.
  II. The practical dimension of Afrocentrism calls for reforming the school curriculum to fit the needs and cultural experiences of African-American children.

A more complex approach is to define the concept you are dealing with, identify its major elements, and illustrate it with specific examples. An excellent instance of this came in a student speech about Islam:

Specific Purpose: To inform my audience of the basic principles of Islam.

Central Idea: The beliefs of Islam can be traced to the prophet Muhammad, are written in the Koran, and have produced a number of sects.

Main Points:
  I. Islam was founded by the prophet Muhammad in the early 600s.
  II. The teachings of Islam are written in the Koran, the holy book of Islam.
  III. Today Islam is divided into a number of sects, the largest of which are the Sunnites and the Shiites.

Yet another approach is to explain competing schools of thought about the same subject. For example:

Specific Purpose: To inform my audience of the major arguments for and against taxing e-commerce.

Central Idea: Supporters and opponents of taxing e-commerce both have legitimate economic arguments.

Main Points:
  I. Supporters of taxing e-commerce maintain that exempting it from taxation gives it an unfair competitive advantage over traditional stores.
  II. Opponents of taxing e-commerce maintain that subjecting it to taxation could hamper the development of business on the Internet.

As you can see from these examples, speeches about concepts are often more complex than other kinds of informative speeches. Concepts are abstract and can be very hard to explain to someone who is learning about them for the first time. When explaining concepts, pay special attention to avoiding technical language, to defining terms clearly, and to using examples and comparisons to illustrate the concepts and make them understandable to your listeners.

The lines dividing speeches about objects, processes, events, and concepts are not absolute. Some subjects could fit into more than one category, depending on how you develop the speech. You could treat the Declaration of Independence as an object—by explaining its history and its role in the American Revolution. Or you could deal with the meaning of the Declaration, in which case you would be speaking about a concept—an idea bound up with freedom and democracy.

To take another example, a speech about the destruction of ancient Pompeii by the eruption of Mount Vesuvius would probably deal with its subject as an event, but a speech on what causes volcanoes to erupt would most likely treat its subject as a process. The important step is to decide how you will handle your subject—as an object, a process, an event, or a concept. Once you do that, you can develop the speech accordingly.

One final word about organizing your informative speech: Regardless of which method of organization you use, be sure to give your listeners plenty of help in sorting out facts and ideas during the speech. One way is by using enough transitions, internal previews, internal summaries, and signposts (see Chapter 8). Another way is to follow the old maxim: "Tell 'em what you're going to say; say it; then tell 'em what you've said." In other words, preview the main points of your speech in the introduction, and summarize them in the conclusion. This will make your speech not only easier to understand but also easier to remember.

Guidelines for Informative Speaking

All the previous chapters of this book relate to the principles of informative speaking. Choosing a topic and specific purpose, analyzing the audience, gathering materials, choosing supporting details, organizing the speech, using words to communicate meaning, delivering the speech—all of these must be done effectively if your informative speech is to be a success. Here we emphasize five points that will help you avoid the mistakes that plague many informative speakers.

Don't Overestimate What the Audience Knows

In a speech about meteorology, a student said, "If modern methods of weather forecasting had existed in 1900, the Galveston hurricane disaster would never have taken place." Then he was off to other matters, leaving his listeners to puzzle over what the Galveston hurricane was, when it happened, and what kind of destruction it wreaked.

The principles of informative speaking are applicable to a wide range of situations. Knowing those principles will help you whenever you need to convey knowledge and understanding.

The speaker assumed that the audience already knew these things. But his classmates were not experts on meteorology or on American history. Even those who had heard of the hurricane had only a fuzzy notion of it. Some were not even sure about the location of Galveston. Only the speaker knew that the hurricane, which killed more than 6,000 people when it unexpectedly struck Galveston, Texas, on September 8, 1900, is still the deadliest natural disaster in American history.

As many speakers have discovered, it is easy to overestimate the audience's stock of information. In most informative speeches, your listeners will be only vaguely knowledgeable (at best) about the details of your topic. (Otherwise, there would not be much need for an informative speech!) Therefore, you must lead your listeners step by step, without any shortcuts. You cannot *assume* they will know what you mean. Rather, you must be *sure* to explain everything so thoroughly that they cannot help but understand. As you work on your speech, always consider whether it will be clear to someone who is hearing about the topic for the first time.

Suppose you are talking about the protective tariff. Although many of your classmates might have heard of the protective tariff, you cannot assume they have a firm grasp of it. So you should start by telling them what it is. How will you tell them? Here's one way:

> A protective tariff is a form of customs duty. It is a tax on imported goods, but it differs from other taxes in that its primary purpose is not financial but economic—not to increase a nation's revenue but to protect its domestic industry from foreign competition.

To someone who knows a lot about business and commerce this is perfectly clear. But someone who does not will probably get lost along the way. The tone of the statement is that of a speaker reviewing information already familiar to the audience—not of a speaker introducing new information.

Here, in contrast, is another explanation of protective tariffs:

What is a protective tariff? Let me explain with an example.

Suppose you make shoes. So does a business in Taiwan. But that business can sell its shoes here cheaper than you can. As a result, you are going bankrupt.

So you appeal to the government for help. The government sets up a tariff to protect you from being ruined by the cheap foreign shoes. This means that the government puts a tariff—a tax—on every shoe that comes into the United States for sale from Taiwan. If the tariff is high enough, the shoes from Taiwan will now be more expensive than yours.

Your business has been protected by the tariff. Hence the name, protective tariff.[3]

This statement is clear and simple. Its tone is that of a teacher unraveling a new subject.

Is it too simple? Will your classmates feel as if you are talking down to them? Almost certainly not. Many students hesitate to speak simply because they are afraid they will sound simpleminded. They think they need big words and complicated sentences to sound intelligent. But nothing could be farther from the truth. The test of a good speaker is to communicate even the most complex ideas clearly and simply. Anyone can go to a book and find a learned sounding definition of a protective tariff like the one above. But to say in plain English what a protective tariff is—that takes hard work and creative thinking.

Also, remember that readers can study a printed passage again and again until they extract its meaning, but listeners don't have that luxury. They must understand what you say in the time it takes you to say it. The more you assume they know about the topic, the greater your chances of being misunderstood.

If you have circulated a questionnaire among your listeners before the speech (see Chapter 5, pages 113–116), you should have a good idea of their knowledge about the topic. If not, you will usually do better to aim for the low end of the knowledge spectrum. Some experts recommend preparing a speech as if the audience had never heard of the subject. That may be a bit extreme, but it is one way to make sure you define every special term, clarify every idea, illustrate every concept, and support every conclusion.[4] You cannot go wrong by following the news reporters' code: "Never *over*estimate the information of your audience; never *under*estimate the intelligence of your audience."

Relate the Subject Directly to the Audience

The British dramatist Oscar Wilde arrived at his club after the disastrous opening-night performance of his new play.

"Oscar, how did your play go?" asked a friend.

"Oh," Wilde quipped, "the play was a great success, but the audience was a failure."

Speakers have been known to give much the same answer in saving face after a dismal informative speech. "Oh," they say, "the speech was fine, but the audience just wasn't interested." And they are at least partly right—the audience *wasn't* interested. Then was the speech fine? Not by any objective standard. A speech is measured by its impact on a particular audience. There is no such thing as a fine speech that puts people to sleep. It is the speaker's job to get listeners interested—and to keep them interested.

Informative speakers have one big hurdle to overcome. They must recognize that what is fascinating to them may not be fascinating to everybody. A mathematician, for example, might be truly enthralled by a perfect equation, but most people wouldn't want to hear about it. Once you have chosen a topic that could possibly be interesting to your listeners, you should take special steps to relate it to them. You should tie it in with their interests and concerns.

Start in the introduction. Instead of saying,

I want to talk with you about stress.

you could say,

Do you get butterflies in your stomach when you have to give a speech? Can you feel your blood pressure rising when you have an argument with your spouse or your roommate? Are you worried sick about finishing the paper you've been putting off all week? If so, you have experienced the symptoms of stress.

Get your audience involved right at the beginning. Notice how one student did this in her speech on the massacre of Chinese democracy protesters in Tiananmen Square. Because this student had grown up in Hong Kong, the massacre was vivid in her mind, but she needed to get her U.S. classmates involved in the topic. She began by saying:

Imagine yourself standing in the middle of a road confronting military troops. You see an endless sea of tanks rolling one after another, jamming the entire road. The series of tanks lines up right before you. If you take one step forward, the lead tank will crush you to death. In China, in 1989, a man actually faced such a scene.

Another approach is to ask a series of questions that arouse curiosity and draw your audience into the speech. One student used this technique especially well in a speech about the medical and culinary uses of dandelions:

What starts out yellow and ends up as a fluffy white ball? If I told you it was *Taraxacum officinale,* would that ring a bell? What if I told you it was of the family *Compositae*—would that excite your senses? If you haven't figured it out by now, the subject of which I am speaking is none other than the common, ordinary dandelion.

View these excerpts from "Tiananmen Square" and "Dandelions: The Uncommon Weed."

CD: VIDEO CLIP 14.1

Don't stop with the introduction. Whenever you can, put your listeners into the body of the speech. After all, nothing interests people more than themselves. Don't just rattle off statistics and concepts as if you were reciting a shopping list. Find ways to talk about your topic in terms of your listeners. Bring your material home to them. Get it as close to them as possible.

Here's an example. Let's say you are explaining how people can discover whether they are "secret southpaws"—that is, people who are naturally left-handed but who have grown up preferring the right hand because they were taught to use it as a child. You have plenty of facts and could recite them like this:

According to *Science* magazine, half of all people who are naturally left-handed assume they are right-handed because that is the hand they use to eat, to write, and to play sports. But how can it be determined whether one is a natural southpaw? According to Abram Blau, author of *The Master Hand,* there are a number of simple tests. For one thing, most natural left-handers can write spontaneously backward or upside down with the left hand. For another, when left-handers clasp their hands in front of themselves, they usually place the left thumb on top. In contrast, when left-handers grab a broom, they normally place their left hand below the right. Finally, when using the right hand, natural left-handers will draw a circle clockwise, while natural right-handers will draw it counterclockwise. People who give a left-handed response on three or more of these tests may well be secret southpaws.[5]

This is fascinating information, but it is not made fascinating to the audience. Let's try again:

Just because *you* use *your* right hand to eat, to write, and to play sports, *you* may assume *you* are naturally right-handed. But, says *Science* magazine, half of all people who are naturally left-handed grow up using their right hands. How can *you* tell if *you* are a natural lefty? Dr. Abram Blau, author of *The Master Hand,* gives some tests *you* can try.

First, on a sheet of paper see if *you* can write backward or upside down with *your* left hand. If *you* are left-handed, *you* can probably do this spontaneously, without practice or training.

Second, clasp *your* hands in front of *you*; whichever thumb *you* place on top usually indicates *your* dominant hand.

Third, grab hold of a broomstick. Odds are *you* will place *your* dominant hand on the bottom.

Finally, draw a circle on a piece of paper with *your* right hand. If *you* draw it counterclockwise, *you* are probably a natural right-hander. But if *you* draw it clockwise, *you* are very likely a natural lefty.

If *you* test left-handed on three of these tests, there is a good chance *you* are a secret southpaw.

Look at all the "you's" and "your's." The facts are the same, but now they are pointed directly at the audience. This is the kind of thing that gets listeners to sit up and pay attention.

Don't Be Too Technical

What does it mean to say that an informative speech is too technical? It may mean the subject matter is too specialized for the audience. Any subject can be popularized—but only up to a point. The important thing for a speaker to know is what can be explained to an ordinary audience and what cannot.

Say your subject is electronic amplifiers. It's no trick to demonstrate how to operate an amplifier (how to turn it on and off, adjust the volume, set the tone and balance controls). It's also relatively easy to explain what an amplifier does (it boosts the sound received from a radio, CD player, tape deck, or live performance). But to give a full scientific account of how an amplifier works—that is another matter. It cannot be done in any reasonable time unless the audience knows the principles of audio technology. You would be better off not even trying. The material is just too technical to be understood by a general audience.

Even when the subject matter is not technical, the language used to explain it may be. Every activity has its jargon. This is true of golf (bogey, wedge, match play); of chemistry (colloid, glycogen, heavy water); of photography (aperture, f-stop, depth of field); of ballet (arabesque, jeté, pas de deux). If you are talking to a group of specialists, you can use technical words and be understood. But you must do all you can to avoid technical words when informing a general audience such as your speech class.

You may find this hard to do at first. Many people are so addicted to the lingo of their subject that they have trouble escaping it. As you give more speeches, though, you will become increasingly adept at expressing your ideas in everyday, nontechnical language.

Here, for instance, are two statements explaining the process of cryonics, which involves freezing people after death in the hope that medical science will be able to restore them to life in the future. The first is heavily laden with specialized language that would have little impact on ordinary listeners:

> Options for cryonic suspension include freezing the subject's head or complete body. In either case, the process entails complex scientific procedures that, for maximum functionality, must be implemented immediately upon the cessation of biological functioning. Measures must be taken to minimize tissue decomposition so as to ensure that the subject can be successfully resuscitated at some undetermined future period.

The second statement is perfectly understandable. It is from the speech on cyronics reprinted at the end of this chapter, and it shows how technical information can be made clear to the average person:

> Currently, when a person who has signed up to be cryonically suspended dies, a specific procedure, which was outlined in the book *Cryonics: Reaching for Tomorrow,* must be carried out.
>
> First, before death, an individual must decide whether to have his or her entire body frozen or just the head. If the whole body is to be frozen, it must be preserved upon death. Immediately after death—ideally within a matter of minutes—the patient is connected to a heart-lung machine and chemicals such as glucose and heparin are circulated with the oxygenated blood to help minimize the freezing damage. At the same time, the patient's internal temperature is reduced as quickly as possible using cold packs.
>
> If only the head will be frozen, a slightly different procedure must be carried out. The head must be surgically detached from the rest of the body and preserved in a separate container. You may be wondering, "Why would I preserve only my head?" The answer is, with some diseases the body is in a very poor condition. If this is the case and you choose to preserve your head only, you do so with the belief that medical science will be able to create a healthy new body for you in the future.

jargon
The specialized or technical language of a trade, profession, or similar group.

View this excerpt from Jayne Richter, "Cryonics."
CD: VIDEO CLIP 14.2

Much clearer, isn't it? The only specialized words in the whole passage are "glucose," "heparin," and "oxygenated blood," and they do not get in the way. The rest of the language is straightforward, the ideas easy to grasp. This is what you should strive for in your informative speeches.

Avoid Abstractions

"My task," said the novelist Joseph Conrad, "is, before all, to make you see." And make the reader see is just what Conrad did. Witness this passage, in which Conrad describes the aftermath of an explosion aboard a ship:

> The first person I saw was Mahon, with eyes like saucers, his mouth open, and the long white hair standing straight on end round his head like a silver halo. He was just about to go down when the sight of the main deck stirring, heaving up, and changing into splinters before his eyes, petrified him on the top step. I stared at him in unbelief, and he stared at me with a queer kind of shocked curiosity. I did not know that I had no hair, no eyebrows, no eyelashes, that my young mustache was burnt off, that my face was black, one cheek laid open, my nose cut, and my chin bleeding.[6]

A speech is not a novel. Still, too many abstractions are tedious—whether in a novel or in a speech. Many informative speeches would be vastly improved by the novelist's bent for color, specificity, and detail.

One way to avoid abstractions is through *description*. When we think of description, we usually think of external events such as the explosion described by Conrad. But description is also used to communicate internal feelings. Here is how one student tried to convey to his audience the sensations he experienced when he first began sky diving:

description
A statement that depicts a person, event, idea, and the like with clarity and vividness.

> As we wait for the plane to climb to the jump altitude of 12,000 feet, my mind races with a frenzied jumble of thoughts: "Okay, this is the moment you've been waiting for. It's going to be great. Am I really going to jump out of an airplane from 12,000 feet? What if something goes wrong? Can I still back out? Come on now, don't worry. It'll be fine."

Even if we have not been sky diving, we have all had the same kinds of emotions on similar occasions. So what happened next?

> Now it is time to jump. My palms are sweating and my heart is pounding so hard I think it may burst. "Get ready," yells the instructor. As I jump into the blue, I wonder, "What am I doing here?"

Yes—and then what?

> The blast of air resistance blows me backward like a leaf at the mercy of an autumn wind. In about ten seconds my body levels out and accelerates to a speed of 120 miles an hour. The air supports my body like an invisible flying carpet. There is no sound except for the wind rushing around my face. The earth appears soft and green, rivers look like strips of silver, and in every direction the scenery forms a panoramic landscape. Any fears or doubts I had are gone in the exhilaration of free flight. Every nerve in my body is alive with sensation; yet I am overcome by a peaceful feeling and the sense that I am at one with the sky.

Whether in the classroom or out, effective informative speakers work on communicating their ideas in clear, nontechnical language that relates the topic to their listeners' background, knowledge, and interests.

As we listen to the speaker, we are almost up there with him, sharing his thoughts, feeling his heart pound, joining his exhilaration as he floats effortlessly through the sky. The vivid description lends reality to the speech and draws us further in.

Another way to escape abstractions is with *comparisons* that put your subject in concrete, familiar terms. Do you want to convey what would happen if a comet or large asteroid struck the earth? You could say this:

> If a comet or large asteroid struck the earth, the impact would be devastating.

True, but "the impact would be devastating" is vague and abstract. It does not communicate your meaning clearly and concretely. Now suppose you add this:

> To give you an idea how devastating the impact would be, it would be like all the nuclear bombs in the world going off at one spot.

Now you have made the abstract specific and given us a sharp new slant on things.

Like comparison, *contrast* can put an idea into concrete terms. Suppose you want to make the point that a person's chances of winning a state lottery are extremely low. You could say, "The odds, for example, of winning a state lottery are an astronomical 7 million to 1." The word "astronomical" suggests that you consider 7 million to 1 long odds, but long in comparison to what? One speaker offered this contrast:

> The odds of picking the correct six-digit sequence in a typical state lottery are more than 7 million to 1. In contrast, the odds of getting hit by lightning are only 2 million to 1. The chances of being dealt a royal flush in a poker game are 650,000 to 1. The

comparison
A statement of the similarities among two or more people, events, ideas, etc.

contrast
A statement of the differences among two or more people, events, ideas, etc.

odds of dying in an automobile accident are about 6,000 to 1. In other words, the odds are much stronger that you will get hit by lightning or be killed in a car crash than that you will win the jackpot in a state lottery.

Now an abstract fact has been put into meaningful perspective. See if you can do something similar in your informative speech.

Personalize Your Ideas

Listeners want to be entertained as they are being enlightened.[7] Nothing takes the edge off an informative speech more than an unbroken string of facts and figures. And nothing enlivens a speech more than personal illustrations. Remember, people are interested in people. They react to stories, not statistics. Whenever possible, you should try to *personalize* your ideas and dramatize them in human terms.

> **personalize**
> To present one's ideas in human terms that relate in some fashion to the experience of the audience.

Let's say you are talking about anorexia nervosa, the eating disorder that affects millions of young women in the United States. You would surely note that 1 in every 100 teenage females in the U.S. suffers from anorexia, that the number is rising every year, and that college-age women make up 45 percent of all cases of anorexia. You would also note that the effects of anorexia include extreme weight loss, brittle bones, decreased pulse rate, and brain damage. In addition, you would note that despite drug therapy, hospitalization, and forced feeding, close to 20 percent of the people who are diagnosed with anorexia die from it.

But these are dry facts and figures. If you really want to get your audience involved, you will weave in some examples of people who have suffered from anorexia. One speaker began by telling about her best friend, Julie:

I was Julie's best friend. I watched her grow from a little girl who was doted on by her parents into a tomboy who carried frogs in her pockets. I watched her become a young woman, fussing with her hair and trying on every outfit in her closet before her first date. I always wanted to be just like her.

But then something went terribly wrong. Julie's shiny hair became dull and brittle. Her eyes lost their sparkle, and she didn't smile that brilliant smile any more. I watched now, as she stepped onto the scale seven times a day, wore baggy clothes to cover her shriveled frame, and kept muttering about losing those last two stubborn pounds. Julie had become anorexic.

During the body of the speech, the speaker mentioned Julie twice more to illustrate different aspects of anorexia. Then, in the conclusion, she brought Julie's story to its tragic end:

We have seen that anorexia is a serious disease with deep-seated causes and devastating, potentially fatal effects. Julie was one of those who couldn't beat anorexia. She died when she was only 17. We will never go to college together and share a dorm room. She will never fulfill her dream of becoming a nurse. And we will never grow old living beside each other and watching our kids grow up together. Anorexia killed my beautiful, vibrant friend.

View these excerpts from Jennifer Breuer, "Dying to Be Thin."

CD: VIDEO CLIP 14.3

It was a powerful ending, and it left the audience stunned. By putting a human face on a familiar topic, the speaker took anorexia out of the realm of statistics and medical jargon and brought it home in personal terms. As one listener said afterward, "Because of your speech, I will never see anorexia in the same way again."

Sample Speech with Commentary

The following classroom speech provides an excellent example of how to apply the guidelines for informative speaking discussed in this chapter.[8] As you study the speech, notice how the speaker takes what could be a highly technical topic and explores it in clear, nontechnical language. Pay attention as well to how crisply the speech is organized, how the speaker uses well-chosen supporting materials to develop her ideas, and how she relates those ideas to her audience at various points throughout the speech.

View the full speech "Cryonics."

CD: VIDEO DISK 2

Cryonics

Commentary	Speech
	Jayne Richter
Beginning with a series of brief hypothetical examples is a fine way to capture attention and interest. In this case, the scenarios work particularly well because they relate the topic directly to the audience.	The time is now. Imagine your mother or father has suffered a heart attack. Deprived of its vital blood supply, a part of their heart is dying. Or imagine your grandmother or grandfather lying nearly motionless in their nursing home bed. Advanced age, complicated by pneumonia, is about to end their lives. Or imagine a close friend has just entered the hospital with a massive systemwide infection. AIDS has left their body ravaged by multiple diseases.
The speaker poses two questions that arouse curiosity and get the audience further involved in the speech. Then she reveals her topic.	For most people, these circumstances would herald the end of life. Today's medicine can no longer help them. But all of you may be able to meet again in the far future. Does this sound like science fiction? Perhaps. But it may one day be possible. How? Through the process of cryonics.
The speaker defines cryonics, establishes her credibility, and previews the main points to be discussed in the body of the speech. An explicit preview statement at the end of the introduction is especially important in speaking to inform.	Cryonics is the process of freezing human beings after death in the hope that medical science will be able to revive them in the future. Intrigued by the prospect of being cryonically frozen, I've spent some time researching the subject of cryonics. After reading dozens of newspaper and magazine articles, I would like to give you a brief overview of the history, methods, and future of cryonics. Let's start with the development of cryonics.

Now the speaker moves into her first main point. The information in this paragraph provides historical perspective on the impulse for immortality that underlies the appeal of cryonics.

The speaker sketches the development of cryonics in our own time. The details in this paragraph add variety, color, and interest. Imagine, for example, how much less effective the paragraph would have been if the speaker had merely said, "The first case of a person being cryonically frozen occurred in the 1970s." The specific names and dates add depth and texture to the speaker's explanation.

This paragraph completes the speaker's first main point. Because cryonics is so often associated with science fiction, the speaker's classmates were especially intrigued to learn that there are four cryonics institutions in the U.S. and that 80 people have already been cryonically frozen.

The speaker uses questions as signposts to let the audience know she is moving into her second main point.

The explanation in this and the next paragraph provides an excellent model of how to explain technical information in everyday, nontechnical language. Because the speaker is not an expert on cryonics, she is careful to identify the source of her information. You can view this portion of the speech on CD-ROM Video Clip 14.2.

Although the idea of freezing people is relatively new, the notion of preserving them is old. In the 1770s, for example, Ben Franklin wrote that he wanted to be "immersed in a cask of Madeira wine, 'til that time when he could be recalled to life." It was not to be, but Franklin's dream lived on to be revived in our time as cryonics.

Cryonics has been a staple of science fiction novels, the plot device in movies such as *Austin Powers* and *Sleepers,* and the subject of countless newspaper and magazine articles. Until 1964, however, cryonics remained firmly in the realm of fiction. It was at this time that physics professor Robert Ettinger argued in his book *The Prospect of Immortality* that cryonics was indeed possible. Three years later, on January 12, 1967, 73-year-old James H. Bedford became the first human being to be cryonically frozen.

Ever since Bedford was frozen, cryonics has steadily increased in popularity. Currently there are four cryonic institutions in the United States—two in California and one each in Michigan and Arizona. So far 80 people have been cryonically frozen from around the world, and another estimated 800 people have signed up to be frozen when they die. Their aim is to remain frozen in a state of suspended animation—perhaps for centuries—in the hope that medical science will be able to revive them in the future at a time when cures exist for virtually all of today's diseases and when restoration to full function and health is possible.

So you're probably wondering how will they do it? How does cryonics work?

Currently, when a person who has signed up to be cryonically suspended dies, a specific procedure, which was outlined in the book *Cryonics: Reaching for Tomorrow,* must be carried out. First, before death, an individual must decide whether to have his or her entire body frozen or just the head. If the whole body is to be frozen, it must be preserved upon death. Immediately after death—ideally within a matter of minutes—the patient is connected to a heart-lung machine and chemicals such as glucose and heparin are circulated with the oxygenated blood to help minimize the freezing damage. At the same time, the patient's internal temperature is reduced as quickly as possible using cold packs.

Notice how the speaker relates the topic directly to her audience by speaking in terms of "you" and by posing the question that listeners are likely asking mentally.

The speaker completes her discussion of how cryonics works. Notice how she clarifies the meaning of "cryoprotectant" by comparing it to an automotive antifreeze. This is a small point, but it illustrates the speaker's efforts throughout the speech to communicate technical terms and concepts in ways her audience can readily understand.

A transition cues the audience that the speaker is moving to her next main point.

Knowing that cost is a common question people have about cryonics, the speaker makes sure to include it in her speech. The quotation at the end of this paragraph adds a bit of wry humor.

A signpost at the beginning of this paragraph gets the speaker into her next subpoint, which deals with the problems involved in rethawing people once they have been cryonically frozen. As in the rest of the speech, the speaker identifies the source of her information and presents that information clearly and forthrightly.

The speaker explains the efforts of scientists to find a way to reduce the damage caused

If only the head will be frozen, a slightly different procedure must be carried out. The head must be surgically detached from the rest of the body and preserved in a separate container. You may be wondering, "Why would I preserve only my head?" The answer is, with some diseases the body is in a very poor condition. If this is the case and you choose to preserve your head only, you do so with the belief that medical science will be able to create a healthy new body for you in the future.

Once the head or body is ready for freezing, a liquid called a cryoprotectant, which works as an antifreeze of sorts to help prevent cell damage, is circulated through the body or head. Over a 20-day period, the patient is prepared for long-term storage by cooling the body or head to a temperature of negative 320 degrees Fahrenheit. When this temperature is reached, the patient is stored in a steel cylinder of liquid nitrogen. According to an article in *Omni* magazine, "At this temperature, biological function ceases and the patient will remain unchanged for hundreds of years."

Now that we have explored the development of cryonics and how the freezing process works, you may wonder about questions such as how much it costs and whether the people that are frozen can be rethawed.

According to an article in *Fortune* magazine, the cost of cryonic suspension ranges from $60,000 to $125,000. It can be creatively paid for by making the cryonics institution the beneficiary of your life insurance policy. These costs may be rather steep, but as one cryonics member states, "Facing my own mortality turned out to be much harder than coming up with the cash to pay for life insurance premiums."

But cost is not the only issue. Even if you can afford the cost of being cryonically frozen, scientists have not yet worked out all the details involved in freezing and rethawing. As explained by *New Scientist* magazine, the problem is that the freezing process itself inflicts a crippling amount of cellular damage by dehydrating cells and puncturing their delicate membranes. So far, there are only a few types of human tissue that can be successfully frozen and rethawed, including sperm, embryos, and bone marrow, which contain relatively few cells. It is not yet possible to freeze and rethaw complicated organs such as the heart or liver—not to mention a complete body or brain.

What scientists need is a procedure that will allow them to reduce the damage inflicted by the freezing process. And in by the freezing process so as to be able to bring frozen patients back to life. This brings her discussion of cryonics fully up to date and completes the body of the speech.

The phrase "In closing" signals that the speaker is moving into her conclusion. She then provides an excellent summary of the main points developed in the body.

The final paragraph relates the topic to the audience once again and unifies the entire speech by referring back to the three hypothetical scenarios mentioned in the introduction. The closing sentence ends the speech on a strong note.

fact scientists are currently working on this procedure. Research is being done in the hope of finding better cryoprotectants—or antifreezes—which will reduce the cell damage caused by freezing. According to the book *Cryonics: Reaching for Tomorrow*, scientists are also developing microscopic machines that are capable of repairing cells at the molecular level. These machines might one day make it possible to repair the cell damage caused by the freezing process and thus bring frozen patients back to full life. Until that time, the people that are already frozen will have to remain in their current state of suspended animation in the hope that science will one day work out solutions to the problems involved with freezing and rethawing.

In closing, we have seen that cryonics is much more than a plot in a science fiction novel. It has developed from a wholly unrealistic fantasy to the point that 80 people have already been frozen and hundreds more have made the choice to be cryonically frozen when they die. If scientists can ever figure out how to rethaw people successfully, we can be sure that cryonics will become much more popular.

So think again of your father or mother suffering a heart attack, your grandmother or grandfather dying of pneumonia, or your close friend stricken with AIDS. If they chose to be buried or cremated in traditional fashion, their physical minds and bodies would be destroyed. That is absolutely certain. By contrast, being cryonically frozen offers some small chance that they may be revived in the future. Even if that chance is small, it's more than no chance at all.

Summary

Speaking to inform occurs in a wide range of everyday situations. Yet it is a difficult task that requires more skill than you might think. Improving your ability to convey knowledge effectively will be most valuable to you throughout your life.

Informative speeches may be grouped into four categories—speeches about objects, speeches about processes, speeches about events, and speeches about concepts. These categories are not absolute, but they are helpful in analyzing and organizing informative speeches.

Objects, as defined here, include places, structures, animals, even people. Speeches about objects usually are organized in chronological, spatial, or topical order. A process is a series of actions that work together to produce a final result. Speeches about processes explain how something is made, how something is done, or how something works. Clear organization is especially important in speeches about processes because listeners must be able to follow each step in the process. The most common types of organization for speeches about processes are chronological and topical.

An event is anything that happens or is regarded as happening. You can approach an event from almost any angle. You might explain its origins, causes, effects, implications, major features, and so on. Usually speeches about events are arranged in chronological, causal, or topical order. Concepts include beliefs, theories, ideas, and principles. Speeches about concepts are often more complex than other kinds of informative speeches, and they typically follow a topical pattern of organization.

No matter what the subject of your informative speech, be careful not to overestimate what your audience knows about it. In most classroom speeches your listeners will be no more than slightly familiar with your topic. Therefore, you cannot assume they will know what you mean. Explain everything so thoroughly they cannot help but understand. Avoid being too technical. Make sure your ideas and your language are fully comprehensible to someone who has no specialized knowledge about the topic.

Equally important, recognize that what is fascinating to you may not be fascinating to everybody. It is your job to make your informative speech interesting and meaningful to your audience. Find ways to talk about the topic in terms of your listeners. Avoid too many abstractions. Use description, comparison, and contrast to make your audience *see* what you are talking about. Finally, try to personalize your ideas. No matter what your subject, you can almost always find a way to dramatize it in human terms.

Key Terms

informative speech (340)
object (341)
process (343)
event (346)
concept (348)

jargon (355)
description (356)
comparison (357)
contrast (357)
personalize (358)

Review Questions

After reading this chapter, you should be able to answer the following questions:

1. What are the four types of informative speeches discussed in the chapter? Give an example of a good specific purpose statement for each type.

2. Why must informative speakers be careful not to overestimate what the audience knows about the topic? What can you do to make sure your ideas don't pass over the heads of your listeners?

3. What should you do as an informative speaker to relate your topic directly to the audience?

For further review, go to the Study Questions for this chapter.

CD: STUDY QUESTIONS

4. What two things should you watch out for in making sure your speech is not overly technical?

5. What are three methods you can use to avoid abstractions in your informative speech?

6. What does it mean to say that informative speakers should personalize their ideas?

Exercises for Critical Thinking

1. Below is a list of subjects for informative speeches. Your task is twofold: (a) Select four of the topics and prepare a specific purpose statement for an informative speech about each of the four. Make sure that your four specific purpose statements include at least one that deals with its topic as an object, one that deals with its topic as a process, one that deals with its topic as an event, and one that deals with its topic as a concept. (b) Explain what method of organization you would most likely use in structuring a speech about each of your specific purpose statements.

hobbies	sports
animals	music
science	cultural customs
education	technology
media	health

2. Analyze the speech in Appendix B by Jennifer Breuer ("Dying to Be Thin"). Identify the specific purpose, central idea, main points, and method of organization. Evaluate the speech in light of the guidelines for informative speaking discussed in this chapter.

*A*pplying the POWER of Public Speaking

As the manager for a local chain of coffee houses, you have been asked to speak to a gourmet group about how to make genuine Italian cappuccino. As you write down ideas for your speech, you find that you have the following main points:

    I. First you must make the espresso.
    II. Grind the coffee beans so they are fine but not too fine.
    III. Place the ground coffee in the filter holder of the espresso machine.
    IV. Tamp the coffee once lightly to level the grind in the filter holder.
    V. Lock the filter holder onto the brew head of the espresso machine.
    VI. Activate the on switch to extract the espresso.
    VII. In addition to making the espresso, you must prepare frothed milk for cappuccino.
    VIII. Fill a steaming pitcher 1/3 full of very cold milk.

IX. Place the steam vent of the espresso machine just below the surface of the milk in the pitcher.

X. Fully open the steam vent.

XI. Keeping the tip of the steam vent just below the surface of the milk, move the pitcher in a circular motion.

XII. Be careful not to overheat or scald the milk, which will ruin the froth.

XIII. Once you have the desired amount and consistency of froth, turn the steam vent off and remove it from the pitcher.

XIV. Now you are ready to combine the espresso and frothed milk.

XV. The normal proportions for cappuccino are 1/3 espresso to 2/3 frothed milk.

XVI. Some people prefer to pour the espresso into the frothed milk in a cappuccino cup.

XVII. Other people prefer to pour or spoon the frothed milk over the espresso.

Having taken a speech class in college, you know this is too many main points for an audience to keep track of. As you look over your list again, however, you realize that it can easily be reorganized into three main points, each with several subpoints. What are those main points and subpoints?

Notes

[1] John R. Johnson and Nancy Szczupakiewicz, "The Public Speaking Course: Is It Preparing Students with Work-Related Public Speaking Skills?" *Communication Education,* 36 (1987), pp. 131–137.

[2] Andrew D. Wolvin and Diana Corley, "The Technical Speech Communication Course: A View from the Field," *Association for Communication Administration Bulletin,* 49 (1984), pp. 83–91.

[3] Adapted from Rudolf Flesch, *The Art of Readable Writing* (New York: Harper & Row, 1949), p. 82.

[4] James J. Welsh, *The Speech Writing Guide* (New York: Wiley, 1968), p. 51.

[5] Adapted from a speech by Kenda Creasy Dean. Used with permission.

[6] Joseph Conrad, "Youth: A Narrative," in Samuel Hynes (ed.), *Collected Stories of Joseph Conrad* (Hopewell, N.J.: Ecco Press, 1991), p. 166.

[7] James Humes, *Roles Speakers Play* (New York: Harper & Row, 1976), p. 25.

[8] Reprinted with permission of Jayne Richter. This speech is also available on the videotape supplement to *The Art of Public Speaking.*

CHAPTER FIFTEEN

SPEAKING TO PERSUADE

The Psychology of Persuasion

Persuasive Speeches on Questions of Fact

Persuasive Speeches on Questions of Value

Persuasive Speeches on Questions of Policy

Sample Speech with Commentary

amon Trujillo began that particular school day by stopping at the library to return an overdue book. "Look," he explained to the librarian, "I know this book was due last week, but I was sick with the flu and couldn't even get out of bed. Do I still have to pay the fine? I can get you a note from my doctor if you need one." The librarian hemmed and hawed. Then he said, "Okay. You don't have a record of any other fines. Just this once."

With a sigh of relief, Ramon went on to his morning classes. At noon he was dashing across campus when a friend stopped him. "How about some lunch?" she asked. "I really can't," replied Ramon. "I have to stand at the table and get signatures on the petition against higher tuition. I'll see you later, though."

During the afternoon, Ramon had a free period, and he used the time to meet with his history professor. "The reason I wanted to see you," he began, "is . . . well . . . I think I deserved a better grade on my last exam. I know you don't like to change grades, but I went back and reviewed all my notes on the Vietnam question, and I really think I got everything you were looking for." The professor agreed to look at Ramon's exam. "Well," she said when she was finished, "it certainly looks good to me. I'm going to raise your grade from a B-plus to an A-minus."

At dinner that evening, Ramon asked his roommate to loan him $20 until the end of the month. "You know," he said, "it was my Mom's birthday last week. In addition to getting a present for her, I had to buy the last book for my biology class. But I'm working some extra hours next weekend at the pizza place, and I'll be able to pay you back without any problem." After checking to make sure he had enough money, Ramon's roommate said, "Sure. After all, what are friends for?"

persuasive speech
A speech designed to change or reinforce the audience's beliefs or actions.

If you asked Ramon how he spent his day, he might say, "I returned a book to the library, I went to classes, I worked the petition table, I talked with my history professor, I ate dinner with my roommate." In fact, he spent a large part of his day *persuading*—persuading people to do things that they were reluctant to do or that had not occurred to them.

Most of us do a certain amount of persuading every day, although we may not realize it or call it that. Public speaking to persuade is essentially an extension of this. It is an attempt to convert a whole group, not just an individual, to your point of view on a particular subject.

The ability to speak (and write) persuasively will benefit you in every part of your life from personal relations to community activities to career aspirations. In a recent study, economists added up the number of people—lawyers, sales representatives, public relations specialists, counselors, administrators, and others—whose jobs depend largely on their ability to persuade people to adopt their point of view. The economists concluded that persuasion accounts for 26 percent of the U.S. gross domestic product![1]

Although persuasion has been studied for the past 2,000 years, it is still the subject of lively debate among scholars. There are a number of respected theories about how persuasion works, a variety of scientific models of the persuasive process, even a wide range of competing definitions of persuasion.[2]

For our purpose it is enough to know that when you speak to persuade, you act as an advocate. Your job is to change listeners' minds—to get them to agree with you and, perhaps, to act on that belief. Your goal may be to defend an idea, to refute an opponent, to sell a program, or to inspire people to action. Because persuasive speakers must communicate information clearly and concisely, you will need all the skills you used in speaking to inform. But you will also need new skills—skills that take you from giving information to affecting your listeners' beliefs or actions.

As with other kinds of public speaking, you will be more effective in persuasion if you approach it systematically. Let us begin by looking at some of the psychological principles involved in the persuasive process.

The Psychology of Persuasion

Persuasion is a psychological process. It always occurs in a situation where two or more points of view exist. The speaker believes irradiating fresh meats and vegetables poses a danger to human health, but many listeners do not. The speaker considers doctor-assisted suicide to be immoral, but some in the audience think it is justified in certain circumstances. The speaker wants everyone in the audience to sign up immediately to learn CPR, but most listeners are inclined to procrastinate and will do it "someday." The different points of view may be completely opposed, or they may simply be different in degree. Whichever the case, there must be a disagreement, or else there would be no need for persuasion.

The Challenge of Persuasive Speaking

Of all the kinds of public speaking, persuasion is the most complex and the most challenging. Your objective is more ambitious than in speaking to inform, and audience analysis and adaptation become much more demanding. In some persuasive speeches you will deal with controversial topics that touch on your listeners' most basic attitudes, values, and beliefs. This will increase your listeners' resistance to persuasion and make your task that much more difficult.

It is much easier, for example, to explain the history of capital punishment than to persuade an audience either that capital punishment should be abolished or that it should be reinstituted in every state. In the persuasive speech you must contend not only with your audience's knowledge of capital punishment but also with their attitudes toward crime and justice, their beliefs about whether capital punishment deters people from committing violent crimes, and their values about the taking of human life. Lines of argument that work with one part of the audience may fail with—or even upset—another part. What seems perfectly logical to some listeners may seem wildly irrational to others. No matter how expert you are on the topic, no matter how skillfully you prepare the speech, no matter how captivating your delivery—some listeners will not agree with you.

This does not mean that persuasion is impossible. It does mean that you should enter a persuasive speaking situation with a realistic sense of what you can accomplish. You cannot expect a group of die-hard Democrats to become Republicans or a steak lover to turn vegetarian as a result of one speech. If listeners are not strongly committed one way or another on your topic, you can realistically hope your speech will move at least some of them toward your side. If listeners are strongly opposed to your viewpoint, you can consider your speech a success if it leads even a few to reexamine their views.

How successful you are in any particular persuasive speech will depend above all on how well you tailor your message to the values, attitudes, and beliefs of your audience. Persuasion is a strategic activity. Just as a businesswoman or a military commander plots a strategy to gain a big sale or to be victorious in battle, so a persuasive speaker must have a strategy to win the audience to her or his side. In Chapter 5 we considered the general principles of audience analysis and adaptation. Here we need to emphasize two additional principles that are crucial to the psychology of persuasion. The first deals with how listeners process and respond to persuasive messages. The second pertains to the target audience for persuasive speeches.

How Listeners Process Persuasive Messages

We often think of persuasion as something a speaker does *to* an audience.[3] In fact, as a great deal of research shows, persuasion is something a speaker does *with* an audience. Although audiences in the United States seldom interrupt a speaker while she or he is talking, they do not just sit passively and soak in everything the speaker has to say.

Instead, they often engage in a mental give-and-take with the speaker. While they listen, they actively assess the speaker's credibility, delivery, supporting materials, language, reasoning, and emotional appeals. They may respond positively at one point, negatively at another. At times they may argue, inside their own minds, with the speaker. This mental give-and-take is especially vigorous when listeners are highly involved with the topic of the speech and believe it has a direct bearing on their lives.[4]

In a sense, the psychological interaction between a speaker and audience during a persuasive speech is similar to what happens vocally during a conversation—as in this example:

Jordan: The federal government really needs to clamp down on hate speech. Publications that demonize homosexuality are inciting violence, sometimes even murder.

Keisha: I agree that violence against gays and lesbians is wrong, but I'm not sure censorship is the right approach. There's no proof these publications actually cause violence. Besides, doesn't the First Amendment guarantee the right to free speech, even for people who support detestable causes?

Jordan: Free speech is important, but people have a right to live without being persecuted. Doesn't our government have a responsibility to do what it can to keep people safe from discrimination?

Keisha: We can't compromise on free speech. It's a very dangerous idea to let someone in government decide what's acceptable speech and what's not. Once we ban hate speech, we might start banning other forms of expression, too.

Jordan: Not necessarily. We already outlaw some kinds of speech because they are dangerous to the community—such as threatening the life of the President or shouting "Fire" in a crowded building. Why is banning hate speech any different?

No matter what the situation, a persuasive speech will be more effective if the speaker delivers the message sincerely and adapts it to the target audience.

Much the same kind of interaction might occur during a persuasive speech except that the listener—in this case, Keisha—would respond to herself rather than out loud.

What does this mean to you as a speaker? It means you must think of your persuasive speech as a kind of *mental dialogue* with your audience. Most important, you must anticipate possible objections the audience will raise to your point of view and then answer those objections in your speech. You cannot convert skeptical listeners unless you deal directly with the reasons for their skepticism.

As you prepare your persuasive speech, put yourself in the place of your audience and imagine how they will respond. For this to work, you must be as tough on your speech as your audience will be. Every place they will raise a question, answer it. Every place they will have a criticism, deal with it. Every place they will see a hole in your argument, fill it. Leave nothing to chance.[5]

mental dialogue with the audience
The mental give-and-take between speaker and listener during a persuasive speech.

The Target Audience

Unfortunately, no matter how carefully you plot your speech, you will seldom be able to persuade all your listeners. Some will be so opposed to your views that you have absolutely no chance of changing their minds. Others will already agree with you, so there is no need to persuade them. Like most audiences, yours will probably contain some listeners who are hostile to your position, some who favor it, some who are undecided, and some who just don't care. You would like to make your speech equally appealing to everyone, but this is rarely possible. Most often you will have a particular *part* of the whole audience that you want to reach with your speech. That part is called the *target audience.*

Concentrating on a target audience does not mean you should ignore or insult the rest of your listeners. You must always keep in mind the ideas and feelings of your entire audience. But no matter how noble your

target audience
The portion of the whole audience that the speaker most wants to persuade.

intentions or how hard you try, you can't persuade all the people all the time. It only makes sense, then, to decide which portion of the audience you *most* want to reach.

Advertising gives us an effective model. Successful commercials are aimed at particular segments of the market, and their appeals are picked to fit the target audience. Mutual funds are now directing many of their advertisements at women. Why? Because more and more women are investing in the stock market. Beer commercials, on the other hand, are directed at men—especially blue-collar men—because they drink the most beer. Soft-drink commercials? They are meant to hook young people, so they feature teenagers, play their kind of music, and echo their values.

For your classroom speeches, you don't have the sophisticated research capability of a large advertising agency. But as we saw in Chapter 5, you can use observation, interviews, and questionnaires to find out where your classmates stand on your speech topic. This is your equivalent of market research. From it you can identify your target audience and the issues you will have to discuss to be convincing. Once you know where your target audience stands, you can tailor your speech to fit their values and concerns—aim at the target, so to speak.

Here, for example, is how one student, Amy Shapiro, determined her target audience for a persuasive speech urging her classmates to pass on the gift of life by signing organ donor cards.

There are 22 students in my audience. My audience-analysis questionnaires show that 3 are opposed to donating their organs under any circumstances. I cannot persuade them no matter what I say. My questionnaires also show that 4 have already signed organ donor cards. I don't need to persuade them. The other 15 students could be persuaded if they knew more about the need for organ donors and about how the process works. They are my target audience.

Not only did Amy pinpoint her target audience, she also knew from her audience-analysis questionnaire the issues she would have to discuss to be convincing:

The members of my target audience break down this way: 7 give "fear of being pronounced dead prematurely" as their main reason for not signing organ cards; 5 are concerned about their body being "cut up or disfigured"; and 3 cite religious reasons for their opposition. The questionnaires also show that 10 of the 15 don't fully understand the need for organ donors.

With all this information, Amy was able to put together a first-rate speech that focused specifically on her classsmates' attitudes and beliefs about signing organ donor cards. In the speech, she showed the need for organ donations by explaining that there are thousands of people whose only hope for life is to receive a heart, liver, or kidney transplant. She also took care to answer her classmates' fears and objections. She showed that there are strict safeguards to prevent doctors from pulling the plug prematurely to make a heart or liver available for transplant surgery, that donated organs are removed as carefully as if the doctor were operating on a live patient, and that almost all religious leaders approve of organ donation as a way to help save lives. As a result, she was able to convince several of her classmates to sign organ donor cards.

In the next chapter, we'll discuss the methods you can use to hit the target in your persuasive speeches. In the rest of this chapter, we focus on the three major kinds of persuasive speeches and how to organize them most effectively. We will look first at speeches on questions of fact, then at speeches on questions of value, and finally at speeches on questions of policy.

Persuasive Speeches on Questions of Fact

What Are Questions of Fact?

What college basketball team has won the most games since 1990? Who was the first African-American to sit on the U.S. Supreme Court? How far is it from New York to London? These questions of fact can be answered absolutely. You can look up the answers in a reference book, and no reasonable person would dispute them. The answers are either right or wrong.

But many questions of fact cannot be answered absolutely. There *is* a true answer, but we don't have enough information to know what it is. Some questions like this involve prediction: Will the economy be better or worse next year? Who will win the Super Bowl this season? Will another major earthquake strike California before the year 2025?

Other questions deal with issues on which the facts are murky or inconclusive. What is the cause of chronic fatigue syndrome? Is sexual orientation genetically determined? Are daily megadoses of vitamins beneficial to human health? Did William Shakespeare really write the plays attributed to him? No one knows the final answers to these questions, but this doesn't stop people from speculating about them or from trying to convince other people that they have the best possible answers.

question of fact
A question about the truth or falsity of an assertion.

Analyzing Questions of Fact

In some ways, a persuasive speech on a question of fact is similar to an informative speech. But the two kinds of speeches take place in different kinds of situations and for different purposes. The situation for an informative speech is *nonpartisan.* The speaker acts as a lecturer or a teacher. The aim is to give information as impartially as possible, not to argue for a particular point of view. On the other hand, the situation for a persuasive speech on a question of fact is *partisan.* The speaker acts as an advocate. His or her aim is not to be impartial but to present one view of the facts as persuasively as possible. The speaker may mention competing views of the facts, but only to refute them.

For example, consider the assassination of John Kennedy. After almost 40 years, there is still much public debate about what really happened in Dallas on November 22, 1963. Did Lee Harvey Oswald act alone, or was he part of a conspiracy? How many shots were fired at President Kennedy and from what locations? If there was a conspiracy, who was involved in it? The informative speaker would merely recite the known facts on both sides of these questions without drawing a conclusion about which side is correct. The persuasive speaker, however, would draw a conclusion from the known facts and try to convert listeners to his or her point of view.

If there were no possibility of dispute on questions of fact, there would be no need for courtroom trials. In a criminal trial there is usually at least one known fact—a crime has been committed. But did the defendant commit the crime? And if so, for what reason? The prosecuting attorney tries to persuade the jury that the defendant is guilty. The defense attorney tries to persuade the jury that the defendant is innocent. It is up to the jury to decide which view of the facts is more persuasive.

Organizing Speeches on Questions of Fact

Persuasive speeches on questions of fact are usually organized *topically.* Consider, for example, the August 1996 presentation by NASA scientists in support of their claim that life existed on Mars several billion years ago. Speaking at a press conference carried live on CNN, the scientists put their case together so that each main point presented a *reason* someone should agree with them. If that case were put in speech outline form, it would look like this:

Specific Purpose:	To persuade my audience that life existed on Mars 3 billion years ago.
Central Idea:	Scientific analysis of a Martian meteorite found in Antarctica indicates that life existed on Mars 3 billion years ago.
Main Points:	I. The meteorite contains a type of molecule that can result from the decomposition of living organisms.

One of the most important public speakers in recent U.S. history, Cesar Chavez often dealt with questions of fact. Here he is seen addressing an audience about dangerous pesticides in the California grape harvest.

    II. Crystals in the meteorite have the same shape as crystals formed by bacteria on Earth.

    III. Crystals in the meteorite also contain other key similarities to crystals found in 3-billion-year-old fossils from Earth.

To take another example, suppose you are trying to persuade your classmates that genetically engineered crops pose serious dangers to the environment and to human health. Your specific purpose, central idea, and main points might be:

Specific Purpose: To persuade my audience that genetically engineered crops pose serious dangers to the environment and to human health.

Central Idea: Genetically engineered crops have the potential to create major environmental and health hazards.

Main Points:
    I. Genetically engineering crops will create environmental havoc by harming beneficial insects while creating superbugs and superweeds that will be very difficult to control.

    II. Genetically engineered crops will create health problems by introducing harmful toxins and allergens into foods without the knowledge of consumers.

Occasionally you might arrange a persuasive speech on a question of fact *spatially.* For example:

Specific Purpose: To persuade my audience that poaching of wild animals is a serious international problem.

Central Idea: Poaching is threatening the survival of animal species throughout the world.

Main Points:
    I. In Africa, poaching has claimed thousands of leopards, cheetahs, rhinoceroses, and elephants.

    II. In Asia, poaching has all but eliminated Bengal tigers, snow leopards, and musk deer.

    III. In South America, poaching has driven jaguars and swamp deer to the brink of extinction.

    IV. In North America, poaching has drastically reduced the number of bald eagles, grizzly bears, timber wolves, and giant otters.

Notice that in all these examples the speaker's purpose is limited to persuading the audience to accept a particular view of the facts. Sometimes, however, the dispute that gives rise to a persuasive speech will go beyond a question of fact and will turn on a question of value.

Persuasive Speeches on Questions of Value

What Are Questions of Value?

Who is the best NFL quarterback of all time? Is the cloning of human beings morally justifiable? What are the ethical responsibilities of journalists? Such questions not only involve matters of fact, but they also demand *value judgments*—judgments based on a person's beliefs about what is right or wrong, good or bad, moral or immoral, proper or improper, fair or unfair.

Take the issue of euthanasia. It can be discussed on a purely factual level by asking questions such as "How long can a person showing no brain activity be sustained on life support systems?" Or "How much does it cost to maintain such a person in a hospital or nursing home for one month?" Or "Are there any countries in which euthanasia is practiced legally?" These are factual questions. The answers you reach are independent of your belief about the morality of euthanasia.

But suppose you ask "Is it morally justifiable to remove life support systems from a living body?" Or "Is it acceptable to burden a family with the cost of maintaining life support when there is no hope for the patient's recovery?" Now you are dealing with questions of value. How you answer will depend not only on your factual knowledge about euthanasia, but also on your moral values.[6]

question of value
A question about the worth, rightness, morality, and so forth of an idea or action.

Analyzing Questions of Value

Contrary to what many people think, questions of value are not simply matters of personal opinion or whim. If you say, "I enjoy bicycle riding," you do not have to give a reason why you enjoy it. You are making a statement about your personal taste—not about the value of biking as a sport or a form of transportation. Even if bicycle riding were the most unpleasant activity ever invented, it could still be one of your favorites.

On the other hand, if you say, "Bicycle riding is the ideal form of land transportation," you are no longer making a statement about your personal enjoyment of biking. Now you are making a statement about a question of value. Whether bicycling is the ideal form of land transportation does not depend on your own likes and dislikes. To defend the statement, you cannot say, "Bicycle riding is the ideal form of land transportation because I like it."

Instead, you must *justify* your claim. The first step is to define what you mean by an "ideal form of land transportation." Do you mean a mode of transportation that gets people where they want to go as fast as possible? That is relatively inexpensive? That is fun? Nonpolluting? Beneficial for the user? In other words, you must establish your *standards* for an "ideal form of land transportation." Then you can show how bicycle riding measures up against those standards.

Whenever you give a speech on a question of value, be sure to give special thought to the standards for your value judgment.

Organizing Speeches on Questions of Value

Persuasive speeches on questions of value are almost always organized *topically*. The most common approach is to devote your first main point to establishing the standards for your value judgment and your second main point to applying those standards to the subject of your speech.

Think back for a moment to the speech about bicycle riding as the ideal form of land transportation. If you organized this speech in topical order, your first main point would identify the standards for an ideal form of land transportation. Your second main point would show how biking measures up against those standards. Here is how your specific purpose, central idea, and main points might look:

Specific Purpose: To persuade my audience that bicycle riding is the ideal form of land transportation.

Central Idea: Bicycle riding is the ideal form of land transportation because it is faster than walking or running, does not exploit animals or people, is nonpolluting, and promotes the health of the rider.

Main Points:
I. An ideal form of land transportation should meet four major standards.
   A. It should be faster than running or walking.
   B. It should not exploit animals or people.
   C. It should be nonpolluting.
   D. It should be beneficial for the person who uses it.
II. Bicycle riding meets all these standards for an ideal form of land transportation.
   A. Bicycle riding is faster than walking or running.
   B. Bicycle riding does not exploit the labor of animals or other people.
   C. Bicycle riding is not a source of air, land, water, or noise pollution.
   D. Bicycle riding is extremely beneficial for the health of the rider.

When you speak on a question of value, you do not always have to devote your first main point to setting forth the standards for your value judgment and the second to applying those standards to the topic of the speech. But you must make sure to justify your judgment against *some* identifiable standards. In the following example, notice how the speaker devotes her first main point to judging capital punishment against moral standards and her second main point to judging it against legal standards:

Specific Purpose: To persuade my audience that capital punishment is morally and legally wrong.

Central Idea: Capital punishment violates both the Bible and the U.S. Constitution.

Main Points: I. Capital punishment violates the biblical
                        commandment "Thou shalt not kill."
                    II. Capital punishment violates the constitutional ban
                        on "cruel and unusual punishment."

As you can see, speeches on questions of value may have strong implications for our actions. A person who is persuaded that capital punishment is morally and legally wrong is more likely to support legislation abolishing the death penalty. But speeches on questions of value do not argue directly for or against particular courses of action. They do not urge listeners to *do* anything. Once you go beyond arguing right or wrong to arguing that something should or should not be done, you move from a question of value to a question of policy.

Persuasive Speeches on Questions of Policy

What Are Questions of Policy?

Questions of policy arise daily in almost everything we do. At home we debate what to do during spring vacation, whether to buy a new cell phone, which movie to see on the weekend. At work we discuss whether to go on strike, what strategy to use in selling a product, how to improve communication between management and employees. As citizens we ponder whether to vote for or against a political candidate, what to do about school violence, how to maintain economic growth and protect the environment.

question of policy
A question about whether a specific course of action should or should not be taken.

All these are questions of policy because they deal with specific courses of action. Questions of policy inevitably involve questions of fact. (How can we decide whether to vote for a candidate unless we know the facts of her or his stand on the issues?) They may also involve questions of value. (The policy you favor on abortion will be affected by whether you think abortion is moral or immoral.) But questions of policy *always* go beyond questions of fact or value to decide whether something should or should not be done.

When put formally, questions of policy usually include the word "should," as in these examples:

What measures should be taken to protect the Internet against cyber terrorism?

Should same-sex marriages be legalized?

What steps should be taken to ensure that all people in the United States receive adequate health care?

How should colleges and universities deal with the problem of hazing on campus?

Should our state institute online voting for all elections?

Types of Speeches on Questions of Policy

When you speak on a question of policy, your goal may be either to gain passive agreement or to motivate immediate action from your listeners. Deciding which goal you want to achieve is crucial, for it will affect almost every aspect of your speech.

Speeches to Gain Passive Agreement

If your goal is passive agreement, you will try to get your audience to agree with you that a certain policy is desirable, but you will not necessarily encourage the audience to do anything to enact the policy. For example, suppose you want to persuade people that the United States should abolish the electoral college and elect the President by direct popular vote. If you seek passive agreement, you will try to get your audience to concur that the President should be chosen directly by the people rather than by the electoral college. But you will not urge the audience to take any action right now to help change presidential election procedures.

Here are some specific purpose statements for policy speeches that seek passive agreement:

> To persuade my audience that affirmative-action programs should not be eliminated.

> To persuade my audience that there should be tougher enforcement of laws to protect the victims of domestic abuse.

> To persuade my audience that the state legislature should ban hospitals from employing unlicensed assistants in positions that require medical expertise.

> To persuade my audience that college scholarship athletes should receive a $250 monthly stipend for personal expenses.

> To persuade my audience that the federal government should require mandatory trunk safety releases on all cars sold in the United States.

In each of these cases, the speaker's aim is to affect the thinking of listeners—to convince them that the speaker's policy is necessary and practical. The speaker is not trying to get listeners to take action in support of the policy.

Speeches to Gain Immediate Action

When your goal is immediate action, you want to do more than get your listeners to nod their heads in agreement. You want to motivate them to action. Beyond convincing them that your cause is sound, you will try to rouse them to take action right away—to sign a petition for abolishing the electoral college, to campaign for lower tuition, to begin a regular exercise program, to contribute to a fund drive, to vote for a political candidate, to donate time to the Special Olympics, and so forth.

Here are some examples of specific purpose statements for policy speeches that seek immediate action:

> To persuade my audience to give blood through the Red Cross.

> To persuade my audience to vote in the next presidential election.

> To persuade my audience to sign a petition against reducing student loans.

> To persuade my audience to donate time to Habitat for Humanity.

> To persuade my audience to boycott clothing made at sweatshops.

Persuasive speeches on question of policy are given whenever people debate specific courses of action. To be effective, such speeches need to deal with the three basic issues of need, plan, and practicality.

Some experts say you should seek action from your audience whenever possible. Although it is much easier to evoke passive agreement than to elicit action, the listener is not making much of a commitment by thinking, "Sure, I agree with you." Within a day or two that same listener may forget entirely about your speech—and about her or his agreement with it.

Action, however, reinforces belief. There is a great deal of research showing that if you can persuade a listener to take some kind of action—even if it is no more than signing a petition, putting a bumper sticker on a car, or attending a meeting to learn about the sorority system—you have gained a more serious commitment. Once a listener acts in behalf of a speaker's position, no matter if the action is minor, she or he is more likely to remain committed to the speaker's position and to take future action in support of it.[7]

When you call for action in a persuasive speech, you should make your recommendations as specific as possible. Don't just urge listeners to "do something." Tell them exactly what to do and how to do it. If you want them to donate blood to the Red Cross, tell them where to go, how to get there, what will happen after they arrive, and how long the whole procedure will take. After the speech give everyone a brochure from the Red Cross to reinforce your message. The more specific your instructions, the more likely your call to action will succeed.[8]

Analyzing Questions of Policy

Regardless of whether your aim is to elicit passive agreement or to gain immediate action, you will face three basic issues whenever you discuss a question of policy—need, plan, and practicality.

Need

There is no point in arguing for a policy unless you can show a need for it:

Is there a need for more student parking on campus?

Is there a need for a system of standardized national tests for graduation from high school?

Is there a need to privatize the U.S. Social Security system?

Your first step is to convince listeners that there is a problem with things as they are. No doubt you have heard the old saying "If it ain't broke, don't fix it." People are not inclined to adopt a new policy unless they are convinced the old one is not working. This is why the *burden of proof* always rests with the speaker who advocates change. If you are speaking in favor of a new policy, you must prove to your listeners' satisfaction that there is a serious problem with existing policy, that the problem will only get worse with time, and that action must be taken now to solve the problem. (Of course, you may be defending present policy, in which case you will argue that there is *no* need to change—that things are already working as well as can be expected.)

need
The first basic issue in analyzing a question of policy: Is there a serious problem or need that requires a change from current policy?

burden of proof
The obligation facing a persuasive speaker to prove that a change from current policy is necessary.

Plan

The second basic issue of policy speeches is plan. Once you have shown that a problem exists, you must explain your plan for solving it.

What can we do to get more student parking on campus?

What subjects should be covered in a system of national education testing, and who will create the tests?

How will money be invested in a privatized Social Security system? Will the government still guarantee benefits to people who need them?

Answering such questions is especially important if you call for a new policy. It's easy to complain about problems; the real challenge is to develop solutions.

In most classroom speeches, you will not have time to describe your plan in detail, but you should at least identify its major features. For example, if you advocate new measures to protect personal privacy against electronic data gathering in our high-tech society, you might follow the lead of some proponents and urge the creation of strict controls over the collection, storage, and sharing of personal information by all businesses and government agencies. When explaining your plan, you might draw upon the experiences of European countries such as England, France, Germany, and Sweden, all of which have curbs on the electronic storage of personal information. But whatever your plan, be sure to explain any aspects of it that might seriously affect your audience's willingness to accept it.

plan
The second basic issue in analyzing a question of policy: If there is a problem with current policy, does the speaker have a plan to solve the problem?

Practicality

The third basic issue of policy speeches is practicality. Once you have presented a plan, you must show that it will work. Will it solve the problem? Or will it create new and more serious problems?

> Building a multilevel parking ramp on campus would provide more student parking, but the cost would require a sharp increase in tuition.

> National testing for all high-school students would create uniform educational standards throughout the United States, but there is no guarantee it would produce better teaching and learning.

> Privatizing Social Security could help keep the system economically sound, but it might leave people who make bad investment decisions without retirement benefits.

These are significant concerns. Whenever you advocate a new policy, you must be prepared to show that it is workable. No matter how serious a problem may be, listeners usually want some assurance that a speaker's plan will actually solve the problem.[9] One way to provide this assurance is to show that a plan similar to yours has been successfully implemented elsewhere. For example, CD-ROM Video Clip 15.1 shows an excerpt from a student speech calling for mandatory foreign-language instruction in elementary schools. As you view the clip, notice how the speaker clearly presents her plan and then points to the effectiveness of similar plans in other states and countries.

View the discussion of practicality in Renee Varghese, "Multicultural, Multilingual."

CD: VIDEO CLIP 15.1

If you oppose a shift in policy, one of your major arguments will be that the change is impractical—that it will create more problems than it can solve. Many parents and educators, for instance, say that imposing standardized national tests for high-school graduation will destroy the autonomy of local school districts and result in federal control of classrooms in every part of the nation. Other opponents say that such tests will discriminate against late bloomers, racial and ethnic minorities, and other children with special needs. If listeners accept these arguments, they will probably decide that a policy requiring standardized national tests for high-school graduation should not be adopted.

How much of your speech should you devote to need, to plan, and to practicality? The answer depends on your topic and your audience. If your audience is not aware of the dangers posed by privacy-invading technology in government and business, you will have to give much of your time to need before covering plan and practicality. On the other hand, if your listeners already know about the problems of the U.S. Social Security system, you can remind them quickly of need and then devote most of your speech to plan and practicality.

Or suppose you advocate increasing the tax on cigarettes to $5.00 a pack in order to reduce smoking among teenagers. Most people agree that teen smoking is a serious health problem, but many would question whether increasing the price of cigarettes will do much to solve the problem. Therefore, you should devote a fair part of your speech to practicality—to showing that in countries which have drastically raised their cigarette taxes, the smoking rate among teenagers has dropped by as much as 60 percent.

Organizing Speeches on Questions of Policy

Effective organization is crucial when you seek to persuade listeners on a question of policy. Although any of the basic patterns of organization explained in Chapter 8 can be used when discussing a question of policy, there are four special patterns that are especially useful for policy speeches. They are problem-solution order, problem-cause-solution order, comparative advantages order, and Monroe's motivated sequence.

Problem-Solution Order

If you advocate a change in policy, your main points often will fall naturally into problem-solution order. In the first main point you demonstrate the need for a new policy by showing the extent and seriousness of the problem. In the second main point you explain your plan for solving the problem and show its practicality. For example:

> **problem-solution order**
> A method of organizing persuasive speeches in which the first main point deals with the existence of a problem and the second main point presents a solution to the problem.

Specific Purpose: To persuade my audience that action is needed to deal with the safety problems caused by motorists' use of cell phones while driving.

Central Idea: Solving the safety problems caused by using a cell phone while driving will require action by individuals and government alike.

Main Points:
    I. The widespread use of cell phones by motorists has made driving much more dangerous.
       A. Studies have shown that motorists are four to eight times more likely to be involved in an accident when they are using a cell phone.
       B. In the past three years, an alarming number of fatalities have been blamed on drivers' use of cell phones.
    II. The problem can be solved by a combination of individual and government action.
       A. Individuals should only use their cell phones while driving for genuine emergencies.
       B. Government should pass legislation restricting the use of cell phones while driving.

You can use the problem-solution format just as easily to organize a speech opposing a change in policy. In such a speech your job is to defend the current system and to attack your opponents' proposed policy. Thus in the first main point you might argue that there is *not* a need for change. In the second main point you might show that even if there were a serious problem, the suggested new policy would *not* solve it and would create serious problems of its own. For example:

Specific Purpose: To persuade my audience that Congress should not pass legislation making English the official language of the United States.

Central Idea: Making English the official language of the United States is neither necessary nor practical.

Main Points:

I. Making English the official language of the United States is not necessary.
   A. Because of its history of immigration, the U.S. has always had considerable linguistic diversity.
   B. Notwithstanding that diversity, in the long run newcomers to the U.S. almost always adopt English as their primary language.

II. Making English the official language of the United States is highly impractical.
   A. It will cost time and money that would be better spent on other issues.
   B. It will reduce the ability of states and localities to adapt to the immediate language needs of their residents.

Problem-Cause-Solution Order

problem-cause-solution order
A method of organizing persuasive speeches in which the first main point identifies a problem, the second main point analyzes the causes of the problem, and the third main point presents a solution to the problem.

For a variation on problem-solution order, you might arrange your speech in problem-cause-solution order. This produces a speech with three main points—the first identifying a problem, the second analyzing the causes of the problem, and the third presenting a solution to the problem. For example:

Specific Purpose: To persuade my audience that, if they choose to drink, they should take action to drink responsibly.

Central Idea: Excessive drinking among college students is a serious problem that can be combatted by choosing activities that are not alcohol-centered and by overcoming social pressure for excessive drinking.

Main Points:

I. Excessive drinking remains a serious problem among college students.
   A. Students who drink to excess tax a community's medical resources.
   B. Students who drink to excess cause serious problems for themselves.

II. Two causes of the problem specific to college life are social pressure and the large number of alcohol-centered activities.
   A. College has an abundance of alcohol-centered activities.
   B. There is also great social pressure on students to drink to excess.

III. There are individual solutions to these problems that you can implement right away.

View the conclusion of Joveta Dixon, "Responsible Drinking."

CD: VIDEO CLIP 15.2

Regardless of how you organize your persuasive speech, you will need strong supporting materials. You can find some materials on the Internet, but specialized sources may only be available at the library.

    A. Choose enjoyable activities that are not alcohol-centered.
    B. Learn to control social pressure for excess drinking.

Some teachers prefer this method of organization because it requires a speaker to identify the causes of the problem. This in turn makes it easier to check whether the proposed solution will get at the causes of the problem.

Comparative Advantages Order

When your audience already agrees that a problem exists, you can devote your speech to comparing the advantages and disadvantages of competing solutions. In such a situation, you might put your speech in comparative advantages order. Rather than dwelling on the problem, you would devote each main point to explaining why your solution is preferable to other proposed solutions.

comparative advantages order A method of organizing persuasive speeches in which each main point explains why a speaker's solution to a problem is preferable to other proposed solutions.

Suppose you want to convince your audience that the U.S. space program should continue to shift its emphasis from highly glamorous staffed flights such as the space shuttle to unstaffed scientific missions that gather information about other planets and the nature of the solar system. Using comparative advantages order, you would compare unstaffed scientific missions with staffed space flights and show why the former is a better choice. Your specific purpose, central idea, and main points might look like this:

Specific Purpose: To persuade my audience that the U.S. space program should continue to put greater priority on unstaffed scientific missions that gather information about the planets and the solar system.

Central Idea:	Unstaffed scientific missions are less costly and more beneficial than staffed space flights.
Main Points:	I. Unstaffed scientific missions are far less costly than staffed space flights.
	II. Unstaffed scientific missions provide many more practical benefits than staffed space flights.

Monroe's Motivated Sequence

Developed in the 1930s by Alan Monroe, a professor of speech at Purdue University, the motivated sequence is tailor-made for policy speeches that seek immediate action. The sequence has five steps that follow the psychology of persuasion:[10]

Monroe's motivated sequence
A method of organizing persuasive speeches that seek immediate action. The five steps of the motivated sequence are attention, need, satisfaction, visualization, and action.

1. *Attention.* First you gain the attention of your audience. You do this in the introduction by using one or more of the methods described in Chapter 9: relating to the audience, showing the importance of the topic, making a startling statement, arousing curiosity or suspense, posing a question, telling a dramatic story, or using visual aids.

2. *Need.* Having captured the interest of your audience, you next make them feel a need for change. You show there is a serious problem with the existing situation. It is important to state the need clearly and to illustrate it with strong supporting materials—statistics, examples, and testimony—that relate directly to the audience's values or vital interests. By the end of this step, listeners should be so concerned about the problem that they are psychologically primed to hear your solution.

3. *Satisfaction.* Having aroused a sense of need, you satisfy it by providing a solution to the problem. You present your plan and show how it will work. Be sure to offer enough details about the plan to give listeners a clear understanding of it.

4. *Visualization.* Having given your plan, you intensify desire for it by visualizing its benefits. The key to this step is using vivid imagery to show your listeners how *they* will profit from your policy. Make them *see* how much better conditions will be once your plan is adopted.

5. *Action.* Once the audience is convinced your policy is beneficial, you are ready to call for action. Say exactly what you want the audience to do—and how to do it. Give them the address to write. Tell them where they should go to join the Young Republicans. Show them how to sign up for counseling. Then conclude with a final stirring appeal that reinforces their commitment to act.

Many students prefer the motivated sequence because it is more detailed than problem-solution order. It follows the process of human thinking and leads the listener step by step to the desired action. One indication of its effectiveness is that it is widely used by people who make their living by persuasion—especially advertisers. The next time you watch television, pay close attention to the commercials. You will find that many of them follow the motivated sequence, as in this example:

Attention:	It is late in the day. We see a business conference room. A project manager and several others are gathered around a table. Some are sitting, others are standing. They are putting the final touches on the company's bid for an important contract. Tightly framed close-ups and quick snatches of conversation heighten the sense of tension and drama.
Need:	"This is great work," says an associate seated to the manager's left. "I don't see how the competition can beat it." "They can't," the manager replies. "Now we have to get it to the coast by tomorrow morning. If we don't, we're all in trouble."
Satisfaction:	The manager and her associate exchange knowing looks. "U.S. Express," they say in unison, nodding their heads in agreement. The announcer, in voice-over, tells us: "U.S. Express guarantees overnight delivery—without fail."
Visualization:	We see the business conference room the next day. The manager is listening to the speaker phone. "Your bid arrived this morning," the voice on the phone announces. "You really put all the pieces together. The competition couldn't come close." The manager and her colleagues smile in satisfaction. One person raises his right arm in a signal of triumph.
Action:	The audience is urged to rely on U.S. Express whenever shipments have to arrive overnight.

Try using the motivated sequence when you want to spur listeners to action. You should find it easy and effective, as did one student who used it in a speech urging classmates to work for passage of a local tenants' rights bill. Here are the highlights of his speech:

Attention:	Have you ever had cockroaches running through the cupboards in your apartment? Have you sweltered in the heat because the air conditioning didn't work? Or shivered in the cold because the furnace was broken? Or waited months for the security deposit you never got back even though you left your apartment as clean as when you moved in?
Need:	Throughout this city students and other apartment tenants are being victimized by unresponsive and unethical landlords. Just last year more than 200 complaints were filed with the city housing department, but no action has been taken against the landlords.
Satisfaction:	These problems could be solved by passing a strong tenants' rights bill that defines the rights of tenants, specifies the obligations of landlords, and imposes strict penalties for violators.

THE
INTERNET
Connection

As a persuasive speaker, you must understand both sides of an issue so you can answer the objections of listeners who do not support your point of view. You can use the Internet to help by visiting the websites of organizations that take opposing views. For example, if your topic is population growth, visit both Zero Population Growth (http://www.zpg.org) and the Population Research Institute (http://www.pop.org). Or, if you are speaking on gun control, access both the National Rifle Association (http://www.nra.org) and the Coalition to Stop Gun Violence (http://www.gunfree.org).

If you want your listeners to take action by writing their U.S. Senator or Representative, encourage them to use e-mail. For a list of Senate e-mail addresses, see Contacting the Senate (http://www.senate.gov/contacting/index.cfm). For assistance in contacting members of the House, log on to Write Your Representative (http://www.house.gov/writerep).

Visualization: Such bills have worked in a number of college communities across the nation. If one were passed here, you would no longer have to worry about substandard sanitary or safety conditions in your apartment. Your landlord could not violate the terms of your lease or steal your security deposit.

Action: A tenants' rights bill has been proposed to the city council. You can help get it passed by signing the petition I will pass around after my speech. I also urge you to help by circulating petitions among your friends and by turning out to support the bill when it is debated in the city council next week. If we all work together, we can get this bill through the council.

Monroe's motivated sequence is entirely compatible with the standard method of outlining discussed in Chapter 10. The following outline shows how one speaker incorporated the sequence into a speech urging her classmates to enroll in a self-defense course. In its full form, the outline included supporting materials for all the points in the speech.

Specific Purpose: To persuade my audience to enroll in a self-defense course.

Central Idea:	Enrolling in a self-defense course is an effective way for college students to protect themselves in potentially dangerous situations.

Introduction

Attention:	I. Have you ever felt unsafe walking home from the library on a dark evening?
	II. No matter where we live, crime affects us all— men and women, students and instructors, young and old.
	III. We need to stop being the victims.
	IV. Today I would like to encourage all of you to enroll in a self-defense course.

Body

Need:	I. College students face many crime issues, both as students and as members of society.
	A. Crime and violence are concerns for people in all walks of life.
	B. College students, many of whom are away from home for the first time, are especially easy targets for crime.
Satisfaction:	II. Enrolling in a self-defense course is one way we can help protect ourselves in potentially dangerous situations.
	A. On campus, the university has a club sport called Shorin Ryu Karate, which emphasizes practical self-defense.
	B. In town, Villari's Self-Defense and Tai Chi Center offers several courses in self-defense.
	C. You can also find self-defense courses by searching on the Internet or looking in the Yellow Pages.
Visualization:	III. After taking a self-defense course, you will be much better prepared to deal with an emergency situation.
	A. As I can testify from my own experience, learning the techniques of self-defense builds your confidence and helps you react correctly when danger threatens.
	B. Many other people have reported the psychological and physical benefits of taking a self-defense course.

View an excerpt from Rebecca Hanson, "Self-Defense on Campus."

CD: VIDEO CLIP 15.3

Conclusion

Action:	I. So I encourage you to enroll in a self-defense course, whether it be on campus or off, here or in your hometown.

II. Taking such a course could make the difference in protecting your property, in defending yourself or a loved one, even in saving your own life.

III. Ask yourself: Do you want to be the victim or the survivor?

Try using the motivated sequence when you seek immediate action from your listeners. Over the years it has worked for countless speakers—and it can work for you as well.

Sample Speech with Commentary

The following persuasive speech was presented in a public speaking class.[11] It deals with a question of policy and provides an excellent example of problem-solution structure.

As you read the speech, notice how the speaker deals with the issues of need, plan, and practicality. Notice also how she anticipates the potential objections of her audience and answers those objections at various stages of the speech. Finally, observe how clear and uncluttered the speech is. There are few wasted words, and the ideas progress cleanly and crisply.

The Problem with Pennies

Commentary	Speech
	Susan Ingraham
The opening quotations capture attention with their clever variations on traditional sayings about pennies.	"A nickel for your thoughts." "A nickel saved is a nickel earned." "Nickels from heaven."
The contrast between the three traditional sayings quoted here and the variations on those sayings presented in paragraph 1 provides a witty way for the speaker to lead into revealing her topic and stating her central idea. The final sentence of this paragraph—"It's time to let the dinosaur of our economy go extinct"—is especially effective.	Okay, maybe these phrases don't have quite the same ring as the original sayings—"A penny for your thoughts," "A penny saved is a penny earned," and "Pennies from heaven." But it's a fact of our nation's economic life that the penny is becoming obsolete. Inflation over the past few decades has been the death of penny candy, penny arcades, and penny bubble gum. The fact is that pennies don't buy much of anything any more. The age of the penny is over. It's time to let this dinosaur of our economy go extinct.
The speaker begins this paragraph with three questions that most listeners have in their minds at this stage of the speech. By stating that she changed her mind about	Sure, most of you say, pennies can be annoying. But why do we have to get rid of them? Why must we change something that's worked for so long? And what would we do without pennies? I had the same questions when I started work on

these questions as a result of her research, the speaker suggests that listeners should change their minds too.

The speaker starts the body of her speech by stating her first main point—that pennies cause problems for individuals, for businesses, and for the nation as a whole. Her repeated use of "you" throughout this paragraph relates the topic to the audience and helps draw them into the speech.

The speaker uses statistics and an example to support her claim that many people don't use pennies. The story from Noel Gunther works well because it is richly textured and recounts a situation with which many college students can identify.

The statistics in this paragraph are presented clearly and come from credible sources. Although most listeners were skeptical at the start of this speech about the need to abolish pennies, the strength of the speaker's evidence won most of them over by the end.

In this and the next paragraph, the speaker presents a combination of statistics and testimony to demonstrate the problems created for the nation as a whole by keeping pennies in circulation.

this speech. But as a result of my research, I'm convinced that the continued use of pennies is a costly problem and that we can get along just fine without them. Today, I hope to convince you of the same thing.

The place to begin is by noting that pennies cause problems for individuals, for businesses, and for the nation as a whole. Many Americans consider pennies a useless annoyance. According to my class survey, about two-thirds of you find pennies bothersome. They take up space and add weight to your pockets, wallets, and purses. They get in the way when you're trying to find other coins. They slow down checkout lines when you have to search for exact change. And most of the time when you really need coins—for copy machines, pay phones, and vending machines—you can't use pennies anyway.

In fact, many people *don't* use pennies. A survey by the U.S. Mint showed that only half of the 12,000 people questioned use pennies on a daily basis. Most of the other half collect pennies around the house, waiting until they have enough to cash in at the bank. It can be a long wait. In a *Los Angeles Times* article, writer Noel Gunther explained that during his last two years in college, he and his roommate saved all their pennies so they could throw a "Pennies from Heaven" party for graduation. They filled six jars with what looked like a fortune. The day before graduation, they emptied the jars and counted out $21.56—barely enough to buy beverages!

Pennies are a nuisance for the business community as well as for individuals. The National Association of Convenience Stores estimates that an average of two seconds is spent handling pennies during each of its members' 10 billion annual cash transactions. That comes out to a total of 5.5 million hours spent handling pennies—at an annual cost of $22 million. According to *Fortune* magazine, some banks charge up to 30 cents for every dollar's worth of pennies they process. This makes it very costly for some businesses to accept pennies.

Keeping pennies in circulation also costs the nation as a whole. Every year the Treasury Department takes about 7 billion pennies out of circulation because they are bent or worn out. According to the Treasury Department, several billion more pennies go into mayonnaise jars, coffee cans, piggy banks, and dresser drawers. Or they are simply thrown away. In the survey mentioned earlier in my speech, the U.S. Mint reported that 6 percent of American adults simply jettison their pennies with the trash!

The evidence in this paragraph is particularly strong and builds cumulatively to the statement, based on testimony from U.S. Treasury officials, that "it costs our society considerably more than a penny to transact a penny's worth of business."

A transition bridging the first and second main points helps listeners keep track of where the speaker is in the speech.

Now the speaker moves into her second main point, in which she presents a solution to the problems caused by pennies. The solution has four steps, each of which is explained clearly and concisely so listeners will understand exactly what the speaker is proposing.

By demonstrating how her plan will work, the speaker answers the potential objections of her audience to the plan. Notice how much less effective the speech would have been if the speaker had failed to explain the procedures by which purchases and sales taxes would be rounded off to the nearest nickel.

The speaker reaches the final step in her plan, which calls for the total elimination of pennies from the economy.

Having presented her plan, the speaker now shows its practicality. In this paragraph, she argues that pennies can be eliminated from the U.S. economy today as easily as half-cent coins were eliminated during the nineteenth-century.

To keep an adequate supply of pennies in circulation, the U.S. Mint creates approximately 12 billion new pennies each year. The cost of manufacturing these new pennies is .66 of a cent apiece, which adds up to almost $80 million a year. As Treasury officials told *U.S. News & World Report,* when you add on storage and handling expenses, it costs our society considerably more than a penny to transact a penny's worth of business.

You can now see the magnitude of the problem with pennies. Fortunately, it's a problem that can be easily solved.

The solution I recommend is similar to a plan supported by the Coin Coalition, a group working to eliminate pennies from our economy. The plan has four basic steps. First, the federal government should legalize and standardize the rounding off of all purchases to the nearest nickel. This rounding off should take place after all items in a given transaction are totaled but before the sales tax is added. Because the number of purchases rounded up would roughly equal the number rounded down, this would not cause any increased cost to consumers.

Second, the sales tax should also be rounded off to the nearest nickel. Both the customer and the state would stand an equal chance of gaining or losing a maximum of two cents on each purchase. In essence, this is no different from what you do when you file your income taxes—except that in computing your income taxes, you round everything off to the nearest dollar.

Because the first two steps of this plan will eliminate the need for pennies, the third step is for the U.S. Mint to stop making new pennies. As we have seen, this will save the taxpayers some $80 million a year in minting costs alone.

The fourth step of this plan is for people to cash in the pennies already in circulation, thereby removing pennies entirely from the money supply.

I admit that it may be hard to imagine a world without pennies, but there is plenty of evidence that this plan will work. James Benfield, Executive Director of the Coin Coalition, notes that when the U.S. stopped minting half-cent coins in 1857, a similar procedure of rounding off purchases and phasing out the coins worked extremely well. None of us miss the half-cent, and in a few years none of us will miss the penny.

Here the speaker reinforces the practicality of her plan by relating it to the everyday experiences of her audience. Dealing with questions of practicality is especially important in a speech such as this in which listeners are likely to be skeptical about the speaker's plan.

The speaker begins her conclusion by summarizing her main points.

The closing sentence of the speech is especially effective. By echoing the introduction in tone as well as content, it gives the speech a strong sense of closure and reinforces the speaker's point that eliminating pennies from the economy can be easily accomplished.

Whether we realize it or not, many of us already round off some of our purchases to the nearest nickel. Think for a moment of the "Take a Penny, Leave a Penny" containers next to the cash registers at local convenience stores. Every time you take a few pennies from the box to pay for your purchase or leave a few pennies from your change, you are actually rounding off the amount you pay to the nearest nickel.

In conclusion, pennies create problems for individuals, for businesses, and for the nation as a whole. The time and money currently wasted in using and minting pennies could be put to more productive ends. By rounding off purchases and sales taxes to the nearest nickel, by ending production of new pennies, and by letting old pennies drop out of use, the problems created by pennies could be eliminated without upsetting the economy. And just as we have gotten used to life without penny candy, penny arcades, and penny bubble gum, so I think, given time, we will also get used to the phrase "a nickel saved is a nickel earned."

Summary

Of all the kinds of public speaking, persuasion is the most complex and the most challenging. When you speak to persuade, you act as an advocate. Your job is to sell a program, to defend an idea, to refute an opponent, or to inspire people to action.

How successful you are in any particular persuasive speech will depend above all on how well you tailor your message to the values, attitudes, and beliefs of your audience. Careful listeners do not sit passively and soak in everything a speaker has to say. While they listen, they actively assess the speaker's credibility, supporting materials, language, reasoning, and emotional appeals. You should think of your speech as a kind of mental dialogue with your audience. Most important, you need to identify your target audience, anticipate the possible objections they will raise to your point of view, and answer those objections in your speech. You cannot convert skeptical listeners unless you deal directly with the reasons for their skepticism.

Persuasive speeches may center on questions of fact, questions of value, or questions of policy. Some questions of fact can be answered absolutely. Others cannot—either because the facts are murky or because there is not enough information available to us. When giving a persuasive speech about a question of fact, your role is akin to that of a lawyer in a courtroom trial. You will try to get your listeners to accept your view of the facts.

Questions of value go beyond the immediate facts to involve a person's beliefs about what is right or wrong, good or bad, moral or immoral, ethical or unethical. When speaking about a question of value, you must justify your opinion by establishing standards for your value judgment. Although questions of value often have strong implications for our actions, speeches on questions of value do not argue directly for or against particular courses of action.

Once you go beyond arguing right or wrong to urging that something should or should not be done, you move to a question of policy. When you speak on a question of policy, your goal may be to evoke passive agreement or to spark immediate action. In either case, you will face three basic issues—need, plan, and practicality. How much of your speech you devote to each issue will depend on your topic and your audience.

There are several options for organizing speeches on questions of policy. If you advocate a change in policy, your main points will often fall naturally into problem-solution order or into problem-cause-solution order. If your audience already agrees that a problem exists, you may be able to use comparative advantages order. Whenever you seek immediate action from listeners, you should consider a more specialized organizational pattern known as Monroe's motivated sequence, whose five steps are based on the psychology of persuasion.

Key Terms

persuasive speech (368)

mental dialogue with the audience (371)

target audience (371)

question of fact (373)

question of value (377)

question of policy (378)

speech to gain passive agreement (379)

speech to gain immediate action (379)

need (381)

burden of proof (381)

plan (381)

practicality (382)

problem-solution order (383)

problem-cause-solution order (384)

comparative advantages order (385)

Monroe's motivated sequence (386)

Review Questions

After reading this chapter, you should be able to answer the following questions:

1. What is the difference between an informative speech and a persuasive speech? Why is speaking to persuade more challenging than speaking to inform?

2. What does it mean to say that audiences engage in a mental dialogue with the speaker as they listen to a speech? What implications does this mental give-and-take hold for effective persuasive speaking?

3. What is the target audience for a persuasive speech?

4. What are questions of fact? How does a persuasive speech on a question of fact differ from an informative speech? Give an example of a specific purpose statement for a persuasive speech on a question of fact.

5. What are questions of value? Give an example of a specific purpose statement for a persuasive speech on a question of value.

6. What are questions of policy? Give an example of a specific purpose statement for a persuasive speech on a question of policy.

7. Explain the difference between passive agreement and immediate action as goals for persuasive speeches on questions of policy.

8. What are the three basic issues you must deal with when discussing a question of policy? What will determine the amount of attention you give to each of these issues in any particular speech?

9. What four methods of organization are used most often in persuasive speeches on questions of policy?

10. What are the five steps of Monroe's motivated sequence? Why is the motivated sequence especially useful in speeches that seek immediate action from listeners?

For further review, go to the Study Questions for this chapter

CD: STUDY QUESTIONS

Exercises for Critical Thinking

1. Look back at the story of Ramon Trujillo at the beginning of this chapter (page 368). Like Ramon, most people do a certain amount of persuading every day in normal conversation. Keep a journal of your communication activities for an entire day, making special note of all instances in which you tried to persuade someone else to your point of view. Choose one of those instances and prepare a brief analysis of it.

   In your analysis, answer the following questions: (1) Who was the audience for your persuasive effort? (2) What was the "specific purpose" and "central idea" of your persuasive message? (3) Did you rehearse your persuasive message ahead of time, or did it arise spontaneously from the situation? (4) Were you successful in achieving your specific purpose? (5) If you faced the same situation again, what strategic changes would you make in your persuasive effort?

2. Below are four specific purposes for persuasive speeches. In each case explain whether the speech associated with it concerns a question of fact, a question of value, or a question of policy. Then rewrite the specific purpose statement to make it appropriate for a speech about one of the other two kinds of questions. For instance, if the original purpose statement is about a question of policy, write a new specific purpose statement that deals with the same topic as either a question of fact or a question of value.

Example:

Original statement: To persuade my audience that it is unfair for judges to favor natural parents over adoptive parents in child custody disputes. (question of value)

Rewritten statement: To persuade my audience that the courts should establish clear guidelines for settling disputes between adoptive parents and natural parents in child custody cases. (question of policy)

a. To persuade my audience to donate time as a community volunteer.

b. To persuade my audience that violence on television is a major cause of violent behavior in society.

c. To persuade my audience that a national sales tax should be adopted to help pay off the national debt.

d. To persuade my audience that it is unethical for businesses to use genetic testing in screening potential employees.

3. Choose a topic for a persuasive speech on a question of policy. Create two specific purpose statements about that topic—one for a speech to gain passive agreement, another for a speech to motivate immediate action. Once you have the specific purpose statements, explain how the speech seeking immediate action would differ in structure and persuasive appeals from the speech seeking passive agreement. Be specific.

4. Analyze the sample speech with commentary at the end of this chapter ("The Problem with Pennies," pages 390–393). Because this is a speech on a question of policy, pay special attention to how the speaker deals with the three basic issues of need, plan, and practicality. Does the speaker present a convincing case that a serious problem exists? Does she offer a clear plan to solve the problem? Does she demonstrate that the plan is practical?

5. Select a television commercial that is organized according to Monroe's motivated sequence. Prepare a brief analysis in which you (a) identify the target audience for the commercial and (b) describe each step in the motivated sequence as it appears in the commercial.

6. Analyze the speech in Appendix B by Jennifer Conard ("The Ultimate Gift"). Because this speech is organized in Monroe's motivated sequence, pay special attention to how the speaker develops each step in the sequence—attention, need, satisfaction, visualization, action. Identify where each step of the sequence occurs in the speech and explain how the persuasive appeal of the speech builds from step to step.

*A*pplying the POWER of Public Speaking

As a local union leader, it is your job to present a contract offer made by management to your striking membership. Though the proposed offer falls short of meeting all of your union's demands, you believe it is a good offer, and in your speech, you will recommend that the union members vote to accept it.

The contract issues have been hotly debated, so you have an idea how some of your 42 members will cast their ballots. One issue is that management has guaranteed to maintain full benefits for current workers but wants to reduce benefits for new workers. Though the proposed offer limits these reductions, you know of 12 members who will vote against any proposal that limits the benefits of future workers. Already with you, however, are the 8 members who voted not to strike at all and who will vote to accept any reasonable offer. Among the undecided voters are those who think that since the strike is only in its second week, a better contract may be offered if this proposal is rejected.

Who is the target audience for your speech? How will you persuade them to vote yes on the contract offer? Which of the following methods of organization will you use for your speech, and why: problem-solution, comparative advantages, Monroe's motivated sequence?

Notes

[1] Amanda Bennett, "Economics + Meeting = A Zillion Causes and Effects," *The Wall Street Journal,* January 10, 1995, p. B1.

[2] On the difficulty of defining persuasion, see Daniel J. O'Keefe, *Persuasion: Theory and Research* (Newbury Park, Calif.: Sage, 1990), pp. 14–17; Deirdre D. Johnston, *The Art and Science of Persuasion* (Dubuque, Iowa: W. C. Brown, 1994), pp. 2–27.

[3] Kathleen Kelley Reardon, *Persuasion in Practice* (Newbury Park, Calif.: Sage, 1991), p. 3.

[4] This view of the interaction between speaker and listener reflects cognitive processing models of persuasion. For an excellent review of these models, see James B. Stiff, *Persuasive Communication* (New York: Guilford Press, 1994), pp. 175–196.

[5] There is a great deal of research confirming the need for persuasive speakers to answer potential objections to their arguments. See, for example, Mike Allen, "Comparing the Persuasive Effectiveness of One- and Two-Sided Messages," in Mike Allen and Ray W. Preiss (eds.), *Persuasion: Advances through Meta-Analysis* (Cresskill, N.J.: Hampton Press, 1997), pp. 87–98.

[6] For further discussion of questions of fact and value and the relationship between them, see David L. Vancil, *Rhetoric and Argumentation* (Boston: Allyn and Bacon, 1993), pp. 26–32.

[7] Although there has been much research on this point in recent years, the most influential study remains James Price Dillard, "Self-Inference and Foot-in-the-Door Technique," *Human Communication Research,* 16 (1990), pp. 422–447.

[8] O'Keefe, *Persuasion: Theory and Research*, pp. 159–161.

[9] Paul Mongeau, "Another Look at Fear-Arousing Appeals," in Allen and Preiss, *Persuasion: Advances through Meta-Analysis*, pp. 53–63.

[10] Raymie E. McKerrow, Bruce E. Gronbeck, Douglas Ehninger, and Alan H. Monroe, *Principles and Types of Speech Communication,* 14th ed. (New York: Longman, 2000).

[11] Reprinted with permission of Susan Ingraham.

METHODS OF PERSUASION

Roger Dawson has a secret. With this secret, Dawson promises, you can get exactly what you want from almost anyone. You can develop "an aura of personal charisma that will have people respect you, understand you, and gladly agree with you." You can acquire "a new power that's so important to you, you'll wonder how you ever got along without it!"

What is Roger Dawson's secret? He calls it the "Secret of Power Persuasion." This secret is so valuable that America's biggest corporations pay Dawson $10,000 a day to share it with them. So valuable that the Book-of-the-Month Club chose Dawson's book *Secrets of Power Persuasion* as one of its offerings. So valuable that thousands of people have purchased Dawson's *Secrets of Power Persuasion* audiocassette.[1]

Can Dawson really give people "magical persuasion techniques" that will transform their lives? Probably not. Persuasion is too complicated for that. Yet, as the popularity of Dawson's book, tape, and business seminars shows, there is a perpetual fascination with the strategies and tactics of effective persuasion.

What makes a speaker persuasive? Why do listeners accept one speaker's views and reject those of another speaker? How can a speaker motivate listeners to act in support of a cause, a campaign, or a candidate? People have been trying to answer these questions for thousands of years—from the ancient Greek philosopher Aristotle to modern-day communication researchers. Although many answers have been given, we can say that listeners will be persuaded by a speaker for one or more of four reasons:

Because they perceive the speaker as having high *credibility*.

Because they are won over by the speaker's *evidence*.

Because they are convinced by the speaker's *reasoning*.

Because their *emotions* are touched by the speaker's ideas or language.

In this chapter we will look at each of these. We will not discover any magical secrets that will make you an irresistible persuasive speaker. Persuasion is a complex activity that cannot be reduced to snappy formulas or simple techniques. But if you learn the principles discussed in this chapter and apply them astutely, you will greatly increase your odds of winning the minds and hearts of your listeners.

Building Credibility

Here are two sets of imaginary statements. Which one of each pair would you be more likely to believe?

The U.S. judicial system needs major changes to deal with the increased number of court cases. (Sandra Day O'Connor)

The U.S. judicial system is working fine and does not need any major changes at this time. (Stephen King)

The horror novel is entering a more sophisticated stage as writers develop new character types and plot devices. (Stephen King)

The horror novel is declining in quality compared with other forms of popular fiction. (Sandra Day O'Connor)

Most likely you chose the first in each pair of statements. If so, you were probably influenced by your perception of the speaker. You are more likely to respect the judgment of O'Connor, U.S. Supreme Court justice, when she speaks about the judicial system, and to respect the judgment of King, author of *Carrie*, *The Shining*, and more than 40 other books, when he speaks about trends in the horror novel. Some teachers call this factor *source credibility*. Others refer to it as *ethos*, the name given by Aristotle.

ethos
The name used by Aristotle for what modern students of communication refer to as credibility.

Factors of Credibility

Over the years researchers have given much time to studying credibility and its effect on speechmaking. They have discovered that many things affect a speaker's credibility, including sociability, dynamism, physical attractiveness, and perceived similarity between speaker and audience. Above all, though, a speaker's credibility is affected by two factors.

- *Competence*—how an audience regards a speaker's intelligence, expertise, and knowledge of the subject.

- *Character*—how an audience regards a speaker's sincerity, trustworthiness, and concern for the well-being of the audience.[2]

credibility
The audience's perception of whether a speaker is qualified to speak on a given topic. The two major factors influencing a speaker's credibility are competence and character.

The more favorably listeners view a speaker's competence and character, the more likely they are to accept what the speaker says. No doubt you are familiar with this from your own experience. Suppose you take a course in economics. The course is taught by a distinguished professor who has published widely in all the prestigious journals, who sits on a major international commission, and who has won several awards for outstanding research. In class, you hang on this professor's every word. One day the professor is absent; a colleague of hers from the Economics Department—fully qualified but not as well known—comes to lecture in the professor's place. Possibly the fill-in instructor gives the same lecture the distinguished professor would have given, but you do not pay nearly as close attention. The other instructor does not have as high credibility as the professor.

It is important to remember that credibility is an attitude. It exists not in the speaker, but in the mind of the audience. A speaker may have high credibility for one audience and low credibility for another. A speaker may also have high credibility on one topic and low credibility on another. Looking back to our imaginary statements, most people would more readily believe Stephen King speaking about horror novels than Stephen King speaking about the judicial system.

Types of Credibility

Not only can a speaker's credibility vary from audience to audience and topic to topic, but it can also change during the course of a speech—so much so that we can identify three types of credibility:

■ *Initial credibility*—the credibility of the speaker before she or he starts to speak.

■ *Derived credibility*—the credibility of the speaker produced by everything she or he says and does during the speech itself.

■ *Terminal credibility*—the credibility of the speaker at the end of the speech.[3]

All three are dynamic. High initial credibility is a great advantage for any speaker, but it can be destroyed during a speech, resulting in low terminal credibility. The reverse can also occur. A speaker with low initial credibility may enhance her or his credibility during the speech and end up with high terminal credibility, as in the following example:

Barry Devins manages the computer and information systems for a major non-profit research foundation. Soon after taking the job, he purchased a highly touted internal e-mail system and installed it on all the foundation's computers. Barry assumed there would be some glitches, but they far exceeded anything he had imagined. It took him almost six months to get the system working properly, and even then people continued to grumble about all the messages they had lost during the phase-in period.

A year later, the foundation was awarded a large contract, and the president decided to purchase a new computer system for the entire organization. She asked Barry to take charge of buying the system and training the staff in its use. She suggested that he outline his plans at a weekly staff meeting.

As you might expect, Barry had low initial credibility when he stood up to address the staff. Everyone remembered vividly the trouble caused by the e-mail system, and they were extremely reluctant to go through such a process again. But Barry realized this and was prepared.

He began by reminding everyone that the president had authorized him to purchase a truly state-of-the-art system that would make their lives easier and improve coordination throughout the office. He then acknowledged that he had told them the same thing before installing the e-mail system—an admission that drew a laugh and helped everyone relax. Using a notebook computer like the ones he intended to purchase, Barry projected a series of PowerPoint slides showing the capabilities of the new system and a time line for installation. He also explained that he had checked with several other organizations that had installed the same system, and they all had told him that it worked flawlessly.

All through his presentation, Barry took the approach, "I know the e-mail system was something of a disaster, and I have worked hard to make sure we don't suffer such an experience again." By the time he finished, most staff members were eager to get their new computers. Barry had achieved high terminal credibility.

In classroom speeches, you will not face the same problems with credibility as do controversial public figures. Nonetheless, credibility is important in *every* speaking situation, no matter who the participants are or where it takes place. In every speech you give you will have some degree of initial credibility, which will always be strengthened or weakened by your message and how you deliver it. And your terminal credibility from one speech will affect your initial credibility for the next one. If your classmates see you as sincere and competent, they will be much more receptive to your ideas.

Enhancing Your Credibility

How can you build your credibility in your speeches? At one level, the answer is frustratingly general. Since everything you say and do in a speech will affect your credibility, you should say and do *everything* in a way that will make you appear capable and trustworthy. Good organization will improve your credibility. So will appropriate, clear, vivid language. So will fluent, dynamic delivery. So will strong evidence and cogent reasoning. In other words—give a brilliant speech and you will achieve high credibility!

The advice is sound, but not all that helpful. There are, however, some specific, proven ways you can boost your credibility while speaking. They include explaining your competence, establishing common ground with the audience, and speaking with genuine conviction.

Explain Your Competence

One way to enhance your credibility is to advertise your expertise on the speech topic. Did you investigate the topic thoroughly? Then say so. Do you have experience that gives you special knowledge or insight? Again, say so.

Here is how two students revealed their qualifications. The first stressed his study and research:

> I never knew much about UFOs until I did a research project on them in my high-school science class. Since then, I have read quite a bit about them, including the latest reports of the highly respected Center for UFO Studies in Evanston, Illinois. As a result, I have decided that the evidence strongly suggests that Earth has been—and continues to be—visited by spaceships from other planets.

The second student, who spoke about the dangers of chewing tobacco, emphasized her background and personal experience, as well as her research. After opening with a story about a 23-year-old man named Tom who died from oral cancer caused by his use of chewing tobacco, she said:

View this portion of Catherine Twohig, "The Dangers of Chewing Tobacco."

CD: VIDEO CLIP 16.1

> Due to the fact that I am currently studying to be a dentist, and because my father is a dentist and I have worked for him as an assistant for over four years, I have actually seen cases similar to Tom's which result from chewing tobacco. I have also attended a number of seminars on this topic, and today I'd like to persuade each of you to feel as strongly as I do about the dangers of chewing tobacco.

In both of these cases, the speakers greatly increased their persuasiveness by establishing their credibility.

Establish Common Ground with Your Audience

Another way to bolster your credibility is to establish common ground with your audience. You do not persuade listeners by assaulting their values and rejecting their opinions. This approach only antagonizes people. It puts them on the defensive and makes them resist your ideas. As the old saying goes, "You catch more flies with honey than with vinegar." The same is true of persuasion. Show respect for your listeners. You can make your speech more appealing by identifying your ideas with those of your audience—by showing how your point of view is consistent with what they believe.[4]

A speaker's credibility has a powerful impact on how the speech is received by the audience. One way to bolster your credibility is to deliver your speeches expressively and with strong eye contact.

creating common ground

A technique in which a speaker connects himself or herself with the values, attitudes, or experiences of the audience.

Creating common ground is especially important at the start of a persuasive speech. Begin by identifying with your listeners. Show that you share their values, attitudes, and experiences. Get them nodding their heads in agreement, and they will be much more receptive to your ultimate proposal. Here is how a businesswoman from Massachusetts, hoping to sell her product to an audience of people in Colorado, began her persuasive speech:

I have never been in Colorado before, but I really looked forward to making this trip. A lot of my ancestors left Massachusetts and came to Colorado nearly 150 years ago. Sometimes I have wondered why they did it. They came in covered wagons, carrying all their possessions, and many of them died on the journey. The ones who got through raised their houses and raised their families. Now that I've seen Colorado, I understand why they tried so hard!

The audience laughed and applauded, and the speaker was off to a good start.

This method of establishing common ground is used often in speeches outside the classroom. Now look at a different approach, used in a classroom speech favoring a tuition increase at the speaker's school—a very unpopular point of view with his classmates. He began by saying:

As we all know, there are many differences among the people in this class. But regardless of our age, major, background, or goals, we all have one thing in common—we are all concerned about the quality of education at this school. And that quality is clearly in danger. Because of budget reductions, faculty salaries have fallen below those at comparable schools, library purchases have been cut back, and more and more students are being crowded out of classes they need to take. Whether we like it or not, we have a problem—a problem that affects each of us. Today I would like to discuss this problem and whether it can be solved by an increase in tuition.

By stressing common perceptions of the problem, the student hoped to get off on the right foot with his audience. Once that was done, he moved gradually to his more controversial ideas.

Deliver Your Speeches Fluently, Expressively, and with Conviction

There is a great deal of research to show that a speaker's credibility is strongly affected by his or her delivery. Moderately fast speakers, for example, are usually seen as more intelligent and confident than slower speakers. So too are speakers who use vocal variety to communicate their ideas in a lively, animated way. On the other hand, speakers who consistently lose their place, hesitate frequently, or pepper their talk with vocalized pauses such as "uh," "er," and "um" are seen as significantly less competent than speakers who are more poised and dynamic.[5]

All of this argues for practicing your persuasive speech fully ahead of time so you can deliver it fluently and expressively. In addition to being better prepared, you will take a major step toward enhancing your credibility. (Be sure to review Chapter 12 if you have questions about speech delivery.)

Speaking techniques aside, the most important way to strengthen your credibility is to deliver your speeches with genuine conviction. President Harry Truman once said that in speaking, "sincerity, honesty, and a straightforward manner are more important than special talent or polish." If you wish to convince others, you must first convince yourself. If you want others to believe and care about your ideas, you must believe and care about them yourself. Let your audience know you are in earnest—that your speech is not just a classroom exercise. Your spirit, your enthusiasm, your conviction will carry over to your listeners.

Using Evidence

Evidence consists of supporting materials—examples, statistics, testimony—used to prove or disprove something. As we saw in Chapter 7, most people are skeptical. They are suspicious of unsupported generalizations. They want speakers to justify their claims. If you hope to be persuasive, you must support your views with evidence. Whenever you say something that is open to question, you should give evidence to prove you are right.

Evidence is particularly important in classroom speeches because few students are recognized as experts on their speech topics. Research has shown that speakers with very high initial credibility do not need to use as much evidence as do speakers with lower credibility. For most speakers, though, strong evidence is absolutely necessary. It can enhance your credibility, increase both the immediate and long-term persuasiveness of your message, and help "inoculate" listeners against counterpersuasion.[6]

Evidence is also crucial whenever your target audience opposes your point of view. As we saw in Chapter 15, listeners in such a situation will not only be skeptical of your ideas, they will challenge them at every step of the speech. They will mentally argue with you—asking questions, raising

evidence
Supporting materials used to prove or disprove something.

objections, and creating counterarguments to "answer" what you say. The success of your speech will depend partly on how well you anticipate these internal responses and give evidence to refute them.[7]

You may want to review Chapter 7, which shows how to use supporting materials. The following case study illustrates how they work as evidence in a persuasive speech.

How Evidence Works: A Case Study

Let's say one of your classmates is talking about the harmful effects of repeated exposure to loud music and other noises. Instead of just telling you what she thinks, the speaker offers you strong evidence to prove her point. As you read the case study, notice how the speaker carries on a mental dialogue with her listeners. At each juncture she imagines what they might be thinking, anticipates their questions and objections, and gives evidence to answer the questions and resolve the objections.

She begins this way:

As college students we are exposed to loud music and other noise all the time. We go to parties, clubs, and concerts where the volume is so loud we have to shout so the person next to us can hear what we are saying. We play our personal stereos so high they can be heard halfway across the room. And we seldom give it a second thought. But we should, because excessive noise can have a serious impact on our health and well-being.

How do you react? If you already know about the problems caused by noise pollution, you probably nod your head in agreement. But what if you don't know? Or don't agree? If you enjoy rock concerts and listening to your personal stereo at high volumes, you probably don't *want* to hear anything bad about it. Certainly you will not be persuaded by the general statement that exposure to loud music and other noises can have "a serious impact on our health and well-being." Mentally you say to the speaker, "How do you know? Can you prove it?"

Anticipating just such a response, the speaker gives evidence to support her point:

The American Medical Association reports that 28 million Americans suffer from serious hearing loss, and that 10 million of those cases are caused by too much exposure to loud noise.

"That's unfortunate," you may think. "But everyone loses some hearing as they grow old. Why should I be concerned about it now?" The speaker answers:

According to *Health* magazine, more and more victims of noise-induced deafness are adolescents and even younger children. Dr. James Snow, director of the National Institute on Deafness, reports that noise-induced hearing loss can begin as early as 10 years of age. Audiologist Dean Garsetcki, head of the hearing-impairment program at Northwestern University, says, "We've got 21-year-olds walking around with hearing-loss patterns of people 40 years their senior."

"These are impressive facts," you say to yourself. "Luckily, I haven't noticed any problems with my hearing. When I do, I'll just be careful until it gets better." Keeping one step ahead of you, the speaker continues:

The problem with hearing loss is that it creeps up on you. *Sierra* magazine notes that today's heavy-metal fans won't notice the effects of their hearing loss for another 15 years. And then it will be too late.

"What do you mean, too late?" you ask mentally. The speaker tells you:

Unlike some physical conditions, hearing loss is irreversible. Loud noise damages the microscopic hairs in the inner ear that transmit sound to the auditory nerve. Once damaged, those hairs can never recover and can never be repaired.

"I didn't know that," you say to yourself. "Is there anything else?"

One last point. Repeated exposure to loud music and other noise does more than damage your hearing. The latest issue of *Prevention* magazine reports that excessive noise has been linked to such problems as stress, high blood pressure, chronic headaches, fatigue, learning disorders, even heart disease. It's easy to see why Jill Lipoti, chief of Rutgers University's Noise Technical Assistance Center, warns that "noise affects more people than any other pollutant."

Now are you convinced? Chances are you will at least think about the possible consequences the next time you are set to pump up the volume on your stereo. Maybe you will use earplugs when you sit in front of the speakers at a rock concert. You may even begin to reassess your whole attitude toward the problem of noise pollution. Why? Because the speaker did not just spout her opinions as if they were common knowledge, but instead supported each of her claims with evidence. You should try to do the same in your persuasive speeches.

Tips for Using Evidence

Any of the supporting materials discussed in Chapter 7—examples, statistics, testimony—can work as evidence in a persuasive speech. As we saw in that chapter, there are guidelines for using each kind of supporting material regardless of the kind of speech you are giving. Here we need to look at four special tips for using evidence in a persuasive speech.

Use Specific Evidence

No matter what kind of evidence you employ—statistics, examples, or testimony—it will be more persuasive if you state it in specific rather than general terms.[8] In the speech about noise pollution, for instance, the speaker did not say, "Lots of people suffer from hearing loss." That would have left the audience wondering how many "lots" amounts to. By saying, "28 million Americans suffer from serious hearing loss," the speaker made her point much more effectively. She also enhanced her credibility by showing she had a firm grasp of the facts.

Use Novel Evidence

Evidence is more likely to be persuasive if it is new to the audience.[9] You will gain little by citing facts and figures that are already well known to your listeners. If those facts and figures have not persuaded your listeners already, they will not do so now. You must go beyond what the audience already knows and present striking new evidence that will get them to say, "Hmmm, I didn't know *that*. Maybe I should rethink the issue." Finding such evidence is not always easy. It usually requires hard digging and resourceful research, but the rewards can be well worth the effort.

Use Evidence from Credible Sources

The Evidence Checklist can help you prepare your persuasive speech.

CD: SPEECH CHECKLIST

There is a good deal of research to show that listeners find evidence from competent, credible sources more persuasive than evidence from less qualified sources.[10] Above all, listeners are suspicious of evidence from sources that appear to be biased or self-interested. In assessing the current state of airline safety, for example, they are more likely to be persuaded by testimony from impartial aviation experts than by statements from the president of American Airlines. In judging the conflict between a corporation and the union striking against it, they will usually be leery of statistics offered by either side. If you wish to be persuasive—especially to careful listeners—you should rely on evidence from objective, nonpartisan sources.

Make Clear the Point of Your Evidence

When speaking to persuade, you use evidence to prove a point. Yet you would be surprised how many novice speakers present their evidence without making clear the point it is supposed to prove. A number of studies have shown that you cannot count on listeners to draw, on their own, the conclusion you want them to reach.[11] When using evidence, be sure listeners understand the point you are trying to make.

Suppose, for example, that you recite the following evidence about the growth of America's coyote population:

> Despite being hunted and trapped relentlessly for over 100 years, coyotes now live in every state of the Union except Hawaii. According to *Smithsonian* magazine, Mississippi has more than 200,000 coyotes, Massachusetts and Pennsylvania both have several thousand, and there is even a good-sized coyote population in parts of New York City.

What is the point of this evidence? That efforts to control America's coyote population should be expanded because there are too many coyotes? Or that programs to control America's coyote population are futile and should be stopped? On the basis of the evidence, a listener could draw either conclusion. To help prevent this from happening, you should be sure to state the conclusion you want the audience to draw.

logos
The name used by Aristotle for the logical appeal of a speaker. The two major elements of *logos* are evidence and reasoning.

Evidence is one element of what Aristotle referred to as *logos*—the logical appeal of a speaker. The other major element of *logos* is reasoning, which works in combination with evidence to help make a speaker's claims persuasive.

The story is told about Hack Wilson, a hard-hitting outfielder for the Brooklyn Dodgers baseball team in the 1930s.[12] Wilson was a great player, but he had a fondness for the good life. His drinking exploits were legendary. He was known to spend the entire night on the town, stagger into the team's hotel at the break of dawn, grab a couple of hours sleep, and get to the ballpark just in time for the afternoon game.

This greatly distressed Max Carey, Wilson's manager. At the next team meeting, Carey spent much time explaining the evils of drink. To prove his point, he stood beside a table on which he had placed two glasses and a plate of live angleworms. One glass was filled with water, the other with gin—Wilson's favorite beverage. With a flourish Carey dropped a worm into the glass of water. It wriggled happily. Next Carey plunged the same worm into the gin. It promptly stiffened and expired.

A murmur ran through the room, and some players were obviously impressed. But not Wilson. He didn't even seem interested. Carey waited a little, hoping for some delayed reaction from his wayward slugger. When none came, he prodded, "Do you follow my reasoning, Wilson?"

"Sure, skipper," answered Wilson. "It proves that if you drink gin, you'll never get worms!"

What does this story prove? No matter how strong your evidence, you will not be very persuasive unless listeners grasp your reasoning. You should know, therefore, how to reason clearly and persuasively.

Many people think of reasoning as an esoteric subject of interest only to philosophers, but we all use reasoning every day in practical life. Reasoning is simply the process of drawing a conclusion based on evidence. Sometimes we reason well—as when we conclude that ice particles forming on the trees may mean the roads will be slippery. Other times we reason less effectively—as when we conclude that spilling salt will bring bad luck. Most superstitions are actually no more than instances of faulty reasoning.

As we saw in Chapter 1, reasoning is an important component of critical thinking, and it permeates all areas of our lives. We are bombarded daily with persuasive messages ranging from television commercials to political appeals. Sometimes the reasoning in those messages is sound, but often it is faulty—as when we are told that drinking Pepsi will make us more youthful or that using a Dell personal computer will turn the drudgery of writing a term paper into an effortless pleasure. Unless you know how to reason clearly, you may be easy prey for unscrupulous advertisers and glib politicians.

Reasoning in public speaking is an extension of reasoning in other aspects of life. As a public speaker you have two major concerns with respect to reasoning. First, you must make sure your own reasoning is sound. Second, you must try to get listeners to agree with your reasoning. Let us look, then, at four basic methods of reasoning and how to use them in your speeches.[13]

reasoning
The process of drawing a conclusion on the basis of evidence.

Reasoning from Specific Instances

When you reason from specific instances, you progress from a number of particular facts to a general conclusion.[14] For example:

Fact 1:   My physical education course last term was easy.

Fact 2:   My roommate's physical education course was easy.

Fact 3:   My brother's physical education course was easy.

Conclusion: Physical education courses are easy.

reasoning from specific instances
Reasoning that moves from particular facts to a general conclusion.

As this example suggests, we use reasoning from specific instances daily, although we probably don't realize it. Think for a moment of all the general conclusions that arise in conversation: Politicians are corrupt. Professors are bookish. Dorm food is awful. Accounting courses are hard. Republicans are conservative. Marines are tough. Where do such conclusions come from? They come from observing particular politicians, professors, Republicans, marines, accounting courses, and so on.

The same thing happens in public speaking. The speaker who concludes that America's drinking water is becoming unsafe because several cities have had major outbreaks of waterborne diseases in recent years is reasoning from specific instances. So is the speaker who claims that commercial air travel is becoming less safe because several major plane crashes have occurred in the past year. And so is the speaker who argues that racial tension is growing because a number of black churches have been burned in the South.

Such conclusions are never foolproof. No matter how many specific instances you give (and you can give only a few in a speech), it is always possible that an exception exists. Throughout the ages people observed countless white swans in Europe without seeing any of a different color. It seemed an undeniable fact that all swans were white. Then in the nineteenth century, black swans were discovered in Australia![15]

Guidelines for Reasoning from Specific Instances

When you reason from specific instances, you should follow a few basic guidelines.

hasty generalization
An error in reasoning from specific instances, in which a speaker jumps to a general conclusion on the basis of insufficient evidence.

First, avoid generalizing too hastily. Beware of the tendency to jump to conclusions on the basis of insufficient evidence. Make sure your sample of specific instances is large enough to justify your conclusion. Also make sure the instances you present are fair, unbiased, and representative. (Are three physical education courses *enough* to conclude that physical education courses in general are easy? Are the three courses *typical* of most physical education courses?)

Second, be careful with your wording. If your evidence does not justify a sweeping conclusion, qualify your argument. Suppose you are talking about the crisis in America's national park system brought on by overuse and commercial development. You document the problem by discussing some specific instances—Yosemite, Yellowstone, the Everglades. Then you draw your conclusion. You might say:

As we have seen, America's national park system is serving almost 400 million people a year, with the result that some parks are being overcome by traffic, pollution, and garbage. We have also seen that more and more parks are being exploited for mining, logging, and other forms of commercial development. It certainly seems fair, then, to conclude that new measures are needed to ensure that the beauty, serenity, and biological diversity of America's national parks are preserved for future generations as well as for our own.

Persuasive speeches need strong evidence to convince skeptical listeners. Finding the best evidence takes hard digging and resourceful research, but it is well worth the effort.

This is not as dramatic as saying, "America's national parks are on the brink of destruction," but it is more accurate and will be more persuasive to careful listeners.

Third, reinforce your argument with statistics or testimony. Since you can never give enough specific instances in a speech to make your conclusion irrefutable, you should supplement them with testimony or statistics demonstrating that the instances are in fact representative. Suppose you are talking about identity theft, in which larcenists use stolen identities to open credit-card accounts, get loans, take over bank accounts, and even establish criminal records in other people's names. You might say:

> One of America's fastest-growing crimes, identity theft is causing havoc for innocent people across the country. Theresa May, an English professor in Georgia, was victimized by a California woman of the same name who obtained her Social Security number and then applied for loans, defaulted on the payments, and filed for bankruptcy—all in the professor's name. In Ohio, a successful businesswoman's Social Security number was stolen by a thief who escaped to another state, where she used the Ohio woman's identity to obtain a driver's license and several credit cards, on which she ran up a slew of charges. As a result, the businesswoman, who had impeccable credit, was denied a mortgage.

The specific examples help make the conclusion persuasive, but a listener could easily dismiss them as sensational and atypical. To prevent this from happening, you might go on to say:

Although these examples are dramatic, they are representative of what is happening around the country. According to a report published in the *Los Angeles Times,* reported identity theft complaints nationally have risen from fewer than 40,000 in 1992 to more than 750,000 this past year. Image Data LLC, a fraud prevention service based in Nashua, New Hampshire, estimates that one in every five Americans or a member of their family have been a victim of some kind of identity fraud. Beth Givens, director of the Privacy Rights Clearinghouse, a nonprofit consumer rights organization, says the problem is so serious that it has reached "epidemic proportions."

With this backup material, not even a skeptical listener could reject your examples as isolated.

When you reason from specific instances in a speech, you can either state your conclusion and then give the specific instances on which it is based or give the specific instances and then draw your conclusion. Look back at the example about national parks on page 410. In that example, the speaker first gives three facts and then draws a conclusion ("It certainly seems fair, then, to conclude that new measures are needed to ensure that the beauty, serenity, and biological diversity of America's national parks are preserved for future generations as well as for our own").

Now look again at the example just given about identity theft. In this example, the conclusion—"One of America's fastest-growing crimes, identity theft is causing havoc for innocent people across the country"—is stated first, followed by two specific instances. It doesn't matter which order you use as long as your facts support your conclusion.

Reasoning from Principle

reasoning from principle
Reasoning that moves from a general principle to a specific conclusion.

Reasoning from principle is the opposite of reasoning from specific instances. It moves from the general to the specific.[16] When you reason from principle, you progress from a general principle to a specific conclusion. We are all familiar with this kind of reasoning from statements such as the following:

1. All people are mortal.

2. Socrates is a person.

3. Therefore, Socrates is mortal.

This is a classic example of reasoning from principle. You begin with a general statement ("All people are mortal"), move to a minor premise ("Socrates is a person"), and end with a specific conclusion ("Socrates is mortal").

Speakers often use reasoning from principle when trying to persuade an audience. One of the clearest examples from American history is Susan B. Anthony's famous speech "Is It a Crime for U.S. Citizens to Vote?" Delivered on numerous occasions in 1872 and 1873, at a time when women were legally barred from voting, Anthony's speech reasoned along the following lines:

1. The United States Constitution guarantees all U.S. citizens the right to vote.

2. Women are U.S. citizens.

3. Therefore, the United States Constitution guarantees women the right to vote.

This, too, is an instance of reasoning from principle. It progresses from a general principle ("The United States Constitution guarantees all U.S. citizens the right to vote") through a minor premise ("Women are U.S. citizens") to a conclusion ("Therefore, the United States Constitution guarantees women the right to vote").[17]

Guidelines for Reasoning from Principle

When you use reasoning from principle in a speech, pay special attention to your general principle. Will listeners accept it without evidence? If not, give evidence to support it before moving to your minor premise. You may also need to support your minor premise with evidence. When both the general principle and the minor premise are soundly based, your audience will be much more likely to accept your conclusion.

Suppose, for example, that you plan to speak about excessive salt in the American diet. You begin by formulating a specific purpose:

Specific Purpose: To persuade my audience to limit their consumption of fast foods, canned goods, and frozen foods because of their excessive salt content.

Next, you decide to use reasoning from principle to help persuade your audience. Your argument looks like this:

1. Excessive consumption of salt is unhealthy.

2. Fast foods, canned goods, and frozen foods contain excessive amounts of salt.

3. Therefore, excessive consumption of fast foods, canned goods, and frozen foods is unhealthy.

To make the argument persuasive, you have to support your general principle: "Excessive consumption of salt is unhealthy." You cite medical evidence and research studies. Part of your speech might go like this:

High salt intake has been linked with hypertension, or high blood pressure, which is a major cause of heart disease, kidney disease, and stroke. In northern Japan, where the typical diet contains enormous amounts of sodium, hypertension is the major cause of death. But among people who eat very little salt, such as the preliterate tribes of New Guinea, hypertension and hypertension-related deaths are virtually unknown.

Having supported your general principle, you now go on to bolster your minor premise: "Fast foods, canned goods, and frozen foods contain excessive amounts of salt." Your evidence includes the following:

The human body needs only 230 milligrams of sodium per day to function efficiently. But many fast foods, canned goods, and frozen foods deliver several times that amount in a single serving. One McDonald's Big Mac has 1,510 milligrams of sodium—

nearly seven times the daily requirement. One serving of canned tomato soup has 1,050 milligrams of sodium—nearly five times the daily requirement. One frozen turkey dinner has 2,567 milligrams of sodium—*eleven* times the daily requirement. No wonder we have a salt overload!

Now you have lined up your ammunition very effectively. You have supported your general principle and your minor premise. You can feel confident in going on to your conclusion.

Therefore, excessive consumption of fast foods, canned goods, and frozen foods is unhealthy.

And you can expect your audience to take you seriously. When used properly, reasoning from principle is highly persuasive.

Causal Reasoning

causal reasoning
Reasoning that seeks to establish the relationship between causes and effects.

There is a patch of ice on the sidewalk. You slip, fall, and break your arm. You reason as follows: "*Because* that patch of ice was there, I fell and broke my arm." This is an example of causal reasoning, in which someone tries to establish the relationship between causes and effects. In this example the causal reasoning is pretty straightforward. You can test it in reverse: "If the patch of ice *hadn't* been there, I wouldn't have fallen and broken my arm."

As with reasoning from specific instances, we use causal reasoning daily. Something happens and we ask what caused it to happen. We want to know the causes of violent crime, of the football team's latest defeat, of our roommate's peculiar habits. We also wonder about effects. We speculate about the consequences of television violence on young children, of the star quarterback's leg injury, of telling our roommate that a change is needed.

Guidelines for Causal Reasoning

As any scientist (or detective) will tell you, causal reasoning can be a tricky business. The relationship between causes and effects is not always as clear as it seems. There are two common errors to avoid when using causal reasoning.

false cause
An error in causal reasoning in which a speaker mistakenly assumes that because one event follows another, the first event is the cause of the second. This error is often known by its Latin name, *post hoc, ergo propter hoc,* meaning "after this, therefore because of this."

The first is the fallacy of false cause. This fallacy is often known by its Latin name, *post hoc, ergo propter hoc,* which means "after this, therefore because of this." In other words, the fact that one event happens after another does not mean that the first is the cause of the second. The closeness in time of the two events may be entirely coincidental. If a black cat crosses your path and five minutes later you fall and break your arm, you needn't blame your accident on the poor cat.

One student in speech class argued that the cold war that existed between the Western democracies and the communist nations of eastern Europe until the demolishing of the Berlin Wall in 1989 was caused by the United States' decision to drop the atomic bomb at Hiroshima and Nagasaki at the end of World War II. His reasoning? Hiroshima and Nagasaki were bombed in August 1945. The cold war began a few months later. Therefore, the beginning of the cold war was caused by the bombing of Hiroshima and

Nagasaki. The student's classmates were not persuaded. They pointed out that the simple fact that the cold war started after the bombing of Hiroshima and Nagasaki does not prove that it was *caused* by the bombing; the cold war would have broken out even if the United States had not dropped atomic bombs on Japan.

A second pitfall when using causal reasoning is assuming that events have only one cause. We all tend to oversimplify events by attributing them to single, isolated causes. In fact, though, most events have several causes. What, for example, causes the election of a presidential candidate? Unhappiness with the incumbent? A good media campaign? Economic conditions? Desire for a change? World affairs? Support of the party regulars? A clever makeup job for a television debate? A solid, intelligent party platform? *All* of these factors—and others—affect the outcome of a presidential election. When you use causal reasoning, be wary of the temptation to attribute complex events to single causes.

You cannot escape causal reasoning. All of us use it daily, and you are almost certain to use it when speaking to persuade—especially if you deal with a question of fact or policy.

Analogical Reasoning

What do these statements have in common?

If you're good at racquetball, you'll be great at Ping-Pong.

In Great Britain the general election campaign for Prime Minister lasts less than three weeks. Surely we can do the same with the U.S. presidential election.

analogical reasoning Reasoning in which a speaker compares two similar cases and infers that what is true for the first case is also true for the second.

Both statements use reasoning from analogy. By comparing two similar cases, they infer that what is true for one must be true for the other. The first speaker reasons that because a person is good at playing racquetball, he or she should also be good at playing Ping-Pong. The second speaker reasons that because the British can elect a Prime Minister with less than three weeks of campaigning, the United States should be able to do the same when electing a President.

Guidelines for Analogical Reasoning

The most important question in assessing analogical reasoning is whether the two cases being compared are essentially alike. If they are essentially alike, the analogy is valid. If they are not essentially alike, the analogy is invalid.

invalid analogy
An analogy in which the two cases being compared are not essentially alike.

Look back, for example, to the analogies at the start of this section. Is playing racquetball the same as playing Ping-Pong? Not really. To be sure, both involve hitting the ball with a racquet or a paddle. But racquetball uses a stringed racquet and a rubber ball. Ping-Pong uses a solid paddle and a smaller, lighter, celluloid ball. Racquetball is played by hitting the ball against the walls or ceiling of an enclosed court. Ping-Pong is played by hitting the ball back and forth over a net stretched across a table. Skill at one is no guarantee of skill at the other. The analogy is not valid.

What about the second analogy? That depends on how much alike the British and American political systems are. Are the countries similar in size and diversity? Is it possible for candidates in both countries to canvass the entire land in less than three weeks? Do both countries have nationwide primaries before the general election? Are the two electorates equally informed about political issues? Does the party system operate the same in both countries? In other words, are the factors that allow Great Britain to conduct campaigns for Prime Minister in less than three weeks also present in the United States? If so, the analogy is valid. If not, the analogy is invalid.

Reasoning from analogy is used most often in persuasive speeches on questions of policy. When arguing for a new policy, you should find out whether a similar policy has been tried somewhere else. You may be able to claim that your policy will work because it has worked in like circumstances elsewhere. Here is how one student used reasoning from analogy to support her claim that controlling handguns will reduce violent crime in the United States:

Will my policy work? The experience of foreign countries suggests it will. In England, guns are tightly regulated; even the police are unarmed, and the murder rate is trivial by American standards. In Japan, the ownership of weapons is severely restricted, and handguns are completely prohibited. Japan is an almost gun-free country, and its crime rate is even lower than England's. On the basis of these comparisons, we can conclude that restricting the ownership of guns will control the crime and murder rates in America.

By the same token, if you argue against a change in policy, you should check whether the proposed policy—or something like it—has been implemented elsewhere. Here, too, you may be able to support your case by reasoning from analogy—as did one student who opposed gun control:

> Advocates of gun control point to foreign countries to prove their case. They often cite England, which has strict gun control laws and little violent crime. But the key to low personal violence in England—and other foreign countries—is not gun control laws but the generally peaceful character of the people. For example, Switzerland has a militia system; 600,000 assault rifles each with two magazines of ammunition are sitting at this moment in Swiss homes. Yet Switzerland's murder rate is only 15 percent of ours. In other words, cultural factors are much more important than gun control when it comes to violent crime.

As these examples illustrate, argument from analogy can be used on both sides of an issue. You are more likely to persuade your audience if the analogy shows a truly parallel situation.[18]

Fallacies

A fallacy is an error in reasoning. As a speaker, you need to avoid fallacies in your speeches. As a listener, you need to be alert to possible fallacies in the speeches you hear.

Logicians have identified more than 125 different fallacies. Earlier in this chapter, we discussed three of the most important: hasty generalization (page 410), false cause (pages 414–415), and invalid analogy (page 416). Here we look at five other major fallacies that you should take special care to guard against.

fallacy
An error in reasoning.

Reasoning is an important part of persuasive speaking. In a legal trial, for example, neither the prosecution nor the defense is likely to sway the jury unless their reasoning is clear and convincing.

Red Herring

The name of this fallacy comes from an old trick used by farmers in England to keep fox hunters and their hounds from galloping through the crops. By dragging a smoked herring with a strong odor along the edge of their fields, the farmers could throw the dogs off track by destroying the scent of the fox.

red herring
A fallacy that introduces an irrelevant issue to divert attention from the subject under discussion.

A speaker who uses a red herring introduces an irrelevant issue in order to divert attention from the subject under discussion. For instance:

How dare my opponents accuse me of political corruption at a time when we are working to improve the quality of life for all people in the United States.

What does the speaker's concern about the quality of life in the U.S. have to do with whether he or she is guilty of political corruption? Nothing! It is a red herring used to divert attention away from the real issue.

Here's another example:

Why should we worry about the amount of violence on television when thousands of people are killed in automobile accidents each year?

The number of people killed in automobile accidents is a serious problem, but it has no bearing on the question of whether there is too much violence on television. It, too, is a red herring.

Ad Hominem

ad hominem
A fallacy that attacks the person rather than dealing with the real issue in dispute.

Latin for "against the man," *ad hominem* refers to the fallacy of attacking the person rather than dealing with the real issue in dispute. For instance:

The governor has a number of interesting economic proposals, but let's not forget that she comes from a very wealthy family.

By impugning the governor's family background rather than dealing with the substance of her economic proposals, the speaker is engaging in an *ad hominem* attack.

Here's another example of the same fallacy:

There is no doubt that American businesses have been hurt by all the environmental regulations passed in recent years. Most of the regulations were dreamed up by ivory-tower intellectuals, nature freaks, and tin-headed government bureaucrats. We can't afford those kinds of regulations.

The speaker's claim is that environmental regulations have hurt American businesses. But instead of presenting evidence to support this claim, the speaker lashes out at "ivory-tower intellectuals, nature freaks, and tin-headed government bureaucrats." In addition to being illogical, this argument is ethically suspect in its use of name-calling to demean the supporters of environmental regulations.

Sometimes, of course, a person's character or integrity can be a legitimate issue—as in the case of a police chief who violates the law, a scientist who falsifies data, or a corporate president who swindles stockholders. In such cases, a speaker might well raise questions about the person without being guilty of the *ad hominem* fallacy.

Either-Or

Sometimes referred to as a false dilemma, the either-or fallacy forces listeners to choose between two alternatives when more than two alternatives exist. For example:

> Either we build a new high school or children in this community will never get into college.

Or:

> The government must either raise taxes or reduce services for the poor.

Both statements oversimplify a complex issue by reducing it to a simple either-or choice. In the first statement, building a new high school may be necessary because the current one is overcrowed or outdated, but failing to build it is not going to keep all students in the community from attending college. With respect to the second statement, is it true that the only choices are to raise taxes or to reduce services for the poor? A careful listener might ask, "What about cutting defense spending or eliminating pork-barrel projects instead of reducing services for the poor?"

You will be more persuasive as a speaker and more perceptive as a listener if you are alert to the either-or fallacy.

either-or
A fallacy that forces listeners to choose between two alternatives when more than two alternatives exist.

Bandwagon

How often have you heard someone say, "It's a great idea—everyone agrees with it"? This is a classic example of the bandwagon fallacy, which assumes that because something is popular, it is therefore good, correct, or desirable.

Much advertising is based on the bandwagon fallacy. The fact that more people use Tylenol than Advil does not prove that Tylenol is a better pain reliever. Tylenol's popularity could be due more to aggressive marketing than to superior pain relieving. The question of which product does a better job of reducing pain is a medical issue that has nothing to do with popularity.

The bandwagon fallacy is also evident in political speeches. Consider the following statement:

> The President must be correct in his approach to foreign policy; after all, the polls show that 60 percent of the people support him.

This statement is fallacious because the only way to prove that the President is correct in his approach to foreign policy is to examine his approach and compare it with other approaches. Popular opinion cannot be taken as proof that an idea is right or wrong. Remember, "everyone" used to believe that the world is flat, that space flight was impossible, and that women should not attend college with men!

bandwagon
A fallacy that assumes that because something is popular, it is therefore good, correct, or desirable.

Slippery Slope

The slippery slope fallacy takes its name from the image of a boulder rolling uncontrollably down a steep hill. Once the boulder gets started, it can't be stopped until it reaches the bottom.

A speaker who commits the slippery slope fallacy assumes that taking a first step will lead inevitably to a second step and so on down the slope to disaster—as in the following examples:

If we allow the government to restrict the sale of semi-automatic weapons, before we know it, there will be a ban on the ownership of handguns and even hunting rifles. And once our constitutional right to bear arms has been compromised, the right of free speech will be the next to go.

Passing federal laws to control the amount of violence on television is the first step in a process that will result in absolute government control of the media and total censorship over all forms of artistic expression.

If a speaker claims that taking a first step will lead inevitably to a series of disastrous later steps, he or she should provide evidence or reasoning to support the claim. To assume that all the later steps will occur without proving that they will is to commit the slippery slope fallacy.

Appealing to Emotions

One year before rising to speak at the 1992 Republican National Convention, Mary Fisher learned that she had contracted the HIV virus from her ex-husband. Resolving to do all she could to fight the disease, she became an outspoken advocate of the need for public understanding and resources in the battle against AIDS. After telling her story to the Republican Platform Committee in May, Fisher, a former staff assistant to President Gerald Ford, was invited to address the party's national convention.

Feeling, as she said later, like "the only HIV-positive Republican," she was deeply concerned about how her message of compassion and awareness would be received—especially since most Americans, at that time, were still in a state of denial about the seriousness of the AIDS crisis.

Speaking with great emotion and conviction, Fisher presented one of the most admired speeches of recent years. The Houston Astrodome fell eerily silent as she spoke, and many of the delegates were moved to tears as they listened. Across the nation, millions watched on television, captivated by Fisher's powerful words and heartfelt delivery. Afterward, most listeners attributed the success of the speech to its emotional power. The *New York Times* deemed it "exceptional for its deep emotion and sharp message."[19]

View the ending of Mary Fisher, "A Whisper of AIDS."

CD: VIDEO CLIP 16.2

Effective persuasion often requires emotional appeal. As the Roman rhetorician Quintilian stated, "It is feeling and force of imagination that make us eloquent."[20] By adding "feeling" and the "force of imagination" to her logical arguments, Mary Fisher produced a compelling address. Although your words may never change the course of national opinion, you too can use emotional appeal to bring your persuasive speeches home to your listeners.

What Are Emotional Appeals?

Emotional appeals—what Aristotle referred to as *pathos*—are intended to make listeners feel sad, angry, guilty, afraid, happy, proud, sympathetic, reverent, or the like. These are often appropriate reactions when the question is one of value or policy. Few people are moved to change their attitudes or take action when they are complacent or bored. As George Campbell wrote in his *Philosophy of Rhetoric*, "When persuasion is the end, passion also must be engaged."[21]

Below is a list of some of the emotions evoked most often by public speakers. Following each emotion are a few examples of subjects that might stir that emotion:

- *Fear*—of serious illness, of natural disasters, of sexual assault, of unsafe aviation standards, of personal rejection, of economic hardship.

- *Compassion*—for the physically disabled, for battered women, for neglected animals, for the unemployed, for starving children in Africa, for victims of AIDS.

- *Pride*—in one's country, in one's family, in one's school, in one's ethnic heritage, in one's personal accomplishments.

- *Anger*—at the actions of political terrorists, at members of Congress who abuse the public trust, at landlords who exploit student tenants, at businesses that sell unsafe products, at vandals and thieves.

- *Guilt*—about not helping people less fortunate than ourselves, about not considering the rights of others, about not doing one's best.

- *Reverence*—for an admired person, for traditions and institutions, for one's deity.

Obviously this list is not complete. There are many other emotions and many other subjects that might stir them. However, this brief sample should give you an idea of the kinds of emotional appeals you might use to enhance the message of your persuasive speech.[22]

Generating Emotional Appeal

Use Emotional Language

As we saw in Chapter 11, one way to generate emotional appeal is to use emotion-laden words. If you want to move your listeners, use moving language. Here, for instance, is part of the conclusion from a student speech about the challenges and rewards of working as a community volunteer with young children:

> The promise of America sparkles in the eyes of every child. Their dreams are the glittering dreams of America. When those dreams are dashed, when innocent hopes are betrayed, so are the dreams and hopes of the entire nation. It is our duty—to me, it is a sacred duty—to give all children the chance to learn and grow, to share equally in the American dream of freedom, justice, and opportunity.

pathos
The name used by Aristotle for what modern students of communication refer to as emotional appeal.

The underlined words and phrases have strong emotional power. By using them, the speaker hopes to produce an emotional response.

There can be a problem with this approach, however. Packing too many emotionally charged words into one part of a speech can call attention to the emotional language itself and undermine its impact. When a sudden barrage of passionate language is inconsistent with the rest of the speech, it may strike the audience as ludicrous—obviously not the desired effect. Remember, the emotion rests in your audience, not in your words. Even the coldest facts can touch off an emotional response if they strike the right chords in a listener.

Develop Vivid Examples

Often a better approach than relying on emotionally charged language is to let your emotional appeal grow naturally out of the content of your speech. The most effective way to do this is with vivid, richly textured examples that personalize your ideas and help pull listeners into the speech emtionally.

Here is how one speaker used a vivid example for emotional appeal. The subject was illegal trapping of wild animals. The audience was a group of citizens and the village board in a semirural town. The speaker was a representative of the Humane Society. Here is what she might have said, stripping the content of emotional impact:

> Trapping of wild animals on town property is not only illegal, it is also dangerous. On several occasions domestic animals have been caught in traps set for raccoons, squirrels, and beavers.

What she actually said went something like this:

> Tina was found dead last week—her neck broken by the jaws of a steel trap. I didn't know Tina, and most of you didn't either. But John and Rachel Williamson knew her, and so did their children, Tyrone and Vanessa. Tina had been a beloved member of their family for 10 years. She was a Samoyed—a handsome, intelligent dog, pure white with soft, dark eyes. When she died she was only 200 yards from her back door.
>
> Tina had gone out to play that morning as usual, but this time she found something *un*usual—an odd-shaped box with delicious-smelling food inside. She put her head inside the box to get at the food. When she did, the trap closed and Tina was killed.
>
> Unless we crack down on illegal trapping within town property, this tragedy will be repeated. The next time it might be *your* family dog. Or your pet cat. Or your child.

People who listen to a speech like that will not soon forget it. They may well be moved to action, as the speaker intends. The first speech, however, is not nearly so compelling. Listeners may well nod their heads, think to themselves "good idea"—and then forget about it. The story of Tina and the family who loved her gives the second speech emotional impact and brings it home to listeners in personal terms.[23]

Speak with Sincerity and Conviction

Ronald Reagan was one of the most effective speakers in recent U.S. history. Even people who disagreed with his political views often found him irresistible. Why? Partly because he seemed to speak with great sincerity and conviction.

What was true for Reagan is true for you as well. The strongest source of emotional power is the conviction and sincerity of the speaker. All of your emotion-laden words and examples are but empty trappings unless *you* feel the emotion yourself. And if you do, your emotion will communicate itself to the audience through everything you say and do—not only through your words, but also through your tone of voice, rate of speech, gestures, and facial expressions.

Ethics and Emotional Appeal

Much has been written about the ethics of emotional appeal in speechmaking. Some people have taken the extreme position that ethical speakers should stick to reason and avoid emotional appeal entirely. To support this view, they point to speakers who have used emotional appeal to fan the flames of racial hatred, religious bigotry, and political fanaticism.

There is no question that emotional appeals can be abused by unscrupulous speakers for detestable causes. But emotional appeals can also be wielded by honorable speakers for noble causes—by Winston Churchill to rouse the world against Adolf Hitler and the forces of Nazism, by Nelson Mandela to call for racial justice, by Mother Teresa to help the poor and downtrodden. Few people would question the ethics of emotional appeal in these instances.[24]

Nor is it always possible to draw a sharp line between reason and emotional appeal. Think back for a moment to the story about Tina, the Samoyed who was killed near her home by an illegal trapper. The story certainly has strong emotional appeal. But is there anything unreasonable about the story? Or is it irrational for listeners to respond to it by backing stronger measures to control illegal trapping? By the same token, is it illogical to be angered by drive-by-shootings? Fearful about cutbacks in student aid? Compassionate for victims of child abuse? In many cases, reason and emotion work hand in hand.

One key to using emotional appeal ethically is to make sure it is appropriate to the speech topic. If you want to move listeners to act on a question of policy, emotional appeals are not only legitimate but perhaps necessary. If you want listeners to do something as a result of your speech, you will probably need to appeal to their hearts as well as to their heads.

On the other hand, emotional appeals are usually inappropriate in a persuasive speech on a question of fact. Here you should deal only in specific information and logic. For example, did Al Gore knowingly engage in illegal fund-raising during the 1996 presidential election? If you say, "No, because I admire Gore," or "Yes, because I have always disliked Gore," then you are guilty of applying emotional criteria to a purely factual question. The events relative to Gore's fund-raising activities are matters of fact and should be discussed on factual grounds alone.

Even when trying to move listeners to action, you should never substitute emotional appeals for evidence and reasoning. You should *always* build your persuasive speech on a firm foundation of facts and logic. This is important not just for ethical reasons, but for practical reasons as well. Unless

While strong evidence and sound reasoning are vital to persuasion, emotional appeals often make a speaker's message come alive. To be most effective, emotional appeals should be delivered with sincerity and conviction.

you prove your case, careful listeners will not be stirred by your emotional appeals. You need to build a good case based on reason *and* kindle the emotions of your audience.[25]

When you use emotional appeal, keep in mind the guidelines for ethical speechmaking discussed in Chapter 2. Make sure your goals are ethically sound, that you are honest in what you say, and that you avoid name-calling and other forms of abusive language. In using emotional appeal, as in other respects, your classroom speeches will offer a good testing ground for questions of ethical responsibility.

Sample Speech with Commentary

View the full speech "Self-Defense on Campus."

CD VIDEO DISK 2

The following persuasive speech was presented in a public speaking class at the University of Wisconsin.[26] It deals with a question of policy and is a good example of how students can utilize the methods of persuasion discussed in this chapter.

Self-Defense on Campus

Commentary	Speech
	Rebecca Hanson
The speaker begins with an extended hypothetical example. Vivid and richly textured, it gains attention and relates the topic	You're tired; you're hungry. You've just spent a long day at College Library and you can't wait to get back to your room. Glancing outside, you remember how quickly it becomes dark. You

directly to the audience. It also contains a strong element of emotional appeal—especially for female students who have experienced the feelings described by the speaker.

When you begin a speech with a hypothetical example, it's a good idea to follow up with statistics showing that the example is not far-fetched. The statistics in this paragraph are especially effective because they come from the city in which the speech was given.

After reinforcing the fact that crime is a concern for all members of her audience, the speaker focuses on the specific issue of enrolling in a self-defense course. She establishes her credibility by citing the benefits she gained from taking such a course. Although she stresses her personal experience here, it becomes clear as the speech goes on that she has also done a great deal of research on the topic.

This speech is organized according to Monroe's motivated sequence. In this paragraph, the speaker begins her discussion of the need for students to enroll in a self-defense course. Notice how she identifies the sources of her statistics and translates the figures into terms that relate directly to her classmates.

Moving from the general crime statistics in the previous paragraph, the speaker focuses on crime issues facing college students. Her questions about students' "bad habits" with respect to crime prevention are especially effective, and her use of "you" helps draw the audience further into the speech.

The quotation at the end of this paragraph is one of several pieces of evidence the

don't think much of it, though, as you bundle up and head out into the gusty wind. Not until you spy the shadows on the sidewalk or hear the leaves rustling beside you do you wish you weren't alone. You walk quickly, trying to stop your imagination from thinking of murderers and rapists. Only when you are safely inside your room do you relax and try to stop your heart from pounding out of your chest.

Can you remember a time when you felt this way? I would be surprised if you never have. The FBI reported last year that there were three murders, approximately 430 aggravated assaults, 1,400 burglaries, and 80 rapes here in Madison alone. And while these statistics are quite alarming, they don't even compare to the numbers of larger metropolitan areas.

No matter where we live, crime affects us all—men and women, students and instructors, young and old. We need to stop being the victims. One way we can do this is by enrolling in a self-defense course. There are many times I can remember when my heart seemed to pound out of my chest, but because I took an introductory course in self-defense, I feel more confident and more prepared to deal with potentially dangerous situations. Today I would like to encourage all of you to enroll in a self-defense course. Let's start by looking at the dangers of crime we face as college students.

College students face many crime issues, both as members of society and as students on campus. These crimes endanger our money, our property, our self-confidence, our psychological well-being, and even our lives. According to the Foundation for Crime Prevention Education, violence and crime have dramatically increased. An American is six times more likely to be assaulted with a weapon today than in 1960. The FBI reports that someone is either murdered, raped, assaulted, or robbed every 16 seconds. This means today, at the end of our 50-minute class period, approximately 187 people will have been victims of a violent crime.

College students, many of whom are away from home for the first time, are especially easy targets for crime. Students often look at campus housing as a secure place. But according to the book *Street Wisdom for Women*, precautions must be taken in a dorm or Greek house, just as in any house or apartment. How many of these bad habits do you have? How often do you leave your room without locking your door, forgetting how easily accessible your room is to anyone? How often do you fall asleep without locking your door? Or how often do you open your door without first checking to see who is there? As speaker located on the Internet. Notice how she identifies the exact source of the quotation, rather than making the general statement, "As I discovered on the Web, . . . "

The speaker completes the need section of her speech by noting that drugs and alcohol increase the crime problems faced by students. Here, as in other parts of the speech, her statistics are clearly presented and come from credible sources.

This paragraph begins with a transition into the satisfaction section of the speech. Notice how clearly the speaker presents her plan and identifies the self-defense classes students can attend right on campus.

Now the speaker looks at options for students who want to enroll in a self-defense class off campus. As in the previous paragraph, she provides specific information about those options. This kind of specificity is vital whenever a speaker seeks to persuade an audience to take immediate action.

Having explained her plan, the speaker moves into the visualization section of her speech, in which she will demonstrate the benefits of her plan. This is one of the most important aspects of any persuasive speech on a question of policy.

the Wake Forest University Police Crime Prevention website states, "Each of us must become aware of the precautions necessary to reduce the likelihood that we will become victims of crime." Those who forget to take these precautions invite trouble.

Although students must watch themselves in campus housing, they must also take care elsewhere. Prevalent use of drugs and alcohol, especially on college campuses, increases the chance of crime. Using drugs or alcohol makes you an easier target because, as we all know, it affects your judgment, influencing your decisions on safety. According to the Pacific Center for Violence Prevention, in 42 percent of all violent crimes, either the assailant, the victim, or both had been drinking. Specifically on campus, 90 percent of all violent crimes involve drugs and/or alcohol. This problem is so serious that testimony by law enforcement officials reprinted on the Security On Campus website indicates that many college campuses are the highest crime areas in their communities.

So now that we see the dangers we face as students, what can we do to protect ourselves? Although there are many ways of dealing with crime, I recommend that you and every college student enroll in a self-defense course. You can choose from a variety of self-defense courses offered right here in Madison. You can find one to fit your schedule and your pocketbook. On campus, the university has a club sport called Shorin Ryu Karate, which emphasizes practical self-defense. They hold their meetings in the evening, after classes, right on campus, and they're open to all university students, faculty, and staff.

Another option is Villari's Self-Defense and Tai Chi Center, which not only offers courses in self-defense, but in tai chi, karate, and kung fu. Villari's location on State Street is convenient for all university students. To find a class that fits your needs, you can also search over the Internet or through the Yellow Pages. I also brought along some brochures today, so if you are interested, please see me after class.

After enrolling in a self-defense course, you will find yourself much better prepared to deal with an emergency situation. Patrick Lee, an instructor for a course called "Self-Defense for Women: Victim or Survivor," claims the biggest thing he teaches in his courses is that you must decide from the beginning whether you want to be the victim or the survivor. Repeating over and over again that "I am a survivor" not only increases your self-confidence but helps you think more clearly in a difficult situation.

In this and the next paragraph, the speaker uses a personal example to illustrate the benefits of taking a self-defense class. The example also boosts the speaker's credibility by showing that she has firsthand experience on the topic. As you can see from CD-ROM Video Clip 15.3, the speaker's credibility is further reinforced by the sincerity and conviction of her delivery.

The speaker's success in repelling the padded attacker adds an element of emotional appeal to this section of the speech.

As in other places, the speaker clearly identifies the source of evidence from the Internet. The quotation from Cindy is an instance of peer testimony, and it provides further proof of the benefits of taking a self-defense class. The final sentence of this paragraph reinforces the point made by the quotation and effectively wraps up the body of the speech.

The speaker moves into her conclusion, in which she develops the action stage of Monroe's motivated sequence. Notice how specific her call to action is and how she ties it directly to her classmates by talking in terms of "you" and "your."

The closing quotation reinforces the speaker's central idea, relates once again to the audience, and ends the speech on a dramatic note.

I didn't realize the importance of this myself until I took an introductory course in self-defense in my high school physical education class. After a few days of practice, each of us faced the notorious padded attacker. Expecting to enjoy fighting the attacker, I prepared to yell, "No; stop; back off," as forcefully as possible. But before I knew it, this man, twice my size, had put me in a hold I could not get out of. My mind was so overcome with fear that I could barely muster out a "No." Immediately, I pictured this as a real situation, one which I probably would not have survived.

But after a few more days of practice, we were able to go against the padded attacker one more time. This time, I no longer felt fear. I felt anger. I was angry that this man felt he could take advantage of me. This time, using what I learned, I yelled, "No; back off," and successfully escaped his move. And this time I survived.

I'm not the only example showing the benefits of taking self-defense. If you're interested, check out "Stories from Self-Defense Classes" posted to the Internet by the Assault Prevention Information Network. Although I don't have the time to share with you the dozens of success stories, I can sum them up with a quote by Cindy, a 23-year-old woman who used her self-defense knowledge to scare off an assailant. Cindy says, "I know deep inside, where it matters most, that I have what it takes to defend myself if need be, and this feeling is one of pure joy." As you can see, self-defense is time and money well invested.

So I encourage you to enroll in a self-defense course, whether it be through a physical education class or through a private organization and whether you do it here or back in your hometown. Even if you do not enroll right away, I encourage you to do so in the near future. Taking such a course could mean keeping your money, protecting your property, defending yourself, your boyfriend or girlfriend, husband or wife. It could even mean the difference between life and death.

Don't ever think, "It could never happen to me." Why not be prepared? As Patrick Lee said, "Ask yourself, do you want to be the victim or the survivor?"

Summary

People have been studying the methods of persuasion since the days of the ancient Greeks. They have found that listeners accept a speaker's ideas for one or more of four reasons—because they perceive the speaker as having high credibility, because they are won over by the speaker's evidence, because they are convinced by the speaker's reasoning, or because they are moved by the speaker's emotional appeals.

Credibility is affected by many factors, but the two most important are competence and character. The more favorably listeners view a speaker's competence and character, the more likely they are to accept her or his ideas. Although credibility is partly a matter of reputation, you can enhance your credibility during the speech by establishing common ground with your listeners and by letting them know why you are qualified to speak on the topic. You can also build your credibility by presenting your speeches fluently and expressively.

If you hope to be persuasive, you must also support your views with evidence—examples, statistics, and testimony used to prove or disprove something. As you prepare your speech, try at each point to imagine how your audience will react. Anticipate their doubts and answer them with evidence. Regardless of what kind of evidence you use, it will be more persuasive if it is new to the audience, if it is stated in specific rather than general terms, and if it is from credible sources. Your evidence will also be more persuasive if you state explicitly the point it is supposed to prove.

No matter how strong your evidence, you will not be very persuasive unless listeners agree with your reasoning. In reasoning from specific instances, you move from a number of particular facts to a general conclusion. Reasoning from principle is the reverse—you move from a general principle to a particular conclusion. When you use causal reasoning, you try to establish a relationship between causes and effects. In analogical reasoning, you compare two cases and infer that what is true for one is also true for the other. Whatever kind of reasoning you use, you want to make sure that you avoid fallacies such as hasty generalization, false cause, and invalid analogy. As both a speaker and listener, you should also be on guard against the red herring, *ad hominem,* either-or, bandwagon, and slippery slope fallacies.

Finally, you can persuade your listeners by appealing to their emotions—fear, anger, pity, pride, sorrow, and so forth. One way to generate emotional appeal is by using emotion-laden language. Another is to develop vivid, richly textured examples that personalize your ideas and draw listeners into the speech emotionally. Neither, however, will be effective unless you feel the emotion yourself and communicate it by speaking with sincerity and conviction.

As with other methods of persuasion, your use of emotional appeal should be guided by a firm ethical rudder. Although emotional appeals are usually inappropriate in speeches on questions of fact, they are legitimate—and often necessary—in speeches that seek immediate action on questions of policy. Even when trying to move listeners to action, however, you should never substitute emotional appeals for evidence and reasoning. You need to build a good case based on facts and logic in addition to kindling the emotions of your audience.

Key Terms

ethos (401)

credibility (401)

initial credibility (402)

derived credibility (402)

terminal credibility (402)

creating common ground (404)

evidence (405)

logos (408)

reasoning (409)

reasoning from specific instances (410)

hasty generalization (410)

reasoning from principle (412)

causal reasoning (414)

false cause (414)

analogical reasoning (415)

invalid analogy (416)

fallacy (417)

red herring (418)

ad hominem (418)

either-or (419)

bandwagon (419)

slippery slope (420)

pathos (421)

Review Questions

After reading this chapter, you should be able to answer the following questions:

1. What is credibility? What two factors exert the most influence on an audience's perception of a speaker's credibility?

2. What are the differences among initial credibility, derived credibility, and terminal credibility?

3. What are three ways you can enhance your credibility during your speeches?

4. What is evidence? Why do persuasive speakers need to use evidence?

5. What are four tips for using evidence effectively in a persuasive speech?

6. What is reasoning from specific instances? What guidelines should you follow when using this method of reasoning?

7. What is reasoning from principle? How is it different from reasoning from specific instances?

8. What is causal reasoning? What two errors must you be sure to avoid when using causal reasoning?

9. What is analogical reasoning? How do you judge the validity of an analogy?

For further review, go to the Study Questions for this chapter.

CD: STUDY QUESTIONS

10. What are the eight logical fallacies discussed in this chapter?

11. What is the role of emotional appeal in persuasive speaking? Identify three methods you can use to generate emotional appeal in your speeches.

Exercises for Critical Thinking

1. Research has shown that a speaker's initial credibility can have great impact on how the speaker's ideas are received by listeners. Research has also shown that a speaker's credibility will vary from topic to topic and audience to audience. In the left-hand column below is a list of well-known public figures. In the right-hand column is a list of potential speech topics. Assume that each speaker will be addressing your speech class.

   For each speaker, identify the topic in the right-hand column on which she or he would have the highest initial credibility for your class. Then explain how the speaker's initial credibility might be affected if the speaker were discussing the topic in the right-hand column directly across from her or his name.

Speaker	**Topic**
Oprah Winfrey	Women in Politics
Jesse Jackson	Talk Shows: Who Needs Them?
Steven Spielberg	The Perils of Broadcast Journalism
Elizabeth Dole	African Americans: The Next Agenda
Peter Jennings	Movies in the 21st Century

2. Identify the kind of reasoning used in each of the following statements. What weaknesses, if any, can you find in the reasoning of each?

   a. According to a study by the American Medical Association, men with bald spots have three times the risk of heart attack as men with a full head of hair. Strange as it may seem, it looks as if baldness is a cause of heart attacks.

   b. Contrary to what the chemical industry argues, limiting pesticide use does not threaten the food supply. Sweden has cut back on pesticides by 50 percent over the last few years with almost no decrease in its harvest. The Campbell Soup Company uses no pesticides at all on tomatoes grown in Mexico, and they reap as much fruit as ever. Many California farmers who practice pesticide-free agriculture have actually experienced increases in their crop yields.

   c. The United States Constitution guarantees all citizens the right to bear arms. Gun control legislation infringes on the right of citizens to bear arms. Therefore, gun control legislation is contrary to the Constitution.

   d. Almost every industrialized nation in the world except for the United States has a national curriculum and national tests to help ensure that schools throughout the country are meeting high standards of education. If such a system can work elsewhere, it can work in the United States as well.

3. Over the years there has been much debate about the role of emotional appeal in public speaking. Do you believe it is ethical for public speakers to use emotional appeals when seeking to persuade an audience? Do you feel there are certain kinds of emotions to which an ethical speaker should not appeal? Why or why not? Be prepared to explain your ideas in class.

4. Analyze the speech in Appendix B by Mary Fisher ("A Whisper of AIDS"). In your analysis, concentrate on how Fisher builds her credibility, employs evidence and reasoning, and generates emotional appeal. In addition, study how she uses the resources of language discussed in Chapter 11 to bring her message home to listeners.

Applying the POWER of Public Speaking

As marketing director, you've helped your small company grow from ownership of one health club to nine in as many years. Now one of your less successful competitors is throwing in the towel and has announced plans to sell its seven clubs. Most members of your company's management team want to make an offer to purchase these clubs. However, some members, including yourself, believe the purchase would jeopardize your company's stability by nearly doubling its size overnight.

At a meeting of the management team, you listen as one of the advocates of purchasing the clubs makes his case. Among his points are the following: (1) The company must either purchase the clubs or abandon any thoughts of future growth; (2) If the company can successfully add clubs one at a time, as it has done in the past, then it should be able to add seven at once; and (3) Because a majority of the management team supports the purchase, it must be a good idea.

In your speech, you will point out the fallacy in each of these points. What are those fallacies?

Notes

[1]Roger Dawson Productions, Incorporated, La Habra, California.
[2]For a review of research on the factors of credibility, see James B. Stiff, *Persuasive Communication* (New York: Guilford Press, 1994), pp. 90–102.
[3]James C. McCroskey, *An Introduction to Rhetorical Communication*, 7th ed. (Boston: Allyn and Bacon, 1997), pp. 91–101.
[4]There is abundant research showing that perceived similarity between speaker and audience enhances the speaker's persuasiveness. For a summary of that research, see Richard M. Perloff, *The Dynamics of Persuasion* (Hillsdale, N.J.: Lawrence Erlbaum, 1993), pp. 145–149.
[5]See Perloff, *Dynamics of Persuasion,* pp. 170–179.

[6]A great deal of research has been conducted on the role of evidence in persuasive communication. For an excellent review of that research, see John C. Reinard, "The Empirical Study of the Persuasive Effects of Evidence: The Status after 50 Years of Research," *Human Communication Research,* 15 (1988), pp. 3–59.

[7]See Mike Allen, "Comparing the Persuasive Effectiveness of One- and Two-Sided Messages," in Mike Allen and Ray W. Preiss (eds.), *Persuasion: Advances through Meta-Analysis* (Cresskill, N.J.: Hampton Press, 1997), pp. 87–98.

[8]Reinard, "Empirical Study of Evidence," pp. 37–38.

[9]Donald Dean Morley and Kim B. Walker, "The Role of Importance, Novelty, and Plausibility in Producing Belief Change," *Communication Monographs,* 54 (1987), pp. 436–442.

[10]See John C. Reinard, "The Persuasive Effects of Testimonial Assertion Evidence," in Allen and Preiss, *Persuasion: Advances through Meta-Analysis,* p. 70.

[11]Daniel J. O'Keefe, *Persuasion: Theory and Research* (Newbury Park, Calif.: Sage, 1990), pp. 159–161.

[12]Adapted from James C. Humes, *A Speaker's Treasury of Anecdotes about the Famous* (New York: Harper and Row, 1978), p. 131.

[13]For fuller discussion, see James A. Herrick, *Argumentation: Understanding and Shaping Arguments* (Scottsdale, Ariz.: Gorsuch Scarisbrick, 1995); George W. Ziegelmueller and Jack Kay, *Argumentation: Inquiry and Advocacy,* 3d ed. (Boston: Allyn and Bacon, 1997).

[14]In classical systems of logic, reasoning from particular facts to a general conclusion was known as induction. Contemporary logicians, however, have redefined induction as any instance of reasoning in which the conclusion follows from its premises with probability—regardless of whether the reasoning moves from specific instances to a general conclusion or from a general premise to specific conclusion. In this scheme, reasoning from specific instances is one kind of inductive argument—as are causal reasoning and analogical reasoning. See, for example, S. Morris Engel, *With Good Reason: An Introduction to Informal Fallacies,* 6th ed. (New York: St. Martin's, 2000); Howard Kahane, *Logic and Contemporary Rhetoric: The Use of Reason in Everyday Life,* 8th ed. (Belmont, Calif.: Wadsworth, 1998).

[15]Lionel Ruby, *The Art of Making Sense* (Philadelphia: Lippincott, 1954), p. 261.

[16]In classical systems of logic, reasoning from a general premise to a specific conclusion was known as deduction. But just as contemporary logicians have redefined induction (see note 14), they have redefined deduction as any instance of reasoning in which the conclusion follows from its premises with certainty. Some deductive arguments move from general premises to a specific conclusion, but others move from specific premises to a general conclusion. Many speech textbooks confuse reasoning from principle—which is one form of deduction—with deductive reasoning in general.

[17]The full text of Anthony's speech is in Karlyn Kohrs Campbell (ed.), *Man Cannot Speak for Her: Key Texts of the Early Feminists* (New York: Praeger, 1989), pp. 289–316.

[18]In an interesting study on this subject, see Bryan B. Whaley and Austin S. Babrow, "Analogy in Persuasion: Translator's Dictionary or Art?" *Communication Studies,* 44 (1993), pp. 239–253.

[19]See Appendix B for the full text of Fisher's speech.

[20]H. E. Butler (trans.), *The Institutio Oratoria of Quintilian* (Cambridge, Mass.: Harvard University Press, 1961), IV, p. 141.

[21]George Campbell, *The Philosophy of Rhetoric,* ed. Lloyd F. Bitzer (Carbondale, Ill.: Southern Illinois University Press, 1988), p. 77.

[22]For an excellent survey of communication research on emotion and persuasion, see Alice H. Eagly and Shelly Chaiken, *The Psychology of Attitudes* (Fort Worth, Tex.: Harcourt Brace Jovanovich, 1993), pp. 431–447.

[23]The power of examples to generate strong responses in listeners is well documented. See, for example, Dean C. Kazoleas, "A Comparison of the Persuasive Effectiveness of Qualitative Versus Quantitative Evidence: A Test of Explanatory Hypotheses," *Communication Quarterly,* 41 (1993), pp. 40–50.

[24]For a strong defense of emotional appeal on ethical grounds, see Craig Waddell, "The Role of *Pathos* in the Decision-Making Process: A Study in the Rhetoric of Science Policy," *Quarterly Journal of Speech,* 76 (1990), pp. 381–400.

[25]Research on fear appeals, for example, has demonstrated that messages devoted exclusively to arousing fear in the audience are less effective than messages that combine fear appeals with reasonable explanations of how to eliminate or cope with the source of fear. See Paul Mongeau, "Another Look at Fear-Arousing Appeals," in Allen and Preiss, *Persuasion: Advances through Meta-Analysis,* pp. 53–68.

[26]Reprinted with permission of Rebecca Hanson.

CHAPTER SEVENTEEN

SPEAKING ON SPECIAL OCCASIONS

Speeches of Introduction

Speeches of Presentation

Speeches of Acceptance

Commemorative Speeches

After-Dinner Speeches

Special occasions are the punctuation marks of day-to-day life, the high points that stand out above ordinary routine. Christenings, weddings, funerals, graduations, award ceremonies, inaugurals, retirement dinners—all these are occasions, and they are very special to the people who take part in them. Nearly always they are occasions for speechmaking. A close friend proposes a toast to the bride and groom; the sales manager presents an award to the sales representative of the year; the president delivers an inaugural address; the basketball coach gives a speech honoring the team's most valuable player; a family member delivers a moving eulogy to the deceased. These speeches help give the occasion its "specialness." They are part of the ceremonial aura that marks the event.

Speeches for special occasions are different from the speeches we have considered so far in this book. They may convey information, but that is not their primary purpose. Neither is their primary purpose to persuade. Rather, they aim to fit the special needs of a special occasion. In this chapter we look at the most common special occasions and the kinds of speeches appropriate for each.

Speeches of Introduction

"Distinguished guests, the President of the United States." If you are ever in a situation in which you have to introduce the President, you will need no more than the eight words that begin this paragraph. The President is so well known that any further remarks would be inappropriate and almost foolish.

speech of introduction
A speech that introduces the main speaker to the audience.

Most of the time, however, a speech of introduction will be neither this brief nor this ritualized. If you are introducing another speaker, you will need to accomplish three purposes in your introduction:

Build enthusiasm for the upcoming speaker.

Build enthusiasm for the speaker's topic.

Establish a welcoming climate that will boost the speaker's credibility.

A good speech of introduction can be a delight to hear and can do much to ease the task of the main speaker. The basic message of such a speech should be "Here is a speaker you will enjoy, and this is why."[1] Usually you will say something about the speaker and about the topic—in that order. Following are some guidelines for speeches of introduction. Most of the points apply also to the other types of special-occasion speeches discussed in this chapter.

Be Brief

During World War I, Lord Balfour, Great Britain's foreign secretary, was to be the main speaker at a rally in the United States. But the speaker introducing Lord Balfour gave a 45-minute oration on the causes of the war. Then, almost as an afterthought, he said, "Now Lord Balfour will give his address." Lord Balfour rose and said, "I'm supposed to give my address in the brief time remaining. Here it is: 10 Carleton Gardens, London, England."[2]

Every speaker—and audience—who has ever sat through a long-winded introduction knows how dreary it can be. The audience is thinking, "Oh, for heaven's sake, get *on* with it." For the speaker, it is even more troublesome. She or he is psyched up. The adrenaline is pumping. But as the introducer drones on, the feeling of readiness begins to drain away. By the time the introducer finally sits down, the speaker may well have lost much of her or his creative energy.

The purpose of a speech of introduction is to focus attention on the main speaker, not on the person making the introduction. Under normal circumstances, a speech of introduction will be no more than two to three minutes long, and it may be shorter if the speaker is already well known to the audience.

Make Sure Your Remarks Are Completely Accurate

Many an introducer has embarrassed himself or herself, as well as the main speaker, by garbling basic facts about the speaker. Always check with the speaker ahead of time to make sure your introduction is accurate in every respect.

Above all, get the speaker's name right. This may seem obvious, but it needs repeating. Remember that nothing is more important than a person's name. When you get a name wrong, you strip that person of identity and importance. If the speaker's name is at all difficult—especially if it involves a foreign pronunciation—practice saying it well in advance. However, don't practice so much that you frighten yourself about getting it wrong. This was the plight of an announcer whose gaffe is now a classic: "Ladies and gentlemen, the President of the United States—Hoobert Heever!"

Adapt Your Remarks to the Occasion

In preparing your introduction, you may be constrained by the nature of the occasion. Formal occasions require formal speeches of introduction. If you were presenting a guest speaker at an informal business meeting, you might be much more casual than if you were presenting the same speaker to the same audience at a formal banquet.

Adapt Your Remarks to the Main Speaker

No matter how well it is received by the audience, a speech of introduction that leaves the main speaker feeling uncomfortable has failed in part of its purpose. How can you make a main speaker uncomfortable? One way is to overpraise the person—and especially to praise him or her for speaking skills. Never say, "Our speaker will keep you on the edge of your seat from beginning to end!" This is like prefacing a joke with the line, "Here is the funniest joke you've ever heard." You create a set of expectations that are almost impossible to fulfill.

Another way to create discomfort is by revealing embarrassing details of the speaker's personal life or by making humorous remarks that are in poor taste from the speaker's point of view. An introducer may think this kind of remark is funny: "Why, I've known Anita Fratello since she was 10 years old and so fat that everybody in the class called her Blimpo!" To the speaker, however, the remark will probably not be a bit funny and may be painful.

Like other speeches for special occasions, a commencement address is part of the ceremonial aura that marks the event and helps to make it special.

Adapt Your Remarks to the Audience

Just as you adapt other speeches to particular audiences, so you need to adapt a speech of introduction to the audience you are facing. Your aim is to make *this* audience want to hear *this* speaker on *this* subject. If the speaker is not well known to the audience, you will need to establish her or his credibility by recounting some of the speaker's main achievements and explaining why she or he is qualified to speak on the topic at hand. But if the speaker is already personally known to the audience, it would be absurd to act as if the audience had never heard of the person.

Also, you will want to tell each audience what *it* wants to hear—to give the kind of information that is interesting and accessible to the members of that audience. If you were introducing the same speaker to two different groups, some of the information in the speeches of introduction might be the same, but it would be slanted differently. Suppose, for example, the police commissioner of a certain city is going to address two groups—an audience of elementary-school children and the members of the city council. The introduction to the schoolchildren might go something like this:

> Children, we have a very important guest with us today. He is the number one policeman in our city, the head of all the other police officers. Besides knowing a lot about crime right here at home, the police commissioner has also spent time working

with Interpol—a special group of police officers who deal with crimes around the world. Today he is going to talk about how all of us can work with our neighborhood police officers to prevent crime. Let's give a big round of applause and listen carefully to Police Commissioner Robert Washington.

But the introduction to the city council would be along these lines:

Members of the city council and distinguished guests: It is my privilege to introduce to you today the police commissioner, who will address us on the subject of the community policing program. Most of you know that the commissioner has a distinguished record as head of our police force for more than 10 years. However, you may not know that he also holds a master's degree in criminology and studied abroad for a year with Interpol, the international police force.

The commissioner first introduced the community policing program six years ago. The idea behind the program is to get police officers out of their cars and into our neighborhoods, where they can talk directly to merchants and residents about the real dynamics of our city. These officers do more than make arrests. They try to find ways to help solve the problems that contribute to crime in the first place. Often that means hooking people up with services offered by other city agencies—schools, hospitals, housing, drug treatment centers.

And the program seems to be working. Crime is down in the neighborhoods with community policing, and our citizens report that they feel more secure. Today the commissioner is going to tell us how this program can be extended to more of the city and made more effective for all of our citizens. Please welcome Police Commissioner Robert Washington.

Try to Create a Sense of Anticipation and Drama

You may have noticed one detail shared by the two speeches introducing the police commissioner: In both cases the speaker's name was saved for last. This is a convention in speeches of introduction. While there may occasionally be a good reason to break the convention, usually you will avoid mentioning the speaker's name until the final moment—even when the audience knows exactly whom you are discussing. By doing this you build a sense of drama, and the speaker's name comes as the climax of your introduction.

Often you will find yourself in the situation of introducing someone who is fairly well known to the audience—a classmate, a colleague at a business meeting, a neighbor in a community group. Then you should try to be creative and cast the speaker in a new light. Try to increase the audience's eagerness to hear the speaker. Talk to the speaker beforehand and see if you can learn some interesting facts that are not generally known—especially facts that relate to the speaker's topic. If possible, interview some of the speaker's close friends or family.

Above all, if you expect to be creative and dramatic, be sure you practice your speech of introduction thoroughly. Even though it is short, there is no excuse for not working out the delivery as fully as possible. You should be able to deliver the speech extemporaneously, with sincerity and enthusiasm.

Speeches of Presentation

speech of presentation
A speech that presents someone a gift, an award, or some other form of public recognition.

Speeches of presentation are given when someone is receiving publicly a gift, an award, or some other form of public recognition. Usually such speeches are relatively brief. They may be no more than a mere announcement ("And the winner is . . . ") or be up to four or five minutes in length.

As with other kinds of speeches, speeches of presentation need to be adapted to the audience and to the occasion. The main theme of a speech of presentation is to acknowledge the achievements of the recipient. You need to tell the audience why the recipient is receiving the award. Point out her or his contributions, achievements, and so forth. Do not deal with everything the person has ever done. Focus on achievements related to the award, and discuss these achievements in a way that will make them meaningful to the audience.

Depending on the audience and the occasion, you may also need to discuss two other matters in a speech of presentation. First, if the audience is not familiar with the award and why it is being given, you should explain briefly—or at least allude to—the purpose of the award. Second, if the award was won in a public competition and the audience knows who the losers are, you might take a moment to praise the losers as well.

Below is a sample speech of presentation. It was delivered by Gregory Peck in presenting the Jean Hersholt Humanitarian Award to Danny Kaye at the Academy Awards ceremony in Los Angeles. Because the Hersholt Award is a special honor bestowed by the academy's board of governors, there are no public competitors for the award. Thus Peck did not need to say anything in recognition of the "losers." His speech focused on Kaye's contributions to UNICEF and to symphony orchestras as the reasons for bestowal of the award.[3]

■ Presenting the Jean Hersholt Humanitarian Award ■

Gregory Peck

It's a long trip from Brooklyn to Buckingham Palace, and it's a far piece from Beverly Hills to an obscure village in Bangladesh. Danny Kaye has made both journeys, sustained by his remarkable gifts, his grace, and his intelligence. He has been a star of the first magnitude since his remarkable talent exploded on the Broadway stage in *Lady in the Dark* in 1941, and one who has had a high sense of priority: His wife Sylvia, and daughter, Dena, have always come first in his life—and then, in no special order, his work, the world's children, and great music.

For UNICEF (United Nations International Children's Emergency Fund), he continues to travel the world, bringing joy and hope to children on all the continents, and initiating programs to save them from hunger and give them a better chance in life. He has been doing this for years, with no pay and without fanfare. No trumpets. No headlines. His reward, the laughter of children.

As forbearing and skillful as he is with children, so he is with symphony orchestras, groups of 70 or 80 highly disciplined artists. He cannot read music, yet he has conducted major orchestras all over the world with musicianship that is sensitive, completely serious, and at times, likely to veer off alarmingly into the hilarious. Danny's irrepressible *joie de vivre* makes his concerts joyous occasions for musicians and audiences alike. Bach and Mozart have no better friend. Nor have the orchestras and their pension funds. Nor have we.

And thus, for his prodigious labors for the children of the world, for the wondrous people who make music, the Board of Governors proudly gives the Jean Hersholt Humanitarian Award to a "Citizen of the World" who does honor to our profession—Mr. Danny Kaye.

Speeches of Acceptance

The purpose of an acceptance speech is to give thanks for a gift or an award. When giving such a speech, you should thank the people who are bestowing the award, and you should recognize the people who helped you gain it.

The acceptance speech that follows is the companion piece to the speech of presentation by Gregory Peck. It was delivered by Danny Kaye in accepting the Jean Hersholt Humanitarian Award at the Academy Awards ceremony, and it exemplifies the three major traits of a good acceptance speech—brevity, humility, and graciousness.[4]

acceptance speech
A speech that gives thanks for a gift, an award, or some other form of public recognition.

■ Accepting the Jean Hersholt Humanitarian Award ■

Danny Kaye

I am terribly excited to be given this great honor. And I'm so delighted that I find myself, as we say, trembling. If I were any more delighted, I think I'd be in an institution.

However, I feel a little bit guilty about all the praise that Greg lavished on me. It was really no hardship at all. Really, I am crazy about children. I am crazy about conducting. And I am crazy about flying.

I am definitely not crazy about disease or famine or neglect. But, then, neither are any of you. And we, all of us in our profession, share a long and wonderful tradition of doing something about it—of giving of our time and our talent wherever and whenever needed—without prejudice, without stint. That's one of the reasons that I am so very proud of our profession and so proud to be one of you.

I share this award with you, with all of you, and I give thanks to the memory of Dag Hammarskjöld and Maurice Pate, with whom I started to work for UNICEF about 28 years ago. And to Gene Ormandy, who put a baton in my hand, my little nervous hand, and made me an offer I couldn't refuse—to stand in front of a symphony orchestra and conduct. Wow! That's the greatest feeling of neurotic power in the world. You ought to try it!

My special thanks to the Board of Governors. I love this and I love you. Thank you.

Commemorative Speeches

Commemorative speeches are speeches of praise or celebration. Eulogies, Fourth of July speeches, testimonial addresses, and dedications are examples of commemorative speeches. Your aim in such speeches is to pay tribute to a person, a group of people, an institution, or an idea.

As in an informative speech, you probably will have to give the audience information about your subject. After all, the audience must know *why* your subject is praiseworthy. They will need to know something about the history of the institution or the life of the person being praised. As in other speeches, you may draw on examples, testimony, even statistics to illustrate the achievements of your subject.

Your fundamental purpose in a commemorative speech, however, is not just to inform your listeners but to *inspire* them—to arouse and heighten their appreciation of or admiration for the person, institution, or idea you are praising. If you are paying tribute to a person, for example, you should not compose a biography that simply recounts the details of the person's life. Rather, you should create a speech that goes beyond biography—that penetrates to the *essence* of your subject and generates in your audience a deep sense of respect.

When speaking to commemorate, you do not exhort like the advocate or explain like the lecturer. You want to express feelings, to stir sentiments—joy and hope when a new building is dedicated or a new President is inaugurated; anticipation and good wishes at a commencement celebration; lament and consolation at a funeral or memorial service; admiration and respect at a testimonial dinner. In some ways, a commemorative speech is like an impressionist painting—"a picture with warm colors and texture capturing a mood or a moment."[5]

But while the painter works with brush and colors, the commemorative speaker works with language. Of all the kinds of speeches, perhaps none depends more on the creative and subtle use of language than does the speech to commemorate. Some of the most memorable speeches in history, including Abraham Lincoln's Gettysburg Address, have been commemorative. We remember such speeches—we continue to find them meaningful and inspiring—largely because of their eloquent use of language.

One of the most effective commemorative speakers in our recent history was President Ronald Reagan. After the explosion of the space shuttle *Challenger* in 1986, Reagan delivered a nationally televised eulogy to the astronauts killed in the blast. Below are two versions of Reagan's closing lines. The first is what he *might* have said, stripping the text of its warm emotional content and poignant language:

> Like Francis Drake, the great explorer of the oceans, the *Challenger* astronauts gave their lives for a cause to which they were fully dedicated. We are honored by them, and we will not forget them. We will always remember seeing them for the last time this morning as they prepared for their flight.

Here is what Reagan *actually* said:

> There's a coincidence today. On this day 390 years ago, the great explorer Francis Drake died aboard ship off the coast of Panama. In his lifetime the great frontiers were the oceans, and an historian later said, "He lived by the sea, died on it, was buried in it." Well, today we can say of the *Challenger* crew: Their dedication was, like Drake's, complete.
>
> The crew of the space shuttle *Challenger* honored us by the manner in which they lived their lives. We will never forget them, nor the last time we saw them, this morn-

ing, as they prepared for their journey and waved goodbye and "slipped the surly bonds of earth" to "touch the face of God."[6]

View the ending of Ronald Reagan's eulogy to the *Challenger* astronauts.

CD: VIDEO CLIP 17.1

Tho final words—"'slipped the surly bonds of earth' to 'touch the face of God'"—are especially effective. Drawn from a sonnet called "High Flight" that many pilots keep with them, they ennoble the deaths of the astronauts and end the speech on an eloquent, moving, and poetic note.

When speaking to commemorate, you will deal for the most part with intangibles. Your success will depend on your ability to put into language the thoughts and emotions appropriate to the occasion. It is easy—too easy—to fall back on clichés and trite sentiments. Your challenge will be to use language imaginatively in order to invest the occasion with dignity, meaning, and honest emotion.

In doing so, you may want to utilize the special resources of language discussed in Chapter 11 to enhance the imagery and rhythm of your prose. Metaphor, simile, parallelism, repetition, antithesis, alliteration—all are appropriate for commemorative speeches. Some highly acclaimed commemorative speeches—including Martin Luther King's "I Have a Dream" and John Kennedy's inaugural address—are distinguished by their creative use of such devices.

Confronted with the evocative speeches of a Kennedy or a King, you may decide that the speech of commemoration is far beyond your abilities. But other students have delivered excellent commemorative speeches—not immortal, perhaps, but nonetheless dignified and moving. The speech on pages 444–445 was given by Andrea Besikof, a student at the University of Wisconsin, in a public speaking class. The assignment was to give a brief speech paying tribute to a person, an institution, or an idea. Andrea spoke about her grandparents and other survivors of the Holocaust during World War II. As you read this speech, notice how effectively Andrea used the resources of language to give her ideas artistic unity and emotional impact.[7]

The aim of a commemorative speech is to pay tribute to a person, a group of people, an institution, or an idea. Here Sam Velasquez addresses listeners during Latino Heritage Recognition Day.

The Survivors

Andrea Besikof

"Work! Harder. Faster. Shovel! Don't just stand there. Shovel!"

And so he shoveled with all of his energy and all of his might. Hour after hour, he shoveled until his body could not shovel any more. Finally, he stopped working, leaned over on his shovel, and let his body limply rest, as his eyes stared at the ground.

The commander looked his way and hollered in a low and penetrating voice, "Shovel!"

But the man did not move. The commander lifted his gun, loaded it with ammunition, and shot him. The man released his hands from the shovel and fell to the ground. He murmured his last words, "How could this happen?"

The commander walked over, lifted his heel, and kicked the man into the mass grave, which he had been digging.

One more Jew was removed from the world. He was one of 6 million who was brought to his death by the Nazi policy to annihilate the Jewish race. The Nazis collected the Jews in the ghettos; they transported the Jews to the death camps; they worked the Jews until they could not work any more. Then they killed them—by gun and by gas, by starvation and sickness, by torture and terror.

Millions of Jews died in the death camps of Buchenwald, Auschwitz, Dachau, and Treblinka. It seems unfathomable that people could have survived the Nazis' wartime atrocities. Yet, by the grace of God, there were survivors. The survivors were the young and the strong, not the old and the meek. The survivors were the lucky and the few.

My grandparents are Holocaust survivors. They are each the only survivors in their families. They witnessed the deaths of their mothers and fathers, brothers and sisters, friends and neighbors. They witnessed the destruction of their lives and homes, towns and country, shops and synagogues. They lived through the death camps. They lived through the excruciating work. They lived to see liberation.

Since I was a little girl, my grandparents have told me about their lives during the Holocaust. They have told me about the persecution, the intolerance, and the injustice so that I could appreciate my freedom, my liberty, and my independence. It has always amazed me that my grandparents don't have spite or malice. After all they suffered, they have only hope and love. They don't want to hate any more.

During World War II, my grandparents were victims of anti-Semitism. Fifty years later, they are victims no longer. Today they fight against the "isms" which plague our communities, our states, our nation, and our world. They tell their story so that we, the younger generation, will understand the horrific force which anti-Semitism was in their lives. They relate their experiences to the struggles which so many people grapple with today. They will tell their story, and they will not rest until all people can live without fear and without denial, until all people can live with pride and with dignity.

And when my grandparents are gone, I will continue to tell their story. I will tell my children about the men and women who were murdered for no cause. I will tell my children about the heroism of the Jews in the Warsaw ghetto who fought strength for strength against the Nazi militia. I will tell these stories to all who will listen.

And I hope that you, too, will tell stories. As the Holocaust survivor and writer Elie Wiesel, once said, "Not to transmit an experience is to betray it."

To the millions who died in the Holocaust, lie peacefully in your graves, for you have not been forgotten.

To the survivors of the Holocaust, rest assured that we have listened to your stories. We have learned by your examples and we, too, will fight for freedom and peace.

May no person around the globe again fall to his or her death murmuring, "How could this happen?"

After-Dinner Speeches

After-dinner speeches may be harder to define than any other kind of speech. While the custom of saying a few words of tribute or celebration following a meal is probably as old as civilization itself, after-dinner speeches as a formal type of speech developed in England during the early nineteenth century.[8] By the 1880s they had become so popular on this side of the Atlantic that one observer called them "the style of oratory most cultivated" in the United States.[9]

At that time they were delivered, literally, after dinner. By the 1920s, however, with the growing popularity of noon meetings for groups such as the Lions and Kiwanis clubs, "after-dinner" speeches could be heard after lunch as well. Because so many organizations now have breakfast gatherings, you are as likely to hear an "after-dinner" speech today at eight o'clock in the morning as at eight o'clock in the evening.

After-dinner speeches are best thought of as a kind of speech to entertain. Whether presented after breakfast, lunch, or dinner—in a formal dining room or at an outdoor barbecue—they usually have a lighter tone than a speech to inform or to persuade. This difference in tone will obviously have some impact on your choice of topic. AIDS, child abuse, drunk driving, sweatshops, gun violence—all are important, but audiences do not expect to hear about such weighty matters in the relaxed atmosphere of the typical after-dinner speech. For the most part, though, any topic suitable for an informative or persuasive speech can be appropriate for an after-dinner speech, as long as you approach it in a lighthearted manner.

Suppose, for example, that your subject is nutrition. If you were giving an informative speech on this topic, your specific purpose might be "To inform my audience of the four basic nutrients in the human diet." If you were presenting a persuasive speech, your specific purpose might be "To persuade my audience that they should reduce their consumption of red meat in favor of more fish, vegetables, and grains." But if you were giving an after-dinner speech on the topic of nutrition, your specific purpose might be "To entertain my audience by showing them the ridiculous extremes some people go to in following special diets."

Or to take another example, say your subject is meteorology. If you were making an informative speech, your specific purpose might be "To inform my audience of the different methods used by meteorologists to predict the weather." If you were giving a persuasive speech on the same topic, your specific purpose might be "To persuade my audience that the federal government should increase the budget for weather-related research." If you

after-dinner speech
A speech to entertain that makes a thoughtful point about its subject in a lighthearted manner.

were giving an after-dinner speech, however, your specific purpose might be "To entertain my audience by showing them how preposterous it is to talk about the 'typical' weather in our state."

As these examples suggest, after-dinner speeches should not be technical or argumentative. They may contain information that is new to the audience, and they may even have a persuasive impact, but their supporting materials should be chosen primarily for their entertainment value. Audiences for after-dinner speeches are seldom in a mood to follow a close train of reasoning, a complicated set of statistics, or a series of abstract concepts. Rather, they are looking for a good-natured speech that stimulates the imagination by approaching the topic in a novel way, treating it lightly, even whimsically.

This is not to say that after-dinner speeches should be rambling or totally frivolous. Like all other speeches, they require careful preparation and organization. They should have a central theme, and they should strive to make a thoughtful point about that theme—whether it is an aspect of human nature (such as vanity or the desire for immortality), of college life (such as final exams or finding a decent apartment), of sports (such as the similarities between modern football and the ancient Roman gladiators), of family life (such as the perils of summer vacations or the experience of being a parent for the first time), of work (such as putting up with the boss or dealing with weird customers), of travel (such as poor service by the airlines or dealing with unusual customs abroad), or even of current events (such as how we choose presidential candidates or jitters over the stock market).

As you might imagine, humor can be an important part of after-dinner speeches. Some of America's finest after-dinner speakers have been humorists, such as Mark Twain and Will Rogers, Art Buchwald and Andy Rooney. This does not mean, however, that you need to be a stand-up comic to be a successful after-dinner speaker. The purpose of humor in an after-dinner speech is more to provoke smiles or chuckles than to convulse the audience with a series of one-liners. Nor is humor used merely to make the audience laugh. In the best speeches, humor grows naturally out of the speech materials and helps the speaker make his or her point by providing special insight into the topic.

One of the best-known instances of humor in a recent public speech occurred in Barbara Bush's 1990 commencement address at Wellesley College. There had been much controversy about the choice of Bush as speaker, and 150 students had signed a petition saying she did not represent the kind of career woman Wellesley seeks to educate.

In her speech, Bush made many serious points about the importance of family and the choices facing modern women, but she softened those points with humor. "Who knows," she said toward the end of her speech, "somewhere out in this audience may even be someone who will one day follow in my footsteps, and preside over the White House as the president's spouse." Then, after a pause, she added, "I wish *him* well!" It was a perfect line, perfectly timed. The audience of 5,400 people roared with laughter and gave Bush a ringing ovation.[10]

View this section of Barbara Bush's commencement speech at Wellesley College

CD: VIDEO CLIP 17.2

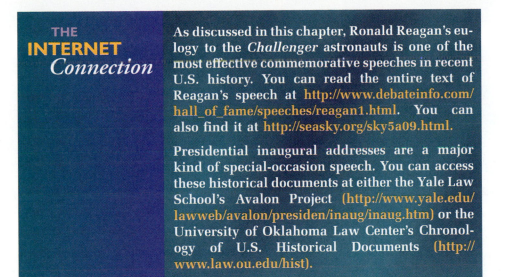

THE INTERNET *Connection*

As discussed in this chapter, Ronald Reagan's eulogy to the *Challenger* astronauts is one of the most effective commemorative speeches in recent U.S. history. You can read the entire text of Reagan's speech at http://www.debateinfo.com/hall_of_fame/speeches/reagan1.html. You can also find it at http://seasky.org/sky5a09.html.

Presidential inaugural addresses are a major kind of special-occasion speech. You can access these historical documents at either the Yale Law School's Avalon Project (http://www.yale.edu/lawweb/avalon/presiden/inaug/inaug.htm) or the University of Oklahoma Law Center's Chronology of U.S. Historical Documents (http://www.law.ou.edu/hist).

Tickling an audience's funnybone, however, can be difficult even for accomplished public speakers. If you don't feel confident working for a laugh, don't worry. Humor can contribute to a successful after-dinner speech, but it is not essential. Indeed, the best approach is usually not to work specifically for laughs. If you deal with the topic creatively, select supporting materials that are interesting in their own right, and use the resources of language to create sharp imagery, vivid descriptions, colorful details, and clever phrasing, you should do just fine.

All of these traits are represented in the following after-dinner speech. It was given by Julie Daggett, a student at the University of Wisconsin, to her public speaking class.[11]

The Horror of It All

Julie Daggett

They never did find his head or hands. I crouched in the corner, peering through my fingers as he moaned and wailed in an endless search for his missing appendages. I was terrified—but not as terrified as poor Bette Davis. They put her in the nuthouse. I simply turned on the light and ran to the safety of my father's lap. As I perched, shuddering, he said the phrase I was to hear over and over through the coming years, "It's okay, it's only a movie." It did not end for me there, however. The movie *Hush, Hush, Sweet Charlotte* was just the beginning of my love/hate relationship with horror movies.

My scaredy-cat tendencies actually began at a very early age. As a young child, I insisted the hall light be kept on when I went to bed—no measly night-light would do for a hard-core chicken. My parents would come upstairs after the news and tell each other to "turn off the l-i-g-h-t." I could be heard miles away screaming, "NO! I know what that spells!" After *The Ghost and Mr. Chicken* with Don Knotts, my bedtime ritual went something like this—look under the bed, look in the closet, turn off the light, and leap into the sack. As time passed, however, this childish nonsense began to subside. I was growing up.

But then it happened. Theater owners offered up *The Exorcist,* a temptation I could not resist. That delicious, horrible feeling of being terrified was renewed. I was hooked. I stayed pretty sane, though, until I read the book, at which time I discovered I was possessed by the Devil. I had six of the ten symptoms, including headaches, nausea, and loss of sleep. It may not have been Satan himself, but there was definitely a demon lurking somewhere.

Over the next several years, the movie industry fed my passion for terror—and my paranoia. The movie *Halloween* ended any possibility of parking on a deserted road after a date. I was not going to fog up the windows making myself a sitting duck for any escaped mental patient. The *Friday the 13th* series put a stop to any thought of camping overnight in the wilderness, while *Night of the Living Dead* put a dent in my car. I was in such a panic to get out of the dark parking lot after viewing this old classic that I slammed into a pole, causing $300 damage to my trusty Chevy.

My fright-flick fanaticism was taking a toll on my everyday life. I began to notice that guys who took me to these movies didn't often ask me out again—apparently my squirming and screaming in the theater embarrassed them a bit. Some people just don't know how to really get into a movie. I no longer took babysitting jobs because I was afraid to be alone in a strange house. I wouldn't do laundry at night because that meant I had to go down to the basement.

My fears weren't even limited to being alone. One Friday night I was home watching HBO with my Mom. Let me explain that our house is situated in the dead center of a very isolated woods. As a kid I remember thinking it would be an ideal place for escaped convicts to hide out and hold hostages. Anyway, there we were, munching away on junk food, when suddenly the lights went out. Keep in mind that this was a calm summer evening—no rain, no lightning, not even any wind. There was only one explanation—we had a madman in the basement.

In my alarm I turned to the woman who had protected me all my life. My Mom looked at me and said the only thing she could say, "Grab the potato chips." Chips and keys in tow, we bolted for the car. But this was not to be the end of our ordeal—no electricity, no electric garage door opener. I looked at my Mom and said the only thing I could say, "Ram it!" Bravely, Mom kept her head. She crept out of the security of the locked car to manually open the garage door and drive us, in our pajamas, to safety. It was then that I knew I was out of control. It was then that I decided to go cold turkey—no more horror films.

It's been two years now, and I can finally look back at these escapades and laugh. It's been two years now, and I pride myself on the fact that I live alone. The only thing that keeps me awake nights these days is writing speeches. I'm not going to end up in the nuthouse like Bette Davis. But I'm not going to get too overconfident, either. Remember all those unsuspecting kids in *Halloween?* They were just out having a good time when, WHAM—and the rest is history.

Summary

Special occasions include weddings, funerals, dedications, award ceremonies, retirement dinners, and the like. Nearly always they are occasions for speechmaking. In this chapter we have considered speeches of introduction, speeches of presentation, speeches of acceptance, commemorative speeches, and after-dinner speeches.

When you make a speech of introduction, your job is to build enthusiasm for the main speaker and to establish a welcoming climate that will boost his or her credibility and confidence. Keep your remarks brief, make certain they are completely accurate, and adapt them to the audience, the occasion, and the main speaker.

Speeches of presentation are given when someone is receiving publicly a gift or an award. The main theme of such a speech is to acknowledge the achievements of the recipient. You need to tell the audience why the recipient is receiving the award.

The purpose of an acceptance speech is to give thanks for a gift or an award. When delivering such a speech, you should thank the people who are bestowing the award and recognize the contributions of people who helped you gain it. Be brief, humble, and gracious.

Commemorative speeches are speeches of praise or celebration. They include Fourth of July speeches, eulogies, testimonial addresses, and the like. Your aim in such a speech is to pay tribute to a person, a group of people, an institution, or an idea. When making a commemorative speech you want to inspire your audience—to arouse and heighten their appreciation of and admiration for the subject. You will deal for the most part with intangibles, and your success will depend on how well you put into language the thoughts and feelings appropriate to the occasion.

After-dinner speeches are best thought of as a kind of speech to entertain, and they usually have a lighter tone than informative or persuasive speeches. Neither technical nor argumentative, they seek to stimulate the imagination by approaching the topic in a novel or unexpected way. Although humor can be an important part of after-dinner speeches, it is not essential. If you do use humor, it should grow naturally out of the speech materials and provide insight into the topic.

Key Terms

speech of introduction (436)
speech of presentation (440)
acceptance speech (441)

commemorative speech (442)
after-dinner speech (445)

Review Questions

After reading this chapter, you should be able to answer the following questions:

1. What are the three purposes of a speech of introduction? What guidelines should you follow in preparing such a speech?

2. What is the main theme of a speech of presentation? Depending on the audience and occasion, what two other themes might you include in such a speech?

For further review, go to the Study Questions for this chapter.

CD: STUDY QUESTIONS

3. What are the three major traits of a good acceptance speech?

4. What is the fundamental purpose of a commemorative speech? Why does a successful commemorative speech depend so much on the creative and subtle use of language?

5. What is the primary difference between an after-dinner speech and a speech to inform or to persuade? What is the role of humor in after-dinner speaking?

Exercises for Critical Thinking

1. Attend a speech on campus. Pay special attention to the speech introducing the main speaker. How well does it fit the guidelines discussed in this chapter?

2. Observe several speeches of presentation and acceptance—at a campus awards ceremony or on a television program such as the Academy Awards, Grammy Awards, Emmy Awards, or Tony Awards. Which speeches do you find most effective? Least effective? Why?

3. Analyze the commemorative speech by Andrea Besikof ("The Survivors," pages 444–445). Assess the speech in light of the criteria for commemorative speaking presented in this chapter.

4. Analyze the after-dinner speech by Julie Daggett ("The Horror of It All," pages 447–448). Evaluate the speech in light of the criteria for after-dinner speaking discussed in this chapter.

Applying the POWER of Public Speaking

Your community's fast-growing youth sports program, now one of the largest in the state, serves 5,000 children and teenagers, including your own son and daughter. Welcome as this success has been, it has led to a serious budget shortfall. While your city can continue to provide a basic annual grant, you and other parents have planned a major fund raiser.

Through a college friend who majored in journalism, you have contacted ESPN sportscaster Robin Roberts, who is known to be an active spaker for charity and civic functions. She has agreed to be the featured speaker at your annual recognition banquet. As program chair, you will introduce Roberts based on information provided by the ESPN publicity department. Through a communication glitch, however, the information has failed to arrive and you are running out of time to prepare your two-minute introduction.

Figuring that there must be information about Roberts on the Internet, you log on to Fast Search (http://www.alltheweb.com) and enter "Robin Roberts" + ESPN in the search box. Using the sources you find, write the first minute of your speech.

Notes

[1]William Norwood Brigance, *Speech: Its Techniques and Disciplines in a Free Society* (New York: Appleton-Century-Crofts, 1961), p. 505.

[2]James C. Humes, *Roles Speakers Play* (New York: Harper & Row, 1976), p. 8.

[3]Reprinted with permission of Gregory Peck and the Academy of Motion Picture Arts and Sciences. Copyright 1982 by the Academy of Motion Picture Arts and Sciences.

[4]Reprinted with permission of Danny Kaye and the Academy of Motion Picture Arts and Sciences. Copyright 1982 by the Academy of Motion Picture Arts and Sciences.

[5]Humes, *Roles Speakers Play,* pp. 33–34, 36.

[6]Ronald Reagan, "Address to the Nation, January 28, 1986," in Richard L. Johannesen, R. R. Allen, Wil A. Linkugel, and Ferald J. Bryan (eds.), *Contemporary American Speeches,* 8th ed. (Dubuque, Iowa: Kendall/Hunt, 1997), pp. 407–408.

[7]Reprinted with permission of Andrea Besikof.

[8]Chauncey M. Depew, *My Memories of Eighty Years* (New York: Scribner's, 1924), p. 378.

[9]Barnet Baskerville, *The People's Voice: The Orator in American Society* (Lexington, Ky.: University Press of Kentucky, 1979), p. 112.

[10]For the full text of Bush's speech, see Appendix B.

[11]Reprinted with permission of Julie Daggett.

CHAPTER EIGHTEEN

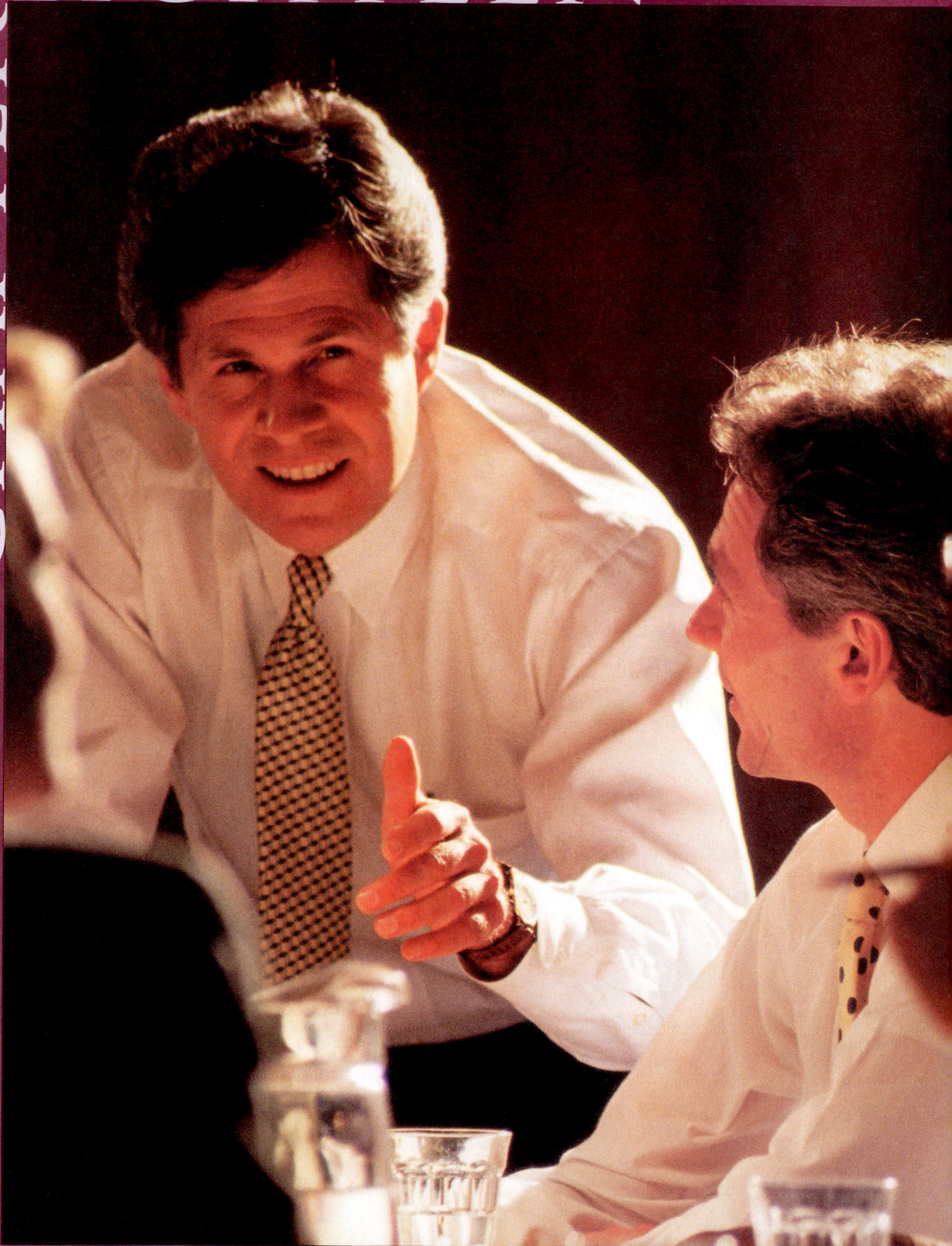

SPEAKING IN SMALL GROUPS

The president of a small company decided to remodel the office space on her management floor. She assigned her youngest vice president, Greg Anapau, to make a plan for remodeling the offices and to carry through the plan.

Greg was very pleased with his plan. He thought he had taken everyone's needs into account, and he had arranged for most of the remodeling to be done over a long weekend so no one's work would be disrupted. On Monday morning, after the remodeling, Greg settled back in his office waiting for congratulations to pour in.

Instead, a crowd of angry people stormed into his office. "There's no telephone jack in my room," said the advertising manager, "and the telephone company says it can't put one in for three weeks. How can I do business without a telephone?"

Right behind him was the administrative assistant. "Do you realize," she said, "how far I have to walk to get to the president's office? It's only 15 feet from my room, but with that new partition, I have to walk halfway around the building!"

Next came the research manager, who said, "What am I supposed to do with my library? All my books are packed up and there's no place to put them."

Angriest of all was another vice president. "For heaven's sake," she said, "why didn't you ask me? The same things happened the *last* time the offices were moved around. I could have told you to watch out for the phone jacks and the research library."

Wearily, Greg went back to his blueprint, making plans to rearrange the offices again.

What went wrong? Greg did not have enough resources on his own to make a successful plan. If a group, instead of a single person, had been assigned to remodel the offices, the problems might have been averted. One person could have taken charge of space needs, another of traffic paths, a third of telephones and other equipment, and so forth. The final plan would have taken *all* factors into account.

Of course, you may have heard the old saying that "a camel is a horse designed by a committee." If you have ever been part of a group that seemed to get nothing done, you may be inclined to say, "Oh, let one person decide and get it over with." The problem in such cases, however, is not that there is a group, but that the group is not functioning properly. A great deal of research shows that if members of a group work well together, they can almost always resolve a problem better than a single person.[1]

This chapter deals with speaking in a particular kind of group—the problem-solving small group.

What Is a Small Group?

dyad
A group of two people.

As its name implies, a small group has a limited number of members. The minimum number is three. (A group of two persons is called a *dyad,* and it operates quite differently from a group of three or more.) There is some difference of opinion about the maximum number of people who constitute a small group. Most experts set the maximum number at seven or eight; some go as high as twelve.[2] The important point is that the group must be small enough to allow free discussion among all members. In small-group communication, all participants are potentially speakers *and* listeners. A manageable number of people permits everyone to shift easily between speaking and listening.

Members of a small group assemble for a specific purpose. They are not just a band of three to twelve people who happen to end up in the same room. Several shoppers milling around the clothing section of a department store are not a small group, even if they speak to one another or comment about high prices and poor service. But if those same shoppers decided to meet together and prepare a formal complaint to the store manager about high prices and poor service, they would then constitute a small group. They would have assembled for a specific purpose.

A *problem-solving small group* is formed to solve a particular problem. Such groups exist in every area of life. Business groups consider ways of increasing sales. Church groups discuss how to raise funds and provide for the needy. Groups of parents work on improving day care facilities. The President's cabinet debates a foreign policy move. A ski club evaluates proposals for the next outing. You will almost surely be a member of many problem-solving small groups during your life.

Although speaking in a small group is not the same as public speaking, it involves many similar skills. Members of a small group influence one another through communication. At times they inform their fellow members. At other times they seek to persuade them. As a participant in a small group, you might influence your colleagues by giving them important information, by encouraging them to speak, by convincing them to change their minds, by leading them into a new channel of communication, even by getting them to end a meeting of the group. All other members of the group have the same opportunity to influence you through effective communication.[3]

small group
A collection of three to twelve people who assemble for a specific purpose.

problem-solving small group
A small group formed to solve a particular problem.

Leadership in Small Groups

We have said that small groups often make better decisions than do individuals. But the word "often" should be stressed here. To make sound decisions, groups need effective leadership.

Kinds of Leadership

Sometimes there is *no specific leader.* In such a situation, members of effective groups tend to have equal influence. When a need for leadership arises, any of the members can—and one probably will—provide the necessary leadership. A typical instance might be a class project, in which you and several classmates are working together. From time to time each of you will help the group move toward its goal by suggesting when and where to meet, by outlining the strengths and weaknesses of a certain viewpoint, by resolving disagreements among other members, and so forth.[4]

In some circumstances a group may have an *implied leader.* For example, if a business meeting includes one vice president and several subordinates, the vice president becomes the implied leader. The same is true if one member of the group is a specialist in the topic at hand and the others

leadership
The ability to influence group members so as to help achieve the goals of the group.

implied leader
A group member to whom other members defer because of her or his rank, expertise, or other quality.

are not. Members will likely defer to the person with the highest rank or greatest expertise, and that person will become the group's implied leader.

Even when a group starts out leaderless, there may be an *emergent leader.* This is a person who, by ability or by force of personality, or just by talking the most, takes a leadership role.[5] The emergence of a leader may or may not be desirable. If the group is stalemated or has dissolved into bickering or making jokes, an emergent leader can put the group back on track. There is a danger, however, that the emergent leader may be not the most effective leader but merely the most assertive personality. Ideally, each member of the group should be prepared to assume a leadership role when necessary.

Finally, there may be a *designated leader*—a person elected or appointed as leader when the group is formed. A group that meets for only one session should almost always have a designated leader who takes care of the procedural tasks and serves as spokesperson for the group. Likewise, a formal committee will usually have a designated chairperson. The chair can perform leadership functions or delegate them, but he or she remains in charge of the group.[6]

A group may or may not need a specific leader, but it always needs leadership. When all members of the group are skilled communicators, they can take turns at providing leadership even if the group has a designated or implied leader. As you develop group communication skills, you should be prepared to assume a leadership role whenever necessary.[7]

Functions of Leadership

An effective leader helps the group reach its goals by fulfilling three overlapping sets of needs—procedural needs, task needs, and maintenance needs.

Procedural Needs

Procedural needs can be thought of as the "housekeeping" requirements of the group. They include:

Deciding when and where the group will meet.

Reserving the room, checking the number of chairs, making sure the heat or air conditioning is turned on.

Setting the agenda of each meeting.

Starting the meeting.

Taking notes during the meeting.

Preparing and distributing any written handouts needed for the meeting.

Summarizing the group's progress at the end of the meeting.

If there is a designated leader, she or he can attend to these needs or assign one or more group members to do so. Otherwise, members of the group must devise ways to split the procedural responsibilities.

emergent leader
A group member who emerges as a leader during the group's deliberations.

designated leader
A person who is elected or appointed as leader when the group is formed.

procedural needs
Routine "housekeeping" actions necessary for the efficient conduct of business in a small group.

Task Needs

Task needs go beyond procedural needs and are substantive actions necessary to help the group complete the particular task it is working on. They include:

Analyzing the issues facing the group.

Distributing the workload among the members.

Collecting information.

Soliciting the views of other members.

Keeping the group from going off on a tangent.

Playing devil's advocate for unpopular ideas.

Formulating criteria for judging the most effective solution.

Helping the group reach consensus on its final recommendations.

Most members will help the group satisfy its task needs. Leadership becomes necessary when some task needs are not being fulfilled adequately, as in this example:

A group of students had undertaken to solve the parking problems on their campus. The group had held several meetings, and most of its task needs had been met. Members had done a good job polling students for their opinions, discussing alternative solutions with the administration, and considering the relative merits of each solution. However, one member of the group, Pilar, noticed that two items had not been given enough attention: No one had investigated potential sources of money for new parking facilities, and no one had studied the environmental impact of constructing additional parking spaces. Therefore, Pilar briefly took a leadership role to perform a task need for the group. She pointed out that these two areas had been neglected and recommended that the group explore them further.

The effective leader—whether permanent or temporary—has a realistic notion of the group's task needs and of how to meet them.

Maintenance Needs

Maintenance needs involve interpersonal relations in the group. They include such factors as:

How well members get along with one another.

How willing members are to contribute to the group.

Whether members are supportive of one another.

Whether members feel satisfied with the group's accomplishments.

Whether members feel good about their roles in the group.

If interpersonal problems dominate discussion, the group will have a difficult time working together and reaching a decision. This is one of the more important areas calling for effective leadership. A leader can do much

task needs
Substantive actions necessary to help a small group complete its assigned task.

maintenance needs
Communicative actions necessary to maintain interpersonal relations in a small group.

Small groups require effective leadership to accomplish their goals. They also require members who participate fully and communicate well with each other.

to create and sustain supportive communication in the group. By helping group members handle conflict, by working out differences of opinion, by reducing interpersonal tension, by encouraging participation from all members, by being alert to personal feelings, and by promoting solidarity within the group, a leader can make a tremendous contribution toward helping the group achieve its goals.[8]

Responsibilities in a Small Group

Every member of a small group must assume certain responsibilities, which can be divided into five major categories: (1) commit yourself to the goals of your group; (2) fulfill individual assignments; (3) avoid interpersonal conflicts; (4) encourage full participation; (5) keep the discussion on track. Some of these responsibilities involve leadership roles, but all five are so important that each participant should take them as personal obligations, regardless of the group's leadership. Let us look more closely at each of these responsibilities.

Commit Yourself to the Goals of Your Group

For a group to succeed, members must align their personal goals with the group's goal. This sounds obvious, but it is not always easy. When you are working with other students on a class project, the group goal—and most likely the goal of each member—is to get a good grade, which should ensure a positive attitude toward the group. There is a strong incentive for members to cooperate and commit themselves to completing the task.

Problems arise when one or more members have personal goals that conflict with the group's goal. Here is the kind of situation that can occur:

Irene Messner is a member of her church's committee to buy new equipment for the parish house kitchen. Because the budget is very tight, the committee's goal is to get the best equipment for the lowest price. But unknown to the other members of the group, Irene's son-in-law is a salesman for a distributor of high-priced kitchen appliances. Privately, Irene has reasoned that if she can sway the committee toward that company, her son-in-law will get a large commission. Irene does not mention this fact to the group. Instead, she argues that *quality*—not price—should be the determining factor in the purchase. The group process breaks down because Irene will not surrender her private goal.

This is an extreme example, but there can be more subtle kinds of private goals, as in the following case:

Jeff and Rachel are part of a group, and Jeff would like to be on closer terms with Rachel. In order to impress her, he may agree with everything she says, regardless of whether he really shares her views. Consequently, Jeff's expressed views are not his actual views. In short, Jeff has a *hidden agenda* in the group meeting. The group's agenda is to solve the problem, but Jeff's agenda is to get a date with Rachel.

Group members may have all sorts of hidden agendas. One may be experiencing personal problems—lowered grades, a breakup with a friend, trouble at home, or just a bad day. Another may have a commitment to a different group whose goals conflict with those of the present group. A third may want to take charge of the group for reasons of personal power, regardless of the group's task.

Remember that what one member of a group does affects all the other members. You should not try to advance your own interests or boost your own ego at the expense of the group and its goals. Beware of hidden agendas—whether yours or someone else's—and participate with a positive spirit. If a group is to work effectively, all members must commit themselves to the goals of the group and cooperate to achieve them.

hidden agenda
A set of unstated individual goals that may conflict with the goals of the group as a whole.

Fulfill Individual Assignments

As mentioned earlier, one of the advantages of the group process is that it divides the workload among several people. Work assignments might involve gathering information, making arrangements for a meeting, researching a particular aspect of the group's topic, taking notes at a meeting, and so forth. Unless every member fulfills his or her assignments, the group's entire project may fail—as in the following example:

Several years ago, one student group decided that as a class project they would bring Easter baskets to the patients in the children's ward of a local hospital. After the project had been approved, assignments were given out. Navid would coordinate with the hospital authorities. Corrine would handle fund-raising for the needed supplies. Jesse would supervise the egg-decorating team. Xunhua would be responsible for buying baskets and chocolate bunnies. Josh would arrange for transportation to the hospital.

Everybody completed their assignments except Josh, who was busy writing a term paper. He asked a friend to pick up a bus schedule and assumed everything would be fine. On Easter morning the group assembled at the bus stop, loaded down with baskets for the children. And they waited and waited. After an hour Josh called the bus company, only to discover that the buses did not run on holidays. By the time Josh had made other arrangements to get to the hospital, visiting hours were over, and the group could not get in.

No matter what other assignments they may have, *all* members of a group have one very critical assignment—listening. If you tune out the person who is speaking, or if you concentrate entirely on what *you* plan to say next, the group is not going to make much progress.

Effective listening is vital to small-group communication. First, it helps you understand what is happening in the group. And unlike a public speaking situation, you can stop the speaker and ask for clarification on any point about which you are confused. Second, listening helps you evaluate the merits of the speaker's position in relation to your own. Third, listening provides support for the speaker and helps establish a positive climate for discussion. In group discussion, as in other kinds of situations, listening is crucial to effective communication.[9]

Avoid Interpersonal Conflicts

If groups were made up of robots, there would be no problem with interpersonal conflicts. But groups are made up of people—people with likes and dislikes and animosities and prejudices and very different personalities. It is vital to the group process that disagreements be kept on a task level, rather than on a personal level.

Suppose you disagree with another member's idea. Disagreement on the personal level could sound like this: "That's the most stupid idea I ever heard of! Do you realize how much money it would cost to do that?" But on the task level, disagreement is aimed at the *idea,* not the person: "Potentially that's a very good solution, but I'm not sure we have enough money to accomplish it."

When disagreements are allowed to become personal, some members may start to see the group as a kind of debating society. Rather than focusing on the task, they may spend their time getting even with other participants, defending themselves, trying to score points, and jumping on people's ideas. Other members—especially those who are shy or soft-spoken—may recoil from the verbal combat and withdraw from active participation in the group's deliberations.

No matter what the group, personal antagonism leaves a bad taste in everyone's mouth and harms the performance of the group. It's essential that someone take a leadership role and bring the discussion back to the relevant issues. Let's say your group is considering the practicality of adding a vegetarian section to the dormitory cafeteria. The discussion might go like this:

Miguel: It seems to me a waste of time, money, and space to make a special section for vegetarians. There are plenty of vegetables on the menu now. Anyone who doesn't want to eat the meat doesn't have to.

Liu: You're not getting the point. Vegetarian menus have to be *balanced* with enough vegetable protein. It's not enough to say, "Don't eat the meat." We need a special section where the menus are planned for a nutritious vegetarian diet.

Miguel: Oh, for pity's sake, you food freaks are all alike. You think you've got the true faith and all the rest of us are sinners just because we eat a hamburger now and then.

Liu: If you want to kill innocent animals to eat, that's none of my business. Go ahead, ruin your health, load yourself up with cholesterol. I don't care. But don't stand in the way of people who really care about their bodies.

Leader: Just a minute. Before we go on with this part of the discussion, don't we have some figures on how many students would actually use the vegetarian section? Lisa, I think that was your department. What did you find out?

None of this is to say that members of a group should never disagree. In fact, a serious problem occurs when members get along so well and are so concerned about maintaining the harmony of the group that they will not disagree with one another about anything. Whenever one member makes a suggestion, everybody else thinks it's a wonderful idea. When this happens, the group misses the benefit of having a group in the first place. There is no chance to reach the best decision by exploring an array of perspectives, opinions, and information. A group that is concerned above all with dodging disagreement will not be any more effective than one that dissolves into personal quarreling.

The point, then, is not that groups should avoid conflict but that they should keep it at the task level and not allow it to degenerate into personal feuding. There is usually little achievement—and even less feeling of satisfaction—when a group is consumed by personal bickering and antagonism.

Encourage Full Participation

If a group is to work effectively, all members must contribute fully and share their ideas with one another. Every member of a group should take responsibility for encouraging other members to participate. You can do this, first of all, by listening attentively. Listening provides support for the speaker. After all, how would you like to speak in a group where everybody else appears bored or distracted?

If there are one or two quiet members in the group, you can draw them into the discussion by asking their opinions and showing your interest in their ideas and information. For instance, you can say something like, "We haven't heard from Jason in a while, and he has some personal experience in this matter. Jason, can you tell the others what you told me about this plan?"

Another way to encourage participation is to help build a supportive environment. When a member speaks, you can say, "That's an interesting idea." Or "I never knew that, can you tell us more about it?" Conversely, try to avoid negative comments that will squelch a speaker before she or he has finished—comments like "Oh, no, that never works" or "What a dumb idea." Supportive comments create goodwill among group members and make everyone feel free to discuss their ideas without ridicule or embarrassment.

If you are shy or afraid your ideas will be taken too critically, you may be unwilling to participate at first. To overcome your diffidence, try to remember that your contribution is necessary to the group. This is why you are there. At the very least, you can help provide a supportive environment for discussion by listening, reacting, and encouraging the free exchange of ideas.

Keep the Discussion on Track

In some groups the discussion proceeds like a stream-of-consciousness exercise. Here is a hypothetical example in which a town planning board is considering installing a new traffic light at a busy intersection:

Ahmed: You know, we're going to have trouble getting cars to come to a full stop even if we do put in a traffic light.

Diana: Tell me about it! I came through there yesterday and hit my brakes, and the car just kept going. Maybe I need the brakes adjusted, though.

Mike: Get ready to pay through the nose. I had a brake job on my car last week, and it was nearly twice as much as last time.

Rico: That's nothing. Have you looked at lawnmowers lately? And if you think lawnmowers are high . . .

Jill: Who mows lawns? I had my yard planted with ground cover and put gravel over the rest. It's . . .

Leader: Excuse me, folks, but weren't we talking about the *traffic light?*

Every member has a responsibility to keep the discussion on track and to intervene if the group wanders too far afield. There is nothing wrong with a little casual conversation to break the tension or provide a brief respite from work, but it shouldn't be allowed to get out of hand. When working in a problem-solving group, make sure the group's ultimate goal is always in the forefront. Do your best to see that discussion proceeds in an orderly fashion from one point to the next and that the group does not get bogged down in side issues.

On the other hand, you need to guard against the tendency to progress to a solution too quickly, without thoroughly exploring the problem. This concern can be especially serious when members of a group are tired or discouraged. If you feel your group is taking the easy way out and jumping at an easy solution, try to make the other members aware of your concern. By suggesting that they talk about the problem in more detail, you may bring out vital information or ideas. One classroom group learned the perils of making a snap decision:

> The group's first job was to decide what they should do for a class project. Near the beginning of their first meeting, someone suggested that they observe an established small group—the city council of their community—to see how the group worked. Everyone thought it was a splendid idea, and the class group wrapped up their session, congratulating themselves on having disposed of the problem so quickly.
>
> But what looked at first like a great idea proved to have some crucial drawbacks. First, it turned out that the city council would not meet again until after the group's class project was due. Second, the city council had 20 people on it—not really an appropriate number to study as a small group. The quick solution turned out to be no solution at all.

Fortunately, there are systematic ways to keep the discussion on track and to avoid hasty group decisions. If your group follows a tested method of decision making, it will have a much better chance of reaching a satisfactory decision.[10] We turn, therefore, to the most common decision-making technique for small groups—the reflective-thinking method.[11]

The Reflective-Thinking Method

The reflective-thinking method is derived from the writings of the American philosopher John Dewey. It offers a logical, step-by-step process for discussion in problem-solving groups. The method consists of five steps: (1) defining the problem; (2) analyzing the problem; (3) establishing criteria for solving the problem; (4) generating potential solutions; (5) selecting the best solution. By following these steps, your group will make its work much easier.

Let's take a closer look at the reflective-thinking method. As we do, we'll illustrate each step by following a single group through the entire process.

reflective-thinking method
A five-step method for directing discussion in a problem-solving small group.

Define the Problem

Before a problem-solving group can make progress, it must know exactly what problem it is trying to solve. Defining the problem may seem easy, but it is not always so. In a sense, defining the problem for group discussion is akin to settling on a specific purpose for a speech. Unless it is done properly, everything that follows will suffer.

The best way to define the problem is to phrase it as a *question of policy*. We discussed questions of policy in Chapter 15 (see pages 378–382).

question of policy
A question about whether a specific course of action should or should not be taken.

Here it is enough to note that questions of policy inquire about the necessity and/or practicality of specific courses of action. Questions of policy typically include the word "should." For example:

What measures should our school take to deal with hazing by athletic teams and other groups on campus?

What steps should the legislature take to protect residents of our state against identity theft?

What policy should the United States adopt with respect to the exploitation of child labor in other countries around the world?

When phrasing the question for discussion, your group should follow several guidelines. First, make sure the question is as clear and specific as possible. For example:

Ineffective: What should be done about fraudulent charities?

More Effective: What should the federal government do to control the activities of fraudulent charities?

Second, phrase the question to allow for a wide variety of answers. Be especially wary of questions that can be answered with a simple yes or no. For example:

Ineffective: Should the city build a new elementary school?

More Effective: What steps should the city take to deal with increasing enrollment in the elementary schools?

Third, avoid biased or slanted questions. For example:

Ineffective: How can we keep the campus bookstore from ripping off students?

More Effective: What changes, if any, should be made in the pricing policies of the campus bookstore?

Fourth, make sure you pose a single question. For example:

Ineffective: What revisions should the college consider in its admissions requirements and in its graduation requirements?

More Effective: What revisions should the college consider in its admissions requirements?

More Effective: What revisions should the college consider in its graduation requirements?

To clarify this first step of the reflective-thinking method, let's see how our model problem-solving group defined the problem:

As a class project, the group set out to discuss the problem of sharply rising costs for attending college. Following the reflective-thinking method, they began by defining the problem. After several false starts they phrased the problem this way: "What steps should our school take to reduce student costs for attending college?"

Analyze the Problem

After the problem has been defined, the group begins to analyze it. Too often, groups (like individuals) start mapping out solutions before they have a firm grasp of what is wrong. This is like a doctor prescribing treatment before fully diagnosing the patient's ailment. If your group investigates the problem as thoroughly as possible, you will be in a much better position to devise a workable solution.

In analyzing the problem, pay particular attention to two questions. First, how severe is the problem? Investigate the scope of the problem. Determine how many people it affects. Assess what might happen if the problem is not resolved. Second, what are the causes of the problem? Check into the history of the problem. Learn what factors contributed to it. Ascertain its major causes.

As you might imagine, analyzing the problem requires research. Effective group decisions depend on having the best information available. You can get this information in the same way you gather materials for a speech. Sometimes you can rely on your own knowledge and experience. More often, you need to get information from other sources—by looking on the Internet, by interviewing someone with expertise on the topic, or by working in the library (see Chapter 6). When meeting with your group, make sure you have done the research assigned to you, so you can offer complete and unbiased information.

Let's return now to our sample group and see how it analyzed the problem of rapidly escalating student costs for attending college:

The group talked first about the severity of the problem. Tuition had risen dramatically, as had outlays for books and incidentals. One member offered statistics to show that the cost of attending college had doubled in the past 10 years. Other members noted that the problem was affecting not only students. Merchants within the college community were being hurt because students had less money to spend on such items as clothes and entertainment. The institution itself was affected since rising costs were driving away students who might otherwise have applied.

To determine the causes of the problem, the group researched articles in the library about the rise in student costs for attending college across the nation. They also interviewed an economics professor and the head of the student aid program on campus. After studying the matter thoroughly, the group identified several major causes, including administrative costs, faculty salaries, the rising price of textbooks, and increased living expenses.

Establish Criteria for Solutions

If you planned to buy a car, how would you proceed? You would probably not just walk into a dealer's showroom and buy whatever appealed to you on the spur of the moment. You would most likely decide ahead of time

criteria
Standards on which a judgment or decision can be based.

what kind of car you wanted, what options it should have, and how much money you could afford to spend. That is, you would establish *criteria* to guide you in deciding exactly which car to buy.

You should do much the same thing in group discussion. Once your group has analyzed the problem, you should not jump immediately to proposing solutions. Instead, you should take time to establish criteria—standards—for responsible solutions. You should work out (and write down) exactly what your solutions must achieve and any factors that might limit your choice of solutions. If, for example, a committee is authorized to spend a maximum of $1,000 on a club's annual banquet, one of the criteria for the committee's decision will be that the banquet cost no more than $1,000.

A common failing of problem-solving groups is that they start to discuss solutions before agreeing on criteria for the solutions. When this happens, a group runs into trouble. Some people will propose solutions based on one set of criteria, while others will propose solutions based on different criteria. You can avoid such conflicts by making sure the group sets up criteria before proposing solutions.

To give a better idea of how this stage of the reflective-thinking method works, let's look at the cost-cutting group we have been following:

After some discussion, the group established these criteria for possible solutions: (1) The solution should significantly reduce students' costs. (2) The solution should come into force at the start of the next school year. (3) The solution should not hurt the prestige of the college. (4) The cost of the solution should be minimal and should be paid by the administration. (5) The human resources needed to implement the solution should come from administrative personnel already working on the school's staff. (6) The solution should involve only actions controlled by the college—not matters controlled by outside individuals or agencies.

Generate Potential Solutions

Once your group has the criteria firmly in mind, you are ready to discuss solutions. Your goal at this stage is to come up with the widest possible range of potential solutions—not to judge the solutions. That comes later. At this stage you are only suggesting possibilities. One member of the group should be responsible for writing down all the solutions proposed at this time.

brainstorming
A method of generating ideas by free association of words and thoughts.

Many groups find the technique of *brainstorming* helpful in this stage. Brainstorming allows a group to generate a variety of solutions without prematurely evaluating them. In Chapter 4 we discussed how brainstorming can work for an individual in choosing a speech topic. Here brainstorming is expanded to the whole group.

The best approach is to begin by having each member of the group list all the possible solutions he or she can think of. One member of the group should then consolidate the individual lists into a single master list. The group should discuss the master list to make sure potential solutions have not been overlooked. At this stage, members often "piggyback" new ideas onto ideas on the master list. For example, if one suggestion is "Establish food co-ops," a group member might say, "Yes, and we could establish cloth-

A problem-solving small group needs accurate, unbiased information if it is to make an effective decision. In a class project, all group members have an obligation to help the group complete its research.

ing co-ops, too." One member should be responsible for writing down these new ideas and adding them to the master list. The brainstorming process continues until the group cannot think of any more solutions.

Brainstorming in this fashion has two advantages. First, it encourages creativity. There is a great deal of research to show that beginning with written lists produces more and higher-quality ideas than when a group tries to generate potential solutions by oral discussion.[12] Second, this method of brainstorming encourages equal participation. Having each member create his or her own list of potential solutions makes it less likely that one or two members will dominate the process or that anyone will hold back ideas for fear of being hooted down.

Let's see how our cost-cutting group handled this stage:

> By brainstorming, the group came up with the following possible solutions: (1) reduce the number of required books for each course; (2) cut some of the "fat" from the administrative staff; (3) make all professors teach more courses; (4) approach landlords about stabilizing rent and utility costs; (5) establish food and clothing co-ops; (6) increase financial aid; (7) decrease the amount of money available for faculty research; (8) boycott businesses around the campus where price markups are highest; (9) increase out-of-state tuition; (10) decrease dormitory expenses; (11) organize fundraising programs with the student union; (12) redirect some money from construction of new buildings to student aid. This was a good yield from a brainstorming session— twelve solid suggestions.

The Reflective Thinking Checklist can help your group keep its discussion on track

CD: SPEECH CHECKLIST

Select the Best Solution

After all potential solutions have been listed, it is time to evaluate them and choose the best solution or solutions. The best way to proceed is to take a particular solution, discuss it with regard to the criteria established earlier in the group's deliberations, then move on to the next solution, and so on. This orderly process ensures that all potential solutions receive equal consideration.

consensus
A group decision that is acceptable to all members of the group.

As each potential solution is discussed, the group should make every effort to reach *consensus*. A consensus decision is one that all members accept, even though the decision may not be ideal in the eyes of every member. In other words, consensus may range from full approval of a decision to "Well, I can live with it." Because it usually results in superior decisions as well as in a high degree of unity within the group, consensus is the ideal of group decision making. It comes about when members have been so cooperative that they reach a common decision through reasoning, honest exchange of ideas, and full examination of the issues.[13]

Like most ideals, consensus can be difficult to achieve. If there are different viewpoints, members of the group will often try to find the easiest way to resolve the differences. Sometimes a member will call for a vote, which is very agreeable to those holding a majority opinion (since they will win) but not so pleasant for those in the minority. Resorting to a vote does resolve the immediate conflict, but it may not result in the best solution. Moreover, it weakens unity in the group by fostering factions and perhaps by creating bitterness among the members who lose on the vote. A group should vote only when it has failed in every other attempt to find a solution agreeable to all members.

What kind of final decision did our model cost-cutting group reach? Let's see:

The cost-cutting group had twelve possible solutions to evaluate. Three were rejected because they violated the group's criterion that an acceptable solution must involve only actions controlled directly by the college. Redirecting building money to student aid could be done only by the state legislature. Approaching landlords about stabilizing rent and boycotting campus businesses were also outside the jurisdiction of college administrators.

Three more solutions were rejected because they were economically impractical. Increasing financial aid would hurt many students because the funds would have to come from student fees. Raising out-of-state tuition would drive away 10 percent of the college's out-of-state students. And decreasing dorm costs would make it impossible to provide minimally acceptable services.

The proposal to reduce funds for faculty research was also rejected since most research money comes from government, corporations, and foundations. Besides, research was recognized as a primary means of maintaining the college's prestige. Finally, the suggestion to reduce administrative "fat" was rejected as too costly because a group would have to be established to audit all administrative duties.

After refining the suggestions, the group finally reached consensus on a solution that included the following provisions: (1) A student should not have to spend more than $80 on required books for any single course. (2) The university should authorize the student union to organize food, book, and clothing co-ops. (3) The student union should conduct five fund-raising projects each academic year. (4) Each professor should teach one more class a year.

Once consensus has been reached on a solution or solutions to the problem, the group is ready to present its findings.

Presenting the Recommendations of the Group

The work of a problem-solving group does not end with the last stage of the reflective-thinking process. Once a group has agreed on its recommendations, it usually needs to present them to somebody. A business group might report to the president of the company or to the board of directors. A special committee of the city council reports to the full council. A presidential commission reports to the President and to the nation at large. A classroom group reports to the instructor and to the rest of the class. The purpose of such reports is to present the group's recommendations clearly and convincingly.

Sometimes a group will prepare a formal written report. Often, however, the written report is supplemented with—or replaced by—an oral report, a symposium, or a panel discussion.

Oral Report

An oral report is much the same in content as a written report. If the group has a designated leader, she or he will probably deliver the report. Otherwise, the group will have to select one person for the job.

If you are picked to present your group's report, you should approach it as you would any other speech. Your task is to explain the purpose, procedures, and recommendations of your group. As with any speech, your report should have three main sections. The introduction will state the purpose of the report and preview its main points. The body will spell out the problem addressed by your group, the criteria set for a solution, and the solution being recommended. The conclusion will summarize the main points and, in some cases, urge that the group's recommendations be adopted.

Also, as with any other speech, you should adapt your report to the audience. Use supporting materials to clarify and strengthen your ideas, and consider whether using visual aids will enhance your message. Make sure your language is accurate, clear, vivid, and appropriate. Rehearse the report so you can deliver it fluently and decisively. Afterward, you—and possibly other members of the group—may be called on to answer questions from the audience. (Review the section on answering questions in Chapter 12, pages 302–306.)

Symposium

A symposium consists of a moderator and several speakers seated together in front of an audience. If the group presenting the symposium has a designated leader, he or she will typically be the moderator. The moderator's job is to introduce the topic and the speakers. Each speaker in turn delivers a prepared speech on a different aspect of the topic. After the speeches, there may be a question-and-answer session with the audience.

The symposium is often used for group reports in speech classes. One way to organize it is to have each member of the group present a brief talk sketching the group's work and decisions during one stage of the reflective-

oral report
A speech presenting the findings, conclusions, decisions, etc. of a small group.

symposium
A public presentation in which several people present prepared speeches on different aspects of the same topic.

Speaking in a small group requires many of the same skills involved in public speaking. Group members may even make formal presentations as part of the group's deliberations or when presenting the group's report.

thinking process. Another way is to have each speaker deal with a major issue relating to the discussion topic. A group dealing with capital punishment, for example, might have one speaker present the group's conclusion on the issue of whether capital punishment is an effective deterrent to crime, another speaker present the group's position on the morality of capital punishment, and so forth.

No matter what kind of symposium your group presents, all the speeches should be carefully planned. They should also be coordinated with one another to make sure the symposium reports on all important aspects of the group's project.

Panel Discussion

panel discussion
A structured conversation on a given topic among several people in front of an audience.

A panel discussion is essentially a conversation in front of an audience. The panel should have a moderator, who introduces the topic and the panelists. Once the discussion is under way, the moderator may interject questions and comments as needed to focus the discussion. The panelists speak briefly, informally, and impromptu. They talk to each other, but loudly enough for the audience to be able to hear. As with a symposium, a panel discussion may be followed by a question-and-answer session with the audience.

Because of its spontaneity, a panel discussion can be exciting for participants and audience alike. But, unfortunately, that spontaneity inhibits systematic presentation of a group's recommendations. Thus the panel discussion is seldom used by problem-solving groups, although it can work well for information-gathering groups.

If you are a participant in a panel discussion, beware of the common fallacy that no serious preparation is required. Although you will speak impromptu, you need to study the topic ahead of time, analyze the major issues, and map out the points you want to be sure to make during the discussion. An effective panel discussion also requires planning by the moderator and panelists to decide what issues will be discussed and in what order. Finally, all panelists must be willing to share talking time. One purpose of a panel is to have all participants voice their ideas, not to have one or two members monopolize the discussion.

Whatever method your group uses to present its findings, you can benefit from the public speaking guidelines given throughout this book. The techniques of effective speech need refinement for different situations, but the principles remain the same whether you are one person addressing an audience, part of a small group of people working to solve a problem, or a participant in a symposium or a panel discussion.

Summary

A small group consists of three to twelve people assembled for a specific purpose. A problem-solving small group, as its name implies, is formed to solve a particular problem. When such a group has effective leadership, it usually makes better decisions than do individuals by themselves. Most groups have a designated leader, an implied leader, or an emergent leader. Some groups have no specific leader, in which case all members of the group must assume leadership responsibilities. An effective leader helps a group reach its goals by fulfilling procedural needs, task needs, and maintenance needs. As you develop your skills in group communication, you should be prepared to assume a leadership role whenever necessary.

Apart from leadership, all members of a group have five basic responsibilities. You should commit yourself to the goals of your group, fulfill your individual assignments, avoid interpersonal conflict within the group, encourage full participation by all members, and help keep the group on track. Meeting these responsibilities is vital if your group is to be successful.

Your group will also be more successful if it follows the reflective-thinking method, which offers a logical, step-by-step process for decision making in problem-solving groups. The method consists of five steps: (1) defining the problem as clearly and specifically as possible; (2) analyzing the problem to determine its severity and causes; (3) establishing criteria to guide the group in evaluating solutions; (4) generating a wide range of potential solutions; (5) selecting the best solution or solutions.

Once your group has agreed on its recommendations, it usually has to present them to somebody. Sometimes this presentation will be in the form of a written report. Often, however, it will be an oral presentation—a report by one member of the group, a symposium, or a panel discussion. Whichever kind of oral presentation your group gives will call for the skills of effective speechmaking explained throughout this book.

Key Terms

dyad (454)
small group (455)
problem-solving small group (455)

leadership (455)
implied leader (455)
emergent leader (456)

designated leader (456)   criteria (466)
procedural needs (456)   brainstorming (466)
task needs (457)   consensus (468)
maintenance needs (457)   oral report (469)
hidden agenda (459)   symposium (469)
reflective-thinking method (463)   panel discussion (470)
question of policy (464)

Review Questions

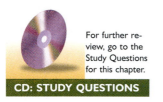

For further review, go to the Study Questions for this chapter.

CD: STUDY QUESTIONS

After reading this chapter, you should be able to answer the following questions:

1. What is a small group? What is a problem-solving small group?

2. What are the four kinds of leadership that may occur in a small group? Explain the three kinds of needs fulfilled by leadership in a small group.

3. What are the five major responsibilities of every participant in a small group?

4. What are the stages of the reflective-thinking method? Explain the major tasks of a group at each stage.

5. What are the three methods for presenting orally the recommendations of a problem-solving group?

Exercises for Critical Thinking

1. Identify the flaw (or flaws) in each of the following questions for a problem-solving group discussion. Rewrite each question so it conforms with the criteria discussed in the chapter for effective discussion questions.

    a. Should all students be required to take two years of a foreign language to graduate from college?
    b. What should be done to prevent the utterly ridiculous shortage of computers for students at this school?
    c. What should be done about sweatshops?
    d. What should our state government do to control taxes and to combat drunk driving?
    e. Should the federal government institute a system of standardized national tests for all schoolchildren?

2. If possible, arrange to observe a problem-solving small group in action. You might attend a meeting of your city council, the school board, the zoning commission, a local business, a church committee. To what extent does the discussion measure up to the criteria of effective

discussion presented in this chapter? What kind of leadership does the group have, and how well does the leader (or leaders) fulfill the group's procedural needs, task needs, and maintenance needs? How do the other members meet their responsibilities? What aspects of the meeting are handled most effectively? Which are handled least effectively?

3. Identify a relatively important decision you have made in the last year or two. Try to reconstruct how you reached that decision. Now suppose you could remake the decision following the reflective-thinking method. Map out exactly what you would do at each stage of the method. Do you still reach the same decision? If not, do you believe the reflective-thinking method would have led you to a better decision in the first place?

4. Attend a symposium or panel discussion on campus. Prepare a brief analysis of the proceedings. First, study the role of the moderator. How does she or he introduce the topic and participants? What role does the moderator play thereafter? Does she or he help guide and focus the panel discussion? Does she or he summarize and conclude the proceedings at the end?

    Second, observe the participants. Are the speeches in the symposium well prepared and presented? Which speaker (or speakers) do you find most effective? Least effective? Why? Do participants in the panel discussion share talking time? Does their discussion appear well planned to cover major aspects of the topic? Which panelist (or panelists) do you find most effective? Least effective? Why?

Notes

[1]Charles Pavitt and Ellen Curtis, *Small Group Discussion: A Theoretical Approach,* 2nd ed. (Scottsdale, Ariz.: Gorsuch Scarisbrick, 1994), pp. 25–62.
[2]For a summary of research on the question of group size, see Richard L. Moreland, John M. Levine, and Melissa L. Wingert, "Creating the Ideal Group: Composition Effects at Work," in Erich H. Witte and James H. Davis (eds.), *Understanding Group Behavior: Small Group Processes and Interpersonal Relations* (Mahwah, N.J.: Lawrence Erlbaum, 1996), II, pp. 12–15.
[3]The importance of communication to effective group discussion is stressed by Charles Pavitt, "Does Communication Matter in Social Influence During Small Group Discussion? Five Positions," *Communication Studies,* 44 (1993), pp. 216–227. For a recent review of scholarship in this area, see Marshall Scott Poole, "Group Communication Theory," in Lawrence R. Frey, Dennis S. Gouran, and Marshall Scott Poole (eds.), *Handbook of Group Communication Theory and Research* (Thousand Oaks, Calif.: Sage, 1999), pp. 37–70.
[4]See David Barry, "The Bossless Team," in Robert S. Cathcart, Larry A. Samovar, and Linda D. Henman (eds.), *Small Group Communication: Theory and Practice,* 7th ed. (Madison, Wis.: Brown and Benchmark, 1996), pp. 411–424.
[5]B. Aubrey Fisher and Donald G. Ellis, *Small Group Decision Making: Communication and the Group Process,* 4th ed. (New York: McGraw-Hill, 1994), pp. 202–207.
[6]For an excellent discussion of the responsibilities of designated group leaders, see John K. Brilhart and Gloria J. Galanes, *Effective Group Discussion,* 9th ed. (New York: McGraw-Hill, 1998), pp. 181–206.

[7]Kevin Barge, "Leadership as Communication," in Lawrence R. Frey and J. Kevin Barge (eds.), *Managing Group Life: Communicating in Decision-Making Groups* (Boston: Houghton Mifflin, 1997), pp. 202–233.

[8]For research on this aspect of group interaction, consult Joann Keyton, "Relational Communication in Groups," in Frey, Gouran, and Poole, *Handbook of Group Communication Theory and Research,* pp. 192–222.

[9]See Larry L. Barker, Kathy J. Wahlers, and Kittie W. Watson, *Groups in Process: An Introduction to Small Group Communication,* 5th ed. (Boston: Allyn and Bacon, 1995), pp. 75–100.

[10]Sunwolf and David R. Seibold, "The Impact of Formal Procedures on Group Processes, Members, and Task Outcomes," in Frey, Gouran, and Poole, *Handbook of Group Communication Theory and Research,* pp. 395–431.

[11]For other decision-making techniques, see Pavitt and Curtis, *Small Group Discussion,* pp. 341–378.

[12]See Carl M. Moore, *Group Techniques for Idea Building,* 2nd ed. (Thousand Oaks, Calif.: Sage, 1994).

[13]Gloria J. Galanes, Katherine Adams, and John K. Brilhart, *Communicating in Groups,* 4th ed. (New York: McGraw-Hill, 2000), p. 100.

APPENDIX A
GIVING YOUR FIRST SPEECH

Preparing Your Speech

Developing the Speech
Organizing the Speech

Delivering Your Speech

Speaking Extemporaneously
Rehearsing the Speech
Presenting the Speech

Sample Speeches with Commentary

Y ou may be surprised to learn that one of your first assignments is to give a speech. You say to yourself, "What am I going to do? I have barely started this course, yet I'm supposed to stand up in front of the whole class and give a speech! I've only read a few pages in the textbook, and I don't know much about public speaking. Where do I begin?"

If these are your thoughts, you aren't alone. Most beginning speech students have a similar reaction. Fortunately, giving your first speech sounds a lot harder than it is. The purpose of this appendix is to help you get started on preparing and delivering your speech.

Preparing Your Speech

Usually a brief, simple presentation, the first assignment is often called an icebreaker speech because it is designed to "break the ice" by getting students up in front of the class as soon as possible. This is an important step because much of the anxiety associated with public speaking comes from a lack of experience giving speeches. Once you have broken the ice by giving a speech, you will feel less anxious and will have taken the first step on the road to developing sound public speaking habits that lead to confidence.

Developing the Speech

There are a number of possible assignments for the first speech. One is a speech of self-introduction that provides insight into the speaker's background, personality, beliefs, or goals. In other cases, students are asked to introduce a classmate, rather than themselves. Some instructors require yet a different kind of speech. No matter which you are assigned, be sure to focus your presentation sharply so it conforms to the assigned time limit. One of the most common mistakes students make on their first speech is trying to cover too much material. You should select a limited number of points and illustrate them clearly.

It would be impossible, for example, to tell your audience everything about your life in a two- or three-minute speech. A better approach would be to focus on one or two major events that have helped define who you are—competing in the state track meet, volunteering to tutor disadvantaged children, getting your first job, and the like. This allows you to make a few well-developed points about a clearly defined subject.

On the other hand, avoid the temptation to narrow the focus of your topic too much. Few listeners would be pleased to hear a two- or three-minute discussion of advanced trumpet-playing techniques. Such a speech would be too specialized for most classroom audiences.

Once you have a topic for your speech, be creative in developing it. Think of ways to make your presentation mysterious or suspenseful. Suppose you are telling the audience about your "brush with greatness," in which you met a celebrity, visited a famous place, or participated in a newsworthy event. Rather than identifying the celebrity at the outset, you might save his or her name for the end of your speech. As your story unfolds, tantalize your classmates with clues about your celebrity's gender, physical characteristics, special talents, and the like, but keep the name a secret until the last moment. The idea is to hold your classmates on the edges of their seats as they listen.

In addition to mystery and suspense, audiences are naturally interested in dangerous situations, adventure, and drama. If your task is to introduce a fellow student, find out if she or he has ever been in danger. Suppose your classmate went on a white-water rafting expedition and fell overboard. The story of how this person was rescued would be very dramatic. Or perhaps you spent a year in Africa with the Peace Corps. The details of such an adventure would make excellent material for a speech of self-introduction.

If you think about it, every person has faced risk, done the unusual, or triumphed over hardship. Try to find ways to include such fascinating experiences in your speech.

You can also make your speech interesting by using colorful, descriptive language. One speaker used this technique when introducing a fellow student, named Reva, to the class. The speaker began by saying:

> Drawers pulled open. Clothes scattered all over the floor. A little girl with white blonde curls is digging through her father's chest of drawers. "At last," she exclaims. "I found you." She pulls the expensive European cigars out from the drawer and holds them triumphantly in the sun. Little Reva was not going to let her father ruin his health. Without hesitation, she hoists the cigars out the open window and skips out of the room.

View the beginning of Kristin Berg, "A Family Tradition."

CD: VIDEO CLIP A.1

This speaker could have said, "When she was young, our classmate Reva threw her father's cigars out the window because she didn't want him to smoke." Instead, the speaker painted a word picture so her listeners could visualize the chest of drawers, the scattered clothes, the little girl's blonde curls, and the expensive European cigars. Colorful and concrete illustrations like this are always more interesting than dull language and abstract generalizations.

You might wonder whether you should use humor to make your first speech entertaining. Audiences love witty remarks, jokes, and funny situations, but like anything else, humor is only effective when done well. It should flow naturally out of the speech content rather than being contrived. If you are not normally a funny person, you are better off giving a sincere, enthusiastic speech and leaving out the jokes. In no case should you include humor that involves obscenity, embarrasses individuals, or negatively stereotypes groups of people. The best kind of humor gently pokes fun at ourselves or at universal human foibles.

Organizing the Speech

Regardless of your topic, your speech will have three main parts—an introduction, a body, and a conclusion. Your first job in the introduction is to get the attention and interest of the audience. You can do this by posing a question, telling a story, making a startling statement, or opening with a quotation. The purpose of all these methods is to create a dramatic, colorful opening that will make your audience want to hear more.

For an excellent example, look at the speech excerpt on CD-ROM Video Clip A.2. The speech is by Gurpreet Paul, a student at the University of Wisconsin. Her assignment was to present a narrative about a significant experience in her life. This is how she began:

View the beginning of Gurpreet Paul, "Kiyomi and Me."

CD: VIDEO CLIP A.2

> Her name was Kiyomi. She was a mysterious Japanese dancer. Last autumn I got to meet her. How, you ask. Well, actually, she was a character in a play. I met her the day I became her. That day was one of the happiest days of my life. I wanted that part so desperately it was all I could think about. Being Kiyomi was one of the most memorable experiences of my life.

After this introduction, the speaker's classmates were eager to hear more about Kiyomi and her role in the speaker's life.

In addition to gaining attention and interest, the introduction should orient your listeners toward the subject matter of your speech. In the longer speeches you will give later in the term, you will usually need to provide an explicit preview statement that identifies the main points to be discussed in the body of your speech. (For example, "Today I will inform you about the symptoms, causes, and treatment of hepatitis C." Or "This afternoon we will explore the problem of sweatshops in the United States and look at some solutions to the problem.")

Because your introductory speech is so short, you may not need as detailed a preview statement. But you still need to give your audience a clear sense of the topic and purpose of your speech. Look back for a moment at the introduction about Kiyomi quoted earlier. Notice how it moves from arousing curiosity about the identity of Kiyomi to letting the audience know that the rest of the speech will focus on why "becoming" Kiyomi was one of the most significant experiences in the speaker's life. By the end of the introduction, there is no doubt about the topic of the speech. (Be sure to check with your instructor to see what kind of preview statement he or she prefers for the introductory speech.)

After getting the audience's attention and revealing your topic, you are ready to move into the body of your speech. In some speeches, the body seems to organize itself. If you have been assigned to tell a story about a significant experience in your life, you will relate the events in the order they occurred. The basic structure for such a speech is chronological: "This happened; then this happened; then this happened."

But not all speeches follow this format. Suppose you have been asked to give a presentation introducing a classmate. You could organize the most important biographical facts about your subject in chronological order, but this might result in a dull, superficial speech: "In 1982 Alicia was born in Cleveland, attended King Elementary School from 1987 to 1994, and graduated from South High School in 2000."

A better way of structuring your remarks might be to discuss three of the most important aspects of Alicia's life, such as hobbies, career goals, and family. This is called the topical method of organization, which subdivides the speech topic into its natural, logical, or conventional parts. Although there are many other ways to organize a speech, your first presentation will probably use either chronological or topical order.

Regardless of the method of organization you use, remember to limit the number of main points in the body of your speech. If you have too many points, your audience will struggle to recognize the most important ideas. In a two-minute speech, you won't have time to develop more than two or three main points.

Once you have selected those points, make sure each one focuses on a single aspect of the topic. For example, if your first point concerns your classmate's home town, don't introduce irrelevant information about her job or favorite music. Save this material for a separate point, or cut it from the speech altogether.

Try to make your main points stand out by introducing each with a transition statement. In a speech introducing a classmate, you might begin the first main point by saying:

> Shannon's family moved a great deal throughout her childhood.

When you reach the second point, you might introduce it like this:

> Moving a lot led to Shannon's outgoing nature and confidence in making friends. In fact, she has friends all around the world with whom she corresponds regularly over e-mail.

You have now let your audience know that the first main point is over and that you are starting the second one. The third main point might begin as follows:

> Corresponding with people all over the world is more than just a hobby for Shannon, since she is majoring in international relations.

Transition statements such as these will help your audience keep track of your main ideas.

When you finish discussing your final point, you will be ready to move into your conclusion. You need to accomplish two tasks in this part of the speech. First, you should let the audience know you are about to finish your speech. Second, you should reinforce the major theme of the speech.

If possible, try to end on a dramatic, clever, or thought-provoking note. For example, in the speech whose introduction we looked at earlier, the student devoted the body of her speech to explaining how she won the role of Kiyomi and what happened when she performed the role on stage. Then, in her conclusion, she wrapped up by saying:

> I needed this experience to appreciate who I was. I realized that I should be myself and not long to be someone else. So what if I'm not the most graceful or feminine person? So what if I don't possess all the wonderful characteristics of Kiyomi? I am still me—not a character in a play. Yet by playing that character, I learned one of the most important lessons of my life. I learned that by becoming a woman who never was, I became proud of who I am.

View the ending of Gurpreet Paul, "Kiyomi and Me."

CD: VIDEO CLIP A.3

The final lines bring the speech to a dramatic close and underscore why the experience of playing Kiyomi was so important to the speaker.

Delivering Your Speech

Once you have selected a subject and organized the content into a clear structure, it is time to work on the delivery of your speech. Because this is your first speech of the term, no one expects you to give a perfectly polished presentation. Your aim is to do as well as possible while also laying a foundation you can build upon in later speeches. With this is mind, we'll look briefly at the extemporaneous method of speech delivery, the importance of rehearsing your speech, and some of the major factors to consider when speech day arrives.

Speaking Extemporaneously

You might be inclined, as are many beginning speakers, to write out your speech like an essay and read it word for word to your listeners. The other extreme is to prepare very little for the speech—to wing it by trusting to your wits and the inspiration of the moment. Neither approach is appropriate for your introductory talk. Reading your speech from a manuscript runs the risk of poor eye contact with the audience and a stiff, unenthusiastic delivery. On the other hand, ad-libbing is a recipe for disaster. The outcome is usually an aimless talk that is either embarrassingly short or rambles on far too long.

Most experts recommend speaking extemporaneously, which combines the careful preparation and structure of a manuscript presentation with the spontaneity and enthusiasm of an unrehearsed talk. Your aim in an extemporaneous speech is to plan your major points and supporting material without trying to memorize the precise language you will use on the day of the speech.

The extemporaneous method requires you to know the content of your speech quite well. In fact, when you use the extemporaneous method properly, you become so familiar with the substance of your talk that you need only a few brief notes to remind you of the points you intend to cover. The notes should consist of key words or phrases that jog your memory, rather than of complete sentences and paragraphs. This way, when you stand up in front of the audience, you will tell them what you know about the topic in your own words.

Prepare your notes by writing or printing key terms and phrases on index cards or sheets of paper. Some instructors require students to use index cards because they are small and unobtrusive, don't rustle or flop over, and can be held in one hand, which allows the speaker to gesture more easily. Other teachers recommend sheets of paper because you can get more information on them and because it is easier to print out computer files on paper. If you are unsure what your instructor prefers, be sure to ask well before your speech is due.

Whether you use index cards or sheets of paper, your notes should be large enough to decipher clearly at arm's length. Many experienced speakers prefer to double or triple space their notes because this makes it easier to see them at a glance during the speech. Write or print on one side only of the index card or paper, and use the fewest notes you can manage and still present the speech fluently and confidently.

You can see an example of extemporaneous delivery on CD-ROM Video Clip A.4. The speaker, Katherine Hillman, is giving a speech of self-introduction using a personal object—in this case, a shoe—to explain something important about herself. As you view the excerpt from Katherine's speech, notice how her points are well planned, yet she is not tied to a manuscript. She walks away from the lectern, holds up her shoe, and points to things on it that reflect different aspects of her life. All the while, she speaks directly to her classmates and makes strong eye contact with them.

At first, it may seem very demanding to deliver a speech extemporaneously. In fact, you already have a great deal of experience using the extemporaneous method in everyday conversation. Do you read from a manuscript when you tell your friends an amusing story or relate the events of a trip or an unusual experience? Of course not. You recall the essential details of your story and tell the tale to different friends, on different occasions, using somewhat different language each time. You feel relaxed and confident with your friends, so you just tell them what is on your mind in a conversational tone. You should try to do the same thing in your speech.

View an excerpt from Katherine Hillman, "A Mile in My Shoes."

CD: VIDEO CLIP A.4

Rehearsing the Speech

When you watch a truly effective extemporaneous speaker, the speech comes out so smoothly that it seems almost effortless. In fact, that smooth delivery is the result of a great deal of practice. As your speech course progresses, you will gain more experience and will become more comfortable delivering your speeches extemporaneously.

The first time you rehearse your introductory speech, however, you will probably struggle. Words may not come easily, and you may forget some things you planned to say. Don't become discouraged. Keep going and complete the speech as well as you can. Concentrate on gaining control of the ideas rather than on trying to learn the speech word for word. Every time you practice, you will get better and better.

For this approach to work, you must rehearse the speech out loud. Looking silently over your notes is not enough. Speaking the words aloud will help you master the content of your talk. Once you have a fairly good grasp of the speech, ask friends or family members to listen and to give constructive feedback. Don't be shy about asking. Most people love to give their opinion about something, and it's crucial that you rehearse with a live audience before presenting the speech in class.

As you practice, time your speech to make sure it is neither too long nor too short. Because of nerves, most people talk faster during their first speech than when they practice it. When you rehearse at home, make certain your speech runs slightly longer than the minimum time limit. That way, if your speaking rate increases when you get in front of your classmates, your speech won't end up being too short.

Don't be surprised if the timing of your speech varies somewhat as you practice. It would be a bad sign if your speech took exactly the same amount of time during each rehearsal, because that would indicate that you were reading it from manuscript or had memorized it verbatim.

Presenting the Speech

When it is your turn to speak, move to the front of the room and face the audience. Assume a relaxed but upright posture. Plant your feet a bit less than shoulder-width apart and allow your arms to hang loosely by your side. Arrange your notes before you start to speak. Then take a moment to look over your audience and to smile. This will help to establish rapport with your classmates from the start.

Once you are into the speech, feel free to use your hands to gesture, but don't worry overly about planning your gestures ahead of time. If you don't normally use your hands expressively during informal conversation, then you shouldn't feel compelled to gesture a lot during your speech. Whatever gestures you do use should flow naturally and spontaneously from your feelings.

Above all, don't let your gestures or bodily actions distract listeners from your message. Do your best to avoid nervous mannerisms such as twisting your hair, wringing your hands, shifting your weight from one foot to the other, rocking back and forth, tapping your fingers on the lectern, or jingling coins in your pockets. No matter how nervous you feel, try to appear calm and relaxed.

During your talk, look at your classmates as often as you can. One of the major reasons for speaking extemporaneously is to maintain eye contact with your audience. In your own experience, you know how much more impressive a speaker is when she or he looks at the audience while speaking.

If you have practiced the extemporaneous method of delivery and prepared your notes properly, you should be able to maintain eye contact with your audience most of the time. Be sure to look to the left and right of the room, as well as the center, and avoid the temptation to speak exclusively to one or two sympathetic individuals. When you are finished speaking, your classmates should have the impression that you established a personal connection with each of them.

Try to use your voice as expressively as you would in normal conversation. Concentrate on projecting to the back of the room. Unless you see your classmates cringing and covering their ears, you will probably not be too loud. Despite your nerves fight the temptation to race through your speech. If you make a conscious effort to speak up, slow down, and project clearly, you will be on the right track to an effective presentation.

As explained in Chapter 1, it is normal to be nervous before delivering a speech. You can deal with nervousness by preparing thoroughly, thinking positively, and visualizing yourself giving a successful speech. If you have butterflies in your stomach before delivering your speech, sit quietly in your chair and take several slow, deep breaths. You can help reduce your tension by tightening and relaxing your leg muscles, or by squeezing your hands together and then releasing them. Finally, remember that although you may be anxious about giving your speech, usually your nervousness will not be visible to your audience.

All the topics discussed in this appendix are developed in much more detail in the rest of this book. As the course progresses, you will acquire more knowledge about how to prepare and present a speech, and you will gain experience as a speaker.

For now, keep your introductory assignment in perspective. Remember that neither your audience nor your instructor expects perfection. You are not a professional speaker, and this is the first speech of the class. Do your best on the assignment and have fun with it. Plan what you want to say, organize the material clearly, practice thoroughly, and use the extemporaneous method of delivery. You may be surprised by how much you enjoy giving your first speech.

Sample Speeches with Commentary

The following speeches were presented by students in beginning speech classes at the University of Wisconsin. The first is a speech of self-introduction; the second is a speech introducing a classmate. As you read the speeches, notice how clearly they are organized and how creatively they are developed.

View the full speeches "Kiyomi and Me" and "A Family Tradition."

CD: VIDEO DISK 2

Kiyomi and Me	
Commentary	**Speech**
	Gurpreet (Priya) Paul
The opening paragraph serves as the speaker's introduction. She gets the attention of her audience by arousing curiosity about the identity of Kiyomi. She then makes clear that the rest of the speech will explain why the experience of acting the role of Kiyomi was one of the most important experiences of her life.	Her name was Kiyomi. She was a mysterious Japanese dancer. Last autumn I got to meet her. How, you ask. Well, actually, she was a character in a play. I met her the day I became her. That day was one of the happiest days of my life. I wanted that part so desperately it was all I could think about. Being Kiyomi was one of the most memorable experiences of my life.
The speaker starts her narrative by identifying the play in which Kiyomi appears and explaining why the speaker was so captivated by the role.	When I first read the script for the play *A Wind of a Thousand Tales,* I couldn't believe it. The description of the character Kiyomi was perfect. She was everything I ever wanted to be in life. She was beautiful, humble, shy, loving, loved, and, most of all, she was graceful. To me, she was the ideal woman. So, obviously, I tried out for the part.
The narrative continues in chronological order. Notice how clearly the speaker moves from event to event as her story proceeds.	I had to wait an entire weekend to find out if I got the part or not. Now I know that doesn't seem like a long time, but to me it felt like an eternity. So when I found out I got the part that Monday, I was so excited that I memorized all my lines that night.
Now the speaker moves from getting the part of Kiyomi to performing the play on stage. She provides enough details for the	Yet it wasn't getting the part that made so much of a difference in my life. The most important experience came after all the rehearsals, when it was finally time to perform the play.

audience to understand what occurred, but not so many as to make the speech run longer than the assigned time limit.

I was performing on stage, when gradually I forgot who I was. I said all the lines and performed all the actions—but not as Priya acting as Kiyomi, but as Kiyomi herself. It was the strangest experience of my life. I had become a completely different person. Even after the play was over, it took me a good five minutes to snap out of it.

The speaker concludes by explaining why her experience playing Kiyomi was so meaningful. The final sentence is especially effective and ends the speech on a dramatic and thought-provoking note.

After finding myself again, I realized why I had this strange experience. I needed this experience to appreciate who I was. I realized that I should be myself and not long to be someone else. So what if I'm not the most graceful or feminine person? So what if I don't possess all the wonderful characteristics of Kiyomi? I am still me—not a character in a play. Yet by playing that character, I learned one of the most important lessons of my life. I learned that by becoming a woman who never was, I became proud of who I am.

A Family Tradition

Commentary

Speech

Kristin Berg

Opening with a brief story is an excellent way to get the audience's attention. Notice how the speaker uses colorful, descriptive language and provides sharply etched details that help bring the story to life.

Drawers pulled open. Clothes scattered all over the floor. A little girl with white blonde curls is digging through her father's chest of drawers. "At last," she exclaims, "I found you." She pulls the expensive European cigars out from the drawer and holds them triumphantly to the sun. Little Reva was not going to let her father ruin his health. Without hesitation, she hoists the cigars out the open window and skips out of the room.

This paragraph completes the speaker's introduction. After identifying the subject of the speech and providing some basic biographical information, the speaker states the central idea she will develop throughout the rest of the speech—that Reva's daring is attributable above all to the values of her family.

Reva's parents were not sure what to make of their five-year-old daughter and her precocious antics. Thirteen years later, Reva, your classmate, continues to astound her parents. She likes to meet new people; she loves to party; and she left her home state of Indiana to come here to the University of Wisconsin. They attribute her daring to the American culture. But I contend that, more than anything, she embodies the values of her family.

The speaker begins the body of her speech by discussing how Reva's parents boldly decided to leave the Netherlands and emigrate to the United States.

Reva's parents were born in a small backwater town in the Netherlands, just 10 miles from the German border. Both parents were raised in traditional Dutch Catholic families where 10 to 12 children were the norm. However, Reva's parents turned out to be anything but traditional. They renounced both Catholicism and traditional Dutch life. Reva's mother had never seen an orange, a person of color, or even a Protestant, yet she decided she was going to America. Knowing little English, the young couple set off to build a new life in a new land.

Vivid, humorous, and richly textured, the story in this paragraph is especially effective. As you can see from CD Video Clip 12.4, it was delivered with excellent vocal variety, gestures, and eye contact.

Surrounded by a new people, a new language, and a new culture, the young couple struggled to make their growing family belong. Reva remembers her father's daring and sometimes dangerous stunts to give her an authentic American childhood. One Christmas Eve, Reva was snuggling under her covers, waiting for the night to pass, when, all of a sudden, a rapid stomping shook the ceiling above. The children screamed as the roof rumbled and roared. They went scurrying down the stairs only to watch as large, dusty bundles dropped down the chimney into the fireplace. Meanwhile, Reva's father was wrestling wind and ice atop the roof, losing several toys and nearly his life in his struggle to give his children a genuine "Santa and Reindeer" Christmas.

The speaker provides additional information about Reva's family.

Today, Reva's family is fully comfortable in American life and society. Her father travels the country in his work as an engineering specialist. Her oldest sister, Amy, attends Washington University Medical school in St. Louis, while her other sister is a junior at MIT. Clearly, Reva's family has accomplished a great deal.

The question at the start of this paragraph gets the audience to think about the experience of Reva's parents in personal terms.

How many of us can imagine leaving our families and everything we own to travel thousands of miles across the ocean to a land where we have no guarantee of success? Furthermore, a land where we don't even speak the language. And yet, once here, Reva's family was able to carve out an extremely successful lifestyle.

The speaker concludes by returning to the central idea announced in the introduction. The last sentence brings everything together and adds a touch of eloquence.

This is why I think Reva's daring nature is not simply a result of an American life. Rather, I would contend that Reva's parents passed on to her their own adventurous spirit, which allowed them to break tradition; their own courage, which enabled them to leave their homeland; and their own creativity, which they used to weave their traditions into the fabric of American society. If, as it's been said, one is inevitably the product of one's own family, then Reva is truly blessed indeed.

Appendix B
Speeches for Analysis and Discussion

Questions of Culture
Sajjid Zahir Chinoy

Choices and Change
Barbara Bush

I Have a Dream
Martin Luther King, Jr.

Dying to Be Thin
Jennifer Breuer

A Whisper of AIDS
Mary Fisher

The Ultimate Gift
Jennifer Conard

Multicultural, Multilingual
Renee Varghese

Questions of Culture
Sajjid Zahir Chinoy

Seldom does a student commencement address upstage the featured speaker—especially when that speaker is a Pulitzer prize winner from Harvard University. Yet that is exactly what happened when Sajjid Zahir Chinoy spoke to his fellow graduates at Richmond University on May 12, 1996.

Born and raised near Bombay, India, Chinoy was selected to speak as the result of a campuswide competition. After describing the jumble of emotions that filled his mind as he came to the United States to attend school, he spoke movingly of the warm reception he received in Richmond and of how cultural differences can be overcome by attempting to understand other people.

Addressing his audience of 3,000 people extemporaneously and without notes, Chinoy received thunderous applause, and his remarks were widely reported in the press. His speech was so inspiring that the main speaker, Harvard psychiatrist Robert Coles, began his address by paying tribute to Chinoy. "I've been to a number of commencements," said Coles, "but I've never heard a speech quite like that."

The text of this speech has been transcribed from a video recording and is reprinted with permission from Sajjid Zahir Chinoy and the University of Richmond. It is also available on the videotape supplement to *The Art of Public Speaking.*

View the full speech "Questions of Culture."

CD VIDEO DISK 2

1 Distinguished guests, faculty, staff, students, ladies and gentlemen, and, most of all, the Class of 1996:

2 I can visualize the scene again and again: 11:30 P.M., Saturday night, the fifteenth of August, 1992, Bombay International Airport, India. I was leaving home for the University of Richmond. And as I said that final goodbye to my parents, my family, and my friends; and as I saw hope, expectation, even a tinge of sadness, in their eyes; and as I stepped aboard the Boeing 747 in front, I knew my life had changed forever.

3 The next 36 hours on board the aircraft were a time of questions, of concerns, of tremendous uncertainty.

4 Had I made the right choice in leaving home? Had I made the right choice in leaving my parents, my family, my home? Had I made the right choice in leaving my country, my culture, my background? Had I made the right choice in choosing the University of Richmond?

5 And then, of course, there was that one nagging question, that one overriding concern: As one of only three Indian students on a Richmond campus of 3,000, would I ever fit in?

6 My country was different. My culture was different. My experiences were different. My background was different. My language was different. My accent was different. Would I ever fit in?

7 And so here I was, high above the clouds, grappling with questions of culture, of interaction, of ethnicity. What I didn't know was that 30,000 feet below, on the ground, the world was faced with these very same questions—the question of culture, the question of interaction, the question of ethnicity.

8 And so whether my aircraft took off from Bombay, where the Hindus and the Muslims lived together in a most fragile peace; or whether my aircraft was over Africa, where the Hutus and Tutsis of Rwanda and Burundi had long-standing animosity; or whether my aircraft was over Bosnia, where

the Serbs, the Croats, the Muslims, and the Bosnians had broken yet another truce, the question was the same—could different cultures ever come together to reinforce one another?

9   Ladies and gentlemen, after that bumpy aircraft ride, this young Indian student had found his answer. He had been witness to the four most spectacular years of his life at the University of Richmond. The academics were great; the extracurriculars were great; his graduate plans were great.

10   But what left an indelible impact on his mind was none of this. No, instead it was those special moments, those moments of human interaction, those human relationships that can never quite be translated into words:

11   The time this young Indian student spent his first Thanksgiving dinner with his debate team coach. That Thanksgiving evening when I ate my first American turkey and saw my first American football game, not knowing the difference between a tackle and a touchdown. And yet, all of a sudden, just like that, this very different Indian student had become an inherent part of the great American tradition of giving thanks.

12   The time I spent my first Christmas Eve with my journalism professor. That Christmas evening when the relationship wasn't of a faculty member and a student anymore, but of two buddies who fought fiercely over every point in Ping-Pong.

13   The time I had a long and honest talk with an American friend on the eve of a calculus exam. I didn't learn much calculus that night, but what I did learn was that as different as we are—different countries, different cultures, different continents—inherently we are still the same.

14   The time in December 1992 when India was hit by communal riots, when violence and bloodshed were but a few hundred yards from my family and my home, and when my fantastic roommate from my freshman year sat up the entire night, giving me hope, strength, and courage at every step.

15   Yes, four years after that bumpy aircraft ride, I have found the answer to the question of culture.

16   I have found that it has taken just a little understanding, just a little sensitivity, just a little open-mindedness, just a little empathy on the part of this community—this University of Richmond community—to change my life like never before.

17   I have found that it makes no difference what culture you follow, what your background is, what your experiences are, what language you speak, what accent you have. The commonality of the human bond far transcends these superficial differences.

18   And yet look around at the world today. Look around at the very regions that were faced with the same question of culture that I was faced with four years ago.

19   Look at Bosnia, where, between 1992 and 1996, 300,000 people had been slaughtered—Bosnians, Serbs, Croats, Muslims—all because they came from a slightly different heritage or culture or history.

20   Look at Bombay, India. In one maddening week in 1992, 2,000 Indians—Hindus and Muslims—lost their lives fighting with one another. They fought over a mosque; they fought over a structure made of brick and mortar. Two thousand human beings lost their lives.

21   Look at Africa, where, between 1992 and 1996, 1 million Hutus and Tutsis lost their lives. Just comprehend that for a moment. Between the time

you were a freshman and a senior, 1 million lost their lives fighting over culture, over history, over background.

22 Yes, just look at the madness. The world has fought hard to highlight its differences. We have forgotten our inherent similarities. All because what was missing was a little understanding. Just a little sensitivity. Just a little open-mindedness. Just a little empathy.

23 Two similar questions of culture in 1992. Two diametrically opposite results in 1996.

24 And so, to the Class of 1996, I say go and distinguish yourselves like never before. Go get the best of jobs, the most rewarding of careers. Go to the best of graduate programs. And make a real difference in your communities.

25 But not for one moment, not for one moment, ever forget the memory of these four years—the memory that just a little understanding, just a little sensitivity, just a little open-mindedness, just a little empathy on your part can mean the difference between complete despair for one young boy in Bosnia and remarkable hope for another young boy at Richmond.

26 Thank you.

Choices and Change

Barbara Bush

Barbara Bush's commencement address at Wellesley College on June 1, 1990, is one of the best known speeches of recent years. Bush was invited to speak by the senior class when their first choice, Alice Walker, author of *The Color Purple,* could not attend. In protest, 150 Wellesley seniors—about one-fourth of the graduating class—signed a petition charging that Bush was not a good role model for career-oriented students at a women's college and had been chosen because of the man she married rather than for her own achievements.

The petition touched off a storm of controversy. Throughout the month before Bush's speech, educators, newspaper columnists, and others debated the petition and the larger issue of women's role in American society. The media spotlight became even more intense when Bush invited Raisa Gorbachev, whose husband would be in the United States for summit meetings on the day of the Wellesley commencement, to join her at Wellesley and also to speak to the graduates.

In her speech, Bush dealt with one of the most important issues facing modern women—how to balance their careers with their commitments to friends and family. She urged her audience to respect difference, to get involved in social issues, and to cherish human relationships as "the most important investments you will ever make." She capped off the speech by suggesting that someone in the audience might follow in her footsteps as the President's spouse. "I wish *him* well," she added, to thunderous cheering and applause.

Bush's blend of humility and humor won many accolades. NBC News anchor Tom Brokaw called her address "one of the best commencement speeches I've ever heard," while the *New York Times* judged it "a triumph." Many Wellesley students who had been skeptical about Bush's appearance also said they were pleasantly surprised by the speech. "She was wonderful and funny," one of them stated. "I think she could have addressed more women's issues. But she was sincere and she touched our hearts."

The text of this speech is taken from a videotape supplied by Wellesley College, and it includes several impromptu comments and other changes from the version published in the press. The speech is also included in the videotape supplement to *The Art of Public Speaking*.

1 Thank you very, very much President Keohane, Mrs. Gorbachev, trustees, faculty, parents, and, I should say, Julia Porter, class president, and certainly my new best friend, Christine Bicknell—and of course the Class of 1990. I am really thrilled to be here today and very excited, as I know all of you must be, that Mrs. Gorbachev could join us. These are exciting times—they're exciting in Washington, and I had really looked forward to coming to Wellesley. I thought it was going to be fun; I never dreamt it would be this much fun. So thank you for that.

2 More than 10 years ago when I was invited here to talk about our experiences in the People's Republic of China, I was struck by both the natural beauty of your campus and the spirit of this place.

3 Wellesley, you see, is not just a place, but an idea, an experiment in excellence in which diversity is not just tolerated, but is embraced.

4 The essence of this spirit was captured in a moving speech about tolerance given last year by a student body president of one of your sister colleges. She related the story by Robert Fulghum about a young pastor who, finding himself in charge of some very energetic children, hits upon the game called "Giants, Wizards and Dwarfs." "You have to decide now," the pastor instructed the children, "which you are—a giant, a wizard or a dwarf." At that, a small girl tugging at his pants leg asks, "But where do the mermaids stand?"

5 And the pastor tells her there are *no* mermaids. And she says, "Oh yes there are—I am a mermaid."

6 This little girl knew what she was and she was not about to give up on either her identity or the game. She intended to take her place wherever mermaids fit into the scheme of things. Where *do* the mermaids stand—all those who are different, those who do not fit the boxes and the pigeonholes? "Answer that question," wrote Fulghum, "and you can build a school, a nation, or a whole world."

7 As that very wise young woman said, "Diversity, like anything worth having, requires effort." Effort to learn about and respect difference, to be compassionate with one another, to cherish our own identity, and to accept unconditionally the same in others. You should all be very proud that this is the Wellesley spirit.

8 Now I know your first choice today was Alice Walker—guess how I know!—known for *The Color Purple*. Instead you got me—known for the color of my hair! Alice Walker's book has a special resonance here. At Wellesley, each class is known by a special color. For four years the class of '90 has worn the color purple. Today you meet on Severance Green to say good-bye to all of that, to begin a new and a very personal journey to search for your own true colors.

9 In the world that awaits you beyond the shores of Lake Waban, no one can say what your true colors will be. But this I do know: You have a first-class education from a first-class school. And so you need not, probably

cannot, live a "paint-by-numbers" life. Decisions are not irrevocable. Choices do come back. And as you set off from Wellesley, I hope that many of you will consider making three very special choices.

10 The first is to believe in something larger than yourself, to get involved in some of the big ideas of our time. I chose literacy because I honestly believe that if more people could read, write and comprehend, we would be that much closer to solving so many of the problems that plague our nation and our society.

11 Early on I made another choice which I hope you'll make as well. Whether you're talking about education, career, or service, you're talking about life, and life really must have joy. It's supposed to be fun!

12 One of the reasons I made the most important decision of my life, to marry George Bush, is because he made me laugh. It's true, sometimes we've laughed through our tears, but that shared laughter has been one of our strongest bonds. Find the joy in life, because as Ferris Bueller said on his day off: "Life moves pretty fast. You don't stop and look around once in a while, you're gonna miss it!" (I'm not going to tell George you clapped more for Ferris than you clapped for George!)

13 The third choice that must not be missed is to cherish your human connections: your relationships with family and friends. For several years, you've had impressed upon you the importance to your career of dedication and hard work—and of course that's true. But as important as your obligations as a doctor, a lawyer, a business leader will be, you are a human being first, and those human connections—with spouses, with children, with friends—are the most important investments you will ever make.

14 At the end of your life, you will never regret not having passed one more test, not winning one more verdict, or not closing one more deal. You will regret time not spent with a husband, a child, a friend, or a parent.

15 We are in a transitional period right now, fascinating and exhilarating times, learning to adjust to changes and the choices we, men and women, are facing. As an example, I remember what a friend said, on hearing her husband complain to his buddies that he had to babysit. Quickly setting him straight, my friend told her husband that when it's your own kids, it's not called babysitting!

16 Now, maybe we should adjust faster; maybe we should adjust slower. But whatever the era, whatever the times, one thing will never change: fathers and mothers, if you have children, they must come first. You must read to your children, and you must hug your children, and you must love your children. Your success as a family, our success as a society, depends not on what happens in the White House, but on what happens inside your house.

17 For over 50 years, it was said that the winner of Wellesley's annual hoop race would be the first to get married. Now they say the winner will be the first to become a CEO. Both of those stereotypes show too little tolerance for those who want to know where the mermaids stand. So I want to offer a new legend: the winner of the hoop race will be the first to realize her dream—not society's dream, her own personal dream. And who knows? Somewhere out in this audience may even be someone who will one day follow in my footsteps and preside over the White House as the president's spouse. And I wish him well!

18 Well, the controversy ends here. But our conversation is only beginning. And a worthwhile conversation it has been. So as you leave Wellesley today, take with you deep thanks for the courtesy and the honor you have shared with Mrs. Gorbachev and with me. Thank you. God bless you. And may your future be worthy of your dreams.

I Have a Dream

Martin Luther King, Jr.

Martin Luther King's "I Have a Dream" speech is widely regarded as a masterpiece. It was delivered August 28, 1963, to some 200,000 people who had come to Washington, D.C., to participate in a peaceful demonstration to further the cause of equal rights for African-Americans. King spoke from the steps of the Lincoln Memorial, in the "symbolic shadow" of Abraham Lincoln, and the crowd filled the vast area between the Memorial and the Washington Monument. In addition, millions of Americans watched the speech on television or listened to it on the radio.

Like most ceremonial addresses, "I Have a Dream" is relatively short. Although it took King only 16 minutes to deliver the speech, he prepared it more carefully than any other speech in his career to that time. His purpose was to set forth as succinctly and as eloquently as possible the guiding principles of the civil rights movement, and to reinforce the commitment of his listeners to those principles.

One of the most interesting features of this speech is King's use of language to make the abstract principles of liberty and equality clear and compelling. Throughout, King relies on familiar, concrete words that create sharp, vivid images. He uses many more metaphors than do most speakers, but they are appropriate to the occasion and help to dramatize King's ideas. Finally, King makes extensive use of repetition and parallelism to reinforce his message and to enhance the momentum of the speech.

If you have heard a tape recording of "I Have a Dream," you know its impact was heightened by King's delivery. In his rich baritone voice, marked by the fervor of the crusader and modulated by the cadences of the Southern Baptist preacher, King gained the total involvement of his audience. As William Robert Miller says, "The crowd more than listened, it participated, and before King had reached his last phrase, a torrent of applause was already welling up."

The text of this speech was taken from a tape recording and is reprinted with permission of Joan Daves. Copyright 1963 by Martin Luther King, Jr. The speech is also available on the videotape supplement to *The Art of Public Speaking*.

1 I am happy to join with you today in what will go down in history as the greatest demonstration for freedom in the history of our nation.

2 Five score years ago, a great American, in whose symbolic shadow we stand today, signed the Emancipation Proclamation. This momentous decree came as a great beacon light of hope to millions of Negro slaves, who had been seared in the flames of withering injustice. It came as a joyous daybreak to end the long night of their captivity.

3 But one hundred years later, the Negro still is not free. One hundred years later, the life of the Negro is still sadly crippled by the manacles of segregation and the chains of discrimination. One hundred years later, the Negro lives on a lonely island of poverty in the midst of a vast ocean of

material prosperity. One hundred years later, the Negro is still languished in the corners of American society and finds himself an exile in his own land. And so we've come here today to dramatize a shameful condition.

4 In a sense we've come to our nation's Capitol to cash a check. When the architects of our republic wrote the magnificent words of the Constitution and the Declaration of Independence, they were signing a promissory note to which every American was to fall heir. This note was a promise that all men—yes, black men as well as white men—would be guaranteed the unalienable rights of life, liberty, and the pursuit of happiness.

5 It is obvious today that America has defaulted on this promissory note insofar as her citizens of color are concerned. Instead of honoring this sacred obligation, America has given the Negro people a bad check—a check which has come back marked "insufficient funds."

6 But we refuse to believe that the bank of justice is bankrupt. We refuse to believe that there are insufficient funds in the great vaults of opportunity of this nation. And so we've come to cash this check—a check that will give us upon demand the riches of freedom and the security of justice.

7 We have also come to this hallowed spot to remind America of the fierce urgency of now. This is no time to engage in the luxury of cooling off or to take the tranquilizing drug of gradualism. Now is the time to make real the promises of democracy. Now is the time to rise from the dark and desolate valley of segregation to the sunlit path of racial justice. Now is the time to lift our nation from the quicksands of racial injustice to the solid rock of brotherhood. Now is the time to make justice a reality for all of God's children.

8 It would be fatal for the nation to overlook the urgency of the moment. This sweltering summer of the Negro's legitimate discontent will not pass until there is an invigorating autumn of freedom and equality. Nineteen sixty-three is not an end, but a beginning. Those who hope that the Negro needed to blow off steam and will now be content will have a rude awakening if the nation returns to business as usual. There will be neither rest nor tranquility in America until the Negro is granted his citizenship rights. The whirlwinds of revolt will continue to shake the foundations of our nation until the bright day of justice emerges.

9 But there is something that I must say to my people, who stand on the warm threshold which leads into the palace of justice. In the process of gaining our rightful place, we must not be guilty of wrongful deeds. Let us not seek to satisfy our thirst for freedom by drinking from the cup of bitterness and hatred.

10 We must forever conduct our struggle on the high plane of dignity and discipline. We must not allow our creative protest to degenerate into physical violence. Again and again we must rise to the majestic heights of meeting physical force with soul force.

11 The marvelous new militancy which has engulfed the Negro community must not lead us to a distrust of all white people. For many of our white brothers, as evidenced by their presence here today, have come to realize that their destiny is tied up with our destiny. They have come to realize that their freedom is inextricably bound to our freedom. We cannot walk alone.

12 As we walk, we must make the pledge that we shall always march ahead. We cannot turn back. There are those who are asking the devotees of civil rights, "When will you be satisfied?" We can never be satisfied as long as the Negro is the victim of the unspeakable horrors of police brutality. We can never be satisfied as long as our bodies, heavy with the fatigue of travel, cannot gain lodging in the motels of the highways and the hotels of the cities. We cannot be satisfied as long as the Negro's basic mobility is from a smaller ghetto to a larger one. We can never be satisfied as long as our children are stripped of their selfhood and robbed of their dignity by signs stating "For Whites Only." We cannot be satisfied as long as a Negro in Mississippi cannot vote and a Negro in New York believes he has nothing for which to vote. No, no, we are not satisfied, and we will not be satisfied until justice rolls down like waters, and righteousness like a mighty stream.

13 I am not unmindful that some of you have come here out of great trials and tribulations. Some of you have come fresh from narrow jail cells. Some of you have come from areas where your quest for freedom left you battered by the storms of persecution and staggered by the winds of police brutality. You have been the veterans of creative suffering. Continue to work with the faith that unearned suffering is redemptive.

14 Go back to Mississippi, go back to Alabama, go back to South Carolina, go back to Georgia, go back to Louisiana, go back to the slums and ghettos of our Northern cities, knowing that somehow this situation can and will be changed. Let us not wallow in the valley of despair.

15 I say to you today, my friends, so even though we face the difficulties of today and tomorrow, I still have a dream. It is a dream deeply rooted in the American dream.

16 I have a dream that one day this nation will rise up and live out the true meaning of its creed, "We hold these truths to be self-evident, that all men are created equal."

17 I have a dream that one day on the red hills of Georgia the sons of former slaves and the sons of former slaveowners will be able to sit down together at the table of brotherhood.

18 I have a dream that one day even the state of Mississippi, a state sweltering with the heat of injustice, sweltering with the heat of oppression, will be transformed into an oasis of freedom and justice.

19 I have a dream that my four little children will one day live in a nation where they will not be judged by the color of their skin but by the content of their character. I have a dream today.

20 I have a dream that one day, down in Alabama, with its vicious racists, with its governor having his lips dripping with the words of interposition and nullification, one day right there in Alabama little black boys and black girls will be able to join hands with little white boys and white girls as sisters and brothers. I have a dream today.

21 I have a dream that one day every valley shall be exalted, every hill and mountain shall be made low, the rough places will be made plane and the crooked places will be made straight, and the glory of the Lord shall be revealed, and all flesh shall see it together.

22 This is our hope. This is the faith that I go back to the South with. With this faith we will be able to hew out of the mountain of despair a stone of hope. With this faith we will be able to transform the jangling discords

of our nation into a beautiful symphony of brotherhood. With this faith we will be able to work together, to pray together, to struggle together, to go to jail together, to stand up for freedom together, knowing that we will be free one day.

23 This will be the day—this will be the day when all of God's children will be able to sing with new meaning, "My country 'tis of thee, sweet land of liberty, of thee I sing. Land where my fathers died, land of the pilgrim's pride, from every mountainside, let freedom ring." And if America is to be a great nation, this must become true.

24 So let freedom ring from the prodigious hilltops of New Hampshire. Let freedom ring from the mighty mountains of New York. Let freedom ring from the heightening Alleghenies of Pennsylvania!

25 Let freedom ring from the snowcapped Rockies of Colorado! Let freedom ring from the curvaceous slopes of California!

26 But not only that. Let freedom ring from Stone Mountain of Georgia!

27 Let freedom ring from Lookout Mountain of Tennessee!

28 Let freedom ring from every hill and molehill of Mississippi. From every mountainside, let freedom ring.

29 And when this happens, when we allow freedom ring—when we let it ring from every village and every hamlet, from every state and every city—we will be able to speed up that day when all of God's children, black men and white men, Jews and Gentiles, Protestants and Catholics, will be able to join hands and sing in the words of the old Negro spiritual, "Free at last! Free at last! Thank God almighty, we are free at last!"

Dying to Be Thin

Jennifer Breuer

Despite receiving a great deal of medical attention in recent years, anorexia remains a serious problem in the United States. In fact, reports the *New York Times,* the rate of anorexia is growing by 5 percent a year, and more than 40 percent of all anorexics are young women.

In the following informative speech, Jennifer Breuer, a student at the University of Wisconsin, explores these and other facts about the symptoms, causes, and treatment of anorexia. As you read the speech, notice how Jennifer organizes her ideas and draws upon the experience of her friend Julie to illustrate the devastating consequences of anorexia.

This speech is printed with permission from Jennifer Breuer. It is also available on the videotape of student speeches that accompanies this edition of *The Art of Public Speaking.*

View the full speech "Dying to Be Thin."

CD VIDEO DISK 2

1 I was Julie's best friend. I watched her grow from a little girl who was doted on by her parents into a tomboy who carried frogs in her pockets. I watched her become a young woman, fussing with her hair and trying on every outfit in her closet before her first date. I always wanted to be just like her.

2 But then something went terribly wrong. Julie's shiny hair became dull and brittle. Her eyes lost their sparkle, and she didn't smile that brilliant smile anymore. I watched now, as she stepped onto the scale seven

times a day, wore baggy clothes to cover her shriveled frame, and kept muttering about losing those last two stubborn pounds. Julie had become anorexic.

3 One in every 100 teenage females in America suffers from anorexia, and the *New York Times* says this number is rising by 5 percent every year. Although this disease does strike men, says the *Times,* 90 percent of its victims are women, and 44 percent of those victims are college-age females.

4 From my research and my personal experience with Julie, I have discovered that anorexia is an extremely serious disease that strikes a large number of Americans. Today I will tell you what anorexia is, what causes it, and what methods are used to treat it. Let's start by examining what anorexia is.

5 Anorexia nervosa, one of a number of eating disorders, is a disorder of self-starvation. Simply put, a person who is anorexic refuses to eat normal amounts of food. An article in *Maclean's* states that there are four characteristics of all anorexics: (1) refusal to maintain normal body weight, (2) loss of more than 15 percent of original body weight, (3) a distorted image of one's own body, and (4) an intense fear of becoming fat.

6 The refusal of anorexics to eat has many serious physical consequences. Hair and skin become dry and brittle, and a fine growth of hair may cover the entire body in an attempt to compensate for a lower body temperature. As the anorexia progresses, lack of calcium causes bones to become brittle and break easily. According to an article in *Sports Illustrated,* "The X-rays of a young person who has been anorexic for five to six years and those of a 70-year-old are almost identical." Lack of nutrition can also cause brain damage, blackouts, and a decreased pulse rate. In the most severe cases, anorexia can prove fatal.

7 In Julie's case, she suffered from many of the symptoms of anorexia. I saw her 5'7" frame drop to 86 pounds. She became weak and pale. Even in the middle of the summer, she was cold all the time. I just wanted to say to her, "Julie, please, can't you see what you're doing to yourself!" But, like most anorexics, she just couldn't see.

8 What causes people like Julie to become anorexic? Scientists have identified three main causes of anorexia. An article in *Newsweek* attributes the rise in cases of anorexia to the pressure in our society to be thin. The media constantly bombards us with images of thin people as ideals. Fat-free products and diet aids have become multimillion-dollar industries. These images and these industries project the idea that being anything but slender is something to be feared and shunned.

9 The second major factor in causing anorexia is the personality of the victim and his or her reaction to the pressures of society. The book *Dying to Please* states that most anorexics fit a basic profile. Many are overachievers or perfectionists. They excel in school and are involved in a variety of extracurricular activities. They seek to please parents, teachers, and friends. Anorexics see being thin as a way to please others. In fact, most will limit their food intake to try to fulfill expectations of perfection from family and friends.

10 A third possible cause of anorexia has only been discovered within the past year. Doctors at the University of Pittsburgh School of Medicine found that when anorexics don't eat, they experience a rise in their level of opiates, natural brain chemicals that produce a sense of happiness. The researchers also found that when anorexics do eat, their bodies produce higher than normal levels of serotonin, a brain chemical that causes a sense of anxiety.

According to the doctors, these chemical changes may make anorexia as physically addictive for the anorexic as alcohol or drugs are for the alcoholic or drug addict.

11 Julie always wanted to be perfect. She was prom queen, a straight-A student, and a member of every team, club, and organization imaginable. But then Julie decided she needed to go on a diet. She started constantly comparing herself to pictures of models in magazines. She was just sure that if she could look like the models, her life would truly be perfect. But losing weight never made Julie's life perfect.

12 What kinds of treatment could have helped Julie and others like her? Treatment of anorexia is a lifetime process. According to Dr. Katherine Halmi, director of the eating disorders clinic at New York Hospital, people think that eating disorders are "minor disorders that can be overcome with a little will power and effort, but these are serious, incapacitating illnesses that require professional intervention."

13 Methods of treatment used to treat anorexia include group therapy, drug therapy, and individual counseling. In severe cases, hospitalization and forced feeding are used to provide nutrition for the anorexic until he or she will eat a sufficient amount. Most anorexics are never cured and must fight the disease daily. Another article in the *New York Times* states that more than 80 percent of anorexics will have several relapses before they are cured. As Angie Melnyk, a 14-year-old who has been anorexic for two years, stated, "If you could cure anorexia in 30 days, it would be a lot less trouble."

14 As I mentioned before, for some anorexics, no treatment is successful. For 18 percent of diagnosed anorexics, the disease proves fatal.

15 We have seen that anorexia is a serious disease with deep-seated causes and devastating, potentially fatal effects. Julie was one of those who couldn't beat anorexia. She died when she was only 17. We will never go to college together and share a dorm room. She will never fulfill her dream of becoming a nurse. And we will never grow old living beside each other and watching our kids grow up together. Anorexia killed my beautiful, vibrant friend.

A Whisper of AIDS

Mary Fisher

Mary Fisher's emergence as an AIDS activist demonstrates how the need for public speaking can touch anyone sometime in her or his life. Only a year before Fisher rose to give the following speech to the Republican National Convention in Houston, Texas, she learned that she had contracted the HIV virus from her ex-husband. Resolving to do all she could to fight the disease, she became an outspoken advocate of the need for public understanding and resources in the battle against AIDS.

After telling her story to the Republican Platform Committee in May 1992, Fisher, a former staff assistant to President Gerald Ford, was invited to address the party's national convention that summer. Feeling, as she said later, like "the only HIV-positive Republican," she was deeply concerned about how her message of compassion and awareness would be received.

It did not take long, however, for Fisher's audience to realize that they were hearing a very special speech. Within a few minutes, the Astrodome turned eerily silent as the delegates stopped their chatting and gave Fisher their undivided attention. Some were moved to tears. Across the United States, millions watched on television, captivated by Fisher's somber words and heartfelt delivery. The *New York Times* deemed the address "exceptional for its deep emotion and sharp message."

One of the most admired public speeches of recent years, Fisher's address has been widely reprinted. The text here is from Fisher's book, *Sleep with the Angels: A Mother Challenges AIDS,* and is presented with permission from Moyer Bell Publishers, Wakefield, Rhode Island. Copyright 1994 by Family AIDS Network, Incorporated.

1 Less than three months ago, at platform hearings in Salt Lake City, I asked the Republican Party to lift the shroud of silence which has been draped over the issue of HIV/AIDS. I have come tonight to bring our silence to an end.

2 I bear a message of challenge, not self-congratulation. I want your attention, not your applause. I would never have asked to be HIV-positive. But I believe that in all things there is a good purpose, and so I stand before you, and before the nation, gladly.

3 The reality of AIDS is brutally clear. Two hundred thousand Americans are dead or dying; a million more are infected. Worldwide, 40 million, or 60 million, or a hundred million infections will be counted in the coming few years. But despite science and research, White House meetings and congressional hearings, despite good intentions and bold initiatives, campaign slogans and hopeful promises—despite it all, it's the epidemic which is winning tonight.

4 In the context of an election year, I ask you—here, in this great hall, or listening in the quiet of your home—to recognize that the AIDS virus is not a political creature. It does not care whether you are Democrat or Republican. It does not ask whether you are black or white, male or female, gay or straight, young or old.

5 Tonight, I represent an AIDS community whose members have been reluctantly drafted from every segment of American society. Though I am white and a mother, I am one with a black infant struggling with tubes in a Philadelphia hospital. Though I am female and contracted this disease in marriage, and enjoy the warm support of my family, I am one with the lonely gay man sheltering a flickering candle from the cold wind of his family's rejection.

6 This is not a distant threat; it is a present danger. The rate of infection is increasing fastest among women and children. Largely unknown a decade ago, AIDS is the third leading killer of young-adult Americans today—but it won't be third for long. Because, unlike other diseases, this one travels. Adolescents don't give each other cancer or heart disease because they believe they are in love. But HIV is different. And we have helped it along—we have killed each other—with our ignorance, our prejudice, and our silence.

7 We may take refuge in our stereotypes, but we cannot hide there long. Because HIV asks only one thing of those it attacks: Are you human? And this is the right question: Are you human? Because people with HIV have not entered some alien state of being. They are human. They have not earned cruelty and they do not deserve meanness. They don't benefit from being isolated or treated as outcasts. Each of them is exactly what God made: a person. Not evil, deserving of our judgment; not victims, longing for our pity. People. Ready for support and worthy of compassion.

8   My call to you, my Party, is to take a public stand no less compassionate than that of the President and Mrs. Bush. They have embraced me and my family in memorable ways. In the place of judgment, they have shown affection. In difficult moments, they have raised our spirits. In the darkest hours, I have seen them reaching not only to me, but also to my parents, armed with that stunning grief and special grace that comes only to parents who have themselves leaned too long over the bedside of a dying child.

9   With the President's leadership, much good has been done; much of the good has gone unheralded; as the President has insisted, "Much remains to be done."

10   But we do the President's cause no good if we praise the American family but ignore a virus that destroys it. We must be consistent if we are to be believed. We cannot love justice and ignore prejudice, love our children and fear to teach them. Whatever our role, as parent or policy maker, we must act as eloquently as we speak—else we have no integrity.

11   My call to the nation is a plea for awareness. If you believe you are safe, you are in danger. Because I was not hemophiliac, I was not at risk. Because I was not gay, I was not at risk. Because I did not inject drugs, I was not at risk.

12   My father has devoted much of his lifetime to guarding against another holocaust. He is part of the generation who heard Pastor Niemoeller come out of the Nazi death camps to say, "They came after the Jews and I was not a Jew, so I did not protest. They came after the Trade Unionists, and I was not a Trade Unionist, so I did not protest. They came after the Roman Catholics, and I was not a Roman Catholic, so I did not protest. Then they came after me, and there was no one left to protest."

13   The lesson history teaches is this: If you believe you are safe, you are at risk. If you do not see this killer stalking your children, look again. There is no family or community, no race or religion, no place left in America that is safe. Until we genuinely embrace this message, we are a nation at risk.

14   Tonight, HIV marches resolutely towards AIDS in more than a million American homes, littering its pathway with the bodies of the young. Young men. Young women. Young parents. Young children. One of the families is mine. If it is true that HIV inevitably turns to AIDS, then my children will inevitably turn to orphans.

15   My family has been a rock of support. My 84-year-old father, who has pursued the healing of the nations, will not accept the premise that he cannot heal his daughter. My mother has refused to be broken; she still calls at midnight to tell wonderful jokes that make me laugh. Sisters and friends, and my brother Phillip (whose birthday is today)—all have helped carry me over the hardest places. I am blessed, richly and deeply blessed, to have such a family.

16   But not all of you have been so blessed. You are HIV-positive but dare not say it. You have lost loved ones, but you dared not whisper the word AIDS. You weep silently; you grieve alone.

17   I have a message for you: It is not you who should feel shame; it is we. We who tolerate ignorance and practice prejudice, we who have taught you to fear. We must lift our shroud of silence, making it safe for you to

reach out for compassion. It is our task to seek safety for our children, not in quiet denial but in effective action.

18 Some day our children will be grown. My son Max, now four, will take the measure of his mother; my son Zachary, now two, will sort through his memories. I may not be here to hear their judgments, but I know already what I hope they are.

19 I want my children to know that their mother was not a victim. She was a messenger. I do not want them to think, as I once did, that courage is the absence of fear; I want them to know that courage is the strength to act wisely when most we are afraid. I want them to have the courage to step forward when called by their nation, or their Party, and give leadership— no matter what the personal cost. I ask no more of you than I ask of myself, or of my children.

20 To the millions of you who are grieving, who are frightened, who have suffered the ravages of AIDS firsthand: Have courage and you will find comfort.

21 To the millions who are strong, I issue this plea: Set aside prejudice and politics to make room for compassion and sound policy.

22 To my children, I make this pledge: I will not give in, Zachary, because I draw my courage from you. Your silly giggle gives me hope. Your gentle prayers give me strength. And you, my child, give me reason to say to America, "You are at risk." And I will not rest, Max, until I have done all I can to make your world safe. I will seek a place where intimacy is not the prelude to suffering.

23 I will not hurry to leave you, my children. But when I go, I pray that you will not suffer shame on my account.

24 To all within sound of my voice, I appeal: Learn with me the lessons of history and of grace, so my children will not be afraid to say the word AIDS when I am gone. Then their children, and yours, may not need to whisper it at all.

25 God bless the children, and God bless us all.

The Ultimate Gift

Jennifer Conard

As the Red Cross states, "Blood is like a parachute. If it's not there when you need it, chances are you'll never need it again." Although Americans take it for granted that they will be able to get a transfusion whenever they need one, blood donations have dipped so low in recent years that a serious, nationwide shortage could result. "When you need surgery, when you need cancer treatment, when a woman gives birth—we all assume the blood will be there," says Dr. Arthur Caplan of the University of Pennsylvania. "You can't make that assumption any more."

In the following speech, Jennifer Conard, a student at the University of Wisconsin, urges her classmates to become regular blood donors. Like many speeches that seek immediate action, this one follows Monroe's motivated sequence. As you read it, study how the speaker develops each step in the motivated sequence. How does she gain the attention of her listeners? Does she present a convincing case that there is a need for blood donors? Is her plan explained in sufficient detail? How does she visualize the benefits of her plan? Does her call for action have strong persuasive appeal?

This speech is presented with permission from Jennifer Conard and is also available on the videotape of student speeches that accompanies this edition of *The Art of Public Speaking*.

View the full speech "The Ultimate Gift."

CD VIDEO DISK 2

1 Are you at least 17 years old? Do you weigh more than 110 pounds? Do you consider yourself fairly healthy?

2 If you answered yes to all of these questions, you should be donating blood every two months. In my survey of the class, I found that only 50 percent of you have ever donated blood and that only 1 out of 13 of you donate on a regular basis. The lack of participation of eligible donors is a serious problem that requires immediate action. Through extensive research and two years of faithfully donating blood, I have come to realize the magnitude of this problem and just how easy the solution can be.

3 Today I would like to show why blood donors are in such desperate need and encourage you to take action to combat this need. Let's first take a look at the overwhelming need for blood donors.

4 The lack of participation of eligible blood donors poses a threat to the lives of many Americans. According to the American Red Cross Web pages, where I obtained an enormous amount of information, in the United States alone someone undergoes a blood transfusion once every three seconds, which amounts to 3,000 gallons of blood every hour, day and night. People who benefit from donations range from cancer patients to organ transplant patients to surgical patients; even premature infants and trauma victims benefit from donations. The need for blood never takes a vacation and neither should donors.

5 Let me tell you about Brooke, a three-year-old girl with long, curly blond hair and bright blue eyes. Brooke is a victim of cancer and had major surgery to remove a large tumor in her abdomen. She has spent approximately half of her life in the hospital receiving chemotherapy and other treatments for infections that resulted from a decrease in her white blood cell count after each session.

6 According to Texas Children's Hospital, Brooke's treatment will require blood products with a replacement value of 508 units of blood, of which only 250 units have been replaced. She still needs more than 250 units of blood to continue her treatment. If she doesn't receive this blood, she will not live to attend kindergarten, to go to the prom in high school, or to get married—luxuries we all too often take for granted.

7 Cases like Brooke's are becoming all too common these days, with only 1 in 20 eligible Americans donating blood and the donor rate dropping steadily at 2 percent annually. These facts are particularly distressing considering that nearly half of us here will receive blood sometime in our lives.

8 You can now see the magnitude of the problem with the lack of blood donations. Fortunately, it is a problem that can be easily solved. Each and every one of you can be part of the solution. All you have to do to save priceless lives is go to the nearest Red Cross and donate your blood.

9 For those of you who have never donated blood before, the process is so simple and easy. First, you fill out a donor information form that asks you questions about your sexual history and health. You will then receive

a miniphysical. They will take a drop of blood from your finger to measure the percent of red cells in your blood. Then they will take your blood pressure, as well as your temperature and pulse. So not only are you saving lives by donating blood, you are also checking on your own.

10   After your physical, you will be asked from which arm you prefer to donate. Then you will be asked to lie on a donor chair. A staff member will clean your arm and insert a sterile, nonreusable needle, so there is no way to contract AIDS from donating blood. After a pint of your blood has been taken, which usually takes about 10 minutes, you will be asked to rest for 10 to 15 minutes while you enjoy juice and cookies. The process is over, and in eight weeks you can donate again.

11   Many of you may be scared at the thought of the anticipated pain and needles. I admit I was terrified the first time I gave blood, but then I realized I was scared over nothing. The extent of the pain as they insert the needle is equivalent to someone scratching your arm for a brief second, and while the needle is in your arm, you don't feel a thing. And as I stated before, it is impossible to contract AIDS from donating blood.

12   Now that you know how easy and safe the solution is to the lack of blood donations, let's take a look at just how much difference your donations can make. Every unit of blood you donate can help save up to three lives. You see, the blood you donate is divided three ways—into red blood cells, white blood cells, and platelets. Each of these are stored separately and used for different types of treatment. Red blood cells are used to treat anemia. White blood cells are used to fight infections, while platelets are important to control bleeding and are used in patients with leukemia and other forms of cancer.

13   The joy you get from helping three people can be increased many times over. You see, you can donate blood six times in a year. Those six donations could help as many as 18 people. Just think, if you donated for 10 years, you could help save the lives of nearly 180 people. Who knows—one of those lives could be that of a friend, a family member, or even your own, since you can now donate in advance of your own surgery.

14   Now that you know what a difference just one donation can make, I want to encourage you to take action. I urge you to take a stand and become a regular blood donor. Forty-five minutes out of your day is a small price to pay for the lifetime of satisfaction you receive by knowing you may have saved a life. If you have never donated blood before, pull deep inside yourself to find some courage and become a proud wearer of the "I am a first time blood donor" sticker. If you have donated before, think back to the feeling of pride you received from making your donation.

15   Finally, I ask all of you to think of a loved one you hold so dear to your heart. Imagine they need a blood transfusion and there is a shortage of donations that day so they can't receive the treatment they so desperately need—just like Brooke, the three-year-old girl I talked about earlier. Go to the nearest Red Cross in Madison, which is on Sheboygan Avenue, or attend the next blood drive here on campus. These drives are held in various parts of campus, including the dorms. In fact, the next drive will be held in the Ogg Residence Hall in two weeks.

16   Please take this opportunity to save lives and make yourself feel like a million bucks. Give the ultimate gift—the gift of life. Donate blood!

Multilingual, Multicultural

Renee Varghese

Washington Irving described Americans in 1804 as "a strange set of fellows that run about all parts of the world without caring to learn the language beforehand." Irving's words were written almost 200 years ago, but they are still true today. Foreign language instruction in the United States lags far behind that in most other nations, and few native-born adult Americans can converse in any tongue other than English.

In the following persuasive speech, Renee Varghese, a student at the University of Wisconsin, argues that knowledge of a foreign language has become essential for a nation that depends on a global economy and is becoming increasingly multicultural. Citing research that shows children learn a foreign language best when they are very young, she advocates mandatory foreign language instruction in all elementary schools.

As you read the speech, study how the speaker uses statistics, examples, and testimony to support her ideas. Does she convince you that knowledge of a second language is essential in today's world? Does she present a workable program for starting foreign language instruction earlier in the educational process? How does she demonstrate the practicality of her program? How could she have made the speech more convincing?

This speech is presented with permission from Renee Varghese.

1   ¿Perdóneme señor; me perdí. Podría decirme cómo ir al Hotel del Sol?

2   A few of you may know I just said, "Excuse me, sir. I'm lost. Could you tell me how to get to the Sun Hotel?" However, some of you may not, even though you had three to four years of Spanish in high school. I have one question for you: Would you be able to get around in a foreign country where the language you studied was spoken?

3   According to a class survey I conducted, all of you said that you studied a foreign language in high school, the majority of you for three to four years. Yet most of you do not have enough knowledge of the language to use it correctly. In addition, 92 percent of you said you thought it would have been more helpful to have started your foreign language study earlier.

4   Today I hope to convince you that knowledge of a foreign language is important and that it would be more beneficial to begin foreign language study earlier in our education. With the world economy globalizing and our country becoming increasingly multilingual, knowledge of a foreign language is now a necessity. Through my own experience and research, I have discovered that starting foreign language instruction in elementary school is most advantageous because our language-acquisition skills are the sharpest at that time. Let's begin with why knowledge of a second language is critical for the world today.

5   The first reason such knowledge is critical is because it is essential for global communication. According to an article in *Current* magazine, Americans both in and out of government proclaim the new global economy the defining reality of our age. With technology growing faster and faster, we have now become closer to our global neighbors than ever before. Governments and businesses will increasingly need workers who can communicate with our global partners in Latin America, Africa, and Europe.

6 According to an article in the *Foreign Language Annals,* "The number of foreign-based industries doing business in the United States has tripled in the last 10 years, while the U.S. has doubled overseas business." A recent issue of *Career World* states that some accountants at Chase Manhattan Bank and National City Bank must have a good grasp of foreign languages because these banks have branched out abroad. One study in the *Journal of Education for Business* showed that among both United States and foreign firms, 51 percent of the responding firms would give hiring preferences to those accounting and business majors skilled in a foreign language.

7 Not only is knowledge of a foreign language necessary for business communication, but the United States itself is a country of mixed cultures, nationalities, and tongues and is growing more multilingual every day.

8 According to Table 57 in the *Statistical Abstract of the United States,* people born in another country make up 9 percent of the American population. An article in the *Population Bulletin* states that 32 million people reported to the last United States Census that they spoke a language other than English at home. This number is larger than the populations of New York, Pennsylvania, and Colorado combined and is six times larger than the number of people that live here in Wisconsin.

9 According to the Census Bureau, more than 17 million people in the U.S. speak Spanish as their primary language. In many parts of the country, knowledge of Spanish has become a vital day-to-day issue. Kathy Lemmons, chairwoman of the foreign language department at Fayetteville High School in Arkansas, says, "When I talk to doctors, they wish they would have taken Spanish; when I talk to lawyers and business people, they say the same thing."

10 But whether Spanish, Japanese, German, Italian, Chinese, or Polish, it is obvious that proficiency in another tongue is needed. To meet this need, I propose a solution that mandates state governments to require foreign language instruction in all elementary schools. The program I advocate is called FLES, the Foreign Languages in Elementary Schools Program. This program is based mostly on the spoken word versus writing and interpretation, and it starts teaching foreign languages as early as the first grade or even kindergarten.

11 It's important to note that much of the foreign language instruction done in this program is very basic. Olwen Bell, a French teacher at an Arkansas elementary school that has implemented the program, states that "There's a lot of role playing, singing, and chanting." Classroom teachers can easily take courses to learn how and what to teach the kids. It's not necessary for teachers to go back to school to get a degree in a foreign language. However, teachers should take instructional courses so they have opportunities for continued professional growth.

12 This program is working in Arkansas and other states. North Carolina, Oklahoma, Montana, and Arizona either have or are planning to institute similar programs. It is time for the rest of the U.S. to follow their lead. This would be a huge change in American education, but it's something that is vital if students are to be prepared for the world they will live in.

13 For years European and Asian countries have begun mandatory English in early grades. Other English-speaking countries such as Australia do extensive foreign language training in the early grades of their schools. Foreign language instruction works in these countries, and it can work in the U.S. as well.

14 In fact, there is abundant evidence that the optimum time to learn a foreign language is before the age of 10 because the brain is most receptive at this time. According to the book *Teaching Foreign Languages to the Very Young,* specific skills such as the ability to distinguish between foreign sounds and to reproduce them are more effective before the age of 10. The same book states that after the age of six the capabilities for pronunciation rapidly begin to deteriorate.

15 John Silber, Chancellor of Boston University and Chairman of the Massachusetts Board of Education, remarks, "It is quite clear that remarkable competence in a language can be achieved in three years—if these years are the ages three, four, and five. There is no question that for the average child trying to become bilingual, the earlier the better."

16 Finally, although some people wonder whether early foreign language instruction gets in the way of learning other subjects, according to the book *Foreign Languages and the Elementary School Child,* experiments done in public schools in Minnesota, Pennsylvania, and New York showed that learning foreign languages had no adverse effects on achievement in subject areas such as math and social studies. In some cases, kids who had foreign language instruction performed better in subjects such as spelling, reading, arithmetic, and language usage.

17 Furthermore, studying a language can help students better understand those outside their own culture and aid them in becoming more tolerant.

18 ¿Cuándo visitamos un país extranjero, estamos suponiendo que alguien habla Inglés? ¿Depende de un diccionario? To put it in English, "When we visit a foreign country, are we to expect that someone will speak English? Depend on a foreign language dictionary?"

19 People from other countries know to expect little from Americans as far as speaking foreign languages is concerned. However, it is time to stop this stereotype.

20 As we have seen, there is strong evidence that knowledge of a second language is vital for interaction both within the United States and on a global scale. We can provide that knowledge by instituting foreign language study in all elementary schools. Evidence shows that this is the best time to begin foreign language acquisition and that instruction in a second language can even help in learning other subjects.

21 With this in mind, hopefully one day when our children are lost somewhere in a foreign country, unlike their parents before them, they will know exactly what to say and do.

GLOSSARY

abstract   A summary of a magazine or journal article, written by someone other than the original author.   (Chapter 6)

abstract words   Words that refer to ideas or concepts.   (Chapter 11)

acceptance speech   A speech that gives thanks for a gift, an award, or some other form of public recognition.   (Chapter 17)

ad hominem   A fallacy that attacks the person rather than dealing with the real issue in dispute.   (Chapter 16)

adrenaline   A hormone released into the blood-stream in response to physical or mental stress.   (Chapter 1)

after-dinner speech   A speech to entertain that makes a thoughtful point about its subject in a lighthearted manner.   (Chapter 17)

alliteration   Repetition of the initial consonant sound of close or adjoining words.   (Chapter 11)

analogical reasoning   Reasoning in which a speaker compares two similar cases and infers that what is true for the first case is also true for the second.   (Chapter 16)

antithesis   The juxtaposition of contrasting ideas, usually in parallel structure.   (Chapter 11)

appreciative listening   Listening for pleasure or enjoyment.   (Chapter 3)

articulation   The physical production of particular speech sounds.   (Chapter 12)

atlas   A book of maps.   (Chapter 6)

attitude   A frame of mind in favor of or opposed to a person, policy, belief, institution, etc.   (Chapter 5)

audience-centeredness   Keeping the audience foremost in mind at every step of speech preparation and presentation.   (Chapter 5)

bandwagon   A fallacy that assumes that because something is popular, it is therefore good, correct, or desirable.   (Chapter 16)

bar graph   A graph that uses vertical or horizontal bars to show comparisons among two or more items.   (Chapter 13)

bibliography   A list of all the sources used in preparing a speech.   (Chapter 10)

Bill of Rights   The first 10 amendments to the United States Constitution.   (Chapter 2)

biographical aid   A reference work that provides information about people.   (Chapter 6)

bookmark   A feature in a Web browser that stores links to websites so they can be easily re-visited.   (Chapter 6)

brainstorming   A method of generating ideas by free association of words and thoughts.   (Chapters 4, 18)

brief example   A specific case referred to in passing to illustrate a point.   (Chapter 7)

browser   A computer program for navigating the World Wide Web.   (Chapter 6)

burden of proof   The obligation facing a persuasive speaker to prove that a change from current policy is necessary.   (Chapter 15)

call number   A number used in libraries to classify books and periodicals and to indicate where they can be found on the shelves.   (Chapter 6)

card catalogue   A catalogue that lists on 3 × 5 cards all the books and periodicals owned by a library.   (Chapter 6)

causal order   A method of speech organization in which the main points show a cause-effect relationship.   (Chapter 8)

causal reasoning   Reasoning that seeks to establish the relationship between causes and effects.   (Chapter 16)

central idea   A one-sentence statement that sums up or encapsulates the major ideas of a speech.   (Chapter 4)

channel   The means by which a message is communicated.   (Chapter 1)

chart   A visual aid that summarizes a large block of information, usually in list form. (Chapter 13)

chronological order   A method of speech organization in which the main points follow a time pattern.   (Chapter 8)

cliché A trite or overused expression. (Chapter 11)

clutter Discourse that takes many more words than are necessary to express an idea. (Chapter 11)

commemorative speech A speech that pays tribute to a person, a group of people, an institution, or an idea. (Chapter 17)

comparative advantages order A method of organizing persuasive speeches in which each main point explains why a speaker's solution to a problem is preferable to other proposed solutions. (Chapter 15)

comparison A statement of the similarities among two or more people, events, ideas, etc. (Chapter 14)

comprehensive listening Listening to understand the message of a speaker. (Chapter 3)

computer catalogue An online listing of the books and periodicals owned by a library. (Chapter 6)

computer-generated graphic A diagram, chart, graph, or the like created with the aid of a computer. (Chapter 13)

concept A belief, theory, idea, notion, principle, or the like. (Chapter 14)

concrete words Words that refer to tangible objects. (Chapter 11)

connective A word or phrase that connects the ideas of a speech and indicates the relationship between them. (Chapter 8)

connotative meaning The meaning suggested by the associations or emotions triggered by a word or phrase. (Chapter 11)

consensus A group decision that is acceptable to all members of the group. (Chapter 18)

contrast A statement of the differences among two or more people, events, ideas, etc. (Chapter 14)

conversational quality Presenting a speech so it sounds spontaneous no matter how many times it has been rehearsed. (Chapter 12)

creating common ground A technique in which a speaker connects himself or herself with the values, attitudes, or experiences of the audience. (Chapter 16)

credibility The audience's perception of whether a speaker is qualified to speak on a given topic. (Chapters 9, 16)

crescendo ending A conclusion in which the speech builds to a zenith of power and intensity. (Chapter 9)

criteria Standards on which a judgment or decision can be based. (Chapter 18)

critical listening Listening to evaluate a message for purposes of accepting or rejecting it. (Chapter 3)

critical thinking Focused, organized thinking about such things as the logical relationships among ideas, the soundness of evidence, and the differences between fact and opinion. (Chapter 1)

delivery cues Directions in a speaking outline to help a speaker remember how she or he wants to deliver key parts of the speech. (Chapter 10)

demographic audience analysis Audience analysis that focuses on demographic factors such as age, gender, religious orientation, group membership, and racial, ethnic, or cultural background. (Chapter 5)

denotative meaning The literal or dictionary meaning of a word or phrase. (Chapter 11)

derived credibility The credibility of a speaker produced by everything she or he says and does during the speech. (Chapter 16)

description A statement that depicts a person, event, idea, and the like with clarity and vividness. (Chapter 14)

designated leader A person who is elected or appointed as leader when the group is formed. (Chapter 18)

dialect A variety of a language distinguished by variations of accent, grammar, or vocabulary. (Chapter 12)

direct quotation Testimony that is presented word for word. (Chapter 7)

dissolve ending A conclusion that generates emotional appeal by fading step by step to a dramatic final statement. (Chapter 9)

dyad A group of two people. (Chapter 18)

egocentrism The tendency of people to be concerned above all with their own values, beliefs, and well-being. (Chapter 5)

either-or A fallacy that forces listeners to choose between two alternatives when more than two alternatives exist. (Chapter 16)

emergent leader A group member who emerges as a leader during the group's deliberations. (Chapter 18)

emphatic listening Listening to provide emotional support for a speaker. (Chapter 3)

ethical decisions Sound ethical decisions involve weighing a potential course of action against a set of ethical standards or guidelines. (Chapter 2)

ethics The branch of philosophy that deals with issues of right and wrong in human affairs. (Chapter 2)

ethnocentrism The belief that one's own group or culture is superior to all other groups or cultures. (Chapter 1)

ethos The name used by Aristotle for what modern students of communication refer to as credibility. (Chapter 16)

event Anything that happens or is regarded as happening. (Chapter 14)

evidence Supporting materials used to prove or disprove something. (Chapter 16)

example A specific case used to illustrate or to represent a group of people, ideas, conditions, experiences, or the like. (Chapter 7)

expert testimony Testimony from people who are recognized experts in their fields. (Chapter 7)

extemporaneous speech A carefully prepared and rehearsed speech that is presented from a brief set of notes. (Chapter 12)

extended example A story, narrative, or anecdote developed at some length to illustrate a point. (Chapter 7)

eye contact Direct visual contact with the eyes of another person. (Chapter 12)

fallacy An error in reasoning. (Chapter 16)

false cause An error in causal reasoning in which a speaker mistakenly assumes that because one event follows another, the first event is the cause of the second. This error is often known by its Latin name, *post hoc, ergo propter hoc,* meaning "after this, therefore because of this." (Chapter 16)

feedback The messages, usually nonverbal, sent from a listener to a speaker. (Chapter 1)

fixed-alternative questions Questions that offer a fixed choice between two or more alternatives. (Chapter 5)

font A complete set of type of the same design. (Chapter 13)

frame of reference The sum of a person's knowledge, experience, goals, values, and attitudes. No two people can have exactly the same frame of reference. (Chapter 1)

gazetteer A geographical dictionary. (Chapter 6)

general encyclopedia A comprehensive reference work that provides information about all branches of human knowledge. (Chapter 6)

general purpose The broad goal of a speech. The three major kinds of general purposes are to inform, to persuade, and to entertain. (Chapter 4)

generic "he" The use of "he" to refer to both women and men. (Chapter 11)

gestures Motions of a speaker's hands or arms during a speech. (Chapter 12)

global plagiarism Stealing a speech entirely from a single source and passing it off as one's own. (Chapter 2)

goodwill The audience's perception of whether the speaker has the best interests of the audience in mind. (Chapter 9)

graph A visual aid used to show statistical trends and patterns. (Chapter 13)

hasty generalization An error in reasoning from specific instances, in which a speaker jumps to a general conclusion on the basis of insufficient evidence. (Chapter 16)

hearing The vibration of sound waves on the eardrums and the firing of electrochemical impulses in the brain. (Chapter 3)

hidden agenda A set of unstated individual goals that may conflict with the goals of the group as a whole. (Chapter 18)

hypothetical example An example that describes an imaginary or fictitious situation. (Chapter 7)

imagery The use of vivid language to create mental images of objects, actions, or ideas. (Chapter 11)

implied leader A group member to whom other members defer because of her or his rank, expertise, or other quality. (Chapter 18)

impromptu speech A speech delivered with little or no immediate preparation. (Chapter 12)

incremental plagiarism Failing to give credit for particular parts of a speech that are borrowed from other people. (Chapter 2)

inflections Changes in the pitch or tone of a speaker's voice. (Chapter 12)

informative speech   A speech designed to convey knowledge and understanding.   (Chapter 14)

initial credibility   The credibility of a speaker before she or he starts to speak.   (Chapter 16)

interference   Anything that impedes the communication of a message. Interference can be external or internal to listeners.   (Chapter 1)

internal preview   A statement in the body of the speech that lets the audience know what the speaker is going to discuss next.   (Chapter 8)

internal summary   A statement in the body of the speech that summarizes the speaker's preceding point or points.   (Chapter 8)

Internet   A global collection of interlinked computer networks.   (Chapter 6)

invalid analogy   An analogy in which the two cases being compared are not essentially alike.   (Chapter 16)

jargon   The specialized or technical language of a trade, profession, or similar group. (Chapter 14)

key-word outline   An outline that briefly notes a speaker's main points and supporting evidence in rough outline form.   (Chapter 3)

kinesics   The study of nonverbal body motions as a systematic mode of communication. (Chapter 12)

leadership   The ability to influence group members so as to help achieve the goals of the group.   (Chapter 18)

line graph   A graph that uses one or more lines to show changes in statistics over time or space.   (Chapter 13)

link   A connection between two documents or sections of a document on the World Wide Web.   (Chapter 6)

listener   The person who receives the speaker's message.   (Chapter 1)

listening   Paying close attention to, and making sense of, what we hear.   (Chapter 3)

logos   The name used by Aristotle for the logical appeal of a speaker. The two major elements of *logos* are evidence and reasoning.   (Chapter 16)

main points   The major points developed in the body of a speech. Most speeches contain from two to five main points.   (Chapter 8)

maintenance needs   Communicative actions necessary to maintain interpersonal relations in a small group   (Chapter 18)

manuscript speech   A speech that is written out word for word and read to the audience. (Chapter 12)

mean   The average value of a group of numbers. (Chapter 7)

median   The middle number in a group of numbers arranged from highest to lowest.   (Chapter 7)

mental dialogue with the audience   The mental give-and-take between speaker and listener during a persuasive speech.   (Chapter 15)

message   Whatever a speaker communicates to someone else.   (Chapter 1)

metaphor   An implicit comparison, not introduced with the word "like" or "as," between two things that are essentially different yet have something in common.   (Chapter 11)

mixed metaphor   A metaphor that combines two or more incompatible or illogical comparisons.   (Chapter 11)

mode   The number that occurs most frequently in a group of numbers.   (Chapter 7)

model   An object, usually built to scale, that represents another object in detail.   (Chapter 13)

monotone   A constant pitch or tone of voice. (Chapter 12)

Monroe's motivated sequence   A method of organizing persuasive speeches that seek immediate action. The five steps of the motivated sequence are attention, need, satisfaction, visualization, and action.   (Chapter 15)

multimedia presentation   A speech that uses special computer software to combine several kinds of visual and/or audio aids in the same presentation.   (Chapter 13)

name-calling   The use of language to defame, demean, or degrade individuals or groups. (Chapter 2)

need   The first basic issue in analyzing a question of policy: Is there a serious problem or need that requires a change from current policy? (Chapter 15)

newspaper index   A research aid that catalogues articles from one or more newspapers. (Chapter 6)

nonsexist language   Language that does not stereotype people on the basis of gender.   (Chapter 11)

nonverbal communication   Communication that occurs as a result of appearance, posture, gesture, eye contact, facial expressions, and other nonlinguistic factors. (Chapter 12)

object Anything that is visible, tangible, and stable in form. (Chapter 14)

open-ended questions Questions that allow respondents to answer however they want. (Chapter 5)

oral report A speech presenting the findings, conclusions, decisions, etc. of a small group. (Chapter 18)

panel discussion A structured conversation on a given topic among several people in front of an audience. (Chapter 18)

parallelism The similar arrangement of a pair or series of related words, phrases, or sentences. (Chapter 11)

paraphrase To restate or summarize an author's ideas in one's own words. (Chapters 2, 7)

patchwork plagiarism Stealing ideas or language from two or three sources and passing them off as one's own. (Chapter 2)

pathos The name used by Aristotle for what modern students of communication refer to as emotional appeal. (Chapter 16)

pause A momentary break in the vocal delivery of a speech. (Chapter 12)

peer testimony Testimony from ordinary people with first-hand experience or insight on a topic. (Chapter 7)

periodical index A research aid that catalogues articles from a large number of journals or magazines. (Chapter 6)

personalize To present one's ideas in human terms that relate in some fashion to the experience of the audience. (Chapter 14)

persuasive speech A speech designed to change or reinforce the audience's beliefs or actions. (Chapter 15)

pie graph A graph that highlights segments of a circle to show simple distribution patterns. (Chapter 13)

pitch The highness or lowness of the speaker's voice. (Chapter 12)

plagiarism Presenting another person's language or ideas as one's own. (Chapter 2)

plan The second basic issue in analyzing a question of policy: If there is a problem with current policy, does the speaker have a plan to solve the problem? (Chapter 15)

positive nervousness Controlled nervousness that helps energize a speaker for her or his presentation. (Chapter 1)

practicality The third basic issue in analyzing a question of policy: Will the speaker's plan solve the problem? Will it create new and more serious problems? (Chapter 15)

preliminary bibliography A list compiled early in the research process of works that look as if they might contain helpful information about a speech topic. (Chapter 6)

preparation outline A detailed outline developed during the process of speech preparation that includes the title, specific purpose, central idea, introduction, main points, subpoints, connectives, conclusion, and bibliography of a speech. (Chapter 10)

preview statement A statement in the introduction of a speech that identifies the main points to be discussed in the body of the speech. (Chapter 9)

problem-cause-solution order A method of organizing persuasive speeches in which the first main point identifies a problem, the second main point analyzes the causes of the problem, and the third main point presents a solution to the problem. (Chapter 15)

problem-solution order A method of speech organization in which the first main point deals with the existence of a problem and the second main point presents a solution to the problem. (Chapters 8, 15)

problem-solving small group A small group formed to solve a particular problem. (Chapter 18)

procedural needs Routine "housekeeping" actions necessary for the efficient conduct of business in a small group. (Chapter 18)

process A systematic series of actions that leads to a specific result or product. (Chapter 14)

pronunciation The accepted standard of sound and rhythm for words in a given language. (Chapter 12)

question of fact A question about the truth or falsity of an assertion. (Chapter 15)

question of policy A question about whether a specific course of action should or should not be taken. (Chapters 15, 18)

question of value A question about the worth, rightness, morality, and so forth of an idea or action. (Chapter 15)

quoting out of context Quoting a statement in such a way as to distort its meaning by removing the statement from the words and phrases surrounding it. (Chapter 7)

rate The speed at which a person speaks. (Chapter 12)

reasoning The process of drawing a conclusion on the basis of evidence. (Chapter 16)

reasoning from principle Reasoning that moves from a general principle to a specific conclusion. (Chapter 16)

reasoning from specific instances Reasoning that moves from particular facts to a general conclusion. (Chapter 16)

red herring A fallacy that introduces an irrelevant issue to divert attention from the subject under discussion. (Chapter 16)

reference work A work that synthesizes a large amount of related information for easy access by researchers. (Chapter 6)

reflective-thinking method A five-step method for directing discussion in a problem-solving small group. (Chapter 18)

repetition Reiteration of the same word or set of words at the beginning or end of successive clauses or sentences. (Chapter 11)

research interview An interview conducted to gather information for a speech. (Chapter 6)

residual message What a speaker wants the audience to remember after it has forgotten everything else in a speech. (Chapter 4)

rhetorical question A question that the audience answers mentally rather than out loud. (Chapter 9)

rhythm The pattern of sound in a speech created by the choice and arrangement of words. (Chapter 11)

scale questions Questions that require responses at fixed intervals along a scale of answers. (Chapter 5)

search box The space provided by a search engine for entering the terms to be used in a keyword search. (Chapter 6)

search engine A program used in combination with a browser to find information on the World Wide Web. (Chapter 6)

sexist language Language that promotes the stereotyping of people on the basis of gender. (Chapter 11)

signpost A very brief statement that indicates where a speaker is in the speech or that focuses attention on key ideas. (Chapter 8)

simile An explicit comparison, introduced with the word "like" or "as," between things that are essentially different yet have something in common. (Chapter 11)

situation The time and place in which speech communication occurs. (Chapter 1)

situational audience analysis Audience analysis that focuses on situational factors such as the size of the audience, the physical setting for the speech, and the disposition of the audience toward the topic, the speaker, and the occasion. (Chapter 5)

slippery slope A fallacy that assumes that taking a first step will lead to subsequent steps that cannot be prevented. (Chapter 16)

small group A collection of three to twelve people who assemble for a specific purpose. (Chapter 18)

spare "brain time" The difference between the rate at which most people talk (120 to 150 words a minute) and the rate at which the brain can process language (400 to 800 words a minute). (Chapter 3)

spatial order A method of speech organization in which the main points follow a directional pattern. (Chapter 8)

speaker The person who is presenting an oral message to a listener. (Chapter 1)

speaking outline A brief outline used to jog a speaker's memory during the presentation of a speech. (Chapter 10)

special encyclopedia A comprehensive reference work devoted to a specific subject such as religion, art, law, science, music, etc. (Chapter 6)

specific purpose A single infinitive phrase that states precisely what a speaker hopes to accomplish in his or her speech. (Chapter 4)

speech of introduction A speech that introduces the main speaker to the audience. (Chapter 17)

speech of presentation A speech that presents someone a gift, an award, or some other form of public recognition. (Chapter 17)

speech to gain immediate action A persuasive speech in which the speaker's goal is to convince the audience to take action in support of a given policy. (Chapter 15)

speech to gain passive agreement   A persuasive speech in which the speaker's goal is to convince the audience that a given policy is desirable without encouraging the audience to take action in support of the policy.   (Chapter 15)

sponsoring organization   An organization that, in the absence of a clearly identified author, is responsible for the content of a document on the World Wide Web.   (Chapter 6)

stage fright   Anxiety over the prospect of giving a speech in front of an audience.   (Chapter 1)

statistics   Numerical data.   (Chapter 7)

stereotype   A widely held, oversimplified opinion or image.   (Chapter 11)

strategic organization   Putting a speech together in a particular way to achieve a particular result with a particular audience.   (Chapter 8)

supporting materials   The materials used to support a speaker's ideas. The three major kinds of supporting materials are examples, statistics, and testimony.   (Chapters 7, 8)

symposium   A public presentation in which several people present prepared speeches on different aspects of the same topic.   (Chapter 18)

target audience   The portion of the whole audience that the speaker most wants to persuade. (Chapter 15)

task needs   Substantive actions necessary to help a small group complete its assigned task. (Chapter 18)

terminal credibility   The credibility of a speaker at the end of the speech.   (Chapter 16)

testimony   Quotations or paraphrases used to support a point.   (Chapter 7)

thesaurus   A book of synonyms.   (Chapter 11)

topic   The subject of a speech.   (Chapter 4)

topical order   A method of speech organization in which the main points divide the topic into logical and consistent subtopics. (Chapter 8)

transition   A word or phrase that indicates when a speaker has finished one thought and is moving on to another.   (Chapter 8)

transparency   A visual aid drawn, written, or printed on a sheet of clear acetate and shown with an overhead projector.   (Chapter 13)

URL (Uniform Resource Locator)   A string of letters or numbers that identifies the location of a given website on the Internet.   (Chapter 6)

visual framework   The pattern of symbolization and indentation in a speech outline that shows the relationships among the speaker's ideas. (Chapter 10)

visualization   Mental imaging in which a speaker vividly pictures himself or herself giving a successful presentation.   (Chapter 1)

vocal variety   Changes in a speaker's rate, pitch, and volume that give the voice variety and expressiveness.   (Chapter 12)

vocalized pause   A pause that occurs when a speaker fills the silence between words with vocalizations such as "uh," "er," and "um." (Chapter 12)

volume   The loudness or softness of the speaker's voice.   (Chapter 12)

World Wide Web   A global hypertext information system that allows users to access text, graphics, audio, and moving images from the Internet.   (Chapter 6)

yearbook   A reference work published annually that contains information about the previous year.   (Chapter 6)

PHOTO CREDITS

Chapter 16
Opposite page 399: Stephen Jaffe/The Image Works; page 404: Joel Gordon; page 411: Michael Newman/PhotoEdit; page 417: Ron Chapple/FPG; page 424: Bob Daemmrich/Stock, Boston.

Chapter 17
Opposite page 435: Arthur Grace/Sygma; page 438: Mark J. Terrill/AP/Wide World Photos; page 443: John Berry/The Image Works.

Chapter 18
Opposite page 453: R.W. Jones/Corbis; page 458: Bruce Ayres/Tony Stone Images; page 467: Loren Santow/Tony Stone Images; page 470: Dan Bosler/Tony Stone Images.

Appendix A
Page A1: Susan Lapides/Design Conceptions.

INDEX

Frames of reference, of listeners,
    17–18
Free speech
  First Amendment and, 48–49
  name-calling and, 40

G

Galaxy Quotations, 142
Gandhi, Mohandas, 64
Gastil, Janet, 182
Gazetteers, 135
Gender, audience analysis and, 103–104
General encyclopedias, 132
General indexes, 128–129
Generalization, hasty, 410
General purpose, defined, 81
General Reference Center, 128–129
Generic "he," 276
Gestures, 299–300. *see also* Body
    movement; Eye contact
Global plagiarism, 43
Goals, for ethical speaking, 36
Goodwill, 223–224
Gore, Al, 274
Government resources, on Web,
    141–142
Graphs, as visual aids, 319–321
Group membership, audience analysis
    and, 107–108
Guinness Book of World Records, 179

H

Hancock, John, 272
Handouts, 331
Hanson, Rebecca, 424–427
Hasty generalization, 410
Hawking, Stephen, 64
"He," generic, 276
Hearing, defined, 56. *see also*
    Listening
Hidden agendas, 459
Hitler, Adolf, 35
Honesty, ethical speaking and, 38–39
How to Lie with Statistics (Huff),
    122–123
Huber, Vicki, 11
Huff, Darrell, 122–123
Humor, in after-dinner speeches,
    446–447
Hunter, Duncan, 182
Hypothetical examples, 167–168

I

Iacocca, Lee, 3
Imagery
  concrete words and, 266–267
  defined, 266
  metaphors and, 268–269
  simile and, 267–268

Immediate action, speeches to gain,
    379–380
Implied leaders, 455–456
Impromptu speeches, 286–287
Inaugural addresses, 447
Incremental plagiarism, 45–46
Indentation
  preparation outline, 239–240
  speaking outline, 246–247
Indexes
  general, 128–129
  newspaper, 130–132
  periodical, 127–128
Inflections, 290
Informative speeches, 81–82,
    340–341
  about concepts, 348–350
  abstractions and, 356–358
  audience and, 350–354
  description in, 356
  about events, 346–348
  example of, 359–362
  guidelines for, 350–359
  about objects, 341–343
  personalizing ideas in, 358–359
  about processes, 343–345
  technical language and, 354–356
  Web resources for, 347
Ingraham, Susan, 390–393
Initial credibility, 402
Interference, in communication
    process, 19
Internal previews, 205–206
  labeling, for preparation outlines,
    241–242
Internal summaries, 206
  for preparation outlines, 241–242
International Listening Association, 65
Internet, 135–136. *see also* World
    Wide Web (Web)
Interviews, for audience analysis, 113.
    see also Research interviews
Introduction, speeches of, 436–439
Introductions, of speeches, 214–226
  arousing curiosity in, 218
  establishing credibility and goodwill
    in, 222–224
  guidelines for preparing, 226
  obtaining audience attention/interest
    in, 214–215
  in preparation outlines, 239
  quotations in, 219–220
  relating topic to audience in, 215–216
  revealing topic in, 221–222
  sample of, 225–226
  startling audience in, 217–218
  stating importance of topic in,
    216–217
  story telling in, 220–221

Introductions, of speeches *(Cont.)*
  using rhetorical questions in,
    218–219
Invalid analogy, 416

J

Jackson, Jesse, 274
Jargon, 355
Johannesen, Richard, 35
Jones, Jenkin Lloyd, 36

K

Kaye, Danny, 440–441
Keller, Helen, 64
Kennedy, Edward, 49
Kennedy, John F., 443
Key-word outline, for note-taking,
    67–70
Keyword searches
  Internet, 139
  online catalogue, 126–127
Kinesics, 297
King, Martin Luther, Jr., 13, 266, 443

L

Language. *see also* Words
  abstract words and, 263–264
  accuracy and, 258–260
  alliteration in, 271
  antithesis in, 271–272
  appropriate use of, 272–274
  clichés in, 268
  concrete words and, 263–264,
    266–267
  dialects in, 295–296
  eliminating clutter in, 264–265
  familiar words and, 261–263
  importance of, 256–257
  metaphors and, 268–269
  nonsexist, 274–277
  parallelism in, 270
  repetition in, 270–271
  rhythm of, 269–270
  simile and, 267–268
Latino/Hispanic Resources, 144
Leadership
  functions of, 456–458
  types of, 455–456
  Web resources on, 462
Lexis/Nexis Academic Universe, 131
Library research, 125–135. *see also*
    Research
  catalogues for, 125–127
  general indexes for, 128–129
  newspaper indexes for, 130–132
  periodical indexes for, 127–128
  reference works for, 132–135
Lincoln, Abraham, 64
Line graphs, as visual aids, 319